THE
MESSAGES OF THE BOOKS

THE

MESSAGES OF THE BOOKS

BEING

DISCOURSES AND NOTES ON THE BOOKS OF THE
NEW TESTAMENT

BY

F. W. FARRAR, D.D., F.R.S.

LATE FELLOW OF TRINITY COLLEGE, CAMBRIDGE
ARCHDEACON AND CANON OF WESTMINSTER; AND CHAPLAIN IN ORDINARY TO THE QUEEN

New York
THE MACMILLAN COMPANY
1927

PREFACE.

On being appointed eight years ago to the charge of a London parish, I endeavoured to carry out a design, long entertained, of taking the Books of the Bible as texts, and preaching a separate discourse on each of the sixty-six treatises which make up "the Library of Divine Revelation." My object was to point out the general form, the peculiar characteristics, the special message of the Sacred Books one by one, because I had found by experience, both as a teacher and as a clergy-man, that this method of studying each part of Scripture as a complete whole was much less common than could be desired. There seemed to me to be no adequate reason why multitudes of Christians should be so little acquainted with the distinctive scope and individuality—the physiognomy and psychology, if I may be allowed the expressions—of each separate part of the living oracles. Until a wider method of studying Scripture is adopted, much of the labour bestowed on isolated texts will be wasted. The true mean-ing of a text is often incomprehensible unless it be considered historically, and unless its original sense be thus disentangled from the misinterpretations to which almost every memorable sentence of the Bible has at some time or other been exposed.

No one who has not given special attention to the subject can have any conception of the extent to which fragments of the Bible have been misquoted and misapplied. It is no exaggeration to say that the majority of the shibboleths which have been bandied about in current controversies are applied in senses entirely apart from those in which they were intended by the original writers. Such texts are associated in most minds with meanings which have assiduously been read into them, but which they do not really contain. A volume of the saddest import, and of the most solemn warning, might be written on the calamities which have ensued in age after age of civil and ecclesiastical history from systematic perversions of Holy Writ. The surest way to cure such evils in the present, and to obviate such disasters in the future, is the study of Scripture as a whole, and the consideration of each part of it in relation to the age and conditions under which it was written. "I am convinced," says Goethe, "that the beauty of the Bible increases in proportion as it is understood; that is to say, in proportion as we consider and perceive that each word which we take generally, has had a peculiar, special, and directly individual application in accordance with given circumstances of place and time."

Surely then among the sermons which are yearly preached in the Church of England, and which treat of so great a variety of subjects, there must be room for some which deal with entire sections of Scripture, with the desire to set forth something of their meaning and history. Yet so far as I am aware, no volume of discourses devoted to this end has been published by any clergyman of the Church of England. The statement might indeed be made much broader. There are many series of sermons devoted to the consecutive exposition of some one book of the Bible, but until this volume was nearly completed, I did not know of any volume of sermons either in Patristic, Scholastic, Reformation, or Post-Reformation theology, from the first century down to the last decade, which contains a series of discourses dealing *seriatim* with "the Messages of the Books." [1] It has always been too much the tendency of Christians to construct their theology and support their spiritual life by means of isolated texts. But it is as impossible to judge of the design or to realise the splendour of a mosaic by picking up some glittering fragment of it, as to judge of Scripture or to apprehend its "many-coloured wisdom" by a few favourite verses. We do not treat even the higher works of human genius in this manner. No one would suppose that a reader understood the mind of Shakspeare merely because he could repeat some of the finest lines of *Hamlet* or *King Lear;* nor should we assume that a man who had never read the *Paradise Lost,* had entered into the heart of Milton merely because he was able to repeat with enthusiasm some of the most familiar passages of the poem. But if this be true of the works of single authors, how much more must it apply to the Bible, which is not a single book, but the collected literature of a whole people written amid the most astonishing varieties of condition and circumstance, by a multitude of different authors, of whom some were separated from others by a space of sixteen hundred years ?

The present volume is devoted to the Books of the New

[1] It was only when my book was very nearly complete that I heard of Dr. Donald Fraser's *Synoptical Lectures,* in which a similar plan is carried out.

Testament, and if it should be found useful it will be followed in time by one on the Books of the Old Testament. As I have spoken of the Gospels and Epistles in previous works, I have inevitably gone, to some extent, over old ground, and in some passages have used the same language. But since the entire setting of the present work, as well as much that it contains, is new, I venture to hope that it may not be wholly unacceptable to those who have my former books in their possession no less than to other readers.

If the present attempt should lead other clergymen to bring the whole of the Bible before their hearers, Book by Book, and to carry out the design in a manner far superior to that which has alone been possible to me, my labour will not have been in vain. I trust that these discourses will be accepted as one more attempt—however humble—to advance the general knowledge of Scripture, and to make known the unsearchable riches of Christ.

F. W. FARRAR.

TABLE OF CONTENTS.

III.

ST. MARK'S GOSPEL.

IV.

ST. LUKE'S GOSPEL.

V.

ST. JOHN'S GOSPEL.

VI.

THE ACTS OF THE APOSTLES.

VII.

FORM OF THE EPISTLES.

VIII.

ST. PAUL'S THIRTEEN EPISTLES.

IX.

THE FIRST EPISTLE TO THE THESSALONIANS.

X.

THE SECOND EPISTLE TO THE THESSALONIANS.

XI.

THE FIRST EPISTLE TO THE CORINTHIANS.

XII.

THE SECOND EPISTLE TO THE CORINTHIANS.

XIII.

THE EPISTLE TO THE GALATIANS.

XIV.

THE EPISTLE TO THE ROMANS.

XV.

THE EPISTLE TO THE PHILIPPIANS.

XVI.

THE EPISTLE TO THE COLOSSIANS.

XVII.

THE EPISTLE TO THE EPHESIANS.

XVIII.

THE EPISTLE TO PHILEMON.

XIX.

THE FIRST EPISTLE TO TIMOTHY.

XX.

THE EPISTLE TO TITUS.

THE CATHOLIC EPISTLES.

XXVII.

THE FIRST EPISTLE OF ST. JOHN.

XXVIII.

THE SECOND EPISTLE OF ST. JOHN.

XXIX.

THE THIRD EPISTLE OF ST. JOHN.

XXX.

THE REVELATION OF ST. JOHN.

THE GOSPELS.

"Sì come luce luce in ciel seconda
    Vennero appresso lor quattro animali
    Coronato ciascun di verde fronda."
                    DANTE, *Purgatorio*, xxix. 91-93.

"Ich halte die Evangelien für durchaus ächt; denn es ist in ihnen der Abglanz einer Hoheit wirksam, die von der Person Christi ausging: die ist göttlicher Art, wie nur je auf Erden das Göttliche erschienen ist."—GOETHE, *Gespräche mit Eckermann*, iii. 371.

" Mag die geistige Cultur immer fortschreiten, mögen die Naturwissenschaften in immer breiterer Ausdehnung und Tiefe wachsen, und der menschliche Geist sich erweitern wie er will; über die Hoheit und sittliche Cultur des Christenthums, wie es in den Evangelien leuchtet, wird es nicht hinauskommen."—*Id*.

THE FOUR GOSPELS.

H ἁγία τῶν εὐαγγελίων τετρακτύς.—EUSEB., *H. E.* iii. 25.

"The beginning of the Gospel of Jesus Christ, the Son of God."
MARK i. 1.

IT will be my endeavour in the following discourses to consider the main object and special peculiarities of each of the twenty-seven books of which the New Testament is composed. Out of the many thousands of sermons which are weekly and sometimes even daily delivered in England, it is I think very desirable that some should be devoted to the scope and meaning of the Books of Scripture rather than to its separate texts. By thus doing we can as it were kneel down to drink of the pure stream as it bursts from the living rock. The Bible teaches us its best lessons when we search its pages as wise and humble learners; when we judge of it by the truths which we learn from it, and not by the prejudices and prepossessions which we bring to it; when we seek in it the elements and bases of our faith, not when we go to it for proof texts of doctrines which we already hold.[1]

We naturally begin with the Gospels. It is true that they do not belong chronologically to the earliest, but to the latest period of the New Testament writings. We will speak of the

[1] "Optimus interpres hic est qui sensum e Scriptura potius retulerit quam attulerit, nec cogat hoc in dictis contentum videri quod ante intelligentiam docere praesumserit."—LUTHER, after Hilary, *De Trinitate*, 1.

other books as far as possible in the order in which they were
written, and we shall find an obvious advantage in so doing.
No inconvenience will, however, result from our speaking
first of the four Gospels, both because they record the life of
Christ, which was the beginning of the good tidings and of
the New Covenant, and because some records more or less
similar to them must have existed in an oral form for many
years before they were reduced to writing by the four
Evangelists.

Let us first of all notice the phrase, " The New Testament."
It is taken from the rendering of Luke xxii. 20, " This cup is
the new testament in my blood." [1]   Strange to say, the title,
like " Old Testament," is founded on a pure mistake, which
is now too deeply rooted to be removed.   Happily it is not a
mistake which does any harm, or conveys any false impression.
In the Revised Version, which in hundreds of verses serves as
an admirable commentary on the true meaning of Scripture,
the verse is rightly rendered, "This cup is the new *covenant*
in my blood."   A "testament" means " a will," and the Jews
knew nothing about "making wills."   They neither possessed
the phrase nor the custom till they had learnt them both
from the Romans.   The word rendered " testament" ($\delta\iota\alpha$-
$\theta\acute{\eta}\kappa\eta$) is the equivalent for the Hebrew word *Berîth* (which
occurs in the name Baal Berith, " lord of the covenant").
Nowhere in the New Testament does it mean " a will," except (for a special reason) in a single passage of the Epistle
to the Hebrews.[2]   What we call the " New Testament " is
the book which reveals to us that fresh ($\kappa\alpha\iota\nu\grave{\eta}$) covenant
which God, in this last epoch of the world's history, has
made with man in Jesus Christ, as He had made His former
covenant with Abraham and with Moses.

In placing the Gospels first in the order of the canon, the
Church has been guided by a right instinct.   For Christianity is an historical religion, and our Christian faith is
faith in God revealed in Christ.   Now the Gospels not only

---

[1] Comp. Matt. xxvi. 28 (in R. V.), 1 Cor. xi. 25.   [2] Hebrews ix. 16, 17.

record for us the historic facts which are the objective bases of our Christian creed, but they are our almost exclusive authority on this subject. They tell us all that we are really permitted to know in detail about the earthly life of the Saviour in whom we believe.[1]

The word Gospel is the Saxon translation of the Greek word *euangelion*.[2] In early Greek the word meant the reward given to one who brought good tidings.[3] In Attic Greek it meant (in the plural) a sacrifice for good tidings.[4] Hence the word became, even among Romans, a kind of exclamation like our " Good news ! "[5] In later Greek it meant the good news actually delivered.[6] Among all Greek-speaking Christians—and at the beginning of the Christian era Greek was universally spoken throughout the civilised world — the word was adopted to describe the best and gladdest tidings ever delivered to the human race—the good news of the kingdom of God. Naturally a word which meant " good news " soon came to be used as the title of the books in which the history of those good tidings was contained.[7] But in the New Testament itself the word Gospel

---

[1] It is this which gives to the Gospels their unique importance. Neither from the classical writers, nor from Christian tradition, nor from the Apocryphal Gospels, nor from the Fathers, nor from the Talmud, do we learn a single new, certain, or valuable fact about the life of Christ. See Keim, *Jesu von Nazara*, i. 8–35.

[2] The word "Gospel," which seems to have acquired currency from Wycliff's translation, is used by euphony for *godspel*, *i.e.* news (*spelian*, "to tell ") about God. So "gossip " is for " godsib," *i.e.* relationship in things pertaining to God ; " and gossamer for *god-summer*, from the legend that the threads of gossamer are fragments of the Virgin's winding-sheet which fell from her when she was taken up to heaven (German *Marienfäden*).

[3] For instance in Homer, *Od.* xiv. 152.

[4] ἐβουθύτει ὡς εὐαγγέλια. Xen. *Hell.* iv. 3, s. 14.

[5] " Εὐαγγέλια ! Valerius absolutus est ! " Cic. *ad Att.* ii. 3.

[6] 2 Sam. xviii. 20 (LXX.) ; Is. lxi. 1 ; Luke iv. 18.

[7] In the address of the Angel to the Shepherds we find the words " *I bring you good tidings* of great joy," where the verb used is εὐαγγελίζομαι. This verb is specially common in St. Luke and St. Paul. The substantive does not occur in St. Luke. In St. John the only instance of either verb or substantive is Rev. xiv. 6 (where it does not refer to the Gospel). In St. Paul it occurs sixty-one times. From this Greek word are derived the French *Évangile*, the German *Evangelium*, the Italian *Evangelio*, the Portuguese *Evangelho*, &c.

always means "the word preached," and is never used for a written book.[1]

The language in which the New Covenant is written is the form of Greek which was everywhere spoken in the first century of the Christian era. It was known as the Macedonian, or "common," or Hellenistic Greek. The growth of this dialect was due to the conquests of Alexander the Great. It was a stage of the Greek language in which decadence was marked by a loss of finish and synthetic power. The purer language of the Athenian writers was largely mingled with poetic, Semitic, and provincial words and idioms, due to the conflux of different forms of civilisation in the city of Alexandria, in which this "common dialect" was mainly spoken. The rapid dissemination of the dialect was due in some measure to the large colonies of Jews engaged in mercantile pursuits, who were to be found all along the shores of the Mediterranean and in almost every region of the ancient world.[2] It was a form of speech simplified in grammar and in the periodic structure of its sentences, but enriched in vocabulary by many convenient additions. What it lost in polish it gained in plasticity. So far from being, as it has been absurdly called, "a miserable patois," it made up by flexibility, energy, and clearness for all that it had resigned in symmetry and grace. In the hands of Apostles and Evangelists it became an instrument of incomparable force. It had been providentially prepared for their use by the studies and labours of three centuries. They found ready to their hands the rich stores of religious and philosophical phraseology which had been invented or adopted to express the truths of revelation by the Septuagint translators of the Old Testament, by the writings of Aristobulus and Philo, by the authors of some of the apocryphal books, and by the whole school of Alexandrian theosophists.

[1] Mark xiv. 9 ; 2 Cor. viii. 18 ; Eph. iv. 11 ; Acts xxi. 8   The earliest use of Εὐαγγέλιον for a book is in Justin Martyr.   Marcion gave the name "Gospel" (without naming any author) to his mutilated St. Luke.
[2] Cicero, *Pro. Arch.* 10.   "Graeca leguntur in omnibus fere gentibus."

Let us pause for a moment to notice the perfectness of the THE FOUR
" evangelic preparation " by which God marked " the fulness GOSPELS.
of the times." The Gospel could never have spread with a
rapidity so amazing but for the concurrence of three vast
and world-wide events, whereby God had so ordered the world
of history as to prepare the way for the revelation of His Son.
Those three events were the career of Alexander the Great,
the rise of the Roman empire, and the dispersion of the Jews.
The conquests of Alexander gave to the civilised world a
unity of language, without which it would have been, humanly
speaking, impossible for the earliest teachers to make the
" good tidings " known in every land. The rise of the Roman
empire secured to the nations a social order and a political
unity which protected and consolidated the growth of the new
faith. The dispersion of the Jews, tending to weaken still
further a decadent Paganism, had prepared the world
for a purer morality and a monotheistic faith. Greeks and
Jews and Romans were the deadly enemies of early
Christianity, yet the Gospel emanated from the capital of
Judæa; it was preached in the tongue of Athens; it was
diffused through the empire of Rome. The tallîth of Shem,
according to the aspiration of one of the wisest of the rabbis,
was thus united to the pallium of Japhet.[1] Thus the New
Testament became a cosmopolitan book—a book for all ages
and all lands. Speaking the tongue of Homer and of Plato
the Jewish preachers of a universal Christian redemption
made their way along the undeviating roads by which the
Roman legionaries—" those massive hammers of the whole
earth "—had made straight in the desert a highway for our
God. Semite and Aryan became the unconscious ministers
of a religion which at first they despised, then hated, and
lastly feared. The Greek conqueror, the Roman emperor,
the Jewish rabbi, the Alexandrian eclectic—Alexander, and

---

[1] " The New Testament," says Dr. Schaff, " has a Greek body, a Hebrew
soul, and a Christian spirit which rules both."—*Hist. of Apostol. Church*,
p. 573.

Augustus, and Gamaliel and Philo—were alike engaged unconsciously, but with momentous influence, in preparing the
"way of the Lord." The letters of Hebrew and Greek and
Latin inscribed above the cross were the prophetic testimony
of the world's three noblest languages to the undying claims
of Him who suffered to unite all nations into the one great
family of God.

Beginning then with the Gospels, let us see what are the
first facts which demand our attention.

i. We see four separate books containing something that
is peculiar to each, much that is common to all; of which
tradition says, and research—even the most recent and the
most thorough—goes far to prove, that the three first were
written within forty,[1] and the fourth within fifty, years of the
death of Christ. Each of these professes to give us some
account of Him. It is probable that the one which stands
first was actually written first, but all of them may alike
have been preceded by fragments of written, as, from the
nature of things, they were all certainly preceded by cycles
of oral teaching. The first then—the Gospel according to
St. Matthew—is the Gospel of God, the good news or glad
tidings of Jesus Christ, in the form of delivery which St.
Matthew adopted. He was by trade a humble "publican,"
not improbably a first cousin to our Lord according to the
flesh, of whom all that we learn from the Bible is, that one
word of Christ transformed him from a despised taxgatherer
into a holy Apostle. He wrote for his fellow-countrymen,
and perhaps originally in Aramaic. His record of what he had
seen of Jesus may have been composed when, after long
living in Palestine, he left his native country to find in some
far land his natural death or his martyr's crown.

The second and third Gospels were written by early disciples;
—not by actual apostles, but, as St. Jerome says, by "Apostolic
men." St. Mark has, by a precarious conjecture, been identified with the young man having a linen sheet cast over

---

[1] See the Discourse on St. Matthew (*infra*).

his naked body, who showed that strange mixture of curiosity and boldness at the Garden of Gethsemane. In later years —though on one occasion he wavered when he was acting as an attendant (ὑπηρέτης, Acts xiii. 5) to Paul and Barnabas— he became the chosen son and companion of St. Peter, by whose sanction and with whose aid his Gospel was probably written.

St. Luke was not a Jew but a Gentile. In his Gospel we have the Gospel of one who came to Christ from Heathendom. Tradition says that he was a proselyte and physician of Antioch, and we learn from his own modest writings that he was the year-long friend and helper of St. Paul in his travels and imprisonment. He narrated the facts which he diligently gathered from oral and written sources. But he, too, like St. Mark, though not an Apostle, was the representative of an Apostle, and illustrates the truths which were most prominently taught by the great Apostle of the Gentiles.

Lastly, St. John in his old age at Ephesus—the disciple whom Jesus loved, who also leaned on His breast at supper, the last survivor of the Apostles as his brother was their earliest martyr—when the first generation of Christians was dead and gone, when the Gospel as it was preached by St. Matthew, St. Peter, and St. Paul was already in men's hands, when Jerusalem was now trodden under foot of the Gentiles—under the guidance of the Holy Spirit, left as his immortal legacy to the Church of God a final picture of the Redeemer in the record of many discourses and many incidents, which, in the other Gospels, had been but partially or not at all revealed.

Let us note in passing that the names of the three first Evangelists are little likely to have suggested themselves to any forger. Any one who desired to palm upon the Church a written Gospel under the shadow of some great name, would have attributed his work to St. Peter or St. James, or one of the greater Apostles, not to the despised publican, the wavering deacon, and the Gentile physician.

The Gospels.

ii. Now, as we look at these four Gospels, one obvious difference between them at once strikes the most careless reader. It is that St. Matthew, St. Mark, and St. Luke are in many respects like each other, and in many respects unlike St. John. The first three dwell mainly and almost exclusively on Christ's ministry in Galilee; the fourth on His ministry in Judea. The first three only narrate at length one of His visits to Jerusalem—the one which ended in the crucifixion; St. John gives us the incidents of four such visits previous to the one in which He was put to death. The first three are occupied mainly and almost exclusively with His miracles, parables, and addresses to the multitude; St. John, with the higher, deeper, more abstract, more esoteric—and in one or two important instances, more individual discourses. The first three give us more of the external incidents of the life of Christ, and hence were called by some early writers the bodily Gospels (σωματικά); the fourth, more of its inmost spiritual meaning.[1] The first three are, to use a convenient modern term, more objective; the fourth, more subjective. The first three deal more with action; St. John with contemplation. The first three speak more of the labour and of the way; the fourth, more of the rest and of the home. Hence the first three are called the Synoptists, because one tabular view can be given of their narratives;[2] the fourth stands in many respects apart. Once more, the first three are more fragmentary than the fourth. The first three "may be compared to a succession of pictures,

---

[1] The remark that St. John's is the spiritual Gospel (πνευματικόν) is as old as Clement of Alexandria (ap. Euseb., H. E. iii. 24).

[2] The Greek word Synopsis has the same meaning as the Latin Conspectus, viz. "a collective view." The first three Evangelists are called "Synoptists" because their Gospels can be arranged and harmonised, section by section, in a tabular form, since they are mainly based on a common outline. The term appears to be quite modern, but has been rapidly brought into general use since its adoption by Griesbach. See Holtzmann in Schenkel, Bibel-Lexicon, s.v. Evangelien; and Ebrard in Herzog, s.v. Harmonie. I am not aware of any earlier use of the word "Synopsis," as applied to a tabular view of the first three Gospels, than Georgii Sigelii Synopsis historiae Jes. Christi quemadmodum Matthaeus, Marcus, Lucas, descripsere in forma tabulae proposita. Noribergae. 1585. Folio.

in which a painter represents a complete history;" the fourth produces the effect of a more ideal unity.[1]

But the fact that the Gospels are, to borrow the phrase of St. Augustine, " various, not contrary," is a distinct advantage. They thus become, as it were, the sacred stereoscope which sets before us the life of our Saviour, not in its bare surface, but in its living solidity. If we had only possessed the three first we should have known much about our Lord, but not the whole. "The Synoptic Gospels contain the Gospel of the Infant Church, that of St. John, the Gospel of its maturity." They give us, for the world, the experience and origin of a society; St. John gives us, for the Church, the inspired intuitions of a disciple.[2]

There is contrast between them, but no contradiction.[3] In Greek literature we have two widely divergent records of Socrates, but we know him all the more thoroughly from the different way in which his personality affected the minds of two men so unlike each other as the busy, active, and practical soldier, and the deep-souled, poet-philosopher. Xenophon sketches for us the outer life of Socrates, Plato gives us an idealisation of his inmost spirit. The Synoptists, it has been truly said, furnish us with pictures like those three separate portraits of Charles I. which Vandyke prepared for the sculptor who was to reproduce in marble the very man.[4] We may borrow an analogy from the physical world, and say that the first three Evangelists give us divers aspects of one glorious landscape ; St. John pours over that landscape a flood of heavenly sunshine which seems to transform its very character, though every feature of the landscape

---

[1] Holtzmann in the *Protestanten Bibel* (Eng. Trans. i. 40). The fragmentariness of the synoptical memoirs is illustrated by the fact already mentioned, that they confine themselves almost exclusively to the Galilean ministry, though they were well aware of the ministry in Judaea (Matt. xxi. 8, 9 ; xxiii. 37 ; xxvii. 57, &c.).

[2] Westcott, *Introduction to the Study of the Gospels*, p. 197.

[3] " Per hujusmodi evangelistarum locutiones *varias sed non contrarias* discimus nihil in cujusque verbis nos inspicere debere nisi voluntatem."—Aug. *De Consens. Evang.* ii. 28.

[4] Westcott, *Introd.* p. 234.

remains the same. Their circumstantial differences recall the
variety of Nature; their substantial agreement resembles
its marvellous and essential unity. For the object of each
and all of the Gospels is that expressed by St. John, "that
ye might believe that Jesus is the Christ the Son of
God, and that believing ye might have life through His
name."[1]

iii. Hence the Church has always been thankful for the
fact that "holy men of old, moved by the Holy Ghost," have
left us four separate, and mainly, if not absolutely, independent Gospels. We are thus furnished with such a
weight of contemporaneous testimony as is wanting to the
great majority of events in Ancient History. A fourfold
cord is not easily broken.[2]

Early Christian writers compared the Gospels to that river
which, flowing out of Eden to water the Garden of God, was
parted into four heads, compassing lands of which the gold

---

[1] John xx. 31.

[2] It is no part of my purpose to enter in detail into the question of the
authenticity or even the canonicity of the various books of the New Testament. To attempt this would require a volume, and the task has already been
most admirably performed by many abler scholars. I may refer the reader to
two English books—Dr. Westcott, *On the Canon of the New Testament*, and
Dr. Charteris, *On Canonicity* (which is based on Kirchhofer's *Quellensamm-
lung*), as well as to the widely different views taken by Dr. Davidson in his
Introduction. I may, however, mention the remarkable confirmation to the
early date of the Gospels, and therefore the refutation of the theories of the
Tübingen school, and of many German scholars, which results from a recent
discovery. The Mechitarist Fathers at Venice have published a translation
from the Armenian of a commentary by Ephraem Syrus in the fourth century
on the work known as the *Diatessaron* of Tatian. From this it is finally clear
that Tatian's Harmony was a close weaving together of *our four present
Gospels*. Now Tatian was a disciple of Justin Martyr, and the fact that the
Gospels had already in his day (*circ.* A.D. 160) received an exclusive recognition,
entirely refutes the hypothesis of many that, in their present form, several
of them are not older than the middle of the second century. Thus Baur
refers the Gospel of St. Matthew to A.D. 130–134, and Volkmar places it not
earlier than A.D. 105. Irenaeus is now proved to have been much nearer the
mark when he placed it A.D. 64 (*Haer*. iii. s. 1). The testimonies of Papias,
Irenaeus, Tertullian, of the Muratorian Canon, and of Clemens of Alexandria,
to say nothing of Justin Martyr, show how early the Gospels had acquired a
position of supreme authority. But, apart from this, the undisputed Epistles
of St. Paul, as well as those of St. James, and the First of St. Peter, and the
Epistle to the Hebrews, are sufficient to confirm the Gospels in every important
particular.

is good, and which have bdellium and the onyx-stone.[1] But
a still commoner symbol of the Evangelists is that derived
from the four living creatures, "the fourfold-visaged four"—
the cherubim which form the chariot of the Lord in the Vision
of Ezekiel by the river Chebar.[2] In almost every church
you find, somewhere depicted, the four symbols of the Evangelists—the man or angel for St. Matthew; the lion of
St. Mark; the calf of St. Luke; the eagle for St. John.
The man was chosen as the emblem of St. Matthew because
he brings out Christ's kingly and human character;[3] the
lion for St. Mark, from the strength and energy of his
delineation;[4] the ox for St. Luke, because he indicates
Christ's priestly and mediatorial office;[5] the eagle for St.
John, because "he soars to heaven above the clouds of
human infirmity, and reveals to us the mysteries of the
Godhead, and the felicities of Eternal Life, gazing on the

[1] " Paradisi hic fluenta
    Nova fluunt sacramenta
    Quae descendunt coelitus :
    His quadrigis deportatur
    Mundo Deus, sublimatur
    Istis arca vectibus."
                    ADAM DE S. VICTORE.

[2] Ezek. i. 5-26. As early as Irenaeus we find the expression "the four-
shaped Gospel." *Adv. Haer.* iii. 11, s. 8. τετράμορφον τὸ εὐαγγέλιον, ἐνὶ
πνεύματι συνεχ'μενον. He fancifully dwells on the number four as that of the
four winds and the four elements. Adam of St. Victor says :—
            " Circa thema generale
            Habet quisque speciale
                Styli privilegium,
            Quod praesignat in propheta
            Forma pictus sub discreta
                Vultus animalium."
Dante symbolises them as—
                    "*quattro animali*
            Coronato ciascun di verde fronda,"
Purgat. xxix. 93. The green leaves which crown the four living creatures are
emblems of the leaves of the Tree of Life.

[3] In the oldest mosaics the type is human (bearded), not angelic.

[4] According to some because St. Mark was specially the historian of the
Resurrection, and the mediaeval notion was that young lions were born dead
and vivified by the parent lion's roar in three days. Rupert of Deutz in
Apoc. iv., and Mark xvi. 16, connects it with the terribleness of this Gospel,
beginning with the voice "crying" (*rugiens*) in the wilderness, and ending
with a curse.

[5] The ox being the emblem of sacrifice.

light of immutable truth with a keen and steady ken." [1]
This, then, is why the Gospels are compared to the Vision
of the Four at the river of Chebar. "Like them the Gospels
are Four in number; like them they are the Chariot of God
Who sitteth between the Cherubim; like them, they bear
Him on a winged throne into all lands; like them, they move
wherever the Spirit guides them: like them they are mar-
vellously joined together, intertwined with coincidences and
differences; wing interwoven with wing, and wheel interwoven with wheel: like them they are full of eyes, and
sparkle with heavenly light: like them they sweep from
heaven to earth, and from earth to heaven, and fly with
lightning speed and with the noise of many waters. *Their
sound is gone out into all lands and their words to the end of
the world.*" [2]

Whatever may be the archaeological and artistic interest
of these universal symbols, it must be admitted that they
are fanciful and arbitrary; and this is rendered more obvious
from the varying manner in which they used to be employed
and justified. But as there is no element of mere fancy in
what has been already said as to the value of having four
Gospels, and as to the differences between St. John and the
three who had preceded him, so there will be none in the

---

[1] Aug. *De Consens. Evang.* i. The union of the four emblems into one
figure was called "the Tetramorph," or *Animal Ecclesiae.* Calvin, in a style
not usual with him, compares the Gospels to a four-horsed triumphal chariot
—the *quadriga* of Christ.

[2] Wordsworth, *Greek Test.*, The Four Gospels, p. xli. The first instance of
this symbolism is found in Irenaeus (*Adv. Haer.* iii. 11, s. 8), who, however,
assigns the eagle to St. Mark and the lion to St. John. St. Augustine assigns
the lion to St. Matthew, the man to St. Mark (*De Consens. Evang.* i. 6).
Pseudo-Athanasius again (*Synopsis Script.*) assigns the ox to St. Mark, the
lion to St. Luke. The distribution sanctioned by St. Jerome is that which has
finally prevailed. "Prima hominis facies Matthaeum significat qui quasi
de homine exorsus est scribere *Liber generationis Jesu Christi, filii David, filii
Abraham.* Secunda Marcum in quo vox leonis rugientis in eremo auditur
(Mark i. 3). Tertia Vituli quae Evangelistam Lucam a Zacharia sacerdote
initium sumpsisse praefigurat. Quarta Evangelistam Joannem qui assumtis
pennis aquilae, et ad altiora festinans, de Verbo Dei disputat." *Praef.
in Comment. Ev. Matth.* (See Lange, *Leben Jesu*, i. 156 ; Mrs. Jameson,
Sacred and Legendary Art, i. 132–143 ; Schaff, *Hist. of Christian Church*,
585–589.)

brief preliminary sketch which will now be given of the THE FOUR GOSPELS.
main characteristics of each separate Gospel.[1]

1. St. Matthew wrote in Judaea, and possibly wrote his
earliest sketch of the Discourses of Christ in the Jewish
language, though in that case, it is obvious for critical
reasons, that he must himself, at a later period, have translated his work into Greek. This very fact goes far to illustrate the specialities of his Gospel. It is the Gospel for
the Jews; it is the Gospel of the past; it is the Gospel of
Jesus as the Messiah. It is the Gospel which reflects the tone
of mind which prevailed in the Church of Jerusalem among
the " Hebrews of the Hebrews" headed by James the Lord's
brother, whose Epistle recalls most frequently the first Gospel,
especially its record of the Sermon on the Mount. That it is
the Gospel for the Jews appears in the very first words, " the
book of the generation of Jesus Christ the son of David, the
son of Abraham ";—the son of David, and therefore the heir to
the Jewish kingdom; the son of Abraham, and therefore the
heir of the Jewish promise. That it is the Gospel of the past
appears in the constant formula—the refrain as it were—
"that it might be fulfilled," which recurs on nearly every
page of the book. This Gospel contains no less than sixty-five
quotations from the Old Testament; nearly three times
more than those in any other Gospel. Even in the first
two chapters the Evangelist sees in five incidents of the
infancy of Jesus the fulfilment of five ancient prophecies.
Another point is that this Gospel is mainly didactic, being
marked by five great continuous discourses—the Sermon on v. vii.
the Mount; the Address to the Apostles; the Parables on x.
the "Kingdom of the Heavens," a Jewish phrase peculiar to
St. Matthew; the Discourse on the Church; and the Discourses xiii.
xviii.
on Judgment;—these discourses all bearing on the work of xxiii.-xxv.

[1] These generic peculiarities were very early noticed. Thus in the *Carmen*
of St. Gregory of Nazianzus we find :—

Ματθαῖος μὲν ἔγραψεν Ἑβραίοις θαύματα Χριστοῦ,
Μάρκος δ' Ἰταλίῃ, Λοῦκας Ἀχαιΐδι,
Πᾶσι δ' Ἰωάννης κῆρυξ μέγας οὐρανοφοίτης.

the Messiah as Lawgiver, as Judge, and as King. The Gospel of St. Matthew was then as it were "the ultimatum of Jehovah to His ancient people : recognise Jesus as your Messiah, or accept Him as your Judge."[1]

2. St. Mark is said to have written in Rome for Latins. It is a very natural supposition that when St. Peter was in his Roman prison, awaiting death, the Roman Christians asked Mark to preserve for them the great Apostle's reminiscences of the life of the Lord. Hence St. Mark's Gospel corresponds to the character of him who first made the great confession. It is the Gospel of the present; the Gospel for the practical Roman world; the Gospel of Jesus as Lord of human society. It is the Gospel which reflects the tone of mind prevalent in that moderate section of the Jewish-Christian Church of which St. Peter was the acknowledged head. So completely does the Evangelist represent the views of St. Peter that St. Peter's speech to Cornelius, in Acts x., has been called "the Gospel of St. Mark in a nutshell." If St. Matthew's is the didactic Gospel, or the Gospel of popular discourses, St. Mark's is the anecdotical; the Gospel of energetic incident.

It is a book of Apostolic memoirs,[2] and is marked by the graphic vividness which reflects the memory of an eye-witness. It is the Gospel which, apart from any special references to theology or to prophecy, simply describes in

---

[1] Godet, *Bible Studies*, Eng. Trans. p. 23. We shall see hereafter that St. Matthew's point of view is so little exclusive that he can admit passages which point to the evanescence of the law and the universality of the Gospel (ix. 16 ; xii. 7, 8 ; xiii. 31 *sq.* ; xxvii. 19, &c.). It should be carefully borne in mind that these characteristics are merely *general* and *relative*. It is not meant that the Evangelists represent our Blessed Lord *exclusively*, but only *predominantly*, under the aspects here mentioned. It must not be supposed that any one of the Evangelists wrote with a *deliberate* subjective bias. They dealt with facts not theories, and in no way altered those facts in the interests of any special view. They neither did, nor could, invent or create ; it was their sole duty to record. It is only from the *grouping* of facts, and from the prominence given to particular incidents or expressions throughout the several Gospels, that we deduce the ruling conceptions of the inspired writers. St. Augustine's expression that they wrote "ut quisque meminerat et ut cuique cordi erat" (*De Consens. Evang.* ii. 5) is not a very happy one.

[1] Ἀπομνημονεύματα, Just. Mart. *Dial.* 103.

brief and startling succession, our Lord's deeds as He lived, and moved among men.

3. St. Luke on the other hand wrote in Greece, for the bright, clever, affable Greek world. Hence his Gospel is in its language the most accurate, in its order the most historical and artistic.[1] It is the first volume of a great narrative, tracing the victorious advance of Christianity from Galilee to Jerusalem, from Jerusalem to Antioch, from Antioch on its westward course to Rome. It reflects the tone of mind which was prevalent in the school of St. Paul. It is the universal Gospel of the Gentile convert.[2] It does not deal with the yearnings of the past,[3] or with the glory of the present, but with the aspirations of the future.[4] It paints Christ's Gospel not as the fulfilment of Prophecy, or as "the Kingdom of the Age," but as the satisfaction of our moral cravings; it describes Jesus to us, not as the Jewish Messiah, or the Universal Lord, but as the Saviour of sinners. One of its keynotes is "My spirit hath rejoiced in God my Saviour." It is a Gospel, not national, but universal; not regal, but human. It is the Gospel, "cleansed from the leprosy of castes," and the blindness of limitations. It is the Gospel for sinners, for Samaritans, for Gentiles. It is "the revelation of divine mercy;" it is "the manifestation of divine philanthropy." It is Christianity for man.

4. It might then have been imagined that the three Synoptic Gospels had exhausted the possible aspects of dawning

[1] The word καθεξῆς, "in order," is peculiar to his writings.
[2] Hence he omits particulars (*e.g.* in the Sermon on the Mount) which would have been less intelligible to Greek readers, and substitutes Ἐπιστάτης or Διδάσκαλος ("Master" or "Teacher") for Rabbi; "lawyer" for "scribe;" "yea" or "verily" for "Amen;" the Greek φόρος for the Latin *census;* the *Lake* for the Sea of Galilee, &c.
[3] Thus St. Luke has only twenty-four Old Testament quotations as against sixty-five of St. Matthew, and (except iv. 18, 19) none which are peculiar to himself, except in the first two (i. 17-25, ii. 23, 24) and the 22nd and 23rd chapters (xxii. 37, xxiii. 31, 46).
[4] Yet St. Luke never excludes passages which speak of the spiritual perpetuity of the Law (xvi. 17) and obedience to it (ii. 22 sq., v. 14, &c.). See too i. 32, ii. 49, xix. 46, xxii. 30. This is of course due to the fact that the Evangelists were primarily faithful recorders, and were never led into dishonest suppression by party bias.

C

Christianity.   It might be asked what remains ?   One infinite thing remains, Eternity; the wants of the spiritual reason.   St. John drops the great keystone into the soaring arch of Christian revelation, when he represents Christ, neither as Messiah only, nor King only, nor even as Saviour only, but as the Incarnate Word ; as Christ, the Life and Light of men, the pre-existent and Eternal Son of God ; not only as the Son of Man who ascended into heaven, but as the Son of God, who descended from heaven to sanctify the world.   The whole circle of Gospel Revelation is as it were rounded into a flawless symbol of eternity, when St. John was inspired to write that " In the beginning was the Word, and the Word was with God, and the Word was God.   And the Word was made flesh, and dwelt among us, and we beheld His glory, the glory as of the only begotten of the Father, full of grace and truth."

We may thus sum up these large, though neither exclusive nor exhaustive generalisations.

St. Matthew wrote in Judaea for the Jews.   His is the Gospel of the Past, the Gospel which sees in Christianity a fulfilment of Judaism, the Gospel of discourses, the didactic Gospel, the Gospel in which Christ is represented to us as primarily the Messiah of the Jew.

St. Mark wrote in Italy for the Romans.   His is the Gospel of the Present; the Gospel of incident; the anecdotical Gospel; the Gospel which represents Christ as the strong Son of God and Lord of the World.

St. Luke wrote, perhaps in Corinth, for the Greeks.   His is the Gospel of the Future ; the Gospel of progressive Christianity ; the Gospel of Universal and free Salvation ; the Historic Gospel ; the Gospel for Sinners ; the Gospel of Jesus as the Good Physician and the Saviour of Mankind.

St. John wrote in Ephesus for all Christians.   His is preeminently the Gospel for the Church : the Gospel of Eternity ; the spiritual Gospel ; the Gospel for the devout and thought-

ful disciple; the Gospel of Christ as the Eternal Son, and
the Incarnate Word.

"Matthew," says Godet, "groups together doctrinal teachings in the form of great discourses; he is a preacher. Mark
narrates events as they occur to his mind; he is a chronicler.
Luke reproduces the external and internal development of
events; he is the historian properly so called." St. John, we
may add, gives the inmost spirit and meaning of the facts
which he narrates; he is the philosopher and the divine.

Now to make our conceptions of the different books of the
Bible clear and definite, and to fix them in our memories,
it is often very desirable, when it is possible, to choose for each
book one characteristic and typical phrase or sentence by
which it is definitely marked, and I think that we can do
this in the case of the four Gospels.

The characteristic phrase for St. Matthew is "*that the saying might be fulfilled,*" which occurs some thirteen times in
his Gospel; the inmost idea of his Gospel is expressed in the
sentences, "This is Jesus, the King of the Jews," and "I am
not come to destroy but to fulfil."

The central conception of Mark might be summed up by
"*Jesus Christ the Son of God,*" or "*What is this? A new
teaching!* With authority He commands even the unclean
spirits and they obey Him." A characteristic of the startling
rapidity and energetic brevity of his Gospel is furnished by
the words "*and immediately*" which occur in him no less
than forty-two times, whereas they occur but three times in
the much longer Gospel of St. John.

The sentences which we might choose as most characteristic
of the joyous and sympathetic tenderness of St. Luke, are
"*Who went about doing good,*" (Acts x. 38), or "*A Saviour
which is Christ the Lord*" (ii. 11.)[1]

---

[1] This verse describes the actual *work* of Jesus as set forth in the Gospel.
The general idea of the Gospel itself may be seen in i. 77. τοῦ δοῦναι γνῶσιν
σωτηρίας τῷ λαῷ αὐτοῦ ἐν ἀφέσει ἁμαρτιῶν αὐτῶν, and xxiv. 47, καὶ κηρυχθῆναι
ἐπὶ τῷ ὀνόματι αὐτοῦ μετάνοιαν καὶ ἄφεσιν ἁμαρτιῶν εἰς πάντα τὰ ἔθνη, ἀρξά-
μενον ἀπὸ Ἱερουσαλήμ.

The Gospels.

The motto for St. John—indicative of the depth of view which pervades all his Gospel—could only be the four most marvellous and epoch-making words ever written, words which concentrate into themselves long centuries of divine history and world-wide speculations, "*The Word became flesh.*"

The extent to which the differences which we have pointed out were felt and recognised is curiously illustrated by the preference given to one or other of the Gospels by different sects of heretics.

Thus, St. Matthew's Gospel was, as we might have expected, the favourite of the sects of Jewish Christians; of the Nazarenes, with their limited and imperfect conceptions of Christian truth, and the Ebionites, with their denial of the supernatural birth of Christ.

St. Mark was preferred by the followers of Cerinthus, the Docetae and other sects who made a distinction between the human Jesus and the Divine Christ.[1]

St. Luke's—or rather a mutilated version of it—was the chosen Gospel of the Marcionites, who were the most extravagant of the anti-Judaic followers of St. Paul.

St. John's Gospel, with its mystic depths, was the accepted Gospel of the Valentinians, and other philosophising Gnostic sects.

The four Gospels are meant to show us what Christ was, and what He meant us to be; and what the salvation was wherewith He saved us from sin, and from Satan, and from ourselves.

If we desire to realise their inner unity we must find it in ourselves. We shall need no further verification of their general testimony if we put on the new man which after Christ Jesus is created in righteousness and true holiness. When we have learnt to read those books aright we shall find their harmony in thoughts purified, in lives ennobled by the spirit of Christ. The glad tidings will help to dissipate our

[1] Iren. *Haer.* iii. 11, § 7.

sadness and brighten our discouragements. We shall look
upon ourselves more hopefully; and we shall look upon our
fellow men with more of patience and of tenderness, because
we shall then regard both ourselves and them in the light of
those words into which surely the spirit of all the four
Gospels may be compressed—as souls—"for whom Christ
died."

NOTE I.

THE ORIGIN OF THE GOSPELS.

THE FOUR
GOSPELS.

THE main phenomenon presented by the Synoptists, when we read them side by side, is the coexistence of minute resemblances with wide divergence.

a. The resemblances extend even to slight peculiarities of language such as the rare and dubious word ἐπιούσιος "daily" in the Lord's prayer; the use of the diminutive ὠτίον "little ear" (John xviii. 10; Matt. xxvi. 51; Luke xxii. 51); the curious adverb δυσκόλως to mean "with difficulty" (Matt. xix. 23; Mark x. 23: Luke xviii. 24); the irregular Doric form of the perfect passive ἀφέωνται (Matt. ix. 2; Mark ii. 5; Luke v. 20); the double augment in ἀπεκατεστάθη (Matt. xii. 13; Mark iii. 5; Luke vi. 10). Too much importance has been attached to these minute resemblances. The reading ἀφέωνται is in some MSS. replaced by ἀφίενται. Ἐπιούσιος is probably a Greek attempt to translate the Hebrew מָחָר (ἡ ἐπιοῦσα ἡμέρα "to-morrow," see Prov. xxvii. 1, LXX.); the double Doric augment in some tenses of ἀποκαθίστημι is widely diffused, and diminutives were common in Hellenistic Greek.

But apart from these minor resemblances, the same forms of expression constantly recur in passages which in other respects diverge considerably from each other. The verbal agreement is chiefly—to the extent of seven-eighths—in the report of words; the divergences are chiefly in the narratives. This is exactly what we should expect.

β. The differences extend to the transposition of whole sections; the omission of entire discourses; the insertion of long narratives; the statement of facts in a way which would lead to mistaken inferences unless such inferences were corrected by *data* derived from the other narrators.

These facts have been minutely examined. It has been ascertained by Stroud that "if the total contents of the several Gospels be represented by 100, the following table is obtained:

St. Mark	has	7	*peculiarities,*	and 93	*coincidences.*	
St. Matthew	„	42	„	„	58	„
St. Luke	„	59	„	„	41	„
St. John	„	92	„	„	8	„

Reuss has further calculated that the total number of verses *common* to all the Synoptists is about 330.; that St. Matthew has 350 verses peculiar to himself, St. Mark 68, and St. Luke 541. The coincidences are usually in the record of sayings : the peculiarities in the narrative portion. In St. Matthew, the narrative occupies about one fourth ; in St. Mark one half ; and in St. Luke one third. The instances of verbal coincidence between all the three Synoptists together are mostly in short sentences and are not very frequent.

Another important fact is that when St. Matthew and St. Luke verbally agree—which is chiefly in the words of Jesus—St. Mark always agrees with them ; that the resemblances between St. Luke and St. Mark are much closer than those between St. Luke and St. Matthew, but are not numerous, being only eight in all,[1] and mostly in short words of the Lord ; that where St. Mark has additional touches St. Luke usually has them also, but less seldom when additions are found only in St. Matthew ; and that where St. Mark is silent, St. Luke often differs from St. Matthew.

St. Luke and St. Mark agree most in the Galilean, and least in the Judean scene of the narrative. Their agreement chiefly is in short "words of the Lord" with the context that leads to them. But the agreement of St. Luke with St. Matthew is often for several consecutive sentences. To give the passages and details would occupy too much space. It is not often that *both* St. Luke and St. Matthew contain passages omitted by St. Mark (*e.g.* the Lost Sheep, Matt. xviii. 12—14; Luke xv. 4—7, and compare Matt. viii. 5 *sq.*, xxii. 1 *sq.* with Luke vii. 1 *sq.*, xiv. 15 *sq.*).

All the Evangelists have in common forty-seven sections. In St. Mark there are not more than twenty-four verses to which no parallel exists in St. Matthew and St. Luke.[2]

The best way to estimate the facts is to examine side by side the text of the Synoptists in any passage which they have in common, such as the Parable of the Wicked Husbandmen (Matt. xxi. 33—44 ; Luke xx. 9—18 ; Mark xii. 1—11), or the Transfiguration and the healing of the demoniac boy (Matt. xvii. 1—21 ; Mark ix. 1—27 ; Luke ix. 28—42). This may very easily be done by studying Rushbrooke's *Synopticon,* in which the matter common to all the Evangelists is printed in red ; the matter common to each pair in black spaced type ; and the matter peculiar to each in ordinary type. The examination will at once illustrate the extraordinary complexity of the problem to be solved. It will reveal the existence of apparent discrepancies intersecting resemblances,

---

[1] Marsh. Renan says : " Les détails que Matthieu ajoute à Marc, Luc ne les a pas ; ce que Luc semble ajouter à Matthieu Marc l'a toujours. Dans les passages qui manquent chez Marc il y a chez Luc une autre recension que chez Matthieu."—*Les Évangiles,* 258.

[2] Westcott *Introd.* ; Schaff. *Hist. of Christian Church,* p. 595.

and of diversities interlacing agreements in every possible variety. It will at the same time leave on every candid mind an irresistible impression that we are reading the truthful narrative of one and the same story by different witnesses, modified only by the individuality, the keenness of observation, and the retentiveness of memory of the narrators.[1]

The various theories which have been invented to account for these facts have been elaborately discussed. They are

1. The "borrowing" theory, or theory of inter-dependence, supported by Eichhorn, Marsh and others, which supposes that one or two of the Evangelists directly borrowed from the other. It was, for instance, long supposed that St. Mark was, as St. Augustine calls him, only an abbreviator and "pedissequus" of St. Matthew. Each of the Evangelists in turn has been regarded as the source from which the others borrowed. Every such theory has broken down under the weight of the accumulated absurdities which it involves.

2. The "Primitive Gospel" theory. It has been supposed that there was some earlier edition—a Proto-Marcus or other Proto-Evangelist— in a form different from our canonical Gospels. Every possible modification of this view has now been abandoned as absolutely untenable. Each theory of the kind requires as many subordinate hypotheses of early editions, later recensions, translations, &c., as the Ptolemaic system of astronomy required orbs and epicycles to account for its theory of the motions of the heavenly bodies.[2]

3. The "Tendency" hypothesis of the Tübingen school, which held

---

[1] Other passages which may most profitably be contrasted are Matt. xxi. 33—44. Mark xii. 1—11. Luke xx. 9—18, or we may compare only single verses, such as :

Matt. xxviii. 7.	Mark xvi. 7.	Luke xxiv. 6.
——— iii. 5.	—— i. 5.	—— iii. 3.
——— xix. 16.	—— x. 17.	—— xviii. 18.

or verses common to two Synoptists (*e.g.* Mark viii. 19, Luke viii. 14 ; or Matt. xiv. 4, Mark vi. 19). It would take a volume to tabulate the results : but by means of such inquiries carried out with the aid of Rushbrooke's *Synopticon*, it seems possible to recover the "Triple Tradition" common to the three—the original and almost continuous narrative which they alike utilised, and which began at the preaching of the Baptist. Dr. Abbott (*Encycl. Brit.* Art. Gospels) as the outcome of such inquiries, regards it as demonstrable that (1) St. Mark did not copy from St. Matthew or St. Luke ; and (2) that St. Matthew and St. Luke may have been influenced by some original form of St. Mark, or of the original tradition which he used.

[2] One specimen may suffice to illustrate the complexity of those arbitrary guesses. Scholten (if I understand his view rightly) supposes a Proto-Mark. followed by our present St. Mark (Deutero-Mark), and a Trito-Matthew, which is our St. Matthew ! But as though this were not enough he supposes that the Proto-Marcus was a sketch by John Mark, which combined a Deutero-Matthew with the *Logia* of Matthew (a supposed collection of "sayings," v. *infra*), and that these *Logia* were in five series ! (see more in Hilgenfeld, *Einleit.* 455). Are such fancies worth refuting, or even worth recording ?

that each of the Gospels was a history modified in the interest of party opinion from some primitive Aramaic source, which is conjectured to have been an early form of the Gospel according to the Hebrews.[1] The ordinary form of the Tübingen theory is that St. Matthew's Gospel is a combination of an Aramaic with a more liberal document; that St. Luke's is a Pauline protest supplemented from Ebionite sources; and that St. Mark copied from both !

4. These hypotheses have little or nothing in their favour, nor do they account adequately for the facts before us. They assume that the Evangelists altered each other's narratives often for the worse, often by changes which would have been to the last degree meaningless and trivial. They depend on the impossible and irreverent assumption that each of the Synoptists felt himself at liberty to alter, or to omit, or to transpose, and in multitudes of ways to manipulate not the facts only of the life of Christ, but even the words which He uttered. Even the Rabbis laid down the rule (*Shabbath*, f. 15, i.) that it was the duty of a pupil to reproduce to the utmost of his ability the *ipsissima verba* of his teachers, lest from any mistake or alteration he should confuse the *Halacha*, or established precedent and opinion, to which appeal was made. It is inconceivable that the Evangelists, if they had any of the Canonical Gospels, or any other faithful record in their hands, should have felt themselves at liberty to subject the sayings and actions of their Master to a process of dogmatic adaptation. Such a theory explains nothing, and accounts for nothing. To mention none of the other difficulties (which are suggested by every page) is it conceivable that the Synoptists, if they had access to each other's writings, should have given different genealogies of Christ, different versions of the Lord's prayer, different formulae of the institution of the Eucharist, even different forms of the inscription on the cross ?

5. The general conclusions to which all recent inquiries seem to point and which are now most widely accepted, are that:

i. There existed—as there naturally must have existed—in the early Church a cycle of authoritative oral tradition, which had become fixed by constant repetition in the preaching of different Apostles. It represented all that they most vividly remembered, or considered most immediately important in the life and teaching of their Lord. This memory of fundamental facts sufficed all the early churches founded by St. Paul.[2] "La tradition vivante," says Renan (ζῶσα φωνὴ καὶ μένουσα) · "était le grand réservoir où tous puisaient."[3] "The eternal youth of the word of Christ," says Holtzmann, "was manifested by the fact that for a

---

[1] This is in the main the view of Baur, Schwegler, Ritschl, Volkmar, Hilgenfeld, Köstlin, Davidson.

[2] It should be borne in mind that in that age and in the East men were trained to rely on memory to a far greater extent than in modern times.

[3] *Les Évangiles*, p. 96.

century it passed through the world of human thought, preserved only by oral tradition, yet unweakened in essence, and still maintaining its freshness and originality."[1] "So full of grace were His lips," Origen had said, seventeen centuries earlier, "that brief as was the period during which He taught, yet the whole world has been filled with His faith and doctrine." [2]

ii. This authoritative tradition, retained for a time in the strong memories of those who frequently heard it, was gradually committed to writing by some of the disciples for the use of wider circles. Earliest among such narratives (διηγήσεις) and utterances would be the genealogy of Christ, His miracles, His discourses, briefer sayings and eschatological prophecies.

iii. These written memorials were early used by those who, more or less unsuccessfully, first attempted to set forth a continuous sketch of the ministry of Christ.

iv. The most authentic and valuable of such attempts were to a certain extent utilised in the narratives of the Evangelists. This is certain. It would be an absolute absurdity to maintain that the many verbal coincidences between the Synoptists could be accounted for except on the supposition that they had access to common sources of information.

6. This hypothesis has three considerations in its favour.

a. It corresponds with the manner in which other sacred writings have originated in ancient days. "Plus un souvenir est grand et sacre," says De Pressensé, "plus il se grave profondément." [3]

β. It comes nearest to the oldest tradition on the subject in the Church as recorded by Papias.[4] Eusebius agrees with him in saying that the work of the Apostles was to preach and to bear witness, and that they paid but little attention to the composition of books.[5]

γ. It closely follows the remarkable facts mentioned by St. Luke in the preface to his Gospel. St. Luke tells us that when he undertook to write his Gospel he found "many" narratives (διηγήσεις) of the life of Christ and the origin of Christianity already in existence. These failed to satisfy him. They were "attempts," and as he implies, inadequate

---

[1] *Protestanten Bibel* (E. T. i. 35). In saying "for a century," he means that (as we see from the remark of Papias, *ap.* Euseb. *H. E.* iii. 24) tradition subsisted till the middle of the second century, side by side with written narratives.

[2] Origen, *De Princip.* iv. 5. Our Lord Himself predicted the vitality of this oral tradition (Matt. xxiv. 14, 34 ; xxvi. 13).

[3] *Hist. des trois prem. Siècles*, ii. 81.

[4] See the remarkable passage of Papias, preserved by Eusebius (*H. E.* iii. 39).

[5] Σπουδῆς τῆς περὶ τὸ λογογραφεῖν μικρὰν ποιούμενοι φροντίδα, Euseb. *H. E.* iii. 24. St. John in his second Epistle (v. 12) purposely puts off writing (οὐκ ἠβουλήθην διὰ χαρτοῦ καὶ μέλανος (γράφειν)) because he prefers to deliver his message orally.

attempts. They professed, indeed, to represent the "tradition" delivered by those who had been "from the beginning eye-witnesses and ministers of the word," but St. Luke felt himself compelled to offer to Theophilus something more perfect. Besides his knowledge and use of this sacred tradition he had made careful investigations of the whole history from the beginning (παρηκολουθηκότι ἄνωθεν πᾶσιν ἀκριβῶς) in order that his friend might fully know (ἵνα ἐπιγνῷς) the actual and certain facts (τὴν ἀσφάλειαν) about all the truths in which he had already been orally instructed. Christ had not commanded His Apostles to write, but to preach. The Gospels were produced to meet a more and more imperious necessity. The same impulse and the same reasonings which weighed with St. Luke may well have influenced the other Evangelists at nearly the same time. That St. Luke did not include these Gospels among the "attempts" with which he was dissatisfied, and indeed that he was not acquainted with them, though he had recourse to traditions and documents which they also had incorporated, is clear from every page of his Gospel.

7. If then this hypothesis of a fixed oral tradition gradually reduced to writing, be insufficient to account for the differences and resemblances of the Evangelists, it is at least certain that no more reasonable suggestion has yet been made.[1]

The Four Gospels superseded all others and won their way into universal acceptance by their intrinsic value and authority.[2] After "so many salutary losses"[3] we still possess a rich collection of Apocryphal Gospels, and, if they serve no other good purpose, they have this value, that they prove for us undoubtedly the unique and transcendent superiority of the sacred records. These bear the stamp of absolute truthfulness, all the more decisively when placed in contrast with writings which show signs of wilful falsity. We escape from their "lying magic" to find support and help in the genuine Gospels. "And here we take refuge with the greater confidence because the ruins which lie around the ancient archives of the Church look like a guarantee of the enduring strength and greatness of those archives themselves."[4]

[1] This is the view which has been adopted in the main by Herder, Gieseler, (who first developed it in 1818) Schulz, Credner, Lange, Ebrard, Thiersch, Norton, Alford, Renan, Godet, Westcott, Schaff, Weiss, and Archbishop Thomson.
[2] "Multi conati sunt scribere Evangelia, sed non omnes recepti," Orig. *Hom. in Luc.*
[3] Keim, *Jesu of Nazara*, i. 45 (E. T.)
[4] Keim, i. 45.

NOTE II.

STYLE, AND DIFFERENT BOOKS OF THE NEW TESTAMENT.

THE FOUR
GOSPELS.

One of the greatest modern stylists has said that there are at least five different styles in the New Testament. Under this head he ranks together

     1. Matthew. Mark. The Apocalypse.
     2. Luke and the Acts.
     3. General Epistles of St. Paul. Hebrews. 1 Peter.
     4. James. Jude. 2 Peter. Pastoral Epistles.
     5. The writings of John.

There is much insight in the remark, though it is open to criticism. But adds M. Renan, what constitutes (in this point of view) the strength of all these writings is that they are written in Greek but conceived in Aramaic. The absoluteness of Old Testament idiom, in which there are no *nuances*, in which all is black or white, shade or sunshine, which instead of saying " I preferred Jacob to Esau," says " Jacob have I loved and Esau have I hated," retains in the New Testament also its startling and overwhelming energy and fascination.

THE GOSPEL ACCORDING TO ST. MATTHEW.

"The book of the generation of Jesus Christ, the son of David, the son of Abraham."—MATT. i. 1.

1. WHEN we desire to know something about a book our first question is, "Who wrote it?" Fortunately we know that the author of the Gospel which stands first in our New Testament was the apostle St. Matthew. We are told but little about him personally. He was a son of Alphaeus, a brother of James the Little ; possibly, as criticism has conjectured, a brother of St. Thomas called Didymus, whose name means "the twin"; possibly, as tradition has said, a kinsman of our Lord according to the flesh. The Gospels, not excepting his own, record nothing about him except his call and his farewell feast.[1] He had been a publican; that is, he had held the low and despised office of collector of the taxes imposed by the conquering Romans on his oppressed fellow-countrymen.[2]

That office was all the baser because of its gainfulness. It was usually stained with dishonesty. In a Jew it bore the stigma of unpatriotic subservience to an alien

---

[1] Matt. ix. 10. The modest reticence of the Evangelist appears in his suppression of his share in this feast. Comp. Luke v. 29.

[2] Herod Antipas may perhaps have been allowed to collect his own taxes, and Matthew may have thought himself comparatively justified in serving as a revenue officer to a semi-Jewish king. On the other hand, as Herod had to pay tribute to the Romans, the discredit which the office attached to a faithful theocratic Jew was just the same ; and it is clear that the tax-collectors were as much detested in Galilee as everywhere else.

ST. MATTHEW. oppression. From a position thus sordid and despised
one word of Christ redeemed him. Touched by the
Matt. viii. 19, Ithuriel spear of His Master's love, he sprang up from a
20. tax-gatherer into an apostle. He who rejected the scribe
accepted the publican, and enabled the subservient
Matt. ix. 11. official to work side by side with the flaming zealot.
One farewell feast, to his old companions, on a Pharisaic fast-
Matt. ix. 10. day—a feast in which the guests were so numerous as to
Mark ii. 15. prove that St. Matthew had something to lose by the abandonment of his functions—and then, forsaking all, he followed
Christ. It is he alone who has appended to his own name
the opprobrious addition of " Matthew the publican."[1] He
need not have done so, for Matthew was a new name. His
old name had been Levi. Matthew means " the gift of
God."[2] The old name Levi had been abandoned with the
old profession.[3] In that single word, " the publican " (x. 3),
and in the absolute suppression of his own personality
throughout the Gospel, we see the deep humility of the
Evangelist. Not one incident, not one question, of his is
recorded. He occupied a very retiring and humble position
in the apostolic band. Tradition only records one saying of
his and one fact about him. The traditional fact is that he
lived the life of an ascetic, on herbs and water.[4] The saying
is that when the neighbour of an elect man sins, he himself
has sinned; for had he lived as the Word commands, his

[1] It has been fancied that St. Matthew shows traces of the matters which
formerly occupied his attention in the use of the word " tribute-money " not
" penny " in xxii. 17—22, and in recording the miracle of the stater.

[2] Ματθαῖος is the Greek form of מַתִּי, shortened from מַתִּתְיָה (perhaps
another form of Amittai, Jonah i. 1) Θεόδωρος. Mattathias, 1. Macc. ii. 1.
Matthias, Acts i. 23.

[3] The identification of Matthew with Levi (Matt. ix. 9, x. 3. Mark ii. 14.
Luke v. 27) has indeed been questioned (what has not been questioned ?),
but it has been all but unanimously accepted from the earliest ages. The chief
exceptions are the Valentinian Herakleon (Chem. Alex. *Strom.* iv. 9, 73) ;
Origen (*c. Cels.* i. 62), Grotius, Michaelis, de Wette, and Ewald (*Christus*, pp.
289, 321).

[4] Ματθαῖος μὲν οὖν ὁ ἀπόστολος σπερμάτων καὶ ἀκροδρύων καὶ λαχάνων ἄνευ
κρεῶν μετελάμβανε. Chem. Alex. *Paed.* ii. 1, p. 16. If so this manner of
life seems to have been adopted in later days (see Matt. ix. 10—14, Matthew's
feast).

neighbours would have so reverenced him as to refrain from sin. These traditional particulars have no intrinsic improbability. It was believed in the early Church that certain ascetic or half-Essene tendencies existed in the circle of our Lord's earthly relatives. We see a certain general resemblance between the Judaic sternness and simplicity of James, "the Lord's brother," and of St. Matthew. The sternness is illustrated by the fact that in this Gospel the idea of punishment and retribution is more prominent than in the others.[1] As to the death or labours of St. Matthew we know nothing. It is said that he went forth from Jerusalem as a missionary;[2] but whither he went—whether to Æthiopia or to Parthia—is uncertain; nor is it known whether he died peacefully, or whether he won the martyr's crown.[3]

2. But out of this life, so discredited in its youth, so unrecorded in its manhood, there flowed a most memorable service—the first Gospel. He thus lived to confer an eternal benefit on that Church of God, which he alone of the Evangelists has mentioned by that name.[4] It is not the only instance in which one who seems to have lived much alone with God and his own soul has, like John Tauler or Thomas à Kempis, embalmèd in one brief book the inmost fragrance of a blessed spirit, to last for a life beyond life.

3. His comparative obscurity, his unpopular profession, help to make his authorship more indisputable. No forger

---

[1] See Matt. vii. 13, 23, 42; xviii. 34, 35; xxii. 13; xxiii. 33; xxiv. 50, 51; xxv. 30, 46.

[2] Euseb. *H. E.* iii. 24; v. 10; Socrates, *H. E.* i. 19.

[3] Herakleon (*ap.* Clem. Alex. *l. c.*) excepts from the number of martyrs Matthew, Philip, Thomas, Levi and many others. In all western works of art he is represented as being slain by the sword. Greek artists uniformly exhibit him as dying in peace, while an angel swings the censer beside his bed; as on the ancient dome of San Paolo at Rome. (Mrs. Jameson.) As to his missionary labours, Eusebius only says that he went ἐφ' ἑτέρους. Eusebius and Jerome have nothing to add to this. Macedonia, Persia, &c., are only specified by later writers, till at last, Nicephorus Callistus (in 1350) specifies the Anthropophagi!

[4] Ἐκκλησία. Matt. xvi. 18; xviii. 17. The fact that this word, so common in the Epistles, where it occurs 112 times, should occur here only in the Gospels, like the fact that the title "Son of Man," so common in the Gospels, is not found in the Epistles, is an interesting but entirely undesigned coincidence, which throws light on the purpose, age, and credibility of the Gospels.

ST. MATTHEW. would have attributed his work to one whose name belonged
to the least distinguished among the Apostles. It would
have been natural to forge an Epistle of St. Peter; no one
would have thought of an Epistle of St. Matthew. And yet
antiquity is unanimous in the belief, both that he wrote this
Gospel,[1] and that he wrote it originally in Aramaic, for his
own countrymen.[2] If so, the Aramaic original has perished[3]
and the Greek translation must, for almost undoubted critical
reasons, have come from the hands of the Apostle himself.[4]

The Gospel of St. Matthew was, in all probability, the
earliest of the four.[5] It is natural to suppose that when the
demand for a written Gospel had arisen, the Church would
desire to possess such a document from the pen of an actual
Apostle. Silent, observant, faithful, belonging to the Lord's
own friends and relations, familiar with the art of writing by
the necessities of his trade, and not otherwise prominently

---

[1] Credner, Volkmar and others, argue that "the Gospel according to (κατά)
Matthew" does not imply direct authorship; but their view is disproved by
usage (Bleek, *Einleitung*, 87; De Wette, § 78), Hilgenfeld (*Einleitung*, 149),
shows that the phrase implies that the one Gospel was set forth in four
Gospels. Thus in 2 Macc. ii. 13, the Book of Nehemiah is referred to as
κατὰ Νεεμίαν, and Epiphanius (*Haer.* viii. 4) has ἡ κατὰ Μωϋσέα Πεντάτευχος.
It is not impossible that the office of St. Matthew involved a familiarity with
the art of writing, and with other forms of literary activity.

[2] This is asserted by Papias (*ap.* Euseb. *H. E.* iii. 39): Irenaeus (*Haer.* iii.
1, s. 1); Origen (*ap.* Euseb. vi. 25); Eusebius (*H. E.* v. 8); Jerome (*De Virr.
illustr.* 3); Cyril of Jerusalem (*Catech.* xiv. 5); Epiphanius (*Haer.* xxx. 3,
li. 3), &c. It is now generally believed (α) that the Greek style of the book, in
spite of the Hebraic colouring which it has in common with nearly all the
books of the New Testament; and (β) the use of the LXX. in the majority of
the quotations, prove our present Greek Gospel to have been an original.
Keim and others suppose that Papias and all who followed him may have
been led into confusion by the existence of the "Gospel of the Hebrews"
which mainly agreed with the narrative of Matthew. See the note at the end
of this discourse.

[3] There would be nothing very extraordinary about this fact. Josephus tells
us that he first wrote his *Antiquities* in Aramaic.

[4] The Greek figure *paronomasia* occurs twice (vi. 16; xxi. 41). It is noticeable too that in the Gospel to the Hebrews the Holy Ghost is feminine ("my
mother the Holy Ghost") because the Hebrew רוּחַ is feminine; but there is
nothing of this kind in St. Matthew.

[5] Ep. Barnab. iv. vii. Iren. *Haer.* i. 26, § 2; iii. 1, §. 1. Euseb. *H. E.*
iii. 27. Origen, *ap.* Euseb. *H. E.* vi. 25. Cerinthus (*circ.* A.D. 110) used the
Gospel (Epiphan. *Haer.* xxx. 14), as also Clement, Hermas, Justin, &c. And
this view is accepted even by Schwegler, Strauss, Hilgenfeld, Keim, &c.
Irenaeus (*Haer.* iii. 1) dates it A.D. 61—64, which is probably a little too early.

engaged in apostolic work, St. Matthew may have been
specially marked out for that high task. He may have
undertaken it when twelve years had elapsed after the death
of Christ. At that time the Apostles—in accordance with a
command which (as tradition says) they had received from the
Lord—began to disperse from Jerusalem to make disciples in
all the world.[1] The written words would supply the void left
by their absence from the Holy City.[2]

And his Gospel is one of pre-eminent importance. We
have already seen that of the entire materials of the evangelic history, two-fifths are common to the Synoptists.
Only one-third of the materials belongs to the others individually and peculiarly. But St. Matthew's Gospel, which is
nearly as long as St. Luke's, contains fourteen entire sections
which are found in him alone. These sections, moreover, are
of the deepest interest. Among the forty-two peculiarities
are ten parables,[3] two miracles,[4] four events of the Infancy,[5]
seven incidents connected with the Passion and Resurrection,[6]
and not a few great passages in our Lord's discourses.[7] Indeed, it is the prominence of our Lord's discourses in St.
Matthew that makes it characteristically "the didactic
Gospel," so that one-fourth of the whole is taken up with

[1] The tradition is first found in the *Preaching of Peter* quoted by Clement
of Alexandria (*Strom.* vi. § 43), and is alluded to by Apollonius (A.D. 180) *ap.*
Euseb. *H. E.* v. 18.

[2] Euseb. *H. E.* iii. 24.

[3] The Tares ; the Hid Treasure ; the Pearl ; the Drawnet (xiii. 24—50) ; the
Unmerciful Servant (xviii. 23—35) ; the Labourers in the Vineyard (xx. 1—16) ;
the Two Sons (xxi. 28—32) ; the Marriage of the King's Son (xxii. 1—14) ;
the Ten Virgins (xxv. 1—13) ; the Talents (xxv. 14—30.)

[4] The Cure of Two Blind Men (ix. 27—31) ; The Stater (xvii. 24—27.)

[5] The Magi ; the Massacre of the Infants ; the Flight into Egypt ; the
return to Nazareth.

[6] The Bargain, and Suicide of Judas ; the Dream of Pilate's wife ; the
departed saints who rose ; the watch at the sepulchre ; the story of the Sanhedrin ; the earthquake on Easter morning.

[7] Ten in all. Parts of Sermon on Mount (v.—vii.) ; the revelation to babes ;
the invitations to the weary (xi. 25—30) ; about Idle Words (xii. 36—37) ; the
prophecy to Peter (xvi. 17—19) ; on Humility and Forgiveness (xviii. 15—35) ;
Rejection of the Jews (xxi. 43) ; the Great Denunciation (xxiii.) ; the Eschatological Discourse (xxv. 31-46) ; the Great Commission and promise (xxviii.
18—20). Hence the frequency of such phrases as "And when Jesus finished
these sayings" (vii. 28 ; xi. 1 ; xiii. 53 ; xix. 1 ; xxvi. 1).

the actual words and sermons of the Son of Man. Meanwhile these minute analyses have established the great result that the Evangelists are, as witnesses, independent of each other, and that as each gave his own testimony in his own way, they weave the separate strands of that fourfold cord of evidence by which the Church is moored to the living Rock of truth.

4. The next question which we ask about a book is, "When was it written?" When we remember that we owe exclusively to the Gospels our knowledge of the life and death of our Saviour Christ; when we recall that our faith centres in a Person and that the Gospels are our sole narrative of His life, we see how much it imports us to know at what date they were penned.[1] Had the records of the life of Jesus, like those of the life of Buddha, been only written long centuries after His death, we could feel no security as to their faithfulness. Tradition may last unimpaired for a generation, but after that time it becomes obliterated and confused. The divine features of our Saviour's life would have been blurred, as in the Apocryphal Gospels, by all kinds of false and puerile traditions, if they had not been committed to writing before the eye-witnesses were dead. We may thank God for the certainty that the three first Gospels, like every other book of the New Testament, even the Gospel and Epistles of St. John, were written in the same generation which had witnessed the death of Christ, crucified as He was in early manhood.[2]

---

[1] Other sources, whether Pagan or Apocryphal, or Oriental, or early Christian, have not preserved for us a single fact. At the best, a few of the unrecorded sayings (ἄγραφα δόγματα) are possibly genuine, as is certainly that preserved by St. Paul (Acts xx. 35). They are deeply interesting, and have often been collected, as by Fabricius, *Cod. Apocr. N. T.* i. 32; Grabe *Spicileg.* i. 12; Körner, *De Sermonibus Christi* ἀγράφοις, 1776; Hess. *Leben Jesu,* ii. 553; Westcott, *Introd. Append.* C. The three most interesting and well-attested of the traditional sayings are, "Show yourselves approved money-changers." (Origen, *in Joann.* xix.) "He who wonders shall reign, and he who reigns shall rest." (Clem. Alex. *Strom.* ii. 9, § 45.) "Near Me near the fire. Far from Me far from the Kingdom." (Origen *in Jer.* iii.). There are interesting traditions in the *Codex Bezae* (D) added to Matt. xx. 28. Luke vi. 4.

[2] It is interesting to notice that the title "Son of Man" is recorded eighty-four times in the Gospels. It is the human, the Messianic title, which

Fortunately the epoch of the Old Dispensation was closed by an event so stupendous that it completely revolutionised the religious history of Judaism, and fundamentally affected the thoughts of Christians. That event, of which the results are still unexhausted, was the Fall of Jerusalem. Had that catastrophe preceded the writing of the Synoptic Gospels and the Epistles of St. Paul, nothing is more certain than that it must have been directly mentioned, and that it must have exercised an immense influence on the thoughts and feelings of the Apostles and Evangelists. No writer, dealing with the topics and arguments and prophecies with which they are constantly occupied, could possibly have failed to appeal to the tremendous sanction which had been given to all their views by God Himself, who thus manifested His Providence in human history, and showed all things by the quiet light of inevitable circumstances.[1] It may then be regarded as certain—it is indeed, admitted by many sceptical critics—that the Gospels were, and from their own internal evidence must have been, published before A.D. 70, and therefore within forty years after our Lord's crucifixion. It is scarcely possible to exaggerate the importance of this fact in estimating the evidences of historic religion. If we had not possessed the records of any who were actually contemporaries of our Lord Jesus, imagine how intense would have been our desire to see such records. Scholars have sometimes regretted that there is no extant account of Socrates from the pen of Kebes or one of his less gifted disciples. But the importance of Socrates is absolutely infinitesimal, even in a purely historic point of

---

Jesus gave to Himself. Nothing is more natural than the fact that it is used to describe our Lord *in the Gospels only.*

[1] Such passages as Matt. v. 35 ; xxii. 7 ; xxiii. 2–34 ; xxiv. 2 ; ("The Holy City," "The Holy Place," "The City of the Great King" &c.) could not have been written after the destruction of Jerusalem. The whole of Chapter xxiv. implies expectations which were indeed fulfilled, and fulfilled in the sense intended, but in a sense very different from that which was understood by the early Christians, or anticipated by the Evangelists and Apostles. See especially xxiv. 15 ; again, such passages as xvi. 28 ; xxiii. 36, 39 ; xxiv. 34 ; xxvi. 64 ; xxvii. 8 ; xvii. 24, are certain proofs that the Gospel was written before A.D. 70.

view, in comparison with the importance of the Christ. Had we not possessed the Gospels we should certainly have been willing to sacrifice whole libraries, nay, whole languages and literatures, in exchange for authentic details, attested by contemporary evidence, of the human life of Him " whose bleeding hand lifted the gates of the centuries off their hinges," and whose words and deeds have stirred to their inmost depths the hearts of men—yes, even of those who believe not on Him.[1]

But here, in the Gospel of St. Matthew, we have the very treasure which we should have so ardently desired. St. Mark was not an Apostle ; St. Luke was not an Apostle. We have reason to believe that they represent the testimonies respectively of St. Peter and St. Paul; but we do not know to what extent St. Mark was an eye-witness, and St. Luke implies that he was not personally an eye-witness at all. St. John, indeed, had lived in the closest intimacy with Jesus; but his Gospel was not so much intended for a record of external facts. But in St. Matthew's Gospel we have a sketch of the life of Christ—and probably the earliest of them—by one who was perhaps the kinsman of Jesus; certainly His Apostle; certainly one of His chosen Twelve ; certainly one of those who had lived in His nearest intimacy ;—by one who had walked and talked with Him in the fields of Galilee, and on the slopes of Olivet ; one who had sat with Him in the synagogue, and sailed with Him in the boat, and prayed with Him under the star-lit sky; one who had seen and heard, and his hands had handled the Word of Life :—and that which he had seen and heard declares he unto us.

And we must count it as a distinct blessing—a circum-

---

[1] Thus Strauss speaks of Christ as something unique, and says "Never at any time will it be possible to rise above Him, nor to imagine any one who should even be equal with Him." Goethe calls him, "the Divine Man, the Saint, the type and model of all men." Channing says, "I believe Jesus Christ to be a more than human being." Renan says, "Between thee and God there is no longer any distinction." J. S. Mill says that there is no better rule than "so to live that Christ would approve our life." Similar testimonies might be indefinitely multiplied. Some of them I have quoted in my Hulsean Lectures on *The Witness of History to Christ.*

stance in which we see the Providence of God—that there st. matthew is no trace whatever that St. Matthew was naturally a highly-gifted man. The glory of his Gospel consists in the inherent glory of the divine events which it was his high mission to narrate. We have already seen that not an act, not a sentence, not a question of his own, is recorded in any of the Gospels. So far as we are aware, he did not possess, either before or after the Crucifixion, a particle of special, still less of preponderant, influence in the apostolic band. His call is mentioned, and after that he is in no way distinguishable from the mass of his brother-Apostles. He was present at Pentecost, and thenceforth he disappears altogether from the pages of New Testament history. We do not know either where he lived, or what he did, or when or how he died. For the world the significance of his life is simply concentrated in his authorship of the Gospel. His writings do not show a trace of that glorious and indefinable quality for which there cannot be found any other name than genius. For the Church it is a happy circumstance that neither he, nor Apostles ten times more gifted than he, had the ability to invent the words, so inexhaustible in their profundity, the character so divine in its power, which on this earth have belonged to Christ alone. On every page of St. John's writings we do see the marks of an individual genius, unique and indisputable. This very circumstance has led many sceptics to discredit his testimony, and depreciate the historic value of his Gospel. They have seen in him a writer who had the high capacity to modify or even in some measure to originate. No such suspicion has ever attached to the Gospel of the less gifted Publican. He gives us exactly what we most needed: he could be a simple and faithful narrator, and he aims at nothing more.

5. We know then who wrote the Gospel, and when; but why did he write it? Every book worth calling a book is written with an object; what is the object of the Gospel of St. Matthew? If the book be part of a revelation, what

does it reveal? We have seen that it is infinitely valuable as a record of Christ's life and work by one who knew Him. But how does it differ from the other Gospels? What was the special conception of the Evangelist? Under what distinct aspect does he represent the Lord of Life?

6. Even apart from unanimous tradition, we should see at a glance that he wrote mainly for his own countrymen.[1] It was plainly his object—his " one literary passion"—to connect the Law with the Gospel; to fling an illuminated bridge of inspired truth between the Old and the New Dispensations; to connect the memories of his readers with their hopes; to show that the Lord of the Christian was the Messiah of the Jew.[2] This Gospel, as we have already seen, is the Gospel in relation to the Past; the Gospel represented as the fulfilment of the long ages of Prophecy; the Gospel designed to prove to the Hebrews, and to all the world, that no chasm of discontinuity separated the New Age from the days of the Fathers. It was a most noble and necessary design thus to show that all Revelation was one unimpeded progress in knowledge and broadening of the light. This Gospel was the eternal witness against those heretical Christians who, like the Marcionites and many Gnostic sects, strove to dissever themselves wholly from the God who had revealed Himself of old time to patriarchs and prophets. It was St. Matthew's task to show that in the Old Testament the New was prefigured, and in the New Testament the Old was revealed. He might have used the words quoted by the old Carthusian monk in answer to the frivolous youth who asked him how he had managed to get through his life, " Cogitavi

---

[1] Τοῖς ἀπὸ Ἰουδαϊσμοῦ πιστεύσασιν. Orig. ap. Euseb. *H. E.* vi. 25, The word "lawlessness" (ἀνομία) occurs four times in St. Matthew (vii. 23; xiii. 41; xxiii. 28; xxiv. 12), but in no other Gospel. The comparison of Mark vii. 3, 4, with Matt. xv. 1, 2, illustrates the difference between one who wrote for Romans and one who wrote for Jews.

[2] This was noticed as early as the days of Irenaeus. τὸ κατὰ Ματθαῖον εὖ πρὸς Ἰουδαίους ἐγράφη οὗτοι γὰρ ἐπεθύμουν πάνυ σφόδρα ἐκ σπέρματος Δαβὶδ Χριστόν. Ὁ δὲ Ματθαῖος ἔτι μᾶλλον σφοδροτέραν ἔχων τοιαύτην ἐπιθυμίαν παντοίως ἔσπευδε πληροφορίαν παρέχειν αὐτοῖς (cd. Stieren's *Iren. fr.* xxix).

dies antiquos, et annos aeternos in mente habui"—"I have considered the days of old, and the years of ancient times."

7. These are not mere theories. St. Matthew alone calls Jerusalem the "Holy City," and the "Holy Place," and the "City of the great King." Seven times he calls our Lord "the Son of David." He derives His genealogy not, as St. Luke does, from Adam the ancestor of mankind, but from Abraham the Jewish forefather, and David the Jewish king. He alone speaks of Christianity as "the consummation of the Ages." He has upwards of sixty references to the Old Testament. His ever-recurring formula is, "that it might be fulfilled," [1] The words "I am not come to destroy but to fulfil," modified by "except your righteousness exceed the righteousness of the Scribes and Pharisees ye cannot enter into the kingdom of heaven," might be regarded as the doctrinal epitome of large portions of his Gospel. He conceived of Christianity primarily as the "bright consummate flower" and perfected fruit of Judaism.[2] The stumbling-blocks of the Jew were the deep humiliation of Jesus; His rejection by their rulers; His death of shame; His depreciation of their oral and Levitic Law. It was St. Matthew's task to show, by the simple testimony of truth, that in all this Jesus had but fulfilled to the letter the ideal of their grandest prophecies.[3] He

---

[1] Thus in quotations used by our Lord we have γέγραπται, ἀναπληροῦται, πῶς πληρωθῶσι (iv. 14 ; xiii. 14 ; xxvi. 54). In other quotations we have ἵνα πληρωθῇ τὸ ῥηθέν (i. 22 ; ii. 15 ; iv. 14 ; viii. 17 ; xii. 17 ; xiii. 35 ; xxi. 4 ; xxvii. 9) ; οὕτω γέγραπται (ii. 5) ; ἐπληρώθη τό ῥηθέν (ii. 18). The verb πληρόω is not thus used by the other Synoptists, but occurs six times in St. John (Mark xv. 28, is omitted in the R. V.). On these quotations see further in Note 2.

[2] St. Matthew's trustworthiness and impartiality are proved by the fact that the broader truths of "Pauline" Christianity are by no means suppressed. At the beginning of the Gospel we have the adoration of the Infant Christ by the Gentile Magi, and in xxviii. 15, the word "Jews" is used even by St. Matthew, as by the other Evangelists, as though he were outside the circle of Jewish nationality. (See *infra*, note 2, on the Unity of the Gospel.) Even into the Genealogy of the "Son of David" he has introduced the names of Rahab the Canaanite and Ruth the Moabitess.

[3] His humiliation, Zech. ix. 9 ; Is. liii. 3 ; Ps. xxii. 6 ; Matt. viii. 17 ; Ps. cxviii. 22, 23 ; His rejection, Is. liii. 1 ; xxix. 13, 14 ; vi. 9, 10 ; Matt. xiii. 14, 15 ; xxi. 42 ; xv. 7—9 ; His death, Zech. xiii. 7 ; xi. 12, 13 ; Matt. xxvi. 31, 14—16 ; xxvii. 3—10 ; His depreciation of their Levitic and oral law, Is xxix. 13 ; Matt. xv. 1—9.

ST. MATTHEW desired to set Jesus forth to them as their very Christ; the Legislator of a new and spiritual Law; the King of a new and spiritual dominion; the Prophet of a new and universal Church; the Divine Messiah who should soon resolve all doubts, returning on the clouds of Heaven to judge and save. Thus in St. Matthew we have the very essence of the Christian faith—the close of the old Æons; the dawn of the last Revelation; the proclamation of that which he alone of the Evangelists calls, in Jewish phraseology, "the Kingdom of the Heavens." [1]

8. Such, then, being his special aim, what is the general idea and outline of his book?

Among the characteristics of this Gospel must certainly be noticed a certain sternness—a certain exclusiveness which is in striking contrast with the tone of St. Luke. It is St. Matthew alone who records, and that twice over (xx. 16, xxii. 14), the remarkable saying of Christ about "the called" and "the chosen." "More than the rest of the Evangelists," it has been said, "He seems to move in evil days, and amid a race of backsliders; among dogs and swine who are unworthy of the words of truth; among the tares sown by the enemy; among fishermen who have to cast back many of the fish caught in the net of the Gospel. The broad way is ever in his mind, and the multitude of those that go thereby; and the guest without the wedding garment; and the foolish virgins; and the goats; and those who cast out devils in the name of the Lord, and yet are rejected." It has been conjectured that Antinomian tendencies may at this time have begun to be developed among the Hellenising Jews. The Evangelist lays special stress on the guilt of hypocrisy and religious ostentation, and viewed in the light of the

---

[1] The use of the Hebraism οὐρανοί (2 Cor. xii. 2) in St. Matthew is peculiar. Ἡ βασιλεία τῶν οὐρανῶν occurs in this Gospel thirty-two times. The other Christian writers use "the kingdom of God." The plural "heavens" is used by St. Matthew where there is a reference to the dwelling-place of God (ὁ πατὴρ ὁ ἐν τοῖς οὐρανοῖς). He uses it even in the first clause of the Lord's prayer. St. John does not use the plural once, and Luke only four times.

approaching Fall of Jerusalem and the wavering or retro-gression of great masses of the nation, the introduction into the Lord's Prayer of "Deliver us from the evil," and of the clause (xxiv. 12) "by reason of the multiplication of law-lessness the love of many is waxed cold," will seem not only appropriate but typical of the character of the whole of the First Gospel.[1]

9. Few have fully realised the antique simplicity, the monumental grandeur with which the Evangelist has carried out his design, the magnificent unity and fine construction of this Gospel. We see throughout an art which is all the more effective from its simple unconsciousness. He begins with the genealogy, to show that Jesus was of royal descent —the root and offspring of David. Then, just as the old religious painters of Italy throw out their exquisite colours on a golden ground, so the Evangelist paints his divine picture on the golden background of the Nativity and the Infancy. Even in doing this he shadows forth the double motive of his picture—which is partly to show that Christ's life, in its every incident, fulfilled the words of ancient prophecy; and, partly, that He came not only to reign but to suffer, not only to reveal but to die. Hence, side by side with the homage of the Magi we have the massacre of the Innocents; side by side with the royal descent the flight into Egypt; side by side with the visions of angels the taunt of "the Nazarene." We see from the first that Jesus was the Messiah by suffer-ing, though He was not only the Son of David, but the Son of God. The plan is carried out with perfect consistency.

I. After the Genealogy and the Infancy begins the Prelude —the ministry of the Forerunner and the preparation of the Christ. Each has its heavenly radiance, each its deepened shadow. The splendid success of the Baptist ends in his melancholy imprisonment; the Saviour's unction from the Holy One is followed immediately by the Temptation in the Wilderness.

[1] Dr. Abbott in *Enc. Britan. s. v.* "Gospels."

II. After this prelude the central mass of the book falls into two great divisions—(A) the Ministry and (B) the Passion: Christ the Redeemer by revelation; Christ the Redeemer by death; Christ the Word of God, making His Father known; Christ the Lamb of God, dying for the sins of the world.

A. The Ministry begins at iv. 12 with a swift preliminary glance at the prophecy which marked out Galilee as its chosen scene.[1] At iv. 23 the Evangelist sums up that ministry under the two great heads of "preaching the Gospel of the kingdom" and "healing all manner of disease." Thus, externally, he divides this long section of his record into the two main divisions of Words and Acts. This part of the Gospel occupies from iv. 17 to xvi. 21. At iv. 17 begins the ministry of life; at xvi. 21 begins the entrance into the path of death. Each section, though their prominence is completely obliterated by our division into chapters, is marked by a repetition of the same emphatic phrase at iv. 17: "*From that time forth began Jesus to preach*"; at xvi. 21, "*from that time forth began Jesus to show unto His disciples how that he must . . . be killed.*"

The first of these two chief sections—that of the Public iv. 17–xvi. 21. Preaching—sets forth the Words and Acts of Christ in four stages. The first stage (*a*) consists of the Sermon on the Mount and ten miracles. First, Christ as the New Prophet and Lawgiver, in the Sermon on the Mount, lays down the v.–viii. high spiritual laws of the kingdom of Heaven. There are no rolling clouds as at Sinai, no crashing thunder, no careering fires, no congregated wings of the rushing angelic host; yet this Galilean hill, with its calm voice, its lowly Teacher, its listening multitude, its lilies sprinkled on the green grass, is the Sinai of the New Covenant. Those beatitudes are its decalogue, those virtues its ritual. Prayer and alms, holiness and humbleness of heart—there you have the Leviticus of Christianity, the Pentateuch of spiritual worship. The

[1] Isaiah ix. 1; Matt. iv. 14—16.

glow of teaching is followed by the blaze of miracle. With st. matthew other words of instruction are interwoven ten successive works of power, which are only selected as specimens of an unrecorded multitude.

Then (β) at chapter x. begins the second stage of Words and Deeds. A wider phase of work is inaugurated by the great Discourse to the Twelve. After this, amid other teachings of ever deepening solemnity—the doubts of John the Baptist, the rejection by the cities of Galilee, the alarm of His own family, the hatred of the Pharisees—there blazes forth the one transcendent and concentrated miracle—the healing of the demoniac, blind and dumb. But even such a miracle as this only kindles in His enemies, not faith, but blasphemy; and we see that it is not by signs either from heaven or on earth that the reason of man can be convinced, or his heart won to faith and love.

(γ) Accordingly, in chapter xiii. a third phase of the ministry of Words and Deeds is ushered in by a new kind of teaching, at once penal and stimulative. There we have seven consecutive Parables, which mark an advance of conflict and opposition. This section ends with the miracles of Feeding the Five Thousand and Walking on the Sea.

Then we have (δ) a fourth stage of Discourses and Miracles. It opens at chapter xv. with the denunciation of the Oral Law, and after a period of flight and wandering even to the limit of heathen lands, it ends with the healing of the Syrophoenician girl; the cure of many sick; the feeding of the four thousand; the mocking disbelief of the Pharisees; and the acknowledgment by Peter and the Apostles, that Jesus is the Christ, the Son of the living God.[1]

---

[1] Keim attaches primary importance to the Gospel of St. Matthew (*Jesus of Nazara*, i. 64—94, E. T.) and his remarks are suggestive. He says, "Notwithstanding individual instances of anticipation or anachronism, we find on the whole a beautiful and continuous development of the history of Jesus. His preaching passes gradually from an approaching kingdom to one that has come, and to one that is yet in the future; from a strong insistence upon the Law to a freer and freer criticism of it; from a calling of all Israel to a calling of babes and sucklings; from a calling of the Jews to a calling of the Gentiles:

I would ask you to observe how through these Acts of
the divine drama—these objective stages of Word and Deed
—there run the undertones of two other deep subjective
contrasts—one, the acceptance of Christ by His chosen,
contrasted with His rejection by the world; the other, a yet
more universal contrast at every stage, the contrast between
the sin and misery of man and the infinite compassion and
love of the Incarnate Lord.   These marvellous and subtle
contrasts are not due to any skill of the Evangelist himself.
It is only because he bears witness to the Truth, and is inspired by the Spirit of Truth, that the simple Galilean
tax-gatherer becomes a divine musician, so that—falling from
concord or sweet accord to discord or harsh accord through
noble yet unsuspected harmonies,—

> " his volant touch,
> Instinct, through all proportions high and low
> Flies and pursues transverse the resonant fugue."

B. Then, with the same formula—" From this time forth
began Jesus "—we enter, in xvi. 21, on the second great
section—the Passion Music of this Divine Tragedy.   The
world has rejected Christ, but the Apostles have confessed
Him.   Henceforth the main task of the Saviour is not the
appeal to the multitudes, but the training of the disciples.
From this point Jesus consciously enters upon the path of
Death.   Henceforth He is recognised by His disciples; but
the struggle for life with the leaders of His people has
begun.   Here, again, we have four stages.   With ever-ad-
vancing clearness at Caesarea; at Capernaum; on the road to
Jerusalem; at Jerusalem itself; the Lord predicts His death,
His betrayal, His mockery, His crucifixion; and each time
with these, His Resurrection.   After the first prediction
comes the Transfiguration; and in each case we have the
" rainbow, like unto an emerald," spanning the black clouds
—the line of glory transfusing or running side by side with

from a preaching of the Messiah to a preaching of the Son and finally to a
preaching of the Cross."   Later on he calls it "antique history," and a
" grand old granitic book."

the line of humiliation. The fourth prediction is preluded
in the 23rd and 24th chapters by two discourses of overwhelming significance, viz. the denunciation in which He
hurls at the Scribes and Pharisees, hypocrites, His thunders
and lightnings of terrible invective; and the eschatological
discourse on the fall of Jerusalem and the end of the
world.

(*b*) After this fourth prediction follows at once the unspeakable tragedy of the closing scenes—the anointing; the betrayal;
the desertion; the arrest; the agony; the denials; the trial;
the mockery; the torture; the cross; the grave. And then,
after this midnight of horror and of mystery, as with one
awful "Now"—from the grey dawn to the rosy flush, to the
bursting splendour, to the risen sun, to the all-pervading
daylight—in pulse after pulse of radiance, in flood after
flood of sunshine—there beam upon us the empty sepulchre;
the angel visions; the triumph over death; the Resurrection;
the appearances to the assembled disciples; the vast commission; the illimitable promise of a Presence with us for
evermore. Language will hardly describe for us the grandeur
of this consummation. We require for its due apprehension
the yearning passion of music. You may have heard
Haydn's oratorio of the *Creation*. You remember there
the fine recitative, " And God said, Let there be light ";
and then how the music begins first as in a rapid flow of
soft and golden ripples, which roll on into wave after wave,
billow after billow, tide on tide of resistless sound, as though
heaved forward by the infinite world of waters behind it,
till at last, in a crashing, overwhelming outburst, which con-
centrates into one crowning note all wonder and all exultation, come forth the words, " And there was Light!" This
alone gives me a faint conception of what must have been,
to those sorrowing and half-crushed disciples, the gladness—
and we may still catch an echo of that gladness in the
page of the Evangelist—of that first Easter Day.

Such, then, is St. Matthew's Gospel—the Didactic Gospel;

ST. MATTHEW the Gospel of the past fulfilled; the Gospel of the Prophesied Messiah; the Gospel of the nine Beatitudes; the Gospel of the seven consecutive Parables; of the ten consecutive miracles; of the five continuous discourses, of which one is the Sermon on the Mount. In reading it, in looking on at this divinest of all tragedies, we, as it were,

> " Sit in a theatre to see
> A play of hopes and fears,
> While the orchestra breathes fitfully,
> The music of the spheres."

We see its five great Acts—the Infancy; the Prelude; the Ministry, in its four stages of Words and Deeds; the Doom, in its four advancing predictions; and then the Triumph. Throughout these scenes there run the elements which constitute all the grandeur of a heavenly drama —variety, progress, contrast, the incomparable depth of pathos relieved and overflooded by the incomparable exultation of final Victory. From the cradle to the Resurrection the action never pauses. Side by side in overwhelming scenes the Teaching advances in depth and clearness, the Power in mercy and miracle. Side by side there is an increasing vehemence of hatred, and an intensified adoration of love and trust. Louder and louder roll over the maddened Pharisees the terrible thunders of His rebuke; softer and more softly are breathed to His disciples the promises of His infinite consolation. In the early brightness of that Galilean spring of His ministry, He is an honoured Prophet; the Disciples follow, the people believe, the Pharisees respect Him. Then the year darkens into gathering and deepening opposition, but meanwhile the Disciples have advanced from love to adoration, until to the people He becomes an excommunicated Wanderer, but to His own the Son of God. Then the pillars of the kingdom of Heaven seem to be shattered to the lowest foundations, as its King descends, amid the derision of raging and triumphant enemies, through shame and anguish, to the Valley of

Death. But, lo! when all seems lost—when the sun and ST. MATTHEW.
moon have shrunk into darkness from the dreadful sacrifice;
when the kings and peoples of the earth seem to have burst
His bands asunder and cast away His cords from them; when
the Powers of Evil seem to have won their last and most
awful victory, suddenly, as with a flash of lightning out of
the blue sky, the Cross becomes the Throne, and the
Sepulchre the portal of Immortality; and shattering the
gates of brass, and smiting the bars of iron in sunder, He
rises from Death to Life, from Earth to Heaven, and sends
forth His twelve poor chosen ones, armed with the implement
of a malefactor's torture, and with "the irresistible might of
weakness," to shake, to conquer, to evangelise, to enlighten,
to rule the world.

10. And thus the book carries with it internal evidence of
its own sacredness. How could the unlettered Galilean
publican have written unaided a book so "immeasurably
effective"? How could he have sketched out a Tragedy
which, by the simple divineness of its theme, dwarfs the
greatest of all earthly tragedies? How could he have composed a Passion-music which, from the flute-like strains of
its sweet overture to the "multitudinous chorale" of its
close, accumulates with unflagging power the mightiest
elements of pathos and of grandeur? Why would the world
lose less from the loss of *Hamlet*, and the *Divina Comedia*,
and the *Paradise Lost* together, than from the loss of this
brief book of the despised Galilean? Because this book is
due not to genius, but to revelation; not to art, but to truth.
The words of the man are nothing, save as they are the
record of the manifestation of God. The greatness of the
work lay, not in the writer, but in Him of whom he wrote;
and in this, that without art, without style, without rhetoric,
in perfect and unconscious simplicity, he sets forth the facts
as they were. He is "immeasurably effective" because he
nowhere aims at effectiveness. He thought of nothing less.
Though we find in his book the "simple grandeur of monu-

mental writing," he brought to his work but three intellectual endowments : the love of truth ; an exquisite sensibility to the mercy of God and the misery of man ; and a deep sense of that increasing purpose which runs through the ages. And thus endowed by the Holy Spirit of God, he has given us this unique History, so genuinely human, and therefore, in all its parts, so genuinely divine ; a mighty, because a simply truthful, record of the words and deeds of Him who was both God and man. The Evangelist held up to the truth a soul which was a sphere of crystal in its purity and its integrity ; and therefore in that crystal sphere we see the King in His Beauty ; the Son of David ; the Messiah of Prophecy ; the Lord and Saviour of all the World—*our* Lord, *our* Saviour. If with all our hearts we truly seek Him, we shall find Him there. God grant that we may find Him to our souls' eternal peace !

NOTE I.
ANALYSIS OF ST. MATTHEW.

The Analysis of St. Matthew may be briefly summed up as follows in its main outline and articulations (omitting minor incidents).

I. The Prelude (i–iv. 12).
    1. The Genealogy (i. 1–17).
    2. The Nativity (i. 18–25).
    3. The Infancy (ii).
    4. The Preaching of the Baptist (iii. 1–12).
    5. The Baptism (iii. 13–17).
    6. The Temptation (iv. 1–11).
    7. The withdrawal into Galilee (iv. 12–16).

II. The Ministry in its period of acceptance—Words and Deeds (iv. 17 ; xvi. 21).
    A. Calling of the Apostles (iv. 18–22).
    Miracles in general (iv. 23–25).

Words.   The Sermon on the Mount (v–viii).
Deeds.   Ten Miracles (interwoven with other incidents) (viii–ix).
Words. B.   Mission of the Twelve, and other discourses (x. i–xi. 8).
Deeds.   The withered hand (xi. 9–21).
    Healing of a dumb, blind, demoniac, with other incidents (xi. 22–45).
    C. The period of opposition.
Words.   Seven Parables (xiii).
Deeds.   Feeding the five thousand (xiv. 13–21).
    Walking on the Sea, and other miracles (xiv. 22–36).
    D. Open rupture with the Jewish authorities.
Words.   Denunciation of the Pharisees (xv. 1–20).
Deeds.   The Syrophoenician woman, and other miracles (xv. 21–31).
    Feeding the four thousand (xv. 32–39).
    The great confession (xvi. 13–20).

III. Entrance on the path of death, with record of other Words, and Deeds.
    First prophecy at Caesarea Philippi (xvi. 21).
    Second prophecy at Capernaum (xvii. 22).
    Third prophecy near Jerusalem (xx. 17).
    Fourth prophecy at Jerusalem (xxvi. 1, 2).

IV. The closing scenes, the death and burial (xxvi. 3–xxvii).

V. The Resurrection (xxviii).

NOTE II.

UNITY OF ST. MATTHEW'S GOSPEL.

ST. MATTHEW.　There is scarcely a book of the New Testament which some German critic has not attempted to disintegrate, by dividing it between various authors, editors, or interpolators. This Gospel, in spite of the grand and obvious unity which underlies the book, is no exception.

1. Thus, one class of critics—Schleiermacher, Köstlin, Weiszäcker, Holtzmann, Ewald and others—have attempted a separation between the *sayings* and the *acts*. But

(i.) The attempt was suggested by the purely mistaken notion that when Papias said that Matthew composed the "oracles" (λόγια; see Rom. iii. 2) in the Hebrew language, he meant by oracles "collections of sayings." It is now understood that "*logia*," as used by Papias and other writers, does not mean merely "sayings" but "records." Indeed in the same passage Papias himself says that St. Mark's Gospel was not a collection of the Lord's *words* (σύνταξις κυριακῶν λόγων, *v.l.* λογίων) though he had just described it as containing "the things either said or done by Christ." [1]

(ii.) It is impossible to separate the Words from the Deeds in the Gospel of St. Matthew. They are inextricably interwoven; they presuppose and explain each other.

We need not therefore linger over a theory "the mechanical shallowness of which is fatal to the organic life of the Gospel, and which falls to pieces in the very hands of its inventor." (Keim.)

2. A second attempt to divide the Gospel between two authors has arisen from the asserted discrepancies of opinion which it contains. [2]

It is said that on the one hand the Gospel is Judaic and particularist, on the other hand universalist and liberal. We have in it alike such Jewish-Christian elements as the Messiah of the Jews, and the sanctity of the Sabbath, and a prohibition to preach the Gospel to the Gentiles, and the characterisation of the Gentiles as "dogs;" (see v. 17, 19; vii. 6; x. 5, 6; xv. 24; xix. 28, &c.); and on the other hand liberal narratives, like the Adoration of the Magi, and the centurion of Capernaum, and such superiority to mere national prejudices as that shown in the record of discourses which placed Tyre and Sidon and Nineveh above Jerusalem. We have also the command to preach the Gospel to all the Gentiles (See viii. 11; xii. 21; xxiv. 2; xxii. 7; xxiii. 38; xxiv. 14; xxviii. 15, 19; the parables of the Husbandman, &c. (xx. 1-16; xxi. 33-44; xxii. 1-14), &c.

---

[1] See Bishop Lightfoot, *Contemp. Rev.* August, 1875.

[2] "Der Evgst. Matthäus hat nun aber einen Januskopf, dessen eines Gesicht in das Griechische, das andre in das Semitische weist." Hilgenfeld, *Einleit.* 495.

Do these differences necessitate the supposition that a Judaic Gospel ST. MATTHEW. has been interpolated, or edited (*überarbeitet*) by a liberal Christian?

The answer is simple. The asserted discrepancy lay in facts which found their synthesis in wider truths. Jesus was both the Messiah of the Jew and the Saviour of the World. He came to the Jew first, and afterwards to the Gentile. The Evangelist was a Jewish Christian, but he could not suppress, nor did he desire to suppress, facts and words which belonged to an order of thoughts infinitely wider than that in which he had been trained. There is no contradiction between these different points of view. They are but various aspects of many-sided truths.

3. A third attempt to divide the Gospel has been based on the fact that of the numerous quotations from the Old Testament some are from the Septuagint, others are rendered from the original Hebrew.

This phenomenon, first noticed by Credner and then by Bleek, Holtzmann and others, has been minutely examined especially by Anger. The result of his investigations is—

(i.) That both kind of quotations are scattered throughout the Gospel.

(ii.) That St. Matthew's *cyclic* quotations (*i.e.* those which he has in common with the general cycle of Synoptic tradition) are from the LXX., but that in his individual quotations—those which involve remarks and inferences of his own—he generally reverts to the Hebrew.

(iii.) That quotations from the LXX. bear the proportion of about thirty to ten to those from the Hebrew.

(iv.) That the quotations from the LXX. preponderate in the narrative, those from the Hebrew in the reflections.[1]

It is not easy to account for this peculiarity. It may have been due to the idiosyncrasy of the writer; to the documents which he used; to the accident of having immediate access to a Hebrew or Greek copy of the Bible, or to many other unexplained causes. The attempt to divide the book between two authors with reference to these quotation is a wholesale failure.

There is then no ground whatever for denying the Unity of the Book, while there are the strongest reasons for asserting it.[2]

---

[1] In the sayings of Jesus only xi. 10 is from the Hebrew; but in the Evangelist's own comments, ii. 6, 15, 23; iv. 15; viii. 17; xii. 18; xxi. 5; xxvii. 9. Yet he reverts to the LXX. even in his own remarks in i. 23; iii. 3. The strange thing is that in some of these instances (*e.g.*, ii. 6, 18; iv. 15; xxi. 5), the LXX. would have served his purpose as well though not in ii. 5; xxvi. 31 (see for fuller details, Hilgenfeld, p. 459–497). Perhaps as a rule the Evangelist thought it right to refer as often as possible to the Hebrew when he applies the Prophecies.

[2] Not only the same essential purpose is obvious throughout the book, but also the same formulae, such as "the kingdom of the heavens" thirty-two times; "Our Father in the heavens" or "heavenly" twenty-two times; "that it might be fulfilled;" the pleonastic, πορευθείς "going;" the frequent καὶ ἰδού; the use throughout of τότε, ἐκεῖθεν, εὐθέως, ἐν τῇ ἡμέρᾳ ἐκείνῃ as formulae of vague transition, &c. See Reuss, *Heilige Schriften*, ii. p. 194.

NOTE III.

THE GOSPEL ACCORDING TO THE HEBREWS.

It is now generally admitted that our present Gospel of St. Matthew is not and cannot be a translation.[1] The opinion that St. Matthew first wrote in Aramaic may, as we have seen, be a mistake of Papias who had heard of the "Gospel according to the Hebrews." Even Origen had only heard by tradition of the Hebrew original. Jerome seems certainly to have fallen into some confusion, for he says, that he had seen the Hebrew original of St. Matthew in the library of the martyr Pamphilus at Caesarea, and among the Nazarenes in the Syrian Beroea (*De Virr. Illustr.* 3). In the previous chapter he says that he had translated into Greek and Latin the Gospel according to the Hebrews. In later life he seems to have had doubts on the subject, to which Origen had often referred. Pantaenus is said to have discovered the original Hebrew Gospel of St. Matthew among the Indians, who had received it from the Apostle Bartholomew (Euseb. *H. E.* v. 10, § 3; Jer. De *Virr. Illustr.* 36). The truth seems to be that the Gospel of the Nazarenes, the Gospel of the Ebionites, the Gospel according to the Twelve Apostles, and the Gospel according to the Hebrews were all more or less heretical, or at the best were unwarrantable *Antilegomena* based upon the genuine Gospel. The Roman Catholic writer, Sepp, without more ado calls the Gospel according to the Hebrews "a Jewish-Christian humbug."

Of the Gospel according to the Hebrews thirty-three fragments remain. They have been collected by Credner, Hilgenfeld, and Nicholson. They are also collected in Canon Westcott's *Introduction to the Gospel* (pp. 433–438), with the fragments of the Gospel to the Ebionites.

[1] See such phrases as κακοὺς κακῶς ἀπολέσει αὐτούς, xxi. 41, and such paronomasias as ὄψονται καὶ κόψονται (xxiv. 30); ἀφανίζειν. . . φαίνεσθαι, vi. 16, αἰτίαν. . . αἰτία, xix. 3, 10. In the Ep. of Barnabas (iv. v.) early as it is, there seem to be two quotations from the Greek (xxii. 14 ; ix. 13).

THE GOSPEL ACCORDING TO ST. MARK.

"This too the elder used to say. Mark having become Peter's interpreter,
wrote accurately all that he (Peter) mentioned [or all that he (Mark) remembered ἐμνημόνευσεν]; he did not, however, (record) in order either the things
said or done by Christ, for he neither heard the Lord nor followed Him, but
(as I said) subsequently (followed) Peter, who used to frame his teaching in
accordance with the needs (of his hearers), but not as though he were making
a methodic narrative of the Lord's discourses. So Mark made no error in
writing down some things as he (Peter) narrated them. For he took heed to
one thing, to omit nothing of what he heard, and to make no false statement
in them."—PAPIAS (in Euseb. *H. E.* iii. 39, § 15).

"What is this? A new teaching! With authority He commandeth even
the unclean spirits, and they obey Him."—MARK i. 27.

1. THE old notion of the Gospel of St. Mark which satisfied
many of the Fathers and Schoolmen, and still satisfies most
readers—is the mistaken and superficial view that the
Evangelist was nothing but a follower and epitomist of St.
Matthew.[1] It is a view which does not look an inch deeper
than the most obvious phenomena.[2] No doubt the Gospel of
St. Mark does present the same general outline as the pre-
ceding Gospel. We have seen that St. Matthew had five great
divisions. St. Mark entirely omits the Genealogy and the
Infancy, but he too has first the Prelude: then the long section of the Ministry with its Miracles and Parables; the
rejection by the world, and acceptance by the Apostles; the

---

[1] So Augustine, *De Consens. Evang.* i. 4, "subsecutus (Matthaeus) tamquam
pedissequus et breviator ejus."
[2] A very large school of modern critics (Ritschl, Volkmar, Ewald, Köstlin,
Reuss, Weiss, &c.) has maintained the priority of Mark; but the Fathers
(Irenaeus, *Haer.* iii. 10, § 6; Clemens Alex. *ap.* Euseb. *H. E.* vi. 14; Tert.
Cont. Marcion. iv. 2; Jerome, *De Virr. Illustr.* 7, 8) and others place
Matthew first, and their view is now being generally adopted.

opening glory and deepening gloom; the year of prosperity in Galilee, the year of flight among the heathen:—then the closing scenes: then the Resurrection.[1] This resemblance in arrangement is due of course mainly to the actual order of facts. The closeness of the general symmetry does not arise from any abbreviation of St. Matthew by St. Mark, but from the actual order of events and the use made by both Evangelists of existing oral or written records of Apostolic preaching. Nor must we forget that the Evangelists were personally known to each other. Mark must have met Matthew in his mother's house, which was the common rendezvous of the early Christians in Jerusalem, and he must have been with Luke in Rome. To a large extent therefore at different periods of their careers they lived in the same circle of ideas and beliefs, and must have frequently conversed with each other. Yet each is quite independent. St. Mark has two miracles and one parable recorded by himself exclusively,[2] and in every incident and in every parable he diverges from St. Matthew repeatedly, both in phraseology and in details. He is in no sense a copyist. He claims the rank of an independent witness. It is extremely doubtful whether he had so much as seen the earlier Gospel of the Publican Apostle.

2. Of St. Mark himself all that is known is the tradition which identifies him with John Mark, the son of that Mary whose house in Jerusalem was a meeting place of the early Church. Hence the home of the Evangelist was perhaps the

---

[1] None of the Apostles could have failed to observe that the scenes at Caesarea Philippi—the confession of Christ's divine Messiahship by St. Peter, and the first "Passion-cry" of approaching death—marked a special epoch in the ministry of Christ.

The outline of St. Mark is as follows:—

1. Introduction (i. 1–13).
2. The Galilean ministry (i. 14–ix).
3. Incidents of the Journey to Jerusalem (x).
4. Closing scenes, Death, and Resurrection (xi. 1–xvi. 8).
5. Conclusion (canonical, but probably added later) (xvi. 9–20).

[2] St. Mark's peculiar sections are iv. 26–29 (the growth of the seed): vii. 32–37 (the multitudes, and the compassion of Jesus); viii. 22–26 (the blind man gradually healed); xi. 1–14 (details about the ass, &c.); xiii. 33–37 (Watch!); xvi. 6–11 (details of the appearance of the risen Christ).

scene both of the Last Supper and of the descent of the Holy Spirit at Pentecost. He was a cousin of Barnabas, and therefore, was of Levitic descent,[1] and as Barnabas was from Cyprus, Mark may have owed his Latin name to this circumstance.[2] He was the companion of Paul and Barnabas in their first journey. Becoming the unwilling cause of the sharp dispute between them, he went with Barnabas to Cyprus. Afterwards we find him in the closest and dearest intimacy with St. Peter in Rome, and completely forgiven and trusted by St. Paul also during his Roman imprisonment. The great Apostle of the Gentiles mentions him in one Epistle with a kindly message, and in another specially wishes for his presence, because he was " profitable to him for ministering." [3] There is no ground for the fancy that St. Mark was the young man in the linen sheet whom he mentions in the unique and characteristic incident of the arrest at Gethsemane.[4] Tradition says that he went to Alexandria ; founded the famous Catechetical school in that city, and there died a martyr's death.[5]

3. The date of his Gospel was certainly before the fall of

[1] Col. iv. 10, ἀνέψιος, not "sister's son," as in A. V. Epiphanius (*Haer.* li. 6) says (without probability) that St. Mark was one of the seventy disciples of Christ, and fell away from Him (John vi. 66) but was brought back by St. Peter.

[2] The name was adopted (after the Jewish fashion) for use among Gentiles. It was one of the commonest Latin names, as John was one of the commonest Hebrew names.

[3] 1 Pet. v. 13 ; Philem. 24 ; 2 Tim. iv. 11. St. Peter uses υἱός, not τέκνον, but evidently the term is one of affection.

[4] This precarious identification has been rendered all the more popular because it falls in with the fancy that each of the Evangelists has, as Godet expresses it, left in a corner of his picture a modest indication of his own personality ; Matthew in the Publican whom Jesus calls by a word from the receipt of toll ; Mark in the young man in the linen garment ; Luke in the companion of Cleopas on the walk to Emmaus ; John in the unnamed disciple whom Jesus loved (St. Luc. ii. 447). If the last supper was held (as is probable) in the house of Mary the mother of Mark, the Evangelist may have been " the man bearing a pitcher of water." To bear a pitcher of water was most unusual for a man, and this man could only have been the master of the family bringing the water for some sacred purpose. Possibly too the signal had been privately agreed on. It must be remembered that our Lord was at that time under the ban, and that there was a price upon His head.

[5] Euseb. *H. E.* ii. 16 ; Epiphan. *Haer.* li. 6 ; Jer. *De Virr. Ill.* 8 ; Chrys. *Hom. in Matt.* ; Nicephor. ii. 43. For numerous legends and their treatment in Art, see Mrs. Jameson, i. 147–154.

Jerusalem. It was probably published within a few years of the Gospels of St. Matthew and St. Luke. Mutual inter-course and the fact that Apostolic teaching was already fixed in its general outline and expressions—can (as we have seen) alone account for the many resemblances combined with the many dissimilarities of these three Gospels. And yet, as a distinct whole, St. Mark's Gospel entirely differs from the others. Though it contains but a handful of verses, which have no parallel in St. Matthew and St. Luke, it was written with a different object, it is stamped with a different individuality.

4. For instance, it is obvious that St. Mark wrote for a code of different readers. St. Matthew wrote for Hebrews, St. Luke for Greeks, St. Mark wrote for Romans,[1] probably in Rome. He has ten Latin words, such as *legio, centurio, quadrans, flagellare, census, sextarius, speculator, praetorium,*[2] some of which are peculiar to himself. He uses several distinctly Latin idioms.[3] He has fewer references to the Old Testament than the other Evangelists, and only one which is peculiar to himself;[4] in other words his quotations are always cyclic, *i.e.* they belong to the narrative, not to the recorder.[5] He always adds a note of explanation to Jewish words and

---

[1] But even Romanists have given up the view of Baronius that he wrote in Latin, a statement which is found in some MSS. The Roman Christians all spoke Greek. Even Clement of Rome wrote in Greek.

[2] κράββατος (*grabatus*), which he, alone of the Synoptists, uses five times, occurs also in John v. 8–12, Acts v. 15 : ix. 33. At the end of the Gospel the Peshito version adds : "End of the Holy Gospel of the preaching of Mark, who spoke and preached in Latin at Rome.

[3] τὸ ἱκανὸν ποιεῖν, xv. 15. He also has συμβούλιον διδόναι, *consilium dare ;* ἐσχάτως ἔχειν, *in extremis esse*—a phrase which Phrynichus says was only used by the vulgar. ὥρα πολλή, vi. 35. No less than eight words which St. Luke avoids are used by St. Mark, and are condemned by Phrynichus as "slang" words (κράββατος, μονόφθαλμος, εὐσχήμων (in the sense of rich), κολλυβισταί, κοράσιον, ὁρκίζω, ῥάπισμα, ῥαφίς). The last word for "needle" is used by Hippocrates, but Phrynichus reprehends it severely, and St. Luke used βελόνη instead (Luke xviii. 25, B. D. L.). His Greek is sometimes incorrect, ὅταν with indicative ; ἵνα first with the conjunctive and then the infinitive (iii. 14, 15).

[4] Mark i. 2, 3. The reference in xv. 28 is omitted in our Revised Version, as perhaps a gloss from Luke xxii. 37.

[5] Seventeen of these quotations (out of nineteen) are from the LXX., and for the most part agree with St. Matthew almost verbally.

Jewish usages.[1] The word "Law" does not occur in his pages, though it occurs eight times in St. Matthew, nine times in St. Luke, and fifteen times in John.[2] Even the style seems to catch something of the energetic brevity, something of the haughty compression of the Romans for whose instruction his Gospel was designed.

5. Then again, in addressing different readers, he wrote for a different purpose. St. Matthew desired to link the Present to the Past; to point to the fulfilment of Old Testament prophecies; to prove that Jesus was the Messiah of the Jew, the Son of David, the Son of Abraham.

St. Luke wrote to connect Christianity with the advancing future; to associate the work of Jesus with Humanity; to set Him forth as the Son of Adam; the Saviour of the World.

St. John wrote to connect Christ with the Eternal; to serve the deepest needs of the soul; to satisfy the most yearning aspirations of the spirit.

The object of St. Mark, in this concise, vigorous, vivid Gospel was more limited, though not less necessary.[3] It was to manifest Jesus as He had been in the present, in daily actual life; Jesus living and working among men, in the fulness of His energy; Jesus in the awe-inspiring grandeur of his human personality as a Man who was also the Incarnate, the wonder-working Son of God.[4]

He narrates eighteen of the Miracles, but only four of St. Matthew's fifteen Parables, and those in briefest form.

---

[1] See vii. 1-5, 11-18; vii. 3, 4; xii. 18; xiv. 12; xv. 42, &c.

[2] St. Mark uses "the commandment" (ἐντολή) eight times (vii. 8; x. 19, &c.).

[3] The brevity of St. Mark's Gospel was early commented on, Jerome, *Cat.* 8. In Hippolytus (*Philos.* vii. 30) we find the curious epithet Μάρκος ὁ κολοβοδάκτυλος, "Mark, the stump-fingered." In later days it originated the legend that St. Mark had maimed one of his fingers to disqualify himself for the priesthood; but it probably arose from the abridged narratives of his Gospel (see Keim, *Jesu of Nazara,* i. 117).

[4] The first words of St. Mark, "The beginning of the Gospel of Jesus Christ, the Son of God," are a most fitting keynote to the whole book. "The Son of God" is here omitted by ℵ, but the same title is given to Christ in seven other passages of the Gospel.

ST. MARK. Unanimous ancient tradition has connected St. Mark's Gospel with the eyewitness of St. Peter.[1] It contains many special allusions to St. Peter. Whole passages look as if they only put into the third person what St. Peter had narrated to the writer in the first person. This Gospel displays the same conciliatory spirit of catholicity as that which marked the great Apostle of the Circumcision. St. Peter's speech in Acts x. to the Roman centurion—in which he describes the essence of Apostolic testimony to be "How God anointed Jesus of Nazareth with the Holy Ghost and with power, who went about doing good, and healing all that were oppressed of the devil; for God was with Him"—has been called by Meyer with happy insight "a programme of the Gospel." "What is this? A new teaching with power! The very demons obey Him." Into these words are compressed the main features of the work of Christ as here revealed to us; its startling originality, its authoritative tone, the astonishment inspired by its supernatural and beneficent ascendency. Such was the Day of Christ as it appeared to St. Peter and to St. Mark.

6. We cannot fail to observe how admirably this Gospel of St. Mark accords with the aim which he had in view.

i. First of all it is characterised by an almost impetuous activity. In St. Matthew the element of discourse is most prominent; in St. Mark that of action. St. Matthew's is the didactic, St. Mark's the energetic Gospel. Nothing can be more characteristic of the fact than the words "immedi-

---

[1] Some have seen an allusion to this in 2 Pet. i. 16. Papias (*ap.* Euseb. *H. E.* iii. 39) calls Mark an "interpreter" (ἑρμηνευτής) of St. Peter. Justin Martyr (*Dial.* 106) quotes Mark iii. 17 under the title of "Memoirs (ἀπομνημονεύματα) of Peter." Irenaeus (*Haer.* iii. 1), Clemens. Alex. (*ap.* Euseb. vi. 14), Tertullian ("Marcus quod edidit evangelium Petri affimatur," *c. Marcion.* iv. 5), Origen, Eusebius (*H. E.* ii. 15) all give evidence to the same effect. St. Jerome says, "Marcum, cujus evangelium Petro narrante et illo scribente compositum est" (*ad Hed.* i. 5: *Epp.* cxx. 10). Minute incidents connected with St. Peter are found in i. 29; ix. 5; xiv. 54, 72; xvi. 7. The remark of Eusebius (*Dem. Evang.* iii. 5) about Peter's silence on matters to his own credit is founded on vii. 27–33 (compare Matt. xvi. 13–23). Mrs. Jameson (*Legends of Sacred and Legendary Art*, i. 149) mentions many early and beautiful representations of the Evangelist writing while Peter dictates.

ately," "anon," "forthwith," "by and by," "straightway," "as soon as," "shortly," which seven words in our version represent the one Greek word εὐθέως "immediately," a word so characteristic of the original that it occurs no less than forty-one times in these few pages, though only eight times in the much longer Gospel of St. Luke. St. Mark has no long discourses, no developed parables. He does not wear the flowing robes of St. Matthew: his dress is "for speed succinct." Swift and incisive, his narrative proceeds straight to the goal like a Roman soldier on his march to battle.[1] In reading St. Mark, carried away by his breathless narrative, we feel like the Apostles who—as he alone twice tells us—among the press of people coming and going, "had no leisure so much as to eat." Event after event comes upon us in his pages with the impetuous sequence of the waves in a rising tide.

ii. Again his Gospel is marked by special vividness. It is full of charm and colour. It is brightened by touches inimitably graphic: the Evangelist is a word-painter. We have repeated details of person,[2] of number, of time, of place, which often throw on the narrative a flood of light. The spies are "scribes from Jerusalem"; the questioners are "Peter and Andrew and James and John"; Simon of Cyrene is "the father of Alexander and Rufus," whom the Roman Christians know. The swine "are in number about two thousand"; the cock crows "twice." The time is "a great while before day"; or "the third hour"; or "eventide." The scene is "over against the treasury"; or "on the sea-shore"; or on the slopes of Olivet, or in the courtyard, or in the porch. The interlocutors speak and answer in the first person. The very looks and accents, and gestures of Jesus are recalled alike in His publicity and in His solitude.[3] They

---

[1] Observe the phrases "And He went out from thence" (vi. 1), "And from thence He arose" (vii. 24; ix. 30; x. 1, 2). Hence the Gospel has been called "inartistic, disproportioned, uncouth, *a string of anecdotes*," yet "full of naïve simplicity and single-mindedness."

[2] Bartimaeus, Boanerges.

[3] i. 28, 35, 37, 45; ii. 1-4, 15; iii. 10-12; vi. 32, 33, &c.

ST. MARK. are painted as it were from the photograph of them on St. Peter's memory. Jesus "looks round" on the worshippers. He " takes the little children in His arms," and (how mothers will thank St. Mark for that detail !) " lays His hand on them and blesses them." He " sits down " and calls the Twelve.[1] His very accents are recorded in their original Aramaic —" Boanerges " " Ephphatha," " Talitha Cumi," " Abba," " Corban."

Take by way of example the description of the storm upon the lake. In St. Mark alone do we see the waves breaking over and half swamping the little ship. In St. Mark alone do we see Jesus in His utter weariness sleeping on the leather cushion of the steersman at the stern. Take another scene, the Feeding of the Five Thousand. St. Mark alone tells us of the fresh green grass on which they sat down by hundreds and by fifties; and, as I have pointed out elsewhere, the word which he uses for "companies" means literally " flowerbeds," as though to St. Peter those multitudes, in their festal Passover attire, with its many-coloured Oriental brightness of red and blue, looked like the patches of crocus and poppy and tulip and amaryllis which he had seen upon the mountain slopes.[2] Again, in the narrative of the Transfiguration it is in St. Mark that we see most clearly the dazzling robes of the Transfigured Lord as they shed their golden lustre over Hermon's snow; and it is St. Mark who shows us most vividly the contrast of that scene of peace and radiance with the tumult and agitation of the crowd below;—the father's heartrending anguish at the foaming and convulsion of the agonised demoniac boy, the trouble of the disciples, and the noble passion of the Lord.

As you gaze on Raffaelle's immortal picture of the Trans-

---

[1] Hence what are called his " pictorial participles "—"looking up," "looking round," " springing up,' " stooping down," "speaking indignantly," " turning round," "groaning," &c.—(ἀναβλέψας, περιβλέψας, περιβλεψάμενος, ἀναπηδήσας, κύψας, ἐμβριμησαμενος, ἐπιστραφείς, ἀποστενάξας, &c. See. viii. 12 ; x. 14.) For details of looks and acts see iii. 5 ; vii. 31-37 ; viii. 22-26 ; v. 41 ; xiv. 36.

[2] See *Life of Christ*, i. 402. The remark has often since been copied.

figuration, you will see at once that it is from the narrative
of St. Mark that it derives most of its intensity, its movement, its colouring, its contrast, and its power.[1] It is these
gifts of the Evangelist which make one writer say of him
that "he wears a richly embroidered garment";[2] and another
—thinking of his bright independence and originality—that
in his gospel we breathe "a scent as of fresh flowers."[3]

iii. Both the characteristics on which we have dwelt are
important, as they tell irresistibly against all theories of the
mythic origin of the Gospels. But once again—what is still
more important—St. Mark's Gospel is memorable for its
special presentation of the life of Christ. It is not Messianic
like St. Matthew's; it is not tenderly and universally
Humanitarian like St. Luke's; it is not mystic and spiritual
like St. John's: but it is essentially realistic. Apart from
all theories of the future, apart from all prophecies in the
past, apart from all deep subjective impressions, he
represents Jesus as He lived in Galilee, at once divine and
human. If St. Matthew wrote specially for the Jew, St.
Luke for the Gentile Christian, and St. John for the
theologian, St. Mark writes for the ordinary practical man.
His Roman readers, in their blunt speech, and rough good
sense, might have said to him, "We know nothing of your Old

---

[1] It is, perhaps, to the desire for vividness that we owe St. Mark's constant
double expressions. See ii. 19 ; iii. 5, 27, &c. Thus in iii. 22 he has *two*
phrases for "He has Beelzebub," and yet another in iii. 30. Papias speaks of
his desire to omit nothing that he had heard. Such an expression as ὀψίας
δὲ γενομένης ὅτε ἔδυσεν ὁ ἥλιος (i. 32) may be taken as a type of these "re-
duplicated phrases," and combines the words separately used by Matt. viii.
16 and Luke iv. 40.

[2] "He is an author in a flower-bedecked garment. He makes the narrative
more effective by the contrast between rapid progression and contemplative
stillness, painting the scenery with a thousand touches, the house, the sea,
the followers, the growing throng, the names of persons, the numbers of the
men, and of the animals, and of the pieces of money, the greenness of the
grass, the pillow in the stern of the boat on Gennesareth—all given with a
preference for affectionate and familiar diminutives, and in the present tense.'
—Keim. The same picturesqueness of style is found in the Epistles of St
Peter, and in narratives which must have come from him. Compare th·
account of the cripple healed by St. Peter—which is full of graphic details—
(Acts iii. 1-11) with the much less vivid account of the cripple healed by St
Paul (Acts xiv. 8-10).

[3] Ewald. Meyer calls him *malerisch, anschaulich.*

Testament : we have no philosophic or speculative genius ; we are not ripe for your dogmas; but tell us what Jesus was, how He looked, what He did. Set Him before us as we should have seen Him had we been centurions in Syria, or soldiers beside the Cross. Before we can believe in the Son of God, we must know something of the Son of Man He must be dissevered from Jewish peculiarities or religious formulae. He must be ' universal as our race; he must be individual as ourselves.' "

iv. Now St. Mark meets these very needs. He shows us a Man indeed; one who is no Docetic phantom—one who needs rest, and sleep, and food; one who can love, and sigh, and pity, and be moved with anger and indignation ; but a Man heroic and mysterious, who inspires not only a passionate devotion, but also amazement and adoration ; one the very hem of whose garment heals the sick; one on whom the multitudes throng and press in their eagerness to touch Him ; one whom the unclean spirits no sooner see than they fall flat with the wild cry, "Thou art the Son of God." Here, for instance, is a single touch of description from Christ's last approach to Jerusalem, found in St. Mark alone—" And they were on the way going up to Jerusalem; and Jesus went before, and they were amazed, and they that followed were afraid." What a unique and marvellous picture ! All hope was now gone. The doom was near. Alone, with bowed head, in deep and awful silence, like the leader of some fatal enterprise, Jesus walked in front. But even in that supreme hour of His desolation and rejection, when He was excommunicate, when a price was on His head, in the lowest deeps of the valley of His humiliation, on the path to His Cross of shame, He inspires not the patronage of compassion, but an awful reverence, a hushed and terrified amaze.[1] No sorrow

---

[1] St. Mark uses five words expressive of fear, wonder, trouble, amazement, extreme astonishment. (i. 27 ; v. 28, ἐθαμβήθησαν πάντες ; ii. 12, ὥστε ἐξίστασθαι πάντας ; iv. 41, ἐφοβήθησαν φόβον μέγαν ; vi. 50, ἐταράχθησαν ; vi. 51, ἐξίσταντο καὶ ἐθαύμαζον ; vii. 37, ὑπερπερισσῶς ἐξεπλήσσοντο.) "The wonder-working Son of God sweeps over His kingdom swiftly and meteor-

was like His sorrow; yet the pomp of empires fades, and the pride of power is dwarfed before this lonely anguish of the Man of Sorrows. Constantine weaves the cross on his banners; Rudolph of Hapsburg seizes on a crucifix as his sceptre. It seems as if kings could only bow before the heir to that crown of thorns, and that sceptre of bulrushes. The Lord, as in the old Septuagint version of the Psalm, "reigns from the tree."[1] Nailed to the Cross amid the execrating multitude, He still seems to us to be

> " High on a throne of royal state, which far
> Outshone the wealth of Ormuz or of Ind,
> Or where the gorgeous East with richest hand
> Showers on her kings barbaric pearl and gold."

7. And now we shall I think see why, out of the fourfold cherubic chariot, the Lion was chosen as the symbol of St. Mark. For the characteristics of a lion are the majesty of its pose,[2] the sternness of its eye, the swiftness and power of its leap. And can we not see what an impression as of leonine majesty this Gospel, more than the others, must have made on the stern and practical Romans? So long as they were ignorant of Christianity the general attitude of Romans towards it was that of the haughtiest disdain. The great Roman writers of that epoch called it a " new," a " malefic," an " execrable " superstition. Tacitus vouchsafes only two lines to it, to say that its Author had been crucified under Pontius Pilate, and that, with everything else which could cause a blush, it had flowed into Rome as into the common sewer of Eastern superstition. Those proud and imperial aristocrats, obstinately clinging to a prejudice which disdained inquiry, could not conceive anything more abject than the worship of one who had died a slave's death of torture.

Lion 2

---

like."—Archbishop Thomson. The strong word ἐκθαμβεῖσθαι is peculiar to St. Mark (ix. 15 ; xiv. 33 ; xvi. 5, 6).

[1] Ἐβασίλευσεν ἀπὸ τοῦ ξύλου. Ps. xcvi. 10. LXX. Just. Mart. *Dial.* p. 298. August. *Enarrat. in Ps.* xcvi. Tert. *c. Marc.* iii. 19.

[2] "Solo guardando
A guisa di leon quando si posa."
     DANTE. *Purgatorio,* vi. 66.

ST. MARK   Already St. Paul had said " I am not ashamed "—not even in
Rome ashamed—" of the Gospel of Christ." But St. Mark
set himself to remove these scornful impressions, to counteract
this ignorant contempt. Instead of the mere "Galilean rebel,"
the mere " crucified malefactor " of Roman scorn,[1] he drew a
picture of one whose simple manhood was infinitely more
divine than that of their deified Caesars. The Romans—
slaves amid their boast of freedom—trembled when a Nero
showed in the streets the pale and bloated features which
were the infamous wreck of his early beauty.[2] They spoke in
terrified whispers when the red face of Domitian—red as
though it were flushed with blood—glared over the amphitheatre.[3] But it was not the men—degraded, abject, cowardly,
corrupt—not the men who inspired their awe, but the
despotism built on their own degradation. It was not the
wretch Nero nor the tyrant Domitian whom they dreaded ; it
was the imperial purple, the glitter of the lictor's naked axe,
the drawn swords of Praetorian guards, the background of
thirty legions, the awful *entourage* of spies and informers,
whose whispers cut men's throats. But St. Mark shows them
a Man who, though he lived in the midst of poverty and
insult, a persecuted Nazarene ; though all His state was in
Himself only ; though His face was marred more than any
man ; though He gave His back to the smiters, and His cheeks
to them that plucked off the hair—was more transcendently
and intrinsically awful than any man of whom they had ever
dreamed. More even than the power of His miraculous
beneficence, the majesty of His innocence and holiness
enthralled the heart. And so, on the page of St. Mark,
" Jesus of Nazareth passeth by," with the step not of a peasant
but of an Emperor, not of a malefactor but of a God. There
was not a good man—there was not even an honest slave—in
Rome, who did not in his heart loathe and despise the wicked

[1] Tac. *Ann.* xv. 44.
[2] Suet. *Ner. ad fin.* " Corpore maculoso et faedo."
[3] "Cum denotandis tot hominum palloribus sufficeret saevus ille *vultus c*.
rubor."—Tac. *Vit. Agric.* 45 ; Suet. *Dom.* 18 ; Pliny, *Paneg.* 38.

human gods of Caesarian infamy.[1] No absolute autocracy, no
oppressive magnificence could for a moment lift out of their
vileness a brutal buffoon like Caligula, or a base-hearted
aesthete like Nero. But St. Mark showed to Romans a Man
who was a Man indeed; crowned by His very manhood with
glory and power; Jesus of Nazareth, but the Son of God; a
Man, but a Man Divine and sinless, among sinful and
suffering men. Him, the God-man, no humiliation could
degrade, no death defeat. Not even on the Cross could He
seem less than the King, the Hero, the only Son. And as he
gazed on such a picture how could any Roman refrain from
exclaiming with the awe-struck Centurion, "Truly this was
the Son of God!"

8. Many other points are noticeable in this Gospel—how,
for instance, in one word, "Is not this *the carpenter?*" it throws
the only flash which falls on the continuous tenor of the first
thirty years—from infancy to manhood—of the Life of
Christ; [2] how in one phrase "This He said . . . making all
meats clean," St. Mark alone of the Evangelists, sets forth
with absolute clearness Christ's abrogation and abolition of
the Levitic law; how in two sentences he alone brings out
the slow, and as it were tentative methods of Christ's later
miracles, when the faith in Him was almost dead; how he
alone of the Evangelists tells us of no less than eleven
occasions amid his work on which Christ retired, either to
escape from His enemies, or in solitude—that best "audience-
chamber of God"—to refresh with prayer His wearied soul.[3]
But perhaps one last comparison may help to illustrate
the specialties of this Gospel. I compared the Gospel
of St. Matthew to the fugue and Passion-music of some

---

[1] See Boissier, *La Religion Romaine*, 122–135.

[2] vi. 3. As the reading ὁ τέκτων is certain, and is moreover in accordance
with the early tradition preserved by Justin Martyr, Origen is mistaken in
saying that Jesus is nowhere called "a carpenter" in the Gospels (*c. Cels.*
iii. 36).

[3] See i. 12; iii. 7; vi. 31, 46; vii. 24, 31; ix. 2; x. 1; xiv 34. "Periods
of pause and rest rhythmically intervene between the victories achieved by
Christ."—LANGE.

mighty master. I should apply no such comparison to the Gospel of St. Mark. I should compare it far rather to one of those pictures, at once so lovely and so awe-inspiring, of one of the early Italian painters—an Angelico da Fiesole, or a Giovanni Bellini—where, in colouring fresh as the flowers of spring, or deep, clear, and transparent as crystal, the Magi from the East present their offerings to the Infant King; or where He hangs on the Cross of shame—and though we see on the canvas the ornaments on every robe, the gleam on every jewel, the colours of every flower, yet the admiration for each separate detail, and almost the sense that they are painted there, is lost in the wonder, in the reverence, in the adoration, in the love, inspired by the intense beauty and unutterable majesty of Him in whom all the motive of the picture is centred, and in whom all its glories blend. So it is with St. Mark's Gospel. Amid the thousand details we see but the one Redeemer. Amid the hurrying procession our eyes rest but on a single figure. Amid the multitudinous accents our attention is absorbed by a single voice. And, as we close the last page of the Gospel, the words which spring involuntarily to our lips are these—

> " Strong Son of God, Immortal Love,
>   Whom we, that have not seen Thy face,
>   By faith, and faith alone, embrace,
> Believing where we cannot prove ;
>
> " Thine are these orbs of light and shade ;
>   Thou madest Life in man and brute ;
>   Thou madest Death ; and lo, thy foot
> Is on the skull which thou hast made.
>
> *   *   *   *
>
> " Thou seemest human and divine,
>   The highest, holiest manhood thou ;
>   Our wills are ours, we know not how ;
> Our wills are ours to make them Thine ! "

NOTE I.

ON THE GENUINENESS OF MARK XVI. 9–20.

It is impossible to read these verses attentively in the original without being struck by very remarkable peculiarities. ST. MARK.

1. In xvi. 2 we are told that the women went to the tomb *very early* in the morning (λίαν πρωΐ) and found that Christ was already risen. We are surprised, therefore, to find again in verse 9 the phrase "having risen *early*."

2. "*On the first day of the week*" (πρώτῃ σαββάτου) is expressed by a phrase for "week" which St. Mark never uses. Even in verse 2 we have τῆς μιᾶς σαββάτων.

3. "He appeared *first*." The "first" is surprising, since in the previous verses we have already been told of an earlier appearance to the women of whom Mary Magdalene was one.

4. "*Out of whom He had cast seven devils.*" This is still more unexpected, since the addition to Mary's name has not once been given when she is mentioned before in this Gospel (three times).

5. "*She.*" Here, and in 11 and 13, we have ἐκεῖνος used absolutely in a way unlike St. Mark's. (There is no similar instance in his Gospel except in iv. 20, where, perhaps, the true reading is οὗτοι.)

6. "*Went.*" This verb, πορεύομαι, is used three times in these few verses; not once elsewhere throughout the Gospel.

7. As we proceed we find a number of words and phrases unknown to St. Mark, such as θεᾶσθαι ὑπὸ, ἀπιστεῖν, ἕτερος, παρακολουθέω, βλάπτω, πανταχοῦ, ἐπακολουθέω, συνεργέω, βεβαιόω, πᾶσα κτίσις, μετὰ ταῦτα, ὕστερον, μὲν οὖν, besides seven words which are unique, but might conceivably be due to the subject; and two remarkable variations from St. Mark's usual construction (ἐν τῷ ὀνόματι for ἐπὶ, ἐπιθεῖναι ἐπί τινα, and ἐκβάλλειν ἀπὸ for ἐκβάλλειν ἐκ).

8. We have the title "*the Lord*" twice; which St. Mark never uses elsewhere.[1] In verse 9 the subject (ὁ Ἰησοῦς) is strangely omitted.

9. The use of the connecting particles in verses 19, 20 is rare in St. Mark, and the omissions of the copula in verses 10 and 14 is unusual.

10. Besides these very numerous and undeniable peculiarities thus *accumulated* into a few verses, the powers promised to "*believers*," in verses 17, 18 (handling of serpents, drinking poison, speaking with "new" tongues) are unparalleled, and suggest difficulties.

---

[1] St. Mark invariably uses the address "Rabbi," or "Rabboni," even where "Lord" is used in the parallel passages of the Synoptists.

ST. MARK.   11. "He that believeth and *is baptised* shall be saved" is an expression unlike any other saying of our Lord.

12. The general style has none of the features and favourite expressions which we recognise throughout the rest of the Gospel.

13. It appeared to some readers in very ancient days to contain statements at variance with those of the other Evangelists.[1]

Supposing that such a mass of surprising facts had met us in the pages of *any secular writer whatever* under similar circumstances, it is hard to believe that any critic would have been able to accept the genuineness of the passages. But when we turn to the external evidence the suspicion about the authenticity of the verses is indefinitely strengthened.

1. It is wanting in two of the best and most ancient Uncials—the Sinaitic, and the Vatican MSS.

2. In other MSS., and in MSS. of Syriac and Latin versions we are told that it was omitted in many ancient copies. It is also absent from some old MSS. of the Armenian version, and from one Arabic version.

3. Eusebius, Jerome, Gregory of Nyssa (or Hesychius), and the Scholia of several MSS., say that in their day it was wanting in almost all the Greek copies of the Gospels.[2]

4. It seems to have been unknown to Cyril of Jerusalem (?), Tertullian, and Cyprian; and is not mentioned by Clement of Rome or Clement of Alexandria.

5. A different, shorter, and unquestionably spurious ending is found in some MSS. and versions (*e.g.* L. and Cod. k. of the Itala, and the margin of the Philoxenian Syriac).

Even if the internal evidence in its favour had been strong, the external evidence against it would have made us at least doubtful as to its authenticity. But when we find it thus deficient in external evidence, while at the same time the internal evidence is so startlingly unfavourable, we can hardly wonder that it is rejected or questioned by such critics as Griesbach, Lachmann, Tischendorf, Tregelles, Schulthess, Schulz, Ritschl, Auger, Zeller, Fritzsche, Credner, Reuss, Wieseler, Holtzmann, Keim, Scholten, Klostermann, Hitzig, Schenkel, Ewald, Meyer, Weiss, Alford, Norton, Godet, Lightfoot, Westcott, and Hort.

The external arguments in its favour are,

a. That it is found in most Uncials, and all Cursives (though in the latter often with an asterisk, or a note mentioning its omission in older copies); in most versions, and in all Greek and Syriac lectionaries, &c.

---

[1] τὰ δὲ ἑξῆς (Mark xvi. 9-20) σπανίως ἔν τισιν ἀλλ᾽ οὐκ ἐν πᾶσι φερόμενα περιττὰ ἂν εἴη, καὶ μάλιστα εἴπερ ἔχοιεν ἀντιλογίαν τῇ τῶν λοιπῶν εὐαγγελιστῶν μαρτυρίᾳ. Euseb. Qu. 1, *ad Marinum.* "*Omnibus Graeciae libris paene* hoc capitulum in fine non habentibus, *praesertim cum diversa atque contraria evangelistis caeteris narrare videatur.*"—Jer. *ad Hedib.* Qu. ii.

[2] Greg. Nyss. *Orat. de Resurrect.* See the previous note.

It is quoted by Irenaeus, possibly by Justin Martyr, and by many of the Fathers.

β. Internal arguments in its favour there are, so far as I can discover absolutely none, with the exception that if this passage be removed, the Gospel would end with ἐφοβοῦντο γάρ. It would, indeed, be a very strange ending, though perhaps it might be paralleled. Considering the characteristic of St. Mark's style, it does not seem to be an *impossible* one; nor is it at all impossible that the original ending should have been lost. The "triple tradition" of the Synoptists, as Dr. Abbott has pointed out, ended with the return of the women from the sepulchre, and St. Mark may have scrupled to make any further addition. In these matters we must make allowance for idiosyncrasy, and cannot judge by modern ideas.

Let the reader compare the phenomena presented by these verses with those found in John xxi. That too is regarded, and in all probability rightly regarded, as an appendix, but there can be no doubt that (with the possible exception of the last two verses) it proceeded from the pen of the Apostle himself. This passage of St. Mark stands on a wholly different footing. It is accepted as canonical—in other words it has been accepted by the Church as having a right to be regarded as a part of Scripture ; but the number of competent critics who still believe it to be genuine is diminishing.

The passage is, however, defended, as genuine by Mill, Bengel, Schleiermacher, De Wette, Bleek, Olshausen, Lange, Ebrard, Hilgenfeld, Scrivener, Wordsworth, McLellan, Cook, Morrison, and Burgon. All who desire further evidence may seek it in the second volume of Westcott and Hort's *Revised Greek Text*, pp. 38, *sqq.* ; and will find everything which can be said in its favour in Dean Burgon's monograph on the subject (Oxford and London, 334 pp.). Having read both sides on the controversy they will be able to estimate the value of Dean Burgon's remark that, "*not a particle of doubt, not an atom of suspicion*, attaches to the last twelve verses of the Gospel according to St. Mark."

THE GOSPEL OF ST. LUKE.

"Utilis ille labor, per quem vixere tot aegri ;
Utilior, per quem tot didicere mori."

"He was a physician : and so, to all, his words are medicines of the
drooping soul."—S. JER. *Ep. ad Paulin.*

"Vidi due vecchi in abito dispari
Ma pari in atto, ognuno onesto e sodo,
L'un si monstrava alcun de famigliari
Di quel sommo Ipocrate, che natura
Agli animali fe' ch' ella ha più cari."
DANTE, *Purg.* xxix.

"Whose joy is, to the wandering sheep
To tell of the great Shepherd's love ;
To learn of mourners while they weep
The music that makes mirth above ;
Who makes the Gospel all his theme,
The Gospel all his pride and praise."
KEBLE, *St. Luke's Day.*

"Thou hast an ear for angel songs,
A breath the Gospel trump to fill,
And taught by thee the Church prolongs
Her hymns of high thanksgiving still."—KEBLE.

"A Saviour, which is Christ the Lord."—LUKE II. 11.

ST. LUKE. I CHOOSE these words as being perhaps the most characteristic which I could find to describe the idea which pervades
the Gospel of St. Luke.

About the Evangelist himself we know but little. Apart
from guesses and traditions, our information respecting him
is exceedingly scanty.

He does not mention himself by name in the Gospel or in
the Acts of the Apostles, though the unanimous voice of

ancient tradition, coinciding as it does with many probabilities derived from other sources, can leave no doubt that he was the author of those books.

There are but three places in Scripture in which his name is mentioned. These are Col. iv. 14, " Luke, the beloved physician, and Demas, greet you ; " 2 Tim. iv. 11, " Only Luke is with me ; " and Philem. 24, where he is mentioned as one of Paul's " fellow-labourers." From these we see that St. Luke was the faithful companion of St. Paul, both in his first Roman imprisonment, when he still had friends about him, and in his second Roman imprisonment, when friend after friend deserted him, and was "ashamed of his chain." From the context of the first allusion we also learn that he was " not of the circumcision." Tradition has always declared that he was a Gentile, and a " proselyte of the gate." [1]

The attempt to identify him with " Lucius of Cyrene " in Acts xiii. 1 is an error, since his name Lucas is an abbreviation not of Lucius but of Lucanus, as Annas for Ananus, Zenas for Zenodorus, Apollos for Apollonius, &c. The guess that he was one of the Seventy disciples is refuted by his own words, nor is there any probability that he was one of the Greeks who desired to see Jesus (John xii. 20) or one of the two disciples at Emmaus (Luke xxiv. 13).[2] Eusebius and Jerome say that he was a Syrian of Antioch, and this agrees with the intimate knowledge which he shows about the condition and the teachers of that Church.[3] If in Acts xi. 28 we could accept the isolated reading of the *Codex Bezae* (a reading known also to St. Augustine), which there adds

---

[1] Acts i. 19.

[2] He implies (Luke i. 1) that he was not an eye-witness.

[3] He speaks of " Nicolas of Antioch " in Acts vi. 5, without mentioning the native place of any other of the six deacons. Mr. Smith of Jordanhill, in his dissertation on St. Luke, points out the interesting parallel that of eight accounts of the Russian campaign, only the two Scotch authors (Scott and Alison) mention that General Barclay de Tolly was of Scotch extraction. Schaff. *Hist. of Christian Church,* p. 651. Some of St. Luke's special information about the Herods may have been derived from Manaen, the foster brother of Antipas of Antioch, Acts xiii. 1.

ST. LUKE. συνεστραμμένων δὲ ἡμῶν, "but while *we* were assembled together," it would prove that St. Luke had been acquainted with the Apostle shortly after his arrival from Tarsus to assist the work of Barnabas. In that case he may well have been one of the earliest Gentile converts[1] whom St. Paul admitted into full rights of Christian brotherhood, and with whom St. Peter was afterwards, for one weak moment, ashamed to eat. We cannot, however, trace his connection with St. Paul with any certainty till the sudden appearance of the first personal pronoun (in the plural) in Acts xvi. 10, from which we infer that he joined the Apostle at Troas, and accompanied him to Macedonia, becoming thereby one of the earliest Evangelists in Europe. It is no unreasonable conjecture that his companionship was the more necessary because St. Paul had been recently suffering from an acute visitation of the malady which he calls "the stake, or cross, in the flesh." Since the "*we*" is replaced by "*they*" after the departure of Paul and Silas from Philippi (Acts xvii. 1), we infer that St. Luke was left at that town in charge of the infant Macedonian Church. A physician could find means of livelihood anywhere, and Luke seems to have stayed at Philippi for about seven years, for we find him in that Roman colony when the Apostle spent an Easter there on his last visit to Jerusalem (Acts xx. 5). There is, however, every reason to believe that during this period he was not idle, for if he were "the brother, whose praise is in the Gospel" (*i.e.* in preaching the good tidings) "throughout all the churches" (2 Cor. viii. 18), we find him acting with Titus as one of the delegates for the collection and custody of the contributions for the poor saints at Jerusalem. The identification of St. Luke with this "brother" no doubt originated in a mistaken notion that "the Gospel" here means the written Gospel;[2] but it is probable on other grounds, and is supported by the tradition embodied in the superscription,

---

[1] In Col. iv. 11, 14, he is distinguished from "those of the circumcision."
[2] Jer. *De Virr. ill.* 7.

which tells us that the Second Epistle to the Corinthians was conveyed from Philippi by Titus and Luke.

From Philippi St. Luke accompanied his friend and teacher to Jerusalem (Acts xxi. 15—18), and there we again lose all record of his movements. Since, however, he was with St. Paul at Caesarea when the Apostle was sent as a prisoner to Rome, it is probable that he was the constant companion of his imprisonment in that town. If the great design of writing the Gospel was already in his mind, the long and otherwise unoccupied stay of two years in Caesarea would not only give him ample leisure, but would also furnish him with easy access to those sources of information which he tells us he so diligently used. It would further enable him to glean some particulars of the ministry of Jesus from survivors amid the actual scenes where He had lived.[1] From Caesarea he accompanied St. Paul in the disastrous voyage which ended in shipwreck at Malta, and proceeding with him to Rome he remained by his side until his liberation, and probably never left him until the great Apostle received his martyr's crown. To him—to his allegiance, his ability, and his accurate preservation of facts—we are indebted for the greater part of what we know about the life of the Apostle of the Gentiles.

We finally lose sight of St. Luke at the abrupt close of the Acts of the Apostles. Although we learn from the Pastoral Epistles [2] that he must have lived with St. Paul for two years beyond the point which his narrative has there reached, he may not have arranged his book until after Paul was dead,

---

[1] But although he may have been gathering materials for his Gospel at Caesarea (A.D. 54) there is good reason to believe that it was not published till a later date. The general *tone* of the Gospel—*e.g.* the use of αὐτός and ὁ Κύριος when speaking of Christ—indicates a later time in the rapid development of early Christianity than we should infer from the tone of the other Synoptists. Κύριος as a substitute for Jesus occurs fourteen times in St. Luke ; but elsewhere in the Synoptists only in Mark xvi. 19, 20. The combination "the Lord Jesus," occurs (if genuine) only in Luke xxiv. 3, though common in the Epistles. This would however be partly accounted for by the fact that St. Luke as a Gentile proselyte, belonged *in point of feeling* even more than in point of time to a later generation of Christians than the original Apostles.

[2] 2 Tim. iv. 11.

ST. LUKE. and the course of the narrative may have been suddenly cut short either by accident or even by his own death. Irenaeus (*adv. Haer.* III. 1) expressly tells us that his Gospel was written after the death of Peter and Paul. The most trustworthy tradition says that he died in Greece; and it was believed that Constantine transferred his remains to the Church of the Apostles in Constantinople from Patrae in Achaia.[1] Gregory of Nazianzus tells us in a vague way that he was martyred, but it is idle to repeat such worthless legends as that he was crucified on an olive-tree at Elaea in the Peloponnesus, &c., which rest on the sole authority of Nicephorus, a writer who died after the middle of the 15th century. The fancy that he was a painter,[2] often as it has been embodied in art, owes its origin to the same source, and seems only to have arisen from the discovery of a rude painting of the Virgin in the Catacombs with an inscription stating that it was "one of seven painted by Luca." It is not impossible that there may have been some confusion between the name of the Evangelist and that of a Greek painter in one of the monasteries of Mount Athos.

But leaving "the shiftless quagmire of baseless traditions" we see from St. Luke's own writings, and from authentic notices of him, that he was master of a good Greek style;— an accomplished writer, a close observer, an unassuming historian, a well-instructed physician, and a most faithful friend.[3] If the Theophilus to whom he dedicates both his works was the Theophilus mentioned in the Clementines

---

[1] On the ancient doors of San Paolo at Rome, he is represented dying peacefully.

[2] Give honour unto Luke Evangelist,
    For he it was, the ancient legends sang,
    Who first taught Art to fold her hands and pray.
                                    —ROSSETTI.

[3] In viii. 43, he omits the severe reflection of St. Mark on physicians "and was nothing bettered but rather grew worse." Dr. Plumptre, in the *Expositor* (No. xx. 1876), has collected many traces of St. Luke's medical knowledge (cf. Acts iii. 7, ix. 18, x. 9, 10, xii. 23, xx. 31, xxvi. 7, xxviii. 8 ; Luke iv. 23, xxii. 44, &c.), and even of its possible influence on the language of St. Paul. The theme has been greatly (and perhaps unduly) expanded by Rev. W. H. Hobart, *On the Medical Language of St. Luke*, Dublin, 1882.

as a wealthy Antiochene, who gave up his house to the preaching of St. Peter, then St. Luke may have been his freedman.[1] Physicians frequently held no higher rank than that of slaves, and Lobeck, one of the most erudite of modern Greek scholars, has noticed that contractions in *as*, like Lucas from Lucanus, were peculiarly common in the names of slaves.[2] One more conjecture may be mentioned. St. Luke's allusions to nautical matters, especially in Acts xxvii., are at once remarkably *accurate* and yet *unprofessional* in tone.[3] Now the ships of the ancients were huge constructions, holding sometimes upwards of 300 people, and in the uncertain length of the voyages of those days, we may assume that the presence of a physician amid such multitudes was a matter of necessity. Mr. Smith of Jordanhill, in his admirable monograph on the voyage of St. Paul, has hence been led to the inference that St. Luke must have sometimes exercised his art in the crowded merchantmen which were incessantly coasting from point to point of the Mediterranean. However this may be, the naval experience of St. Luke as well as his medical knowledge would have rendered him a most valuable companion to the suffering Apostle in his constant voyages.

Turning to the Gospel itself, we may first notice that it sets before us that conception of the life and work of Christ which was the basis of the teaching of St. Paul. The views of the great Apostle of the Gentiles are no less represented in the Gospel of St. Luke than are those of the great Apostle of the Circumcision in the Gospel of St. Mark.[4] By the

---

[1] He calls him κράτιστε in Luke i. 4. It is a title either of rank (given to Procurators, &c., Acts xᵣiii. 26 ; xxvi. 25) or of friendship. It is omitted in Acts i. 1.

[2] Renan (*Les Évangiles*, 255) and Dean Plumptre speculate on a possible connection of some kind between Luke and the poet Lucan, nephew of Gallio (Acts. xviii. 14–17) and of Seneca. This possibility was inferred from the apocryphal correspondence between St. Paul and Seneca, and other very slight indications (see Bishop Ellicott's *Commentary*, i. 257, 288).

[3] He uses in this chapter seven compounds of πλέω, and at least ten other correct nautical terms.

[4] Irenaeus, *adv. Haer.* iii. 1 and iii. 14. Tertullian, *adv. Marc.* iv. 2, 5. Origen *apud* Euseb. *H. E.* vi. 25, and *id.* iii. 4. Jerome, *De Virr. illustr.* 7.

ST. LUKE. providence of God we find such holy and beautiful friendships in formative epochs of the Church, as at the Reformation between Luther and Melanchthon, Calvin and Beza, Cranmer, Latimer, and Ridley.[1] How much should we have lost but for the friendship between St. Paul and the loved physician, between St. Peter and "Marcus my son"!

St. Luke's is the longest of the Gospels. A third of the facts it contains is wanting in the other Synoptists. It is enriched by so many beautiful characteristics, produced by the modifying influence and "varying emphasis of subjective ideas," that it deserves the remarkable eulogy which has been given to it of being "*le plus beau livre qu'il y ait.*" It is the most literary of the Gospels. It is dominated throughout by a spirit large and sweet and wise, and "joins the emotion of the drama to the serenity of the idyll. It is full of tears and songs and laughter; it is the hymn of the new people, the hosanna of the little ones and of the humble introduced into the kingdom. A spirit of holy infancy, of joy, of fervour, the evangelistic sentiment in its first originality pervades it with an incomparable sweetness."

It has been the common belief that it was written for the

A long list of words and phrases which are common to St. Luke and St. Paul may be seen in Davidson's *Introd. to the New Test.* ii. 12–19. The student may compare the following:

St. Luke—	St. Paul—
iv. 22.	Col. iv. 6.
iv. 32.	1 Cor. ii. 4.
vi. 36.	2 Cor. i. 3.
vi. 39.	Rom. ii. 19.
ix. 56.	2 Cor. x. 8.
x. 8.	1 Cor. x. 27.
xi. 41.	Tit. i. 15.
xviii. 1.	2 Thess. i. 11.
xxi. 36.	Eph. vi. 18.
xxii. 19, 20.	1 Cor. xi. 23–29.
xxiv. 45.	Acts xvii. 3.
xxiv. 34.	1 Cor. xv. 5.

Sections of St. Luke which are in peculiar accordance with the Gospel of St. Paul (Rom. ii. 16) are iv. 16–30; vii. 36–50; xv. 1–32; xix. 1–10; xxiii. 39–43; and especially the institution of the Lord's Supper. See too 1 Cor. xv. 45, and the constant mention of the Resurrection with the Passion.

[1] Schaff. *Hist. of the Christ. Church*, p. 649.

Greeks, and Jerome says that it was written in Achaia.[1]
One single sentence, to dwell on no other argument, would
be sufficient to show the early date of the Gospel. It is the
prophecy—"This generation shall not pass away till all
things shall be fulfilled" (xxi. 32).

Among the characteristics of this Gospel we may observe
the following:—

I. St. Luke is the first Christian hymnologist. One of
the sacred hymns which he alone has preserved—the
Benedictus, or Song of Zacharias, "Blessed be the Lord God
of Israel"—we constantly sing in our Morning Service; two
more, which he alone has preserved for us—the *Magnificat,*
or song of Mary, "My soul doth magnify the Lord;" and the
Nunc Dimittis, or song of Simeon, "Lord, now lettest Thou
Thy servant depart in peace"—are always used in our Evening Service. To these we may add the *Ave Maria* (i.
28-33) and the *Gloria in excelsis* (ii. 14).[2] How rich a contribution to our Christian Psalmody is this! How great
was the privilege of the Evangelist in having been thus
permitted to hand down to us the words sung daily by
myriads of Christian lips! St. Matthew represents the
Gospel as the accomplishment of the Old Dispensation; but, on the very threshold of St. Luke's Gospel,
the songs of Mary and of Zechariah set forth more
decisively the character of the New, as a kingdom of the
Spirit; as a spring of life and joy opened for human beings;
as a mystery, prophesied of, indeed, because it is eternal, but
now, in the appointed time, revealed to men. The Gospel

---

[1] "In Achaiae Boeotiaeque partibus volumen condidit." *Praef. in Matt.*
"Evangelium Graecis scripsit." Ep. xx. 4, *ad Damas.* The Greek of the
Gospel is pure when St. Luke is writing in his own person; it is only Hebraistic
when he is closely following Aramaic documents. The resemblance of his
vocabulary (not his style) to that of the writer of the Epistle to the Hebrews,
is natural when we remember that they were friends of St. Paul, and of one
another.

[2] The *Benedictus* seems to have been thus used as early as the fourth century,
the *Nunc Dimittis* in the fifth. The *Magnificat* is found as a part of the Evening
Service as early as A.D. 507 in the rule of Caesarius of Arles. The *Gloria*
seems to have been used in the second century.

of the Saviour begins with hymns and ends with praises; and, as the thanksgivings of the meek are recorded in the first chapter, so, in the last, we listen to the gratitude of the faithful.[1]

II. St. Luke's Gospel gives special prominence to prayer, not only by recording (as St. Matthew also does) the Lord's Prayer, but also by alone preserving to us the record how in no less than six instances during our Lord's ministry—at His baptism, after cleansing the leper, before calling His twelve Apostles, at His transfiguration, on the cross for His murderers, and, with His last breath,—our Saviour prayed. Though He was the Lord of heaven and earth, yet as a Man He prayed to His Father in heaven. It is in St. Luke (as in St. Paul) that we find twice repeated, the thought and the rule, that men ought to pray always, to pray without ceasing, and not to faint. And this exhortation is emphasised by the two parables (preserved by St. Luke alone)[2] which encourage us to a persistent energy, a holy importunity, a storming of the kingdom of heaven by violence, a victorious refusal to be denied the granting of our prayers—the parables of the friend at midnight and of the unjust judge. Thus the Gospel of eucharistic hymns is also specially the Gospel of unceasing prayers.[3]

III. Passing over minor characteristics, this Gospel is marked in many details by two main features—the presentation of the Gospel in its gratuitousness and in its universality. "By grace ye are saved through faith," might be the motto of St. Luke as of his great friend and teacher St. Paul. The word "grace," the word "Saviour" or "salvation," the words "to tell glad tidings," often recur in it;[4] and these rich words are applied not exclusively to the Jews, but universally to all. The angels in their opening song announce a Saviour

---

[1] Westcott, *Introd.* p. 354. Maurice, *Unity of the New Test.* p. 236.

[2] Luke xviii. 1 ; xxi. 36 ; xi. 5–13.

[3] It is also the Gospel of thanksgiving. Mention is made no less than seven times of "glorifying God" by praise (ii. 20 ; v. 25 ; vii. 16 ; xiii. 13 ; xvii. 15 ; xviii. 43 ; xxiii. 47).

[4] Χάρις eight times ; εὐαγγελίζομαι ten times.

and good will towards men. Jesus is not only the Son of David, or even the Son of Abraham, but the Son of Adam, the Son of God. It is St. Luke alone who ends the prophecy of Isaiah about the Baptist with the words, " And *all flesh* shall see the salvation of God." He alone records the sermon on the text which prophesied that Jesus should heal the brokenhearted and preach deliverance to the captive. Lastly (to omit many other instances), in him alone does the Lord ascend to His Father in heaven blessing His people with uplifted hands. Tradition says that the Evangelist was a painter; a painter in the common sense he was not, but in another sense he was; and what a picture of our Saviour Christ does this great ideal painter set forth to us—how divine, how exquisite, how circled, as it were, with a rainbow ! He comes with angel carols ; He departs with priestly benedictions. We catch our first glimpse of Him in the manger cradle of Bethlehem ; our last, as from the slopes of Olivet, He vanishes into the cloud of glory with pierced hands upraised to bless.

IV. These two grand dominant ideas of the gratuitousness and universality of the Gospel, as this beloved and loving Evangelist records it, are applied in various ways—every one of which is full of instruction.

a. The Judaism of that day had degenerated (as all spurious religion tends to degenerate) into a religion of hatreds. Then, as in many ages, religion had come to be identified with a partisanship, which clothed its own egotism under the guise of zeal for God, and lost itself in a frenzy of persecuting zeal against all opinions and all practices which were not its own. The Pharisaic Jews hated the Gentiles, hated the Samaritans, despised the poor, oppressed womanhood, insulted publicans, would have called down fire from heaven on all who differed from themselves. Far different is the spirit of the Gospel as set forth by St. Luke. In his pages, towards every age, towards either sex, towards all nations, towards all professions, towards men of every opinion and all shades of character, our blessed Lord

ST. LUKE. appears as *Christus Consolator*, the Good Physician of souls, the Gospeller of the poor, the Brother who loves all His brethren in the great family of God, the impartial Healer and Ennobler of a sick and suffering humanity, the Desire of all nations, the Saviour of the world.

β. St. Luke's is the Gospel of the infancy. St. Matthew too tells us something of the Saviour's birth; but he does not record the birth and infancy of the Baptist, nor the Annunciation, nor the meeting of Mary and Elizabeth, nor the song of the herald angels, nor the Circumcision, nor the Presentation in the Temple, nor the growth of Jesus in universal favour and sweet submission, nor, above all, that one anecdote of His Confirmation at twelve years old, which is " the solitary flower gathered from the silence of thirty years." All three Evangelists indeed tell us how " they brought young children to Christ," and how He laid His sacred hands upon the little heads; but by narrating the infancy and boyhood of Christ, St. Luke teaches us more effectually that even in infancy, even in boyhood, Humanity at every period of its brief life is sacred, for it is Humanity redeemed and consecrated from the cradle to the grave. The valley of its utmost weakness, no less than its valley of the shadow of death, has been illuminated by the footsteps of its heavenly King.[1]

γ. St. Luke's is the Gospel to Gentiles as well as Jews. He dwells on Christ's ministry to the world. At the very beginning of the ministry he records the sermon at Nazareth (iv. 16-30), which overthrows all exclusive Jewish hopes; records the hymn about Christ as " a Light to lighten the Gentiles ; " the prophecy that " all flesh shall see the salvation of God ; " the destined end that repentance and remission of sins should be preached unto all nations, beginning at Jerusalem ; the parallels of Elijah sent to the heathen Sarepta, and

---

[1] Hence this Gospel is preeminently *anti-docetic*. The Docetae denied the true humanity of Christ, and treated His life on earth as an illusory semblance. St. Luke alludes to the human existence of our Lord before birth (i. 40) ; as a babe (ii. 16); as a little child (ii. 27) ; as a boy (ii. 40) ; and as a man (iii. 22).

Elisha healing the heathen leper; the fuller details of the mission of the seventy who, by their number, typified the supposed number of the nations of the world. The same thought appears in the carrying back to Adam the genealogy of Him whom St. Paul calls, "the second Adam." In the other Evangelists this point of view is not passed over, but it acquires its fullest prominence in the Gospel of St. Luke. And thus the third Gospel becomes one great comment on the truth enunciated by St. Paul at Athens, that "God hath made of one blood all nations of men . . . . that they should seek the Lord, if haply they might feel after Him and find Him, though He be not far from every one of us." [1]

δ. It is also the Gospel of womanhood.[2] St. Luke alone records the special graciousness and tenderness of Jesus to women. He alone tells of the raising of the dead boy for whom the heart of Jesus was touched with compassion, because he was "the only son of his mother, and she was a widow;" he alone that Jesus was accompanied in His mission journeys—not by warriors like David, not by elders like Moses, not by kings and princes like the Herods—but by a most humble band of ministering women. He alone preserves the narratives, treasured with delicate reserve and holy reticence in the hearts of the blessed Virgin and of the saintly Elizabeth—narratives which show in every line the pure and tender colouring of a woman's thoughts. He alone tells us how honest Martha was cumbered with much serving, and how Mary of Bethany—the gentle and the lowly—chose, sitting humbly at the feet of Jesus, the better part; he alone how the Lord once addressed to a poor, crushed, trembling, humiliated sufferer the tender name of "daughter"; he alone how, when the weeping women mingled with the crowds who followed Him as He passed to Calvary, He turned and said, "Daughters of Jerusalem, weep not for me, but weep for yourselves and for your children." The Scribes

---

[1] The word γυνὴ occurs nearly as often in St. Luke as in both the other Synoptists put together.

[2] Acts xvi. 14.

ST. LUKE. and Pharisees gathered up their robes lest they should touch
a woman in the streets or synagogues; they pretended that
it was a disgrace to look at, much more to talk to, a woman; [1]
but He, the holy and the sinless, knew that in the normal
life of pure humanity it is only the twofold heart which beats
with one full life; that man and woman must together walk
this world

> "Yoked to all exercise of noble end,
> And so through those dark gates across the wold
> Which no man knows."

V. Again, St. Luke's is the Gospel pre-eminently of the poor
and of humble people, whom the world despises and ignores.
In his Gospel it is to the poor peasant-girl of Nazareth
that the angel comes. It is she who represents humanity
in its lowest, simplest form, and the only "*sancta, sanc-
tissima*" that she can claim is in the pure and sweet submission of "Behold the handmaid of the Lord." Nor is it
to kings or priests or Pharisees that the herald angels sing,
but to simple "shepherds, abiding in the field, watching
over their flocks by night." Nor is it Hillel or Shammai, or
Annas or Caiaphas—not rabbis white with the snows of a
hundred winters, or pontiffs with "gems oracular" upon
their breasts—who take the infant Jesus in their arms, but
unknown men [2] and widowed women, waiting only, in devout
hope, for the Consolation of Israel. And there is so much
about the poor and the hungry in St. Luke, that his has
ever been called (though very erroneously) the Gospel of
Ebionites.[3] He alone reports the parable of Dives and
Lazarus; he alone that of the rich fool; he alone the calling
of "the poor, the maimed, the halt, the blind" to the great

---

[1] John iv. 27, ἐθαύμασαν ὅτι μετὰ γυναικὸς ἐλάλει.

[2] Luke ii. 25, ἄνθρωπος ᾧ ὄνομα Συμεών.

[3] The word *Ebionite* is derived from the Hebrew *Ebion*, "poor." The
Ebionites were Jewish Christians who maintained the eternal validity of the
Jewish law, and the Messiahship but not the Divinity of Christ. They
gradually dwindled into a sect on the shores of the Dead Sea. On the
imaginary relation of St. Luke to the Gospel of the Hebrews, see Keim,
i. 104.

supper; he alone the warning not to choose chief seats, and of the humble exalted; he alone the counsel to the Pharisees to "give alms"; and to the disciples to "sell what they have:" and the advice of St. John the Baptist to part with one of two coats.[1] It is not by any means that he reprobates the mere possession of riches. He recognises the faithfulness of a Nicodemus and a Joseph of Arimathaea; but he saw the special necessity, in such days as those, to admonish the rich men who were grasping and oppressive and illiberal. Like St. James, he felt it to be his duty to warn all who were tempted, as the rich in all ages are tempted, to trust in uncertain riches, instead of being "rich towards God." It is not that he holds poverty in itself to be a beatitude, but only that kind of poverty which is "not voluntary nor proud, but only accepted and submissive; not clear-sighted nor triumphant, but subdued and patient—partly patient in tenderness of God's will, partly patient in blindness of man's oppression—too laborious to be thoughtful, too innocent to be conscious, too long-experienced in sorrow to be hopeful; waiting in its peaceful darkness for the unconceived dawn, yet not without its sweet, complete, untainted happiness, like intermittent notes of birds before the daybreak, or the first gleams of heaven's amber in the eastern grey." Which is there of us all who does not need this lesson? "Who is there almost," as Milton asks, "who measures wisdom by simplicity, strength by suffering, dignity by lowliness?" And if we need that this lesson should be brought home to us, where can we find it more tenderly and more affectionately expressed than in St. Luke?

VI. But, more than this, St. Luke's Gospel is the Gospel not only of children and of the Gentiles, and of the humble and the despised, of the blind, the lame, the halt, the maimed, but even of the publican and the harlot, the prodigal and the outcast; not only of Mary, but of the Magdalene;

---

[1] See iii. 10, 11; x. 38-42; xiv. 12-24; xvi. 14-31. We find in the Acts the same fondness for the Gospel of self-denial.

not only of Zacchaeus, but of the dying thief. There are two conditions of human life;—the one is pompous, critical, independent, self-satisfied. It is represented in the world by the airs of little, brief authority, and in the Church by the boastful tone, the censorious arrogance, the broad phylactery. It is human life as seen in the rich and haughty Pharisee of to-day, no less than it was seen 2,000 years ago;—the life and bearing of the person who has succeeded in trade, or made a good marriage, or of whom people are afraid; of the man who "holds his head high, and cares for no man, he." And there is quite the other side of human life;—the condition of the depressed, the poor, the unprosperous; of the man who has not made a success of life, as men count success; of the weak, who feel themselves weak. It is the life of failure which recognises itself as failure, for which no hope dawns on this side the grave. Or, much sadder even than this! There is the humanity that is conscious of its shame: crushed by its evil, accepting as its due the contempt poured upon it; not turning like even the trampled worm; which knows that it has squandered all, and made of health a shipwreck, and of character a byword, and of all life a blank mistake. How pitiless is the world to these! How it exults over a man that has once slipped! How it rakes out of his past years his buried faults! How it evokes from the unforgetting tomb the pale ghosts of his past delinquencies! The lessons of this Gospel should make us blush if ever we are eager to point the first finger, or to fling the first stone. To delight in blame, to revel in depreciation, is the characteristic of the very basest of mankind. And are we more sinless than the sinless One? more indignant at wrong than He? Yet, while He had plain thunderings and lightnings for impenitent Pharisaism and triumphant wickedness, how did He treat the sinful who knew that they were sinful, and the fallen who did not deny their fall? Now it is a tax-gatherer of bad reputation, and He says, "He also is a son of Abraham." Now it is a gay young fool, who has devoured his living with harlots, and comes all ragged and ST. LUKE. degraded from the far land and the feeding swine; and while he is yet a great way off, his father has compassion on him, and falls on his neck and kisses him. Now it is a broken-down woman who has touched Him, and He tenderly shields her shrinking anguish from the scorn of the unsympathising crowd. Now it is a coarse bandit, dying in agony upon the cross, and He says, " To-day shalt thou be with Me in Para-dise." Now it is a miserable castaway, her soul full of seven devils, who steals behind Him to kiss His feet as she weeps amid her tangled hair; and, while the proud, hard Pharisee scoffs, and comments, and sneers, He says, "Simon, seest thou this woman? I came into thy house; thou gavest Me no water for My feet, but she hath wetted My feet with tears and wiped them with the hairs of her head. Thou gavest Me no kiss; but this woman, since the time I came in, hath not ceased to kiss My feet. My head with oil thou didst not anoint; but this woman hath anointed My feet with ointment. Wherefore, I say unto thee, her sins which are many, are forgiven; for she loved much. And He said unto her, Thy sins are forgiven."

VII. Lastly, this divine and gracious universality of tender-ness is extended—which seems among Christians to be the hardest thing of all—even to those who differ from us in religious opinions. St. Luke's is pre-eminently the Gospel of tolerance.[1] Even against the Jews he does not breathe a single harsh syllable. It shows how deeply he has grasped the truth that Christ hath " other sheep which are not of this fold," though they all form the one flock. St. Luke may teach us the deeply-needed lesson that all religious rancour—whether it call itself Protestant or Catholic, Evan-gelical or Ritualist—is not religious but irreligious; not Christian, but un-Christian and anti-Christian. Hear what Christ says. The Samaritans were held by the Jews to be

[1] " On ne fut jamais moins sectaire. Tout y révèle un esprit large et doux." —Renan, *Les Évangiles*, p. 282.

deadly heretics, and Jesus Himself told them that they " worshipped that which they knew not : " [1]—yet how does He commend the gratitude of the Samaritan leper ! How does He choose as His type of love to our neighbour, not the indifferent priest, or the peering Levite, but the Good Samaritan ! " Let us call down fire from heaven as Elijah did," cry the religious controversialists of all times; and to all times comes the meek rebuke of the Saviour, " Ye know not, ye, what manner of spirit ye are of ; [2] for the Son of Man is not come to destroy men's lives, but to save them."

" We forbad him, because he followeth not us ; " so have the champions of party dogmatism fiercely exclaimed, age after age, hampering and hindering many a grand discovery of science and many a holy work of good ; to whom comes across the centuries, the mild, healing word of the tolerance of Jesus, " Forbid him not; for he that is not against us, is for us."

VIII. Such, then, is the Gospel of St. Luke ;—the Gospel of the Greek and of the future; of catholicity of mind; the Gospel of hymns and of prayers ; the Gospel of the Saviour ; the Gospel of the universality and gratuitousness of salvation ; the Gospel of holy toleration ; the Gospel of those whom the religious world regards as heretics ; the Gospel of the publican, and the outcast, and the humble poor, and the weeping Magdalene, and the crucified malefactor ; the Gospel of the lost piece of money and the lost sheep ; the Gospel of the good Samaritan and of the prodigal son ; [3] the Gospel of the saintly life, of pity, of forgiveness obtained by faith, of pardon for all the world ; the Gospel of grace and of the glad tidings of free salvation ; the Gospel of Him who was, as we all are, the Son of Adam, and who died that we all

---

[1] John iv. 22   [2] Luke ix. 55, οὐκ οἴδατε. . . . . ὑμεῖς.
[3] It is remarkable that St. Matthew's formula for parables is " The kingdom of Heaven is likened unto." That of St. Luke is more "human and humane " viz., " A certain man," " A certain rich man," &c. See x. 30 ; xiv. 16 ; xv. 11 ; xvi. 1, 19 ; xviii. 2 ; xix. 12.

might be the sons of God. Such are its lessons.[1] Have not some of us very much misread and mistaken them? Has the best Christian among us all done more than just begin to spell out their meaning?

---

[1] "Das Evangelium des Menschensohnes, der Humanität Christi, der Verklärung aller Humanität," Lange, *Bibelkunde*, p. 187 ; "Le son pur et clair d'une âme tout argentine," Renan. The word χαρά occurs in this Gospel no less than eight times (Luke i. 14 ; ii. 10 ; viii. 13 ; x. 17 ; xv. 7, 10 ; xxiv. 41, 51). Such terms as ἔλεος, πίστις, δικαιοσύνη, πνεῦμα ἅγιον, γνῶσις, &c., are common to St. Luke and St. Paul.

NOTE I.

FURTHER CHARACTERISATION OF ST. LUKE.

ST. LUKE. Besides the ten characteristics of St. Luke's Gospel which we have pointed out, we may notice further that St. Luke's Gospel is differentiated by

(xi.) Its careful chronological order (1—3). The bias of St. Luke is historical, as that of St. Matthew is theological. " Luke is like a botanist who delights to study each flower in the very spot where it has sprung up, and amidst its native surroundings. Matthew resembles the gardener who is culling splendid bouquets for some special purpose which he has in view."—Godet, *New Test. Studies*, p. 16.

(xii.) Its very important preface. This preface tells us that St. Luke had read previous " attempts" to write Gospels, and deeming them inadequate, had used all diligence to secure completeness ($\pi\hat{a}\sigma\iota\nu$), accuracy ($\dot{a}\kappa\rho\iota\beta\hat{\omega}s$),[1] chronological order ($\kappa\alpha\theta\epsilon\xi\hat{\eta}s$), and earlier commencement ($\check{a}\nu\omega\theta\epsilon\nu$).

(xiii.) Its command of the Greek language.[2]

(xiv.) The prominence given to the *antithesis* between light and darkness, forgiveness and non-forgiveness, God and Satan (iv. 13 ; viii. 12; x. 17-20 ; xiii. 10-17 ; xxii. 3, 31-34).

(xv.) The familiarity with the LXX. ($\dot{\epsilon}\pi\iota\beta\dot{\alpha}\lambda\lambda o\nu$, $\dot{\epsilon}\pi\iota\sigma\iota\tau\iota\sigma\mu\dot{o}s$, $\check{v}\psi\iota\sigma\tau os$, $\sigma\tau\iota\gamma\mu\dot{\eta}$, $\dot{a}\nu\tau\iota\beta\dot{a}\lambda\lambda\epsilon\iota\nu$, $\epsilon\check{v}\theta\epsilon\tau os$, $\pi\epsilon\rho\iota\sigma\pi\hat{a}\sigma\theta\alpha\iota$, $\delta o\chi\dot{\eta}$, $\lambda v\sigma\iota\tau\epsilon\lambda\epsilon\hat{\iota}$, &c.) and the Apocrypha (see xii. 19 ; xviii. 8 ; vi. 35 ; i. 42).

(xvi.) The numerical concinnity which marks the arrangement of the sections. In the sections and sub-sections we find a constant recurrence of the sacred numbers 3 and 7.

Although there is an Hebraic tinge in the hymns and speeches which St. Luke merely records, and in narratives where he is following an earlier or Aramaic document, his own proper style abounds in isolated phrases and words chiefly classical,[2] and his style is more flowing than

---

[1] "Lucam tradunt veteres. . . magis Graecas literas scisse quam Hebraeas. Unde et sermo ejus. . . . comptior est, et saecularem redolet eloquentiam." —Jer. *ad Damas. Ep.* 20. Where the style is less pure, and abounds in Hebraisms, we find internal evidence that St. Luke is closely following some Aramaic document in which the oral tradition had been reduced to writing. The preface shows in what a perfect Greek style he *could* have written.

[2] Instances are—$\nu o\mu\iota\kappa o\iota$ for $\gamma\rho\alpha\mu\mu\alpha\tau\epsilon\hat{\iota}s$, $\dot{\epsilon}\pi\iota\sigma\tau\dot{a}\tau\eta s$ for $\text{P}\alpha\beta\beta\dot{\iota}$, $\lambda\dot{\iota}\mu\nu\eta$ for $\theta\dot{a}\lambda\alpha\sigma\sigma\alpha$, $\check{a}\pi\tau\epsilon\iota\nu$ $\lambda\dot{v}\chi\nu o\nu$ or $\pi\hat{v}\rho$ for $\kappa\alpha\dot{\iota}\epsilon\iota\nu$, $\pi\alpha\rho\alpha\lambda\epsilon\lambda v\mu\dot{\epsilon}\nu os$ for $\pi\alpha\rho\alpha\lambda v\tau\iota\kappa\acute{o}s$, $\kappa\lambda\dot{\iota}\nu\eta$ for $\kappa\rho\dot{a}\beta\beta\alpha\tau os$, $\pi o\rho\epsilon\acute{v}o\mu\alpha\iota$ for $\dot{v}\pi\dot{a}\gamma\omega$, (except in one or two places), the particles

that of St. Matthew and St. Mark. His peculiar skill as a writer lies rather
in "*psychologic comments*," [1] and the reproduction of conversations with
their incidents, than in such graphic and vivid touches as those of St.
Mark. He is also a great master of light and shade, *i.e.* he shows remarkable skill in the presentation of profoundly instructive personal
contrasts—*e.g.* Zacharias and Mary; Simon and the Sinful Woman;
Martha and Mary; the Pharisee and the Publican; the Good Samaritan,
Priest, and Levite; Dives and Lazarus; beatitudes and woes; tears and
Hosannas; and the penitent and impenitent robber. [2]

It is the presence of these characteristics that has earned for this
Gospel the praise (already mentioned) of being "the most beautiful book
that has ever been written." [3]

μὲν οὖν and τε, the combination αὐτὸς ὁ, the more frequent use of the optative,
τὸ εἰρημένον for τὸ ῥηθέν, &c. He avoids the Latinism κοδράντης, and the
word "metamorphosis" (μετεμορφώθη) which the Greeks might have misunderstood (ix. 29). He uses Ἱεροσόλυμα only three times, but Ἱερουσαλήμ
twenty-six times. A long list may be found in Dr. Davidson's *Introd. to
the New Test.* ii. 57–67, and in Dr. Abbott's article "Gospels" in the *Encycl.
Britannica.* In some instances St. Luke corrects an awkward phrase found in
the other Synoptists, *e.g.* by using φιλούντων for θελόντων ἀσπασμούς (xx. 46);
by the addition of τασσόμενος after ὑπ᾽ ἐξουσίαν (vii. 8); by saying πεπεισμένος
ἐστὶν Ἰωάννην προφήτην εἶναι (xx. 6) for ἔχουσι τὸν Ἰωάννην ὡς προφήτην;
by substituting οἱ κατεσθίουσι (xx. 47) for οἱ κατέσθοντες; by using πενίχρα
(xxi. 2) for πτωχή (except when quoting Christ's words), and ὑστερήματος for
the less accurate ὑστερήσεως (xxi. 4). For other instances of St. Luke's
editorial changes see iv. 40; vii. 25; viii. 1; xi. 13, 36, 39, 49, 51, xii.
51, 55. Expressions of St. Mark which might have been cavilled at (*e.g.*
"He *was not able*," Mark vi. 5; "to lay hands on Him," iii. 21) were
omitted, or softened; see the tentative miracle (Mark viii. 24).

[1] iii. 15; vi. 11; vii. 29, 30, 39; xvi. 14, &c. Bishop Ellicott, *Hist.
Lect.* p. 28.

[2] Satan is mentioned six times; only three times in St. Matthew and
once in St. John. It is a curious circumstance, showing the common use
made by the Synoptists of a fixed oral tradition that they only use δαίμων
in the Gadarene narrative (Matt. viii. 31; Mark v. 12; Luke viii. 29);
but δαιμόνιον forty-five times. It is much to be regretted that our revisers did
not keep up the marked distinction between haunting "demons" and "devils."
"Devils" occurs many times in our Bibles, but not once in the New Testament, except in the sense of "slanderers" (2 Tim. iii. 3; Tit. ii. 3); and
"Devil" is only used by St. Paul in Eph. iv. 27; vi. 11; 1 Tim. iii. 6;
2 Tim. ii. 26.

[3] This praise is the more striking because of the source from which it
comes. The writer adds that it shows "un admirable sentiment populaire,
une fine et touchante poésie." "C'est surtout dans les récits de l'Enfance et
de la Passion que l'on trouve un art divin. . . Le parti qu'il a tiré de Marthe
et de Marie sa soeur est chose merveilleuse; aucune plume n'a laissé tomber
dix lignes plus charmantes. L'épisode des disciples d'Emmaus est un des
récits les plus fins, les plus nuancés qu'il y ait dans aucune langue." "Son
livre est un beau récit bien suivi, à la fois hébraïque et hellénique, joignant
l'émotion du drame à la sérénité de l'idylle. Tout y rit. tout y pleure, tout y
chante; partout les larmes et les cantiques; c'est l'hymne du peuple nouveau,
l'Hosanna des petits et des humbles introduits dans le royaume de Dieu."—
Renan.

The Miracles peculiar to St. Luke are—

1. The miraculous draught of fishes.   v. 4-11.
2. The raising of the widow's son at Nain.   vii. 11-18.
3. The woman with the spirit of infirmity.   xiii. 11-17.
4. The man with the dropsy.   xiv. 1-6.
5. The ten lepers.   xvii. 11-19.
6. The healing of Malchus.   xxii. 50, 51.

The Parables peculiar to St. Luke are—

1. The two debtors.   vii. 41-43.
2. The good Samaritan.   x. 25-37.
3. The importunate friend.   xi. 5-8.
4. The rich fool.   xii. 16-21.
5. The barren fig-tree.   xiii. 6-9.
6. The lost piece of silver.   xv. 8-10.
7. The prodigal son.   xv. 11-32.
8. The unjust steward.   xvi. 1-13.
9. Dives and Lazarus.   xvi. 19-31.
10. The unjust judge.   xviii. 1-8.
11. The Pharisee and the publican.   xviii. 10-14.

The two first chapters and the great section, ix. 51—xviii. 14, are mainly peculiar to St. Luke.   This section, descriptive of the incidents in the Journey of Christ, has sometimes, but inadequately, been called "the Gnomology" or collection of moral teaching.   No place is mentioned by name (ix. 52; x. 38; xi. 1—xvii. 12).   Besides the "greater insertion" there is a lesser insertion (vii. 11—viii. 3).

And in addition to those already noted above, other remarkable incidents or utterances peculiar to him are John the Baptist's answers to the people (iii. 10-14); the weeping over Jerusalem (xix. 41-44); the conversation with Moses and Elias (ix. 28-36); the bloody sweat (xxii. 44); the sending of Jesus to Herod (xxiii. 7-12); the address to the Daughters of Jerusalem (27-31); the prayer, "Father, forgive them" (xxiii. 34); the penitent robber (40-43); the disciples at Emmaus (xxiv. 13-31); particulars of the Ascension (xxiv. 50-53). Additional touches which are sometimes of great importance may be found in iii. 22 ("in a bodily shape"), iv. 13, ("for a season"), iv. 1-6 ; v. 17, 29, 39; vi. 11 ; vii. 21, &c.

As Jesus was "born under the Law," the Law is more often mentioned in Chap. ii. (*vv.* 22, 23, 24, 27, 29) than in the rest of the Gospel.

NOTE II.

THE GOSPEL OF MARCION.

Marcion (about A.D. 140) not only knew the Gospel of St. Luke, but ST. LUKE.
adopted it as the basis of his own Gospel with such mutilations as
suited his peculiar opinions. This fact is not only asserted by Irenaeus,
Tertullian, Epiphanius, &c., but may now be regarded as conclusively
proved, and accepted by modern criticism. Marcion omitted chapters
i. ii. and joined iii. 1 with iv. 31. His Gospel, in fact, was a Gospel,
" written *à priori.*"

Marcion, the son of a bishop of Sinope, was expelled from that city
by his father, went to Rome about A.D. 143, and becoming an adherent
of the Syrian heretic Cerdo, founded a formidable schism. There were
in his system Gnostic elements of dualism and docetism. He wrote a
book called *Antitheses* to contrast the teachings of the Old and New
Testaments, and his total rejection of the Old Testament necessitated
his rejection of a large part of the New which bears witness to the Old.
Consequently he only accepted the authority of ten Epistles of St. Paul
(discarding the Pastoral Epistles) and of a mutilated gospel of St. Luke,
in which about 122 verses were excinded. Our knowledge of Marcion's
gospel is chiefly derived from Tertullian (*Adv. Marcionem*) and
Epiphanius (*Haer.* 42). Volkmar (*Das Evang. Marcion*) demonstrated
that Baur and Ritschl were mistaken in supposing that Marcion's gospel
represented an *earlier* form of St. Luke's. He proves that it was merely
a copy with a few dubious readings (*e.g.* in x. 22 ; xi. 2 ; xvi. 17 ; xvii. 2 ;
xviii. 19 ; xx. 2, &c.), and arbitrary omissions of all that tended to
overthrow Marcion's special heresies. On this subject see Canon Westcott's *Introd. to the Gospels*, Appendix D, iv. pp. 441–443, *Canon of the
New Test.* pp. 312–315 ; Sanday, *Gospels in the Second Century*, c. viii.,
and *Fortnightly Rev.* June, 1875. For a reproduction of Marcion's
Gospel see Thilo. *Cod. Apocr.* i. 401. The strangest omission by Marcion
is that of the Parable of the Prodigal Son. As regards the *readings*,
modern opinion inclines to the view that some at least of these may be
worthy of consideration, especially as they often affect no doctrine or
point of importance.

NOTE III.

ANALYSIS OF THE GOSPEL.

ST. LUKE.   The general outline of St. Luke's Gospel is as follows:

1. Introduction. i. 1–4.
2. The Preparation for the Nativity. i. 5–80.
3. The Nativity. ii. 1–20.
4. The Infancy. ii. 21–38.
5. The Boyhood. ii. 30–52.
6. The Manifestation. iii. 1–iv. 13.
7. Early Ministry. iv. 14–vii. 50.
8. Later Ministry in Galilee and its neighbourhood. viii.
9. Close of Galilean Ministry and Journey northwards. ix. 1–50.
10. Incidents and Teachings of the Journey to Jerusalem. ix. 51–xviii. 14.
11. Incidents and Teachings of the last stages of the Journey, xviii. 14–xix. 46.
12. Closing Scenes and Death. xix. 47–xxiii. 49.
13. The Burial and Resurrection. xxiii. 50–xxiv. 49.
14. The Ascension. xxiv. 50–53.

The keynote of the Gospel is struck in i. 77, "*To give knowledge of salvation unto His people in the remission of their sins.*"

Compare the first public declaration of Jesus Himself: "The Spirit of the Lord is upon me, because *He hath anointed me to preach glad tidings to the poor*," iv. 18, 19.

And His last declaration, "Thus it is written, that the Christ should suffer, and rise again from the dead; and *that repentance and remission of sins should be preached in His name unto all the nations* beginning from Jerusalem." xxiv. 47.

NOTE IV.

THE MURATORIAN FRAGMENT ON LUKE.

The allusion to St. Luke at the beginning of the Muratorian fragment in as follows "Tertio Evangelii librum secando Lucan Lucas iste medicus post acensum Xρι cum eo Paulus quasi ut juris studiosum

secundum adsumsisset numeni suo ex opinione concriset dmn tamen nec
ipse dvidit in carne et ide pro asequi potuìt ita et ad nativitate iohannis
incipet dicere." Corrected from the gross blunders of an ignorant scribe,
and conjecturally emended, this seems to mean "the third Book of the
Gospel according to Luke. This Luke, a physician, after the ascension
of Christ when Paul had chosen him as a companion of his journey
wrote in his own name as he heard (ex opinione ἐξ ἀκοῆς, or possibly
κατὰ τὸ δόξαν, Luke i. 3.) Yet neither did he himself see the Lord in
the flesh, and he too did as he best could (?) so he began his narrative
even from the birth of John."

THE GOSPEL OF ST. JOHN.

WRITTEN PROBABLY AT EPHESUS ABOUT A.D. 90.

> " Sed Joannes alâ binâ
> Caritatis, aquilinâ
> Formâ fertur in divina
> Puriori lumine."
>
> ADAM DE STO. VICTORE.

"Sumtis pennis aquilae et ad altiora festinans de Verbo Dei disputat."— JER. *Prol. in Matt.*

"Aquila ipse est Johannes sublimium praedicator et lucis internae atque aeternae fixis oculis contemplator."—AUG. *in Joh. Tr.* 36.

" St. John revealed to the world in his three works the threefold picture of the life in God :—in the Person of Christ (the Gospel), in the Christian (the Epistle), and in the Church (the Apocalypse). He anticipated more perfectly than any other the festival of eternal life."—GODET.

" And the Word became flesh."—JOHN i. 14.

ST. JOHN.
EVERY one who knows anything whatever of Biblical studies is aware that of late years there have been many formidable attacks on the authenticity of the fourth Gospel. Happily it does not belong to my present object to enter into the interminable controversies which have arisen around that question.[1] It has of course been my duty to

---

[1] The discussion began with Evanson's *Dissonance of the Evangelists* in 1792. It was continued by Vogel, Bretschneider (1820), Strauss (1835), Weisse (1838), Bruno Bauer (1840), F. C. Baur (1844), and since that time by a host of writers, especially Zeller, Schwegler, Volkmar, Keim, and Hilgenfeld. The latter tried " to throw light by the torch of Gnosticism on the sanctuary of Johannine theology," and was followed by Réville, D'Eichthal, and others. The position recently adopted by Keim, Scholten, &c., is that St. John was never in Asia at all ; but this view has been amply refuted. An excellent

study all that can be urged against the Gospel by the ablest followers of Baur, and by those who in this particular have accepted their conclusions; but neither in Baur, nor Strauss, nor Hilgenfeld, nor Reuss, nor Keim, nor any other of the able critics who have persuaded themselves that the Gospel was the work of a Gnosticising dreamer in the second century, have I met with any argument that does not seem to me to have been fully and fairly answered. So long as the arguments of such writers as Ewald, Luthardt, and Weiss, in Germany; Godet in France; Bishop Lightfoot, Dr. Westcott, and Dr. Sanday in England remain unrefuted, we may still hold to the conviction that we have before us in this Gospel a genuine work of the beloved disciple. Dr. Westcott especially, in his invaluable commentary, has proved in a most decisive manner that the writer was a Jew; a Jew of Palestine; an eyewitness; an Apostle : and when this is established the inference becomes irresistible that he was the Apostle John. The direct evidence, the indirect evidence, the external evidence, the internal evidence, all combine, and severally suffice, not indeed to clear the subject from difficulties, many of which are inevitable and must remain insoluble, but to prove that the hypothesis of spuriousness is encompassed with difficulties far more formidable. No one has ever doubted the

sketch of the controversy is given by Holtzmann (in Bunsen's *Bibelwerk*), Reuss (*Gesch. d. heil. Schrifts.* i. 2 and 7), and by Godet in his *St. John* (Introd. c. ii.). John the Presbyter—a sort of "spectral duplicate" of the Apostle, who, as has been shown elsewhere (by Zahn, Riggenbach, and Professor Milligan, and in my *Early Days of Christianity*, ii. *ad fin.*) is none other than the Apostle himself—has been evoked as the author. The reader will find powerful defences of the genuineness of the Gospel in the editions of the Gospel by Lücke, Meyer, Hengstenberg, Ewald, Luthardt, Lange, Godet, Westcott, and in Bishop Lightfoot (*Contemp. Rev.* February, 1876); in Dr. Sanday's *Fourth Gospel;* in Weiss's *Leben Jesu;* and in Dr. Ezra Abbott's *Authorship of the Fourth Gospel.* The Johannine literature in this century alone would fill a library; but the objections urged against the genuineness of the Gospel have been met point by point, and nothing can invalidate the mass of external and internal evidence in its favour from early, varied, and unanimous testimony; from the proof that in the second century it was not only widely known, but various readings had already risen in the text; from the style, the knowledge of Palestine, the depth of insight displayed, the many subtle indications that we are reading the words of an eye-witness; and from multitudes of conspiring probabilities derived from the most opposite quarters.

ST. JOHN. depth and the beauty of this Gospel. No one can reasonably doubt that it was written by the author of the First Epistle. If St. John did not write it, it was written by one whose spiritual insight it would be hardly possible to exaggerate Where, whether within the Apostolic circle or outside of it, is such a writer to be found unless we find him in St. John? Above all, where are we to look for such a writer in the second century? The extant Christian literature of that century is before us. Except to those who have studied the writings or fragments of Clemens Romanus, the pseudo-Barnabas, Papias, Hegesippus, Hermas, Irenaeus, Justin Martyr, Ignatius, and other writers,[1] it would be impossible to convey a conception of the immeasurable inferiority by which they are separated from the Gospel of St. John. In that literature there is scarcely a gleam of the exalted genius, of the profound thought, of the indescribable charm which in all ages has won the homage of mankind to this Gospel; and which, even in this age, has extorted the often unwilling eulogies of sceptical critics.[2] To which of the second century writings would Luther have applied the glowing language which he uses of the Fourth Gospel? Which of the Fathers was even remotely capable of giving forth what Herder beautifully calls "this echo of the older Gospels in the upper choirs?" Keim is one of the most devout, and learned of the assailants of this Gospel, yet when he tries to meet this argument his embarrassment becomes almost ludicrous. He does not attempt to face it except in one brief note, and all that he has to say is that there is in the literature of the second century "one pearl" in the Epistle to Diognetus, and "much that is fine in the Apologists," and "even on Roman soil there are Minucius Félix with the splendid scenery of his beautiful dialogue, and the clever and beautiful composition in the Clementine Homilies." If this is all that can be said by a

[1] To these must now be added the newly-discovered and very important Διδαχὴ τῶν δώδεκα Ἀποστόλων.

[2] Almost the sole exception is John Stuart Mill (*Three Essays*, p. 253).

writer like Keim in answer to such an objection, we can only say *cadit quaestio.* Who can forbear a smile when he hears of Justin Martyr, or Minucius Felix with his pretentious prettinesses, or even the anonymous writer of the extravagantly estimated Epistle to Diognetus, spoken of as even remotely comparable to St. John? The forgery—I would use the word in its least invidious sense, and only because there is no other—of this Gospel in the second century would involve a literary problem indefinitely more difficult than would the appearance of Dante's *Divine Comedy* or Milton's *Paradise Lost* in the days of Walafrid Strabo or Alcuin. If, in the middle of the second century there had been any man who could have produced such a book, is it conceivable that one who towered so immeasurably above all his contemporaries should have remained a nameless forger—unnoticed and unknown? Further, supposing that such a person could have existed, would he with such beliefs as this Gospel indicates have dared or wished to palm upon the world an audacious fiction respecting the Divine Word? If the Fourth Gospel be the work of a *falsarius,* then the discourses which centuries of saints have regarded as the divinest parts of their Lord's teaching were the work of a pseudonymous romancer, who wrote with the deliberate intention to deceive. What could be more base than his solemn asseverations— which would in that case be not only shameless, but little short of blasphemous falsehoods—that he is a truthful witness? Renan, with skilful euphuism, talks of the composition of the Gospel in the name of St. John as "a little literary artifice, resembling those of which Plato is fond!"[1] Without pausing to show that the reference to Plato is here profoundly misleading, it suffices to say that the matter in question assumes the proportions not of "a little literary artifice," but of a monstrous and inexcusable deception. And this deception is not only in this case a literary miracle, it is also a spiritual impossibility. Weiss[2] says

[1] Renan, *L'Église Chrétienne,* p. 53.   [2] *Leben Jesu,* i. 124.

with perfect truth that "if it be the poetry of a semi-gnostic philosopher in the second century, the Fourth Gospel is not only an illusive will of the wisp, but in reality a huge lie." But the man who had the intellectual capacity to forge this book, must have been little short of a portent if he also had the spiritual baseness and the reckless audacity to thrust upon the Church his own fancies as the record and revelation of the Living Christ. I do not think that any one has ever had the courage to charge the author of the Fourth Gospel with gross irreverence and fundamental insincerity. No one has ever ventured to hint that he did not believe heart and soul in the Christ of whom he wrote, as the Incarnation of the very God. If then this were so, could there be any presumption so monstrous as that of a writer who, with the Gospels in his hands, devised a deliberate falsification and invention of the words and works of Him whom He proclaimed to be the Son of God? This at least was a course on which the worst and boldest of the Gnostic heresiarchs would hardly have ventured—much less the holy and humble disciple who gave to the world "the spiritual Gospel." It has been well said by Gustave Schwab—

> " Hat dieses Buch, das ew'ge Wahrheit ist,
> Ein lügenhafter Gnostiker geschrieben,
> So hat seit tausend Jahren Jesus Christ
> Den Teufel durch Beelzebub vertrieben." [1]

Are we to believe that the writer who gave its supreme and final form to the theology of the New Dispensation—who, in the judgment of nineteen Christian centuries, saw most deeply into the heart of the Lord Jesus,[2] and expressed most perfectly His inmost teaching,—the writer who, more even than St. Paul, has moulded the thoughts of all Christendom in its conception of what is the very essence

---

[1] Lines given to, and quoted by, Dr. Schaff. The interesting and not improbable legend of the circumstances which led St. John to write his Gospel at the entreaty of the Ephesian elders is related in the Muratorian fragment, in Victorinus of Pettau (Migne, *Patrol.* v. 333), and in Jerome (*Com. in Matt. Prol.*).

[2] " In reading St. John's writings I always seem as if I saw him before me at the Last Supper, leaning on his Master's breast."—CLAUDIUS.

of Christian truth — was a man who, while defiantly re-
constructing Christ out of his own consciousness, was capable
of impudent and wicked asseverations that he was bearing a
true and personal witness to things which he had seen and
heard ? What Christian would have dared to fancy that the
ideal Christ of his own invention was to be preferred to the
Son of Man ? Have we been misled by the phantom of a
dreamer ? If that be so, then the Christian who has built
his faith and his hopes on teaching which he believed to be
that of St. John, the bosom friend of the Lord, will be
tempted to exclaim in despair that—

> " The pillared firmament is rottenness,
> And earth's base built on stubble."

Let us, then, with such convictions, take the Gospel as it
is and consider its plan and outline ; its object ; its characteristics ; and its relation to the other Gospels.

I. It falls at once into two divisions, the Prologue, which
contains the essence of all that the Evangelist intends to set
forth, and the Narrative, in which the truths of the Prologue
are illustrated and proved.

(1) The Prologue occupies not only the first five, but the
first eighteen verses. It sets forth the Word of God—that is,
Christ the Son of God—(*a*) absolutely as pre-existent ; as in
perfect communion with God ; as being God ; and (*b*) in relation
to the universe as its source, its agent, its quickening ; and (*c*)
in relation to created beings, as life and light. Then he tells
us that there is a conflict between light and darkness (5), and
that John bore prophetic witness to the manifestation of the
light in the darkness (6—8). This light had shone even
before the Incarnation in the heart of every man (9), but had
shone unrecognised (10). When it was more fully revealed
at the Incarnation, He, the Incarnate Light, was rejected by
His own people (11), but accepted by those who, in receiving
and believing on Him, became by a new and divine birth
"children of God" (12, 13). The reader is now prepared for
the consummate declaration, which contains the essence of

St. John's Gospel and of all Christianity, that the Word became Flesh; tabernacled among men; and was witnessed by them, as being full of grace and truth. To this Incarnate Word John bore the witness of prophecy (15); believers experienced His full grace (16); and His revelation superseded the old Law (17), for it is the only vision of God which is possible to man (18).

II. Having in this Prologue set forth with unequalled depth and fulness the Eternal Truths which it is the object of his testimony to establish, St. John passes at once to life and to history, in order to show the revelation of God by His Word to men.

(2) The whole subsequent narrative is based on the fundamental antithesis between Faith and Unbelief, between the World and the Disciples. It narrates Christ's Revelation of Himself to the World (i. 19—xii. 50), and His Revelation of Himself to His Disciples (xiii.—xxi).

The Revelation to the World is divided into three parts, (A) the Proclamation (i. 19—iv. 54); (B) the Recognition (iii. iv.): (C) the Antagonism (v. 1—xii. 50).[1]

A. The Proclamation again falls into two divisions, namely, (a) the Testimony to Christ (i. 19—ii. 11), and (β) the Work of Christ (ii. 13—iv. 54).

a. The Testimony to Christ is threefold.

(i.) That of John the Baptist, which is the Testimony of the Old Dispensation in its closing prophetic utterance (i. 19—34).

(ii.) That of the Disciples, who recognise Him (35—51).

(iii.) That of miracles, which St. John calls "Signs" and "Works" (ii. 1—11).

---

[1] It will be seen that I have been mainly guided by Dr. Westcott (*St. John* vii. and *passim*), Keim (*Jesu of Nazara*, i. 156-160), and Reuss (*La Théologie Johannique*, 22-25), in their view of the divisions into which the Gospel falls: but also that I have varied from them. Godet's outline is very simple. He divides the Prologue into three parts—the Word (1-5); the Word rejected by unbelief (6-11); the Word accepted by faith (12-18); and he thinks that the Gospel has three corresponding sections—the Son of God; Jewish unbelief; Christian faith—namely, i.-iv.; v.-xii.; xiii.-xvii. Then follow the consummation of unbelief (xviii., xix.) and of faith (xx.).

B. The initial recognition of Christ is threefold: (a) by the learned Pharisee (ii. 13—iii. 36); (β) by the ignorant and heretical Samaritans (iv. 1—32); (γ) by the Galilean courtier (iv. 43—54).

C. But the opposition soon began, and it runs its course side by side with works ever more decisive, and testimony ever more and more emphatic. In Jerusalem Jesus heals the impotent man, and reveals His relation to God (v.). In Galilee He feeds the five thousand, and reveals in anticipated sacramental teaching, His relation to men (v.). In Jerusalem, at the Feast of Tabernacles He holds His great controversy with the wavering multitudes and proclaims Himself as the Light of the World (vii. viii.); at the Feast of Dedication He heals on the Sabbath the man born blind, and gives to the hostile Pharisees His clear testimony to Himself as the Door and the Good Shepherd, and as one with the Father; He is in consequence compelled to escape to Peraea (ix. x.).

Then comes the final sign—the Raising of Lazarus—and the Revelation of Himself, to those who love Him, as the Resurrection and the Life. But the sign is in vain. It is followed by the final and most deadly antagonism. Jesus is condemned to death, and conceals Himself in the little town of Ephraim (xi.).

The twelfth chapter gives us three closing scenes of the public ministry—the Feast at Bethany; the triumphal entry into Jerusalem; and the request of Greeks to see Jesus. His answer to the request is followed by a voice from heaven; by His last warning to the Jews to walk in the Light while they had the Light; by a summary (37—43) in which the Evangelist points out that the rejection of Christ's ministry was in accordance with ancient prophecy; and by another summary (44—50) in which Jesus Himself utters His judgment respecting those who believe and those who do not believe on Him, and His emphatic testimony to the truth of His words, as being the commandment of the Father which is life eternal (50).

III. The next great division of the Gospel shows us Christ among His own. It occupies in point of time but one single evening. The period of conflict and antagonism with the multitude and with their leaders is practically over. Jesus has been rejected by the world; He now has to reveal Himself to His disciples in such a way as through them—after they have been endued with power by the Holy Ghost—to win the world unto Himself.

It falls like the former division into three sections:—*A.* the last supreme revelation by acts of humility and love. *B.* the last discourses. *C.* the prayer of consecration. These discourses have been called The Sermon in the Chamber. "The Sermon on the Mount sets forth the New Law of Christ, the Sermon in the Chamber vivifies the New Law with the New Spirit."

A. In the first of these sections the Lord washes the Disciples' feet, and separates the last element of antagonism by dismissing the traitor into the night.

B. The discourses fall into two groups—those in the Upper Chamber (xiii. 31—xiv. 31); and those on the way (xv. xvi). This double group of discourses corresponds to the double preamble. The former discourses mainly arise from the questions of individual Apostles, and deal with the Lord's approaching departure, His relation to the Father and the Disciples, and the promise of the Holy Ghost. The discourses on the way dwell on the living union with Christ, with its issues as regards the Disciples and the world; the fuller promise of the Paraclete; and the promise of final victory and joy (xv. xvi.).

C. Then follows the Great High-Priestly Prayer—the Prayer of Consecration—in which the Son pours forth His heart to the Father (*a*) for Himself (1—5); (*β*) for His Disciples (6—19), and (*γ*) for the whole Church (20—26).

IV. The next division shows us "the *dénouement* of the two relations previously established—the double supreme

peripety of the divine tragedy."[1] Jesus has revealed Himself
to the world, and the world has rejected Him. He succumbs
to that opposition and remains dead to unbelief. But He
triumphs for faith, and His death becomes the source of life.
These chapters are much more than a narrative. Through
the narrative they set forth the Person and the Idea. With
the history they suggest the interpretation of its inner
meaning.[2] They show us that the sufferings of the Lord
were voluntary, were predetermined, and in no wise obscured
His majesty. The narrative, as usual, falls into three sections
—(i.) the Betrayal ; (ii.) the Trial; (iii.) the End.

V. The last division tells us of the victory over death,
as evinced by the Resurrection, and believed by St. John, by
the Magdalene, by the disciples, by Thomas, and by many
who have not seen and yet have believed. The chapter "lays
open a new Life in Christ, and a new life in men." This
narrative of the Resurrection is "the counterpart and com-
plement to St. John's narrative of the Passion. His history
of the Passion is the history of the descent of selfishness to
apostasy ; his history of the Resurrection is the history of
the elevation of love into absolute faith."[3] The exclamation
of Thomas, "My Lord and my God," shows that the
Word had finished His work by winning the perfect recognition of Himself as being that which the prologue had set
forth.[4]

VI. The last chapter is obviously an appendix or epilogue.
The Gospel, so far as the original plan of the Evangelist is
concerned, clearly terminates with xx. 31. The main object
of St. John in adding this chapter apparently was to correct
an error which had gained currency respecting himself. In
doing so the Apostle gives us an exquisite narrative of an
appearance of Christ to some of His disciples by the Lake of

---

[1] Reuss, p. 26. [2] Westcott, p. 249. [3] Westcott, p. 287.
[4] Reuss (*Heilige Schriften*, i. § 221) summarily divides the Gospel as
follows :—1. Prologue. 2. First Section (i. 6–xii.). Manifestation in the
World, with recapitulation (xii. 37–50). 3. Opposition and Acceptance
(xiii.–xv.). 3. History of the Passion (xviii.-xx.).

Galilee, in which He teaches them by a living allegory that
work for Him is work which is always blessed, and then
indicates the future duties and destinies of His two chief
Apostles, of whom the one is to feed His sheep and little
lambs (*ἀρνία*), the other is to tarry till He comes.

The Gospel ends with two verses which some have supposed
to be an attestation of the Ephesian elders to whom, in
accordance with a very probable tradition, the Gospel was
originally intrusted. After this attestation the scribe, or the
Apostle himself, explains in a boldly hyperbolical expression
the reason why the written Gospel was, and must inevitably
have been, of a fragmentary character.

2. Such is the Gospel of St. John. Of its object happily we
need not have a moment's doubt, for the Apostle distinctly
foreshadows it in his prologue, and states it at the conclusion.
He admits that the book is a selection; that Jesus did many
other signs which are not written in this book: " but these,"
he says, " are written that ye may believe that Jesus is the
Christ, the Son of God; and that believing ye may have life
in His name." [1]

This statement of the writer's threefold object is at once
terse and extraordinarily comprehensive.

i. In very early days there began a fatal tendency (as we
shall see hereafter) " to sever Jesus," *i.e.* of the two *natures* to
make two *persons;* to draw a distinction between the human
Jesus and the eternal Christ; to represent the life of Jesus
on earth as purely phantasmal; to say that the Divine nature
only united itself with Him at His baptism, and abandoned
Him at the Cross.[2] It was St. John's object to testify that

---

[1] Reuss (*Heilige Schriften*, ii. p. 222) divides the scheme of St. John's system
into three parts. 1. Theological premisses—God and the Son. 2. Historic
premisses—The Incarnate Son and the world. 3. Mystic theology—Faith
and Life : or Light, Love, Life as corresponding to the Being of God ; which
the world lacks, but which are offered by the Son and received by the elect.
John iii. 15 ; 1 John iv. 9.

[2] See the remarks of Irenaeus about Cerinthus (*Haer.* i. 26), and the note
on 1 John iii., iv. 3 *infra*, and for further information see *Early Days of
Christianity*, ii. 446-451.

Jesus was indivisibly and distinctly (ἀδιαιρέτως, ἀσυγχύτως) *the Son of God.*[1]

ii. But it was his object, further, to connect this Revelation with all the past. Jesus, the Son of God, *was also the Christ,* the Jewish Messiah. Christianity was no sudden break, no startling discontinuity in the course of God's revelation. Christianity did not dissever itself from the glorious annals and holy foreshadowings of Judaism. To St. John as to St. Matthew the old dispensation was the new prefigured; the new dispensation was the old fulfilled.

iii. But this twofold polemic or demonstrative object was subordinate to the high moral and religious object. If St. John wrote to show that the present was the consummation of all that was blessed, and the universalisation of all that was narrow in the past, he did so that in this belief *we might have life:*—" these signs have been written that ye may believe that Jesus is (i.) the Christ, (ii.) the Son of God, and that (iii.) believing ye may have life in His name." God who, in time past, spake fragmentarily and multifariously in the prophets, hath at the end of the days spoken unto us in the Son; and if we be one with Him as He is thus set forth we shall have life—true life, eternal life. The thesis of the Epistle to the Hebrews, and the central conception of St. Paul—which was mystic union with Christ and life "in Christ"—are in these few pregnant words united with the Messianic theme of the first Evangelist, St. Matthew. The words have that stamp of supreme finality which a vaulting criticism would vainly attribute to an unknown, second-century Gnostic forger, but which we believe to have been the consummate glory of the bosom Apostle.

3. The characteristics of the Gospel are very clearly marked. First it is eminently the spiritual Gospel, the

---

[1] In his prologue St. John shadows forth the outline of a great philosophy of religion. 1. The contradiction between God and the world, with the Logos as mediator. 2. The coming of the Logos into the world (but never fully recognised) in the form of an illuminating revelation. 3. The Incarnation of the Logos. 4. The coming of the Spirit, as the highest and final blessing. See Keim, pp. 148-153.

Gospel of Eternity, the Gospel of Love. This feature was observed in the earliest days. The other Gospels were called in contradistinction to it the " bodily " gospels. The Synoptists represent the objective teaching of the Apostles (Acts xi. 49); this Gospel represents the deeper and more developed thoughts of St. John. The fourth Gospel is distinguished from the other three, in that it is shaped with a conscious design to illustrate and establish an assumed conclusion. If we compare the purpose of St. John with that of St. Luke (i. 1—4) it may be said with partial truth that the inspiring impulse was in the one case doctrinal, and in the other historical. But care must be taken not to exaggerate or misinterpret this contrast. Christian history is doctrine, and this is above all things the lesson of the fourth Gospel. The Synoptic narratives are implicit dogmas, no less truly than St. John's dogmas are concrete facts. The real difference is that the earliest Gospels contained the fundamental words and facts which experience afterwards interpreted, "while the latest Gospel reviews the facts in the light of their interpretation."[1] It is only in this sense that the Gospel can be called "a theological treatise," or that St. John can be regarded as being, in a technical sense, what the early fathers called him, " the theologian," " the divine."

These views tend at once to correct and to absorb the counter theories that the Gospel was didactic;[2] or supplementary;[3] or polemical;[4] or an *Eirenicon*. It is all of these in its effects, but none of these in exclusive design. It is *didactic* only because the interpretation lay in the facts recorded. It is *supplemental*, and even avowedly supplemental, in so far as the author constantly assumes that certain facts are already in the knowledge of his hearers,[5]

---

[1] Westcott, p. xli.
[2] Muratorian Fragment, and Clement. Alex. *ap*. Euseb. *H. E.* vi. 14.
[3] Clem. Alex. *ap*. Euseb. *H. E.* iii. 24.   [4] Iren. *Haer.* iii. 11.
[5] i. 32, 46 ; ii. 1 ; iii. 24 ; vi. 70 ; vii. 3, &c. Hence St. John, though he speaks at such length of the Last Supper, does not narrate the Institution of the Eucharist. On the one hand *that* was universally known and practised ; on the other he has already given its inmost idea in ch. vi.

and adds other facts out of the abounding specialty of his own information;[1] but at the same time it expressly disclaims all intention to be complete.[2] The object of the Evangelist is not so much the historic record of facts as the development of their inmost meaning. It is *polemical*, since it is incidentally a correction of incipient errors by the statement of truth. It is an *Eirenicon* only because St. John had attained to the apprehension of the one consummate truth —"the Word became Flesh"—in which all religious controversies are reconciled. Every truth which is so supreme and final in character is the synthesis of minor oppositions.[3] For instance, the early Church was profoundly agitated by the question about the Law; St. John, without so much as touching on the question, sets it aside and solves it for ever by the one sentence, "The Law was given by Moses; grace and truth came by Jesus Christ."

4. It is emphatically and preeminently the Gospel of the Incarnation. Matthew had set forth Christ's Messianic function; Mark His active work; Luke His character as a Saviour; St. John sets forth His Person.[4] Christ fills the whole book, and absorbs the whole life of the drama of which He is the centre.[5] The informing idea of every page and chapter is "the Word made flesh." The idea of the Logos, as Godet says, very far from being the mother of the narrative is the daughter of it. The title of Logos is not used by Christ Himself or in the body of the Gospel. He is nowhere, like the Philonian Logos, a vague, changeful, bodiless abstraction, but He is a living human being. St. John sets forth to us that there is no vast unspanned abyss between God and man, but that God became man; that

[1] See ii. 23; iv. 45; x. 32; xi. 2; xii. 37, &c. For many special points of information see as to names vi. 71; xii. 1; xiii. 26; xviii. 10; xix. 13, &c. He supplies our knowledge of the first cycle of the teaching of Jesus, His Judaean ministry, His greatest miracle.
[2] xx. 30, "many other signs . . . *which are not written in this book.*" It is therefore absurd to say that, if any point is omitted it is disparaged.
[3] See especially Westcott, xli. xlii.
[4] Godet, St. John, *Introd.*
[5] Keim.

ST. JOHN. there is nothing inherently evil in the bodily nature of man, but that the Word became Incarnate Man. Jesus is the Son of God, and yet is no Docetic phantom, but hungers and thirsts and is weary, and knows human anguish and human joy.[1] This is the characteristic which led Origen to speak of this Gospel as the consummation of the Gospels, as the Gospels are of all the Scriptures; and Luther to say that it is the unique, the tender, the true master-Gospel, which, with the Epistle to the Romans and the First Epistle of St. Peter made up a New Testament sufficient for his needs. Yet it is entirely untrue to assert that St. John represents a different Christ, "another Jesus" than the Christ of the Synoptists. The scenery, indeed, in which He is placed is partly different, and the form and time, and to some extent the substance of His teaching. But there is no difference as regards His Divinity, and the Emperor Julian[2] was totally wrong when he said that "John, in declaring that the Word was made flesh, had done all the mischief." Christ is the same Christ, though looked at from a different point of view; and (externally) the coincidences in the twofold delineation are to be counted by scores. They are coincidences in place, dates, duration, incident, words, doctrines, imagery; and they have been pointed out again and again.[3] There are in St. John no scribes, no lepers, no publicans, no demoniacs; there is little or nothing which can be called anecdotic. This is accounted for by the avowed character of the book, which also explains why the miracles are here narrated in the light of symbolic acts; not as portents ($\tau\epsilon\rho\alpha\tau\alpha$), nor as exhibitions of power ($\delta\upsilon\nu\alpha\mu\epsilon\iota\varsigma$), nor as deeds which excited wonder ($\theta\alpha\upsilon\mu\alpha\tau\alpha$), nor as contrary to expectation ($\pi\alpha\rho\alpha\delta o\xi\alpha$), but as "deeds" ($\epsilon\rho\gamma\alpha$) perfectly natural to the Doer, and as signs ($\sigma\eta\mu\epsilon\hat{\imath}\alpha$) of His power, and manifestations of His glory (ix. 3, xi. 4). The difference

---

[1] i. 18; iii. 13; x. 18; xvii. 11, &c.; compared with iv. 6, 7; xi. 38; xii. 27; xv. 11; xix. 28.   [2] *ap.* Cyril *c. Julian.*
[3] See Schaff, *History of the Christian Church,* 697; Godet, i. 197; Westcott, lxxix.–lxxxiii.

in the form of His teaching is due to the difference of circumstances and of interlocutors. That teaching is given not in the form of apophthegms, or parables, or eschatologies, or even (often) of continuous discourses, but generally in the form of conversations, which are perpetually interrupted by the misunderstandings—always unspiritual, often simple, sometimes almost grotesque—of those who heard Him.[1] The difference, so far as there is any, in the substance of the teaching arises from the deeper apprehension of St. John. The method in which the teaching is set forth of course reveals the writer's individuality, but it has been repeatedly shown that the teaching itself diverges in no single particular from that of the Synoptists. St. John was a mystic, and delighted in mystic symbolism. Hence, while he does not narrate a single parable, he brings out another side of the doctrine of Jesus, parabolic indeed in character, but less easy of popular apprehension—namely, the allegoric. In the allegoric discourses about bread and wine, about light, the door, the gate, the vine, the shepherd, St. John brings out in a different manner the same essential truths. When Keim talks of St. John as " going over to Paulinism with drums beating and colours flying," and of the Jewish-Christian Apostle as "having broken with all the sacred principles of his youth, his manhood, and his ministry,"—so much of fact as corresponds to this violent exaggeration is accounted for when we remember that St. John wrote latest of the sacred writers; wrote as the last of those Apostles whose brows had reflected the lambent gleams of Pentecost; wrote as the bosom disciple who had enjoyed a most intimate communion with his Lord. When he penned his Gospel a flood of light had been cast on the truths of the New Covenant by the full absorption of Gentile Christians into the Church, by the development of Christian thought, by the antagonism of anti-Christian error, above all

---

[1] See Reuss, p. 8. This feature recurs no less than twenty-five times (ii. 20; iii. 4, 9; iv. 11, 15, 33; vi. 28, 31, 34, 52; vii. 27, 35; viii. 19, 22, 33, 39, 41, 52, 57; ix. 40; xi. 12; xiv. 5, 8, 22; xvi. 29).

ST. JOHN. by the Destruction of Jerusalem, and that Second Coming of Christ to close for ever the Old Dispensation. Many of the same essential doctrines are common to the Apocalypse and the Gospel, and if there be also a deep difference between them it is a difference due to the lapse of twenty years marked by events of unparalleled importance, and by a religious development rich and rapid beyond that of any other epoch in the history of the world.

5. It is the Gospel of Witness.

In accordance with the symbolic character of the book we find throughout it—as has been so admirably shown by Canon Westcott [1]—a sevenfold witness to Christ.

    i. The Witness of the Father (v. 34, 37, viii. 18).

    ii. The Witness of the Son (viii. 14, xviii. 37).

    iii. The Witness of His works (x. 25, v. 36 &c.).

    iv. The Witness of Scripture (v. 39—46).

    v. The Witness of the Forerunner (i. 7, v. 35).

    vi. The Witness of the Disciples (xv. 27, xix. 35).

    vii. The Witness of the Spirit (xv. 26, xvi. 14).

6. It is the Gospel of "the Logos," [2] of Christ the Word of God.

The profound insight—let us say rather the spiritual illumination—which led the Evangelist to use this title for Jesus Christ the Son of God has been recognised in all ages. In the use of it St. John stands alone. Other Apostles seem, as it were, to hover on the verge of it, but they do not definitely adopt it, still less do they dwell prominently upon it. Whether St. John borrowed it from the Logos of Philo,[3] or

---

[1] Westcott, *l. c.* xlv.

[2] When Epiphanius says that the Gospel was rejected by the Alogi, he probably means to imply by paronomasia that the sects which rejected it and the doctrine of the Logos were "without reason." (Comp. Iren. *Haer.* iii. 11.)

[3] Some of Philo's strongest and most remarkable expressions about the Logos are as follows. He calls the Logos "the second God" (*De profug.*, *De Monast.* Opp. ii. 225); "the archetype of the visible world;" the ideal unity of all things; the "idea of ideas;" "the image of God, by whose means the whole universe was created;" "the bond of all things;" the manna; the source of life and holiness; "the soul of the world." See Gfrörer, *Philo*, i. 176–248; Siegfried, *Philo*, 219-228.

from the Memra or Debura of the Jewish schools (afterwards used in the Targums), his adaptation of it infused into the title a majesty and a depth of meaning which were absolutely original. In Philo the Logos is, at the best, a dim abstraction in whose wavering outlines it is impossible to affirm that any absolute hypostasis is meant. In the Jewish schools the use of Memra and Debura (meaning "the word") was due to the desire to soften the simple anthropomorphic and anthropopathic phrases of the Old Testament — phrases which attributed to God human parts and human passions. Thus both in Philo and in the Rabbis the object was to make God seem more distant rather than more near; to interpose lower agencies between Him and the material world; to bridge by imaginary conceptions the infinite chasm which seemed to separate the Divine from all created things. The object of St. John was the very reverse. It was to show that God had come down to man in order that man might arise to God. The Manichean dread of all matter as essentially evil, the Agnostic desire to regard God as unspeakably remote and incomprehensible, were fundamentally overthrown by the immortal utterance that "the Word became flesh." To make such a use of the title "the Word" was to slay those conceptions which lay at the heart of Alexandrian theosophy and of Jewish scholasticism with an arrow winged with feathers from their own nests. It was to adopt their most cherished watchwords in order to substitute for their favourite idols an eternal truth.

And this being the case the title Logos receives all the fulness of its meaning. It means all that the Rabbis implied by the Shechinah and the Metatron, and the Targumists by Memra and Debura. It means both uttered reason and immanent speech, both the spoken word (λόγος προφορικός) and the inner thought (λόγος ἐνδιάθετος) of the Stoics and of Philo. It means all that is included in the Latin words used by different Fathers and translators to express it— *Verbum, Sermo, Ratio.* It means alike (as in the famous lines of

Goethe), "das Wort," "der Sinn," "die Kraft," "die That" the Word, the Thought, the Power, the Act. It fixes and, so to speak, crystallises all that had been said in the Sapiential books of the Old Testament and the Apocrypha about the Word, the Angel of the Presence, and the Wisdom of God, as well as all the speculations of Gentile, Rabbinical, and Alexandrian philosophy. At the same time it supersedes and transcends all those dim approximations to half-apprehended truths. It infuses into them a life which raises them into a loftier sphere of being. More epoch-making words— words which more express the inmost meaning of all revelation in all ages—were never written than the four words of this Gospel, "The Word became flesh," which modern writers are content to assign to an unknown forger of the second century.[1]

7. It is the Gospel of symbolism; and mystic numbers prevail even throughout the arrangement of the topics.

"The clothing of the book is Greek, but the body is Hebrew."[2] The arrangement of the book is throughout constructed with direct reference to the sacred numbers three and seven. Almost all the sub-sections run in triplets. "Jesus is thrice in Galilee, thrice in Judea, twice three feasts take place during His ministry, and particularly three Passover feasts—in the beginning, the middle, the end— which either foretell or procure His death. He works three miracles in Galilee and three in Jerusalem. Twice three days is He in the neighbourhood of John; three days are covered by the narrative of Lazarus, and six by the fatal Passover. He utters three sayings on the Cross, and appears thrice after His Resurrection."[3]

---

[1] See *Early Days of Christianity*, i. 273–276.

[2] Godet, p. 20. See too Keim, p. 157. Of all the Greek connecting particles St. John only uses δὲ, καὶ, οὖν, ὡς, and κάθως. Godet strangely says that he only uses μὲν *once;* but it occurs only *eight* times.

[3] Unless the walking on the sea be regarded as a part of the great scenic miracle of the loaves, there are seven miracles (at Cana ; the nobleman's son ; the paralytic ; the loaves ; walking on the sea ; the man born blind ; Lazarus), together with the draught of fishes in the supplementary chapter (xxi.). Keim's triplets require to be carefully criticised.

The grouping round the three Passovers is part of St. John's original plan (ii. 13, vi. 4, xi. 55). And it can hardly be an accident that Christ utters seven times "I am," and so reveals Himself as the Bread of Life, the Light of the World, the Door of the Sheep, the Good Shepherd, the Resurrection and the Life, the Way, and the True Vine.

In reading the Gospel and First Epistle of St. John we are reading the last words of special revelation; we catch, as it were, the final whisper of the voice of Christ as it was echoed in the heart of the disciple whom He loved. And the tone of the speaker's mind is worthy of the charm which we find in its accents. "Here we have rest and harmony—peace, joy, and blessedness such as the Christian seeks for; and though struggle is not wanting, varied and intense—heat want, trouble, zeal, anger, irony—yet the struggling Christ is a part of the Christian life which seeks to find expression in him; and Christ's finale, at the parting supper, on the cross, after the resurrection, is peace, victory, glory."[1]

[1] Keim, p. 159.

NOTE I.

SPECIAL WORDS AND PHRASES IN ST. JOHN'S GOSPEL.

ST. JOHN.

On the style of St. John, see *infra.* He has been called "a master of lucid obscurity,"[1] and the remark, though meant as a sneer, is a happy one. His style is pre-eminently lucid ; his thoughts are somewhat obscure. Their spirituality and profundity make them "dark with excess of light." We find both in the Gospel and the Epistle the same "emphatic remoteness," the repeated words, the simple constructions, the positive and negative statements (i. 7, 8, 20 ; iii. 15, 17, 20, &c.) of the same truth.[2]

We see in the Gospel, as in the Epistle, the ideality which regards all subjects in the light of their absolute antitheses :—" Light and darkness, God and the world, heaven and earth, spirit and flesh, life and death, truth and error, love and hatred, eternal and transitory, Christ and Satan, the Church and the world, present Christianity attaining to victory through contest." [3]

It is obviously an undesigned coincidence—an unconscious trace of personality—that the Evangelist speaks of the Baptist as "John" without adding his title, as the other Evangelists do. An interesting sign of the later date at which he wrote is that he alone speaks of the Sea of Galilee as the Sea of Tiberias (vi. 1 ; xxi. 1). Thirty years earlier, when the other Evangelists wrote, Herod's new town of Tiberias had not yet succeeded in giving its name to the lake, and superseding its older designation.

It is a very remarkable fact that every one of St. John's peculiar phrases and expressions is found also in his reports of the teaching of our Lord.[4]

It has been often made a serious difficulty that the style remains essentially the same alike in the discourses of John the Baptist, of our Lord, and of the Evangelist himself. Much has been written on this subject, but no further explanation can be given than that the writer

---

[1] Strauss, who compares him to Correggio.

[2] There is not in St. John (taking the best text) a single optative, or a single instance of oblique narration. " La langue de l'évangeliste n'a pas d'analogue dans toute la littérature profane ou sacrée ; simplicité enfantine et transparente profondeur, sainte mélancolie et vivacité non moins sainte : par dessus tout, suavité d'un amour pur et doux."—GODET.

[3] Davidson, *Introd.* ii. 348.

[4] See an interesting note in Huidekoper's *Indirect Testimony of History to the Gospels,* pp. 93–102.

was intensely influenced, and, if the expression be allowed, magnetised by what he had heard from the lips of Jesus as it was reflected in his own subjectivity. Though the style differs, even opponents of the genuineness of the Gospel admit the close and constant identity of the teaching of our Lord as represented by the Synoptists and by St. John. Every reader may verify this fact for himself again and again.[1]

Words which specifically mark St. John's tone of thought are—

"*Saying*" (παροιμία 4 times, λόγος many times). He does not use "parable" once.

"*To gaze upon*" (θεωρεῖν). This occurs 23 times, and only 15 times in all the three Synoptists.

"*The Light*" (i. 4, 5, 7-9, &c., 23 times; "*Glory*," 20 times). "*Glorify*," 22 times.

"*Darkness*," 9 times.

"*The Truth*," 25 times.

"*Love*," 6 times. "*To love*," 12 times.

"*The World*," 78 times (only 15 times in the Synoptists).

"*Flesh*," 8 times.

"*Eternal Life*," 15 times.

"*To abide in*," 18 times.

"*To manifest*," 8 times.

"*To judge*," 19 times; "judgment" 11 times.

"*To believe*," 98 times; twice as often as all the Synoptists.

"*The last day*," 7 times.

"*Witness*," 47 times.

"*To know*," 55 times

"*Works*," 23 times.

"*Name*," 25 times.

"*Signs*," 17 times.

Thus the vocabulary is certainly poor. John uses fewer words than any one of the Synoptists, very far fewer than St. Luke, but "these expressions soon make amends to the reader for their small number by their intrinsic wealth." They are few in number, but divine in quality. They deal with celestial glories.

---

[1] See Reuss, *Heilige Schriften*, ii. p. 224.

NOTE II.

THE MURATORIAN FRAGMENT.

ST. JOHN.   Corrected and conjecturally emended the passage in this ancient fragment on the canon seems to mean, "The fourth book of the Gospels, John,
one of the disciples (wrote). On being exhorted by his fellow-disciples and
bishops, he said, 'Fast with me to-day for three days, and let us mutually
relate what shall have been revealed to each.' That same night it was
revealed to Andrew, one of the Apostles, that John should set forth all
things in his own name, while all revised. Hence, though various
points of importance are taught in separate Gospels, it still makes no
difference to the faith of believers, since all things about the Nativity,
Passion, Resurrection, intercourse with His Disciples, and about His
twofold coming, first in the humility of contempt, which has been, then
glorious in royal power, which is to be, have been set forth in them
all by one supreme Spirit. . . . What wonder is it then if John so
consistently brings forth each point also in his Epistles, saying about
himself, 'What we have seen with our eyes, and heard with our ears,
and our hands have handled, those things we have written.' For thus
he proclaims himself not only an eye-witness, but a hearer too, and
also a writer of all the wonderful things of the Lord in order."

NOTE III.

EXTERNAL EVIDENCE.

It would be absurd here to enter into evidence which it would require
a whole volume of controversy to sift and establish, but it may, I think,
be most fairly asserted that the admission of the weight of external
evidence is gaining ground. The practical certainty that the Gospel
was incorporated in Tatian's *Diatessaron* has now been established by
the commentary of Ephraem Syrus.[1] Even Keim, though he rejects the
genuineness of the Gospel, has made the important admission that "the
actual indication of its existence extends about as far back as those of

[1] Hence Renan's assertion that by Διὰ τεσσάρων Tatian meant "perfect
accord," and that he borrowed the phrase from Greek music (*L'Églis Chrétienne*,
p. 503) falls to the ground.

the other Gospels" (*Jesu of Nazara*, Eng. Trans., i. 187), and allows that it was known to Justin Martyr, and even to the Pseudo-Barnabas, and that Hermas was acquainted with the first Epistle. Bishop Lightfoot (see quotations from his unfinished work in Plummer's *St. John*, p. 19) shows that allusions to it are found even in the shorter Greek forms of the Ignatian Epistles. The first Epistle (and, therefore, probably the Gospel) was known to Hermas and to Polycarp. When such a writer as Keim rejects the attempts of the Tübingen school to bring down its date till after the middle of the second century, and places it as far back as A.D. 100-117, the weight of the external evidence can hardly any longer be questioned, and the immense force of the internal evidence, added to the impossibility of finding or imagining a forger, will be duly felt. Among the most recent and powerful contributions to the arguments in favour of the Gospel are the Commentaries of Canon Westcott, and the chapters in Weiss's *Life of Christ* (v.-vii.).

THE ACTS OF THE APOSTLES.

THE ACTS OF THE APOSTLES.

WRITTEN PROBABLY AT ROME BEFORE A.D. 61.

"The best evidences for the truth of the Gospel are Christianity and Christendom."

"*Multitudinis credentium erat cor unum et anima una.* Quand on a écrit cela on est de ceux qui ont lancé au coeur de l'humanité l'aiguillon qui ne laisse plus dormir jusqu'à ce qu'on ait découvert ce qu'on a vu en songe et touché ce qu'on a rêvé."—RENAN.

"Dieses Buch wohl möchte heissen eine Glosse über die Episteln St. Pauli."
—LUTHER *Vorrede.*

"So mightily grew the word of God and prevailed."—Acts xix. 20.

THE preciousness of a book may sometimes best be estimated if we consider the loss which we should experience if we did not possess it. If so, we can hardly value too highly the Acts of the Apostles. Had it not come down to us there would have been a blank in our knowledge which scarcely anything could have filled up. The origin of Christianity would have been an insoluble enigma. We should have possessed no materials out of which it could be constructed, except, on the one hand, a few scattered remnants of ecclesiastical tradition, and on the other hand shameless misrepresentations, like the pseudo-Clementine forgeries. We might then have had no escape from wild conjectures, such as may be found in the later writings of the followers of Baur, who represent Paul and James as irreconcilable enemies, and consider that the Epistle of St. Jude and parts of the

Apocalypse of St. John were envenomed attacks of Jewish Christians on the authority and character of the Apostle of the Gentiles. It is only from the Acts of the Apostles that we are enabled to understand that union between Judaism and Christianity, for which, as has been said, it would otherwise have been as impossible to account as for a junction of the waters of the Jordan and the Tiber. To very few since the world began has it been granted to render two services so immense as those which have been rendered by St. Luke in his Gospel and the Acts of the Apostles.[1] In the one he has given us the most exquisite and perfect sketch of the Saviour of Mankind; in the other he has enabled us to watch the dawn of the Gospel which the Saviour preached as it broadens gradually into the boundless day. In his earlier work St. Luke had many predecessors, and his task was to sift the materials which they presented, and to combine them with all that he had been able to learn by personal inquiry. In his second work he was at once an historian and in great measure an eye-witness, and he took no small part in the events which he narrates. We have in the Acts a picture of the origins of Christianity drawn by one who was himself a leading actor in the early evangelisation of the world. Quiet, retiring, unobtrusive, the beloved physician has yet so used for us his sacred gifts of calm observation, of clear expression, of large-hearted catholicity, of intelligent research, that he has won for himself a conspicuous place among the benefactors of mankind.

Let us first look at his treatise as a whole, and then endeavour to grasp its special peculiarities.

We see at the first glance that it falls into two great sections, of which the first (i.—xii.) is mainly occupied with the doings of St. Peter, and the second (xiii.—xxviii.) is exclusively devoted to the missions and sufferings of St. Paul; or, dividing

---

[1] Eusebius, *H. E.* iii. 25; reckons the Acts among the *Homologoumena.* The extraordinary fact that in St. Chrysostom's day there were many who were unaware of its existence (Hom. i.) was perhaps due to its having been addressed to one person.

it on another principle, we may say that the first section (i.—
ix. 30) records the establishment of the Church in Palestine,
and the second (ix. 31—xxviii. 31) its extension as far as Rome.

The first fourteen verses are introductory. They describe *I: 1-14.*
the final interview of the risen Lord with the disciples, and
they give fuller details of His Ascension than were known to
—or, at any rate, were recorded by—the Evangelist when he
wrote his earlier volume. Here alone we learn that forty
days elapsed between the Resurrection and the Ascension.
The Gospel was a narrative of all that Jesus began both to do
and to teach as the inauguration of His kingdom. The Acts
furnishes the continuation of that beginning. Prominent in
those last words of Christ are "the promise of the Father"
and "the baptism of the Holy Ghost." The eighth verse
might stand as the motto of the whole book, "Ye shall
receive power when the Holy Ghost is come upon you; and
ye shall be my witnesses both in Jerusalem, and in all Judea,
and Samaria, and unto the uttermost part of the earth." The
first section of the book narrates the fulfilment of the earlier
part of this promise; the later sections show its complete
accomplishment.

In the meeting of the Apostles with the disciples and the *I: 15-26.*
holy women in the upper chamber where they were abiding
we see the cradle of the infant Church. That upper chamber
belonged in all probability to the mother of St. Mark the
Evangelist. If so it must have been within those hallowed
walls that Jesus had partaken with His disciples of the Last
Supper; and they were destined to be shaken not many days
after when, at the Descent of the Holy Spirit, suddenly there
came from heaven a sound as of the rushing of a mighty
wind. The first act of the little community was to select,
partly by lot, a new Apostle in place of the traitor Judas.
Even in the brief notice of these earliest meetings, we learn
three facts of the deepest interest. One, that the disciples were
only 120 in number; a second, that even then the beginning
of a new epoch was indicated by the presence among them of

Mary the mother of Jesus and other women, not separated from them as in the seclusion of the synagogue, but in the midst of them as in the worship of the church; the third, that the brethren of the Lord, who hitherto had been at the best but partial believers, had by this time been fully convinced by the Resurrection, and from henceforth cast in their lot, no longer with the world—which therefore from thenceforth hated them—but with the obscure and persecuted followers of the Nazarene, the Crucified.

The next chapter explains all that follow by telling us of the outpouring of the Holy Spirit at Pentecost, and of the instantaneous results in the conversion of 3,000 souls after the first Apostolic sermon. It also gives us a glimpse of the sweet and simple lives of the first believers in Jerusalem, and their interesting experiment of communism which, as experience soon proves, is neither possible nor desirable in the existing conditions of the world (i.).

The next two chapters narrate the cure of the lame man, which was the first Apostolic miracle; the death of Ananias and Sapphira; and the beginnings of persecution which resulted from the many conversions caused by the first Apostolic sermon, the preaching, and the miracles of Peter. We see the spread of the Gospel in Jerusalem, and the antagonism —at once perplexed and futile—of the Jewish Sanhedrin, which was checked partly by divine interpositions and partly by the wise counsel of the Rabbi Gamaliel, who herein proved himself a worthy descendant of his grandfather, the noble and gentle Hillel (iii.—v.).

The next two chapters narrate the election of deacons; the widening of the sympathies of the Church by the preaching of the Hellenists; and the career, trial, and defence of the first martyr, St. Stephen, the precursor of St. Paul. It was in all probability from St. Paul—who, as a Sanhedrist,[1]

---

[1] St. Paul must have been a Sanhedrist (and therefore married) if we take literally the words of Acts xxvi. 10, "when they were being put to death, I *gave my vote* against them" (ἀναιρουμένων τε αὐτῶν κατήνεγκα ψῆφον).

must have been present at the trial of St. Stephen, and who, as we can trace in his Epistles, had been deeply, though at the time unconsciously, influenced by his words—that St. Luke derived the outlines of that noble speech in which the protomartyr furnishes us with the first sketch of a philosophy of Jewish history (vi. vii.).

VIII.

The next chapter tells us of the first great persecution which proved that the blood of martyrs is the seed of the Church.[1] The scattering of the Christians of Jerusalem led directly to the conversion of Samaria by the labours of Philip the Evangelist. In this chapter also—which is essentially a chapter of memorable beginnings—we are told of the first confirmation; the first instances of heresy and simony in the person of Simon Magus; and the first baptised Gentile convert, the eunuch chamberlain of Candace, queen of Ethiopia.

IX. 1-31

The ninth chapter narrates the event which was to have supremest importance for the whole future of Christianity— the conversion of St. Paul. It tells us of his work at Damascus (after his Arabian retirement); his escape from a plot of the Jews; his introduction by Barnabas to the naturally reluctant and suspicious Church of Jerusalem; his second escape from a plot of the Hellenists; and his retirement to Tarsus.

IX. 32 - X. 18.

Meanwhile, during the divine education of this hero of faith for his great work as the Apostle of the Uncircumcision, St. Peter, in accordance with his Lord's promise, was intrusted with the glorious privilege of admitting uncircumcised Gentiles, not only to baptism, but to the full and unfettered participation in all Jewish and Christian privileges. After the miracles which Peter was permitted to work at Lydda and Joppa, he had that memorable vision on the roof at Joppa, which first fully revealed to him the universality of the Gospel, and the abrogation of all the jealous and exclusive prerogatives of Jewish particularism. He had the courage to act up to the enlightenment which he had thus received. He

[1] "Semen est sanguis Christianorum," Tert. *Apol.* 50.

faced, and for a time allayed, the storm of jealous indignation
which the act of eating with uncircumcised Gentiles had
roused in the breasts of the Circumcisionists, whose narrowness would have made of Jewish institutions not only the
bands in which Christianity was to be nursed, but also cords
whereby it should be strangled (ix. 32—xi. 18).

XI:19 - 21

At the close of the eleventh chapter are brief sections of
the utmost importance. One of these (xi. 19—21) records no
less an event than the practical transference of the capital of
Christianity from Jerusalem to Antioch. It shows that the
conversion of the Gentiles had now passed beyond the region
of timid initiatives. Hitherto the scattered members of the
Church of Jerusalem had only ventured in Cyprus and
Phœnice to preach the Gospel to Jews. At Antioch, encouraged probably by what they had heard of the conversions
of the eunuch and of Cornelius, the wandering missionaries
preached boldly to the Gentiles, and their words were crowned
with a success which was their completest justification, proving
as it did that their work was blessed by God.

XI:22 — 26.

The next paragraph (22—26) tells us how the Elders of
Jerusalem, alarmed by the free admission of Gentiles into the
Church, sent Barnabas to Antioch to see what was going on, and
to report to them. The choice of such an emissary was a very
happy one. A narrow ecclesiast would in that day, humanly
speaking, have ruined the destinies of the infant Church.
The large-heartedness of Barnabas tended to counteract the
Pharisaism of the more bigoted Judaists. His position as a
Levite and a man of wealth, who had so wholly thrown in
his lot with the brethren as to sell his estate for their support,
gave him a deserved influence. He had already shown his
magnanimous breadth of insight by taking Paul by the hand
and introducing him to the Apostles and the Elders; he
now showed it still more conspicuously by two memorable
acts. He gave his entire approval to the work among the
Gentiles at Antioch, and feeling the need of some one who
would be adequate to help him, he made a journey to Tarsus,

and summoned from his retirement the man whose thoughts were thenceforward to shake the world. The gradual growth of the Church, the grandeur of its ever-broadening and brightening horizon, and its destined emancipation from the yoke of Mosaism, were illustrated by the fact that at Antioch the brethren first received their new and distinctive name of " Christians." That cosmopolitan name—which clothed a Hebrew conception in a Greek word ended by a Latin termination—though first given in scorn, was soon accepted with triumph. At first it was almost synonymous with malefactor and was everywhere spoken against, first with ridicule, then with angry scorn, at last with furious execration; and yet it was destined to hold its own against all the forces of philosophy and of empire until the lords of the nation were proud to claim it, and it became the ideal term for all that is great and good and wise in the nature and faith of man. At first the bold profession *Christianus sum* was the answer to the yells of *Christianos ad leones.* But four centuries had not elapsed when it became the murmur of the courtier and the hypocrite as well as the confession of the persecuted saint.

The last paragraph of this chapter (27-30) gives us a glimpse of Christian prophets, and in the subscription raised by the Antiochene Christians on behalf of their brethren who were suffering from the famine in Jerusalem, it shows us how the Gentiles began to repay by material services the spiritual benefits which they had received from the Jews. Side by side with the work of the Church pastoral, and the Church militant, and the Church evangelistic, we have here our first developed specimen of that Christian sympathy shown by almsgiving, which has henceforth continued to be so conspicuous a part of the work of the Church beneficent.

In the twelfth chapter we see Christianity for the first time in antagonism with kings. Our Lord had promised the two sons of Zebedee that they should drink of His cup and be baptised with His baptism. In this chapter we read how James, the elder of them, became the first apostolic martyr.

We are told also of the imprisonment and deliverance of
St. Peter, and of the agonising death of the first royal persecutor (xii.). Herod Agrippa I. thus furnished the earliest
instance of the *mortes persecutorum*, and experienced the
truth of the prophecy, " He that falleth on this stone shall be
broken to pieces ; but on whomsoever it shall fall it will
scatter him as dust."

II. From this point forward the narrative is mainly
occupied with the work of St. Paul.

The thirteenth and fourteenth chapters narrate the first
mission-journey of Paul and Barnabas. They detail their
successes among Gentiles and their persecution by Jews in
Cyprus, at the Pisidian Antioch, at Iconium, Lystra, and
Derbe, and their happy return to the Syrian Antioch from
this first eagle-flight of the mission spirit to preach an
eternal Gospel.[1]

The fifteenth chapter, in a conciliatory narrative, tells us of
the liberal compromise or concordat which for a time restored
peace to the agitated partisans of Jewish and Gentile
Christianity after the first Church synod. In this synod the
genius of Paul, the gentle dignity of Barnabas, and the daring
impetuosity of Peter so completely won over the hesitations
of St. John and of St. James, the Lord's brother, that the
Gentiles were set free by direct and unanimous apostolic
authority, from the necessity for circumcision and from
the crushing and now useless burdens of the Levitic law
(xv. 1—35).

Soon afterwards St. Paul, in spite of his unhappy quarrel
with Barnabas, started with Silas for his second great missionary journey. He passed through Syria and Cilicia, and
then, taking with him from Derbe the young Timotheus,
traversed Phrygia, Galatia, and Mysia till they arrived at
Troas. At that point, immediately after the vision which
determined the great missionary to carry the Gospel for the
first time into Europe, there begins that use of the pronoun

[1] Rev. xiv. 6

"we" (xvi. 10), which shows that at Troas St. Luke joined the travellers. We then follow the fortunes of St. Paul, rejoicing in his successes, and filled with admiration for the indomitable courage and endurance with which he braved all perils and difficulties as he founded church after church in Philippi, in Thessalonica, in Berea, in Athens, in Corinth, and in Ephesus, until he once more pays a brief visit to Jerusalem (xv. 36—xviii. 22).

After a short stay at Antioch he began his third missionary journey. Revisiting Galatia and Phrygia he came to Ephesus. In that great city he stayed for nearly three years. After he had worked with eminent success, his departure was precipitated by a riot of interested partisans. He then went through Macedonia to Corinth, and after spending three months there made his way overland (to escape a Jewish plot for his assassination) to Philippi. Thence he proceeded to Troas and Miletus; and thence to Tyre, Ptolemais, Caesarea, and Jerusalem (xviii. 23—xxi. 17). This interesting journey, so full of touching incidents, is narrated with the graphic details which mark an eye-witness. St. Luke seems to have rejoined his friend at Troas (xx. 5), and was henceforth his constant companion.

At Jerusalem, following the unfortunate counsel of James and the other elders to take part in a Nazarite vow, he became entangled in a fierce tumult of bigoted Jews, and, after a powerful speech, was nearly torn to pieces by them. Rescued by Lysias; tried before the Sanhedrin; escaping by a *ruse* which he afterwards seems to have regretted;[1] again rescued, despatched to Caesarea, and there imprisoned, he was tried before Felix, before Festus, and before Agrippa, and appealing to Caesar was sent as prisoner to Rome, where he arrived after a long and stormy voyage culminating in a shipwreck at Malta. This disastrous voyage is minutely described in what is evidently an extract from the diary of

---

[1] Acts xxiv. 21. His respite was due to the latent animosities which he roused among his accusers.

St. Luke, who was his companion during all those weary months of imprisonment, peril, and adventure (xxi. 18 — xxvii. 44).

After a stay of three months in Malta he was taken on to Rome, and there handed over by the centurion Julius to Burrus, the Praetorian Praefect. After three days he called the Jews together to state his case and to preach to them the Gospel. Some of them believed, but the hostility of the majority was so evident that in stern words of rebuke St. Paul warns them that thenceforth the salvation of God was sent unto the Gentiles, and that *they* would hear it.

At Rome he was allowed to live in his own hired house, and there he stayed two years, receiving all that came to him and preaching to them with all confidence, unimpeded.

In that one word—ἀκωλύτως—a cadence evidently chosen for its emphatic weight, which is expressive of motion succeeded by rest, of action settled in repose [1]—the genial, and skilful writer who has thus far accompanied us suddenly drops the curtain. It is impossible to explain why he ends his sketch of the Apostle at that period. Did he do so deliberately or accidentally? Did he carry down his narrative to the period at which he first wrote his book? Did some remarkable change in the prisoner's condition take place at the close of those two first years in Rome? Did St. Luke intend in yet another book to say what more he knew respecting St. Paul and other Apostles and Evangelists; and was he prevented from writing such a book by the Neronian persecution, or by want of leisure, or by death? These questions can never be answered. All that can be said is that after the fire of Rome and the outbreak of the persecution which resulted from the false accusation of the Christians, the whole condition of Christianity was for a time profoundly altered. To write a book about the progress of Christianity while yet it was a *religio licita*, and under the great protecting wings of the

---

[1] Acts xxviii. 31 ; the word is an epitrite ($\smile$ – – –). See Bishop Wordsworth's note on this verse.

Roman eagle, was a very different thing from writing a book in which the author could only have dwelt with horror on the cruel atrocities of Roman imperialism. During that spasm of violence, when every Christian, merely because he was a Christian, was liable to arrest and death, the only kind of treatise which could circulate without the danger of involving a whole community in indiscriminate ruin if it were denounced by an informer, or given up by some weak *traditor*, was some cryptograph, unintelligible to the heathen, like the Apocalypse of St. John. Even a few lines more, were it only to tell us that St. Paul was liberated before the blood of martyrs began to flow like water in the world's capital, would have been most valuable to us and would have saved the necessity for endless discussions. That they should never have been written is for us an irreparable loss. But a thousand circumstances—the intention to compose a third book in better and safer times, or even his own death—may have made it impossible for Luke to write them. Meanwhile by leaving off at this point he has given to his whole purpose a magnificent unity; he has exactly fulfilled the object which he had in view; he has shown us how, in a space of thirty years, the Gospel reached to the far West; [1] how it was made known to the Samaritans, to the Greeks, to the Asiatics, to the Romans; how the sceptre of righteousness was transferred from the hands of the Jew to those of the Gentile; how the centre of gravity of the Christian Church as an outward organisation was shifted from Jerusalem to Antioch, from Antioch to Rome.

Let us now consider some of the chief features of this invaluable and deeply-interesting book.

1. The title, "Acts of the Apostles," does not come from

---

[1] The four *points de repère* for the chronology of the Acts are xi. 28 ; xii. 23 ; xviii. 2 ; xxiv. 27.

The Famine in the Days of Claudius, A.D. 44, 45.
The Death of Agrippa I. A.D. 44.
The Decree for the Expulsion of Jews from Rome, A.D. 49.
The Recall of Felix, A.D. 60.

the author, and is misleading.   He probably called his book
by the then common title of "Acts" only.[1]   The Apostles in
general are only mentioned once.   St. John only appears on
three occasions in an entirely silent and subordinate capacity.
Of St. James the elder we learn nothing except his martyrdom.
On the other hand, non-Apostles, like Stephen, Philip, and
Barnabas, are prominent.   It is clear, therefore, that the
record is essentially fragmentary.   Although so much of the
book is devoted to St. Paul it tells us but a tithe of his
manifold adventures.   That portion of the Acts which
narrates St. Paul's mission-labours has been called "the
Christian Odyssey," but it is an Odyssey at once imperfect
and discontinuous.   Not one of St. Paul's five scourgings with
Jewish thongs, one only of his three beatings with Roman
rods, not one of the three shipwrecks which preceded the one
so elaborately recorded, are mentioned by St. Luke.   He tells
us nothing of that day and night in the deep.   He mentions
two only of seven imprisonments.[2]   There are even whole
classes of the Apostle's perils and hardships—perils of rivers,
perils of robbers, perils in the wilderness, perils among false
brethren, and miseries of hunger, thirst, fasting, nakedness,
of which St. Luke says nothing.   He does not so much as
allude to the fact that St. Paul wrote a single letter.   He
never even gives the name of so beloved, faithful, and able a
companion of St. Paul as Titus.   Of the council of Jerusalem
he gives us but a partial conception.   It is clear that the
Acts does not pretend to be a complete history.   Its omission
of events and circumstances can be largely supplemented by
the information furnished in the Epistles to the Corinthians,
Romans, and Galatians, in the Pastoral Epistles, in the first
Epistle of St. Peter, and in the earlier chapters of the
Apocalypse.   It is only by combining these with what
St. Luke tells us that we can form any adequate conception
of all that the Apostle of the Gentiles was and did.

[1] There were "Acts of Pilate;" "Acts of Philip;" "Acts of Paul and
Thecla," &c.
[2] Ἑπτάκις δεσμὰ φορέσας.   Clem. Rom. *Ep. ad Cor.* 5.

2. But though thus fragmentary it is a book of the highest importance. St. Luke is writing with a special purpose and is selecting materials on which he could rely. In spite of its marked *lacunae* his book is more valuable than if it had been constructed out of looser elements. As it is St. Luke only narrates that which suits his immediate object, and which he knew by eye-witness or from trustworthy sources.[1]

3. The "Acts" is the earliest sketch of Church history. It is, as we have seen, a book of origins. It tells us of the first apostolic miracle; the first apostolic sermon; the first beginnings of ecclesiastical organisation; the first persecution; the first martyr; the first Gentile convert; the first ecclesiastical synod; the first mission journey; the first European Church.

4. It is also an *Eirenicon,* a "tendency-writing," a book with an object. It sets forth the exquisite ideal for which the writer yearned—simplicity, holy gladness, entire unselfishness, a cheerful activity, unanimity of heart and soul.[2] This has been urged to its discredit.[3] The fact that it exhibits a mediating tendency has been supposed to diminish its credibility. There is not the least reason why St. Luke should be less trustworthy because of his desire to be catholic. Let it be granted that he wished to prove that there was no irreconcilable opposition between St. Paul and the Twelve, between the Churches of Antioch and Jerusalem, between Jewish and Gentile Christians. Let it be granted that the allusion to the synod of Jerusalem in the Epistle to the Galatians gives a glimpse of severer struggles and keener heart-burnings than we might have divined from the narrative of St. Luke. Let it be assumed that subjective and artificial considerations played their part in the selection and arrangement of the narratives which are here brought together. These conces-

---

[1] The "*we* sections" are xvi. 10–xvii. 1 (St. Luke seems to have been left at Philippi, and St. Paul found him there again seven years later), xx. 5, to the end. St. Luke was with St. Paul during his Caesarean and both his Roman imprisonments.

[2] See Acts ii. 44–47; iv. 32, &c.

[3] Especially by Baur, Schwegler, Zeller, and the Tübingen critics in general. See Hilgenfeld *Einleitung,* 575.

sions in no wise detract from the credit due to St. Luke as a genuine historian. They only show that he was too earnest to be a sceptic or a neutral. His bias, if bias it were, was a truly noble one. Real history can never be written by those who look with philosophic indifference on the great passions which it brings into play, nor is truth the less truth because it can and indeed must be regarded under different aspects by different minds. St. Luke has misrepresented nothing. There were divisions of opinion in the Apostolic Church as there always have been in all religious communities ; St. Luke has not concealed the existence of those conflicting views. But under this partial divergence there was an essential and fundamental unity. To the beautiful spirit of the historian this unity appeared to be more real as well as more important than the superficial disagreement, just as the ocean is more important than the ripples upon its surface. He wished to show us the movement of the great universal tide, not the advance or recession of this or that individual wave. It is to his glory and not to his discredit that his sympathies were so large as to dwell rather on the reconcilement of brethren than on the disunion of schools of thought. There must always be a difference between the impressions left by the same events upon different minds, but there is not a single event which St. Luke narrates which can be shown to be inconsistent with the evidences derived from other sources.

5. And we are happily able to declare without any qualification that St. Luke, in every instance where we can absolutely test his assertions, triumphantly establishes his claim to be regarded as a conscientious and accurate historian.

a. He can be tested in numerous points of minute allusion. He certainly wrote the Acts without any intentional reference to any of the Epistles ; and yet in scores of circumstances there are coincidences between the Acts and St. Paul's letters of the subtlest character and wholly undesigned. No one can read even Paley's *Horæ Paulinæ*—which now could be greatly enlarged—without seeing at once that any writer

who was not thoroughly acquainted with the facts which he
details would have fallen into multitudes of contradictions
and discrepancies in dealing with events so complicated
as the incessant journeys and troubles of St. Paul. This
evidence of genuineness is the more convincing because (as
we have seen) St. Luke not only does not use any single
Epistle, but does not mention the fact that St. Paul ever
wrote an Epistle at all. And yet St. Luke not only agrees
with the indications given by the Apostle in an immense
number of small particulars, but can be proved to do so
even when there might seem, at first sight, to be obvious
contradiction. The proof of his credibility, which is founded
on these undesigned coincidences, is at once striking and
beyond the reach of dispute.

β. But further than this, St. Luke touches on many points
of secular history, and geography, and archaeology, and
biography. We can test him again and again from the most
unsuspected sources.[1] He introduces sketches of historical
personages, both Jews and Gentiles, of whom comparatively
little is known—of Jews, like Gamaliel and the High Priest
Ananias; of Idumeans, like Herod Agrippa I., Agrippa II.,
Bernice, and Drusilla; of Romans, like Felix, the brother of
Pallas, Festus, Gallio the brother of Seneca, and Sergius
Paulus [2]—and in each instance his sketch, incidental as it is,
has been confirmed by all that we can learn from non-Christian
sources. He mentions strange and obscure titles, like the
Protos of Malta, the Recorder, and the Asiarchs at Ephesus,
the local Praetors at Philippi, and the Politarchs of Thessalonica; and his accuracy is proved by rare coins and broken
inscriptions. He speaks of a Proconsul of Cyprus, of Asia,
and of Achaia, and his correctness, though challenged, has
been absolutely established. He tells us of the famine in
the days of Claudius; of the popularity-hunting policy, and

---

[1] There is an unsolved difficulty about Theudas (v. 36) but St. Luke is at
least as likely to be accurate as Josephus who contradicts him.

[2] Even the name of this Cyprian Proconsul has been discovered in an
inscription at Soli by General Cesnola.

sudden death of Agrippa I.; of the cosmopolitan *insouciance* of Agrippa II.; of the cultured disdain exhibited by Gallio; of the Italian Band at Caesarea; of the decree for the expulsion of the Jews from Rome; of Candace, Queen of Meroe; of the sale of purple at Thyatira; of the dialect of Lycaonia; of the traces left by the local legends of Baucis and Philemon; of the survival of the old cult of Zeus and Hermes; of the silver *aediculae*, which formed a staple trade of Ephesus; of the famous Ephesian amulets and books of magic; of the colonial privileges of Philippi; of many details of ancient navigation; of the modes of dealing with Roman prisoners; of the inviolable rights of the Roman citizen. In all these minute facts, as well as in many others, extending even to the description of Fair Havens and Lasaea in Crete, and the actual soundings and nature of the bottom off Point Koura on the north-east side of Malta,[1] it has been demonstrated that he is writing with minute knowledge and careful reproduction of tested facts.[2]

6. The book records the rapid growth and triumphant progress of Christianity in the midst of deadly opposition. Its epitome is given in the words: "So mightily grew the Word of God."

In the *Agamemnon* of Aeschylus there is a magnificent description of the fire-signals by which the Greek hero made known to his queen at Argos the capture of Troy. The poet tells us how the courier flame flashed from mountain to mountain, leaping over the plains and seas from Ida to the scaur of Hermes in Lemnos, thence to Mount Athos, then to Makistus, Messapium, Cithaeron, and so at last to the roof of the Atridae.

Even so does St. Luke, a poet, and more than a poet, tell us how the beacon-lights of Christianity flashed from Jerusalem

---

[1] This is strikingly proved in the monograph on the voyage and shipwreck of St. Paul by Mr. James Smith of Jordanhill; and in recent works.

[2] Every one of the discoveries made by Mr. J. T. Wood in his excavations at Ephesus tended to establish the accuracy of St. Luke. See Bishop Lightfoot in the *Contemp. Rev.* for May, 1878.

to Antioch—from Antioch to Ephesus, and to Troas, and to Philippi—from Philippi to Athens and Corinth, until at last it was kindled in the very palace and Praetorian camp of the Caesars at Imperial Rome. The Light of the World dawned in the little Judean village, and brightened in the Galilean hills, and then it seemed to set upon Golgotha amid disastrous eclipse. The book of "Acts" shows us how, rekindled from its apparent embers, in the brief space of thirty years, it had gleamed over the Aegean and over Hadria, and had filled Asia and Greece and Italy with such light as had never shone before on land or sea.

7. And it gives us at the same time the secret of this progress, in which the new faith by "the irresistible might of weakness" shook the world.

That secret, as we learn from the first verses, was the promise of the Father, the power of the Resurrection, the outpouring at Pentecost, and afterwards, of the Holy Spirit of God. "The Spirit"—the "Holy Spirit"—is mentioned more often in this book than in any other part of Scripture.[1] It is a comment on the old prophecy: "Not by might nor by power, but by My Spirit, saith the Lord of Hosts."

8. Lastly, the book is beautifully stamped with the individuality of the writer in its amiable catholicity, its "sweet reasonableness," its abounding geniality, its zeal, and hope and love. In these respects as it is the earliest, so too it is the most unique and attractive of all Church Histories. Ecclesiastical history is not always pleasant to read. It is too often the record of supine indifference on the one side and on the other of daring usurpation. It abounds too often in sanguinary episodes, it is disgraced too often by fierce partisanships and arrogant passions. It furnishes melancholy proofs of insidious corruption; of the hollow compromise between spirituality and worldliness; of the deadly facility with which ritual and organisation can take the place of manly freedom and heart religion. It tells us how Christians,

[1] No less than seventy-one times.

out of careless ignorance and the eternal Pharisaism of the human heart, submit to the reimposition of abrogated tyrannies and thrust priests and formulæ, and all sorts of external infallibilities between themselves and the Spirit of the Lord. There are many centuries—especially when Christianity began to lose more and more of its true simplicity—in which Church History is only exhilarating to those who love to trace the growth of formalism and the decadence of faith. But in the *Origines Christianae* of St. Luke we see a spectacle which is in all respects worthy of the faith of Christ. We see irresistible advance; we see indomitable resolution; we see the conciliatory spirit which leads to mutual accommodation; we see the Spirit of God triumphing not only over the idolatrous corruptions of Paganism, but also over the more subtle and dangerous opposition of false types of orthodoxy, and false types of Christian life. We read the ultimate doom of Antichrist, alike in his semblance to Christ, and in his enmity against Him. We see that when men are faithful their deadliest foes may be those within as well as those without the fold which they would defend; but that, however feeble God's servants may be, and however furiously they may be hated, God still strengthens them to the pulling down of invincible strongholds. It can never be ill with the Church of God so long as she remains true to the high lessons of hope, of courage, and of sweetness, which she was meant to learn from this brief and fragmentary, but faithful and glowing, history of her earliest days.[1] Her best and most persecuted sons— not those who swim with, but those who stem, the tide of her current insincerities; not those who spread their sails to the summer breeze, but those who are ready to face the storm; men like Wiclif, Huss, Savonarola, Luther, Wesley, Whitfield —may read in the story of how it fared with St. Peter and

---

[1] The word χάρις "grace" (akin to χαίρω "I rejoice") is characteristic of St. Luke and St. Paul. It occurs in John i. 14–17, in St. Luke's Gospel, eight times, in the Acts seventeen times, and incessantly in St. Paul. Χαρίζομαι occurs twice in St. Luke's Gospel, three times in the Acts, and often in St. Paul; but not elsewhere in the New Testament.

St. Paul, that the servant must still be as his Master, and that they can never be exempt from the hatred of false Apostles, like Judas, and false princes, like Herod, and false rulers, like Pilate, and false religious parties, like the Pharisees and Sadducees, led on by false priests, like Annas and Caiaphas;—but that nevertheless, the foundation of God standeth sure, having this seal, "The Lord knoweth them that are His," and "Let him that nameth the name of Christ depart from iniquity."

THE EPISTLES.

THE EPISTLES.

FORM OF THE NEW TESTAMENT EPISTLES.

Der Schlachtruf, der St. Pauli Brust entsprungen
Rief nicht sein Echo auf zu tausend Streiten!
Und welch ein Friedensecho hat geklungen
Durch tausend Herzen von Johannis Saiten!
Wie viele rauhe Feuer sind entglommen
Als widerschein von Petri Funkengaben!
Und sieht man Andre still mit Opfest kommen
Ist's weil sie in Jakobi Schul gegraben:—
Ein Satz ist's der in Variationen
Vom ersten Anfang forttönt durch Aeonen.—Tholuck.

"Letters weighty and strong."—2 Cor. x. 10.

THE New Covenant is the Revelation of the Gospel of Jesus Christ. A large part of that revelation is conveyed to us in the form of letters. Those letters are twenty-one in number. The New Testament is indeed entirely composed of a collection of letters, together with five historical books and one Apocalyptic Vision.

In this respect the records of Christianity are absolutely unique in the religious history of the world. Of all the sacred books which the world has seen there is not one which is composed mainly, or at all, of letters, with the single exception of the New Testament. The Bibles of the world—the Vedas, the Zend Avesta, the Tripitaka, the Koran, the writings of Confucius—are poems or rhythmic addresses, or legendary histories, or philosophic discourses. In this, as in all other respects, the ways of God's Providence differ

FORM OF THE NEW TESTAMENT EPISTLES.

Der Schlachtruf, der St. Pauli Brust entsprungen
Rief nicht sein Echo auf zu tausend Streiten?
Und welch ein Friedensecho hat geklungen
Durch tausend Herzen von Johannis Saiten!
Wie viele rasche Feuer sind entglommen
Als widerschein von Petri Funkensprühen!
Und sieht man Andre still mit Opfern kommen
Ist's weil sie in Jakobi Schul' gediehen :—
Ein Satz ist's der in Variationen
Vom erstem Anfang forttönt durch Æonen.—Tholuck.

"Letters weighty and strong."—2 Cor. x. 10.

THE New Covenant is the Revelation of the Gospel of Jesus Christ. A large part of that revelation is conveyed to us in the form of letters. Those letters are twenty-one in number. The New Testament is indeed entirely composed of a collection of letters, together with five historical books and one Apocalyptic Vision.

In this respect the records of Christianity are absolutely unique in the religious history of the world. Of all the sacred books which the world has seen there is not one which is composed mainly, or at all, of letters, with the single exception of the New Testament. The Bibles of the world—the Vedas, the Zend Avesta, the Tripitaka, the Koran, the writings of Confucius—are poems or rhythmic addresses, or legendary histories, or philosophic discourses. In this, as in all other respects, the ways of God's Providence differ from man's expectations. We may thank God that we derive some of the deepest truths of our belief from documents so simple, so individual, so full of human interest and love—written, most of them, "in a style the most personal that ever existed."

Yet it may perhaps be doubted whether there are ever many persons in an ordinary congregation who, if asked to explain what is the special scope and outline—the characteristic meaning and tenor—of any one of those deeply important letters, would be able to do so with any definiteness. But surely it is necessary for an intelligent acquaintance with "the oracles of God"—for a real knowledge of, and reverence for the Bible, and a power to read it aright—that we should know something of its books as well as of those isolated fragments which we call "texts." That is the reason why it seems desirable, in a very simple way, to make clearer, for those who need such help, the totality and general bearing of the books of Scripture. And the best result which we could desire would be that, like the noble Bereans of old, we should all be stimulated to read and to inquire—searching the Scriptures for ourselves whether these things are so.

1. Now the twenty-one letters, which occupy more than a full third of the New Testament, fall into well-marked groups. Two of them—the Epistle to the Hebrews and the 1st Epistle of St. John—to some extent also the Epistle to the Romans—are more like treatises than letters; of the remainder, four are Catholic—that is, addressed to the Church in general; nine are addressed to separate Churches; and six are written to private persons. These twenty-one letters represent the thoughts of at least six writers. Thirteen of them are by St. Paul, who had the chief share in moulding Hellenistic Greek for the purpose of expressing Christian truth; three by St. John; one, and perhaps indirectly two, by St. Peter; two by St. James and St. Jude, both brethren of the Lord; and one—the Epistle to the

Hebrews—by an unknown writer, probably Apollos.[1] There is an inestimable advantage in this rich variety. The glory of Christianity—the sevenfold perfection of undivided light— was too bright to be adequately reflected by any single human mind. It is an infinite privilege that, by divers and manifold reflexions, we are thus enabled not only to see the commingled lustre of the jewels of the ephod, but also the separate hues of each oracular gem. We are thus enabled to realise what St. Paul beautifully describes as the many-coloured, the richly-variegated wisdom of God. We see Christianity from the first in its manifold diversity, as well as in its blended simplicity. We can judge of it as it appeared to men of differing temperaments, and as it was understood in divergent yet harmonious schools of thought. In the letters of St. Peter we see it in its moderate, its conciliatory, its comprehensive, its Catholic aspect. In St. James and St. Jude it is presented in its more limited and more Judaic phase. In the Epistle to the Hebrews we see how it was regarded by the philosophic school of Alexandrian students. In the letters of St. Paul we have the Christianity of freedom; of complete emancipation from Levitic externalism;—the Gospel to the Gentile world. In those of St. John we have Christianity in its intensest spirituality, in its abstractest essence, as the religion of spiritual purity, love, and adoration. And with all these glorious sources from which to learn, we may well feel a humble thankfulness and exclaim with the poet,

> "Oh that I knew how all thy lights combine
> And the configurations of their glorie;
> Seeing not only how each verse doth shine,
> But all the constellations of the storie!

My object in this discourse will be twofold: First of all, to show the advantage of this epistolary form for the

---

[1] That God chose His own fit instruments and that the sacredness of the books was due to the prior position of these writers is clear from the fact that only four of the writers were Apostles. Most of the Apostles lived and died unknown.

conveyance of divine truth; secondly, by getting a clear conception of what Christian letters were, to study the method adopted in nearly all of them, and especially in those of the great Apostle St. Paul. These Pauline letters occupy more pages than the first three Gospels put together, and, if we count the Epistle to the Hebrews, which is also Pauline in its general tone, are more than three times the bulk of all the other letters.

I. As to the first point, the epistolary form of the New Testament, it might perhaps strike us as strange that the deepest truths and the highest arguments of our religion should have been conveyed to us in casual letters. For casual, humanly speaking, they were. They are only preserved to us out of many which must have perished.[1] Every Christian will feel that they were preserved by a special divine Providence; but it is none the less true that their preservation was owing to causes which, in ordinary language, might be called accidental. Nor, again, were they predetermined letters, but they rose, for the most part, out of the circumstances of the day. St. Paul wrote one letter because in a previous letter of his to the same Church he had been somewhat misunderstood; another because he had been secretly calumniated and opposed; a third to check an incipient apostasy; a fourth to express his warm gratitude for

---

[1] This must have been so from the nature of the case, and is now generally admitted. We can hardly see any other form in which the care of all the churches could have come upon St. Paul daily (2 Cor. xi. 28). There is no more reason to believe that every word which an Apostle wrote was "inspired" than every word which he spoke. Traces of letters written by St. Paul which have now perished are found in 1 Cor. v. 9. "I wrote to you *in the letter* not to associate with fornicators;" and in 2 Cor. x. 9, 10, "That I may not seem as though I would frighten you by my letters" (διὰ τῶν ἐπιστολῶν). Another lost letter may be alluded to in Eph. iii. 3; and another, which may however be an Epistle to the Ephesians, in Col. iv. 16. It is impossible to suppose that St. Paul never wrote to thank the Philippians for the contributions which they twice sent to him to Thessalonica (Phil. iv. 16); or that he dictated no line to the Thessalonians when he despatched Timothy to them from Athens (1 Thess. iii. 5). In 2 Thess. iii. 17, he speaks of his signature as the authentication "in *every* letter"; could he have used this expression, if, as yet, he had only written one? The preservation of brief Epistles written on fugitive materials in troublous times is far more surprising than that others (perhaps undoctrinal and unimportant) should have perished.

a pecuniary contribution while he was in prison; a fifth be- cause he wished to intercede for a runaway slave ; a sixth because, in his last days, he longed to be cheered by the society of a beloved convert. St. John wrote one letter—a little note, as we should call it—to convey a kindly message to a Christian lady ; another to a hospitable friend to warn him against the presumption of an intriguing presbyter. We see then that Providence has ordained that many of the documents from which we derive our faith should be in the form of unconstrained epistolary intercourse. And this, so far from being a matter of regret, was a happy circumstance. We might, indeed, assume *a priori* that the form chosen for the dissemination of the Gospel by the Providence of God was the best that could be chosen; and it may be safely asserted that the hold which the New Testament has taken on the minds of men has been due in great measure to its personal element. Christian theology would have been immeasurably less effective if it had been conveyed to the world in canons, or articles, or liturgies, or scholastic treatises.[1]

II. The epistolary form of Christian instruction was, then, a providential arrangement, first of all—I say it without hesitation—because that form of writing is essentially unsystematic. It might well seem an astonishing circumstance that we should have been left to learn almost all that we know, not only about Church organisation, but even about many deep theological mysteries from forms of writing so apparently unpremeditated. But the method of the Bible is alien from the spirit of elaborate, technical, all-explaining theological systems, which attempt to store away the infinite in the little cells of the finite, and to soar up to the secrets of the Deity on the waxen wings of the understanding. We may thank God that it has not pleased Him to

[1] The same human and personal interest, in other forms, reigns throughout the Old Testament. Letters, indeed, are naturally rare (though we find a prophet's letter in 2 Chron. xxi.) because Palestine was a small country, and personal intercourse was easy. It was a different matter when Christian communities were scattered over hundreds of miles of sea and land.

express the plan of salvation in dialectics. The technical terminology, the rigid systematisation of divine mysteries is due to exigencies caused by human error—sometimes even to the pride of human reason—far more than to the initiative set us by the sacred writers.[1]

III. Again, the epistolary form of so much of the New Testament was better adapted than all others to the individuality of the great Apostle of the Gentiles. It suited that impetuosity of feeling—that warm, emotional nature which modern cynicism would have sneered at as " gushing " or " hysterical "—which could not have been fettered down to the composition of formal treatises. A letter could be taken up or dropped, according to the necessities of the occasion or the moods of the writer. It permitted of a freedom of expression far more vigorous, and far more natural to the Apostle, than the regular syllogisms and rounded periods of a formal book. It admitted something of the tenderness and something of the familiarity of personal intercourse. Into no other literary form could have been infused that intensity of feeling which made Casaubon truly say of St. Paul that he alone of writers seems to have written, not with fingers and pen and ink, but with his very heart and vitals, and the very throb of his inmost being; which made St. Jerome say that his words were so many thunders; which made Luther compare them to living creatures with hands and feet. A letter is eminently personal, flexible, spontaneous; it is like " a stenographed conversation." It best enabled Paul to be himself, and to recall most vividly to the minds of his spiritual children the tender, suffering, inspired, desponding,

---

[1] St. Paul's letters, with their numerous antimonies, as much resist the process of formal and scholastic systematisation as the Sermon on the Mount. "Tracts for the time they were tracts for all times. Children of the fleeting moment, they contain truths of infinite moment. They compress more ideas into fewer words than any other writings, human or divine, except the Gospels. They discuss the highest themes which can challenge an immortal mind. And all this before humble little societies! And yet they are of more real and general value to the Church than all the systems of theology, from Origen to Schleiermacher. For 1800 years they have nourished the faith of Christendom and will do so to the end of time."—Schaff. *Hist. of Christian Church,* p. 741.

terrible, impassioned, humble, uncompromising teacher who, in courage and in trembling, in zeal and weakness, in close reasonings and strong appeals, had first taught them to be imitators of himself and of the Lord. His Epistles came fresh and burning from the heart, and therefore they go fresh and burning to the heart.[1] Take away from them the traces of individual feeling, the warmth, the invective, the yearning affection, the vehement denunciations, the bitter sarcasms, the distressed boasting, the rapid interrogatives, the frank colloquialisms, the private details, the impassioned personal appeals—all that has been absurdly called their " intense egotism "—and they would never have been as they are, next to the Psalms of David, and for something of the same reason, the dearest treasures of Christian devotion;— next to the four Gospels, the most cherished text-books of Christian faith. St. Paul was eminently and emphatically a man; a man who had known much of life; a man who, like the legendary Ulysses, had seen many cities and knew the minds of men. He was no narrow scribe, no formalising Pharisee, no stunted ascetic, no dreaming recluse, no scholastic theologian, no priestly externalist, who could suppose that the world depended on the right burning of the two kidneys and the fat;—he was a man, full of strength and weakness, full of force and fire. He was not a man to mistake words for things, or outward scrupulosity for true service, or verbal formulae for real knowledge. Whether it is with a burst of tears or in a flame of indignation that he seizes his

---

[1] Of the special style of St. Paul I have spoken fully elsewhere, and I have shown the extreme probability that he had attended classes of rhetoric in his early years at Tarsus. Otherwise, considering the thoroughly Semitic cast of his mind, it would be difficult to account for the fact that there is scarcely a figure of Greek rhetoric which he does not familiarly use. The same remark would apply to no other writer of the LXX. or of the New Testament. Here it will be sufficient to refer to his Enumerations (Asyndeta 1 Cor. xiii. 4-8; 2 Cor. vi. 4-10; xi. 22-28 &c.); Antitheses (2 Cor. iv. 7-12; v. 21); Climaxes, (1 Cor. xiii., 2 Cor. vii. 11); Rapid interrogatives (Rom. viii. 31-34; 1 Cor. ix. 1-9; Gal. iii. 1-5); Irony (1 Cor. iv. 8; 2 Cor. xi. 16, &c.); Multiplication of Synonyms (2 Cor. vi. 14-16; Rom. ii. 17-23); Oxymora (2 Cor. ii. 2, viii. 2, xii. 10); and Paronomasias (Rom. i. 29, 30; 2 Cor. iii. 2; Phil. iii. 2, 3, &c.)

THE EPISTLES. pen or begins his dictation, he will always speak out the very thing he thinks. The mere form of these writings led to blessed results. When we remember that the Christians of the first one or two decades after the Crucifixion had no Christian books at all, and that all, or nearly all, the letters of the Apostles were the very earliest books of the New Testament, and were known to Christians before the Gospels, we cannot doubt that to their fresh individuality is due, at least in part, the radiant simplicity, the glad enthusiasm of the early Church. What can be more free, and buoyant, and varied than St. Paul's letters? Brilliant, broken, impetuous as the mountain torrent freshly filled; never smooth and calm, but on the eve of some bold leap; never vehement, but to fill some pool of clearest peace; they present everywhere the image of a vigorous joy. Beneath their reasonings and their philosophy there may ever be heard a secret lyric strain of glorious praise, bursting at times into open utterance and asking others to join the chorus. His life was a battle, from which, in intervals of the good fight, his words arose as the song of victory.

2. Such, then, is the epistolary form in which, by God's Providence, a large part of His latest dispensation has been handed down to us. It must be borne in mind that letters between Churches and their teachers were no new things.[1] From very early times the Jewish communities had thus corresponded with each other by epistles which were carried by travelling deputations. These epistles, which were often upon disputed points of doctrine, were called *iggerôth* (אִגְּרוֹת). The intercourse between various communities in the cities of Italy, Greece, and Asia was immensely developed. Emissaries, "Apostles" in the original sense of the word, the synagogue—ministers whom the Jews called Sheloochim,[2] were in constant employment. Inscriptions

---

[1] Baruch vi. is a (spurious) letter of Jeremiah to the Babylonian exiles, 2 Macc. i. gives us an ancient specimen of such a letter.

[2] The "delegate" or "*messenger* of the congregation" was known as Sheliach Zibbur.

tell us of the scores of times that a merchant or agent had sailed between the coast of Asia and Corinth or Brundusium. Even in St. Paul's little circle we observe the incessant activity of missionary work which occupied the time of Luke, Timothy, Titus, Crescens, Apollos, Mark, Aristarchus, Stephanus, and others. And it is probable that they rarely went from Church to Church without carrying at least a few lines of written greeting, or instruction, or consolation, or, at the very least, of introduction and authentication. Thus, and thus only, was St. Paul able to sate the ardour of his missionary zeal.

3. And what is the uniform outline of almost every one of these Epistles? Amid all their rich exuberance of detail we find in them all a general identity of structure.[1] St. Paul's Epistles to the Churches fall, almost invariably, into these six divisions.

i. First, a greeting, sometimes very brief, sometimes extending over several verses, in which he generally manages with consummate skill, to strike the keynote of the whole letter.

ii. Secondly, a thanksgiving to God for the Christian gifts and graces of his converts.

iii. Thirdly, a doctrinal part, in which he argues out or explains some great topic of Christian truth, specially required by the condition of the Church to which he is writing.

iv. Fourthly, a practical section, in which he applies to daily moral duties the great doctrines which he has developed.

v. Fifthly, personal messages, salutations, and details.

---

[1] Reuss, *Théologie Chrét.* ii. 11. It is an interesting subject of inquiry to what extent there was at this period an ordinary form of correspondence which (as among ourselves) was to some extent fixed. In the papyrus rolls of the British Museum (edited for the trustees by J. Forshall) there are forms and phrases which constantly remind us of St. Paul. Renan is probably right in comparing the journeys of the Christian delegates, so far as their outward circumstances are concerned, to those of Ibn Batoutah or Benjamin of Tudela.

vi. Sixthly, a brief autograph conclusion to ratify the genuineness of the entire letter.

This or that division may be wanting, or may be subordinate, in one or other of the letters to the Churches, but this is the almost invariable outline—the scheme and form so to speak—of them all.[1]

Now though the mere salutations at the beginning of the letters might seem to be a small matter, we should observe the beautiful element of novelty, of universality, and of depth which they involve. The ordinary salutation of a Greek letter was "joy" ($\chi\alpha\iota\rho\epsilon\iota\nu$);[2] of a Jewish letter "peace" (*Shalôm*). The Apostles unite both, and into each they infuse a far deeper intensity of meaning. Into Hellenism and Hebraism they struck the divine spirit of Christianity.[3] The Christian has a right to the joy of the Greek and to the peace of the Jew, and to both in supreme measure. The "grace" is the Greek's bright joy embathed in spiritual blessing; the "peace" is a peace hitherto hardly dreamed of; a peace of which there is scarcely the faintest trace in all the golden realms of heathen literature; a peace which passeth all understanding. And thus, as it were, by one touch, in a single phrase, does the Apostle show, quite incidentally, yet with finest significance, that Christianity is not only for individuals, not only for nations even, but for the world;—that in Christ the distinctions of castes and nations are done away; that in Him there is neither Greek, nor Jew, nor barbarian, nor bond, nor free; that for us the blessings of Hellenism and Hebraism may be severally intensified and mutually combined.

---

[1] Something not unlike this general form may be seen even in the letters to the Seven Churches in the Apocalypse.

[2] See the letter of Lysias to Felix, Acts xxiii. 26; and (which is curious) the letter of the Synod of Jerusalem to the Gentile Church (Acts xv. 23), and even the letter written to Jews by the Judaist St. James (Jas. i. 1).

[3] "'Grace' which is the beginning of every blessing; 'Peace' which is the end of all blessings." St. Thomas Aquinas. In his later Epistles he made the touching addition of "mercy." The salutation of the Roman world—from which our word "salutation" is derived—was "health" (s.p.d. *salutem plurimam dicit.*)

4. Another noteworthy point in these initial greetings is that THE EPISTLES. in his later letters St. Paul addresses his words, "not to the Church," but to "the saints." Let us not carelessly overlook the deep lesson involved in this. Whatever we are we are called to be, we are meant to be, saints, *i.e.* holy. No Church can be bound together, no worship can be arranged, no rules of Christian living laid down on any other supposition. The very word for "Church" in the original means "called out"[1]—summoned forth from the world to higher aims and holier aspirations. We may fall indefinitely short of our ideal; we may be very wavering in our pledged allegiance; but let us never forget that the Gospel is addressed to those who, even if they be sinners, are yet called of God, called to sanctification. In Christians an unholy life is not only neglect but rebellion; not only indifference but desertion; not only ignorance but apostasy. Does not the whole tone of St. Paul's letters, even to such Churches as Corinth, does not the whole tone of our own Prayer Book proclaim to us that we are by our very birthright Christians, *i.e.* a chosen generation, a royal priesthood, a holy nation, a peculiar people?[2]

5. Then how remarkable is the thanksgiving which St. Paul places after the greeting in the letter to every Church except that impetuous rebuke which he addressed to the Galatians. What a spirit of hopefulness does it display—

[1] The word Ἐκκλησία is used in the Gospels by St. Matthew alone (Matt. xvi. 18; xviii. 17). It corresponds to the Hebrew קָהָל. St. James still characteristically retains the word "synagogue" to describe even a Christian place of worship. Jas. ii. 2.

[2] The peculiarities of the opening salutations of St. Paul's Epistles may be summed up as follows. (i.) In all his Epistles after his two first (1, 2 Thess.) written at a period before the Judaisers had questioned his Apostolic authority —he calls himself "*an Apostle*"; except in the private letter to Philemon, and in the letter to his beloved Philippians to whom the designation was needless. (ii.) In his five earliest Epistles (1, 2 Thess. 1, 2 Cor. Gal.) he addresses himself to "*the Church*." (iii.) In 1, 2 Thess. he writes "to the Church *of the*"; in later letters "to the church *which is in*" (1, 2 Cor. Gal). (iv.) In all the later letters he addresses himself "*to the saints.*" (v.) He wishes them "*grace and peace*" in all but the Pastoral Epistles which have "*grace, mercy, and peace.*"

hopeful trust in man, hopeful trust in God! We know, for instance, what a factious, conceited, ungrateful, unfaithful Church was that of Corinth; yet even in his letters to Corinth St. Paul begins by thanking God, not indeed for their moral graces (that he could not do), but at least for their intellectual gifts. Even to them he says that "his hope of them is steadfast." These "thanksgivings" are neither an insincere compliment nor a rhetorical artifice (*captatio benevolentiae*). We may see in them the bright virtues of Christian hope. Never let us despair of ourselves; never let us despair of others. There is a light which lighteth every man that cometh into the world; we may dim it as with the darkness of the mine; we may make it burn low as in the vapours of the charnel-house—but quench it quite finally and utterly we cannot. "Our lamps are gone out," say the foolish virgins in the parable, but it is in the original not "our lamps are gone out," but our lamps are being quenched, are going out; and even then they are bidden not utterly to lose heart, but to go to buy fresh oil, that even for them at last their care may be—

> "Fixed and zealously attent
> To fill their odorous lamps with deeds of light,
> And hope that reaps not shame."

6. I will not here speak specially of the third and fourth divisions—the doctrinal and the practical sections of St. Paul's letters—because the special aim of the doctrinal portion varies in each Epistle; but it is important to notice how, in St. Paul's view, doctrine and practice are inseparably blended. There is no divorce between them; no attempt to treat either as superfluous. On the loftiest principles are based the humblest duties: from the sublimest truths are deduced the simplest exhortations. One swift beat of the wing is sufficient to carry the Apostle from the miserable factions of squabbling Corinth to the sunlit heights of Christian charity, and like the lark whose heart and eye, even in its highest flight, are with its nest on the dewy ground, so in one moment—as in

the Epistle to the Ephesians—he can drop at will from the
most heavenly spheres of mystic vision to the commonest
rules of Christian intercourse :—

> " Type of the wise, who soar, but never roam,
> True to the kindred points of heaven and home."

But from this interweaving of doctrine and practice we
may learn a great lesson. Does it not teach us that noble
thoughts make noble acts, that a soul occupied with great
ideas best performs the smallest duties ;—that, as has well
been said, "the divinest views of life penetrate into its
meanest emergencies "? Nothing less than the Majesty of
God and the powers of the world to come can sustain the
sanctity of our homes, the serenity of our minds, and the
patience of our hearts ! [1]

7. Even the final salutations have their own deep human
interest. In themselves, indeed, there is nothing specially
sacred about them. The names Asyncritus, Phlegon,
Hermas, Olympas, &c. have nothing in them more intrinsically mysterious or important than the names of Smith and
Jones. Many of them were names of slaves and artisans,
undistinguished and ordinary persons. Some of them, like
Tryphaena and Tryphosa ("the wanton," "the luxurious"),
could have been little less than insulting; Nereus, Hermes,
Phoebe were names of heathen deities in whom men believed
no longer, grotesquely bestowed on slaves; Stachys "wheat-
ear," Asyncritus "incomparable," Persis, a poor slave-girl
brought from the Persian slave-market—all these names, even
when not ridiculous, involved more or less of a stigma. They
were not the sort of names which were borne by the wise and
mighty and noble. In any case the salutations sent to these
poor persons have no more inherent importance than the
salutations which any modern clergyman might send in a
letter to any poor pensioners or aged widows in his flock. Felix
Neff, "the apostle of the Hautes Alpes," two days before

---

[1] " Paulus ad Romam xi capitibus fidem fundit, et v capitibus deinde mores
superaedificat. . Sic in aliis quoque epistolis facit."—LUTHER.

his death, "being scarcely able to see, traced the following lines at different intervals, in large and irregular characters, which filled a page, "Adieu, dear friend, André Blanc; Antoine Blanc; the Pelissiers whom I dearly love; François Dumont and his wife; Isaac and his wife; Aimé Desbois, Emilie Bonnet, Alexandrine and their mother; all, all the brethren and sisters at Mens. Adieu, adieu." Now this is exactly the style of St. Paul's final salutations; and yet how rich are they in value and interest!

They illustrate Paul's affectionateness; his honour for women; his respect even for slaves; the way in which he esteemed man as simply man; his nice discrimination of character. They are interesting too for the immortality which they bestowed on those obscure and humble Christians whose names, though they were less than nothing to the world, were eternally inscribed in the Lamb's book of life.[1] Very interesting too is that autograph message and benediction which the Apostle always adds. Afflicted in all probability with ophthalmia, it was impossible for him, without pain and difficulty, to write his own letters. He therefore employed the aid of an amanuensis.[2] But, partly to express his own personal interest in the last few words of blessing and greeting, partly to prevent the disgraceful forgeries which existed even at that early time, he authenticated

---

[1]   "There is a Book
By seraphs writ in beams of heavenly light,
On which the eyes of God not rarely look,
A chronicle of actions just and bright;
There all thy deeds, my faithful Mary, shine,
And since thou own'st that praise I spare thee mine."

—COWPER.

[2] The use of an amanuensis partly accounts for the constant "we" which St. Paul interchanges with "I." He does not mean to make those whom he associates with himself in the opening salutations at all responsible for his words, for he sometimes uses "we" when he can only be speaking of his individual self (1 Thess. ii. 18 "we. . . even I, Paul.") The use of "we" is partly due to the modesty which in all languages dislikes the needless prominence of "I." "We" is chiefly characteristic of 1, 2, Thess. In 2 Thess. the only passage which relapses into "I" is ii. 5. Silas and Timothy are associated with him in 1, 2 Thess. Sosthenes in 1 Cor., Timothy in 2 Cor. Phil. Col. Philem. Paul writes in his own name only to the Romans and Laodiceans (Eph.), which Churches he had not personally visited.

every letter with his own signature and written benediction and thus secured to future ages also a proof that they are reading the words of him who was indeed "a vessel of election." [1]

Such then, in the most rapid and summary view, is the general structure of the Epistles of the New Testament; and such, in the briefest possible form, suggested rather than worked out, are some of the lessons which that structure suggests. Any one who will read the Epistles through, each at a sitting, to verify these facts will more and more realise what a hid treasure we may find in the field of these sacred letters. We may thus become more earnest, more intelligent, and more faithful students of the Book of God.

---

[1] St. Paul first adopted this final authentication (γνώρισμα) or badge of cognisance—in 2 Thess. iii. 17 ; and implies that he means henceforth to use it. (ὅ ἐστι σημεῖον ἐν πάσῃ ἐπιστολῇ).

a. In 1 Thess. 1 Cor. we have "The grace of our Lord Jesus Christ be with you;" to which the word "all" is added in 2 Thess. Rom. Phil.

β. In Philem. and Gal. we have "The grace of our Lord Jesus Christ be with your spirit," ("brethren" Gal.)

γ. In Col. 1, 2 Tim. Tit. "Grace be with you" ("thee") ("all" Tit.)

δ. Eph. "Grace be with those that love the Lord Jesus Christ in sincerity."

ε. 2 Cor. "The grace of our Lord Jesus Christ, and the love of God, and the fellowship of the Holy Ghost be with you all."

On authenticating signatures see Cic. *Ad. Att.* viii. 1 ; Suet. *Tib.* 21, 32.

NOTE

ON EARLY CHRISTIAN PSEUDEPIGRAPHY.

Pseudepigraphy—the adoption of an honoured name which was not the name of the author—was common in ancient Jewish literature. It must not be called by the hard name of literary forgery. In many instances it was not at all intended to deceive. A man wrote in the name of some great and well known person because he desired to call attention to what he had to say ; because he desired to claim the sanction of high authority ; because he believed his teaching to be in accordance with that of the writer whose name he assumed. It is (for instance) extremely unlikely that the Alexandrian author of the Book of Wisdom, intended for a moment that any one should be misled to suppose that the old Jewish king was the actual author of the book which he called *The Wisdom of Solomon.* He simply wrote in the person of Solomon, because the pseudepigraphy furnished him with a convenient and recognised form of sapiential literature.

Of this kind of pseudepigraphy we have many instances in early Christian literature ; such as the Epistle of Barnabas (if "Barnabas" was meant to be "the Apostle") ; the Gospels of James, of Thomas, of the Twelve Apostles ; the Testaments of the Twelve Patriarchs ; the Acts of Thomas, Thaddaeus, Andrew, Philip, John ; letters ascribed to Ignatius ; the Clementine Homilies and Recognitions ; the Apostolic Constitutions ; and hundreds more, of which many are extant.

But some of these were not merely pseudepigraphical. There are very early traces of downright forgery. In 2 Thess. ii. 2, St. Paul more than hints that some letter had reached the Thessalonians, which purported to come from him, or at least to express his sentiments, by which they had been misled ; and it is against this danger of having his views misrepresented that he put them on their guard by the promise to add an autograph conclusion to every letter of his (2 Thess. iii. 17). Again, in 2 John 12, St. John seems to express some dislike to epistolary communion where personal intercourse could be had ; and in 3 John 9, he hints (apparently) that letters might be withheld or otherwise tampered with (see Ewald, *Sendschreiben*, p. 51). Hence St. Paul "adjures" the Thessalonians "by the Lord" that his letter be read to the entire community.

There is something startling in the solemnity of the curse with which St. John tries to deter any one from attempting to curtail or interpolate his Apocalypse. But early Christian history shows that the adjuration was very necessary. Dionysius of Corinth (*ap.* Euseb. *H. E.* iv. 23)

deplores the falsification of his own letters. So too Irenaeus ends one of
his books with an adjuration to the copyists "by the Lord Jesus Christ
and by His glorious coming to judge the quick and dead" to compare
and carefully correct their copies by their exemplar, and likewise to place
this adjuration in their copies (*Opp.* 1, 821, ed. Stieren). A similar
passage is found at the end of Rufinus's prologue to his version of
Origen *De Principiis* (Huidekoper, *Judaism at Rome*, p. 289).

There was even a forged letter purporting to be addressed by our Lord
to Abgarus, king of Edessa.

There are spurious letters of Paul to the Laodiceans, and another
Epistle to the Corinthians preserved in the Armenian ; and a spurious
correspondence of Paul and Seneca.

Among other Fathers Origen suffered severely from the falsification of
his writings.

Even in modern times the danger has not wholly ceased. The glaring
and wretched sermon of a Spanish Jesuit Nieremberg on "the Pains of
Hell" is often attributed (even by Mr. Lecky and Mr. Alger) to Bishop
Jeremy Taylor.

ST. PAUL'S THIRTEEN EPISTLES.

Σκεῦος ἐκλογῆς.—ACTS ix. 15.

Παῦλος γενόμενος μέγιστος ὑπογραμμός.—S. CLEM. ROM.

Εἰ καὶ Παῦλος ἦν ἀλλ' ἄνθρωπος ἦν.—ST. CHRYS.

> " Andovvi poi lo vas d'elezione
> Per recarno conforto a quella Fede
> Ch' è principio alla via di salvazione."
>
> DANTE, *Inf.* ii. 8.

> " Monstrava l'altro [1] la contraria cura
> Con una spada [2] lucida ed acuta
> Tal che di qua del rio mi fe' paura."
>
> *Purgatorio*, xxix. 139.

> " Bearing a sword whose glitterance and keen edge,
> E'en as I viewed it, with the flood between,
> Appalled me."—CARY.

"The divine assurance of the old prophets, the all-transcending glory and spiritual presence of the eternal Lord, and all the art and culture of a ripe and wonderfully excited age, seem to have joined, as it were, in bringing forth the new creation of these Epistles of the times, which were destined to last for all the times."—EWALD.

"Even as our beloved brother Paul also, according to the wisdom given unto him, hath written unto you; as also in all his Epistles speaking in them of these things."—2 PET. iii. 15, 16.

THE EPISTLES. WE profess to regard the Bible as the one sacred book. We profess to derive from it, almost exclusively, the doctrines of our faith, and the rules of our conduct. We turn to it in hours of temptation; we find in it the songs of our purest

[1] St. Paul.   [2] The Epistles.

rejoicing; the memory of the dead—(to quote well-known words)—passes into it; the potent traditions of childhood are stereotyped in its verses; it speaks to us with a music that can never be forgotten; we read it—(and seem as if we could read nothing else)—by the bedsides of the dying, and over the graves of our beloved. Yet how many of us even approximately understand it? How many of us obtain from this one Book of God the treasure, and the joy, and the peace which we might obtain from it, better, and in larger measure, than from all the books which fill the world?

I. In this discourse we shall glance generally at the Epistles of St. Paul, which occupy about a fourth of the New Testament. We will consider in outline the four clearly-marked groups into which they fall, and point out what is the key-note, the dominant conception, the central message, of each one of those thirteen Epistles.

1. For any one who desires to gain a real historical conception of their meaning; and of the vast part which they play in the development of Christian doctrine, the first thing necessary is to ascertain and remember their chronological order. It has been a real misfortune for our right comprehension of them, that, during all these centuries, they have been arranged in our Bibles in an order so haphazard and accidental. It is specially to be regretted that this defect has not been remedied even in our Revised Version. It may be slightly doubtful what was the sequence of them in one or two small details, but of the order in which they fall into groups there is no doubt whatever. Nor does it even admit of question that those groups differ from each other in their general characteristics. No one doubts that we best understand the mind, the character, the teachings of any author when we study his writings with some reference to the age at which, and the order in which he wrote them. Most of all is this desirable in the case of one who was always growing in grace, and in the knowledge of our Lord and Saviour Jesus Christ as was St. Paul, whose thoughts,

M

under the guidance of the Holy Spirit, went on deepening and expanding even to his death. Take the case of any secular writer. The importance of observing the chronology of his works is greater in proportion to his greatness. What should we think of an edition of Shakespeare which led us to imagine that he wrote the *Two Gentlemen of Verona*, or *Love's Labour's Lost* in his maturest age, or that he wrote *Hamlet* and *Julius Caesar* when he was a mere youth? What should we think of an editor of Milton who left us to suppose that the *Samson Agonistes* was written at College, and the *Lycidas* when he was a blind old man? But if the bearing of a man's life, and spiritual growth upon his writings be important in such a case, it must (except on the most mechanical and unscripturally superstitious dogma about "verbal dictation") be infinitely more so when those writings are among the sacred books of God's final revelation. And yet we continue to place first the Epistle to the Romans, and we arrange even the Epistles to Ephesus and Colossae before those to the Thessalonians which were written at least ten years earlier, and are in fact the earliest books of the whole New Testament. And this chance order is merely due to the supposed importance of the Churches addressed. The letters to the Romans and Corinthians are put first (apparently) because Rome and Corinth were large and important cities. But such a method of arrangement, it need hardly be said, is no method at all.

2. Many years of the Apostle's ministry elapsed before he wrote a single line that has come down to us. He was converted probably about the age of thirty. His first letter (the First to the Thessalonians) was not written till his second great missionary journey, when he was forty-six years old. All his letters fall into four distinct groups, separated from each other roughly by a period of four or five years each, and covering a space in his life from the age of forty-six to the age of sixty-one. Those four groups are the letters of his second missionary journey, namely the two to

Thessalonica;[1] those of the third missionary journey, the
Epistles to the Corinthians, Galatians, and Romans; those
of the first imprisonment at Rome—namely, the four to
Philippi, Ephesus, Colossae, and Philemon; and those between his liberation and his martyrdom, namely, the letter
to Titus, and the two to Timothy, of which the last was written
in his last Roman imprisonment and when he was expecting,
almost daily, the stroke of death.

3. A rapid sketch will suffice to show the events in
St. Paul's life which coincide with the writing of these letters,
and also to point out, first the general characteristic of each
of the four groups, and then the dominant thought of each
separate Epistle.

(i.) The first group, those to Thessalonica, are the *Eschatological* Epistles; those that is, which bear on the last things;
the Epistles, as they may be called, of the Second Advent;
of Christ's personal return to glorify the saints and to judge
His foes.

A glance at St. Paul's life will show how natural it was
that, at the period in which the Apostle wrote them, such
thoughts should fill the entire horizon of his mind. Consider what he had endured! Beginning as a Pharisee and a
persecutor—appearing first on the scene as the young man
at whose feet the witnesses laid their clothes while they were
stoning St. Stephen—he had been grasped by a resistless
hand as he went to Damascus to hale Christian men and
women to prison, and, by one flash of Christ's light into his
erring but noble heart, he had been made "a fusile Apostle."
Thenceforth, with the exception of brief retirements in
Arabia and Tarsus, his life had been one long martyrdom.
In a basket, by night, down the wall, he had escaped from a
plot to murder him at Damascus; another such plot had
driven him from Jerusalem; another from Antioch in Pisidia;

---

[1] It is a curious circumstance that St. Paul either never wrote to the
Churches founded in his first journey, or that his letters are no longer extant.
It has been ingeniously conjectured that he left those Churches to the care of
Barnabas.

another from Iconium. At Lystra he had been actually stoned and left for dead. Then, not to mention all his troubles, from enemies without and false brethren within, and all the agitating scenes which he had gone through at the Syrian Antioch and Jerusalem in his defence of the liberty of the Gentiles—in his second mission tour he had been seized with illness in Galatia; had been worn with long journeys over the wild, cold hills and glaring uplands of Asia; had been scourged, and imprisoned, and shamefully entreated at Philippi; had nearly fallen a victim to mob violence at Thessalonica; had been hunted from Berea; had been derided at Athens; had been arrested at Corinth. And all this, besides insults, and controversies, and anxieties, and perils from murderers and brigands, from shipwreck and river floods, in the city, in the wilderness, in the sea. Can you wonder that after, and in the midst of, scenes like these, the one thought prominent in his mind—the sole thought that inspired and sustained him—was this—"All this is but for a little time. Soon shall the Lord return again;" and that, when he reached Corinth from Athens, this—the near coming of Christ—was the thought which filled his first two extant letters, the two to his beloved Thessalonians? There could be no more natural topic of consolation in letters from the persecuted Apostle to his persecuted converts.

(ii.) Yet, hard as had been his lot hitherto, a still more troubled phase of his life was to begin;—a phase when he was burdened beyond measure; when he "fought with beasts" at Ephesus; when he seemed to be dying daily, amid fightings without and fears within. If his delicate, nervous frame had been torn by Jewish thongs, and Roman rods, and crushing stones, his sensitive and shrinking soul had to endure an equal or perhaps severer martyrdom from anathema, and calumny, and the oppression of a perpetual hissing. It had come home to him in his first great journey that the Gospel was a Gospel of liberty; that the Gentiles were not to be bound by the yoke of the Levitic law; that though Judaism, had been the cradle of Christianity it was not to be suffered to be its grave. He was already despised by the Gentiles as an enthusiast; detested by the Jews as an apostate; but now he had to accept the additional burden of hatred and suspicion even from many Jewish Christians. They organised something like a counter-mission against him; they led back his foolish Galatians to rites and ceremonies; they maligned his name and undermined his authority among the restless, conceited, and turbulent Corinthians; they even tried to poison against him the minds of the Christians at Rome. Hence the second group of letters, written, during his third journey, at Ephesus and Corinth, are St. Paul's four most powerful, most argumentative, most impassioned Epistles. They were wrung from him at the period of most vehement storm and stress in his life, under great mental anxiety and physical suffering. This second group consists of the letters to the Corinthians, Galatians, and Romans. They may be characterised as the letters of controversy with Judaism— Judaism from within and from without—whether as disturbing his Churches, impugning his authority, enjoining circumcision, or insisting on Mosaic ordinances, which did but nullify the effects of the death of Christ. The first three are marked by all the vehemence and agony of eager warfare; the last is a calmer and more comprehensive review and statement of the results attained. The doctrinal and universal importance of these four Epistles can hardly be exaggerated. The particular details of the controversy are obsolete. The then "burning questions" have "burnt themselves out." The flames of heated discussion about circumcision and "tongues" are now not even as the tails of smoking firebrands. But the principles developed are eternal. In them St. Paul fought out and won, for all time, the battle of full and free salvation; of faith, as against works; of mercy, as against sacrifice; of the obsolescence not only of Levitism itself, but of the whole sacerdotal spirit. He showed for ever that the true worship of the Christian consists in spirituality, not in ceremonialism; in heart service, not in outward ritual; in the religion of the life, not in forms of service; in being, not in doing; in love, not in orthodox formulae, or rubrical niceties, or sacrificial vestments, or sacramental theories. In these letters we have the grandest phase of the struggle of the teaching of the prophets against the usurpation of the priests; the proofs of the groundlessness and nullity of all those persecuting tyrannies and of all that theological intolerance which spring from the pride and ambition of the human heart.

(iii.) After the Epistle to the Romans, which was the last of this great group, nearly five years elapse before we come to the third group. Again escaping from a plot to murder him at Corinth, he made his way to Jerusalem in the voyage so graphically described for us in the Acts of the Apostles. He went overland to Macedonia, spent Easter at Philippi, restored Eutychus in the memorable midnight service at Troas, made that touching farewell speech to the Ephesian elders at Miletus, and then we trace his barque over the blue waters of the Ægean as it threaded its way among

> " The sprinkled isles,
> Lily on lily that o'erlace the sea,
> And laugh their pride when the light wave lisps Greece,"

till he reached the kind friends with whom he knelt in tears and prayer on the sea-shore of Tyre. Then he stayed for some days in the house of Philip at Caesarea, with the virgin prophetesses his daughters, and, amid warnings of peril and imprisonment, continued dauntlessly on his journey to Jerusalem. Nearly torn to pieces by the mob in the Temple, nearly flagellated by the hasty but honest Lysias, rescued from the rage of the Sanhedrin, and the murderous plot of the Sicarii, he was hurried in the night by an armed escort to Caesarea. There he was imprisoned for two dreary years. He was tried before Felix, tried before Festus, tried before Agrippa. Agitated by these scenes, in which the fury and pertinacity of his assailants had become more and more

clear, he appealed to Caesar, hoping to find some protection
from provincial bribery and injustice in the stern majesty of
Roman law. In consequence of this appeal he was forced to
journey amid months of storm and shipwreck to Rome.
There, chained by the wrist to a soldier day and night, he
remained in custody for two years more, and there he wrote
his third group of letters. They also are four in number : the
two to the Philippians and Philemon, dictated by personal
affection and special incidents—and the two great Christological Epistles—those to Ephesus and Colossae—in which, to
counteract a dreamy, subtle, incipient heresy, he develops and
expands, in all its splendour, the doctrine of the Prae-
existence, the Divinity, the Eternal Headship and Supremacy
of our Risen and Ascended Saviour the Lord Jesus Christ.

(iv.) Some four years again elapse during which he wrote his
fourth and last group of letters—the three Pastoral Epistles.
Liberated just in time to escape martyrdom in the Neronian
persecution, he again travelled to Asia Minor and Western
Greece. It was at some time during the wanderings which
followed—wanderings which, unhappily, no Luke has recorded
for us—that he wrote his letter to Titus whom he had left to
govern the Church of Crete ; and the first to Timothy, who
was acting as his delegate at Ephesus. Then, once more
arrested, and sent to a second Roman imprisonment—aged,
lonely, worn-out, forsaken, daily expecting death—he penned
his last brave, bright words to his dearest convert and companion, the beloved and gentle Timotheus. Almost immediately afterwards he was put to death. He was, in all
probability, led out along the Ostian Road, and there, in a
scene so lonely and so obscure, that scarcely even the faintest
gleam of tradition has fallen on it—there, at the close of a
life which the world would have called a hopeless and disastrous failure, but which has been crowned by the Lord,
whose cross he bore, with everlasting victory, and the love of
all generations—the sword flashed, and the life of one of the
noblest of the sons of God was shorn away.

II. Such then are the four groups of Epistles: the first two mainly Eschatological; the next four mainly controversial; of the next four, two occasional, and two Christological; the last three Pastoral.

But, further, every one of these thirteen Epistles, of which we have thus seen the order, has its own special characteristic, its prominent idea—generally its central passage, often even its dominant word or key-note.

a. The first group—those to the Thessalonians—were, we said, the Eschatological group—the Epistles of the Second Advent.

The first is characterised by its extreme sweetness; both are eminently full of consolation. The whole idea of the first is—look to Christ as a comfort in tribulation. Maranatha —the Lord is near.

The second was written to correct the error that Christ's coming would be instantaneous, and to obviate the neglect of daily earthly duties which sprang from that exciting expectation. Its most characteristic, and indeed all but unique, section is that in the second chapter about the Apostasy and the Man of Sin.

β. The second group is the Anti-Judaic group—the group of controversy—written in the great period of distress and conflict. The First to the Corinthians is the Epistle of Church Discipline. It decides by great principles the little details of life and worship. Its fundamental idea is Christian unity; and its chief passages—the unparalleled 13th and 15th chapters—in one of which the Apostle develops his magnificent argument for the Resurrection, and in the other, like some great poet, " with his garland and singing robes about him," pours forth his inspired, impassioned paean to the glory of Christian love.

The Second to the Corinthians falls into two main divisions. The key-note of the first nine chapters is consolation in sorrow; that of the other chapters is boasting—the boastings of his adversaries which drove him into a " boasting " which would have been abhorrent to him had it not been that his boast was in his infirmities and in the Cross of Christ his Lord. The Epistle is specially marked by its intense emotion; it is full of haunting words—now "tribulation," now "commendation," now "boast." It is the Epistle of personal details; the *Apologia pro vitâ suâ* of the great Apostle.

In the Epistle to the Galatians we find him again in a far different mood. It is the Epistle of indignant warning; the only Epistle which he wrote throughout with his own hand. It is his gage of defiance to the Judaists; his triumphant note of exultation over abrogated ordinances and freedom perfected. Here, more than in all the rest, as Luther said, "*meras flammas loquitur!*"—"he speaks mere flames!"

In the Epistle to the Romans, the same theme—justification by faith and not by works; the universality of sin and the universality of grace—is again developed in its positive rather than its antithetic aspect. The theme is handled doctrinally and systematically, not, as in the Galatians, with impassioned controversy, but with irresistible logic and calm and sympathetic strength.

γ. St. Paul had gone through much by the time we come to the third group. It is the Christological and Anti-Gnostic group. In personal force he was a shattered man. He was calmer, he was sadder, he was yet wiser; he sat thinking and praying in his lonely prison. Yet the key-note of the Philippians is joy. There is one little outburst of anger in it, but its one leading thought—the leading thought of the poor, suffering prisoner, so full of gratitude for the pecuniary help which the Philippians had sent to him is—" Rejoice in the Lord alway ; again I will say, Rejoice."

The key-note of the Colossians is Christ all in all; Christ Head over all.

The magnificent Epistle to the Ephesians is rich in many leading thoughts. It is the great Epistle of the Church— the Church in Christ. It is the Epistle of Catholicity; the Epistle of the Ascension ; the Epistle of the Heavenlies ; the

Epistle of the " mystery " and " riches " of the Gospel. Its key-note is grace.

The letter to Philemon is a little satellite and annex to the planet of the Colossians. It is a letter to a private Christian gentleman, to ask pardon for a runaway Laodicean slave.

δ. In the last group, the Pastoral Epistles, again we see a change. The thunderstorms of continuous controversy seem to have rolled far into the distance. The foundations of Christian truths have been laid for ever. St. Paul is writing to Timothy and Titus how they should govern the Churches of Ephesus and Crete. Though here and there we find a grand and pregnant summary of doctrine, the main theme is duty not doctrine, ethics not theology, the holy and wise walk of a Christian pastor in the guidance of his flock.

Lastly, in the Second to Timothy, we have, as it were, the last will and testament of Paul—" the song of the dying swan "—and through it though there runs the old man's wailing undertone to his beloved disciple—" Come to me ; " " Come quickly ; " " Come before winter ; " " Come and cheer me a little ere I die "—yet, drowning this low chord of sorrow, rings the paean of quenchless hope and undaunted trust, as to the dear but timid racer he hands the torch of the Gospel, which in his own brave grasp no cowardice had hidden, no carelessness had dimmed, no storms had quenched.

What an inexhaustible treasure have we here ! The First and Second to the Thessalonians, Epistles of the Second Coming ; the First to the Corinthians, the Epistle of Christian unity and love ; the Second, the Epistle of consolation, and a glimpse into the Apostle's very heart ; the Galatians, the Epistle of Christian liberty ; the Romans, of justification by faith ; Philippians, the Epistle of joy in sorrow ; Colossians, of Christ all in all ; Ephesians, of Christ in His Church ; Philemon, the Magna Charta of emancipation ; the First to Timothy and Titus, the pastor's manual ; the Second to Timothy, the Epistle of courage, and exultation, and

triumph in deep, apparent failure—of victory in the defeat
of lonely death. Again, I say, what a treasure have we here !
May we go to it to learn humility, to learn tolerance, to learn
duty, to learn charity, to learn that man is our brother, to
learn that God is love, to learn that Christ died for our
worst enemies no less than for ourselves. If we fail to learn
such lessons from the Epistles we might as well shut them
up for ever. If God will enlighten the eyes of our hearts by
His Holy Spirit, then indeed shall we know His Word ; find
in it a Urim and Thummim, ardent with precious stones, and
every gem of it, under the mystic glory, bright with the
oracles of God.

NOTE I.

ST. PAUL'S EPISTLES.

"Considering these Epistles for themselves only," says Ewald, "and apart from the general significance of the great Apostle of the Gentiles, we must still admit that, in the whole history of all centuries and of all nations, there is no other set of writings of similar extent, which, as creations of the fugitive moment, have proceeded from such severe troubles of the age, and such profound sufferings of the author himself, and yet contain such an amount of healthfulness, serenity, and vigour of immortal genius, and touch with such clearness and certainty on the very highest truths of human aspiration and action. From the smallest to the greatest they seem to have proceeded from the fleeting moments of this earthly life only to enchain all eternity ; they were born in anxiety and bitterness of human strife to set forth in brighter lustre their superhuman grace and beauty."

NOTE II.

BAUR, who rejected the authenticity of all St. Paul's Epistles except four, classifies them as follows :—

1. *Homologoumena.*—Four. Those of the second group (1, 2 Cor., Gal., Rom.).
   ii. *Antilegomena,* or of uncertain authenticity.—Six. Namely, those of the first group (1, 2 Thess.), and the Epistles of the Captivity (Phil., Eph., Col., Philem.).
   iii. *Notha,* or Spurious. The three Pastoral Epistles.

2. RENAN classes them as follows :—
   i. Incontestably genuine. 1, 2 Cor., Gal., Rom.
   ii. Authentic, though disputed. 1, 2 Thess., Phil.
   iii. Probably authentic, though doubtful. Col. and Philem.
   iv. Probably spurious. Ephes.
   v. Spurious. The Pastoral Epistles. 1, 2 Tim., Tit.
3. They may be arranged according to their form, as by Reuss :—
   i. Circular letters. Ephesians and Romans.[1]

---

[1] These are rather treatises than letters. They were elaborate statements intended to be read by many Churches. Some MSS. *leave a blank* for the words "in Rome" (Rom. i. 7), "in Ephesus" (Eph. i. 1).

ii. Letters to special Churches. Thessalonians, 1, 2 Cor., Philippians,
Colossians, and Galatians.[1]

iii. Letters to spiritual friends.

4. Accepting the thirteen Epistles of St. Paul as authentic, and also the Epistle to the Hebrews, St. Thomas Aquinas made an ingeniously elaborate but entirely untenable attempt to classify them by the grace of Christ, as it is in itself, as it is in the Sacraments, and with regard to its effects.[2]

5. Olshausen's classification of them as i. Dogmatic ; ii. Practical ; iii. Friendly, is inadequate and confusing.

6. Lange classifies them very well as :—
    i. Eschatological. 1, 2 Thess.
    ii. Soteriological. Gal., Rom.
    iii. Ecclesiastical. *a.* Polemically. 1 Cor.
                     β. Apologetically. 2 Cor.
    iv. Christological. Col., Eph.
    v. Ethical. Phil.
    vi. Pastoral (or rather to Individuals). 1, 2, Tim., Tit., Philem.

NOTE III.

CHRONOLOGY OF THE EPISTLES.

The approximate dates and sequence of the Epistles of St. Paul are as follows :—

SECOND MISSIONARY JOURNEY.

FIRST GROUP.—*Eschatological.*

1 Thessalonians. Late in A.D. 52. Written at Corinth.
2 Thessalonians. A.D. 53.

THIRD MISSIONARY JOURNEY.

SECOND GROUP.—*Epistles of Judaic Controversy.*

1 Corinthians. A.D. 57 (early). Written at Ephesus.
2 Corinthians. A.D. 58 (early). Written at Philippi (?).
Galatians. A.D. 58. ⎫
Romans. A.D. 58. ⎭ Written at Corinth.

---

[1] Some of these (1, 2 Cor., Gal.) were addressed to little *groups* of Churches in Achaia, Galatia, &c.

[2] See a paper by the author in the *Expositor*, July, 1883.

EPISTLES OF THE FIRST IMPRISONMENT.

THIRD GROUP.—*Personal and Christological.*

Philippians. circ. A.D. 62. Written at Rome.

Colossians. ⎱
Philemon. ⎰ circ: A.D. 63.

Ephesians. circ. A.D. 63.

EPISTLES OF CLOSING YEARS.

FOURTH GROUP.—*Pastoral Epistles.*

1 Timothy. A.D. 65 or 66. Written in Macedonia (?).

Titus. A.D. 66. Written in Macedonia (?).

2 Timothy. A.D. 67 or 68. Written in Rome.

The following dates (of which some can only be approximate) may be found useful :—

A.D.

GAIUS (Caligula), A.D. 37.

St. Paul's conversion and martyrdom of St. Stephen	37
St. Paul's first visit to Jerusalem	39

CLAUDIUS, A.D. 41.

St. Paul summoned from Tarsus to Antioch	41
Famine. Second visit to Jerusalem	44
First Mission journey	45
Expulsion of Jews from Rome	49
Third visit to Jerusalem	51
" 1 Thessalonians "	52
" 2 Thessalonians "	53

NERO, A.D 54.

Fourth visit to Jerusalem	54
" 1 Corinthians "	57
" 2 Corinthians "	58
" Galatians "	58
" Romans "	58
St. Paul at Rome	61
" Philippians "	62
" Colossians " and " Philemon "	63
" Ephesians "	63
Paul liberated	63
" 1 Timothy "	64
" Titus "	65 or 66
" 2 Timothy "	67
Martyrdom	68

THE
FIRST EPISTLE TO THE THESSALONIANS.

WRITTEN FROM CORINTH, A.D. 52.

> " He came who was the Holy Spirit's vessel,
> Barefoot and lean."—DANTE, *Parad.* xxi. 119.

" *Habet haec epistola meram quandam dulcedinem*, quae lectori dulcibus affectibus non assueto minus sapit quam caeterae severitate quâdam palatum stringentes."—BENGEL.

"Im ganzer ist es ein Trostbrief."—HAUSRATH, *N. Test. Zeitgesch.* ii. 299.

"Paul and Silvanus and Timotheus, unto the 'Church of the Thessalonians."—1 THESS. i. 1.

1. AT the north-western angle of the Archipelago, the ancient Aegean Sea, lies the beautiful city of Saloniki, an important commercial emporium of 70,000 inhabitants. Rising with its white domes and minarets, its vines and cypresses, up the sides of a steep hill, between two ravines, it presents a splendid appearance as the traveller sails into the deep blue waters of its noble bay, and gazes from it upon the snowy mountain-crests of Olympus and Pelion. But when you enter the town all its beauty disappears. Its streets are tortuous, filthy, and neglected, like those of most towns which are blighted by the curse of Islam. It is oppressed by the greed, withered by the atrophy, and unsettled by the fanaticism of Turkish misrule. Known in old days as "the Orthodox city," and for centuries the bulwark of Christendom against

the Turks, it was taken by Amurath II. in 1430, and the majority of its 70,000 inhabitants are now Mohammedans and Jews. It was the outbreak of rage and massacre in this city in the year 1876 which was the first prominent event in the later phases of that Eastern question which has now for so long a period engrossed the attention of the civilised world.

2. In the first century, Thessalonica, the ancient Thermae, the capital of Macedonia Secunda, and the residence of a Roman Proconsul, shared with Ephesus and Corinth the commerce of the Aegean. Into this busy emporium, 1,800 years ago, there entered by the great Egnatian road three travellers. One was a grave elder from Jerusalem, another was a timid and youthful deacon from the bleak highlands of Lycaonia, the third was a worn and suffering Jew of Tarsus. The names of these three poor wandering missionaries were Silas, Timotheus, and Paul. Two of them, only a few days previously, had endured a terrible flagellation with Roman rods in the open market-place, and had then been thrust into the lowest dungeons of Philippi, from which they had been saved by a manifest interposition of Divine power. The whole aspect of the persecuted wanderers bespoke their poverty, their sufferings, and their earthly insignificance. Hated as the Jews were in classical antiquity, it is probable that these wayworn and afflicted wanderers would be met on all sides by suspicious glances and expressions of contempt. Yet their object was the most nobly disinterested which it is possible to conceive. A famine was at that time raging in the Roman empire, and the commonest necessaries of life had risen to six times their proper value. But these missionaries had determined to be independent. Their first object, therefore, was to find a lodging in the Jewish quarter and the means of earning their daily bread. Paul, the most worn, the most suffering of the three, had, as a boy, according to the admirable Jewish custom, learnt a trade. It was the humble mechanical trade of weaving the black goats' hair of his native province into tent-cloth; but even by toiling at this

mean occupation night and day he could barely earn sufficient for their common maintenance, and but for a kindly contribution from his converts of Philippi the three devoted Evangelists must have nearly starved. If this alone had not been sufficient to damp the Apostles' ardour, it might well have been thought that the peril and agony of their recent experiences in Macedonia would at least have induced them to give up all thoughts of mission effort. But their hopes, their aims, were not selfish, or worldly, or commonplace. They were not swayed by the vulgar motives, the narrow domesticities, the self-seeking purposes which are the dominant forces in all ordinary lives. The first three Sabbaths saw them duly in the Jewish synagogue delivering their dangerous message to angry and suspicious Jews. After that, seeing in all probability the uselessness of such appeals, they turned from the large Jewish community and worked among the Gentiles.

The Gentiles had long lost all practical belief in the Pagan religion. Their ancient poets had imagined that awful deities met amid the clouds that rolled over "the azure heights of beautiful Olympus;" but now men had long grown sceptical, and, as Cicero had sadly said when he was an exile at Thessalonica, he saw nothing there but snow and ice. But the human soul cannot live in a vacuum. Man must have some belief in the future and the unseen to save his life from destruction and despair. Hence many of the Gentiles, and above all the gentler and more faithful souls of Gentile women, eagerly embraced the message of a Lord and Saviour Jesus Christ.

The success among the Gentiles of these Jewish teachers of a new faith kindled among the Jews a bitter jealousy.[1] The deadly hatred which, with incessant plots of murder, had

---

[1] That the church of Thessalonica was predominantly *Gentile* is clear from 1 Thess. i. 9, 10, and is implied in Acts xvii. 4, if we read " and of the proselytes *and* of the Greeks a great multitude " (τῶν τε σεβομένων καὶ Ἑλλήνων, A.D. Vulg. Copt. Lachmann, Tregelles, &c.). ii. That they were a *small community* appears from ii. 11, where St. Paul speaks of exhorting them one by one (ἕνα ἕκαστον ὑμῶν). (iii.) That they were mainly slaves and artisans appears from iv. 11, 12.

N

already chased Paul from city to city—from Damascus, from Jerusalem, from Antioch of Pisidia, from Iconium, from Lystra, from Philippi, as it drove him afterwards from Beroea and from Corinth—broke out once more against the bearers of the glad tidings of peace. The Jews themselves were afraid to act, but they enlisted in their bad cause the services of "certain lewd fellows of the baser sort"—the rabble which can always be assembled for mischief from the scum of great cities. This worthless mob set the city in an uproar and assaulted the house of Jason in which the missionaries lived. The rioters were too late. Their intended victims had received timely notice and had escaped into safe concealment. But the mob dragged Jason and one or two other Christians before the magistrates.[1] St. Luke calls those magistrates "politarchs," a name which is not found in a single ancient author, and which would certainly have been set down as a blunder by sceptical criticism but for the happy providence which has preserved it on a large inscription of St. Paul's day, and which St. Paul's own eyes must have seen carved on the entablature of a triumphal arch which once spanned the main street of Thessalonica. The Turks, with their usual disregard and ignorance, recently destroyed this arch; but the stones on which ran the inscription were happily preserved by our British consul, were shipped to England during the outbreak of 1876, and are now safe in the British Museum. They furnish an interesting confirmation of the accuracy of the Evangelist. The politarchs made Jason and his companions give bail, and since their mission labours were thus rudely disturbed, Paul and Silas, leaving Timothy to teach the converts of Thessalonica, made their escape secretly

---

[1] The specific charge was (practically) *laesa majestas*, the creation of disturbances by proclaiming "a different emperor" (ἕτερον βασιλέα). Christianity being "the Gospel of the kingdom" (Matt. iv. 23, &c.) could be easily thus misrepresented. St. Paul not unfrequently uses the term kingdom (1 Thess. ii. 12, and altogether fourteen times in his Epistles) ; but the obvious danger of misapprehension prevented the Apostles from using it so frequently as in the Gospels where it occurs 124 times. Thessalonica was an *urbs libera*, and the Greek cities were slavishly loyal to the Emperor.

by night. Such was the manner in which Christ had been preached in the Church of Thessalonica—the second Church founded in European Christendom.

3. St. Paul felt so deep an interest in these earlier European Christians that in his absence from them he felt like a man bereaved.[1] He longed to visit them again, and made vain attempts to do so from Beroea, from Athens, and from Corinth. At the latter city Timothy came back to him, and while giving a most favourable account of the Church in general, told the Apostle two special facts about them. The one was that they were subjected to severe persecutions both from Jews and Gentiles; the other that many of them were deeply discouraged by the deaths of some members of their little community, who, they seemed to think, would be terrible, and perhaps hopeless, losers from not having survived till that second advent of their Lord, which all Christians at that day supposed to be immediately imminent.

4. It was under these circumstances that, being unable to go to them in person, Paul determined to send them a letter. It was his twofold object to console them under persecution and to explain the groundlessness of their lack of hope about their brethren who had died before seeing the second coming of Christ. With a heart full of solicitude, longing to guide and comfort them, he bade Timothy, who had just arrived from his visit to them,[2] to sit down and write while he dictated. Doubtless he would have written a letter with his own hand, as he did to the Galatians, but the chronic weakness of his eyesight rendered it difficult and painful for him to do so. Whether that letter—the First to the Thessalonians—was the first he ever wrote we do not know, but it is at any rate the first that has come down to us; and since it was written some time before the Gospels, in reading the First Epistle to the Thessalonians, we are reading the oldest book of the New Testament, the earliest document of the Christian religion,

---

[1] ii. 17. ἡμεῖς δὲ ἀδελφοὶ ἀπορφανισθέντες ἀφ' ὑμῶν.
[2] iii. 6. ἄρτι δὲ ἐλθόντος Τιμοθέου πρὸς ἡμᾶς ἀφ' ὑμῶν.

the first extant written testimony of any Christian after the death of Christ. Surely this fact alone ought to give to this brief letter an imperishable interest. What a moment was that in the religious history of the world when Paul first began to entrust to the fugitive papyrus words which were destined to possess so eternal a significance!

5. The circumstances under which the little letter was written explain its object. We can without difficulty understand its general characteristics, its main outline, and its special lesson for ourselves.

i. Its general characteristics can be explained in very few words. It is of all St. Paul's letters the gentlest. There is not a word of controversy in it. It is written almost exclusively to Gentiles, and hence has no controversy, no difficult reasoning, no developed doctrine. Its style is unusually simple. With the exception of one very severe remark about the Jews in the second chapter, it is marked by an extreme sweetness of tone. A loving fatherly spirit breathes in every line. It is in all respects a letter of consolation. Two words strike the key-notes of its two most important sections—"affliction," "advent." He has preached to them in affliction; he has warned them that they would suffer affliction, and that warning has been fulfilled. But he has also preached to them of the coming of Christ, and in that hope all sorrow vanished; so that by a splendid and daring paradox, which was not a rhetorical figure but a blessed truth unknown to the world before, they had received the word in tribulation, yet with joy—in much tribulation yet with joy of the Holy Ghost. That joy was like a green isle of peace in the world's troubled and storm-swept sea, on which the waves might beat, but on which they must for ever beat in vain.

ii. Now look for a moment at the outline of this gentle letter of consolation. It will be seen at a glance that it falls into two main divisions—one personal and retrospective, the other practical and hortatory. It is also clear that it has the six features which occur in nearly all St. Paul's letters to

Churches, namely : (1) the greeting, (2) the thanksgiving, (3) a doctrinal section, (4) a practical section, (5) personal messages, and (6) a final salutation. In this Epistle, however, the personal and the practical elements prevail throughout and blend with each other. The only specially doctrinal portion is that from iv. 13—v. 11. In that section St. Paul speaks of Christ's advent and its bearing on the dead. It should, however, be carefully noted that although only one doctrinal topic receives full treatment, the letter abounds with germs of thought which are developed in later Epistles,[1] and also that the Christology of the Epistle implies though it does not elaborate the most advanced Christology of even the Epistles to the Colossians and Ephesians.[2] The first three chapters are mainly personal and historical, the last two mainly hortatory. Each division ends with an earnest prayer. After greeting them in his own name and that of his two fellow-missionaries, he thanks God that the news of their faith had sounded like a trumpet-blast (ἐξήχηται) throughout Macedonia,[3] and that they had become "imitators" (μιμηταὶ) of their teachers and of the Lord. The second chapter is occupied with reminiscences of his ministry among them and their hearty response. It is clear that calumny had been busily at work, or the self-defence of this chapter would not have been necessary. Happily, however, the missionaries— slandered as good men have been in all ages of the world's history—needed only to appeal to the knowledge of their converts.[4] Whatever enemies might say, the Thessalonians knew that their teachers had borne no resemblance to the mercenary quacks who in that day swarmed throughout the cities of the empire ; that no deceit, no avarice, no flattery,

[1] *E.g.* 1 Thess. v. 8, "the armour of righteousness" (Eph. vi. 13–17) ; iv. 16, "the trump of God" (1 Cor. xv. 52) ; 1 Thess. v. 12, the duty towards ministers (1 Cor. ix. 2–15 ; 2 Cor. xi. 8–10) ; self-defence (1, 2 Cor.).

[2] See 1 Thess. i. 1 ; iii. 11, 12 ; v. 28.

[3] The position of Thessalonica as a much-frequented commercial city is amply sufficient to account for this phrase.

[4] This point comes out remarkably and repeatedly, i. 4, "*knowing.*" ii. 1, "for ye yourselves *know.*" ii. 9, "for ye *remember.*" ii. 11, "even as ye *know.*" iii. 3, "for ye yourselves *know.*" iv. 2, "for ye *know.*"

1 THESS.　no subterranean motives had mingled with the exhortations. They knew the diligence, the unselfishness, the disinterested independence, the affectionate enthusiasm in which the mission to them had been characterised. And the Thessalonians had believed their message, and in spite of bitter persecutions had stood fast in the faith. At this point the incidental mention of the Churches of Judaea, who had been equally faithful amid similar tribulations, makes St. Paul "go off at a word" and digress into a severe denunciation of the Jews which must have arisen from the bitter, though momentary exacerbation caused by their conduct towards him at Corinth.[1] But after this outburst he instantly recovers his calm of mind. He continues to thank God for converts who were "his glory and his joy." He had sent Timotheus to encourage them, since he had himself been twice hindered by Satan from coming to them in person. That dear fellow-worker with God had brought back an almost unexpectedly encouraging report of their steadfastness, which had been to the Apostle amid his own heavy trials a fresh spring of life. St. Paul's feelings towards his little Churches were those of all true pastors since. "Oh how rich a prisoner were I," wrote Samuel Rutherford to his flock at Anworth, "if I could obtain of my Lord the salvation of you all! My witness is above: your heaven would be two heavens, and the salvation of you all as two salvations to me."[2]

ii. Thess. 14-16.

Acts xviii. 5-28.

The third chapter ends with a fervent prayer for them, and

---

[1] The transient nature of this feeling is shown by the tenderness of such passages as Rom. ix. 1–5, written only a few years afterwards. But the feeling must have been strong at the moment, since it led St. Paul to speak of his fellow countrymen in terms which recall the bitter scorn of Tacitus (*Hist.* v. 5), and Juvenal (*Sat.* xiv. 100), where Jews are charged with "hatred of the human race." This is one of the passages which led Baur to treat the letter as spurious. But he mistakes the meaning of 1 Thess. ii. 16, "but the wrath is come (ἔφθασεν) upon them to the uttermost." St. Paul means that their guilt involves their doom ; that their rejection of Christ is Christ's rejection of them ; their wrath against Christ was His wrath against them. Their doom was consummated (Matt. xxvii. 25) in the fulness of their criminality, though the final punishment was for seventeen years longer postponed. St. Paul must have heard from the Apostles about the great eschatological discourse of Christ (Matt. xxiii. 37–39 ; xxiv. *passim*). Ewald speaks of "Christusworten die ihnen gewiss auch schriftlich vorlagen."

[2] Quoted by Dr. Donald Fraser, *Synopt. Lectures*, iii. 98.

then (iii. 11—13) begins the practical section of the Epistle. These converts had grown up amid the impure laxity and manifold temptations of Paganism. St. Paul has, therefore, to warn them first of the high duty of purity (iv. 1—8), then of brotherly love (iv. 9, 10) and a calm frame of mind. Quietness, he tells them, should be their ambition (φιλοτιμεῖσθαι ἡσυχάζειν), and faithful diligence (iv. 11—12). St. Paul would evidently have had a strong dislike for all fanatical excitement, for all holy mendicancy, for all consecrated idleness. From this duty he passes to the feeling which had disturbed their calm, namely, a needless despondency about those of their body who had died without seeing the second coming of the Lord. This (iv. 13—18) forms the doctrinal kernel and chief motive of the Epistle. And yet that it did not furnish St. Paul with the *original* motive for the Epistle is incidentally but decisively shown by the word " finally " in iv. 1 ; showing that even at that point he was thinking of bringing his letter to a conclusion. By the suddenness and awfulness of that coming he exhorts them to maintain an attitude of armed watchfulness (v. 1—11), cheerfulness, and vigilance, and hope. They were to abandon for ever the Gentile views which, in spite of dim hopes and splendid guesses, looked on the world beyond the grave as being at the best " a dolorous gloom," and to adopt that bright Christian confidence which in later years filled even the catacombs with emblems of peace and music and beauty—the dove, the green leaf, the Good Shepherd, the Orphean harp.[1]

---

[1] Here again these few casual words of St. Paul mark an epoch. Rarely, as in the lovely lines of Pindar about the sunlight and golden flowers in the islands of the Blest, had any ancient poet spoken hopefully of the world beyond the grave. And the Islands of the Blest were only for the few, the prevalent conception is that of even Agamemnon in the Shades :—

> " Talk not of reigning in this dolorous gloom,
> Nor think vain words, he cried, can ease my doom ;
> Better by far laboriously to bear
> A weight of woes, and breathe the vital air
> Slave to the meanest hind that begs his bread,
> Than reign the sceptred monarch of the dead."

A despairing Roman epitaph says, " Mortuus nec ad Deos nec ad homines acceptus est " (*Corp. Inscr.* i. 118). Le Boissier, *La Rel. Rom.* i. 304.

From that point—the eleventh verse of the fifth chapter—he ends the Epistle with moral exhortations of extraordinary force, freshness, and beauty. There were traces of insubordination among them, and he bids them respect and love, for their work's sake, their spiritual pastors.[1] There were traces of despondency among them, and he bids them encourage the faint-hearted and take the weak by the hand. There were traces of impatience and quarrelsomeness among them, and he bids them to seek peace among themselves, to avoid all retaliations and seek after all kindness (v. 12—15). Then follow little arrow-flights of sentences, unique in their orginality, and pregnant in meaning: "Rejoice always," "Pray unceasingly," "Give thanks in everything," "Quench not the Spirit," "Despise not preachings," [2] "Test all things," "Hold fast the honourable," "From every kind of evil refrain." [3] Then he breathes his last prayer for them that God would sanctify them wholly in spirit, soul, and body—a prayer remarkable as being the earliest passage in which the trichotomy of our human nature is recognised in Scripture. He asks their prayers, bids them salute one another with the kiss of charity, adjures them ($\delta\rho\kappa\iota\zeta\omega$ $\dot{\upsilon}\mu\hat{a}s$) that his letter be read to all the holy brethren, and ends his letter with an Apostolic blessing.[4]

6. Such then is the oldest book, or tract, or letter of the New Testament; the first extant written communication addressed by Christians to Christians; the first dawn of that glorious Christian literature which was to enshrine during nineteen following centuries so many immortal names; the first brief flight, as it were, of the young eagle from the ark

---

[1] The vagueness of the ecclesiastical organisation here indicated is one of the proofs of the early date of the letter.

[2] It has been fantastically supposed that in these two profound but brief and casual exhortations lies the whole motive of the letter.

[3] This, and not "from every appearance of evil," is the true rendering ($\dot{\alpha}\pi\dot{o}$ $\pi\alpha\nu\tau\dot{o}s$ $\epsilon\check{\iota}\delta o\upsilon s$, v. 22).

[4] The tender and affectionate relation in which St. Paul stood to these little Churches may be seen in these salutations and in such passages as 1 Cor. iv. 15; 2 Cor. vi. 11–13; Gal. iv. 12–21. See 1 Thess. ii. 7–11; where St. Paul compares himself both to a father and a mother.

of Christ's Church, which, over a world where at least the hilltops were beginning to emerge out of the deluge of iniquity, was to soar hereafter with supreme dominion through the brightening air. It may easily be imagined with what delight such a letter would be received by the little storm-tossed community of recent converts. In its tenderness, in its simplicity, in its sincerity, in its sanctity, it marked a new aeon in the world's history. It was worthy to be read to all the holy brethren; worthy to be read to all time. Letter-writing has been in all ages a branch of literature. From the letters of the Greek philosophers down to those of Cicero and Pliny, and from these down to those of Cowper and Carlyle, we have hundreds of specimens of letters; yet I doubt whether mankind would not consent to part with every one of them rather than part with this simple missive, dictated perhaps in a few hours, partly as a personal appeal against prevalent calumnies, partly as a Christian consolation under real trials and needless despondency. There are tones, in the human voice which, when once heard, we can never forget; which from their own natural quality vibrate for ever in the memory. So it is with the voice of inspired Christian wisdom. We need no proof of its inspiration. It thrills straight to the inmost heart, and its accents can never be forgotten. What illimitable hopes, what holy obligations, what golden promises, what lofty ideals, what strange renovation of the whole spirit and meaning of life lie hidden in these simple words![1]

Respecting the main doctrinal section of this brief letter—that which relates to Christ's Advent—a more favourable opportunity for speaking will be offered by the Second Epistle. We may, however, notice the fact that the views of St. Paul in later and more important letters grew and widened amid

---

[1] There can be no more touching illustration of these remarks than the fact that when in the earthquake at Manilla in 1853, the cathedral fell on the clergy and congregation the voice of one of the dying sufferers, whom it was impossible to rescue was heard calmly uttering the words of 1 Thess. iv. 16. (See the Bishop of Derry, *ad. loc.* in *Speaker's Commentary.*)

the divine teaching of events which constituted the spiritual education of his life. Here, writing to recent converts, his main points are (i.) Flee from idolatry and the pollutions of heathendom; (ii.) Wait for the return from heaven of the Risen Christ.[1] He had not yet been called upon (as in 1, 2, Corinthians) to defend against Jewish Christians his Apostolic commission; or as in the Galatians to prove the abrogation of circumcision and the annulment of the law; or as in the Romans to establish the great doctrine of justification by faith; or as in the Pastoral Epistles, and those of his imprisonment at Rome, to dwell on the conception of the Church as the visible establishment of Christ's kingdom. In the course of these controversies, as time sped on and the horizon of his thoughts was widened, and Christianity spread, and the Lord did not visibly return, he was naturally led to think more—though not exclusively[2]—of our present union with Christ, and of our still nearer union with Him when death should set us free.

The two practical duties on which St. Paul thought it right to offer a special warning may however be here fitly noticed.

a. The first is Purity. St. Paul was one of the very few men to whom it has been granted to speak on this painful subject, with stainless delicacy, yet with absolute precision. To him the Spirit of God seems more especially to have intrusted the high task of raising the world out of the depths of vileness to which it had sunk down. In what few words, in a tone how solemn and how fatherly, with arguments how weighty, does he speak at the opening of the fourth chapter. These Thessalonians had been Gentiles; and the life of the Gentiles was socially a life of almost unblushing sin, scourged yet unenlightened by sin's natural retributions. Therefore he entreats and exhorts them to walk as he had taught them to walk, and to abound more and more. He tells them of

[1] See 1 Thess. i. 9-10.
[2] See especially Phil. iii. 20.

the deep sin of sensual indulgence, because the will of God was their sanctification. He bids them each learn how to possess their bodies in sanctification and honour—that is to obtain a holy and noble mastery over themselves and the impulses of their lower nature. If they neglect this, he tells them—and this they knew full well—that they rendered themselves liable to the awful and inevitable consequences of permitted sin; and he tells them further, what they had not yet learnt so well, that to despise these injunctions was to despise not man but God, who had given to them that Holy Spirit who loves "before all temples the upright heart and pure."

And these loving and awful admonitions are not for the Thessalonians only, but for all time. What Paul said more than 1800 years ago one of the greatest writers of our day—not a clergyman, not a Puritan, not in any sense a Churchman—felt constrained to say in a great work a few years ago, namely, that "to burn away in mad waste the divine aroma and plainly celestial elements from our existence; to change our Holy of Holies into a place of riot; to make the soul itself hard, impious, barren;—surely a day is coming when it will be known again what virtue is in purity and continence of life; how divine is the blush of young human cheeks; how high, beneficent, sternly inexorable, if forgotten, is the duty laid . . . on every creature in regard to these particulars. Well, if such a day never comes again, then I perceive that much else will never come. Magnanimity and depth of insight will never come; heroic purity of heart and of eye; noble pious valour to amend us, and the age of bronze and lacquer, how can they ever come? The scandalous age . . . of hungry animalisms, spiritual impotencies and mendacities will have to run its course till the pit swallows it." So writes the great English moralist Thomas Carlyle, and this passage has often been noticed for its eloquence and power. Yet, though written eighteen centuries later, how incomparably does it fall below the few solemn, simple, weighty words of

St. Paul to his Thessalonians at the beginning of the fourth chapter! How far more spiritually religious are St. Paul's words! How far more deeply do they go to the very heart of the matter! And how superior are they in this respect above all, that St. Paul does not only warn, does not only remind of duty, does not only recall to us a sense of the dignity of our being, as having the image of God stamped upon it, and as being highly ransomed and ennobled to a filial relationship with Him, but he also points out to us the source of strength, the secret of victory, without which all warning is useless,—which source of strength lies in the awful words that " He that despiseth, despiseth not man, but God, who has also given to us His Holy Spirit."

b. Of the second virtue on which he here touches—that of brotherly love—we need not dwell. But let it be observed how infinitely new all this was. To us it is as familiar as household words, but there is nothing whatever even remotely resembling it in the vast field of Pagan literature. On the darkness of heathen immorality sentence after sentence of this simplest of the Epistles must have fallen like a sunbeam from God—a ray out of eternity. Imagine the joy of that young, tried, perplexed community as they received it! It was a blessing to be comforted and inspirited by the words of the dear teacher who had changed the current of their lives. It was much to know that he was still with them in heart, healing their incipient disagreements, silencing their needless fears. But to be told truths so utterly new, so divinely precious, as that there could be "joy of the Holy Ghost" even amid "much affliction"; that God had "called them to His kingdom and glory"; that they should, after death, be for ever with Him; that they were all the children of light and of the day; that the Spirit of God dwelt in them—surely such truths transfigured all life, as much as sunlight transfigures the dark cold world. If such words and thoughts shine brightly to us through the indurated dust of age-long familiarity, how must they have sparkled for them,

in their fresh originality, with heaven's own light! How
must they have rejoiced to know that they might use, for
their daily wear, such glory and holiness of thought as had
scarcely been attained by the greatest spirits of their race at
their rarest moments of inspiration; and therewith that
grandeur of life, which, in its perfect innocence towards God
and man, was even to these unknown!

NOTE I.

LEADING IDEA OF THE FIRST EPISTLE TO THE THESSALONIANS.

The leading words of these Epistles are ADVENT (Παρουσία) and AFFLICTION (Θλίψις). The word *Parousia* for advent occurs six times, and St. Paul only uses it once elsewhere (1 Cor. xv. 23).

Its key-note is Hope.

It first expressed the Christian possession of spiritual joy in the midst of calamity. " Much affliction, with joy of the Holy Ghost" (i. 6). This was no rhetorical *oxymoron*, but the sign of a new epoch in the history of human souls.

Its main theme is CONSOLATION from the near hope of the Second advent.

" *The dead in Christ shall arise first; then we that are alive, that are left, shall, together with them, be caught up in the clouds to meet the Lord in the air; and so shall we ever be with the Lord. Wherefore comfort one another with these words.*"—1 Thess. iv. 17, 18.

NOTE II.

The general outline of 1 Thess. is as follows :
It falls into two main divisions.

I. Retrospective (i. ii. iii.)
II. Hortatory (iv. v.)

I. Retrospective.

　　Greeting (ii.).
　　Thanksgiving (i. 2–10).
　　Appeal to them as to the character of his ministry (ii. –112).
　　Thanksgiving for their constancy ; and bitter complaint of the Jews (ii. 13–16).
　　Personal messages, and prayer (ii. 17 ; iii. 13).

II. Hortatory.

　　Warnings and exhortations : Be pure, Be diligent (iv. 1–12).
　　Doctrinal kernel of the Epistle : Be comforted. The Dead and the Advent (iv. 13–v. 11).
　　Further exhortations : Be watchful, Be helpful, Be glad, prayerful, thankful, tolerant, aim at perfectness (v. 12-24).
　　Last words and blessing (v. 25-28).

In this Epistle the personal, doctrinal, and practical sections are intermingled ; and there are no special salutations.

NOTE III.

ON THE GENUINENESS OF 1 THESSALONIANS.

This may be regarded as finally established. The Epistle is thoroughly supported by external testimony, and probably alluded to even by Polycarp and Ignatius. The first to hint a doubt, was J. E. C. Schmidt, *Einleit.* ii. 256, who has subsequently been followed by Baur, Hilgenfeld, and others. Baur's arguments (*Paulus*, cap. vii. and *Theol. Jahrb.* xiv. 141) are mainly based—1. (*a*) On the "colourlessness" and theological unimportance of the Epistle, which he says is (*β*) built on the Acts, with (*γ*) the help of reminiscences from the Epistles to the Corinthians. 2. On supposed traces of a later age. 3. On an "un-Pauline" Apocalypse in iv.

The answer is simple.

1. Why should we suppose that St. Paul could write nothing less important than Epistles to the Romans ?[1] (*β*) So far from being built on the Acts, it is not at first sight easy to reconcile the data of the Epistle with the events narrated in the Acts. (*γ*) May an author have no recurrent phrases ?

2. The supposed traces of a later date are exaggerated inferences from i. 7-9 (this needs no explanation, since Thessalonica was a centre of commerce from which travellers went in all directions ; and Paul himself may have spread the good fame of the Church) and iv. 13 (as though there were any difficulty in supposing that several deaths might have occurred at Thessalonica during the intervening months !).

3. The assertion that the Apocalyptic verses (iv. 13-18) are "un-Pauline" simply assumes that St. Paul's opinions were stereotyped ; not to mention that there is nothing in them which *conflicts* with what he writes elsewhere.

4. The outburst against the Jews, which some have regarded as suspicious, is closely analogous to that in Phil. iii. 2, and is sufficiently accounted for by Acts xviii. 2-13. The whole Epistle was an answer to the secret calumnies of Jews who charged him with "deceitfulness, uncleanness, guile." In this way they began the controversy which did not end till his death (see Lipsius, *Stud. u. Krit.* 1854).

[1] "Der Apostel schrieb nicht lauter Römerbriefe."—Hofmann.

NOTE IV.

DATES IN THE HISTORY OF THESSALONICA.

B.C.

(?)   Founded in ancient days, and known as Emathia, Halia, and, from its hot springs, Therma.

421   Occupied by the Athenians in the Peloponnesian war.

315   Rebuilt by Cassander and called Thessalonica after his wife, a daughter of Philip.

168   Surrenders to the Romans after the battle of Pydna, and becomes the capital of Macedonia Secunda.

42   Made a free city by Antony and Augustus.

A.D.

51   Christianity founded by St. Paul.

389   Massacre by Theodosius.

904   Taken by Saracens.

1185   Retaken by Tancred.   Eustathius Bishop.

1876   Outbreak of Turkish fanaticism.   Destruction of the arch of the "Politarchs."

Saloniki is now the third city of the Turkish Empire with 85,000 inhabitants, of whom about half are Jews.

THE SECOND EPISTLE TO THE THESSALONIANS.

WRITTEN FROM CORINTH, A.D. 52, OR EARLY IN A.D. 53
(SOME MONTHS AFTER THE FIRST).

" Ergo latet ultimus dies ut observentur omnes dies."—AUG.

" Utraque Epistola ad Thessalonicenses fere singula capita singulis suspiriis obsignata habet."—BENGEL.

" These things must first come to pass, but the end is not immediately."—Luke xxi. 9.

VERY shortly after St. Paul had despatched his first letter to the Thessalonians he received further news of their condition. It was on the whole favourable. In his first letter he had urged them to still greater advance in faith, and in brotherly love, and had encouraged them to steadfastness amid the heavy persecutions to which it appears that they were constantly liable. He had also urged on them the duties of purity and diligence, and of due submission to those who were set over them in the Lord. He had, above all, shown the groundlessness of their fears as to any irreparable loss of those who had died without seeing the advent of Christ. In all these matters his letter had produced excellent effects. He has no need to repeat his solemn warnings about chastity and obedience, and he can begin his second letter by thanking God with unusual fervour for the exceeding increase of their faith and charity.

O

1. But yet there was one new and serious danger—over-excitement about the coming of the Lord; a mistaken notion as to its immediate instancy; and a consequent spirit of disorderliness, which sprang from the neglect of daily duties. A restless feeling of alarm had even spread into the heathen world, and the gravest historians of the epoch recount the portents and prodigies which made many hearts faint with fear.[1] It is this attitude of mind that he now mainly endeavours to counteract. His second letter—so brief and simple that it probably cost him no effort—must have been written within a few months of the first. It has all the six usual divisions—the greeting of the first two verses; the thanksgiving, which, with its accompanying prayer and description of the Advent, occupies the first chapter; the doctrinal part, which, with exhortations and a concluding prayer, takes up the second chapter; the practical section, which, with mingled prayers and commands, forms the third chapter; and the final salutation and benediction in the last two verses. But the main point and object of the whole letter could not be better summed up than by those words of our Lord which I have placed at the head of this discourse. That object is clearly stated in the first verse of the second chapter, which literally rendered runs as follows: " Now we beseech you, brethren " (not " by," but) " as regards the presence of our Lord Jesus Christ, and our gathering together unto Him, that ye be not quickly tossed as by a flood, from your intelligence, nor be alarmed, either by spirit, or by word, or by letter professing to be mine, into the supposition that the day of Christ is here." It appears that they had thus, as it were, drifted from their moorings; been tossed out of their sound sense. They had been excited, filled with reprehensible panic and disturbing exultation, by spirit, *i.e.* by some among them professing to speak under inspiration, or with the gift of tongues; and by word, *i.e.* by some rumoured expression

---

[1] Tac. *Ann.* xii. 64. Suet. " Claud." xlvi. &c. and comp. 4 Esdras, *passim ;* Orac. Sib. iv. &c.

of the Apostle's opinions; and by letter, as though coming from St. Paul, *i.e.* either by mistaking what he really had said to them; or by believing in a forged letter, or in some letters which professed to give his sentiments, but misrepresented them. He had told them in his first Epistle to "prove all things"; and it was clear that they had not sufficiently done so. They needed to observe that not every man was infallible who claimed infallibility; or inspired who asserted his inspiration. What they required was "discerning of spirits." That there was a possibility of their being misled by forged letters or spurious messages appears from the close of the Epistle, where St. Paul appends his autograph signature to what had been written by his amanuensis, in order to furnish them with a specimen of his handwriting as an authentication for this and all future Epistles.[1] But besides this liability to be deceived, the eschatological enthusiasm of the Thessalonians had evidently attributed exaggerated importance to one expression which St. Paul had undoubtedly used. He had said that at Christ's coming "we who are alive and remain shall not anticipate," not get the advantage of, "them that sleep." Did not that little word "*we*" show decisively the Apostle's expectation that he personally should survive to see the Second Advent? And if so, of what use were the petty details of daily routine, the petty energies of daily effort? So the Thessalonians seem to have argued. They began the unfortunate example of extravagant literalism. They unduly pressed the sense of a mere passing expression. St. Paul does not, indeed, tell them that they were mistaken in their general inference as to the nearness of the Advent. He probably did expect, at this period of his life, though not later, to see in person the return in glory of his Lord. In common with all the early Church, as we see in almost every one of the Epistles,[2] St. Paul

---

[1] The energetic adjuration in 1 Thess. v. 27, seems to show some misgiving that his letters might be suppressed or tampered with.

[2] 1 Thess. i. 9, 10; 1 Cor. i. 7, xv. 51; Jas. v. 8, 9; 1 Pet. iv. 7; Rev. xxii. 20.

believed that the close of the Age, the end of all things, the visible Epiphany of Christ in judgment, would occur very soon ; that literally, as well as metaphorically, the Lord was at hand ; that universally, as well as individually, the time was short ; that not merely in national judgments, and new revelations, but in flaming personal Apocalypse, they should see the Risen and Returning Christ. In the truest and deepest sense those early Christians were not mistaken. The divine and steady light of History soon made it clear to the Church that our Lord's great Prophecy of the last things had referred in the first instance, and in its primary fulfilment, not to His visible but to His spiritual return in the destruction of Jerusalem and the full inauguration of the last aeon of God's dealings with mankind. It was the winding up of all the Past; the starting point of all the Future. It was at once the death-blow to Paganism, and the annulment of the Jewish Law. Within seventeen years of the date at which St. Paul was writing (A.D. 52 or 53) the Pagans saw an awful sign of the anger of their gods, which Tacitus calls "the saddest and most shameful blow." It was nothing less than the burning of the great Temple of the Capitolian Jupiter in the war between Vitellius and Vespasian, on December 19, A.D. 69. Six months afterwards the Jews saw a yet more awful sign that God had forsaken them, when a soldier of Titus flung the brand which consumed to ashes the Temple of Jerusalem, whereby the very possibility of obeying their worshipped "Law" sank into ashes for ever. These events were a coming of the Lord. The heirs of both Temples, the Capitoline and the Jewish, were the worshippers in the Universal Temple which is the Church of God—the handful of women, slaves, and artisans to whom were written the Epistles of St. Paul.[1] Now, so far as the anticipations of Christ's visible reappearance by the early Christians were mistaken, they were so only on a subject as to which they professed no certainty, and on a subject which their Lord

[1] Döllinger, *Judenth. u. Heindenthum.*

Himself had emphatically told them that it was not given to them, or even to the angels of God, to know. But as to St. Paul's expression, "*we* who are alive and remain," the Thessalonians had, in any case, emphasised its meaning unwarrantably. They had mistaken a generic phrase for a specific and individual one.[1] St. Paul had used the word "we" to mean "we, the living," as opposed to the dead. Even if he *implied*, he had not meant to lay the slightest stress on his own possible survival to that great day. He merely shared the feeling which prevailed even through the Gentile world, that some awful catastrophe was near at hand.[2]

2. He writes to them therefore with two great objects, one doctrinal and one practical. As a matter of doctrine, he wishes to remind them that the second coming of Christ, though he held it to be near ($\dot{\epsilon}\gamma\gamma\dot{\upsilon}\varsigma$)[3] was not instant ($\dot{\epsilon}\nu\dot{\epsilon}\sigma\tau\eta\kappa\epsilon\nu$), had not, so to speak, actually begun; and as a matter of practice he wishes to instruct them how it was their duty to live whether that day was near or far. He does not write to explain away what he had said before, but only to bring out its true meaning.

i. The doctrine forms, as I have said, the one prominent topic of the second chapter; and is in fact the celebrated passage about the Man of Sin. Now about this passage whole volumes of controversy have been written, which have for the most part only succeeded in darkening counsel by the multitude of words without knowledge. What St. Paul says is perfectly plain, though he spoke with an obvious caution which makes his reference obscure. Do not be startled, he says, out of your sound sense by any assertion, whatever its supposed source—not even if it claims to be inspired, or professes to come from me—as that the Day of the Lord is

---

[1] 1 Thess. iv. 15 : $\dot{\eta}\mu\epsilon\hat{\imath}\varsigma \ldots$ οὐ περὶ ἑαυτοῦ φησιν .. ἀλλὰ τοὺς πιστοὺς λέγει. S. Chrys.

[2] Tac. *Ann.* vi. 28 ; xii. 43, 64 ; xiv. 12, 22 ; xv. 22, *Hist.* 1, 3 ; Suet. *Ner.* 36-39, &c.

[3] Maranatha : ὁ Κύριος ἐγγύς.

here. It may come very soon; but two things must happen first, namely, "the Apostasy" (erroneously rendered in our version "a falling away"), and the revelation of a human Satan [1]—the Man of Sin, the Son of Destruction, whose characteristic is blasphemous self-exaltation against God.[2] He reminds them that he had already set forth these facts when he was with them. Now the mystery of this lawlessness was beginning to work, but there was something which withheld, some man who withheld—a restrainer and a restraint—interposed between Christ's Advent and this preliminary Apocalypse of Antichrist, "the Messiah of Satan." When that restrainer and that restraint were "done away with" ($\kappa\alpha\tau\alpha\rho\gamma\eta\sigma\epsilon\iota$, ii. 8) [3] by the far-off shining ($\epsilon\pi\iota\phi\alpha\nu\epsilon\iota\alpha$) of Christ's coming, then the opening bud of the Apostasy should rush into its scarlet flower. The lawless one should be revealed, whom, when revealed, Christ should destroy with the breath of His mouth and the manifestation of His presence.

Now one thing may be regarded as all but certain, namely, that by "the restrainer" St. Paul meant some Roman Emperor,[4] or succession of Roman Emperors; and that by "the restraint" he meant the Roman Empire, regarded as Daniel's fourth kingdom. This is all but certain, both because it has been the explanation current in the Church from the earliest age, derived doubtless from those who heard it from St. Paul; and also because the fact at once accounts for the obvious mystery, and reticence, and almost embarrassment of the Apostle's language. He dared not write more plainly. His letter would be read in public to the Church, and as the meetings of the Church were open to Jews and Gentiles, to enemies as well as to friends, any open reference to the Roman Emperor or the Roman Empire as doomed to pass away, would lead at once to terrible dangers. Already the

---

[1] δ $\dot{\alpha}\nu\tau\iota\kappa\epsilon\dot{\iota}\mu\epsilon\nu\sigma$.

[2] $\dot{\upsilon}\pi\epsilon\rho\alpha\iota\rho\sigma\mu\epsilon\nu\sigma$ $\dot{\epsilon}\pi\dot{\iota}$. Comp. Dan. xi. 36, δ $\beta\alpha\sigma\iota\lambda\epsilon\dot{\upsilon}s$ (Antiochus Epiphanes) $\dot{\upsilon}\psi\omega\theta\dot{\eta}\sigma\epsilon\tau\alpha\iota$ $\kappa\alpha\dot{\iota}$ $\mu\epsilon\gamma\alpha\lambda\upsilon\nu\theta\dot{\eta}\sigma\epsilon\tau\alpha\iota$ $\dot{\epsilon}\pi\dot{\iota}$ $\pi\dot{\alpha}\nu\tau\alpha$ $\theta\epsilon\dot{\sigma}\nu$.

[3] Comp. $\ddot{\epsilon}\omega s$ $\dot{\epsilon}\kappa$ $\mu\dot{\epsilon}\sigma\sigma\upsilon$ $\gamma\dot{\epsilon}\nu\eta\tau\alpha\iota$, ii. 7.

[4] Just as Daniel (xi. 36) refers to Antiochus Epiphanes.

fact that St. Paul, in preaching at Thessalonica, had dwelt much on the Second Coming of Christ as the Universal King had caused the tumult and charge of high treason which drove him from the city.[1] But if we go on to ask who "the Man of Sin" is, and what "the Apostasy" is, we can only reply that after so many volumes have been written, no conclusion can be arrived at. Some Roman Catholics have declared that the Apostasy is Protestantism, and the Man of Sin, Luther. Many Protestants assert that the Apostasy is Romanism, and the Man of Sin the Pope. I repudiate all such interpretations as provincial, as obsolete, as useless, as uncharitable. It would be easy no doubt to talk to any extent about Apocalyptic symbols; about the Little Horn of Daniel; about the Beast; about Gnosticism; about Mahomet; about bad Popes. We might record a multitude of cheap, irresponsible explanations of the past, and yet cheaper and more irresponsible guesses about the future. I regard all such disquisitions as being for the most part intrinsically false, and at any rate highly dubious and useless. They may feed intellectual conceit; they may minister to spiritual self-satisfaction; they may amuse aimless curiosity; they may give plausible excuse for archaeological research; but what other end they serve I do not know. After having read much that has been written on the subject, I am only the more convinced that most of the uses which have been made of this passage about the Man of Sin are supremely unprofitable. Had further details been essential for the good of the Church St. Paul would have supplied them. As it is, he never again so much as refers to the Man of Sin at all; and indeed, as any one can verify for himself, he dwells in succeeding letters less and less on the Personal Return of Christ, more and more on that spiritual Union with Him which is Eternal Life. And if any inquire further about the Man of Sin, I answer in the words of one of the most eloquent of all the Fathers, St. Augustine: "I confess that I" (and

[1] Acts xvii. 7.

indeed the whole Church of Christ) " am entirely ignorant what the Apostle meant." [1]

ii. But the main point on which St. Paul is dwelling is perfectly clear, and its moral significance is of eternal validity. It was important for the Thessalonians to be made to understand that they were mistaken in supposing each morning that, ere sunset came, there would be, as it were, three sudden flashes of lightning out of the rosy sky, and that then with one tremendous " Now," and one great blast from the Archangelic trump, the rocks should be rent, and the whole earth, with all the works of man, smitten into indistinguishable ruin. It was also most important for them to know that however near that terrible event might be, it in no wise diminished the urgency and sacredness of individual duty. St. Paul expresses strong disapproval of those of whom he says in the original with a somewhat scornful play of words, that their only business was to be busybodies.[2] The Advent to which he had bidden them look as a source of heavenly consolation was not to be desecrated into an excuse for prating guesswork and gadding curiosity. A story is told of the old American Puritans, that at one of the gatherings of their statesmen the daylight was suddenly obscured by some deep and unusual darkness; and at last the assembly became so alarmed, that one of them got up and moved that the meeting should at once be adjourned, because it seemed as if this would be the Judgment Day. Whereupon another, and a wiser senator, got up and said : " If this be indeed the Judgment Day, it cannot find us better employed in any respect than in quietly doing our duty. I move simply that candles be lighted." [3] Now that calm old man unconsciously

---

[1] " Ego prorsus quid dixerit fateor me ignorare."—St. Aug. The inquiry is so far exhausted that now we have no books written to decide who " Antichrist" was. Malvenda in 1604 wrote eleven books on Antichrist. Is the world much the wiser for them ?

[2] 2 Thess. iii. 11, οὐκ ἐργαζομένους ἀλλὰ περιεργαζομένους.

[3] Since writing the above I find the anecdote partially quoted by the Bishop of Derry from a letter of General Lee's. He adds the story that St. Francis de Sales being asked whilst playing a game of whist what he would do if Christ were at hand, answered, " Finish the game ; for His glory I began it."

gave an epitome of the advice which constitutes the very
essence of the second Epistle to the Thessalonians.

3. The one practical lesson which, among its many blessed
teachings, this Epistle has for us, may be summed up by saying
that it proves the sacredness, the importance, the necessity of
quiet, everyday duties. Of the " How ? " of Christ's return we
know nothing but a few obvious symbols. This is almost the
only passage in which St. Paul even distantly alludes to any
such details. It is also the only passage in which he speaks
about the destruction of the ungodly. He says that the
Lord Jesus shall be revealed " from heaven in flaming fire,
taking vengeance on those that know not God, who shall be
punished with eternal destruction from the presence of the
Lord." This, in all his thirteen epistles, is the only passage
which even *seems* to refer to the final destiny of the wicked.
Its meaning is much misunderstood. The flaming fire
($\pi\nu\rho\grave{\iota}\ \phi\lambda o\gamma\acute{o}s$) of this Apocalypse has not, to the minds of
those who have really studied the passage, the remotest con-
nexion with hell or with penal fire. The words " in fire of
flame " are to be joined with " revelation," not with " inflicting
retribution." They allude to the light of Christ's coming
(Dan. vii. 9 ; Ex. iii. 2) ; the glory of the Shechinah ; the
Sinaitic splendour of the clouds that burn into gold and
crimson before His Advent feet. The words " taking vengeance " are a severe exaggeration of a rare Greek phrase,
which means rather " assigning retribution for the sake (f
others " ($\delta\acute{\iota}\delta o\nu a\iota\ \grave{\epsilon}\kappa\delta\acute{\iota}\kappa\eta\sigma\iota\nu$, 2 Sam. xxii. 48, LXX.). Those
who are punished are not poor ordinary sinners, but wilful
rejecters and hardened persecutors. The punishment is not
" everlasting destruction," but spiritual cutting-off, in the
period between the Advent and the Judgment, from the
Presence of the Lord ; in other words, an exclusion from
the Beatific Vision at Christ's First Advent, not at the final
Judgment Day.

But passing from this, we may add, that if of the " How ? " of
Christ's Advent we know little, of the " When ? " of the Advent

we know nothing. We believe that Christ will come to judge both the quick and the dead ; but it would not be true of any one of us that we are living in special expectation of that coming. For 2,000 years the world has waited. We know not—no human being professes to know—whether the world may not last any number of thousands of years more. Any one who says that he is now living, as the early Christians did, in daily expectation of Christ's visible return, must (to say the least) be a man of exceptional views. No ! we do look for His coming to us in the constant daily calls and providences of life ; we do look for His coming to us at the hour of death ; we do look for His coming to us in the judgments and destinies of nations :—but, since the Bridegroom delayeth His coming, if we do but keep our loins girded and our lamps burning, we, like even the wise virgins, so far as immediate expectancy is concerned, may blamelessly slumber, provided that when He comes we be but ready to spring up at once, and to meet His call. The lessons, then, not to be disorderly ; not to eat any man's bread for nought ; to earn with quietness our own living ; not to be weary in well-doing ; are as essential to us as to the poor artisans of Saloniki 1,900 years ago. A sailor once leapt overboard to save a comrade at peril of his own life, in a stormy and dangerous sea, and was asked when rescued " if he had thought that he was fit to die ? " " I should not have been made more fit," he answered, "·by declining to do my duty ; " and he, too, like the old Pilgrim Father, gave, unconsciously, the very essence of the Second Epistle of St. Paul to the Thessalonians.

4. Christ comes in many ways. In some way, we know not How ; some day, we know not When : it may be this very day ; it may be (for to Him a thousand years are but as one day), it may be long aeons hence, He shall return in Visible Presence on the rolling clouds of heaven, with ten thousands of His saints. But meanwhile to each of us, in one way or other, in mercy or in judgment ; like the falling dew or the flaming fire ; by natural retributions, or in special providences ;

in the events of life, or at the hour of death, Christ comes.   2 THESS.
There are for us but two lessons as regards His coming, which
this Epistle, and which all Scripture teaches; the first is,
Be ready for Him; the second is, Be ready by the faithful
performance of your duties, whatever they may be, in that
state of life to which God has called you.

i. Be ready. To us, as to the world, Christ shall come as
thieves [1] in the night—"In an hour when ye know not the
Bridegroom cometh." "The last day is hidden, that all days
may be observed." The attempt to calculate the day by
Apocalyptic dates is distinctly anti-scriptural, as well as foolish.
Christ "puts down the childish fingers that count the number
of the days." [2] The lesson to us, the lesson to all, is, Watch.
One of those old Jewish Rabbis—the Rabbi Joshua Ben
Laive—whose lives were spent in watching for the coming of
that Messiah, whom, alas! though He had come, they knew
not, tells how once in vision he asked the Prophet Elijah
when should Messiah come? "Go and ask Him," said Elijah
to the Rabbi. "Where shall I find Him?" "He sits
among the beggars at the gate of Rome." The Rabbi went
and found Him, and asked when He would come. "To-day,"
was the answer. The Rabbi returned to Elijah the Prophet
and told him the story; but even while he was telling it, the
day was over, and the sun had set. "How?" exclaimed the
Rabbi. "The day is past, and He has not come! Has He
then spoken falsely to me?" "No," answered the Prophet;
"what he meant was, 'To-day if ye will hear His voice.'"
Yes, and that too is a summary of the Second Epistle:—"To-
day if ye will hear His voice, harden not your hearts." [3]

ii. Be ready then! And how are we to be ready? Not
by religious excitement; not by intrusive curiosity; not by
feeble heresy-hunting; not by cheap prophesying the exact
year in which the world is to end; not by going about and

---

[1] Κλέπτας, B.
[2] "Omnes calculantium digitos resolvit," Aug. on Matt. xxiv. 36;
quoted by the Bishop of Derry in *Speaker's Commentary.*
[3] Sanhedrin, f. 98, 1.

2 THESS. asking people, "Are you converted?" or, "How is your soul?" No; but by humbly, faithfully, cheerfully doing what God makes it clear to us that we ought to do. Religion is neither a diseased self-introspection; nor an intrusive impertinence; nor an agonising inquiry. What is it? It is the way of the supreme good, plain and indisputable, and ourselves travelling on it. It should be "an all-embracing heavenly canopy, an atmosphere, a life-element;" not always spoken of, but always presupposed. It should be as the bottom of the ocean, always there, always necessary, though not always seen. "It was the custom of this young lady," says a great writer of fiction (and how simply beautiful a description of the spirit of true religion it is), "it was the custom of this young lady, to the utmost of her power, and by means of that gracious assistance which Heaven awarded to her pure and constant prayers, to do her duty." Let us do our duty, and pray that we may do our duty here; now; to-day; not in dreamy sweetness, but in active energy; not in the green oasis of the future, but in the dusty desert of the present; not in the imaginations of otherwhere, but in the realities of now. "Man never is, but always to be blessed," says the poet; but if we do not wring our happiness out of the fair, peaceful, humble duties of the present, however great its trials, we shall never find it in the weakened forces, in the darkened rays of the future. Our duty lies, not in regrets; not in resolutions; but in thoughts followed by resolves, and resolves carried out in actions. Our life lies, not in retrospect of a vanished past; not in hopes of an ambitious future; our life is here, now, to-day; in our prayers; in our beliefs; in our daily, hourly conduct. If we have realised this we have learnt the lesson of St. Paul's second letter to the Thessalonians. If we have learnt this we are not far from, yea, we are *in* the Kingdom of Heaven. If we have learnt this we are both looking for, and hasting unto, the coming of our Lord.

NOTE I.

LEADING FACTS ABOUT THE SECOND EPISTLE TO THE THESSALONIANS.

This is the shortest of St. Paul's letters to any Church.

The general idea is patient and quiet waiting for the day of the Lord.

The key-note is ii. 1, 2, "that ye be not quickly shaken (σαλευθῆναι) from your mind, nor yet be troubled . . . as that the day of the Lord is now present" (ἐνέστηκεν).

The peculiar doctrinal section is that on the Man of Sin.

NOTE II.

OUTLINE OF THE SECOND EPISTLE TO THE THESSALONIANS.

i. The Greeting (i. 1, 2).

ii. The Thanksgiving, mingled with exhortations and prayers (i. 3-12 ; ii. 13-17) ; in which is inserted

iii. The doctrinal section ; the Man of Sin (ii. 1-12).

iv. The practical section (iii. 1-16) mingled with messages, and ended by a prayer.

v. The autographic conclusion and benediction (iii. 17, 18).

The sections flow into each other with no marked separations. Each of the prayers (ii. 16 ; iii. 16) begins with Αὐτὸς δὲ ὁ Κύριος.

The authenticity of the Epistle is all but universally accepted, though Hilgenfeld sees in it "a little Pauline Apocalypse of the last year of Trajan" (*Einleit.* 642). A few critics (Grotius, Ewald, Baur, Bunsen, Davidson) think that the second Epistle was really the first ; but they have found hardly any followers. External and internal evidence are alike against them.

NOTE III.

THE MAN OF SIN (2 Thess. ii. 1-12).

This passage is not well rendered in the A. V. *By the coming*, should be "touching (ὑπὲρ) the Presence." *In mind* should be "from your sense." *Is at hand* should be "is here." *A falling away* should be "the Apostasy." *Above all* should be "against every one." *As God* is

2 THESS. probably spurious, not being in ℵ A. B. D. "Ελεγον should be "I used to tell you;" τῷ ψευδεῖ "the (not *a*) lie;" κριθῶσι, "be judged" (not "damned"); τοῖς ἀπολλυμένοις "the perishing," &c. These inaccuracies are mostly corrected in the R. V.

"No man," says Paley, "writes unintelligibly on purpose." St. Paul wrote this passage in a way which his Thessalonians could understand because they had his oral instructions to help them.[1] But the passage is intentionally written so enigmatically as to render it obscure to any chance "informer" (*delator*) who might drop in to the Thessalonian synagogue. So far as it is of doubtful meaning it can have no special significance for us. In any case it dwells on a topic to which St. Paul never again recurred. Henceforth he spoke scarcely at all on the Second Personal Advent, but very much on our mystic union with Christ.

The most natural supposition about the passage is that by "the checker" (ὁ κατέχων, *qui claudit*) St. Paul meant the reigning Emperor Claudius; and by "the check" the Roman Empire.

This view—besides the fact that St. Paul is speaking not of the Pope, Protestantism, Mahomet, &c., but of something near at hand—has in its favour,

1. Early Christian tradition. "Quis nisi Romanus status ?" Tert. *De Resurr. Carnis*, 24 ; comp. *Apol.* 32 ; Iren. *Haer.* v. 25, 26 ; Aug. *De Civ. Dei*, xx. 12 ; Jerome, Qu. xi. *ad Algas.*; Lactant. *Div. Instt.* vii. 15, &c.

2. Early Rabbinic notions. "The Messiah will not come till *the world* has become all white with leprosy" (*i.e.* has embraced Christianity), Sanhedrin, f. 97, 1. Soteh, f. 49, 2 (Amsterd. ed.). The Jews gave to Antichrist the name Armillus, by which they seem to mean the braceleted Caligula (*Armillatus*, Suet. "Calig." 52).

3. The resemblance to the language of Daniel about Antiochus Epiphanes (Dan. vii. 25, xi. 36, 37), who is also called a "Man of Sin" (ἀνὴρ ἁμαρτωλός, 1 Macc. ii. 48, 62). The touches of description ("sitteth in the temple of God," &c.) are evidently suggested by the insane attempts of Caligula to place his statue in the temple at Jerusalem, and to the stories that he used to go into the Temple of Jupiter at Rome, and pretend to hold conversation with him, during which he would sometimes get angry and frown at him.

4. The fact that St. Paul is evidently touching on a perilous subject on which he could not without danger to his readers speak more plainly.

5. The fact that the oral teaching to which he alludes had already caused a charge of high treason to be brought against him (Acts xvii. 7, ἀπέναντι τῶν δογμάτων Καίσαρος πράττουσι).

6. The prophetic resemblance to the actual course of events. John in

---

[1] "Nos qui nescimus quod illi sciebant pervenire labore ad id quod sensit Apostolus cupimus nec valemus."—S. Aug.

the Apocalypse saw the Antichrist in Nero. To this day, as Renan points out, the Armenian name for the Antichrist is *Neren*, and Nero's death was followed by the fall of Jerusalem—the coming of Christ to close the Old Dispensation.

7. The exact analogy presented by the cautious language of Josephus in explaining Daniel (Jos. *Ant.* x. 10, § 4). He stops short in order to avoid the necessity of explaining that the fourth Empire (which he takes for Rome) is to be dashed to pieces by the stone cut without hands.

The perilous jealousy and suspiciousness of Roman officialism drove the Christians from the first to the use of secrets and dim allusions ($i\chi\theta\tilde{v}s$, 666, &c.), just as the Talmudists were driven to similar cryptographs by similar persecution in later centuries. The mystery lay not in the facts alluded to, but in the symbols by which it had to be partially concealed from those who were not in the secret.

Baur, who is always suggestive even when his views are most untenable, has an interesting parallel between these passages and the Revelation of St. John (*Paul.* ii. β, 24, f. E. T.).

THE FIRST EPISTLE TO THE CORINTHIANS.

WRITTEN FROM EPHESUS, ABOUT APRIL, A.D. 57.

" *Ecclesia Dei in Corintho :* laetum et ingens paradoxon."—BENGEL.

" Est enim haec periculosa tentatio nullam Ecclesiam putare ubi non appareat perfecta puritas."—CALVIN.

" Epistola prior ad Corinthios tota contra securitatem humanorum cordium scripta est."—LUTHER.

" Paul—to the Church of God which is in Corinth."—1 Cor. i. 1, 2.

1 CORINTH.
THE First Epistle to the Corinthians comes next in chronological order after the two to the Thessalonians. It was written some four or five years later. After writing to the Thessalonians, St. Paul had paid a brief visit to Jerusalem, and had then lived for nearly three years at Ephesus.[1] He had thus been nearly four years absent from his Corinthian converts; and when he wrote to them he had to deal with so many topics that it will be impossible to do more than briefly indicate the characteristics of this, the longest, and in some respects the most magnificent, of his Epistles. We saw that the leading idea of the First Epistle to the Thessalonians might be summed up in the thought of hope in the nearness of the Second Advent; and of the Second, in warning against unprofitable religious excitement arising from the fancy that that Advent would instantly occur. The First Epistle to

[1] See Acts xix. 10 ; 1 Cor. xvi. 3–8.

the Corinthians is capable of no such swift summary. It
deals, on the contrary, with eleven or twelve distinct topics,
and it intermingles those topics with weighty and memorable
digressions. In it we see the method of St. Paul in handling
questions of Christian casuistry—in dealing with many
difficulties of belief and practice. The endeavour to guide,
amid these difficulties, the little Christian communities which
he had founded, formed no small part of that heavy burden
which daily rested on him, "the care of all the Churches."

While St. Paul was at Ephesus, Apollos returned to
Corinth, and the news which he brought of the condition of
the Church was very grave. The converts, let us remember,
were but a small body in a large city of some 400,000 inhabitants.[1] When we speak of the Apostolic Churches, we
are apt to forget that they occupied the position now held by
solitary ghettos, or small Moravian settlements, or isolated
dissenting communities. The members of these little bodies
were mostly of low position, and some of them of shameful
antecedents;[2] and they were left in the midst of a heathendom which, at Corinth, presented itself under the gayest and
most alluring aspects. The past history of the city, the beauty
of its situation, which made it "the star of Hellas," the
splendour of its buildings, the activity and variety of its
commerce, arising from its being "the gate of the Pelopon-
nese"[3] and the "bridge of the sea;"[4] the multitude of
slaves, the actual slave-market, the mongrel and hetero-
geneous population of Jews, Greeks, Romans, Asiatics, and
Phoenicians; the confluence of sailors and merchants from
all parts of the civilised world, the absence of ennobling
traditions, the general smattering of popular philosophy, the
aesthetic tastes, the sale of spurious antiquities, the Isthmian
games, above all, the consecration of impurity in the worship
of Aphrodite Pandemos, the thousand Hieroduli in her

---

[1] 1 Cor. i. 26, οὐ πολλοὶ εὐγενεῖς.
[2] 1 Cor. v. 9, 10; vi. 11; ταῦτά τινες ἦτε; 2 Cor. xii. 21.
[3] Pind. *Nem.* vi. 44.   [4] Xen. *Ages.* 2.

temple on Acrocorinthus, all contributed to this result. Corinth was the Vanity Fair of the Roman Empire; at once the London and the Paris of the first century after Christianity. In the Gentile world it was famous-infamous for dishonesty, debauchery, and drunkenness.[1]

It is not in a day that the habits of a life can be thrown aside. Even the most sincere of the converts had a terrible battle to fight against two temptations—the temptation to dishonesty ($\pi\lambda\epsilon\upsilon\epsilon\xi\acute{\iota}a$), in their means of obtaining a daily livelihood, and the temptation to sensuality ($\dot{a}\kappa a\theta a\rho\sigma\acute{\iota}a$), which was entangled with the very fibres of their individual and social life. So long as Paul was with them they were comparatively safe. The noble tyranny of his personal influence acted on them like a spell. But when he had been so long away ;—when they were daily living in the great, wicked streets, among the cunning, crowded traders and the abandoned proletariat—in sight and hearing of everything which could quench spiritual aspiration and kindle carnal desires, in " a city the most licentious of all that are and have ever been "[2]—when the careless, common life went on around them, and the chariot wheels of the Lord were still afar, it was hardly wonderful if the splendid vision of the life of heaven on earth waxed gradually dim. And so it began to be with some of them as it was with Israel of old when Moses was on Sinai ; they sat down to eat and to drink, and rose up to play. Many of them, very many—some in the shame and secrecy of a self-wounded conscience, others openly justifying their relapse by the devil-doctrines of perverted truth [3] —had plunged once more into the impurity, the drunkenness,

---

[1] Even in modern languages " Corinthians " meant profligate idlers. "I am no proud Jack, like Falstaff, but *a Corinthian*, a lad of mettle."— Shakspeare, *I. Henry IV*. ii. 4.

In Greek $Ko\rho\iota\nu\theta\iota a\zeta\acute{\epsilon}\sigma\theta a\iota$ meant "to play the profligate."—Pollux, ix. 6, § 75. Plato, *Rep.* iii. p. 404. Further, see my *Life of St. Paul*, ii. 553-573.

[2] Dion. Chrysost. *Orat. Corinth.* (opp. ii. 119, ed. Reiske.)

[3] 1 Cor. xi. 30, $\pi o\lambda\lambda o\grave{\iota}$ $\dot{a}\sigma\theta\epsilon\nu\epsilon\hat{\iota}s$ $\kappa a\grave{\iota}$ $\check{a}\rho\rho\omega\sigma\tau o\iota$, xv. 32. $\phi\acute{a}\gamma\omega\mu\epsilon\nu$ $\kappa a\grave{\iota}$ $\pi\acute{\iota}\omega\mu\epsilon\nu$, 2 Cor. ii. 17, $\dot{\omega}s$ $o\acute{\iota}$ $\pi o\lambda\lambda o\acute{\iota}$ (or $o\acute{\iota}$ $\lambda o\iota\pi o\acute{\iota}$), xi. 18, $\pi o\lambda\lambda o\grave{\iota}$ $\kappa a\upsilon\chi\hat{\omega}\nu\tau a\iota$, xii. 21, $\pi\epsilon\nu\theta\acute{\eta}\sigma\omega$ $\pi o\lambda\lambda o\acute{\upsilon}s$.

the selfishness around them, as though they had never heard the heavenly calling and never tasted of the eternal gift.[1]

So much at least Apollos must have told St. Paul; and he at once wrote them a brief letter, now lost. It was probably a mere businesslike memorandum, informing them that he meant to pay them a double visit, and asking them to make a collection for the poor saints at Jerusalem; but it contained one passage which in a short, stern phrase bade them not to keep company with fornicators. They had understood him to mean "with *any*" fornicators; and a strict obedience to this command would have involved nothing less than absolute withdrawal from the heathen world. He explains in this Epistle that he had only meant "any *Christians*" who still continued to live unclean lives.[2]

Shortly after this, a letter reached him from the Corinthians themselves. It was a discreditable letter, at once pompous and reticent. So far from dwelling on the ruinous disorders which had sprung up among them, it was entirely self-complacent in tone, and while showing much doctrinal and practical perplexity, touched on questions which, in spite of its self-importance, betrayed the existence of the divisions, the restlessness, and the errors which the Church had so disingenuously concealed.

I. By a careful study of the First Epistle to the Corinthians we are curiously able to reconstruct this letter, and even to recall some of its very phrases. We see too that St. Paul was able to read between the lines of its half-confidences and

---

[1] It is not a very important, though a voluminously debated, question, whether during his three years' stay at Ephesus St. Paul had paid any visit to Corinth. If he had, it could only have been brief and eventless, and St. Luke at any rate leaves it unrecorded (Acts xix.). The notion that he had paid this visit is founded on needless straining of popular expressions in 1 Cor. xvi. 7; 2 Cor. i. 15, 16; ii. 1; xii. 4–14, 21; xiii. 1, 2. "Let us give up the fiction of a journey for which we can find no reasonable grounds."—(Baur, *Paul.* ii. 320.) It is however fair to add that Neander, Meyer, Reuss, W. Grimm, Ewald, and Hausrath accept this supposed unrecorded visit.

[2] See 1 Cor. x. 1–14. A spurious letter of the Corinthians to Paul and his answer are preserved in Armenian. They have been published by Wilkins, Fabricius, and Whiston, and have been translated into English (among others by Lord Byron, see Moore's *Life*, vi. 274); but they are valueless forgeries.

whole concealments. The inflated self-assurance of its tone did not disguise from him the uneasy indication that his new converts were in a perilous moral state.[1]

(i.) After greeting, and saying that they remembered him in all things, and kept the ordinances as he delivered them (1 Cor. xi. 2), the Corinthian Church had first asked their great teacher a series of questions about celibacy and marriage. Was married life wrong? Was celibacy a superior condition? Were second marriages permissible? Were mixed marriages to be allowed? Ought fathers to give their daughters in marriage, or to keep them as the virgins of Christ?[2]

(ii.) Then, with the conceited remark that "they all had knowledge" (1 Cor. viii. 1), they asked him about meats offered to idols. They "knew that an idol was nothing in the world;" might they then, with their superior "knowledge," go to heathen festivals?

(iii.) They disagreed about the rules to be observed in public assemblies. Ought men to cover their heads when they worshipped, after the Jewish custom; or to keep them uncovered, according to the Greek custom? Might women appear with their heads uncovered in the religious meetings?

(iv.) Then as to spiritual gifts. Which was the more important—speaking with tongues or preaching? and how were both to be regulated?[3]

(v.) Further, they had great doubts about the Resurrection. Some, perplexed with material difficulties, maintained

---

[1] The Epistle is full of the word "inflation" by which St. Paul stigmatises the vice of a conceited opiniativeness (φυσιοῦσθε, iv. 6; ἐφυσιώθησαν, 18; πεφυσιωμένων, 19; πεφυσιωμένοι, v. 2; ἡ γνῶσις φυσιοῖ, viii. 1; ἡ ἀγάπη οὐ φυσιοῦται, xiii. 4; φυσιώσεις, 2 Cor. xii. 20. Elsewhere the word only occurs in Col. ii. 18.

[2] The Corinthians could hardly have asked these questions unless they had been visited by some teacher from Jerusalem of Essene proclivities. St. James, the Bishop of Jerusalem, was, according to Hegesippus, a Nazarite, and both to him and to his kinsman St. Matthew, Essene practices are attributed (Hegesippus *ap.* Euseb. *H. E.* ii. 23; Clem. Alex. *Paedag.* ii. 1). Now one branch of the Essenes looked on marriage as necessarily and essentially degrading. It was probably in the self-styled "Christ-party" that these notions were rife.

[3] St. Paul, in writing from Corinth, had already laid down in 1 Thess. v. 19, 20, two pregnant principles which might have solved these difficulties.

that the Resurrection was purely spiritual, and that it was past already. Would Paul give them some solution of the difficulties with which the subject was surrounded?

(vi.) Paul, in his (lost) letter, had asked them to establish an offertory for the poor at Jerusalem. What plans would he recommend to them about this?

(vii.) Lastly, would he send Apollos back to them? They had enjoyed his knowledge and eloquence. Would Paul try to persuade him to return, and also pay them his own promised visit?

Such were the seven main inquiries of a letter which had been conveyed to St. Paul at Ephesus by Stephanas, Fortunatus, and Achaicus, the worthy slaves of a Greek lady named Chloe. The letter was in itself sufficient to awaken some deep misgivings in his mind, both by the self-complacent assumption of its tone, and by the restless intellectualism of its speculations. But this was not all. St. Paul had heard from Apollos some hints about the innovations and turbulence of the Achaian Church. But when he came to talk further with the slaves of Chloe, and they, no doubt reluctantly, bit by bit, in answer to his questionings, had told him all the truth, then he stood simply overwhelmed with grief and horror.

For he learnt (viii.) that the Church was split up into deplorable factions, with the usual accompaniment (so sadly illustrated in many Churches) of "strifes, heartburnings, rages, factions, backbitings, inflations, whisperings, disorderliness."[1] Some prided themselves on their breadth, and culture,

---

[1] 2 Cor. xii. 20 ; ἔρεις, ζῆλοι, θυμοί, ἐριθεῖαι, καταλαλιαί, ψιθυρισμοί, φυσιώσεις ἀκαταστασίαι. Hillel had said "many teachers, much strife." The factiousness at Corinth had been first caused by the visit of Apollos, and then increased (probably) by wandering missionaries from the rank and file of parties at Jerusalem who represented (respectively) the views of Peter, and of James "the Lord's brother." St. Paul in his impetuous way reminds them that though they had "ten thousand pedagogues (1 Cor. iv. 15, μυρίους παιδαγωγοὺς) in Christ," yet after all he was their sole spiritual father. This "detestable and unholy spirit of faction," as it is called by St. Clement of Rome, continued long afterwards (Clem. Rom. *Ep. ad Cor.* i.), and was "carried to a pitch of dementation" of which the world has seen many subsequent specimens.

and philosophical views, and said, " I am of Apollos ; " others
on their sacerdotal pretensions and ecclesiastical correctness,
and said, " I am of Cephas ; " others on their unsophisticated
orthodoxies, and said, " We alone preach the Gospel; we
are the only Christians—we are of Christ."

(ix.) Then not unnaturally these party factions, which rent
and deracinated the unity and wedded calm of the Church
at Corinth, had led to the grossest irregularities in their very
worship :—egotisms of rival oratory, mutual recriminations
in sacred places, the utterance of angry and even blasphemous
language even in their Sabbath gatherings, abuses of gloss-
olaly so extreme that half-a-dozen enthusiasts would be on
their legs at once, each pouring forth a jargon of unintelligible sounds.[1] So bad was the state of things that there
was danger lest any chance Gentile listener should set
them down as a number of maniacs.[2] Even their women
—Christian matrons—got up in the assemblies and gave
their opinions with a positiveness and an assurance as im-
perturbable as though they were masters in theology. So
far from being a scene of peace, the Sunday services of the
Corinthian community were a battle-ground of contending
factions.

(x.) There was worse behind. Even in their social
gatherings—the Agapae or love feasts—the deadly leaven of
selfishness had worked. The kiss of peace was interchanged
by Christians who were going to law with one another, and
that before the heathen, about matters of ordinary honesty.
The rich greedily devoured their luxurious provisions at the
common table, in presence of the poor, half-starved slaves—
the hungry-eyed Lazaruses—who had little or nothing of their
own to bring ; and these, indignant and discontented, watched
with hatred and envy their full-fed brethren. To so terrible
an extent had gluttony and worldly pride thrust themselves
into the most sacred unions, that men nominally Christian

---

[1] 1 Cor. xii. xiii. xiv. *passim.*
[2] 1 Cor. xiv. 23 ; οὐκ ἐροῦσιν ὅτι μαίνεσθε ;

had been seen to stretch drunken hands to the very chalice
of the Lord.[1]

(xi.) Last and worst; there existed among them a depraved
casuistry—a reckless Antinomianism. Not only had uncleanness found open defenders, but one prominent, and probably
wealthy, member of the Church had been guilty of a sin on
which the very heathen cried shame; and yet, blinded by we
know not what strange Rabbinic sophistries,[2] or perverted by we
cannot tell what plausibilities of perverted liberty, the Church,
in which too many were impenitently guilty of the impurity
which was the besetting sin of Corinth, had actually con-
doned this glaring crime![3]

Such was the state of a Church in which St. Paul had
toiled personally for eighteen months, and in which his fervent
energies had been seconded by such loyal workers as Silas,
and Timothy, and Titus, and Apollos, and Sosthenes, and
Erastus. Truly if the ideal Church be the spotless bride of
Christ, here in Corinth, at any rate, "the glory of the orange
flower had faded," the whiteness of the virgin robe was stained!
We often hear the early Church spoken of as though we had
nothing to do but to sit at her feet, and learn, and weep because we have fallen so far short of her example. That is
the conventional fiction; very different is the hard reality,
as Scripture faithfully reveals it to us. The early Church, as
represented by so important a brotherhood as that at Corinth,
though Paul had laboured there so long, was in a worse condition than the worst of our Christian congregations. The
early Church was the Church of the mustard seed; ours is
the Church of the full-grown tree.

Thus, then, like stroke after stroke of some death-knell to
all his hopes, the evil tidings about this turbulent, conceited,

---

[1] 1 Cor. xi. 21, ὃς μὲν πεινᾷ ὃς δὲ μεθύει.
[2] The Rabbis held that proselytism put an end to all previous relationships;
and possibly some Jewish Christians had casuistically applied this *Halacha* of
the Scribes.
[3] 2 Cor. xii. 21. In no Epistles are his warnings against uncleanness more
solemn and emphatic, 1 Cor. v. 11; vi. 15–18; x. 8; xv. 33, 34, &c.

party-shaken, clever, restless, backsliding Church of Corinth fell on the ears of St. Paul. It seemed like the shipwreck of every fond anticipation which had sprung up in his mind during his mission labours of a year and a half. It might well have caused in him extreme passion, or unmitigated despair. He might have sat down at once to write an apocalyptic letter, full of burning denunciation, against these impure, disunited, self-satisfied disgracers of the name of Christian,—rolling over their startled consciences thunders as loud as those of Sinai. Or, suffering and harassed as he already was by the trials and persecutions of Ephesus, he might have folded his hands in utter despair, and, proclaiming his whole life to be a failure, he might have fled like Elijah into solitude, saying "Now, O Lord, take away my life, for I am not better than my fathers." He did neither—this great, this indomitable man. He first took the practical steps which were immediately necessary. He at once gave up for the present his intended visit to Corinth. He sent a messenger to Timothy to tell him not to proceed on the journey to Corinth overland,[1] on which he had been already despatched. In place of Timothy he commissioned the bolder and more active Titus to make what arrangements were most immediately pressing.[2] Then, calling Sosthenes to his side as his amanuensis, he began to dictate to him this astonishing and eloquent Epistle. He tells us himself that he wrote it with throbbing heart and streaming eyes;[3] and yet, suppressing his emotion to the utmost, he proceeded to deal with the eleven questions and topics —the party factions, the notorious offender, the law-suits, the questions about marriage, about meat offered to idols, about headdresses, about speaking with tongues, the Lord's Supper, the offertory, and the Resurrection—which the Corinthian missive and the news which he had heard had forced upon his attention.

---

[1] 1 Cor. iv. 17 ; xvi. 10.

[2] 2 Cor. xii. 18 ; viii. 6.

[3] 2 Cor. ii. 4, ἐκ γὰρ πολλῆς θλίψεως καὶ συνοχῆς καρδίας ἔγραψα ὑμῖν διὰ πολλῶν δακρύων.

Nothing could be more varied than the elements of thought and practice with which he was thus suddenly called upon to deal. He had to heal the ravages made by Greek culture, and Greek rhetoric, and Greek philosophy upon the simplicity of faith. He had to rebuke alike the admixture of casuistical immorality with Christian liberty, and the encroachments of "voluntary humility" upon Christian holiness. He had to rebuke Judaic narrowness and spiritual license. He had in the same breath to deal with Hellenic sensuality and Ebionite exaggeration. For the first time he was called upon to apply the principles of Christianity alike to the most opposite perplexities of thought and to the wildest diversities of practice. How is it that he thus shows himself perfectly at ease whether he is moving in the rarefied ether of dogmatic theology, or steering his steady course amid the concrete and complicated realities of daily administration? It is because problems however dark, details however intricate, become lucid and orderly in the light of eternal distinctions. "The eagle which soars through the air does not worry itself how it is to cross the rivers."

If this letter of St. Paul be compared with the somewhat similar letter which Gregory the Great sent to St. Augustine in answer to inquiries which are of much the same character as to arrangements about the English converts, we see at once how immeasurably more decisive and minute the Pope is than the Apostle.[1] But for this very reason, as Mr. Maurice says, the First Epistle to the Corinthians is "the best manual for the *ductor dubitantium*, because it teaches him that he must not give himself airs of certainty on points where certainty is not to be had."[2] Thus in the very difficult questions about marriage—which seem to have been suggested by members of the Church who had perhaps imbibed an admiration for the practices of the Essenes, and who may have been led to their particular view by the fact that our Lord lived a celibate

[1] The letter is preserved in Bede.
[2] Maurice, *Unity of the New Testament*, p. 423. See Kuenen, *Profeten*, ii. 67 ; Lord Lyttelton in *Contemporary Review*, xxi. 917.

life—St. Paul answers hesitatingly. He does not wish to elevate his own personal leanings into a rule of faith. It would have been well for many of the early and mediaeval ascetics if they had imitated in this respect the moderation and humility of the great Apostle.[1]

And yet we see at once that his letter was not, as a whole, uncertain and laborious, but swift and perfectly spontaneous. St. Paul had no need to burn the midnight oil in long studies. He had that divine enlightenment which enabled him at once to see to the heart of moral difficulties. Even his most elaborate letters were not in reality elaborate. Their most eloquent passages leapt like vivid sparks from a heart in which the fire of love to God burnt until death with an ever brighter and brighter flame.

Before we proceed a step further, what a lesson does his conduct teach us! What practical good sense does he display! What noble and perfect self-control! What power to shake off a despondency which would have been so perfectly excusable, and to crush down deep within his heart a passion and resentment which could hardly have been blamed! What a lesson to us who are so easily depressed and discouraged if our little plans fail, and our little efforts are less successful than we could desire! And again, what a model of controversy and of wisdom does he furnish to the Christian Church of all ages—a model, alas! how little imitated! How clear do practical details become in the light of absolute principles! How different is the perspective under which we see the hard and jarring collisions of Christian opinion, when we only see them under the light of that brotherly love to which, infinitely more than to orthodoxy or knowledge, is granted the vision of all things in God! May we not all learn from this fine example? When difficulties surround us; when, after all our labours, nothing

---

[1] The way in which asceticism has tampered with the Greek text in vii. 3, 5, and the comments of St. Jerome on the passage show how different a spirit prevailed at a later period.

seems to be done and everything remains to be done; in
the midst of apparent failures, in the midst of very real perplexities, in the midst of the babble of criticism and the
strife of tongues, let us like St. Paul sit down bravely at once
and always to embrace the first plain, practical step of duty
which seems wisest at the moment. In quietness and confidence, undeterred and undiscouraged, let us take the best
part our adult spirits can. A great statesman once said, " I
do not know what is meant by painful responsibility. I do
the best, the wisest, the utmost thing I can; and no man can
do more. My moral responsibility ends with the use of my
best endeavours." That too was the brave and practical
spirit of St. Paul. God had given him work to do, and he felt
that he must do it, and ought not to yield to discouragement
in it. Duties were his; results were God's.

It is not here our object to enter fully into the manner
in which St. Paul deals with the eleven topics or problems
presented to him. They must be studied by each reader for
himself. We only now need to consider the outlines of the
letter.

After the greeting, and a guarded thanksgiving which
dwells on spiritual gifts, not on moral graces, St. Paul proceeds at once to rebuke and correct the fatal party spirit of
the Church; but he prepares the way for this even in his
greeting by "nailing them down" (to quote St. Chrysostom's
expression) to the name of Christ. If a Church be truly " in
Christ," there may be differing opinions, but there cannot be
the shameful and shameless wranglings of party hatred and
party faction. Hence in no Epistle is the name of Christ so
continuously introduced. It occurs no less than nine times
in the first nine verses. This correction of Church partisanship, of the conceit of knowledge which springs from it, of
the want of love by which it is fomented, occupies the first
four chapters. One of the many things which are remarkable in their holy irony and impassioned appeal is that,
though one of the parties took his own name, St. Paul will

not say one word to identify himself with any of the parties, nor will he say which section of wrangling Churchmen or wrangling theologians is most in the right or most in the wrong. All that he insists upon is that he had preached the Cross of Christ, because he knew that " by the foolishness of the thing preached " [1] it pleased God to save mankind. What he rebukes is *the spirit* of party. So far as they had yielded to that, they were all alike in the wrong. He shows them that where there is the humility of true wisdom—where there is the simplicity of the Gospel of Christ—where there is a right estimate of Christian ministers as of mere human instruments of whom nothing is required but simple faithfulness—where there is a due appreciation of the royal privileges of every Christian soul—where there is sufficient modesty to prevent every ignorant Christian from assuming that he alone possesses an absolute monopoly of truth—there the spirit of party melts away in the pure air of Christian love.

In the fifth and sixth chapters he deals with the case of the notorious offender. He passes on him, out of mercy, and solely to secure his amendment, a stern sentence, and warns them to shun, and to exclude from the brotherhood of Christ, all whose lives notoriously disgrace it. After an incidental rebuke of their litigious spirit, he gives them with awful emphasis those arguments against impurity which had never before been so clearly stated.

Having thus far corrected disorders, he now proceeds to reply to inquiries.

In the seventh chapter he answers their questions about marriage. The principles are stated with special reference to the persecutions and peculiarities of that epoch. We are here furnished with Paul's opinions not in the abstract, but as a question of immediate expediency in a perilous time when the coming of Christ was near.

The eighth, ninth, tenth, and the first verse of the eleventh chapter are all devoted to the question of meats offered to

[1] Cor. i. 21, διὰ τῆς μωρίας τοῦ κηρύγματος.

idols. It was a problem of immense importance to converts from heathendom, because they could hardly buy meat in the market, or go to any social entertainment, without being confronted by it. It was in fact one of those burning questions on which timid, conventional men usually avoid speaking, because it is not possible to speak without giving offence to one side or the other. St. Paul's principles are clear. An idol is nothing in the world. A Christian is free. He may buy in the market what he will, and eat what is set before him where he will, without morbid worry or servile scrupulosity. Thus we see at once how completely St. Paul, Jew though he was, abandoned those rules about meat ceremonially clean (*Kashar*) which to this day are so burdensome to the modern Jews. In spite of his Rabbinic training he rose indefinitely superior to the micrology of Rabbinism. Yet he would not let his own breadth of view be a stumbling-block to less instructed brethren. If, by his claim of liberty, others were led to assert an emancipation which wounded their weaker consciences, then since kindness is nobler than knowledge, and Christian love more sacred than even Christian liberty, every good man ought to be ready to give up his own personal rights rather than endanger his brother's soul.[1]

The ninth chapter is designed to prove that he practised what he preached; for though, as an Apostle, he had the fullest right to claim maintenance at their hands, he had waived the right in order to cause no offence.

In the tenth he warns them that not only is it wrong to show deficient regard to the tender consciences of weak brethren, but also that it is very easy to use liberty in such a way as to underrate the difficulties and temptations which beset our earthly life. He begs them therefore to imitate himself in abridging their own rights, and so to avoid the peril of themselves perishing or of causing others to perish by permitted things.

---

[1] St. Paul does not even refer to the decision of the synod of Jerusalem, which was a local and temporary compromise.

In the eleventh chapter he settles the question about covered and uncovered heads,[1] and sternly rebukes the gross disorders which had defiled their Eucharistic feasts.

In the twelfth, thirteenth, and fourteenth chapters, of which the thirteenth, the paean to Christian charity, is the most glorious even in the writings of St. Paul, he shows that the loftiest spiritual gifts are not those which are the most dazzling, but those which tend most to edification; and that the simplicity of holy love constitutes the golden perfectness of the whole Christian life.

The fifteenth chapter is the magnificent passage in which he exposes their errors and resolves their doubts about the Resurrection—the chapter so familiar to us as we hear it in our Burial Service,

> "When our heads are bowed with woe,
> When our bitter tears o'erflow,
> When we mourn the lost, the dear."

It is but a casual chapter. In other words, it is no elaborate and premeditated treatise like the *Phaedo* of Plato, but the ready response to some suggested perplexities. Yet who would not give the *Phaedo* of Plato in glad exchange for this simple section of St. Paul's Epistle?[2]

St. Paul ends the letter with messages, salutations, and a final benediction.

Such then is the First Epistle to the Corinthians. It is full of priceless gems. It abounds in rich digressions. Besides the two immortal passages on charity and on the

---

[1] This passage (xi. 2–16) is not a mere detached paragraph. The fact that women claimed the right to appear with uncovered heads was part of the self-assertion which he is combating.

[2] It is a remarkable and interesting fact that the question of the Resurrection had at this epoch received fresh prominence from the asserted re-appearance of the Phœnix in Egypt twenty years before the letter was written, (Tac. *Ann.* vi. 28,) and the exhibition of a live Phœnix (!) in the *Comitium* of Rome in A.D. 47, exactly ten years before this letter was written. (Plin. *H. N.* x. 2.) Clement of Rome in his Epistle to the Corinthians actually appeals to the fable of the Phœnix as a collateral proof of the Resurrection. At that epoch all Gentiles and therefore many Christians believed in the existence of the Phœnix. It is impossible not to recognise a grace of superintendence in the fact that the New Testament is not discredited by any such allusion.

Resurrection, there is the ironic contrast between earthly wisdom and heavenly folly in chapter one; the passage about the Christian race in chapter nine; the sketch of the labours of the Apostles in chapter four; the enumeration of the appearances of the risen Christ in chapter fifteen; and many other paragraphs which ever since have been inestimably dear to the Christian Church.

It would require many a thoughtful hour of personal study to master its manifold doctrines, to win but a few of its rich treasures. But three main lessons which dominate the Epistle—not, however, including the splendid episode on the Resurrection — may be summed up as being (1) practical unity amid divergent opinions; (2) little details decided by great principles; and (3) life in the world, yet not of it.

(1) Divergent opinions in Christian communities there will ever be, and they will be harmless if only they be blended, like the intentional discords of some great piece of music, in the vast harmony of love. We may belong to parties; but let us remember that the more of partisanship we display, the less Christian shall we be. If our party spirit be bitter and unfair, it is not only not religious, but anti-religious—irreligious —yes, even though it dwell on religious themes. Partisanship is generally far fiercer in the cause of error than in the cause of truth; but Truth herself rejects and repudiates with majestic scorn the crude and bitter champions who, in thrusting themselves forward for her defence, wound to the death her sister Charity.

(2) Little details can only be regulated by great principles. Little details to this day—be they even so little as the position of a celebrant or the manner of a genuflexion, and even after eighteen centuries of Christianity—may sometimes give trouble. Little questions may arise about the authenticity of clauses and the value of manuscripts, which yet kindle great conflagrations. If we would be scholars of St. Paul, never let us squabble about them with personal recriminations and railing indictments. Let us refer them to great

principles and they will cease to be perplexing. St. Paul refers the questions which had risen in his day to two great principles: (i.) Be fully persuaded in your own mind; *i.e.*, never do what your conscience tells you is wrong; and (ii.) Let all things be done with charity; *i.e.*, in all but the first essentials it is better to waive your rights and your opinions than to insist on them. Follow this method of controversy, and you will pass, with one sweep of the wing, from the small exacerbations of petty differences to those great ethereal realms where all dark clouds and all human colourings are lost in the boundlessness of light.

(3) Lastly, we must live in the world, and in the world we must often come in contact with low standards and sinful ways. But though we be in the world, we need not be of it. A diamond may fall even into the mire, but it will be a diamond still; or, as the good emperor expressed it—" Whatever any one does and says, I must be good and true, as though the gold, or the purple, or the emerald were always saying thus: whatever happens I must be emerald and keep my colour."

Here surely are great lessons, and they may all be summed up in this one great truth—that the life of the Christian is a life in Christ, and that a life in Christ is a life of peace, a life of order, a life of humility and self-repression, a life of purity, a life of love.

NOTE I.

LEADING IDEAS OF THE FIRST EPISTLE TO THE CORINTHIANS.

The Epistle is occupied with questions of morality and Church discipline. The Apostle dwells on,

i.   Love and unity amid divergent opinions.
ii. The decision of small details by great principles.
iii. Life *in* the world, not *of* it.

It is specially interesting as showing us the conditions of life in an early Christian Church in all their variety and fulness ; and the masterly powers of government and prompt decision displayed by St. Paul.

NOTE II.

OUTLINE OF THE LETTER.

1. Greeting (i. 1-3).
2. Thanksgiving (i. 4-9).
3. The sin of party spirit (i. 10-iv. 21).
4. Disorders in the Corinthian Church.

   i.   The incestuous offender (v. 1-13).
   ii. Lawsuits, &c. (vi. 1-11).
   iii. Impurity (vi. 12-20).

5. Answers to the Corinthian inquiries, and cognate matters.

   i.   Concerning marriage and celibacy (vii. 1-40).
   ii. Concerning things offered to idols (viii. 1-x. 33) illustrated by St. Paul's own example of foregoing his own just rights (ix.) and warnings against the abuse of Christian freedom (x.)
   iii. Regulations about gatherings for worship.
      a. As to covering the head (xi. 1-16).
      $\beta.$ As to the Agapae and the Lord's supper (xi. 17-34).
      $\gamma.$ As to the abuses of glossolaly (xii.-xiv. 40) which would be rendered impossible if Christians recognised the supremacy of love.
   iv. Concerning the Resurrection (xv.)
   v.   Concerning the collection for the poor saints (xvi. 1-4).

6. Personal messages and exhortations (xvi. 5-18).
7. Salutations (xvi. 19-20).
8. Autograph conclusion (xvi. 21-24).

NOTE III.

DATES IN THE HISTORY OF CORINTH.

The main previous moments in the history of Corinth were,

B.C.

243. Aratus and the Achaean League.

197. Battles of Cynocephalae. Corinth occupied by a Roman garrison.

146. Corinth taken and burnt by L. Mummius.

46. The Colonia Julia Corinthus founded by Julius Caesar, and peopled with old Italian veterans (Corinthienses not Corinthii).

A.D.

52. St. Paul founds Christianity in Corinth. Gallio Proconsul of Achaia.

57. St. Paul's letter to the Church of Corinth.

95. Clement of Rome writes to the Church of Corinth.

135. The Church of Corinth visited by Hegesippus. (Euseb. *H. E.* iv. 22)

174. Corinth visited and described by Pausanias.

For ancient descriptions of the city, see Livy, xiv. 28 ; Stat. *Theb.* vii. 106 ; Claudian, *De Bell. Get.* 188 ; Pausanias, ii. 2 ; Strabo, viii. p. 379. For modern, see Leake, *Peloponnesiaca,* p. 392 ; *Morea,* iii. 229 ; Curtius, *Peloponnesos,* ii. 514 ; Byron, *Siege of Corinth;* and Clark, *Peloponnesus,* pp. 42-61.

THE SECOND EPISTLE TO THE CORINTHIANS.

WRITTEN AT PHILIPPI (?) A.D. 57 (LATE) OR A.D. 58 (EARLY).

"There are three crowns; the crown of the Law, the crown of the Priesthood, and the crown of Royalty; but the crown of a Good Name mounts above them all."—Pirke, *Avoth*. iv. 19.

"I write these things being absent, lest being present I should use sharpness."—2 Cor. xiii. 10.

CIRCUMSTANCES sometimes arise in life which induce, and almost compel men, who are otherwise of the most reserved and retiring disposition, to draw aside the veil of natural reticence, and, at the cost of whatever pain, to speak to the world of themselves, of their motives, and of their claims. A man who occupies a prominent public position, who wields a large, and desires to wield a beneficent influence, who, whatever may be his imperfections in the sight of Him before whom the very heavens are not clean, has an honoured, and as far as man is concerned a deservedly honoured name —is not altogether his own. His life, his actions, his motives are to a certain extent public property. It may not, therefore, be in all cases right, or even possible, for him to leave slanderous imputations to perish of their own inherent rottenness. That is no doubt, in ninety-nine cases out of every hundred (as every sensible man is aware), the only wise and proper course. No man, who emerges ever so little above the crowd, has ever, since the world began, wholly escaped attacks. The thistles gather, in their tangled growth, round the foot of the cedars of Lebanon, and fires which come forth from the crackling brambles scathe often, if they cannot wholly devour, the forest trees. The stainless purity of Joseph did not save him from accusation; nor the perfect meekness of Moses; nor the splendid services of Samuel. Elijah was a glorious patriot, and his king met him with the question, " Art thou he that troubleth Israel ? " Shimei cursed and flung dust at David. Of the Baptist's stern, self-denial men could only say " He hath a devil;" of the Saviour's boundless sympathy, "Behold a gluttonous man and a winebibber." And if they called the Master of the house Beelzebub, how much more them of His household ? The early Christians were accused on all sides of infant-murder and Thyestean banquets. Athanasius, Calvin, Luther, were charged with the most flagrant iniquities. The life of Richard Hooker, the most honoured divine of the Church of England, was embittered by a wicked lie. The saintly Francis de Sales was charged with levity and impurity. St. Vincent de Paul long laboured under an imputation of theft. George Whitefield spent his life amid a roar of execration. Four years ago died one of our noblest and bravest prelates, and he, in the colony to which he had devoted his vast self-sacrifice, knew what it was to be greeted by the cry " Three groans for Bishop Selwyn." Few modern statesmen, few modern writers, few public men of any kind, are so fortunate as to escape misrepresentation. Most of them take it as a matter of course,—as much a matter of course as sickness, or old age, or bereavement, and wisely and quietly let it alone. A good man's life is generally sufficient to defend itself; and sooner or later in the justice of Heaven the curse and the falsehood rebound upon the head of him who uttered them. "They say ! What say they ?—Let them say,"—is the best attitude to adopt in an age ignobly pre-eminent for gossip. "My accuser says that I have taken

bribes from the enemy. I, M. Aemilius Scaurus, deny it.
Utri creditis, Quirites? Which of the two do you believe,
gentlemen?" A noble Roman considered that to be a sufficient
defence ; and a good man may usually do the same.

But, as I have said, it is sometimes necessary for the sake
of others, to enter upon self-defence. We have a conspicuous
example in this generation. One of its most honoured and
saintly characters, stung by what he regarded as an undeserved
taunt, wrote an *Apologia pro Vitâ Suâ*, which has added a
valuable book to the treasure-house of Christian literature. In that book he gives a sketch of his biography, and
of his opinions, so far as seemed desirable for the public
advantage. In such conduct there is neither vanity nor
egotism. It is the answer of a good conscience towards God,
declared also to men, that they may be ashamed who falsely
accuse our good conversation in Christ.

I have touched on these considerations because the Second
Epistle to the Corinthians is, in the first century, a writing of
exactly the same origin and character as Cardinal Newman's
Apologia in the nineteenth. It is the Apostle's answer to
them that accused him. It is St. Paul's *Apologia pro Vitâ
Suâ*—his self-defence against an outburst of opposition and
calumny. It was necessary to defend himself because he
was only attacked out of hatred to the Gospel which he
preached to the Gentiles. His present object may be summed
up in the tenth verse of the fifth chapter—" For we commend
not ourselves again unto you, but give you occasion to glory
on our behalf, that ye may have somewhat to answer them
which glory in appearance, not in heart."

2. Soon after St. Paul had written his first extant letter to
Corinth, there occurred at Ephesus that terrible riot which is
described in the Acts of the Apostles, and which (as we
gather from scattered allusions) was even more perilous and
agitating to the Apostle than we might at first have supposed.[1]

[1] Lang, in the *Protestanten Bibel*, conjectures from 2 Cor. i. 8–10, compared
with iv. 8, 9, that in the tumult at Ephesus, St. Paul, hunted through the

2 CORINTH. Rescued from this terrible danger by the devotion of Aquila, Priscilla, and other friends, who risked their own lives for his, he went straight to Troas, and once more began to preach (2 Cor. ii. 12, 13). But though his preaching was blessed— though "a door was opened for him in the Lord"—he forgot himself in anxiety about the feelings of his converts. He could not stay at Troas from extreme anxiety to know the effect produced upon the Corinthians by the severity of his letter, and especially by his sentence upon the notorious offender. He had told Titus to rejoin him there, and bring him news; but either Titus had been delayed, or the precipitation of Paul's escape from Ephesus had brought the Apostle to Troas earlier than Titus had expected. At any rate at Troas he had no rest for his spirit, because he found not Titus his brother. And since he grew more and more uneasy, at length (ii. 13), his oppression of spirit became so intolerable that he could work no more, and hurried from Troas into Macedonia. There—at last—probably at Philippi he met Titus. What Titus said to him the Apostle, in his eagerness, forgets to tell us; but it appears, from the burst of thanksgiving at the close of the chapter, that he brought news which, though chequered, was on the whole favourable. The effect of the severe letter had been to a great extent satisfactory. It had caused among the Corinthian Christians a salutary grief which had shown itself in yearning affection and remorseful endeavour to amend. Titus himself had been received cordially, yet with fear and trembling. The offender, if he had not been dealt with exactly as Paul had ordered [1]—which was perhaps rendered unnecessary by his repentance—had still been visited by the majority with severe reprobation. Accordingly, he sent Titus back—and

streets, driven into a corner, and dashed to the ground, had barely escaped with his life, and had suffered severe bodily injuries from which he had scarcely yet recovered.

[1] This seems clear from a comparison of 1 Cor. v. 3–5, with 2 Cor. ii. 5–10. Had Titus been the bearer of another short letter, no longer extant? It is a question which we cannot answer.

with him Luke—to finish the good work which he had begun.[1]

On the other hand, there had arisen against St. Paul a defiant and influential opposition from the two Judaic factions which called themselves the Cephas-party and the Christ-party, who attacked him with every weapon of fanatical religious hatred. His change of plan in not paying them a double visit had led to much unfavourable criticism. Many injurious remarks on his character and mode of action had been industriously disseminated, especially by certain itinerant Judaic teachers, who were unhappily countenanced, or at any rate professed to be so, by commendatory letters from Christian Pharisees in the Church of Jerusalem. These factious partisans, as we see from the undercurrent of self-defence which runs so strongly throughout the letter, had said, or at least insinuated, that Paul was a man who was so capricious as not to know his own mind; that he wrote private letters to intrigue with individual members of his congregation; that there were good reasons why he had no commendatory letters to show ; that there was a great deal in his antecedents which would not bear examination ; that he walked craftily, and adulterated the Word of God. Now St. Paul had a human heart, not an artificial one ; and he does not even pretend that such calumnies did not sting and wound him. They stung him, and all the more because they came upon him at a time of great mental discouragement and physical prostration (iv. 8—12), when, as he said, " our flesh had no rest, but we are troubled on every side ; from without fightings, from within fears" (vii. 5). We can understand the phenomena of a letter written under such circumstances. If Hope is the key-note of the Epistle to the Thessalonians, Joy of that to the Philippians, Faith of that to the Romans, the Heavenlies of that to the Ephesians, "tribulation " is the one predominant word, and " consolation under tribulation" the one predominant topic of the first

[1] 2 Cor. vii. 6-11, 13-15 ; viii. 6. 18. 23.

2 CORINTH. great section of the second Epistle to the Corinthians. These two words, though unfortunately varied by synonyms in the English version, occur again and again inextricably intertwined in the first chapter. Thus, in the third and fourth verses we read, "Blessed be the God and Father of our Lord Jesus Christ, the Father of Mercies, and God of all consolation, who consoleth us in all our tribulation, that we may be able to console those in all tribulation, by the consolation wherewith we are ourselves consoled by God." This incessant recurrence of the same words—now "tribulation,"[1] now "consolation,"[2] now "boasting,"[3] now "weakness,"[4] now "simplicity,"[5] now "manifest" and "manifestation"[6] now "folly,"[7]—are characteristic of the extreme emotion of mind in which the letter was written. The manner in which thankfulness and indignation struggle with each other, the difficult expressions, the abrupt causal connections, the labouring style, the iteration of taunting words, the interchange of bitter irony with pathetic sincerity—only serve to throw into stronger relief the frequent outbursts of impassioned eloquence. The depth of tenderness which is here revealed towards all who are noble and true, may serve as a measure for the insolence and wrong which provoked, in the concluding chapters, so stern an indignation.[8] Of all the Epistles this is the one which teaches us most of the Apostle's personality. It enables us, as it were, to lay our hands upon his breast, and feel the very throbbings of his heart. If you would know St. Paul as he was, you must study the Epistle again and yet again.

3. Hence of all his letters this is the least, as the First

---

[1] θλίψις, θλίβομαι, i. 4, 6, 8; ii. 4; iv. 8, 17; vi. 4; vii. 4; viii. 13.

[2] παράκλησις, eleven times; the verb 17 times.

[3] Twenty-nine times in 1 and 2 Cor.

[4] ἀσθένεια, 2 Cor. xi. 30; xii. 5, 9, 10; xiii. 4, &c.

[5] ἁπλότης, i. 12; viii. 2; ix. 11, 13; xi. 3.

[6] φανερόω, ii. 14; iii. 3; iv. 10; v. 10, 11; vii. 12; xi. 6.

[7] 2 Cor. xi. 1, 16, 17, 19, 21; xii. 6, 18.

[8] St. Paul assumes that he may rely on the loyalty of the majority; hence his appeal to ὑμεῖς πάντες (ii. 3–5; iii. 18; v. 10; vii. 13; xiii. 13), whereas the opponents are only τινες (iii. 1; x. 2, 7, 12; xi. 4; xiii. 21, &c.).

Epistle to the Corinthians is the most systematic. Indeed the order of its thoughts might almost be called geographical, as he passes in memory from the dangers of Ephesus to the anxiety of Troas, to the afflictions of Macedonia, and to the dark prospect of his coming visit to Corinth.[1] But this historical thread of the Epistle is interwoven with digressions. After the greeting, the thanksgiving and an allusion to the fearful trials through which he had just passed in Asia, he proceeds at once to defend himself from accusations of levity and insincerity in having postponed his intended visit. He tells them that if, on this account, they charged him with saying now " yes," and now " no," with the shiftiness of an aimless man, there was at any rate in his teaching one emphatic " yes," and one unchangeable " Amen "; the infinite " yes " of God in Christ, and the everlasting Amen of the Christian to all God's promises. And then he calls God to witness that it was to spare them that he had not come; because he did not like to visit them in grief. As for the offender, he had repented, and their obedience had been tested. If they forgave the man, Paul forgave him too. Then he tells them of his anxiety as to the effects of his letter, and ends the second chapter with a paean of eucharist to God who led him in triumph through the willing captivity of his weary life.

Then in the third chapter he asks, Is this self-commendation ? does he need commendatory letters to them ? Nay, they were themselves his commendatory letter; a letter which he had himself administered. And since this reminds him of the grandeur of his ministry, he compares its eternal glory with the evanescence of the transient glow on the face of Moses, and proceeds to contrast the splendour of the ministry with the weakness of the ministers. Like the torches hid in Gideon's pitchers, their treasure of light was in earthen vessels, that the glory might be God's, not theirs. This was why they were in everything " afflicted yet not crushed;

---

[1] " Tota Epistola itinerarium sapit."—BENGEL.

perplexed, but not in despair; persecuted, but not forsaken; cast down, but not destroyed." This theme—defending himself against charges of folly and insincerity—he pursues to the sixth chapter, in which he breaks out into a noble appeal.[1] He says that he and his friends strove to commend themselves as ministers to God " in much endurance, in tribulations, in necessities, in pressure, in blows, in prisons, in tumults, in toils, in spells of sleeplessness, in hungerings, in pureness, in knowledge, in long-suffering, in kindness, in the Holy Spirit, in love unfeigned, in the word of truth, in the power of God; by the arms of righteousness on the right hand and on the left; by ill report and good report; as deceivers, and yet true; as being ignored, and yet recognised; as dying, and behold we live; as being chastened yet not being slain; as being grieved and yet rejoicing; as paupers, yet enriching many; as having nothing, and yet as having all things in full possession."

4. He may well appeal, as he does in the eleventh verse of the sixth chapter, to this fervid rush of spontaneous eloquence as a proof that there is no narrowness, no insincerity, no want of affection, no " crypts of shame" in his heart towards them. Taken alone, passages like these might seem painfully personal; we might have thought that the man had got the better of the ambassador. But the man and the ambassador are one, and what he wants from them is not a cold and critical appreciation of his eloquence, but the sympathy of Christians, if not the affection of sons.[2] He proceeds therefore to tell them that if he had written to them severely in his former letter it was only to inflict upon them a holy and a healing pain. Then he ends the seventh chapter with the generous assurance that he had good heart about them in all things.

As a proof of this confidence, he appeals to their generosity

---

[1] The passage, vi. 4–vii. 1, is a powerful appeal to them against incongruous fellowship with evil. It is somewhat parenthetic in character, and some have regarded it as a marginal note.

[2] Maurice, *Unity of the New Testament*, 488.

in a matter dear to his heart—the offertory for the poor at 2 CORINTH.
Jerusalem. The churches of Macedonia, hard pressed as
they were, had contributed with generous self-denial. Their
liberal collection was already finished, though Achaia and
Corinth had begun to collect before them. He had therefore
sent Titus and two dear brethren to Corinth, to look after
and hasten this matter. He had boasted to the Macedonians
about the readiness of the Corinthians, because he had relied
on their promises. The simple fact was (though St. Paul
only hints it in the most delicate manner) that he had been
misled by the glib professions of these most unsatisfactory
Corinthians, which there was only too much reason to fear
would evaporate in talk. As to the value and importance of
the offertory he need surely say nothing; but, anxious that both
he and they should not be ashamed of a charity which lagged
far behind its own promises, he reminds them that " He who
soweth sparingly, sparingly shall also reap; and he who
soweth bountifully—or, as it is literally, with blessings—
shall also reap with blessings." [1] And then, identifying
himself with the grateful recipient who, he says, would
glorify God for this proof of genuine religion, he ends the
ninth chapter with the words " Thanks be to God for His
unspeakable gift." [2]

5. At that point there comes a complete break, an absolute
dislocation, so to speak, in the letter. In the last four
chapters—the tenth, eleventh, twelfth, and thirteenth—
the whole tone of the letter so completely changes that
many have imagined the chapters to be not only a separate
letter, but even to be the stern missive alluded to in
the eighth and following verses of the seventh chapter,
about the reception of which he had suffered so much cruel
anxiety.[3] It is difficult to accept this theory in defiance of

---

[1] ix. 6 ; ἐπ' εὐλογίαις, *i.e.* in a large, liberal spirit.
[2] These two chapters are memorable as being the fullest exposition of the
duty and plan of almsgiving in the Bible.
[3] The Αὐτὸς δὲ ἐγὼ Παῦλος of x. 1, at once marks the change of tone,
(comp. Gal. v. 2 ; Eph. iii. 1). There is a similar, but less marked change

the evidence of the manuscripts, and yet something must have happened to make the tone of these chapters so different from all that had gone before. What happened appears to have been this. After he had despatched Titus, some one seems to have come from Corinth who brought the disastrous intelligence that the party of his opponents had been reinforced and animated by the arrival of an obtrusive emissary with introductory letters from Jerusalem,[1] whose opposition to St. Paul had been more marked, and more unscrupulous than any with which he had yet had to deal.[2] Incited by this Judaic sophister, some of the Corinthians had been passing their censures on St. Paul still more freely than before. They had been saying—as this new messenger from Corinth, perhaps unwisely and unnecessarily told St. Paul— that his presence was mean; that he was untutored in speech; that he was only bold in letters and at a distance; that he walked according to the flesh—that is, that his motives were worldly, not spiritual; that there was in him a vein of folly, or even of insanity;[3] that he had sinister designs in suggesting the offering for the saints at Jerusalem; that his sending of Titus was only a crafty cloak for his own avarice;[4] that his apparent self-denial rose from the fact that he had no commendatory letters to show;[5] that he had never known Jesus, and had misrepresented him altogether;[6] that he was not to be regarded as a true Apostle. The fact that such calumnies should have been current among the converts whom he loved made him at once wretched and indignant. Dazzled by the outrageous pretensions of this

in Rom. xiv. xv., and we notice a similar phenomenon in Demosth. *De Corona.*

[1] 2 Cor. iii. 1 ; x. 13–17.

[2] iii. 1 ; v. 11 ; vii. 2, 3 ; x. 2, 7, 10, 11, 12, 18 ; xi. 18–20. It is possible that the attack on St. Paul's authority was fomented by some who resisted his sentence on the offender.

[3] v. 13, 16 ; xii. 6 ; xi. 16, 17, 19 ; comp. the blunt "Thou art mad, Paul," of Festus.

[4] xii. 16.

[5] 2 Cor. iii. 1–6 ; the taunt that he had none of those " commendatory letters" stung St. Paul deeply (iv. 7–vi. 10).

[6] 2 Cor. xi. 4, ἄλλον Ἰησοῦν . . . ἕτερον εὐαγγέλιον, comp. 1 Cor. ix. 1.

Pharisee, benumbed by the torpedo-touch of his avarice, the Corinthians were beginning to repudiate their true teacher.[1] The absolute necessity of refuting such attacks rose from the importance of his position, and is further illustrated by the extreme vitality of the Ebionite hatred of St. Paul, which smouldered on for a century later, and even in the pseudo-Clementine writings shows its treacherous and sullen fires.[2] From this point of his letter onwards the tender effusiveness and earnest praise to which we have hitherto been listening is replaced by a tone of suppressed indignation, in which love, struggling with bitter irony, renders the language constrained, like the words of one who with difficulty checks himself from saying all that his emotion might suggest. One characteristic of these chapters is the constant recurrence of the word "boast" and "boasting," which occurs twenty-nine times in these Epistles, and only six times in all the rest. Now "boasting" was a thing of which the most distant resemblance was abhorrent to the nature of the Apostle. But something which his enemies might have characterised as "boasting" was simply wrung from him by the injustice of his opponents, and the defection of his flock. To three things especially he could appeal—to his Apostolic activity, to his spiritual gifts, to the Churches which he had founded.[3]

---

[1] See x. 18 ; xi. 8 ; (οὐ κατενάρκησα, "I did not benumb you like a torpedo" one of St. Paul's "cilicisms" according to Jerome) xi. 20 ; xii. 13, 14. Theodoret thought that St. Paul wrote x. 12–18, with kind and intentional obscurity (ἀσαφῶς). St. Chrysostom saw that many expressions in this section are quotations from the sneers of his enemies (κατ᾽ εἰρώνειαν φησὶ τὰ ἐκείνων φθεγγόμενος).

[2] On these insinuations see x. i. 10, 12 ; xi. 6, 16, 17, 19, &c., and note 2, at the end of this discourse.

In the Pseudo-Clementine Homilies Paul is surreptitiously attacked under the name of Simon Magus. In the spurious letter of Peter to James, he is called "the lawless one." In the *Recognitions* he is evidently meant by "the enemy" sent by Caiaphas to arrest St. Peter at Antioch, who also threw St. James down the Temple steps. A pestilent fiction called the "Ascents of James" is believed to have been the source of the notable story that he was a Gentile who had accepted circumcision in hopes of marrying the High Priest's daughter, and who apostatised when his hopes were disappointed. See Epiphan. *Haer.* xxx. 16. Ps. Chem. *Recogn.* iv. 34. *Hom.* xi. 36. Baur, *First Three Centuries*, (E.T.) i. 89–98 ; *Life of St. Paul*, i. 673–678.

[3] ii. 14 ; iii. 2 ; xi. 20-23 ; 1 Cor. ix. 1 ; xv. 10, &c.

2 CORINTH. It would be impossible to summarise this long and passionate appeal, of which the varying tones are changeable as those of an Aeolian harp, but we may be deeply thankful that to it we owe the one famous passage which shows us that, many and various as are the trials and afflictions of the Apostle narrated for us in the Acts of the Apostles, we have not there one tithe of the story of the long martyrdom of the life of Paul—I mean the passage in the eleventh chapter in which, with a mere allusive glance at but a part of what he had endured, he says that he had been "in toils more abundantly, in stripes above measure, in prisons more abundantly, in deaths oft; of the Jews five times received I forty stripes save one; thrice was I beaten with rods; once was I stoned; thrice I suffered shipwreck, a night and a day have I spent in the deep; in journeyings often, in perils of rivers, in perils of robbers, in perils from my own race, in perils from Gentiles, in perils in the city, in perils in the wilderness, in perils in the sea, in perils among false brethren, in toil and weariness, in sleeplessness often, in hunger and thirst, in fastings often, in cold and nakedness—besides the things additional to all these, the care which daily besets me, my anxiety for all the Churches. Who is weak and I share not his weakness? Who is made to stumble, and I do not burn with indignation? If I must boast, I will boast of this my weakness. The God and Father of our Lord Jesus Christ knoweth that I am not lying. In Damascus the ethnarch of Aretas the king was guarding the city of Damascus, wishing to seize me, and through a window, in a basket, I was let down through the wall, and escaped his hands."

Surely this is the most marvellous fragment ever written of any biography. We may read the lives of many of the saints of God, and such reading is eminently profitable; but this is a fragment beside which, not merely the ordinary biographies of comfortable Christians, but even the most imperilled lives of the most suffering saints shrink into

insignificance. It is the very heroism of unselfishness—
the life of an "Apostle of the Third Heaven."

6. Such then is the Second Epistle of St. Paul to the
Corinthians. It is as rich as all the Epistles are in all moral
and spiritual truth. In a very few words we may emphasise
its main and general, as apart from its special, lessons.

a. First, then, let this Epistle teach us to beware of
judging others, and above all to beware of judging and con-
demning them because of their religious opinions. Let us
do rather what St. Paul bids his critics do—test ourselves,
prove our own selves. There are few things more saddening
than the self-sufficiency of religious ignorance. If nothing
else will teach us modesty, let us bear in mind that the
so-called "religious world" has unanimously anathematised
some of the greatest saints, and some of the wisest thinkers,
that ever pleaded the cause of God. Let us remember that
Paul, the greatest of the Apostles, the most glorious of the
saints, was all his life long, and continued to be for a century
after his death, a victim of the abuse—sincere perhaps in its
own narrow region, but grossly and obstinately ignorant—of a
self-styled orthodoxy. Let us beware of thinking that God's
ark is always tottering, or that, if it is, it needs our poor
and feeble hands to hold it up. It can at any rate never be our
duty to slander, to rail, to blacken, to misrepresent, to lie for God.
How many an Eliphaz the Temanite, Bildad the Shuhite, and
Zophar the Naamathite, who holds himself to be an uncompromising champion of imperilled truth will be shamed and
astonished hereafter to hear God's awful disavowal and stern
reproof, and to find that, all the while, they were not worthy
to touch the very skirt of the garment of those whom they
denounced as heretics and sinners.

β. This, then, for the large class of religious accusers who,
in the original Greek are called "devils" (διαβόλους).[1] And
for the accused this. The cases are rare in which it is wise
for any man, as it was for St. Paul, to refute sneers, or expose

---

[1] 1 Tim. iii. 11 ; 2 Tim. iii. 3 ; Tit. ii. 3.

calumnies against ourselves. The wisest way is simply to entrust our cause to God.

> " What idle whispers here concern thee aught ;
> Follow thou me, nor heed what others say ;
> Be like a tower that never stoops its head,
> Bellow the tempests fiercely as they may." [1]

It is said that an eminent person of the present day has treasured up in a book all the fiercest attacks which have been made upon him and, without ever having answered one word either good or bad, keeps that book for the amusement of his friends. Better perhaps was the observation of another, " They cannot harm me by what they say of me. I am too near the Great White Throne for that ! " At any rate we can all imitate the forgiving spirit of good Archbishop Tillotson. Among his papers, at his death, was found a bundle of all the worst lampoons which had ever been written against him, with the pathetic memorandum, " May God forgive them ; I am sure I do." And there is one way at any rate to rob all criticisms of their sting. It is to prove their falsity by the innocence and simplicity of our lives. If we be sure of God's smile, men may say what they will. Moral nobleness is the one shield of adamant against the arrows of intolerable wrong.

γ. One brief lesson more. What had Paul that we have not ? He was weak, he was sensitive, he was uncomely, he was hated, he was poor ; even religious persons in churchly circles at Jerusalem and in Syria looked on him askance. And yet, amid the world's storms of hate and persecution, he carried the lighted torch of truth till it had flashed from Damascus to Jerusalem, from Jerusalem to Rome. If this Jew, whom Gentiles despised, whom Jews detested, did so much, can we, the richly-blessed sons of imperial England do so little ? Let us look at our lives. Are we living for self ? for

---

[1] " Che ti fa ciò che quivi si pispiglia ?
Vien dietro a me, e lascia dir le genti ;
Sta come torre, fermo, che non crolla
Giammai la cima per soffiar di venti."
DANTE, *Purg.* v. 12-15.

pleasure? for gold? for ambition? What a misery, what a vanity of vanities, what a failure of failures is such a life! Are we of any use at all in the world, beyond our mere mechanical routine with its variations of sleeping and eating? "O my God, grant me" (so they are taught to pray in some monasteries in France), "grant me that to-day I may be of some use to some one." If God, for our good, see fit to deny us all else, may He, as His best gift of all, grant us this, to be of some real, of some deep use to our fellow men, before we go hence and are no more seen.

NOTE I.

GENERAL CHARACTERISTICS OF THE EPISTLE.

"The whole Epistle reminds us of an itinerary, but it is interwoven with the noblest precepts."—BENGEL.

"Non mihi videtur digitis calamo et atramento scripsisse, verum ipso corde, ipso affectu et denudatis visceribus."—CASAUBON.

"This Epistle is the most striking instance of a new philosophy of life poured forth not through systematic treatises, but through occasional bursts of human feeling."—STANLEY.

"God exhibits death in the living, life in the dying."—ALFORD.

The Epistle is St. Paul's *Apologia pro Vitâ Suâ.*

The importance of this letter in the Antijudaic controversy was great, for unless St. Paul effectually established his Apostolic authority, his arguments in the Epistles to the Galatians and Romans would not have counterbalanced the leanings and prejudices of the Jewish Christians who claimed the sanction of St. James and the Church of Jerusalem.

The two Epistles to the Corinthians have a special value.

The first gives us our chief insight into the character and condition of the early Churches; the contests by which they were agitated; the practices which were struggling for existence in their worship; the manifold thoughts and speculations which were seething in the midst of them. We see Christianity, under the guidance of the Holy Spirit, endeavouring "to grasp and to set its seal upon life in all its variety."

The second gives us our chief insight into the life and character of the great Apostle. Here, in self-defence, he opens the most secret recesses of his heart. We see his keen logic, his nervous excitement, his deep indignation, his constant self-denial, his strong sense of independence, his immeasurable love. We see his sympathy with the strong combined with his tenderness for the weak; his fire and passion; his practical good sense and tact; his religious fervour; his immense devotion to the cause of Christ in which he was ready to spend and to be spent.[1]

---

[1] "Nirgends finden wir die Subjectivität des Apostels in so hohem Grade und so verschiedener Weise angeregt wie in diesem Briefe, nirgends die rednerische δεινότης so häufig hervortretend (iv. 8–11; vi. 4–10; vii. 11; xi. 22–29)." Immer, *Theologie des N. T.* p. 240. Hausrath *Neut. Zeitg.* ii. 710.

The First Epistle deals with the elements of peril which sprung up for the most part in the Hellenic section of the Church—inflated culture, spurious liberty, &c. The second is aimed almost exclusively at Judaic antagonists.

NOTE II.

OUTLINE OF THE EPISTLE.

It falls into three main divisions.

i.-vii. Personal and ministerial.
viii.-ix. About the collection for the poor.
x.-xiii. Direct personal self-defence.

1. Greeting (i. 1-2).
2. Thanksgiving (i. 3-7).
3. Hortatory and retrospective. An endeavour to come to a better understanding with the Church of Corinth. An undercurrent of apology (i. 8-vii.) darkened by suppressed indignation. Concerning the contribution for the poor saints (viii., ix.) ; suggestions coloured by sorrowful emotion.
4. Indignant defence of his Apostolic position (x.-xiii.).
5. Farewell greetings. "Farewell ; be perfect, be comforted ; be united ; be at peace."
6. Autograph blessing. As though to make up for the severity of the letter this is the fullest form of the Apostolic blessing "thence adopted by the Church in all ages as the final blessing of her services."

This is the least systematic, as the first is the most systematic, of St Paul's writings.

The thread of the Epistle is historical, but it is interwoven with digressions. The broken threads of narrative will be found in i. 8, 15 ; ii. 1 (Ephesus) ; 12 (Troas) ; 13 (arrival in Macedonia) ; vii. 5 (Macedonia) viii. 1 ix. 2 (*id.*) ; xiii. 1 (intention to visit Corinth).

NOTE III.

EFFECTS PRODUCED BY THE EPISTLE.

In the New Testament we hear no more about the state of the Church of Corinth ; but we have two glimpses of it within the century which ensued. One is furnished by the letter of Clement of Rome to the Corinthians (circ. A.D. 95). We see from this letter that the Church of

The Epistles.

Corinth was still in much the same condition as when St. Paul wrote—full of tendencies to faction, insubordination, and doubt. In A.D. 135, the church was visited by Hegesippus, who stayed there some days on his way to Rome. The account which (from a Jewish-Christian point of view) he gives is more favourable. The Corinthian Christians were under an excellent and active bishop named Primus ; women like Phœbe and Priscilla had found a successor in Chrysophora ; and the Church was well spoken of for liberal almsgiving.

NOTE IV.

ATTACKS UPON ST. PAUL, AND HIS REPLIES.

This Epistle is so largely motived by the determined assault upon St. Paul's authority that it is worth while to track out the indications of what calumny had to say of him.

I. The calumnies were aimed, (i.) at his person, (ii.) his teaching, (iii.) his character.

i. As to his PERSON.

    a. He is "abject" (ταπεινός, x. 1.)

    β. Weak (ἀσθενής, x. 10.)

    γ. A contemptible speaker (ὁ λόγος ἐξουθενημένος, x. 10), only big and strong in his letters when he is at a safe distance (ἰδιώτης ἐν λόγῳ, xi. 6.)

ii. As to his TEACHING.

    a. He arrogates too much to himself (ὑπερεκτείνει, x. 12–18).

    β. He is no true Apostle, and that is why he does not dare to claim the privilege of maintenance as an Apostle (1 Cor. ix. 1–23 ; 2 Cor. xi. 7–12 ; xii. 13).

    γ. He has nothing to boast of like the true Apostles, the "out and out Apostles" (οἱ ὑπερλίαν ἀπόστολοι, xi. 5) and is in fact "nothing" (xi. 16–33 ; xii. 11).

    δ. His Gospel is a hidden, crafty, mysterious one (iv. 3) ; a charge founded on 1 Cor. ii. 7.

    ε. The Jesus and the Gospel he preaches is not the true Jesus or the right Gospel (xi. 4).

    ζ. He falsifies the word of God (ii. 17, iv. 2).

    η. He preaches himself and not Christ (iv. 5).

iii. As to his character.

   a. He cannot produce any commendatory letters.[1]

   β. He is fickle and changeable; altering his announced plan; first he says "Yes" and then "No" (i. 15–17).

   γ. The reason is that he is afraid of having his pretensions put to the test; He *dare* not come (xiii. 3; x. 9–11; xii. 20, 21; 1 Cor. iv. 18–21).

   δ. He boasts of his disinterestedness, but this collection about which he is so eager is very suspicious. He sends Titus to get the money out of you, and "suck you dry" (2 Cor. xii. 16–19; viii. 20–23).

   ε. The only excuse for him is that his mind is hardly sound (v. 13; xi. 16–19; xii. 6), and hence he has only visions to appeal to, never having really known Christ (xii. 2; v. 16).[2]

II. To all this the Apostle's answer is indignant and complete: indeed to some of the charges he hardly deigns to give any further answer than a passing word.

i. As to his *person* it matters little or nothing.

   a, β. God is no respecter of persons (Gal. ii. 6). He comforts the "abject" (vii. 6). He strengthens the weak (xiii. 4). They ought not to look at men's faces (x. 7), but at their hearts (v. 12).

   γ. Whatever he was in speech, he was not contemptible in knowledge; and he would answer in person the sneers that he was afraid to come (x. 11; xi. 6; i. 23; xiii. 1–3, 10).

ii. As to his teaching,

   a. It is his opponents who are obtrusive and arrogant, not himself (x. 12–18).

   β. He is an Apostle of Christ's own calling (x. 18); he has only foregone his right to maintenance at their hands that he might not "benumb" or burden them (xi. 7–12; xii. 14–16).

   γ. If he *must* boast he has done more than the "out and out" Apostles of whose countenance and letters the Judaic missionary boasted (xi. 23–33). He has had divine visions (xii. 1–10). He has shown all the signs of an Apostle (xii. 11–13). The Apostles possess no single privilege of which he is destitute (xi.

---

[1] This was remembered against St. Paul by the Ebionites long afterwards. See Ps. Clem. *Recogn.* iv. 3, 5, where Peter is made to give directions that every one is to be regarded as a false Apostle who cannot produce a "testimonial" from James the Bishop of Jerusalem.

[2] Even in the Clementines we find a surreptitious sneer at St. Paul's visions as being mere subjective fancy, or deceit of the devil. Ps. Clement *Hom.* xvii. 13, *seq.* πῶς δὲ σοὶ καὶ πιστεύσομεν αὐτό; . . . πῶς δέ σοι καὶ ὤφθη, ὁπότε αὐτῷ τὰ ἐνάντια τῇ διδασκαλίᾳ φρονεῖς ·

22), and if he be "nothing" he is at any rate not inferior to them (xii. 11).

δ. His Gospel is absolutely open, honest, and manifest except to the wilfully blind (iv. 1-6).

ζ, η, θ. He preaches the true, and the only Christ, not himself (ii. 17, 18; iv. 1-6, 13-18; xi. 1-4).

iii. As to his character,

a. He stands above the need for "commendatory letters." They were themselves his commendatory letter (x. 18; iii. 1-6).

β. If he be "fickle," at any rate his preaching is absolutely fixed (i. 18); but in point of fact his change of plan was due to deliberate kindness towards them that he might not visit them in anger (i. 15-24; xiii. 1, &c.).

γ. They shall judge whether he is afraid or no (xiii. 1-10).

δ. He indignantly disclaims the charge of interested conduct and appeals to plain facts (xii. 14-18; xi. 7-10; vii. 2-4).

ε. To the insinuation that he is not in his right mind he only opposes a few allusions of tender irony (v. 13; xii. 6; xi. 16-19, &c.).

EPISTLE TO THE GALATIANS.

WRITTEN AT CORINTH ABOUT A.D. 58

Διδακτικόν, ἀνεξίκακον.—2 Tim. ii. 24.

"For *charuth* "graven" (Ex. xxxii. 16) read *cheruth* "freedom."—
R. MEIR.

"Principalis adversus Judaismum Epistola."—MARCION (*ap.* Tert. *adv. Marc.* v. 2).

> "He is a freeman whom the truth makes free,
> And all are slaves beside."

INTRODUCTORY.

IT may be regarded as certain that by "Galatians" St. Paul meant the inhabitants of Galatia proper (the Trocmi, Tectosages, Tolistoboii, with their three capital towns of Tavium, Pessinus, and Ancyra). To speak of the Neo-Galatians of the Roman province, which included Iconium, Lystra, and Derbe as Galatians, would be like writing a letter "to the Prussians," which was specially intended for the people of Schleswig-Holstein, or Alsace and Lorraine. St. Luke never dreams of calling Pisidia and Lycaonia by the name Galatia (Acts xiv. 6, 11).[1]

[1] See Hilgenfeld, *Einleit.* p. 251, Hausrath, *Zeitg.* ii.

GALATIANS. St. Paul had founded these Churches A.D. 52, in the visit of which we learn the particulars from Acts xvi. 6, Galatians iv. 13—16. When he paid them a second visit, in A.D. 55, he saw some ground for misgiving, and seems to have been much more coldly received (Acts xviii. 22, 23, iv. 16—20)

The date of the Epistle to the Galatians is, within narrow limits, fixed both by external and internal evidence.

It was evidently written within a short time of the Second Epistle to the Corinthians; for—especially in the self-vindication of chapters i., ii.—it greatly resembles that Epistle in tone, feeling, style, and mode of argument, as well as in many casual expressions.

It must have slightly preceded the Epistle to the Romans, since it is preoccupied with the same order of thought. It is the rough sketch of which the Epistle to the Romans is the finished picture. It is an impassioned, controversial, personal statement of the relation of the Gentiles to the Jews, especially as regards circumcision. The Epistle to the Romans is a full, systematic, general treatise on the relation of the Gospel to the Law (see Bishop Lightfoot, *Galatians*, pp. 44—46). The difference between the two is that Galatians was written in deep emotion, Romans with calm, mature reflection.

At no long period after St. Paul's second visit ("so soon") the Galatians had been "fascinated," "bewitched," by the Jewish emissaries, partly from their natural levity of character and fondness for novelty, and partly because the Judaising ritual bore some resemblance to their own Asiatic and semi-Phrygian cults. The elaborate and orgiastic character of these local superstitions made the Gauls feel discontented with the simple spirituality of Christian worship.

"It was necessary," says Baur, "that the particularisms of Judaism, which exposed to the heathen world so repellent a demeanour, and such offensive claims should be uprooted, and the baselessness of its prejudices and pretensions fully

exposed to the world's eye. This was the service which the
Apostle achieved for mankind by his magnificent dialectic."[1]

The tactics of the Jewish emissaries were very simple.
They began with the Psalms and pure monotheism, and so,
when they had made their "proselytes of the gate," they put
forward so strongly the desirability of further advances, and
the peril of not accepting legal observances that they gradually
got to the knife of circumcision and the whole yoke of the
Levitic Law,[2] and so made them "proselytes of righteousness," and in some cases, as our Lord said, twofold more the
children of Gehenna than themselves.

It was thus that they had treated the royal family of
Adiabene, some of whom lie buried in "the tombs of the
kings" near Jerusalem. Queen Helena, in performance of a
Nazarite vow (twice renewed), spent twenty-one years in
Jerusalem, and during the famine of Claudius's reign fed its
paupers with dried figs imported from Cyprus. The family
had been converted to Judaism by a liberal-minded Jewish
merchant named Abennerig, who wisely told them that
circumcision was not essential. Then came a bigoted
Pharisee, R. Eliezer of Galilee, who so worked on the fears of
the princes Izates and Monobazus that they both had themselves secretly circumcised. Josephus tells us many particulars
about this interesting family.[3]

Josephus had the greatest difficulty in preventing the
circumcision by force of "two great men" who came to him
from Trachonitis; and they had to save their lives from the
fury of the Jewish bigots by a hasty flight (*Vit. Jos.* 23, 31).

The Rabbis say that "Rabbi" (Juda Hakkodesh, who
edited the Mishna) induced the Emperor Antoninus to be
circumcised. The story is none the less significant though it
is a fable, and it is uncertain which emperor is meant by
Antoninus.[4]

[1] *First Three Centuries*, i. 73.
[2] See Hausrath, *Neut. Zeitg.* ii. p. 263.
[3] See Jos. *Antt.* xx. 2, § 2, B. J. v. 6, § 1, vi. 6, § 3.
[4] *Jer. Megillah.* c. 1. *Avoda Zara.* f. 10, 2.

It was an advantage to St. Paul that he was able in this Epistle to concentrate the force of his argument on the single point of circumcision. For

a. The Jewish teachers put it in the forefront. They said that " but for circumcision heaven and earth could not exist " (Nedarim, f. 32, 1); that it was equivalent to all the commandments of the Law (*id.*); and that angels so detest an uncircumcised person that, before Abraham was circumcised, God spoke to him in Aramaic, which the angels do not understand. (*Yalkut Chadash*, f. 117, 3.)

β. If therefore St. Paul could show that for Gentiles circumcision was worse than useless, it became unnecessary to enter on further questions. With circumcision fell the whole Levitic law.

In vehemence, effectiveness, and depth of conviction this Epistle is only paralleled by Luther's *De Captivitate Babylonica*, in which he realised his saying that his battle with the Papacy required "a tongue of which every word is a thunderbolt."

St. Paul did his work so completely that thenceforth in the Christian Church the question as to the need of circumcision for Gentiles was at an end. In the Epistle of Barnabas circumcision is even treated with contempt, and its institution attributed to the deception of an evil angel (*Ep. Barnab.* c. ix.). In the Ignatian letter to Philadelphia we read of "the false Jew of the earthly circumcision" (*Ep. ad. Philad.* 6). Even in the Ebionite pseudo-Clementine homilies they who desire to be de-Hellenised (ἀφελληνισθῆναι, "to be un-Greeked") must be so not by circumcision, but by baptism and the new birth. Of circumcision not a word is said, even by these extreme Judaists.

The leading thoughts of the Epistle are the Freedom of the Gospel; Justification by Faith, not by works of the Law; circumcision nothing and uncircumcision nothing, but a new creation in Christ.

EPISTLE TO THE GALATIANS.

"Stand fast therefore in the liberty wherewith Christ has made us free, and be not entangled again with the yoke of bondage."—GAL. v. 1.

1. IN the history of mankind ages of torpor and oppression GALATIANS. are often ended by a sudden crisis of deliverance, due to the bright genius and burning courage of one man. The man whom God appoints to this high task has, in most instances, to face the fury of a world suddenly awaked from the deep slumber of decided opinions; and by that fury he is always persecuted, and sometimes slain. It is astonishing to note how nations and Churches can be smitten for centuries with a paralysis of mental inactivity; how they can suffer custom to lie upon them with a weight "heavy as frost, and deep almost as life" —how they can allow themselves to be crushed under false systems of belief and morals, without so much as once inquiring on what those systems rest. We are sometimes driven to think that men in general will endure anything rather than the honest pain of facing great questions for themselves. Of how many an age has it been a true description that "the prophets prophesy falsely, and the priests bear rule by their means, and my people love to have it so!" Is not Israel in this respect a type of all mankind? Released from the sensual serfdom of Egypt, and led—a free people—into the eager air of the wilderness, did they not murmur, and rebel, for their lost fleshpots, and leeks, and onions, and full-fed ease? Even so do men love the indolent Egypt of intellectual servitude.

> "They bawl for freedom in their senseless mood,
> But still revolt when truth would set them free;
> License they mean when they cry liberty,
> For who loves that, must first be wise and good."

The Bible, rightly used, is eminently the book of freedom. All the noblest and most inspiring parts of its history tell of

the struggles of a free people against colossal tyrannies. All
the most glorious pages of its prophets are like the blasts of
trumpets blown to awaken men from immoral acquiescence
and apathetic sloth. Its spiritual law is a perfect law of
liberty. The very spirit of its gospel is "Ye shall know the
truth, and the truth shall make you free." And yet, so
innate and perverse is the propensity of mankind to prefer
their familiar fetters to the perils and the pains—the
ennobling perils, the glorious pains—of freedom, that they
have managed to degrade the very Scripture into an instrument of oppression, and have manufactured out of its misinterpretation the subtlest engines of tyranny. But since
this is so, since phrases of Scripture have been made so
dangerous to mankind, since oftentimes the dead letter of it
has been an instrument of murder in the hands of ignorance,
a firebrand of bigotry in the grasp of folly, an arrow of death in
the quiver of fanaticism—they for whom God has "illuminated
the eyes of the understanding," [1] they who know that the
very Scriptures of God, as St. Peter says, may be wrested, by
the unlearned and the unstable, to their own perdition [2]—are
more than ever bound to use the Bible on behalf of that
liberty—that civil, that social, that intellectual, that moral,
that spiritual liberty—of which it was meant by God to be
the shield and sword. The letter of the Bible, if it have
been used to wound, may also, thank God—like the fabled
spear of Achilles—be used to heal. By the help of the
Bible, in time, we freed the slave, though vested interest
quoted Moses and St. Paul to prove the sacredness of slavery.
By the help of the Bible, in time, we shall make England
temperate, though men quote the Epistle to Timothy to
defend the system which maddens men and women with
ardent spirits into desperate crimes. By the help of the
Bible, in time, the English nation shook to the dust a system
of despotism, though priests quoted the Apostles to prove the

---

[1] πεφωτισμένους τοὺς ὀφθαλμοὺς τῆς διανοίας.—Eph. i. 18.
[2] 2 Pet. iii. 15, 16.

duty of passive obedience. A thousand years of papal GALATIANS.
usurpation had been built, like a pyramid upon its apex, on
the inch of argument seized by Romanism in the text "Thou
art Peter, and on this rock will I build my church." But, in
time, by reading the Epistle to the Galatians, a light burst
upon the soul of Luther, and he nailed his theses to the
cathedral door of Wittenberg, and flung the papal bull into
the flames. Every nail he used that day was a nail in the
coffin of tyrannous priestcraft; every flame he kindled that
day was a flame to consume the chaff of false inferences from
false assumptions. What he burnt was the right of designing
tyrannies to build themselves upon isolated texts.

I have said that it was the Epistle to the Galatians which
thus became to Luther a weapon for the emancipation of mankind. He said himself, in his own rough way, "The Epistle
to the Galatians is my epistle. I have betrothed myself to it.
It is my wife." Its very characteristic is that it is the Epistle
of Freedom. In writing it, Paul stood as it were alone upon
a mountain-top, and shouted "Liberty." Eleven times in
these short chapters, and in this connection more often than
in all the other Epistles put together, the thought occurs,
"Stand fast in the liberty wherewith Christ hath made us
free," and "Brethren, ye have been called unto liberty."
"Jerusalem which is above is free, which is the mother of us
all."[1] Those words are the summary and key-note of the
Epistle. "Free from what?" you will ask. Free, I answer,
from all things which enslave the body and the soul; free
from morbid scrupulosities of conscience; free from morbid
anxieties of service; free from the manifold rules of "Touch
not, taste not, handle not;" free from the encroachments of
a spiritual usurpation; free from the strife of contending
sects, which make religion consist of shibboleths or badges;
free from timorous ritualisms and small ceremonial punctu-
alities; free from anything and everything but the law of faith,
the law of grace, the royal law of liberty, the law of those

---

[1] Gal. ii. 4; iii. 28; iv. 22, 23, 26, 30, 31; v. 1, 13.

who are not slaves, but sons; the law which is fulfilled in one word even in this, " Thou shalt love thy neighbour as thyself."

But this freedom is " in Christ." Forty-three times in this Epistle does the name Christ occur, and thirty-nine of these times it is Christ, not "*the* Christ;" Christ the personal name, not Christ the descriptive appellative; Christ the Saviour, the man Christ Jesus.

2. What St. Paul was principally thinking of—the freedom in which, to him, all other freedom was involved—was freedom from Judaism; freedom from the petty and intolerable yoke of circumcision, washings, fasts, feasts, sacrifices, new moons, sabbaths, incessant assemblies, sacerdotal micrology, and all wearing and fretting externalism; freedom from all, save what was of eternal, moral significance in the Mosaic law. Perhaps you may think that it was indeed necessary to deliver Christianity from this yoke, but that now the work is done; so that this Epistle has no longer any concern for us. It is indeed the principal letter against Judaism; but Judaism, you will say, is dead. It was a splendid service to cut Christianity loose from the decaying corpse of obsolete traditions; but it was a service which has for us nothing more than an historical interest. Alas! such a notion is greatly mistaken. Judaism was something more than a dead system; it is a living tendency. There is a Judaism in the secret heart of every one of us, of which we must be aware; and the more you study this Epistle, the more you will recognise that the significance of its teaching is as great for the nineteenth century as for the first. The early Apostles were Jews, all of them circumcised, all of them attending the Temple three times a day, all of them offering sacrifices, and keeping that Levitical law which was indeed necessary, at first for a stiffnecked nation of sensual slaves, who were hankering in their hearts for the specious renewal of Egyptian idolatries under Jewish forms, but which, now that Christ had died, was for the Jews half meaningless, and for the Gentiles wholly pernicious. Christ, in accordance with

the divine economy had not, in so many words, abrogated the Mosaic law; but He had taught spiritual truths which involved the necessity for its abrogation. He had left the consummation of His teaching to that light of God which "shines on patiently and impartially, showing all things in the slow history of their ripening." Now the Law was, as St. Peter said, a yoke, which neither the Jews nor their fathers were able to bear; but the Law alone was as nothing to the mass of infinitesimal minutiae, at once preposterous and puerile, which Scribes, and Rabbis, and Pharisees, had built upon it. By arguments and inferences, and inferences from those arguments, and arguments from these inferences, they, by the spirit which has been the besetting sin of theologian and commentator in all ages, had darkened God's whole heavens with the smoke of an attenuated exegesis which curled " out of the narrow aperture of single texts." Religion is a broad, deep, free, bright, loving, universal spirit: broad as the path of God's commandments, deep as the ocean of His love, free as His common air, bright as His impartial sunshine, loving as His all-embracing mercy, universal as His omnipotent rule. For the centre, and head, and heart of Christianity is Christ, and there was nothing narrow, nothing scholastic, nothing jealously exclusive, in Christ. But, in the craft and subtlety of the devil and man, Religion has ever tended to wither away into Judaism, into Rabbinism, into scholasticism, into ecclesiasticism, into Romanism, into sectarianism, into dead schemes of dogmatic belief, into dead routines of elaborate ceremonial, into dead exclusiveness of party narrowness, into dead theories of scriptural inspiration, into dead formulae of Church parties, into the dead performance of dead works, or the dead assent to dead phrases. Now it was just this fatal tendency of human supineness against which Paul had to contend. Judaic Christians—apparently one man in particular [1]—had come

---

[1] v. 10; St. Paul here speaks of his opponents as οἱ ἀπὸ τῆς 'Ιουδαίας, οἱ ἐκ τῶν Φαρισαίων. The synagogue had, as it were, been honourably buried in the

GALATIANS. from Jerusalem to his fickle and ignorant Galatians with the hard, ready-made Biblical dogma "Unless ye be circumcised, and keep the whole law, ye cannot be saved." [1] They wanted to substitute external badges for inward faith ; legal bondage for Christian freedom ; observance of practices for holiness of heart. They were striving to put the new, rich, fermenting wine of Christianity into their old and bursten wine-skins of Levitism. In their hands, Christianity would have decayed into exclusiveness, self-congratulation, contempt of others, insistence upon the outward, indifference to the essential—a Christianity of the outward platter, a Christianity of the whitened grave. It would be interesting to tell how St. Paul had converted the Galatians, and how and why these formalists and Pharisees had perverted them ; but we can only mention the bare fact. Suffice it that, in order to pervert them, the Judaisers (as at Corinth) had indulged in surreptitious innuendoes against the authority and teaching of St. Paul. Moses, they said, was inspired ; Moses gave the Law at Sinai ; Moses wrote the Holy Book by verbal dictation ; Moses laid down all the rules of Leviticus. Who is this Paul who teaches you that you are free from these things ? What ? deny the inspiration of the Bible ? What ? fly in the face of a divine revelation ? Read for yourselves, they said to the Galatians. The Bible bids you to be circumcised ; the Bible says "Cursed be he that abideth not by all the things written in the book of the law to do them." How dare you disobey Moses and listen to this sceptic, this rationalist, this unorthodox, unsound Paul ? And further than this, they used the two bad arguments of every bad cause— personality and persecution. Paul was not there for them to persecute, but they could abuse him. "He is no Apostle ; he is quite inferior to the Apostles ; he is disobedient to the

Synod at Jerusalem (see Carpzov, *De Synagogâ cum honore sepultâ*, 1716), but these Christian Pharisees were engaged in its resuscitation.

[1] Exactly as the Jew Trypho in Justin Martyr's dialogue (c. viii. p. 226) says "*First be circumcised*, then keep the Sabbaths, and the feasts of the new moons of God, and in a word, do all the things written in the law, and then perhaps (!) you will find mercy from God."

Apostles; he is inconsistent; all Scripture (by which they
meant, *more ecclesiastico*, all their interpretations of Scripture)
is against his views; he is heretical; he is dangerous." So,
blinded by the conceit of ignorance, and the violence of
party, many professing Christians spoke of Christ's saints and
servants then, as many professing Christians speak of Christ's
saints and servants now.

3. St. Paul saw that it was time to speak out, and speak
out he did. The matter at issue was one of vital importance.
The Gospel did not mean that the Gentiles were to be converted into Jews. The essence of the Gospel, the liberty
which Christ had given, the redemption for which He had
died was at stake. The fate of the battle—of the battle of
spirituality against historic tradition—hung apparently upon
his single arm. He alone was the Apostle of the Gentiles.
To him alone had it been granted to see the full bearings of
this question. A new faith must not be choked at its birth
by the past prejudices of its nominal adherents. The hour
had come when concession was no longer possible. It was
necessary to prove once and for ever the falsity of the position
that a man could not become a perfect Christian without
becoming a partial Jew. Accordingly he flung all reticence
and all compromise to the winds. There was in St. Paul
none of that timid pettiness and effeminate conventionality
which has been too often the bane of priests. Hot with
righteous anger he wrote the Epistle to the Galatians. It
was his gage of battle to the incompetence of traditionalism,
his trumpet-note of defiance to the usurpations of Pharisaism;
and it gave no uncertain sound. Against all slavery to the
outward—all reliance on the mechanical—he used words
which were battles. If he had given grounds for the charge
of "inconsistency" by his indifference to trifles, and his
willingness to sacrifice details to principles, there should at
least be no further doubt as to what he meant and taught.
He would leap ashore among his enemies and burn his ships
behind him. He would draw the sword against this false

gospel, and fling away the scabbard. What Luther did at Wittenberg, and at Worms, and at Wartburg, that, and more than that St. Paul did when he wrote the Epistle to the Galatians. It was the manifesto of that spiritual reformation which was involved in the very idea of Christianity. More than any book which was ever written these few pages marked an epoch in history. It was, for the early days of Christianity, the Confession of Augsburg and the Protest of Spires in one. But it was these combined with intense personality and impassioned polemics. His weakness of eyesight usually compelled him to employ an amanuensis ; but in this instance he felt driven, at all costs, to write with his own hand, though it could only be in large, awkward, uneven characters. To the Churches of Galatia he never came again ; but the words scrawled on those few sheets of papyrus were destined to wake echoes which have lived, and shall live for ever and for ever. Savonarola heard them and Wiclif, and Huss, and Luther, and Tyndale, and Wesley. They were the Magna Charta of spiritual emancipation.

4. It requires much thought and study to feel the force and beauty of a letter of which almost every sentence is a thunderbolt, and of which every word, when one understands it, is alive. It has six chapters. Roughly speaking, the first two chapters are an autobiographic retrospect, written to establish his Apostolic independence ; the next two prove the dogmatic position ; the two last are the practical application.

The opening salutation, and the closing words of an Epistle, often furnish us with its main purport. It is so in this instance. "Paul an Apostle—not from men, nor by the instrumentality of any man—but by Jesus Christ, and by God our Father, and all the brethren with me" (for he writes from Corinth, where he had many with him[1]) "to the churches of Galatia.[2] Grace to you and peace from God the

---

[1] Timothy, Gaius of Derbe, Aristarchus, Trophimus, Titus, Justus, Sosthenes, &c.

[2] The separate nationality of the Churches of Galatia bound them very

Father, and our Lord Jesus Christ, who gave Himself for our
sins that He may deliver us from this present evil world."
Notice, first, the stern compression of the salutation. It is
not, as in other Epistles, to "the beloved of God;" not to
"the saints in Christ Jesus;" not to "the saints and faithful
brethren;" but, in his impetuous desire to deal at once with
their errors, simply "to the Churches of Galatia." Notice
too, the emphatic assertion of his Apostolate, as though he
had said, "Speak not to me of the authority of James, or of
the Twelve—the 'super-exalted Apostles' of your Judaic
seducers[1]—I am not responsible to them. I owe to them no
allegiance. My commission is not through them, but direct
from Christ.[2] Then notice, thirdly, how he strikes the key-
note of the Epistle in the word "deliver."[3] Your circumcisions,
and your Judaisms are vain. In Christ alone—only by faith
in Him—does salvation come.

Then, without a word of the thanksgiving which is found
in every other Epistle, he bursts, with startling abruptness,
into the subject of which his mind is so indignantly full. "I
am amazed that you are so quickly shifting from the grace of
Christ into a different Gospel." The very word "shifting"
may perhaps, as Jerome says, be a sharp paronomasia—a
reference to their name Galatae, as though it were derived
from a Hebrew word meaning "to move." "Your *galatising*"

closely into one community. Bleek, *Einleit.* 5, 155. The Church was composed both of Jews (iii. 13, 23, 25; iv. 3, 5) and Gentiles (iii. 29; iv. 8, 12,
17, 21; v. 2; vi. 12).

[1] Acts xv. 24, τινὲς ἐξ ἡμῶν ἐξελθόντες . . . ἀνασκευάζοντες τὰς ψυχὰς ὑμῶν
. . . ἃς οὐ διεστειλάμεθα.

[2] A candid reader can hardly fail to see that St. Paul writes almost in a
tone of irritation at the use made of the names of the Twelve to disparage
himself. Otherwise he would hardly have invented and used twice over, the
strange and ironical phrase, οἱ ὑπερλίαν ἀπόστολοι, "the out-and-out," or
"over-exceedingly" Apostles. He was a man of like passions with ourselves,
and even our Lord's example shows that "the spirit of meekness" must
sometimes give place to indignation. There was scarcely a Church apparently
which Paul founded with such infinite toil and peril, into which these easy
and comfortable missionaries, with their exalted pretensions, did not thrust
themselves. But we must bear in mind that when they had unwarrantably
used the names of James and of the Twelve at Antioch they had been *expressly
repudiated* by those Apostles in the synodical letter from Jerusalem.

[3] Gal. i. ὅπως ἐξέληται ἡμᾶς. See Bishop Lightfoot, *ad. loc.*

GALATIANS.   is but too like your name.[1] Your Jewish teachers have told
you that I am shifty and inconsistent; that I try to please
men. The blame applies to you rather than to me. But no
one shall at any rate mistake what I now say, which is, that
if man or angel preach a different gospel, let him be
anathema—let the ban fall on him. Is that clear? If not I
repeat again, "Let him be anathema."[2] He then plunges to
the end of the second chapter into a personal narrative, to
prove the absolute independence of his own authority. He
proves it negatively by showing, from his education and
conversion, how small had been his intercourse with any of
the Apostles. He proves it positively, by showing that the
Apostles had been compelled by facts to recognise his
mission; and that, on one very memorable occasion, he
had, before the whole Church[3] withstood and condemned
Peter to his face, and proved to him that if the works of the
law were necessary, then Christ had died in vain.

5. He then turns, in the third chapter, from personal self-
defence to the defence of the truth he had preached. He
shows them that their new ceremonialism, so far from being

---

[1] Μετατίθεσθε, Gal. i. 6. Jerome thinks that St. Paul mentally connected
Galatae with בֹּלָל. If so, there is an indignant play on the name as though
it implied inherent fickleness. St. Paul insists that the teachings of the
Judaists do not constitute a mere subordinate school of thought. It is not merely
"another" (ἄλλο) but a "*different*" Gospel (ἕτερον).

[2] St. Paul's impetuosity of feeling is here indicated, not only by the emphatic repetition of ἀνάθεμα ἔστω, as though he were determined that there
should be no mistake about it ; but also by the way in which he almost passes
an anathema on an imaginary angel. We must remember that in spite of all
he had endured (ἔτι) St. Paul had been accused of complaisance (i. 10), and
even that his truthfulness had been called in question (i. 20). His enemies
had represented him as a sort of ecclesiastical demagogue (1 Thess. ii. 4-6)
serving no ends but his own and Satan's.

[3] This was an offence for which the Ebionites never forgave St. Paul. "If
you call me flagrantly in the wrong, (κατεγνωσμένον)," says St. Peter (Ps. Clem.
Hom. xvii. 19), "you accuse God who revealed Christ to me." The *Praedicatio
Petri* says that the two Apostles were not reconciled till death. Even the
fathers tried to explain away the passage. Origen (*ap.* Jer. *Ep.* cxii.), Chrysostom, and (at first) Jerome treated it as a pre-arranged scheme between the
Apostles (κατὰ σχῆμα) ; and Clemens of Alexandria (*ap.* Euseb. *H.E.* i. 12)
tries to make out that Kephas does not mean St. Peter. St. Peter's weakness
bore other bitter fruit, long years afterwards. It was one ultimate cause of
Ebionite attacks on St. Paul ; of Gnostic attacks on Judaism ; of Porphyry's
slanders against the Apostles (comp. Celsus *ap.* Orig. v. 64) ; and of Jerome's
quarrel with Augustine (see Lightfoot, pp. 123-126).

an advance, was a mere retrogression. It was a retrogression
from the spirit to the flesh, from faith to works, from the
Gospel to the law, from the eternal to the transient, from
Christian manhood to childish tutelage. "Dull Galatians!
who bewitched you with his evil eye?—you, before whose
eyes Jesus Christ crucified was conspicuously painted." I
held up before you a banner, as it were, blazoned with the
Cross of Christ;[1] and lo! under some strange sorcery of
sinister influence, you are apostatizing to Judaic rituals!
And then, throughout these two chapters, he proceeds to
show them that the law of which they boasted so much, on
which they relied so much, really placed them under the
curse which it had itself pronounced on its imperfect fulfilment; that the promise to the faith of Abraham preceded the
Law; that the Law—so far from being supreme and final—
had a mere pedagogic function for those in an inferior condition; that it was meant only to be "an usher to Christ"
(iii. 24),[2] meant to educate men into the sense of their own
sinfulness and helplessness, and thus lead them to Christ. So
far from being permanent and perfect, the Law was but
supplementary,[3] parenthetical,[4] provisional,[5] mediate;[6] a
means not an end; a relative purpose of God taken up
and lost in His absolute purpose; a training for infants; a
harsh incident in a necessary tutelage; a fetter for slaves who

---

[1] Just as Augustine of Canterbury, with his monks, carried an embroidered
banner with the monogram of Christ when they came before King Ethelbert.

[2] St. Paul puts the Promise to Abraham in all respects above the Law, and
indeed regards it as an anticipated Gospel (iii. 14–18). The difficult verse
iii. 16 seems merely to be a specimen of what the Rabbis would have called
sôd, the *mystic* explanation of Scripture. St. Paul says that the word "seed"
(σπέρμα) is a singular and collective term, and points to Christ. It is true
that to use either the Hebrew *Zeraim* or the Greek σπέρματα for "offspring"
would be a barbarism, for either plural could only mean "kinds of grain" as
St. Paul was perfectly aware (1 Cor. xv. 38). But the illustration (it is no
more, comp. Rom. iv. 13-18) depends on the fact that the collective singular
term (*Zerah*, σπέρμα) was used in Genesis, and not "sons" or "children."

[3] ἐπιδιατάσσεται, iii. 14 ; προσετέθη, iii. 19.

[4] παρεισῆλθεν, Rom. v. 20.

[5] τῶν παραβάσεων χάριν, ἄχρις οὖ κ.τ.λ. iii. 19. This passage requires
Rom. vii. 7-13 for its comment.

[6] Given mediately by Angels, not by God (Deut. xxxiii. 2, &c.); and
received mediately from Moses, not direct from God.

had to be educated into a yearning for liberty.[1] They must choose between Christ and the Law. If the Law sufficed, Christ had died in vain. If Christ sufficed, the Law was needless. And then, with many a tender reproach and appeal, he adopts the Rabbinic fashion of exegesis, in which he had been trained, and proves by the allegory of Sarah and Agar[2] that we are no longer slaves but sons; that the physical seed of Abraham may be the spiritual seed of Ishmael; that circumcision may in God's sight be uncircumcision, and uncircumcision the only true circumcision;[3] that the actual Jew may be in God's sight the Gentile, and the actual Gentile the spiritual Jew. And all this, remember, he had the daring to urge at a time when Judaism was growing ever narrower and narrower in its haughty exclusiveness; ever more and more damnatory in its rigid demands; ever more and more idolatrous of its deified Law. Imagine the feelings of a prejudiced Jew, who should thus hear one of his own blood arguing that his prized nomocracy was valueless; that his haughty particularism was usurpation; that his Levitic law consisted of " weak and beggarly elements; "[4] that, in them-

---

[1] It is here that we have the famous verse, " Now a mediator is not a mediator of one; but God is one " (iii. 20), with its "300 different explanations." This diversity of interpretation arises from isolating the words from their context, and mistaking the simple meanings of " mediator " and " one." The obvious, and now generally-accepted meaning of the passage seems to be—the Promise to Abraham is not only *antecedent* to the Law of Moses, but intrinsically *above* it. The Law is of the nature of a contract which requires *two* contracting parties; but in the promise God *stood alone*, and no " mediator " (no intermediate agency like that of Moses or the Angels) was necessary.

[2] But the immense superiority of St. Paul's allegorising over that of Philo is shown by his plain acceptance of the literal history in which he traces a divine law. He does not with Philo make Abraham a symbol of " the soul," Sarah of " Divine Wisdom; " Isaac of " Human Wisdom; " Ishmael of " Sophistry," &c.

[3] It was all the more necessary for St. Paul to speak thus plainly because his opponents (owing to his circumcision of Timothy, and as I believe, of Titus also), had taunted him with having himself, at one time, preached circumcision (v. 11). Similarly in Ps. Clement (*Hom.* ii. p. 3), St. Peter charges " the enemy " (*i.e.* St. Paul) with having represented *him* as preaching the abolition of the Law.

[4] iv. 3, 9. The word $\sigma\tau\text{οιχεῖα}$ either means " rudiments " the A B C of religion ; or " physical elements" material and sensuous symbols invested with religious significance.

selves, his ritualisms were as unavailing as the ritualisms of
heathendom; that his vaunted circumcision was now as
useless and as indefensible as the ghastlier concisions of the
Priests of Dindymus.[1] To the bigoted few every one of these
propositions would seem to be a startling and offensive
paradox. It requires no small knowledge of history fully to
realise the splendid originality, the superb courage, required
for the enunciation of such opinions. And let us never forget
that, as St. Paul differed from all other saints and martyrs in
the intensity and prolongation of his sufferings, so too did he
differ from them in being not only an heroic sufferer, but a
man of such fearless and leading genius as the world has
rarely seen. But he knew what he was doing. He had fully
counted the cost. His enemies charged him with hunting
for popularity by suppressing his real convictions. "Am I
now seeking to please men?" he asks (i. 10) He might
have said with Luther, "In former days I used to be most
safe. Now I have loaded myself with the hatred of all the
world."[2]

6. From these personal and doctrinal sections he passes to
the practical part of the letter. The two last chapters are
rich in counsel, as are all similar parts of St. Paul's teaching.
Here you have the law of Christian love; the works of the
flesh, and the fruit of the Spirit; the duty of meek forgiveness,

[1] Nothing would have been more exasperating to the Judaisers than this
suggested analogy between *their* ceremonies and those of heathendom. But,
as Hausrath points out (*N. Zeitg.* ii. 268), St. Paul at least seems to *imply*
that there is no *essential* difference between observing the new moon in the
synagogue, and observing it in the temple of Mên; between living in
booths in autumn, or wailing for Altis in spring; between circumcision and
the self-mutilation of the Galli. Nearly all critics are now agreed that
Ὄφελον καὶ ἀποκόψονται in v. 12 means "since they attach so much importance
to circumcision, would that they would go a little further and make eunuchs
of themselves altogether." (Comp. ἀποκεκομμένοι, Deut. xxiii. 1.) Reuss calls
this "*une phrase affreuse qui revolte notre sentiment.*" But Paul says elsewhere
that "circumcision" would be to the Gentiles a mere "*concision,*" a mere
"cutting the flesh" (Phil. iii. 2, 3), and we must not judge a writer by the
taste of nearly two millenniums later. What modern feeling would stigmatise
as coarse, ancient feeling would accept as justifiable plain-speaking.
[2] Luther went through the same experiences as St. Paul. "Ministerium
Ecclesiæ," he adds, "omnibus periculis expositum est; diaboli insultationibus,
mundi ingratitudini, sectarum blasphemiis."—*Colloq.* i. 13.

GALATIANS. the noble rule "bear ye the burdens (βάρη)" of one another's cares and weaknesses; the solemn warning "each one shall bear his own load (φορτίον)" of moral responsibility; lastly, the unchangeable duties of liberal generosity,—"While we have time let us do good unto all men, but especially to them that are of the household of faith."

Then came the conclusion, "Look at the large letters in which I have written to you with my own hand:"[1] the polemical summary of what he had been teaching—that circumcision is nothing (vi. 12-15); the doctrinal thesis that Christ is all in all (14—16); the flash of personal feeling, "Henceforth let no man trouble me, for I bear in triumph on my body the brand-marks of Jesus"[2]—the brands which mark me as his deserter, his recruit, his slave. What he means the Galatians to understand is that as the Hieroduli in many heathen temples, and the priests of Mithras and the Pessinuntian goddess were branded with physical marks, so he too was branded for the sacred service of Christ his Lord. Then he adds the last word of peace and love, "The grace of our Lord Jesus Christ be with your spirit, brethren.[3] Amen."

7. Notice, in conclusion, the historic importance of the letter, and its practical significance.

i. Its historic importance. It did a work once and for all time. It put an end to the circumcision party and the circumcision controversy.[4] It showed that if a man wanted

---

[1] The size of the scrawled uneven letters was probably due to the painfulness of the effort to write. Many congruent circumstances besides the Apostle's habitual use of an amanuensis tend to prove that he suffered from shortsightedness and probably from ophthalmia.

[2] τὰ στίγματα τοῦ Ἰησοῦ. "Stigmata" were brands generally inflicted as a punishment on slaves. Hence *stigmatias* means "a rascal." Brands might be marked either on a slave; a Hierodoulos (Herod. ii. 113); a deserter; or a recruit (Rönsch. *Das N. T.*, *Tertullian*, p. 700). Hence for the first time in Rom. i. 1, as in later Epistles (Phil. Tit.) St. Paul calls himself "a *slave* of Jesus Christ." Justified by faith in Christianity he has been sanctified by crucifixion with Christ to the world.

[3] The deeply-moved tenderness of the Apostle breaks out in the unusual addition of the word "brethren." We notice as the Epistle advances a growing mildness of tone towards the community (iv. 12-20), but a deepening indignation towards their perverters (v. 7-12, vi. 12, 13).

[4] οἱ περιτεμνόμενοι (vi. 13).

to be a Christian, he must give up all reliance on exclusive-ness and on externalism. The very inmost spirit of Chris-tianity is comprehensive, not exclusive; spiritual, not external; catholic, not sectarian; tolerant, not partisan. A Christian must rely, not on dogmas, not on observances, not on works of any kind, but on Christ alone. This letter was the death-blow of that Judaic tyranny which is constantly endeavouring to reassert itself over Christian freedom. It was the proof for ever that the spirit of faithful godliness is the spirit not of the slave, but of the son. "Judaism was the narrowest (*i.e.* the most special) of religions; Christianity was the most human and all-embracing. In a few years the latter was evolved out of the former, taking all the intensity of its fore-runner, with none of its limitations." Without St. Paul's Epistles, and especially the Epistle to Galatians, to show us how the chasm was bridged "the change would seem as violent and inconceivable as a convulsion which should mingle the Jordan and the Tiber." By the Epistle to the Galatians Paul was God's great instrument for saving Christianity from being stifled at its birth by theories and rituals. It ranks him among the greatest liberators of mankind. It places him at the head of those saints of God who, in differing tones, have, in all great ages, proclaimed the same great truth, that God is love; and that what He wants of us is neither metaphysical theology, nor elaborate ritual, nor ascetic practices, but love to Him our Father in Christ Jesus, and love for His sake to our brother man :—

> "Of all the truths that from Thee shine,
> Lord, Thy philanthropy divine
> Next to my heart still lies,
> And turns my spiritual eyes
> From all ill-natured schemes designed
> To bound what Thou hast to no bounds confined."

ii. And as to the practical meaning of the Epistle, may it not teach us, if we study it aright, what religion is, and what it is not? It is not to wash the cup and the platter. It is not to wear the broad phylacteries of profession. It is not to go to any number of services, or to partake of any number of fasting communions. It is not to have shibboleths upon the lips, or to be the fuglemen of parties, or to condemn our neighbours because they think otherwise than we, or to look askance at every little deviation from our own particular orthodoxy, or to call ourselves by party names, or to rush into current controversies, or to repeat " Lord, Lord," or to say or do many other things which popular religionism requires as tests. It is a much harder, and rarer, and fairer, and sweeter thing than these. It is to love the Lord Jesus Christ in sincerity and truth, and to love one another as He gave us commandment. It is to love God with all our heart, and our neighbour as ourselves. It is to walk in the Spirit, so that we cannot fulfil the lusts of the flesh. It is to pray with humblest sincerity, and try to live in accordance with our prayers. It is to be, to the utmost of our power, gentle, forgiving, generous, brave, pure, as Jesus was. It is to be fearlessly and faithfully true to the best we know. It is, as St. Paul says, " the end of the commandment," which is charity out of a pure heart, and of a good conscience, and of faith unfeigned. " For " (in the closing words of this Epistle) " in Christ Jesus neither circumcision availeth anything, nor uncircumcision, but a new creature; and, a? many as walk according to this rule, peace be on them, and mercy, and upon the Israel of God."

NOTE I.

OUTLINE OF THE EPISTLE.

It falls into three marked divisions,

I. Personal.
II. Doctrinal.
III. Practical.

I. PERSONAL.

1. Greeting (i. 1-5).
2. Instead of the thanksgiving a complaint of their fickleness (i. 6-10).
3. A vindication of his personal independence and authority.
   i. *Negatively.* He was an Apostle before he had any intercourse with the Twelve (i. 11-24).
   ii. *Positively.* (a) The Twelve had acknowledged his equal mission (ii. 1-10) ; and
   (β) He had openly withstood Peter at Antioch (ii. 11-21) ; including his argument against St. Peter's conduct in holding aloof from the Gentiles.

II. DOCTRINAL.

Our justification by faith not by external observances as proved
(a) By the Christian consciousness (iii. 1-5).
(β) By the Old Testament (iii. 6-18).

Hence the true position of the Law is shown to be secondary.
(a) *Objectively.* By the very nature and universality of Christianity (iii. 19-29).
(β) *Subjectively.* By the free spiritual life of Christianity (iv. 1-18).
(γ) After affectionate warnings against those by whom they had been misled, he illustrates his arguments by the allegory of Sarah and Agar (iv. 11-30).

III. PRACTICAL.

(a) The nature of Christian Freedom (v. 1-12).
(β) Warnings against its abuse, both general (13-18) and special (v. 19-vi. 10).

Closing summary of his main theses (ii. 17), polemical (12-13), personal (14-17), and doctrinal (15-16). Blessing (18).

The letter contains the germ of the Theological system which St. Paul develops more fully in the Epistle to the Romans.

Bengel calls ii. 19-21 "*Summa ac medulla Christianismi*" ; and of v. 1-6, he says, "In these stands all Christianity."

THE EPISTLE TO THE ROMANS.

WRITTEN AT CORINTH, A.D. 58.

"First of all (he wrote) to the Corinthians forbidding schismatic factiousness; to the Galatians forbidding circumcision; but to the Romans at greater length, according to the general tenor of the Scriptures (? ordine Scripturarum), but showing that the foundation of the Scriptures is Christ."—MURATORIAN FRAGMENT.

"Tota illa Epistola meo judicio totius sacrae Scripturae tum commentarius, tum epitome, immo lux et Apocalypsis."—LUTHER.

"Christus in homine ubi fides in corde."—S. AUG.

"But to the Cross He nails thy enemies,
The law that is against thee, and the sins
Of all mankind; with Him these are crucified
Never to hurt them more who rightly trust
In this His satisfaction."—MILTON, *Par. Lost*, xii.

"Justification and sanctification cohere, but they are not one and the same. It is faith alone which justifies, and yet the faith which justifies is not alone; just as it is the heat alone of the sun which warms the earth, and yet in the sun it is not alone, because it is always conjoined with light."—CALVIN.

"The righteousness wherewith we shall be clothed in the world to come is both perfect and inherent; that whereby we are justified is perfect but not inherent; that whereby we are sanctified inherent but not perfect."—HOOKER.

"Faith doth not shut out repentance, hope, love, dread, and the fear of God, to be joined with faith in every man that is justified; but it shutteth them out from the office of justifying."—*Homily of Salvation*, p. ii.

INTRODUCTORY.

JEWS had been introduced into Rome in large numbers by Pompeius the Great (B.C. 63), and soon began to multiply and flourish. Augustus, influenced by friendship for the first Herod, had improved their condition, and assigned them the quarter of Rome beyond the Tiber, which they have occupied for ages.[1] They were always hated with the deep hatred which it has too often been their lot to inspire.[2] Sejanus, the bad minister of Tiberius, tried to get rid of them.[3] Claudius, when quarrels arose between them and the Christians, passed a futile decree for their banishment.[4] But they had established themselves too strongly to be repressed, and when the letter to the Romans was written in A.D. 58 they were a large and powerful community.

Christianity was early introduced into Rome. Although even when this letter was written the Church presents but few traces of organisation. Neither the Church as a whole nor bishops nor deacons are mentioned, and it is even possible that the Jews and Gentiles met under different presbyters in different houses. In the Neronian persecution, A.D. 64, the Christian martyrs formed (as Tacitus says) "a great multitude." The first chance seeds of Christianity may have been wafted to Italy by the Jews and proselytes from Rome who heard St. Peter on the day of Pentecost,[5] or by those who had listened to St. Stephen in the synagogue of the Libertini.[6] Probably the early Christian Church at Rome thus casually founded, was without any very regular organisation, for of any such constitution this Epistle offers no trace. It was composed of both Jewish and Gentile elements, who may possibly have met in separate communities. We can hardly say which element preponderated.[7] St. Paul seems to address both. In xi. 13, he says, "I speak unto you Gentiles," and yet, in vii. 1, he says, "I speak to them that know the law." In i. 6-13, xv. 15, 16, he writes as an

---

[1] Jos. *Antt.* xiv. 4, §§ 1–5 ; β, α, i. 6, § 9, Cic. *pro Flacco*, xxviii. Tac. *Hist.* v. 9 ; Plutarch, *Pompeius*, xxxix.; Orosius, vi. 6, &c.

[2] See *Seekers after God*, p. 168. Mart. *Epp.* i. 42, 109 ; vi. 93, &c. Juv. *Sat.* xiv. 96, 134, 186, 201 ; iii. 14, 296 ; vi. 542 ; Peri. v. 184, &c.

[3] Tac. *Ann.* ii. 85 ; Sueton. *Tit.* 36 ; Jos. *Antt.* xviii. 3, § 5.

[4] Acts xviii. 2 ; Suet. *Claud.* 25 ; "impulsore *Chresto* tumultuantes."

[5] Acts ii. 9. [6] Acts vi. 9.

[7] Hence Neander, Meyer, De Wette, Olshausen, Tholuck, Reuss, &c., say that the letter was mainly addressed to Gentiles ; Baur, Schwegler, Thiersch, Davidson, Wordsworth, &c., to Jews.

ROMANS. Apostle of the Gentiles; in x. 1, he speaks of the Jews in the third person (ὑπὲρ αὐτῶν "for them," not, as in the received text, "for Israel"), and in ix.—xi. he is not so much addressing the Jews as arguing about them. In the later chapters he seems to be addressing Gentiles of liberal views. On the other hand, in iv. 1, he speaks of "Abraham our father;" he assumes that his readers have an intimate knowledge of the Old Testament, and he says that he is writing "to them that know the law;" and in ii. 17-24, he speaks directly to Jews. Tregelles points out that there are more quotations from the Old Testament in this letter than in all the rest put together. The reconciliation of these apparent contradictions lies in the fact that the nucleus of the Church was Jewish, and that even the Gentiles were mainly proselytes who at Rome were very numerous.[1]

The Church of Rome claims St. Peter as its actual founder. For that claim there is not only no historic evidence, but such evidence as we have, and, indeed, the whole tenor of this letter, as well as of the Acts of the Apostles, point the other way. Early Church tradition is indeed almost unanimous in asserting that St. Peter was *martyred* at Rome, but his visit to the city probably did not long precede his death. If there were two branches of the Romish Church, one Jewish and one Gentile, each with its own bishops or presbyters, it is quite possible that the Jewish section should have regarded St. Peter as its head.

Further, it may now be regarded as highly probable that while this letter was primarily intended for the Christians at Rome it was at the same time an encyclical letter, which was sent with varying terminations to other Churches such as those of Ephesus and Thessalonica.

St. Paul writes as a stranger to strangers. He has no

---

[1] Tac. *Hist.* v. 5 ; Seneca, ap. Aug. *De Civ. Dei,* vii. 11. The fact is proved by old inscriptions in the Jewish cemeteries, "Die römische Christengemeinde, judenchristlich-essenischen Stammes, aber schon damals durch Heidenchristen, auch paulinisch gesinnte, vermehrt, hat die umfassendste Darlegung der paulinischen Lehre erhalten."—HILGENFELD.

known or avowed antagonist among the Roman Christians; he could therefore enter with perfect calmness and lucidity upon this systematic exposition of the specifically Pauline Gospel. The tone of the Epistle is essentially conciliatory, and this conciliatory spirit is reflected in the "not only but also," of iv. 16. He speaks both of the Jews and of the Law in a tone far more tender than in other Epistles.[1]

He writes in Greek, because Greek was universally understood among the half-foreign poorer classes of the imperial city.[2] Ignatius, Dionysius of Corinth, Irenaeus, Justin Martyr, Clement, Hermas. all wrote in Greek for Roman Christians. All writers agree in recognising the greatness of the Epistle. Calvin said that "every Christian man should feed upon it as the daily bread of his soul." Luther calls it "the chief book of the New Testament, and the purest Gospel." Melanchthon made it the basis of the first scientific treatise of Reformation theology—the *Loci Communis*, 1521. Coleridge calls it "the profoundest book in existence." Meyer, "the greatest and richest of all the apostolic works." Tholuck, "a Christian philosophy of human history." Godet, "the cathedral of the Christian Faith." According to Melanchthon, De Wette, and others, it was meant to be *didactic*—a compendium of Pauline dogma in the form of an apostolic letter—a system of dogmatic theology. This view is in any case too broad. The letter contains an exposition of the doctrines of sin and salvation *Hamartiology, Soteriology)*, but it contains none of the eschatology of the Epistles to the Thessalonians, or of the specific Christology of Ephesians and Colossians.

According to Mangold and others it was meant to be apologetic—a defence of his Apostolate, his general preaching,

---

[1] Compare Rom. iv. 16 ; xi. 26 ; with Gal. iv. 3 ; 2 Cor. iii. 6 ; 1 Thess. iv. 14–16.

[2] "Latin Christianity was born in Africa, not in Italy, and its first eminent writer was Tertullian."—FRASER. Even in writing to Rome, St. Paul classifies mankind as "Greeks and barbarians" (i. 14), and "Jews and Greeks" (i. 16, ii. 9 &c.) "The Churches of the west," says Milman, "were Greek religious colonies. Their language was Greek, their organisation Greek, their orders Greek."

and of his missionary labours. The letter itself shows that this is at the best an exceedingly partial view of the Apostle's aim in writing it. According to Baur and others it is *polemical*, and intended to counteract anti-Pauline tendencies among the Jewish Christians. This view again is too purely historical. It regards chapters ix.-xi. as the pith and kernel of the whole letter; and the whole dogmatic treatment of the Epistle as meant to be "nothing but the most radical and thoroughgoing refutation of Judaism and Jewish Christianity."

The true view perhaps is that the Apostle, after the establishment of his authority at Corinth, began to look westwards, and used an interval of unwonted calm to prepare the way for his missionary labours at Rome. His thoughts were still occupied with the truths of Christian freedom and the universality of the Gospel, which he had maintained against the Judaisers of Galatia, and he wished to prove that Christ was the Messiah of the Gentiles no less than of the Jews. The Gentiles were pressing far more eagerly than the Jews into the Church of Christ (ix. 1; x. 3). Was God then rejecting Israel? His answer to that solemn question was, (1) that spiritual worship does not depend on natural descent, and that justification by faith is equally open to the Gentile and the Jew (ix.); that (2) the Jews are not the rejected but the rejectors (x.); but that (3) the rejection is (*a*) only partial, not absolute; and (*β*) only temporary, not final (xi.).

But if these were the thoughts with which perhaps the Apostle started,[1] he worked backwards from them to thoughts to which he here first gives full and formal expression. He passes from the relative to the absolute; from the abolition of exclusive privileges to God's plan for universal salvation. That plan is "Justification by Faith." In order to prove it

[1] This view was first suggested by Baur (*Paulus*, i. 310), and though it has been keenly criticised by Schott and others still seems to me inherently probable. Baur and Volkmar, however, adopt too exclusively the view that it was mainly addressed to Jewish Christians (see i. 13). The ascetics alluded to in xiv. 2-21 seem to have shared the views of the Therapeutæ (Philo, *Vit. Contemp.* iv.).

St. Paul has to show that neither Jew nor Gentile can attain salvation by any law of works, and that Christ is the only common foundation, the bond of all human society, the root of all human righteousness. The thought which runs through the whole Epistle is the universality of sin, and the universality of grace.

Its four main positions are :

1. All are guilty before God.
2. All need a Saviour.
3. Christ died for all.
4. We are all one body in Him.[1]

The fundamental theme of the Epistle is in 1. 16, 17. We are there told that the Gospel is a progressive manifestation to the world that God's inherent righteousness may become man's justification. By accepting the reconciliation to God offered to us by the death of Christ man may attain salvation. His trustful acceptance of Christ passes into mystic union with Christ, and this is life. Justification becomes sanctification ; faith passes into faithfulness ; and this is an earnest of future glory.

Thus the Epistle to the Romans is St. Paul's Homily of the Salvation of Mankind.

Some leading words in the Epistle :

" *All* " ($\pi \hat{a} s$). Free Salvation *offered* to all, because *needed* by all.

Imputing ($\lambda o \gamma i \zeta o \mu a \iota$). The word occurs ten times in the fourth chapter alone.

Righteousness, Δικαιοσύνη ($\delta \iota \kappa a \iota \delta \omega$, $\delta \iota \kappa a \iota \omega \mu a$, $\delta \iota \kappa \eta$). God's inherent righteousness becoming man's justification ; the new relation of reconcilement between God and man. The righteousness of God, not the righteousness of the law.

God forbid ! ($\mu \dot{\eta} \gamma \acute{\epsilon} \nu o \iota \tau o$). The *horror naturalis* which rejects false inferences from accepted theses (ten times, iii. 4, 6, 31 ; vi. 2, 15 ; vii. 7, 13 ; ix. 14 ; xi. 1, 11. Elsewhere only in 1 Cor. vi. 11, Gal. ii. 17, iii. 21).

---

[1] Bishop Wordsworth, *Epistles*, p. 200.

Leading thought :

" The just shall live by faith."

The verse has already been quoted by St. Paul in Gal. iii. 11. In the LXX. it is " the just shall live by my faith " (ἐκ πίστεως μου) in some MSS. In its original context, the verse meant " the just man shall live (*i.e.* shall be delivered from peril) by his fidelity ; " but St. Paul reads a deeper meaning into " faith " and " live." Habakkuk ends where Paul begins.

The religious history of man may be regarded objectively and historically under four phases :

1. The Sin of Adam. 2. The Promise to Abraham. 3. The Law of Moses. 4. The Redemption of Christ.

And subjectively and individually in four phases :

1. Relative innocence.   2. Awakened consciousness. 3. Imputable transgression. 4. Free justification.

EPISTLE TO THE ROMANS.

" How then can man be justified with God ? "—JOB XXV. 4.
" The just shall live by faith."—HAB. ii. 4, and ROM. i. 17 ; GAL. iii. 11 ; HEB. X. 38.

1. THIS text of Job asks a question to which in those memorable **six** words which occur in four places of Scripture the Prophet and the Apostles furnish the answer.

St. Paul's visit to Corinth seems to have been so far successful that he triumphantly re-established that apostolic authority which had been so rudely impugned.   Towards the close of his few months in this city, having cowed by his presence a factious opposition, he seems to have enjoyed one of those brief but bright interspaces of repose and calm which occur in even the most troubled life.   It was at Corinth that

he had received the news from Galatia which called forth the
burning letter to the waverers of that unstable Church; and
his mind naturally continued to work on the great problems
of the relation of the Law to the Gospel, of Judaism to
Christianity, of faith to works, on which he had been forced
to speak. His thoughts were now turned to Rome, because,
after one more visit to Jerusalem, he meant to stop at the
Imperial City on his way to Spain. It was only too probable
that the Roman Christians would have heard false or distorted
views of him and of his teaching, and he was therefore
anxious, before visiting them in person, to let them know
what his teaching really was. But he was able to tell them
this calmly and fully as a great logical whole. There was no
need for the fiery outbursts of indignation which had marked
his Epistle to the Galatians, for he was writing to a stranger
Church, in which he was not called upon to deal with special
opponents. Hence it was evidently in a peaceful mood that
he dictated to Tertius this inestimable treatise of Christian
theology.[1] In this Epistle, more systematically than in any
other, he gives a lucid and closely-reasoned statement of what
he calls "his Gospel":[2] the special aspect of that mystery
which he was commissioned to reveal. More fully, therefore,
and less polemically than in the Epistle to the Galatians he
here invites an ideal reader to follow him in the discussion
of great abstract truths, and those truths are nothing less
than what may be called the philosophy of the plan of salvation. Phoebe, the humble deaconess of Cenchrea, when she
conveyed this letter to Rome or to Ephesus, was carrying under
the folds of her robe, "the whole future of Christian theology."
Such a statement of his teaching by the Apostle himself was
supremely necessary. Both his social position in the Church
and his theological views were greatly open to attack. He
was not one of the Twelve. He had never been a personal

---

[1] The date of the Epistle, written from Corinth a little before Easter, A.D.
58, appears by comparing Acts xix. 21; xx. 3, 6, 16, with Rom. xv. 25-28 or
1 Cor. xvi. 1-5, 2 Cor. viii. 1-4.
[2] Rom. ii. 16; xvi. 25; Gal. ii. 2; 1 Cor. xv. 1.

disciple of Christ. He was looked on, if not with suspicion yet without cordiality, by many prominent members of the mother Church in Jerusalem. Unfavourable remarks about his aims and his character were freely disseminated. Hence in the Epistles to the Thessalonians and Corinthians he had been compelled to vindicate his character, and in that to the Galatians to establish his independent authority. This was the easier part of his task, and it had been already accomplished. To those who had any further doubts on the subject it was sufficient to reply that his Apostolic rank and mission had in the synod at Jerusalem been fully acknowledged by the Twelve themselves. It was far more difficult to establish dialectically the theological opinions at which he had himself arrived by processes quite different. Our Lord had not openly abrogated the Law. Nay, more, some of His deep sayings were quoted to maintain its eternal validity. St. Paul appealed to visions and revelations, but his opponents asserted that these could only be dubious; or, at the best, that they could only serve to ratify his convictions for himself individually. Both St. Paul and his opponents appealed to the Old Testament; but the letter of the Pentateuch seemed to be indisputably in favour of the literalists, and his attempt to read new and opposite meanings into the old revelations appeared to all bigoted Judaists as so much sophistry. They looked upon it as " the most bare-faced denial of the Divine Word in the Old Testament, which only in mockery could parade itself as a deeper under-standing of that Divine Word itself." [1] To them he appeared as " one who did not believe in the Bible," and " flew in the face of inspired authority."

Further than this, the old narrow traditional school sincerely regarded St. Paul's "innovations" as being morally dangerous, and that in a high degree. To them he seemed to be throwing down all religious barriers and opening the door to antinomianism. Their moral sense was utterly shocked by

[1] Prof. Lipsius, *Protestantenbibel.*

the notion that their divine and cherished law was only given "to multiply transgressions." They looked on St. Paul's teaching as nothing short of scandalous.

And yet, because he loved them, because the letter killeth and the spirit quickeneth, because his heart was full of courage, and his soul of spiritual illumination, he was able in the Epistle to the Romans to develop his peculiar Gospel with such power as to get rid of all objections and to carry with him the grateful assent and conviction of the universal Church.

2. In the few words of introduction I have touched on the origin of Christianity in Rome, on the share which St. Peter may or may not have had in preaching it, and on the question whether the Church was predominantly Jewish or Gentile. We will now take the Epistle as it is, and try to grasp its central idea. We have already seen that critics differ as to its main purpose; but whatever else it may be, it is unquestionably the clearest and fullest statement of the doctrine of sin and the doctrine of deliverance as held by the greatest of the Apostles. It is St. Paul's definition of what he understood as the Gospel of Christ. At the time when St. Paul wrote it he could not fail to see the to him painful and perplexing fact that the Gentiles were pressing into the kingdom of heaven and taking it by storm, and that consequently the inheritance of the vine-yard was being taken from its ancient husbandmen. As he was writing to a mixed Church, this problem—which occupies the ninth, tenth, and eleventh chapters—was probably the earliest in St. Paul's thoughts; but from it he passed to the consideration of wider truths, which made it sink into a subordinate position. For it led him at once to the thought that spiritual sonship depends in no wise on natural descent, and that the only justification possible to man is justification by faith. In that one formula, so often abused into a mere badge of Protestantism, and so often entirely misunderstood, may be summed up the chief thesis of the letter. But the word "faith" in that memorable formula does not mean what it is

popularly taken to mean. It does not mean a mere expression of belief; it does not even mean an actual belief; still less does it mean any body of doctrines; least of all does it mean something opposed to reason—the abnegation of all inquiry—the smiting back the understanding, as with a bar of iron, in order to coerce it, in spite of itself, into the acceptance of a series of dogmatic propositions. "Faith" was used by St. Paul in a sense absolutely original. What he meant by it in its full and ultimate significance was nothing less than that oneness with Christ, that death with Him unto sin and that life with Him unto righteousness, which are its final result and richest flower. One of the key-notes, then, of the letter is the word "all." He wishes to show that the universality of sin is counterbalanced by the universality of grace. And thus in this Epistle, as in every other, the real basis is not a forensic theory, not a metaphysical expression, but "Christ as the common foundation on which Jew and Gentile can stand, the bond of human society, the root of human righteousness." And St. Paul's idea of faith, in the highest of his ascensive uses of it, is best found in Galatians iii. 20. "I am crucified with Christ, nevertheless I live; yet not I, but Christ liveth in me; and the life which I now live in the flesh I live by the faith of the Son of God who loved me, and gave Himself for me."

3. It is of course impossible to give in a few words an exhaustive sketch of a letter which deals with not a few of the vastest problems which have ever occupied the mind of man. A perfect library of theology has been written to expound this letter. Sects have argued, and controversies have raged about it from century to century. All that I shall here attempt is first to give an outline of it, and then with the utmost brevity to set forth the view which it gives of the Gospel as the power of God unto salvation.

4. The outline of the letter is as follows. After the full, solemn, and digressive greeting and thanksgiving of the first

fifteen verses, St. Paul passes, in the most natural manner, to state, in the sixteenth and seventeenth verses, his great theme, which he sums up in those words of Habakkuk, "The just shall live by faith." Since the necessity of this mode of salvation arises from the universality of sin which deserves God's wrath, he proceeds to prove his statement that all have sinned. Of the sinfulness of the Gentiles he gives a truly fearful picture in the rest of the first chapter; and then (to the twentieth verse of the third chapter) he enters on the proof that the Jews have sinned no less fatally.[1] In the twenty-first to the thirty-first verse of the third chapter he once more gives a condensed, yet elaborate summary of the Gospel remedy for sin, viz. justification by free grace through the redemption which is in Christ Jesus. Aware of the extreme novelty of these conclusions, he devotes the fourth and fifth chapters to illustrating them from Scripture; and to the proof that the ruinous work of Adam has been reversed by the healing work of Christ. Then he divides human history into three epochs—the state of innocence or of "unconscious morality;" the state of law; and the state of grace.[2] In the sixth chapter he shows that, so far from encouraging sin, the grace of Christ involves the annihilation of sin; and in the seventh and eighth chapters he shows that the Law was only meant to lead men to the Gospel, and that its deathful commandments are superseded

---

[1] The guiltiness of heathendom was too patent. It required no proof. The Pagans are condemned by the tone of all their literature, by their poets, historians, and orators no less than by their satirists and romancers. Their sins were open, going before to judgment. "Omnia sceleribus et vitiis plena sunt," says the contemporary Seneca (*De Irâ,* ii. 8) "nec furtiva jam scelera sunt." It was far more necessary to show the Jews that they were no less guilty, though their guilt was of a different kind. It was specially important to show them that their privileges, so far from saving them, might only tend to aggravate their condemnation. The Rabbis can hardly persuade themselves that any circumcised son of Abraham can ever perish (Yevamoth f. 47, 2; Avoda Zara, f. 3, col. 1-3). And yet that generation of Jews was so bad that, in the opinion of the Jewish historian, earthquake and lightning must have destroyed them if the Romans had not done so (Jos. *B.G.* iv. 3; v. 9 § 4; x. § 5; xiii. § 6).

[2] See the Introductory Note, and an interesting excursus (F.) "on *St. Paul's view of the Religious History of Mankind,*" by Dr. Sanday, in Bishop Ellicott's *Commentary,* ii. 278.

ROMANS. for the believer, by the Spirit of God quickening the heart of man.[1] This naturally leads him to a serious appeal to his readers to live worthily of their changed nature, an appeal which, at the close of the eighth chapter becomes a magnificent outburst of gratitude, rising at last into a climax of impassioned praise.

Then in the ninth, tenth, and eleventh chapters—which are in one sense an episode, but probably contain the thoughts which suggested the whole Epistle—he deals with the apparent rejection of Israel, and faces the great problems of predestination and free will.[2]

The next four chapters deal with the practical consequences of this Gospel—the duties of self-dedication, humility, unity, hope, love, subordination to human authority, toleration of

---

[1] Conciliatory as is the tone of St. Paul, he here uses the startling expression that the Law "came in" (παρεισῆλθεν, Vulg. *subintravit*, "supervened" Gal. iii. 19, προσετέθη) "that the trespass might abound," *i.e.* to multiply transgressions, which in Gal. iii. 19, he had more obscurely expressed by "for the sake of transgressions" (παραβάσεων χάριν). He justifies his position by a deep psychological analysis showing that the Law stimulates the impulse to sin (*nitimur in vetitum semper*) and intensifies the subsequent remorse; but that it only does this with the merciful purpose of bringing sin to a head and so of curing it. Thus the use of the law is, as the Reformers said, 1. Civil. 2. Educational. 3. Formative. Augebatur morbus ; crescit malitia ; quaeritur medicus, et totum sanatur."—AUG. in Ps. cii.

> "And therefore Law *was given them to evince*
> *Their natural pravity* by stirring up
> Sin against law to fight ; that when they see
> *Law can discover sin but not remove,*
> Save by those shadowy expiations weak
> The blood of bulls and goats, they may conclude
> Some blood more precious must be paid for man.
>   MILTON, *Paradise Lost,* xii. 285.

Into these lines Milton has compressed something of the main conception, both of the Epistle to the Romans and of the Epistle to the Hebrews.

[2] To the difficulty about the rejection of Israel St. Paul furnishes two answers.

1. A theologic answer :—God predestinates.

2. An historic answer :—the rejection of the Jews was due to their own obstinacy.

He does not attempt to reconcile the antinomy because it is irreconcilable. He would have said with R. Akiva, "Everything is foreseen and free will is given. And the world is judged by grace and everything is according to works" (*Pirke Avoth.* iii. 24). He was not oppressed by the problem of God's foreknowledge because (1) He believed absolutely in God's infinite love ; and (2) He apparently looked forward to the redemption of the Universe and of the race (Rom. viii. 19-24 ; xi. 32 ; 1 Tim. ii. 3-6).

scruples, strict conscientiousness, and generally the imitation of Christ. He closes the Epistle with personal messages, with twenty-six greetings, and with a splendid doxology in which, in a form almost resembling the antiphons of a liturgy, he once more repeats the revealed mystery of his Gospel, the deliverance of man by obedience and faith in Christ.

5. The grand fundamental theme of the Epistle is given in i. 16, 17. "For I am not ashamed of the Gospel of Christ, for it is the power of God unto salvation to every one that believeth, to the Jew first and also to the Greek. For in it the righteousness of God is being revealed from faith to faith, even as it is written, But the righteous shall live by faith; for the wrath of God is being revealed from heaven against all impiety and unrighteousness of men who suppress the truth in unrighteousness." The great central truth of our religion, thus stated, is much more than a mere " doctrine of sin," a mere "theory of imputation," a mere watchword of party. It is, on the contrary, a practical truth of momentous importance. On the one side we have man, on the other God; on the one side man's guilt, on the other that consequent suffering, that retributive loss, that profound alienation of man from his Maker, which works, and can only be described, as " the wrath of God." That wrath is being revealed from heaven day by day in the deep misery and anguish of mankind wrought by the Nemesis of violated laws. God is righteous and man is guilty : how then is the gulf between righteousness and guilt to be bridged over? Without holiness we know, we feel, our consciences tell us, that we shall never see God. Shall we then never see Him ? Can God bring a clean thing out of an unclean? Can there be any destiny before the race of man except lamentation, and mourning, and woe ? Clearly there can be no hope unless God—even while we are yet sinners, yet disobedient, yet alienated—interferes on behalf of the wretched and fallen race. Does God interfere, and how ? The Gospel is the answer to that question. If the Gospel answer be not the

true answer, then there is none. And St. Paul gives the answer by saying that if there be a revelation of wrath, there is also a revelation of righteousness; that the righteousness of God towards the sinner is being revealed by the pure steady light of the Gospel, no less clearly than the wrath of God towards sin is being revealed by the lurid blaze of punishment. The word for righteousness and for justification is one and the same word, because God has provided the means whereby His righteousness can become our justification; whereby He can so impart to us His righteousness that it becomes ours; whereby the guilty can be not only forgiven but sanctified, and the quality of a Holy God become the condition of guilty man.

6. How can this be?

I am painfully aware that the mere statement of these truths will seem dry and abstract. This will cease to be the case if we bring the question home to ourselves by putting it into the concrete. Let us take a single case. A man is guilty; he is tied and bound by the chain of some sin, perhaps of many sins; he is absorbed by avarice; he is goaded by ambition; he is the victim of passion. He wants indeed to be pardoned, but he wants also (and this is impossible) to retain the offence. He knows, until his soul has become utterly callous, and his conscience utterly seared, he knows, and it is his daily misery to know, that he is not at one with himself, because his lower nature has gained the disastrous victory over his better nature. In a word, he is not at one with God, because, while he is impure, and false, and evil, God is holy, just, and good. What can save him? No mere change of circumstances, no violent miracle of transformation. The change must be in himself. While his heart is still corrupt he desires to fly from God, and so long as he is what he is, his soul must (so to speak) be left in hell, because heaven itself would be hell to him, and he must say with the evil spirit,

"Which way I fly is hell, myself am hell."

How then is a sinful man to attain to holiness? how is God's righteousness to become his justification? That is the problem.

There is a passage in one of the noblest moral poems of modern days—the *Idylls of the King*—a poem which, from beginning to end—is an allegory of a conscience at work among the warring senses—in which Arthur's greatest knight, entangled in the shame of a deadly sin, and finding more bitterly every day that the taste of sin's corroded fruit is like dust and ashes in the mouth, goes and sits alone, beside a little brook that runs into a river; and as he watches the high reed wave, he cries in the deep anguish of moral despair—

> " ' Mine own name shames me, seeming a reproach.
> For what am I? what profits me my name,
> To make men worse by making my sin known,
> Or sin seem less, the sinner seeming great.
> Alas! for Arthur's greatest knight, a man
> Not after Arthur's heart! I needs must break
> These bonds that so defame me . . . .
> . . . . but if I would not, then may God
> I pray Him, send a sudden Angel down
> To seize me by the hair, and bear me far,
> And fling me deep in that forgotten mere
> Among the tumbled fragments of the hills.'
> So groaned Sir Launcelot in remorseful pain,
> *Not knowing he should die a holy man.*"

But there is the awful question, *How* shall a guilty become a holy man?

The answer is—partly by the free grace of God, partly by the free will of man.

i. Partly, I say, by the free grace of God. That free grace of God was manifested once and for all in the death of Christ. This element in the plan of salvation you will see more fully in the twenty-fifth and twenty-sixth verses of that third chapter, which have been called by Olshausen "the Acropolis of the Christian faith." There you will read that God has provided a way whereby all may attain to the glory of God, "being justified freely by His grace, by means of the redemption which is in Christ Jesus, whom God set forth as a

propitiation by means of faith by His blood to show His righteousness, because of the praetermission of former sins in the
forbearance of God ; . . . . that He might Himself be
righteous, and the justifier of him whose life springs from
faith in Jesus." [1]

Here then is the history of salvation on the part of God.
Guilty as we are, utterly as we deserved punishment, God
sent His Son to live for us, to die for us, to save us ; and by
the death of Christ, God, viewing our whole race as redeemed
in Him, pronounced a judgment of acquittal upon all who
(consciously or unconsciously) are found in Him. This is the
divine paradox by which God can both condemn and pardon.
In the Law God is just and condemns ; [2] in the Gospel He is

---

[1] The elements of this great statement are as follows :

1. JUSTIFICATION.—The Righteousness of God imputed to man (δικαιοσύνη).

2. FAITH :—(a) man's belief ; rising (β) to self-surrender ; (γ) to mystic
union with Christ, which becomes in man (δ) the spirit of a new life.

3. This plan of salvation offered to ALL ; (εἰς πάντας καὶ ἐπὶ πάντας τοὺς
πιστεύοντας).

4. It has been finished and made known (πεφανέρωται) in accordance with
continuous testimony (μαρτυρουμένη).

5. This grace, a free gift not earned by man (χωρὶς νόμου), nor to be earned
(δωρέαν).

6. The object of this faith,—Jesus Christ, His life and death ; which is a
ransoming (ἀπολύτρωσις) and a propitiation (ἱλαστήριον) as regards ·its results
for man. (The word ἱλαστήριον seems here to be used in the sense of ἱλασμός.)

7. The reason for this,—the vindication of God's righteousness which
might otherwise have been questioned because of His praetermission (πάρεσιν)
of previous sins.

8. The end to be obtained—that God might justify every man whose new
life has its root (ἐκ) in faith in Christ.

Thus the Gospel—what the Apostle called specifically *his* Gospel (Rom. ii.
16 ; xvi. 25 ; Gal. i. 7, ii. 2 ; 2 Tim. ii. 8)—is grounded on the grace of God
(χάρις) ; the Redemption in Christ (ἀπολύτρωσις) ; and the faith of man
(πίστις).

St. Paul expresses the conclusion in verse 28. "We reckon therefore
that a man is justified by faith, apart from works of Law." This is the verse
into which Luther, by inference (but unwarrantably) admitted from the Genoese
and Nuremberg Bibles the word "alone," "by faith only" (*vox sola tot
clamoribus lapidata*, Erasm.) Hence the name *Solidifian.* Luther was not
guilty of the foolish error that "faith" (*Glaube*) means merely "belief." *Glaube*
implies not merely belief but *trust.* Knowing that in St. Paul, "faith" ultimately means "union with Christ" (Phil. i. 21 ; Gal. ii. 20), Luther knew
that faith of necessity included works.

The word ἱλαστήριον is always used by the LXX. for *capporeth,* the "mercy-
seat" or "propitiatory ;" and though Fritzsche says "*Valeat absurda expli-
catio,*" it cannot be regarded as certain that that meaning of the word is not
here applied to Christ by a metaphor.

[2] Bengel.

just and pardons. The fact that His judicial righteousness
both condemns and pardons is "the divine theodicy for the
past history of the world." [1] This is all that we know or can
know (and that only by most imperfect metaphor) of the
nature of the redemptive act as regards God. We know no
more because we need to know no more. But this we know,
that if we are in Christ, "such we are in the sight of God
the Father, as is the very Son of God Himself. Let it be
counted folly, or fury, or frenzy, or whatsoever. It is our
wisdom and our comfort: we care for no knowledge in the
world but this, that God hath made Himself the sin of men,
and that men are made the righteousness of God." [2]

ii. But though God has thus provided the remedy, man
must apply it; and if we ask how, Scripture has but one
answer, "by faith." The salvation is freely given, it is freely
given to all; but if man reject it, then, so long as he rejects
it, it is rendered vain. God saves the sinner, but he cannot
save the sin; nor can He save the sinner so long as he
continues in the wilful, willing, defiant, disbelieving choice
of sin. The whole education of life is an education meant to
make us give up sin. All life is meant to teach us, even if it
be by the desperate teaching of evil and its consequences
that good is best. By early training, by inward calls, by the
voices of father and mother, by the worship of His Church,
by His Scriptures, by His sacraments, by the teaching of His
ministers, by the experiences of life, by falls and recoveries, by
sternness and by tender mercy, by bereavements, by sick-
nesses, by disappointments, by mental distress, by physical
pain, by loneliness, by shame, and by success; by thwarting
us, and by letting us have our own way; by not letting us
have the good things of earth while we thanklessly and fruit-
lessly weary ourselves as in the very fire to win them, or by
letting us have them and feel bitter with weariness and sick
with sin, even while we possess them; by the shattering blow
of the lightning of punishment, and by the golden brooding

[1] Tholuck.   [2] Hooker, *Serm.* ii. 6.

ROMANS.

of the dove of peace, He designs, from the first moment that the soul goes astray, to wean us from the fatal fascination and deadly slavery of sin, to obey and trust in Him. Thus to trust in Him is the first step of faith. Faith is not dead belief, but inspiring confidence. And when we have once thus in truth believed with the heart, then begins on the side of man also, the history of the salvation of the Christian soul. Belief becomes self-surrender; self-surrender becomes self-conquest; self-conquest rises into mystical incorporation with Christ in unity of love and life, and this passive union soon passes into an active force, the life in Christ, the life not in the flesh, but in the Spirit. And thus all true faith is inseparable from works. Justification becomes sanctification. The law of our human spirit becomes the law of the spirit of life in Jesus Christ. The guilty man has become a holy man. The wicked man has turned from his iniquity and lives. The leper is cleansed. The prodigal has come home. The soul is saved. The man is fit for heaven.[1]

7. The essence, then, of St. Paul's evangelical theology may be expressed far better by the two words "in Christ," than even by the formula "Justification by faith." The

[1] The right understanding of the word "faith" in its highest sense is essential to the understanding of St. Paul. There are ascensive degrees and qualities of faith.

1. There is dead faith—faith which produces no works—*fides informis.*

2. There is "belief," theoretic persuasion (*assensus*) Rom. iv. 18; x. 14 (Heb. xi. 1).

3. There is faith which has been touched by emotion and has become *faithfulness* by producing self-surrender (Rom. x. 9), xii. 3.

4. Faith passes into *unio mystica,* incorporation with Christ, Rom. i. 17; Phil. i. 21; Gal. ii. 20.

5. It passes from receptivity into spontaneous activity, and becomes a living impulse and power—the spirit of life (1 Cor. vi. 17). Hence, as Luther says, "Faith is a divine work in us, which changes us, and creates us anew in God."

It is only in the later Pastoral Epistles that "Faith" is used in the modern sense of "a body of doctrines."

As to the origin and growth and object of faith,—it begins with hearing (Gal. iii. 2); and since Christ is the essence of the Gospel it becomes "faith in Christ" (Gal. ii. 16; iii. 26). More specially it is faith in Christ's blood (Rom. iii. 24-27); and growing more intense as it narrows from stage to stage, it passes from theoretic assent to dominant conviction (Baur. *Paul.* ii. 149; Pfleiderer, *Paulinism,* § v. Hooker, *Eccl. Pol.* 1, xi. 6).

former phrase occurs thirty-three times, the latter phrase only three or four times. What then shall we say to these things? We might say many things. We might lose ourselves in endless perplexities; we might entangle ourselves in interminable controversies ; we might, by rash logical inferences and syllogistic intrusions into the secret things of God, injure and harden our own souls; and, trying to measure the arm of God by the finger of man, we might lose ourselves in the mazes of defiance and blasphemy. We might take the phrase as a sort of test of the heresy of others, instead of a blessed truth intended for ourselves. Let us reject all such rash conclusions, such repellent inferences, such uncharitable presumption! Let us put forth the hand of faith to receive this white robe of God's righteousness which shall admit us into the marriage supper of the Lamb. God loves us, sinners though we be. Christ died to save us from our sins. We are not asked to reason, but to accept a loving Saviour, and yield ourselves to a loving will. If we do this, then we shall be able to fling away all foolish arguments and horrible conclusions about reprobation, and predestination, and election, as St. Paul himself does, with the one energetic phrase which occurs no less than ten times in this single Epistle, Perish the thought! "God forbid"! ($\mu\grave{\eta}$ $\gamma\acute{\epsilon}\nu o\iota\tau o$). Whatever else the Epistle to the Romans may be, it is transcendently an Epistle of hope. It is the Epistle which says that where sin abounds, there grace superabounds; that God giveth freely to all, and freely calleth all; that though Israel is rejected, yet all Israel shall be saved ; that God shut up all into disobedience that He might pity all. Limit the "all" *if* you will, and *as* you will, but the more we trust God, the more we shall hope in Him. It was this hope that inspired the bursts of rapture which close the eighth and the eleventh chapter. "We are more than conquerors through Christ that loved us. For I am convinced that neither death, nor life, nor angels, nor principalities, nor powers, nor things present, nor things to come, shall be able to separate us from the love of God manifested towards us in Christ Jesus our Lord." And " oh the depth of the riches, and wisdom, and knowledge of God ! How unsearchable his judgments, how untrackable his ways!" For all things are from Him, and all things are by Him, and all things tend to Him. No man need despair, for despair is not only the loss of hope, but also the most perilous abandonment of the soul to faithlessness. The Gospel is good tidings; it is a message of peace to all who will receive it. It tells us how we may be found in Christ, not having our own righteousness, but that which cometh from God by faith in Christ, even the righteousness which begins with the faith of simple trust in God, and ends in the faith of union with His Spirit, and fulfilment of His will.

NOTE I.

ANALYSIS OF THE EPISTLE.

The Epistle falls into two great divisions. i.-xi. mainly Doctrinal; xii.-xvi. mainly Practical.

It also falls into seven clear sections.

i.-v. Statement of the doctrine.

vi.-viii. Answers to objections.

ix., xi. The question of the rejection of Israel.

xii., xiii. Practical exhortations.

xiv.-xv. 13. Mutual duties of the strong and the weak.

xv. 14-33. Personal.

xvi. Salutations.

The closer analysis of the Epistle is as follows:

1. GREETING (i. 1-7). This is the first letter which St. Paul addresses *to the saints,* and the first in which he calls himself *a slave of Christ.*

2. THANKSGIVING (i. 8-15).

3. DOCTRINAL SECTION.

 A. Fundamental thesis (i. 16, 17).

  i. *All equally guilty* (i. 18-iii. 20).

   α. The Gentiles (i. 18-32).

   β. The Jews, in spite of their privileges (ii. 1-iii. 20).

  ii. *All equally redeemed* (iii. 21-30). Justification by faith.

  iii. Illustration from the faith of Abraham (iii. 31· iv. 25).

  iv. The nature and blessedness of the doctrine (v.).

 B. Answers to objections.

  i. Objection: that free grace would multiply sin (vi.).

  Answer: Grace annihilates sin.

  ii. Objection: the doctrine discredits the Law.

  Answer: the Law is spiritual, but we are now dead to the Law (vii. 1-6) which at once provokes to sin (7-12) and gives the sting to disobedience (13-24). But Christ gives us the victory over sin (vii. 25-viii. 11).

 C. Moral appeal founded on these truths, and thanksgivings for them (viii. 12-35).

 D. Episode on the rejection of Israel (ix. x. xi.).

  i. St. Paul's love for Israel (ix. 1-5).

  ii. Spiritual sonship independent of natural descent (6-9).

  iii. God's free will illustrated in the rejection of Esau and Pharaoh (10-18).

  iv. Yet God is not unjust, for justification by faith is open to all (19-33); but Israel rejected God's righteousness (x.).

U

    v. The rejection is, *a.* only partial not absolute (**xi. 110**) ;
       β. Temporary, not final, and meant for the blessing of
       the Gentiles (11–32).

    vi. Burst of thanksgiving (33–36).

4. PRACTICAL. (La foi justifie quand il opère, mais il n'opère que par la charité.—QUESNEL.)

    i. Exhortations to holiness, humility, unity, faithfulness,
       hope, love (xii.), obedience to civil authority, love, and
       watchfulness (xiii.).

    ii. Exhortations to mutual forbearance between the liberal
       and the narrow Christians (with retrospective allusions
       to the doctrine already established, xiv.-xv. 13).

5. Personal apology for having thus addressed them (xv. 13–21) with remarks on his future plans.

6. SALUTATIONS (xvi. 1–24) (15–33).

7. FINAL BLESSING (25–27).

NOTE II.

ON THE INTEGRITY OF THE EPISTLE.[1]

THERE is great reason to doubt whether the last chapter was addressed to the Roman Church. It has been suggested with some probability that it is really an appendix to the letter when it was sent to the Church of Ephesus.[2]

i. The urgency of the recommendation of Phœbe to a strange Church three times as distant from Corinth as Ephesus, is hardly what we should expect (Rom. xvi. 1, 2).

ii. It is strange that St. Paul should salute twenty-six people of an entirely strange Church when he only salutes one or two, or none, in Churches which he founded.

iii. Aquila and Priscilla were *not at Rome but at Ephesus,* a few months before St. Paul wrote this letter (1 Cor. xvi. 19), and again some eight or nine years later (2 Tim. iv. 19).

iv. There are no salutations to such well-known Roman Christians as Eubulus, Pudens, Linus, Claudia (2 Tim. iv. 21).

v. How comes Epaenetus, "the first-fruits of Asia," to be at Rome, and with him so many "kinsmen" and ardent supporters, and fellow

---

[1] The reader may see different views as to this subject, by Bishop Lightfoot, *Journal of Philology,* vi. (1871) ; Dr. Hort (*id.* v. 1870), and Dr. Gifford, *Speaker's Commentary,* iii. 20-30. The view adopted in this note was suggested by Schulz, and has been adopted by Ewald, Renan, Reuss and others.

[2] Semler as far back as 1707 wrote a pamphlet *De Duplice Appendice Ep. ad Rom.* Ewald also thought that xvi. 1-20 was part of a letter to *Ephesus* written from Rome.

prisoners" of St. Paul (xvi. 7, 9, 12, 13) ? Had all the Ephesian Church made a rendezvous at Rome ? [1] Where (unless it was in the scantily recorded perils at Ephesus) could Aquila and Priscilla have run such risks for St. Paul, and Andronicus and Junias have been his fellow-prisoners (συναιχμάλωτοι) ? [2]

vi. If St. Paul had so many kinsmen, and warm friends, and benefactors at Rome, how came it that there was not a single Roman Christian to stand by him in his hour of need ? (2 Tim. iv. 16.) And that not one of them is among the three Jewish friends who were faithful to him in his first Roman imprisonment (Col. iv. 10, 11) ?

vii. How comes the fraternal reproachfulness of xvi. 17–20 to be so unlike the distant politeness of xv. 15–20 ?

viii. How come so many of St. Paul's friends to send greetings to distant and unvisited Rome ?

ix. How come there to be three or four different terminations to this Epistle at xv. 33, xvi. 20, 24, 27 ? Even conservative critics like Bishop Lightfoot have been led by these phenomena to suppose that St. Paul himself circulated this letter in one form without the two last chapters.

x. How comes it that the body of the Epistle does not show the slightest trace of the "divisions," "stumbling-blocks," "beguilers," mentioned in xvi. 17–20 ? Such elements only sprang into existence in Rome at a *later* time (Phil. i. 15–17).

xi. How are we to account for the MSS. phenomena :—the absence of the final doxology from F.G. and MSS. mentioned by Jerome ? its position after xiv. 23, in L. &c. ? its double recurrence (xiv. 24 ; xvi. 25) in A. ? Why have we all this "omission, repetition, transposition" ?

xii. Why did Marcion, for no apparent dogmatic reason, omit these two last chapters?

xiii. Lastly, why does G., which is an important MS. founded on a very ancient copy, leave *a blank* for the words *in Rome*, in i. 7, 15 ?

This last remarkable phenomenon probably affords us a solution of all the others, by indicating that the main body of the letter *was sent to different Churches* with different terminations.

All that can be said on the other side is that

a. Rome swarmed with Asiatics, and was specially full of Greeks ("Non possum ferre Quirites *Graecam* urbem," Juv. *Sat.* iii. 61–73). The names of those saluted are chiefly Greek. (Yet Garucci found that Latin names were twice as numerous as Greek in the old Jewish cemetery at Rome.)

β. Seven of the common names are found on inscriptions in the Roman *Columbaria* (see Bishop Lightfoot, *Philippians*, p. 172–175) ;

[1] Renan, *St. Paul*, p. lxviii.
[2] Elsewhere this word is only applied to Epaphras (Philem. 23) and Aristarchus (Col. iv. 18), who at a later period shared St. Paul's Roman imprisonment.

three of the rarer ones (Tryphaena, Tryphosa, Patrobas); and even
Philologus and Julia in connection. (But the slaves in Caesarian and
other great households were to be counted by thousands, and the names
are mostly common ones.)

NOTE III.

THE JEWS IN ROME.

B.C. 101. First embassy of Jews to Rome sent by Judas Maccabeus.[1]

B.C. 144, 141, 129. The league between Jews and Rome renewed by
Jonathan, Simon, and John Hyrcanus.[2]

B.C. 63. Many Jews taken prisoners to Rome by Pompey.[3]
Their speedy manumission.[4]

B.C. 48-44. The Jews favourably treated by Julius Caesar.[5]

B.C. 27-A.D. 14. The Jews protected by Augustus out of friendship to
Herod.[6]

B.C. 4. A Jewish Embassy to Rome, after the death of Herod the
Great, met by 8,000 Jews living at Rome.[7]

A.D. 19. The Jews banished to Sardinia by Tiberius [8] for their share in
the nefarious practices of the Temple of Isis.

A.D. 34. Probable founding of the Church of Rome about this time by
"strangers of Rome," Libertines and others.[9]

A.D. 40. Philo; embassy to Gaius (Caligula).[10]

A.D. 49. The Jews expelled from Rome by Claudius, because *impulsore
Chresto* (through Messianic excitement? or disputes about Christianity?) they were *assidue tumultuantes.*[11]

A.D. 58. Their influence at Rome is so strong that Seneca says "the
conquered race gave laws to the conquerors."[12]

---

[1] Jos. *Antt.* xii. 10, § 6.   1 Macc. viii. 17.

[2] 1 Macc. xii. 1; xiv. 24.

[3] Jos. *Antt.* xx. 10, § 1.   Tac. H. v. 9.   Cic. *pro Flacco*, xxviii.

[4] Philo, *Leg. ad Gaium*, 23. Yet the Jews were hated from the first.
Cicero, who in *pleading for Flaccus* had to speak low, for fear of these tumults,
calls them a race born for slavery, and speaks of their religion with abhorrence.
Pro Flacco, 28, comp. Hor. *Sat.* 1, iv. 143; x. 69-72.

[5] Jos. *Antt.* xiv. 10, § 1, 5–8, *c. Apion*, ii. 4. Macrobius, *Saturn.* i. 12.
Appian, *Bell. Civ.* ii. 106.

[6] See Jahn, *Hebrew Commonwealth*, §§ cxvii. *fy.*

[7] Jos. *Antt.* xvii. 9–11. B. J. ii. 6.

[8] The growing fear, jealousy, and detestation, inspired by the Jews at Rome
is indicated by the intensely scornful remark of Tacitus on this occasion,
"Si ob gravitatem coeli interissent, *vile damnum.*"—*Ann.* ii. 85.

[9] Jos. *Antt.* xviii. 3, § 5, 1, and Acts ii. 10. Tac. *Ann.* xv. 44.

[10] See Philo, *Legatio ad Gaium;* and *Contra Flaccum.*

[11] Acts xviii. 2. Suet. *Claud.* 35.

[12] Sen. ap. Aug. *De Civ. Dei.* vi. 11.

THE EPISTLE TO THE PHILIPPIANS.
(WRITTEN IN PRISON AT ROME, CIRC. A.D. 62.)

"Summa Epistolae—*gaudeo, gaudete.*"—BENGEL.

"An Epistle of the heart."—MEYER.

"That man is very strong and powerful who has no more hopes for himself, who looks not to be loved any more, to be admired any more, to have any more honour or dignity, and who cares not for gratitude; but whose sole thought is for others, and who lives on for them."—HELPS.

INTRODUCTORY.

THERE cannot be the shadow of a doubt as to the genuineness of the Epistle to the Philippians. Baur, who was the first to suggest any suspicion on the subject (*Paulus*, i. 458), on very insufficient grounds, has been decisively answered by many scholars.[1] It is amply supported by external evidence, and the objections brought against it are more than usually weak, fantastic, and untenable.

The unity of the Epistle is equally established. Stephen Le Moyne's division of it into two Epistles only rose from the expression of Polycarp, who, writing to the Philippians, says, "Neither I, nor any one like me, can reach the wisdom of the blessed and glorious Paul, who also, when absent, wrote to you letters into which if ye look ye will be able to edify yourselves in the faith which has been given to you." But (1) ἐπιστολὰς (Thuc. viii. 51, Jos. *Antt.* xii. 4, 6, 10) may mean "a letter" just as *literae* does in Latin, and, indeed, a little further on Polycarp speaks of only one letter (xi.); (2) St.

---

[1] De Wette, Schenkel, Reuss, Lünemann, Brückner, Ernesti, Meyer, Wilibald Grimm, B. Weiss, Pfleiderer, Hilgenfeld, Lightfoot, &c.

PHILIPPIANS. Paul may have written other letters to the Philippians—indeed, he probably did (iii. 18). All attempts to divide the letter into two (Heinrichs, Paulus, Weisse, &c.) have signally failed, and Phil. iii. 1 has no bearing on the question.

Few now suppose that it was written in the imprisonment at Caesarea. (1) In that imprisonment he could not have hoped for a speedy liberation for he had appealed to Caesar. (2) He was not chained at Caesarea till Felix left; but in this Epistle (i. 7, 13, 16, 17), and in the others, he constantly refers to "his bonds." See further Bleek, *Einl.* p. 161.

The certainty that this Epistle is authentic is a strong additional argument in favour of the authenticity of those to the Ephesians and Colossians to which this letter forms the connecting link. It marks the beginning of Paul's "later manner," and shows traces of the new conceptions—less individual and more universal, less national and more cosmopolitan, less relating to special Churches and more to the whole Church, less impassioned and more severe in their maturity, less relating to Judaic questions and more to the questions which rose from Gentile speculation, less Judaic and Hellenic and more Roman—which were certain to have resulted from the growth of the Church, and from the change in St. Paul's circumstances, when he was no longer the wandering missionary engaged in daily controversies, but the prisoner at Rome, chained to Roman soldiers and expecting his trial before the Emperor of the world. The Church of Philippi was itself an illustration of the confluence of nationalities at this epoch. It was a Church founded by two Jewish missionaries and the Jewish son of a Gentile father (Timothy) in a Roman colony which had occupied the old Greek city of "the Fountains" (Crenides); and as Meyer says, "the town thus vindicated its original name in a higher sense for the entire West." We may collect the general manliness of the inhabitants from the military metaphors (i. 27, ii. 25, iv. 7), and their culture from such terms as αἴσθησις, μορφή, αὐταρκής.

THE EPISTLE TO THE PHILIPPIANS.

" I joy and rejoice with you all."—PHIL. ii. 17.

1. IT was during St. Paul's detention at Rome in a sort of PHILIPPIANS.
military custody for two years, and in the later and severer phase
of it, that he wrote the four letters which constitute his third
group of Epistles—those to the Philippians, Colossians,
Philemon, and Ephesians. The Epistle to the Philippians,
written some four years later than that to the Romans, is
the first which breaks the silence of his sad captivity.[1]

2. It arose directly out of one of the few happy incidents
which diversified the dreary uncertainties of the prisoner's
lot. Just as gleams of sunshine brighten the incessant
showers of an April day, so God sometimes touches with
brightness the tears of life. The incident which thus cheered
the brave heart of the imprisoned Paul was the visit of
Epaphroditus, a leading presbyter of the Church of Philippi.

---

[1] I can feel little or no doubt that this is the earliest of the Epistles of the
Captivity. For (1) when St. Paul wrote it he was quite uncertain as to what his
ultimate fate would be (i. 20–25 ; ii. 23), though he hoped to be acquitted
(ii. 24). On the other hand, when he wrote the letter to Philemon (and therefore those to the Colossians and Ephesians) he was sufficiently sanguine of·
acquittal to ask Philemon (v. 22) to prepare him a lodging. Further (2) the
order of thought in this Epistle has an affinity with that of the letters
to the Galatians and the Romans. It breathes the same *tone* as the letter
to the Romans, and has many parallels of thought and expression. On the
other hand, when he wrote to Ephesus and Colossae, a new set of experiences,
and the necessity for dealing with problems of a wholly different character
from those which he had hitherto faced, had carried him into wholly different
subjects. Seeing the delicate susceptibility of St. Paul's mind, and its tenacity
of recent phrases and impressions, I hold it to be a psychological impossibility
that he should have written Philippians after Colossians and Ephesians, and yet
have shown no traces of the special thoughts with which he had been so recently
and so powerfully occupied. It could not have been written at the *beginning*
of St. Paul's imprisonment, because time must be allowed for the news of St.
Paul's arrival at Rome to reach Philippi ; for the journey of Epaphroditus
from Philippi to Rome ; for his illness ; for the reception of the news of that
illness at Philippi ; and for the return of their expressions of sorrow and
sympathy. But this would not require more than a year. Philippi is about
700 miles from Rome, and the journey occupied about a month.

PHILIPPIANS. He brought with him no less than the fourth pecuniary contribution by which that loving and generous Church had ministered to his necessities. At Rome the Apostle was unable with his fettered hands to work, as he had done elsewhere, for his own livelihood. One would have thought that the members of the Roman Church—some, for instance, of those brethren who a year or two earlier had thronged forth as far as Appii Forum to meet him [1]—were sufficiently numerous and sufficiently wealthy to have saved the great Apostle from the wearing degradation of pecuniary anxiety; but they treated him with the same unaccountable indifference of inconsiderate selfishness [2] with which, to this day, in thousands of English parishes, ministers are left to struggle unaided with the anguish of scanty means. And it was an additional source of sorrow to him that even in the Roman Church the party spirit of the Judaists and others was so bitter that some were preaching Christ of strife and envy. Nothing but the Apostle's splendid magnanimity could have helped him to bear this trial. It was something that, in any way whatever, the name and the Gospel of Christ should be made known. It was being made known in the *best* way by the courage which his bonds inspired and by the intercourse with Praetorian soldiers which those bonds necessitated.[3] " In every way," he says, " whether in pretence or in truth the story of Christ is being told ($\kappa\alpha\tau\alpha\gamma\gamma\acute{\epsilon}\lambda\lambda\epsilon\tau\alpha\iota$), and therein I rejoice, yea and I will rejoice." [4]

---

[1] Acts xxviii. 15.

[2] In ii. 21 he says with deep sadness that "all ($o\acute{\iota}$ $\pi\acute{\alpha}\nu\tau\epsilon\varsigma$) seek their own interests."

[3] He says (i. 13) that "his bonds became manifest in Christ, $\grave{\epsilon}\nu$ $\H{o}\lambda\psi$ $\tau\H{\psi}$ $\pi\rho\alpha\iota\tau\omega\rho\acute{\iota}\psi$," not (as in A.V.) "throughout the whole *palace*," but (as in R.V.) "throughout the whole praetorian guard," *castrum praetorianum* (Suet. *Tib.* 37) ; and he adds, " to all the rest." Even in Caesar's household (iv. 22) some had been converted. The ingenious speculations which try to connect St. Paul with Seneca through Gallio and Burrhus have no real base. The resemblances to Stoic doctrines as enunciated by Seneca, which are found in this Epistle, are of a general character, and refer to truths which, so to speak, were "in the air." See Bishop Lightfoot's Essay on St. Paul and Seneca (*Philippians*, pp. 263–326).

[4] It may be that St. Paul would hardly have used such mild words in the earlier stages of his Judaic controversy. But as Hitzig says the age of the

Amid neglect, misery, and opposition St. Paul felt all the keener appreciation for the kindness of one truly generous community. From the Philippians he could accept the aid which they on their parts esteemed it a privilege and a blessing to be allowed to give. Philippi was specially dear to him. It was the first of all the Christian Churches which he had founded in Europe. "See! what a yearning he feels for Macedonia!" says Chrysostom. He liked the manly independence and affectionate enthusiasm of the Roman citizens of Macedonia. His use of the word "citizenship" and "play the citizens" shows how he shared with them the honourable pride of a claim to the franchise of the empire. Perhaps the wealth of a few converts like Lydia made it less difficult for him to avail himself of their bounty.

It was about autumn when Epaphroditus arrived from Philippi, with the offering,[1] which supplied the suffering Apostle with all that was immediately necessary for his simple needs. Flinging himself into the work of the Gospel at Rome at that unhealthy and malarious season, Epaphroditus was soon prostrated by a dangerous and all but fatal sickness. The news of this illness caused great sorrow at Philippi, and Paul too felt that the death of "his brother Epaphroditus," as he tenderly calls him, would have plunged him in yet heavier sadness. No miracle was thought of. The cases of Epaphroditus and of Trophimus show that, in ordinary life, the Apostles never dreamt of exerting any supernatural power. But those were days in which all Christians had an unfeigned belief in prayer. Paul and the Philippians pleaded with God for the life of their sick friend,

Apostle, which was now perhaps approaching sixty years, and the trial of his imprisonment tended to soften his feelings. Further, these Roman Jews may not have belonged to the "ultramontane" Judaists, who demanded that the Gentiles should be circumcised. Calvin was not a man of very mild disposition, yet he said of Luther, "he may call me 'a beast,' and 'a devil,' but I shall always think of him as a good servant of Jesus Christ."

[1] They had ministered to his necessities twice before at Thessalonica (iv. 16) and once at Corinth (2 Cor. xi. 9).

as Luther and the Reformers pleaded for the life of Melanchthon.[1] God heard their supplication. Epaphroditus recovered; and deeply as St. Paul, in his loneliness and discouragement, would have liked to keep this dear friend by his side, yet, with his usual unselfishness, he yielded to the yearning of Epaphroditus for his home, and of the Christians of Philippi for their absent pastor. He therefore sent him back, and with him he sent this letter, in which he expressed his heartfelt gratitude for the affection which had so happily cheered the monotony of his sorrows.

Thus the Epistle to the Philippians is what we should call an occasional letter. There is nothing systematic or special about it. It is not a trumpet-note of defiance like the Epistle to the Galatians. It is not the reply to a number of questions like the First to the Corinthians. It is not a treatise of theology like the Epistle to the Romans. It has more of a personal character like the Second Epistle to the Corinthians; but it is poured forth, not to those towards whom he had little cause for gratitude and much need for forbearance —not to jealous critics and bitter opponents—but to the favourite converts of his ministry, to the dearest children of his love. It is a genuine and simple letter—the warm, spontaneous, loving effusion of a heart which could express itself with unreserved affection to a most kind and a most beloved Church. That Church of Philippi seems to have been eminently free from errors of doctrine and irregularities of practice. One fault, and one alone, appears to have required correction, and this was of so personal and limited a character, that St. Paul only needs to hint at it gently and with affectionate entreaty. This was a want of unity between some of its members, especially between two ladies, whom St. Paul entreats to be reconciled to each other. I have already mentioned that in the greeting or thanksgiving of each of St. Paul's letters we almost always find a hint of their main

---

[1] " Allda musste mir unser Herr Gott herhalten. Denn ich rieb Ihm die Ohren mit allen *promissionibus exaudiendarum precum.*"—LUTHER.

motive or object.[1] In this letter we find it in the predominance PHILIPPIANS.
of the word " all " in the thanksgiving of the third verse—" I
thank my God in all remembrance of you, always in all my
supplication for you all, making my supplication with joy at
your united work for the Gospel."   This *general* unity had
existed from the first day he had visited them, ten years ago,
until now. He recurs to the same topic at the beginning of the
second chapter,[2] where he again urges them to unity.   " Fulfil
my joy that ye may think the same thing ; having the same
love ; heart-united ; thinking one thing. Nothing for partisanship, or for empty personal vanity ! but in lowliness of mind,
each of you thinking others his own superiors, not severally
keeping your eye on your own interests, but also severally on
the interests of others.   Be of the same mind in yourselves that
Christ Jesus was in Himself, who, existing in the form (*i.e.* in
the very nature, $\mu o \rho \phi \hat{\eta}$) of God, deemed not equality with God
a thing for eager seizure, but emptied Himself, taking the
form (the very nature, $\mu o \rho \phi \grave{\eta} \nu$) of a slave, revealing Himself
in human semblance ($\acute{o} \mu o \iota \acute{\omega} \mu \alpha \tau \iota$) ; and being found [3] in
figure ($\sigma \chi \acute{\eta} \mu \alpha \tau \iota$) as a man, humbled Himself, showing Himself obedient unto death, ay, and that death the death of the
Cross."   And so having, for our example, in lowliness and
unselfishness, descended from the infinite summit of glory to
the most abysmal depths of self-humiliation, He was again
exalted by God to a throne above all thrones, and a dominion
above all dominions.[4]

[1] An interesting feature of this greeting is that here alone he makes special
mention of the " bishops and deacons."   From the word "bishops" we must
exclude all modern connotations of the word.   At this period "bishops" were
simply "presbyters."   The plural form of the word shows the date of the
Epistle before the separation of the office of the "Episcopos" from that of the
"Presbuteroi."

[2] There are two sections in the letter which are devoted to the subject of
unity—i. 27–ii. 18 ; and iv. 1–9. Unity was all the more essential in the
presence of persecution ($\grave{\alpha} \nu \tau \iota \kappa \epsilon \acute{\iota} \mu \epsilon \nu o \iota$, i. 28).

[3] See John i. 45.

[4] It is characteristic of the extreme depth and fulness of the mind of St.
Paul, that even into an exhortation to the common Christian duty of unity he
thus casually introduces a passage so theologically important. The chief
truths of the profoundest Christology could not have been expressed more
grandly, and at the same time more tersely than in this swift outline of

3. This exhortation to perfect unity, founded upon the absolute humility and self-sacrifice of Christ, was the most serious object of this letter. Its infinite charm rests in its exquisite spontaneity. It is not of course such a letter as that to the Romans, but it is in all respects worthy of St. Paul, and shows him in some of the sweetest aspects of his character. St. Paul cannot always wear the majestic cothurnus, yet his lightest words are full of dignity. He could never be colourless. Even his briefest and most casual letters derive their colouring from those rich hues of the writer's individuality, which made it impossible for him to write five lines without giving us some of those jewels of spiritual thought or noble expression "which on the stretched forefinger of all time sparkle for ever."

The outline of this delightful letter of thanks to a loving Church is simply as follows. The exhortation to unity occupies sixteen verses of the second chapter, and, with this exception, after the greeting and thanksgiving, the rest of the first two chapters is filled with personal details about his feelings and work at Rome, especially the touching words about his difficulty of choosing between life and anticipated death. The letter, in fact, is mainly composed of two factors—personal details (i. 12—26 ; ii.

Christ's passage downwards, step by step, from the infinite heights into the uttermost abyss of self-humiliation (ii. 6–8), and then His re-ascent upwards into the super-exaltation [*] of unimaginable dominion (ii. 9-11). Each word of the passage is full of meaning. Around the single verb "He *emptied* Himself" [†] has risen a wide controversy known as "the *kenosis* controversy," and there is much significance, though no shadow of Docetism, in the contrast between the expressions "form" and "fashion"—the abiding and essential form or inmost nature ($\mu o \rho \phi \eta$) of God, in which Christ eternally was, and the outward transitory fashion ($\sigma \chi \hat{\eta} \mu a$) of a man in which He was found.

In this passage the "thought it not robbery to be equal with God" of the A.V. is an unfortunate mistranslation which almost reverses the real meaning. The whole context proves the meaning to be that "He counted it not a prize" —$\dot{a} \rho \pi a \gamma \mu \acute{o} \nu$ colloquially, perhaps incorrectly, used in the sense of $\ddot{a} \rho \pi a \gamma \mu a$— or "a thing to be grasped" to be on an equality with God. We can only mention it as a literary and theological curiosity that so able a critic as Baur fancied that this was an allusion to Wisdom (Sophia) the last Æon of the Pleroma in the Valentinian system, whose offspring sank back into the Emptiness (*Kenoma*) when she attempted to unite herself to the Absolute !

---

[*] ii. 9. $\dot{v} \pi \epsilon \rho \acute{v} \psi \omega \sigma \epsilon$.　　　　[†] ii. 7, $\dot{\epsilon} a v \tau \grave{o} \nu \dot{\epsilon} \kappa \acute{\epsilon} \nu \omega \sigma \epsilon \nu$.

17—30; iv. 10—15) and exhortations to unity (i. 27; ii. 16; PHILIPPIANS. iv. 1—9). But in the second verse of the third chapter the Apostle is suddenly interrupted and disturbed by we know not what bitter gust of feeling, caused by we know not what machination of Jewish malice. Apparently he was on the point of ending his letter. He had said "finally," and "farewell," when, with a sudden burst, as it were, he breaks into a digression singularly unlike the calm, sweet, tolerant tone of the rest of the letter. It is like coming across a stream of molten lava in the midst of green fields. He warns the Philippians in words of intense severity against Jewish and immoral opponents, whom he calls dogs and evil workers, and of whom he says that their god is their belly and their glory in their shame. With the vain boastings and unhallowed worldliness of these Judaists—this "mutilation party," as he calls them—he contrasts his own trust (in spite of all his privileges of birth and life) in Christ alone.[1] He tells them that, so far from counting himself perfect, he aims at resembling one of those wild-eyed charioteers of whom his soldier-guards told him so often when they had come from witnessing the races in the Circus Maximus. He too was a charioteer on the road to righteousness, leaning forward, as it were, in his flying car; bending over the shaken rein and the goaded steed, forgetting everything—every peril, every competitor, every circling of the *meta* in the rear, as he pressed on for the goal by which sate the judges with the palm, which should be the prize of his heavenly calling of God in Christ.[2]

---

[1] This passage (iii. 2–19) is, with the famous passage about Christ's self-inanition (ii. 5–11), the most distinctive and doctrinally important in the letter. Having begun the chapter, "Finally, my brethren, farewell in the Lord, to write to you the same things"—*i.e.* these constant exhortations to unity, or perhaps to joy—"is for me not burdensome, but for you it is safe," he stops, and adds with startling suddenness, "Beware of the dogs, beware of the evil workers, beware of the concision." There is nothing un-Pauline in the words. In 2 Cor. xi. 13, he had spoken of Judaists as "*deceitful* workers," and if "concision"—a word which implies that circumcision may be a mere physical mutilation—be a very severe expression, it is at any rate less so than the (perhaps half-humorous) sternness of the expression ὄφελον ἀποκόψονται in Gal. v. 12.

[2] iii. 14, σκοπὸς "goal" occurs here alone in the New Testament.

PHILIPPIANS. This long digression is, as it were, the spent wave, the dying echo of the Judaic controversy. Beginning in strong indignation, it calms itself down into pathetic appeal. At the close of it, in the third chapter, he addresses his earnest appeal to the two ladies Euodia and Syntyche.[1] After one more exhortation to Christian joy and steadfastness, he ends with warm expressions of gratitude for their generous kindness, and with the salutation and blessing with which he invariably concludes.[2] How richly must the Philippians have felt themselves repaid for their generosity by the receipt of a letter so gentle and so precious !

4. We have seen that the letter originated in an act of Christian liberality, and that its most marked characteristic is that of Christian joy. These two topics, which bear on the origin and the speciality of the letter, require a few words of further consideration.

i. We are often doubtless exhorted to Christian liberality. Yet when we notice the urgency with which St. Paul in letter after letter pleads for the poor saints at Jerusalem, we may well doubt whether this great duty is pressed home to us so plainly, so fearlessly, and so decisively as is desirable. Out of the circle of our own immediate families, beyond

---

[1] Schwegler and Volkmar see in Euodia and Syntyche, not two ladies, but two parties—the orthodox or Petrine party, and the Gentile Christians. Hitzig also thinks that Εὐωδία is a feminine form, invented from Εὐόδιος (LXX. Gen. xxx. 13 = Asher) and Συντύχη, for ἐν τύχῃ = Gad) to show that they were not really women !

[2] In iv. 3, we have "Yea and I beseech thee, also, true yokefellow" (γνήσιε σύζυγε). Who is this unnamed yokefellow ? Renan (*S. Paul*, 165) thinks that it was Lydia, and Clemens of Alexandria (*Strom.* iii. 6, 53) that she was Paul's wife ! Baur thinks that it was meant (by the forger) to indicate St. Peter. It is so unusual to salute a person without mentioning his name that I believe we have here a paronomasia, and that the Philippian's name was Syzygus. It would be quite in St. Paul's manner to address him as Syzygus "yokefellow" in heart as in name. The Tübingen school suppose the Philippian Clement who is here saluted to be meant for Clement of Rome, and they identify him with the martyred Consul, uncle of Domitian ! Clemens was a very common name, and there is nothing to show that he was not a member of the Philippian Church.

Another question occurs to us, why does he add to the salutation of the saints, "*especially* they of Caesar's household " ? That question cannot be answered. "They of Caesar's household " were probably a handful out of the *thousands* of slaves who filled the palace of Nero.

the edge of what may be called a somewhat selfish domes-
ticity, over the verge of the slightly expanded egotism of
the private home, how many of us do anything appreciable
to alleviate the distresses, to lessen the misery, to heal the
open sores of the world, to visit Christ in His sickness,
to relieve Christ in His hunger, to comfort Him in His
imprisonment, or clothe Him in His nakedness ? And if this
be so, if it be not ours to visit the fatherless and widows in
their affliction, or to discharge in person the high duties of
Christian charity, we can only fulfil these duties at all by
generous giving. How many are there who adequately
discharge this duty ? May we not all learn from these
Philippians, the depths of whose poverty abounded to the
riches of their liberality ?

ii. Notice, lastly, the speciality of this letter in its fine
throbbing undertone of spiritual joy. It has been said that
the sum of the whole letter is " I rejoice, rejoice ye." When
Paul and Silas lay in the deepest dungeons of Philippi, scored
and bleeding from the flagellation which the local " Praetors "
had inflicted upon them in the forum, they had sung songs
in the night. Another song now emanates from the Apostle's
Roman prison. His letter is like one of those magnificent
pieces of music which, amid all its stormy fugues and mighty
discords, is dominated by some inner note of triumph which
at last bursts forth into irresistible and glorious victory. It is
new and marvellous. What was there thus to fill the soul
and flood the utterance of St. Paul with joy ? The letter
was dictated by a worn and fettered Jew, the victim of gross
perjury, and the prey of contending enmities ; dictated by
a man of feeble frame, in afflicted circumstances, vexed
with hundreds of opponents, and with scarce one friend
to give him consolation. Could any one have been
embittered with deeper wrongs, or tormented by deadlier
sufferings ? Before we look upon this serene cheerfulness,
this unmurmuring resignation of St. Paul as a matter of
course, compare him for a moment with others whose circum-

stances were a thousandfold less pitiable than his. I will not take the case of Ovid and the wailing agony of his *Tristia,* for Ovid was a poet whose genius had been debased by the enervation of long-continued sensuality. But let us compare St. Paul with men of finer fibre and purer life. Cicero was, for a short time, exiled. His exile had every mitigation. He was not imprisoned. He could choose his own home. He was surrounded wherever he went with wealth, luxury, admiration, troops of friends. He knew that the great and the powerful were using all their influence on his behalf. And yet, though he claimed to be a philosopher, though he had published whole volumes of lofty exhortation, there is scarcely one of the many letters which he wrote during that short exile which is not full of unmanly lamentations.

Take another instance. Seneca was a contemporary of St. Paul; he may even have seen him. He was a man of immense wealth, of high rank, of great reputation; a man who wrote books full of the most sounding professions of Stoic endurance and Stoic superiority to passion and to pain. He too was, for a short time, exiled to Sardinia. He too was free, and rich, and he had powerful friends. How did he bear his exile? He too broke into abject complaints, and in spite of his Stoicism was not ashamed to grovel with extravagant flatteries at the feet of a worthless freedman, to induce him to procure his return.

Take another instance, and this time a Christian—Dante. We know what he thought and felt about "the hell of exile, that slow, bitter, lingering, hopeless death, which none can know but the exile himself." We know how, when the monk who opened for him the door of the monastery of Santa Croce asked him "What seek you here?" he gazed round him with hollow eyes and slowly answered "*Pacem!*" "Peace."

We might take other instances. We might compare St. Paul in exile with Clarendon, or Atterbury, or Bolingbroke. His lot was incomparably worse than theirs, for he was not only an exile, he was cold and hungry, and a prisoner PHILIPPIANS. and lonely, and suffering and distressed by the constant machinations of bitter opponents, and with the sword of the headsman hanging, as it were, by a thread over his neck. Yet his magnanimity stands out in bright contrast with even the best and greatest of these. He does not, like Cicero, weary his friends with complaints and importunities. He does not, like Seneca, fawn upon the worthless. He does not, like Dante, yield to a brooding melancholy. No such gloom comes over him as that which fell on our own great exiles. Yet he was more guiltless than any of these, and his sufferings were infinitely more unmerited. Amid poverty and imprisonment, with the frown of the tyrant bent on him, death seeming to stare him in the face, the fundamental note in the many-toned music of his letter is the note of joy. He recalls to our minds the runner who, at the supreme moment of Grecian history, brought to Athens the news of Marathon. Worn, panting, exhausted with the effort to be the herald of deliverance, he sank in death on the threshold of the first house which he reached with the tidings of victory, and sighed forth his gallant soul in one great sob, almost in the very same words as those used by the Apostle, χαίρετε, χαίρομεν, "Rejoice ye, we too rejoice!" The whole letter bears "the impress, at times almost elegiac, of resignation in view of death with high apostolic dignity, unbroken holy joy, hope, and victory over the world."[1] Here at least is one grand example for us all to follow, one glorious lesson for us all to learn. Let us try to attain to the secret of this peace which is like the deep peace in the heart of ocean in spite of all its surface agitations. Let us try to catch this glowing spirit which, even in the midst of sorrow, gives to the Christian a pure and incommunicable joy. Amid the gloom, amid the vapours of the charnel house, let our heavenly hope be still "Like the lone lamp which trembles in the tomb." They talk of the

[1] Meyer.

X

PHILIPPIANS. depression of the age. Pessimism is becoming a popular philosophy. In its luxury, and in its struggles, and in its sensuality, and in its very successes, the age is sad. We deserve and we receive the punishment of those whom the great Italian poet described as duly punished for this guilt, since—

> "Once we were sad
> In the sweet air made gladsome by the sun,
> Now in this mirky darkness, we are sad."

But the inward joy of the Christian, if brightest in the sunshine, is unquenched even by the storm. The true Christian, the perfect Christian, the saint of God, can be glad even in adversity, and rich in poverty, and calm in the prospect of death. Why? Because he has a freedom which no fetters can coerce, and a treasure which makes as nothing the loss of all; and because death, which guilty men regard as the most awful of penalties, is to him the sleep which God sends to His beloved when their day's work is done. St. Paul stood on a rock which no lightning could shatter, no billow shake. He stood high above the need of riches, above the dread of enemies. In a sense infinitely truer than the vaunt of the Stoic, he superabounded on the verge of hunger; he was a king in the slave's dungeon; in the midst of desertion he had many friends. "Hath he not always treasures, always friends"—the holy Christian man? Yes!

> "Three treasures, life, and light,
> And calm thoughts, regular as infant's breath,
> And three firm friends, more sure than day and night,
> Himself, his Maker, and the angel Death."

NOTE I.

OUTLINE OF THE EPISTLE.

1. Greeting. i. 1, 2.

2. Thanksgiving and prayer. i. 3–11.

3. Personal details, and messages, and thanks (i. 12–26 ; ii. 17–30 ; iv. 10–19).

4. Exhortations to unity (i. 27–ii. 16 ; iv. 1–9).

5. Digression and warning concerning false Judaising teachers (iii. 2–21).

6. Doxology, salutations, and blessing (iv. 20–23).

The letter is the least systematic of all the Epistles, but it contains several very striking and beautiful passages. Such are—

i. 19–26. The doubt respecting the choice of life or death.

ii. 5–11. The appeal to the example of Christ, in His "inanition" (*kenosis*) which was followed by exaltation.

iii. 7–11. His readiness to sacrifice everything for Christ.

12–16. His continued sense of imperfection.

As regards the phraseology of the Epistle we may notice the expressions—

iv. 8. *If there be any virtue.* This is the only place where the word ἀρετή occurs in St. Paul.

That ye may approve the things that are excellent (εἰς τὸ δοκιμάζειν ὑμᾶς τὰ διαφέροντα). Lit. "that ye may discriminate the transcendent," *i.e.* that even in good things you may discern what things are best. Comp. Rom. ii. 8.

i. 13. *In all the praetorian camp.* The *residence* of a king or governor might be called a Praetorium in the Provinces (Matt. xxvii. 27), but we may be sure that this term (properly "general's tent") was not used at Rome, where it would have been insultingly suggestive of a military despotism.

i. 25. *I shall bide and abide with you all* (μενῶ καὶ συμπαραμενῶ) ; the play of words is quite in St. Paul's manner (Rom. i. 28, 29, 30 ; ii. 1 ; xii. 3 ; 2 Cor. iii. 2 ; vi. 10 ; vii. 31 ; xi. 29 ; 2 Cor. iv. 8, &c.)

i. 27. *Live as citizens,* worthily of the "Gospel of Christ" (πολιτεύεσθε comp. πολίτευμα, iii. 20). The Philippians enjoyed the Roman franchise as St. Paul himself did. The substantive "citizenship" does not occur again in the New Testament ; the verb only in Acts xxiii. 1.

ii. 1. *If there be any tender mercies and compassions.* The reading of nearly all the Uncials is εἴ τις σπλάγχνα καὶ οἰκτιρμοί, "if any one be tender mercy and compassion." This has been treated as a mere clerical error, but St. Paul may have written it as he writes ἐνδύσασθε σπλάγχνα. Col. iii. 12.

ii. 17. *If I am poured out upon the sacrifice and offering of your faith.* The metaphor is taken from the drink-offering poured over a sacrifice. 2 Tim. ii. 6. Seneca when dying (Tac. *Ann.* xv. 64) sprinkled the bystanders with his blood, saying, "Libare se liquorem illum Jovi Liberatori." So too Thrasea, "Libemus, inquit, Jovi Liberatori." Id. xv. 35.

ii. 19. *Hazarding his life.* The reading of the best MSS. is παραβολευσάμενος. The word was technically used of *parabolani*, who as it were "played the gamblers" with their lives in attending on the sick.

iii. 1. *Rejoice in the Lord.* The word χαίρετε means both "farewell," and "fare ye well."

iii. 9. *A righteousness which is through faith in Christ, the righteousness which is of God by faith* (διὰ πίστεως ... ἐκ Θεοῦ ... ἐπὶ τῇ πίστει), i.e. a righteousness by *means of faith*, coming from God, *based on* faith.

iv. 10. *Ye have revived your thought for me* (ἀνεθάλετε τὸ ὑπὲρ ἐμοῦ φρονεῖν). Lit. "Ye *bloomed again* to think on my behalf." Here the A.V. keeps the metaphor "your care for me *hath flourished again.*" It was a "fresh springlike outburst" of old kindness.

ii. 25. *Your messenger.* ("Apostle" in the lower and untechnical sense of the word. 2 Cor. viii. 23.)

iii. 21. *Our vile body.* Happily this is, in the A.V., a mistranslation of τὸ σῶμα τῆς ταπεινώσεως ἡμῶν, "the body of our humiliation." Scripture nowhere sanctions the Manichean notion of the vileness of the body or the inherent evil of matter.

iv. 5. *Let your moderation be known unto all men* (ὑμῶν τὸ ἐπιεικὲς). Rather your "courtesy," Tyndale; *modestia*, Vulg.; "softness," Cranmer; "your *reasonableness.*"

iv. 7. *The peace of God shall guard your hearts.* God's peace shall stand armed—shall keep sentry over (φρουρήσει) your hearts.

iv. 12. *I have learned.* Rather, "I have been initiated," "I have learnt the secret" (μεμύημαι).

THE EPISTLE TO THE COLOSSIANS.

WRITTEN DURING THE FIRST ROMAN IMPRISONMENT. ABOUT A.D. 63.

"Christ all in all."

"Per Me venitur, ad Me pervenitur, in Me permanetur."—Aug. *In Joann.* xii.

"'Εν αὐτῷ περιπατεῖτε. In eo ambulate; in illo solo. Hic Epistola scopus est."—BENGEL.

"Walk in Him."—COL. ii. 6.

ST. PAUL'S Epistles—as we have already had occasion to observe—generally grew out of what (in ordinary language) would be called "accidental circumstances." To the Christian, however, there is no such thing as "chance" or "accident." Even the word Τύχη does not once occur in the New Testament. It is therefore only with the limitations which every Christian can supply for himself that the Apostle's writings can be called, in the phrase of a French writer, "*des écrits de circonstance*."

It is, however, perfectly true that he never seems to have written without some express reason or immediate occasion for doing so. Of the four letters despatched during his three years' imprisonment, the letter to the Philippians was caused by the arrival of Epaphroditus from Philippi with a pecuniary gift. The letter to Philemon was written to secure a kindly reception for a runaway slave. The letter to the Ephesians and Colossians rose out of the visit of Epaphras, a Colossian

COLOSSIANS. presbyter, who came to St. Paul at Rome, and whom he calls his "dear fellow servant," and "fellow prisoner."

St. Paul says that the Colossians had never "seen his face in the flesh." But he felt a deep interest in them, and the news which Epaphras brought of their condition was so strange and serious that he felt himself impelled to write to them, in order, if possible, to prevent irreparable mischief.

Among the tributaries of the Maeander in Asia Minor is the river Lycus, a river which, like the Anio, clothes its bed and valley with calcareous deposits, and forms for itself natural bridges of gleaming travertine, of which the fantastic effect is increased by the earthquakes to which this region has been peculiarly liable. On the banks of this strange river were three populous cities, Hierapolis, Laodicea and Colossae. Hierapolis is famous as the birthplace of Epictetus, whose moral teaching is the fairest flower of heathen philosophy; and as the See of Papias, whose writings were of much importance to the early Church. Laodicea, wealthy and magnificent, was the oldest and least faithful of the Seven Churches of the Apocalypse. Colossae, or (as the name appears on coins and inscriptions) Colassae, afterwards called Chonos, was an ancient but dwindling township, "the least important to which any letter of St. Paul is addressed." [1]

Although he was within such easy reach of these three interesting cities, St. Paul, strange to say, had never visited them during his long residence at Ephesus.[2] Perhaps his labours "night and day" among his Ephesian converts had detained him almost exclusively in the great city of Artemis. Yet, indirectly, he had become the founder of the Churches of the Lycus. For among his hearers at Ephesus had been Philemon, and Epaphras of Colossae, and Nymphas of Laodicea; and they, acting on the grand principle that every Christian is God's missionary, seem to have founded these

[1] In the days of Herodotus (vii. 20) and Xenophon (*Anab.* i. 2, § 6) it had been great and flourishing. In the days of Strabo it had sunk into a πόλισμα (xii. 17).
[2] Col. ii. 1.

daughter Churches of the Ionian metropolis.[1] St. Paul was
writing on a private matter to the Colossian Philemon. He
took the opportunity of addressing the Church of that place
and the Churches in the more splendid neighbour-cities which
were in the same valley, and within easy reach of each other.
He was all the more eager to seize this opportunity because
Epaphras brought with him the disturbing tidings that the
germs of a new heresy were there springing into life.

This heresy—new yet old, local yet universal—was but
another of the Protean forms assumed by the eternal
gravitation to erroneous extremes. In outward features it
differed from that tendency to apostatise into Judaism, from
which St. Paul had finally saved the Church by his Epistles
to the Galatians and Romans, nor was it mixed up with
that personal antagonism which adds so much additional
sting and bitterness to his previous controversies. It was
more insidious, but less violent. It was an incipient form of
those dangerous and inflating heresies—bred in the decay and
the ferment of new faiths, and mixture of old creeds—which
were soon to be known under the name of Gnosticism.

The strange district, "sombre and melancholy," rent by
earthquakes, and "burnt up, or rather incinerated by volcanic
catastrophes," seemed to invite its inhabitants to a dreamy
mysticism. Their religiosity was full of formalism and fear.
It may have sprung up among Jewish Essenes, influenced by
subtle Asiatic speculations.[2] It was a mixture of ascetic
practices and dreamy imaginations. It combined a crude
theosophy with a hard discipline and an elaborate ritual. It
made much of meats, and drinks, and new moons, and
sabbaths. It laid down valueless rules of "Touch not, taste
not, handle not." While professing to debase the body with
hard mortification, it was no real remedy for self-indulgence.

---

[1] The true reading of i. 7 is ὑπὲρ ἡμῶν. Epaphras had been a missionary
to these cities *on Paul's behalf.*

[2] On the Colossian heretics, see Bishop Lightfoot's Essay in his edition of
the Epistle, and an excellent note of Nitzsch in Bleek's *Einleitung,* § 163.
Vorlesungen, pp. 15–17.

COLOSSIANS. Under the guise of a voluntary humility, it concealed an extravagant pride. But worse than this, being tainted with the heresy that evil resides in matter, and therefore that the body is essentially and inherently vile, the adherents of this perverted doctrine were perhaps led to hint at some distinction between the human Jesus and the divine Christ. They were certainly trying to thrust all kinds of intermediate agencies, especially angels, between the soul and God. Such were the crafty errors—swiftly germinating in the "loose fertility" of the Asiatic intellect—which St. Paul had to combat in writing to Christians, of whom the majority were personal strangers to himself. He met them, not by indignant controversy, for as yet these errors were only undeveloped; nor by personal authority, for these Christians were not his converts; but by the noblest of all forms of controversy, which is the pure presentation of counter truths. To a cumbrous ritualism he opposes a spiritual service; to inflating speculations a sublime reality; to hampering ordinances a manly self-discipline; to esoteric exclusiveness a universal Gospel; to theological cliques an equal brotherhood; to barren systems a new life, a new impulse, a religion of the heart.

But most of all, he adopts the one best way of meeting the aberrations of Christianity, which is to lead back the soul to Christ. Already to the Thessalonians he had spoken of Christ as the Judge of quick and dead; to the Corinthians as the Invisible Head and Ruler of the Church; to the Galatians as the breaker of the yoke of spiritual bondage; to the Romans as the Deliverer from sin and death. He had now to develop a new truth more nearly akin to that revelation of Christ which we find in St. John. He has to set Christ forth as the eternal and yet Incarnate Word; as the Redeemer of the universe; as the Lord of matter, no less than of spirit; as one who, being the fulness of God's perfections, is the only Mediator, the only Potentate, the sole source of life to all the world. The sum, the whole scope of the Epistle to the Colossians is that Christ is the Pleroma—

the Plenitude—at once the brimmed receptacle and the total colossians. contents of all the gifts and attributes of God; Christ is all in all; walk in Him and in Him alone.

The style of the Epistle is somewhat laboured. It lacks the spontaneity, the fire, the passion, the tender emotion, which mark most of St. Paul's Epistles. The reason for this is twofold. It is partly because he is addressing strangers, the members of Churches which he had not directly founded, and to whom his expressions did not flow forth from the same full spring of intimate affection. It is still more because he is refuting errors with which he was not familiar, and which he had not witnessed in their direct immediate workings. He had only heard of these errors secondhand. He only understood so much of their nature as Epaphras had set before him in his Roman prison. In dealing with them he was engaged upon a new theme. When he was a little more familiarised with the theme—when he is writing of it a second time in the Epistle to the Ephesians, and when he is addressing converts whom he had personally won to Christ—he writes with more fervency and ease. The difference between the Epistles is analogous to that between the Epistles to the Galatians and the Romans. In the close similarity between the letters to Ephesus and Colossae, and yet in the strongly marked individuality of each, we have one of the most indisputable proofs of the genuineness of both. The two are different, but each has its own greatness. If this Epistle has less of the attractive personal element, and the winning pathos of other letters of St. Paul, it is still living, terse, solid, manly, vigorous; and brief though it be, it still, as Calvin says, contains the nucleus of the Gospel.

It falls into five well-marked sections : the introduction, and the doctrinal, the polemic, the practical, the personal sections.

1. After a brief greeting (i. 1, 2), the Apostle utters a full thanksgiving to God for the faith, and love, and fruitfulness, which sprang from their hope of heavenly blessedness (i. 3-8). He then tells them of his ceaseless prayers for

them, that they may be filled with full knowledge and spiritual understanding, still bearing fresh fruit, and being strengthened with fresh power, and perpetually giving thanks to God, who rescued us from the power of darkness, and qualified us for our share of the inheritance of the saints in light, and transferred us into the kingdom of the Son of His love, in whom we have our redemption, the remission of our sins (1-13).

2. This leads him gradually to the great doctrinal passage respecting the nature and office of Christ, as supreme alike in relation to the Universe and to the Church, alike in the natural and in the moral creation (ii. 15-17). It is this passage which constitutes the theological germ of the Epistle, and stamps it pre-eminently as the Christological Epistle. In the following verses St. Paul characteristically dwells on the thoughts at once exalting and humiliating, that the full, absolute, and universal revelation of this long-hidden mystery should have been intrusted *to him;* and he expresses his earnest desire that the Churches of the Lycus valley, though they had not seen his face in the flesh, may be helped by him to the full knowledge of that mystery of God, which is Christ, in whom are hidden all the treasures of wisdom and knowledge, to be by us sought for and enjoyed (i. 11; ii. 3). His object in writing is that they may be founded and firm in their faith, like pillars and temples which are exempt from the earthquake-shocks,[1] of which they saw the terrible traces on every side, and which at last shook their city into the dust.

3. From this he passes to the direct polemic against the encroachments of the error by which the letter had been occasioned (ii. 4-iii. 4). There was (he implies) at Colossae a certain Essene mystic, whom he will not name, who, with his seductive plausibility,[2] was making a prey of them by a so-called "philosophy," which was nothing else but vain deceit

---

[1] i. 23, μὴ μετακινούμενοι, "not earthquake-shaken."

[2] ii. 8, ὁ ὑμᾶς συλαγωγῶν διὰ τῆς φιλοσοφίας. ii. 4, μή τις ὑμᾶς παραλογίζηται ἐν πιθανολογίᾳ.

in accordance with human traditions and earthly rudiments, COLOSSIANS.
not in accordance with Christ. After exposing the special
errors which this man was trying to inculcate (ii. 4—23), he
shows them, in a powerful passage, that the true remedy for
carnal temptations was to be found in thoughts and practices
far different from the worrying scrupulosities of ceremonialism
and asceticism (iii. 1—4).

4. Leaving the regions of doctrine and controversy he
passes to the direct moral applications of the practical part of
his letter. This consists partly of general (iii. 5—17), partly
of special precepts (iii. 18; iv. 6). As general precepts he
bids them slay at a blow [1] by the new life which is in Christ,
and which *is* Christ, the sensual passions of their heathen
past, together with all the hatred and falsehood of the old
man with his deeds, and to put on at once the new man, who
is being ever renewed to full knowledge according to the
image of the creator in that region where all earthly distinctions are done away. Above all, love, in all its forms, is to be
a part of this new being, and peace and spiritual fervour are
to dominate in all their words and deeds (iii. 5—17). Passing
to special precepts,[2] he has a word of exhortation for women,
for men, for children, for fathers. Thinking perhaps of
Onesimus and Philemon, he impresses faithfulness on slaves,
and justice on masters. He urges on them the duty of earnest
and constant supplication, and specially asks their prayers on
behalf of his own labours in the Gospel. He further bids
them walk in wisdom, earnestness, and holiness of speech.

5. The rest of the letter is personal (iv. 7—17). Tychicus
the bearer of the letter, and their fellow townsman Onesimus
would tell them all about him. He sends them greetings
from Aristarchus his fellow captive, Mark the cousin of
Barnabas, and Jesus Justus, his Jewish comforters and fellow
workers. Their pastor Epaphras, Luke the physician, the

---

[1] iii. 5. Νεκρώσατε . . . 8. ἀπόθεσθε. All that was evil was to be blown up
at once, but all good habits were to be continually built up.
[2] These are all in the present imperative, implying continuous duties.

beloved, and Demas—about whom there is a somewhat ominous reticence—greet them. They are to salute the Laodicean Christians and Nymphas and his friends, and to see that this letter and the one which he is writing to Laodicea be interchanged and read in both Churches.[1] Archippus, perhaps the son of Philemon and chief pastor of Laodicea, is to be stirred up to more earnest efforts.

The letter closes with the brief autographic salutation of St. Paul, in that shorter form—" Grace be with you "—which is characteristic of his later Epistles. But St. Paul rarely wrote even a single paragraph without adding some individual touch, and here he inserts the pathetic words " Remember my bonds." Perhaps as he rose to take the reed from his amanuensis—Timothy or Tychicus—the coupling-bond which bound him by the wrist to the Praetorian soldier clanked upon the floor, and he was reminded (as when he wrote to Philemon) that he presents the strange anomaly of " an ambassador in a chain."

Even in the dust of St. Paul's writings there is gold, and there is not a single clause of this Epistle which has not its own beauty, value, or interest. Clearly however the two most specific and important passages are the Doctrinal and the Polemical—in which combined he presents the loftiest possible Christology as the only effectual counterpoise, both morally and intellectually, to Gnostic error.

Let us glance at these two passages.

I. In the first (i. 19—ii. 3), after thanking God for the redemption and remission of sins wrought by the Son of His Love, he proceeds to set forth Christ in His unmistakable, unapproachable, eternal divinity. In relation to God He is God's image, alike His representation and manifestation. In relation to the Universe He is the Mediator between

---

[1] It is called τὴν ἐκ Λαοδικείας because it would come to Colossae from Laodicea, which was lower down the Lycus valley nearer to Ephesus. The " Laodicean " letter is probably the circular letter to " the Ephesians." The extant letter " to the Laodiceans " is a spurious and valueless cento of Pauline phrases.

God and all created things, being *prior to* all creation, and COLOSSIANS. *sovereign over* all creation. Mystic dreamers might invent Angelologies, and thrust intermediate agencies between man and God, thus interfering with man's most blessed privilege of immediate access; but Christ is all in all. All things— in heaven and on earth, visible and invisible—whether "thrones," or "lordships," or "principalities," or "powers,"— all things were created (ἐκτίσθη) by His agency; all things continue their being (ἔκτισται) with reference to Him; His divine prae-existence (αὐτὸς ἔστιν) precedes all things, and in Him as the band of the universe all things cohere. Such is His relation to God, and to all the natural Universe. The constant repetition of the words "all things"[1] shows with what absolute jealousy St. Paul would exclude His universality of pre-eminence from every encroachment, whether of Angels or of Æons.[2] However great they may be in themselves "thrones, dominations, virtues, princedoms, powers," are nothing in respect to His all-completeness. St. Paul will hear of none but

"Him first, Him last, Him midst, and without end."[3]

For, being thus in Himself, what is He to the Church? The Church is the body of which He is the Head. He is the Beginning, the Firstborn from the dead, the presiding power in all things, because God thought good that in Him the whole Plenitude—the totality of the divine attributes and agencies—should take its dwelling. "In Him," he adds a little later on—in a passage which is the nearest approach of any other writer to St. John's "the Word became flesh"—"in Him resides[4] all the Plenitude of Godhead bodily." The human Jesus is one with the Eternal Christ.

But if He be so immense, if He be the Consummation,

---

[1] πάσης κτίσεως, 15. τὰ πάντα . . τὰ πάντα, 16. πρὸ πάντων . . τὰ πάντα, 17.

[2] The Valentinians, according to Irenaeus (*Haer.* i. 4, § 5), talked not only of "thrones" and "lordships," but even of "godships" (θεότητες). St. Paul has already warned the Colossians in this Epistle that the plenitude of Godship is in Christ.

[3] Col. i. 15–17.

[4] κατοικεῖ. St. John uses the word ἐσκήνωσεν (i. 14).

the Fulfilment, the Pleroma, if He be what the Jewish
theosophists called " the Place "—(Makôm)—the Universe,
of which they said "God is not the Makôm, but all the
Makôm is in God" —there was an obvious danger that
speculating errorists might try to *disunite* Jesus—to separate
the human, the suffering Jesus from the Divine, Eternal
Son. St. Paul at once guards against such heresies by adding
that it was also God's will by His means to reconcile all
things to Himself, making peace by the blood of His cross.
St. Paul does not shrink from a juxtaposition of these two
words—the Supreme, the Pleroma on the one hand, who is
the summit of all exaltation, and on the other the lowest
depths of the most abysmal degradation, the gibbet of a
malefactor's shame. He therefore emphatically repeats the
words that " By Him" God thus reconciled all things to
Himself—yea, by His cross—whether the things on earth or
even those in the heavens (i. 15—20). And having thus
compressed into a few lines the description of Christ's work
generally, he proceeds to speak of His work specially for the
redeemed Colossians (21, 22), if only they abide in the faith,
and are not shaken away from the moorings of their hope.

This is the mystery—the truth long hidden now
revealed—of the wealth and glory of which St. Paul became
a steward and a minister, that he might preach it, not to
chosen *mystae*, and not with esoteric reserve, but completely
and universally, warning every man, teaching every man in
all wisdom, to present every man, as fully initiated, to Christ
(i. 23—29).[2]

II. Turning to the polemic against the incipient heresy
(ii. 4—iii. 4) we find from the counter truths presented by
St. Paul that—

---

[1] There is clearly some analogy between the Makôm of this Jewish proverb
and the Pleroma. The Kabbalistic method of Gematria or assigning numerical
equivalents to words (the Greek *isopsephia*) aided this usage. For יהוה
(Jehovah) $= 10 + 5 + 6 + 5 = 26$; and *Makôm* $= 10^2 + 5^2 + 6^2 + 5^2 = 186$. See Philo, *De Somn.* i. p. 575. Bereshith Rabba, § 68.

[2] πάντα ἄνθρωπον, thrice repeated, ἐν πάσῃ σοφίᾳ, i. 28. τέλειον, a word
belonging to the Greek mysteries.

The system of the new teacher interfered with the conception of this supremacy of Christ. He therefore reminds them at the outset not to be plundered by an empty, illusory semblance of "philosophy," which was merely traditional and worldly, and not according to Christ, since in Christ abides, bodily, the Plenitude of Godhead, and they are in Him, fulfilled with the plenitude of Him who is the head of every "principality" and "power." Their beguiling heresiarch, with his subtlety and intellectualism, wished at once to Judaise them, and to make ascetics of them. Thus :—

i. He tried to insinuate the meritoriousness if not the necessity of circumcision. But of what use is external circumcision to those who in baptism have been buried with Christ, and so have stripped off the body of these sins ? Spiritually dead, spiritually uncircumcised, they had been quickened into life, and without circumcision had been freely forgiven all their transgressions by Christ (iv. 11—13).

ii. Again, the false teacher had tried to reintroduce Judaic ordinances—distinctions of clean and unclean food, feasts new moons, Sabbaths (ii. 16).

But how would these avail them ? They were but shadows of which the substance is Christ. All that bond which was once valid against them by its ordinances—that "killing letter"—Christ had blotted out, had torn, had cancelled, had nailed its fragments to His cross (ii. 14—17).

iii. Further, there had been an attempt to remove God so far away as to render it necessary (a) to insert various ranks of angels between Christ and man ; and (β) apparently also to create a formidable demonology.

As to the latter (β)—the dynasts of wickedness—St. Paul says that Christ had "stripped them away from Him," that He had, as it were, torn Himself free from their assaults, which would otherwise have clung to Him like a robe,[1] and had, in perfect confidence, made a show of them, by leading them in triumph upon that same cross to which He

---

[1] ii. 15, ἀπεκδυσάμενος.

had nailed the ordinances of an abrogated bondage. And thus the Eternal Conqueror had made the gibbet of the slave the *feretrum* of the spoils of spiritual victory (ii. 15).[1]

And (*a*) as to angels, no one, by delighting in abjectness, and in service of angels, was to snatch from them the price of their Christian calling. To do this was to walk in the airy void of visions,[2] not on the solid ground of truth. Such fancies sprang from the inflations of the carnal intelligence, aided by the ecstasies of an ill-regulated asceticism. They would be secure from such voluntary self-humiliation if they held fast to Him who is the Head from whom all the life of the body flows" (ii. 18, 19).[3]

iv. Once more their new teacher had tried to entrammel them in the bonds of a rigid and formal asceticism. Like some of the Rabbis he had laid down rules that men should only eat a morsel with salt, and drink water by measure. He had dogmatised over them [4] as though they were living in the world, not in God's kingdom, by such rules as "Handle not, nor taste, nor even touch"—rules affecting mere perishable material things which had no connection with that which really defiles,[5] and which were of purely human origin (ii. 20—23).

What had they to do with such unauthorised bondage? When, in their baptism, they died and were buried with Christ, did they not die at the same time to all these illusory scrupulosities (σκία) and mundane rudiments (στοιχεῖα)? Besides which, all these regulations were useless for the end proposed. They did not in reality tend to the mortification of the evil passions. They were mere volunteered works of

---

[1] *Id. θριαμβεύσας αὐτοὺς ἐν αὐτῷ, i.e.* in the cross.

[2] ii. 18, ἃ ἑόρακεν ἐμβατεύων, "dwelling in," and "walking upon," the things which he has seen ; or as some MSS. read, "which he has *not* seen." There is some corruption or obscurity in the words, but they seem to allude to visions real or imaginary.

[3] The adoration of angels was a Jewish (Epiphan. *Haer.* xxv. 3, 16, and a fragment of the Κήρυγμα πέτρου) and specifically an Essene aberration (Jos. *B. J.* ii. 8, § 7).

[4] ii. 20, τι . . . δογματίζεσθε ;

[5] Mark vii. 1–23.

supererogation; they were a needless ill-usage of the body; their asserted wisdom—their pretence that they sprang from deeper knowledge and higher holiness—was mere assertion. Such oral traditions looked well; they wore a semblance of humility and self-denial, but in reality they were valueless; they did not at all avail to overcome the indulgence of fleshly impulses.

We cannot but regret that, in the original, the verse in which St. Paul lays down this weighty opinion is so difficult that it has been very little understood. Even in our Authorised Version it was rendered in terms which were in part unintelligible, and which entirely failed to make clear the lesson which they convey. Had their meaning been better grasped many a poor monk and anchorite, tormented and half maddened by emaciation and self-torture, might have been spared the bitter experience that the virulence of temptation, so far from being diminished, is intensified almost to madness by morbid self-introspection and unnatural asceticism.[1]

When St. Paul has thus doctrinally and controversially pronounced against the tendencies of which Epaphras had informed him—when he had thus vindicated the supremacy of Christ, the universality of the Gospel, the freedom of Christian life, against the mysticising ecstasies of an ascetic Jewish theosophy—he proceeds to tell the Colossians the true remedy against concupiscence. It is heavenly-mindedness.[2] They were dead : dead to the flesh, dead to passion, dead to their old selves, dead to the world. Their life has been hidden with Christ in God. It is a hidden life, a divine life, which at Christ's manifestation should become a life of manifested glory. Hence the Apostle, in closing the controversial aspect of the truths which he desires to inculcate, bids them to strike

---

[1] Compare the remarkable experiences of St Antony, St. Jerome, Hugo of Avalon, and many others. The monkish commentators almost unanimously explained the "thorn in the flesh" to mean "carnal temptations"—a fact which speaks volumes.

[2] iii. 1. τὰ ἄνω ζητεῖτε οὗ ὁ Χριστὸς. 2. τὰ ἄνω φρονεῖτε μὴ τὰ ἐπὶ τῆς γῆς, κ.τ.λ.

COLOSSIANS. dead[1]—not by regulated ordinances and innovating asceticism, but by the power of the new spiritual life—those earthly temptations which are perpetually bringing the wrath of God upon the children of men. Thus the Epistle is a protest against the invasion of religion by superstitions which were nourished partly by Judaisers, partly by oriental dreamers.[2]

The rest of the Epistle is comparatively simple and easy. It consists of practical rules which spring at once from the great doctrinal truths which have been laid down with so firm a hand. But the specific significance of the Epistle is concentrated into the two passages on which we have been dwelling. It is the Epistle which more fully and clearly than any other sets forth the supreme divinity of Christ Jesus. It is the Epistle which more decisively than any other lays down for us the rule that it is by union with Christ, not by ceremonial observances or self-mortifying practices that we can win the victory over the sinful impulses of our lower nature.

---

[1] iii. 5, Νεκρώσατε οὖν.

[2] In the Acts we read of "magicians" (viii. 9 ; xiii. 8), cheats and quacks and sorcerers (γόητες, 2 Tim. iii. 13) ; exorcists (Acts xix. 13) ; prophets (xvi. 16). The Golden Ass of Apuleius, the story of Apollonius of Tyana, and of Alexander of Abonoteichos, the constant references of writers of that age to Chaldaeans, mathematicians, casters of horoscopes, &c., show the prevalence of oriental superstition.

NOTE I.

SOME SPECIAL EXPRESSIONS AND PASSAGES IN THE EPISTLE.

Among the prominent words of the Epistle are :

"*Bearing fruit*" (i. 6, καρποφορούμενον. 10, καρποφορουντες).

"*Mystery*," i. 27 ; ii. 2 ; iv. 3.

"*Full knowledge*" (ἐπίγνωσις), i. 9, 10 ; ii. 2 ; iii. 10. In the latter passage this full knowledge is a characteristic of the new man. It is a discovery of the mysteries of Christ, of the treasures hidden in Him. It is the wealth of the completeness of the understanding (ii. 2). It holds to the Head, and so differs from the false heretical *Gnosis* with its dreams, and inflations and rituals.

The word "*philosophy*" occurs nowhere in the New Testament except in ii. 8 ; and then only to express the false system of the Gnosticising Essene.

"*To be dogmatised over*" occurs only in ii. 20. "Dogma" in ii. 20, and in all the other places where it occurs, refers to Jews, heathens, and heretics, in the sense of "decree" or "rule."

"*To be umpire*" and "*to decide against*" (βραβεύω, καταβραβεύω) in ii. 18 ; iii. 15.

In i. 23, "Who *translated* us into the kingdom of His dear Son," (μετέστησεν) Bishop Lightfoot sees a possible allusion by way of contrast to the hateful and violent "translation" of 2,000 Jewish families by Antiochus the Great, from Babylon into Lydia and Phrygia, Jos. *Antt.* xl. 3, § 4. The verb is used for wholesale deportations by the LXX. 2 Kings xvii. 23 ; xxiii. 33.

The words *full knowledge of the mystery* (ii. 2) ; and *the riches of the glory of this mystery*, i. 27 ; and *walk in Him* (ii. 6), are keynotes of the Epistle.

The most remarkable passages have been explained in the discourse.

In i. 24 we have a suggestive conception : "Now I rejoice in my sufferings for your sake, and fill up on my part *that which is lacking* (τὰ ὑστερήματα) *of the afflictions of Christ in my flesh*, for His body's sake which is the Church."

We might be startled by such a phrase as "that which is lacking in the sufferings of Christ," and still more at the notion that any can fill up that which so lacks. But though Christ's death was "a full, perfect and sufficient sacrifice for the sins of the whole world," and though no human sufferings can be vicarious in the sense in which His were, yet

COLOSSIANS. the sufferings of His saints may be *ministrative*, and thus, as continuing Christ's work on earth, they are able personally to supplement in His stead (*ἀνταναπληροῦν*), for His Church, what is still required.

———————

It is curious that, in this Epistle alone, eminently Christological as it is, the salutation "Grace be unto you, and peace from God the Father" is *not* associated with the name of Christ, since the following words "and the Lord Jesus Christ" are omitted by the best MSS. On the other hand in iii. 15, the true reading is "Let the peace *of Christ*" (not "of God," as in the A.V.) "arbitrate" ("be umpire" *βραβενέτω*) "in your hearts."

THE EPISTLE TO THE EPHESIANS.

WRITTEN AT ROME, A.D. 63.

"Nulla epistola Pauli tanta habet mysteria tam reconditis sensibus involuta."
—JER. IN EPH. iii.

"To sum up all things in Christ."—EPH. I. 10.

THE slightest glance at St. Paul's letters shows us how
deep and varied were his services to Christian truth, not only
by his life, but even more, if possible, by his writings. They
are a fountain from which streamed many a deep and fertilising
river. No succeeding teacher has been able to understand
them in all their fulness, or even duly to present a single
part of them. We have seen that Luther said of the
Epistle to the Galatians, "It is my epistle; it is my wife,
my Catherine von Bora." The learned and gentle Melanchthon, on the other hand, founded his manual mainly on the
Epistle to the Romans. The stern, clear-sighted, logical Calvin
follows in his *Institutes*, though in a very different spirit and
with infinitely less of sweetness and tenderness—the lines
marked out by the Epistle to the Ephesians. And these
three great Reformers, though so unlike each other, are yet
one in heart and in system; and both in their resemblances
and their differences they severally and yet imperfectly
reflect the many-sided teaching of St. Paul, as he reflected
what he calls in this Epistle the many-coloured—the richly-
variegated—wisdom of God.[1]

[1] Eph. iii. 10, ἡ πολυποίκιλος σοφία τοῦ Θεοῦ. Comp. ποικίλη χάρις, 1 Pet.
iv. 10.

1. There was in St. Paul's mind a peculiar sensibility. He was susceptible to every spiritual influence. Montanus compared the soul of man to a lyre, struck by the *plectrum* of the Holy Spirit. The soul of St. Paul was such a harp—a harp of infinite delicacy and yet with vast compass of music. When once it was touched by the light and breeze of heaven it answered, now in thundering reverberations like the Epistle to the Galatians, and now in soft trembling notes, like those to the Philippians or Philemon. And the strings of that exquisite instrument, when once stirred, continued long to vibrate. Each chord, if ever so lightly touched, continued thrilling with the touch. In minor details we notice this in the way in which St. Paul is haunted and taken possession of by single words and dominant conceptions, each lasting till its full force is spent. We notice it still more in the influence exercised by one Epistle over another. The echo of the Galatians continues to resound in Romans, and only trembles into silence in Philippians. The echo of Colossians is still heard quivering through every chord of Ephesians. There could be no stronger proof of the genuineness of these two Epistles, eagerly as it has been disputed, than their likeness to each other in the midst of unlikeness. To change the metaphor, they are twin sisters of close resemblance yet marked individuality, whose faces, alike yet different, can only be explained by their common parentage. They resemble each other in general structure—one half of each being theological, the other half practical. They are like each other in diction. Seventy-eight verses out of 155 have the same phrases. Yet they are unlike. The characteristic phrase, "the heavenlies" which occurs five times in Ephesians does not occur once in Colossians. Five sections in Ephesians—that which states the fore-ordained unity of the redeemed Universal Church (i. 3—14); that about living in a way worthy of this ideal unity (iv. 5—15); that which contrasts the deeds of darkness and light (v. 7—14); that about the mystery of Christian marriages (v. 23—33); and that about

the Christian armour (vi. 10—17), have no parallel in
Colossians. Ephesians has seven Old Testament allusions,
Colossians has only one. Again, Colossians is brief and
logical, Ephesians more lyrical and diffuse. In Colossians
St. Paul is the soldier, in Ephesians the builder. Colossians
is "his argument, his process, his caution;" Ephesians is
instruction passing into prayer, a Creed soaring into an
impassioned Psalm. Ephesians develops with magnificent
generality the truths which are directed in Colossians against
a special error. Once more, even their fundamental themes
though cognate, are not identical. In Colossians it is Christ-
hood; in Ephesians Churchhood. The topic of Colossians is
Christ all in all; the topic of Ephesians is Christ ascended,
yet present in His Church.

This union of close resemblance and radical dissimilarity is
one of the strong proofs of the authenticity of the Epistle.
The writer shows far too marked an originality to allow of
the supposition that he borrowed from some one else. Any
writer who was reduced to borrow could never have been
capable of so rich and independent an originality of thought
and style.[1]

2. To many it has seemed that in Ephesians St. Paul is
at his best and greatest. Luther called this Epistle one of
the noblest in the New Testament. Witsius calls it a

---

[1] The occurrence of *two* Epistles on almost the same themes, yet widely different
in details, is found in the indisputably genuine Epistles to the Romans and Galatians. The relations between those two Epistles are closely analogous to the
phenomena presented by Colossians and Ephesians. Galatians and Colossians
are specific, impassioned, and polemical: Romans and Ephesians are calm and
independent expositions of the truths involved in the letters which had immediately preceded them. To speak with De Wette of the "verbose expansion"
of the Ephesians; to say with Schneckenburger that it shows "a mechanical
use of materials;" to speak with others of the "colourless character" of this
Epistle is to be blind to the most obvious phenomena. And one of the fundamental weaknesses of the Tübingen and other foreign schools of critics is the
strange facility with which they assume a multitude of "forgers" equal or
even superior to Paul himself in power and spiritual depth, who, though their
writings were transcendently more valuable than all the other literature of the
second century, lived unheard of and died unknown! Could one who remained a
nameless forger have written in these few pages a better refutation of the essence
of Gnosticism, than Irenaeus in his five books against heresy, and Hippolytus
in his ten books of *Philosophomena*, and Tertullian in his *Scorpiace* combined?

ESIANS. divine Epistle, glowing with the flame of Christian love and the splendour of holy light, and flowing with fountains of living water. Alford calls it "the most heavenly work of one whose very imagination is peopled with things in the heavens, and even his fancy rapt into the visions of God." Coleridge said of it, "In this, the divinest composition of man, is every doctrine of Christianity; first, those doctrines peculiar to Christianity; and secondly, those precepts common to it with natural religion." It is emphatically the Epistle of the Ascension. We rise in it, as on wings of inspiration, to the divinest heights. Word after word—and thought after thought—now "the heavenlies," now "spiritual," now "riches," now "glory," now "mystery," now "plenitude," now "light," now "love," seem as it were to leave behind them "a luminous trail" in this deep and shining sky.[1] It is the most sublime, the most profound, the most advanced and final utterance of St. Paul's Gospel to the Gentiles. There we deal no longer with a material advent, nor with arguments about the nullity of ceremonialism, nor with personal vindications, nor even with a system of theology : but we are told of a scheme predestined before earth began; of the all-pervading supremacy of God in Christ; of the universal quickening of spiritual death by the union with the Risen Christ; of the glory and dignity of the Universal Church as the Temple, the Body, the Bride of her Ascended Lord. The motto of the whole Epistle might be, "There is one Body and one Spirit,"—the Body is the Universal Church of God, the Spirit is the Spirit of the Christ.

3. The letter was probably a circular letter to the Churches of Asia, and was not intended for Ephesus alone. This accounts for the exclusion of all private salutations, and for the absence of affectionate intimacy and personal appeal by which it is marked.[2] It falls as distinctly

---

[1] See Introductory Remarks.

[2] It may doubtless have been meant for the Ephesians *among others*, and all personal messages and salutations to the special Church could have been sent in a separate note, or conveyed by Tychicus. The distance and generality of

as Colossians into two marked divisions—three chapters
being doctrinal and Christological; and three chapters moral
and practical. After the salutation follows a singularly rich
compressed and beautiful thanksgiving, in which by the
thrice repeated phrase "the praise of His glory" (i. 6, 12,
14), he reveals that the great fore-ordained plan of man's
deliverance and glorification was the work alike of Father
(i. 3), Son (i. 7), and Holy Spirit (i. 13). He then utters an
earnest prayer that the eyes of their hearts may be illuminated,[1]
that they might fully know the wealth and glory of their
heritage, and the power of God in raising Christ from the
dead, and making Him the Head of His Body the Church
which is the fulness (Pleroma)—the brimmed receptacle—of
Him who filleth all things with all things.[2] The second
chapter shows that these privileges were intended for all
mankind, Gentiles as well as Jews, who had alike been
seated in the heavenlies in Christ by grace, and had alike
been built on the cornerstone of Christ as stones in the one
Spiritual Temple.[3] The third chapter is a further exposition
of this "mystery" or finally revealed truth of divine predestination. He is awestruck when he thinks that the preach-

---

the tone, the absence of the word "brethren," which in vi. 10, is wanting in
some of the best MSS., the twice repeated "if" in iii. 2 ; iv. 12 ; would be
inexplicable if the "*in Ephesus*" of the first verse expressed the sole destination
of the letter. But these words are *omitted* in ℵ B, and St. Basil says that they
were wanting in the ancient MSS. Marcion, merely on critical grounds, and
following tradition, thought that this Epistle was the letter to the Laodiceans
(see Col. iv. 16). The phrase *And ye also* (καὶ ὑμεῖς i. 13 ; vi. 21), is probably
due to the encyclical character of the letter. See Bleek, *Einl.* § 168–170.

[1] i. 18, πεφωτισμένους τοὺς ὀφθαλμοὺς τῆς καρδίας ὑμῶν.

[2] The word Pleroma is here used in a different sense from Col. i. 19, where
it means "the totality of the Divine attributes and agencies." There is
nothing strange in the supposition that St. Paul should use in two senses a
rare, undefined, and technical word which is not one of his own words, but is
borrowed from the terminology of others.

[3] St. Paul is so anxious in these first three chapters to raise the conception
of the Church into that of absolute unity of Gentiles with Jews in the
heavenlies, *i.e.* in the realm of the Ascended Lord—that he not only uses such
words as "coheirs" (συγκληρόνομα), and "built together" (συνοικοδομεῖσθε),
but adopts the late unclassical word "co-citizens" (συμπολῖται), and invents
such strange terms as "con-corporate" (σύνσωμα), "comparticipant"
(συμμέτοχα), "compaginated" (συναρμολογουμένη), "compacted" (συμβιβαζόμενον), ii. 19, 21, 22 ; iii. 6 ; iv. 16.

EPHESIANS. ing and comprehension of that mystery has been specially
assigned to himself the less than least of all saints.[1] The
chapter ends with a prayer for the fuller comprehension
of this mystery, and this prayer passes into an expression
of earnest thanksgiving. Throughout these three sublime
chapters, in which the writer seems to labour with the
fulness and grandeur of his own thoughts, there runs the
broken thread of one continuous petition.[2]

4. With this thanksgiving he closes the doctrinal part of
the Epistle, and begins the practical—" I then "—and how
vast is the significance of that word "then," building as it
does the simplest of all duties on the sublimest of all truths !
—" I then the prisoner of the Lord beseech you to walk
worthily of the vocation wherein ye were called." That is
the key-note of the remainder of the Epistle. St. Paul was
not conscious of any descent of thought when he passed from
the sublimest spiritual mysteries to the humblest practical
obligations. The first duty which he impresses is that of
Unity; the unity of the Spirit in the bond of peace; unity
in the unity of the faith amid the diversity of different gifts
of grace; unity as exemplified in those virtues of lowliness,
meekness, long-suffering, forbearance, which the heathen
had hitherto ranked with vices. He then contrasts this
their Christian vocation with their old heathen life, and so
passes from the dominant conception of Love (i. 3—13) to
that of Light (v. 8—15). As Gentiles, their hearts had been
dark and callous; they had sinned away the very sense of
sin;[3] but now they were clothed in the new nature which
Christ bestowed. Let them then put away lying, and wrath,
and bitterness, dishonesty, and unclean speech, which are all sins
against our oneness in Christ.[4] And especially as children of

---

[1] τῷ ἐλαχιστοτέρῳ, iii. 18.

[2] i. 17 ; iii. 13, 14.

[3] Hence the expression "callosity of heart" (πώρωσιν, iv. 18), and "past-
feelingness" (ἀπηλγηκότες, iv. 19, "*qui postquam peccaverint, non dolent*).

[4] Among other words St. Paul uses the Aristotelian expression εὐτραπελία,
"cultivated impertinence," (*Rhet.* ii. 12)—the consummate skill of the pro-
fessional liar and paid slanderer.

light let them walk in the light, and bring forth the fruits of EPHESIANS.
light,[1] in goodness, righteousness, and truth, in the spirit of
an exhortation which is perhaps a fragment from some early
Christian hymn.

> " Awake thee thou that sleepest,
> And from the dead arise thou,
> And Christ shall shine upon thee."[2]

Then, lest the freedom and enthusiasm of Christianity, the
new fermenting wine of the Gospel, should lead to any disorder,
he specially urges on them the duties of mutual submission[3]
in the three great social relations of wife to husband, and
husband to wife (v. 22—33); children to parents, and parents
to children (vi. 1—4); of masters to servants, and servants
to masters (vi. 5—9). And since this life in the light of
Christ pervades every sphere of duty, he bids them to grow
strong in the Lord and in the might of His strength.

5. That exhortation brought into his mind the image of
armour with which the worn and aged prisoner was so familiar.
The long coupling-chain ($ἅλυσις$) which bound his right
wrist to the left of a Roman legionary clanked continually as
it touched some part of the soldier's arms. Among the few
objects on which St. Paul could daily gaze were the baldric,
the military boot, the oblong shield, the cuirass, the helmet of
his Prætorian guardsmen. Doubtless the Apostle, in his
tender yet manly breadth of sympathy with his fellowmen in
all things human, often conversed with these soldiers. That
was how it came about that the Gospel was heard of through-

---

[1] v. 9. $ὁ καρπὸς τοῦ φωτός$.

[2] The lines

> $Ἔγειραι ὁ καθεύδων$
> $Ἀνάστα ἐκ τῶν νεκρῶν$
> $Ἐπιφαύσει σοι ὁ Χριστός$.

There is evidently something rhythmical in these lines. We see, from Col. iii.
16, Rev. xix. 1-4, that hymns and antiphonal congregational singing already
existed. Hippolytus quotes these words as coming from "a prophet;" $ὁ δὲ$
$προφήτης λέγει,$ $Ἔγειραι, κ.τ.λ.$ (*De Christo et Antichr.* 65.)

[3] The mental association between fervent singing and the duty of subjection
is perhaps to be found in a reminiscence of disorderly public worship at Corinth.
How often has the perfervid shouting of revivalists degenerated into unseemly
uproar !

out the Praetorian barracks. It was the beginning of the days when there should be in the Roman army a Thundering Legion; of the days when the host of Maxentius should be flung into wild panic by the cross on the Labarum of Constantine at the battle of the Milvian Bridge. The Roman soldiers would forget their contempt for a miserable Jew, and the weariness of the thankless office in the performance of which they were as much prisoners as the prisoner himself, when they began to realise the high courtesy of St. Paul, and what a wealth of power and wisdom lay in the words of this poor but far-travelled prisoner. He would ask them of Gaul, and Britain, and Germany; the stations in which they had wintered; the fields which they had fought. They would tell him in what tumult the helmet got its fracture; in what battle the shield was dinted; what blow made that hack in the sword, and how under the walls of what besieged fortress their armour had got those marks of fire from the falaricae or malleoli—the darts, which had been flung down upon them wrapped in flaming tow. And with these images in his mind, drawn from the daily spectacle of his prison, he tells his Christians since they too are soldiers, not of Caesar but of Christ, in what panoply they may resist "the world-rulers of this darkness," the spiritual powers of wickedness in the heavenlies.[1] He tells them of the baldric of sincerity; the breast-plate of moral righteousness; the war-boots (*caligae*) of ready zeal in the cause of the Gospel; the covering shield of faith, to quench flaming arrows of the wicked one; and, as their one weapon of offence, the

[1] The vague expression "the spirituals (*i.e.* the spiritual *hosts*, R.V.) of wickedness in the heavenlies" is startling. We should have expected "in the sublunaries" (ἐν τοῖς ὑπουρανίοις), since throughout the Epistle *the heavenlies* has been used for the realms of the Risen Christ. Probably here (if the reading be right) the word is used in a purely physical sense (A.V. "in high places") to denote the upper regions: just as in 2 Cor. iv. 4, St. Paul calls Satan "the prince of the power *of the air*." The expression "world-rulers" (κοσμοκράτορες) is even transliterated in the Rabbis from the Greek. "The spirituals" here means the band of demon-powers (*Geisterschaft*). St. Paul was familiar with this conception from his Rabbinic studies. In the Talmud *Thacksiphid* and *Ibalgannith* (Berachoth, f. 51, 1) are used for bodies of Shedîm or evil spirits.

sword of the Spirit which is the Word of God.[1] In this armour
they were to stand fast. "Blessed," says David, "is the man
that walketh not in the counsel of the ungodly; nor standeth
in the way of sinners ; nor sitteth in the seat of the scornful."[2]
St. Paul has told the Ephesians that they must sit with
Christ in the heavenlies;[3] that they must walk in love, walk
not as other Gentiles walk, walk as children of light, walk
accurately, walk not as unwise but as wise ;[4] he tells them
now that clad in heavenly armour they are to stand fast in
the Lord, to stand against the wiles of the devil, and having
done all to stand.[5]

And then he ends with asking for their prayers—not
that he may be set free; for his thoughts are never for
himself, always for his Master's work—but that he may
boldly make known this mystery of the Gospel for which
he is an ambassador, not like the world's ambassadors,
splendid and inviolable—but an " ambassador in a coupling-
chain," an ambassador with fettered hands.[6] He sends no
personal messages because they will be carried by the beloved
and faithful Tychicus, but he ends with a blessing singularly
full and sweet, " Peace to the brethren, and love with faith
from God the Father, and the Lord Jesus Christ. Grace be
with all who love our Lord Jesus Christ in incorrupt
sincerity."

6. Such is a most imperfect sketch of this rich, many-sided
circular letter. Not a tenth part of its beauty and wealth of
truth is here indicated. Its fervour, intensity, and sublimity ;
the unifying power of imagination over the many subordinate
truths which are ever struggling for utterance ; the eager and
exultant conviction which hurries the Apostle onward in spite
of the deeply important thoughts which crowd themselves
into long parentheses and almost interminable paragraphs ;

---

[1] Comp. Is. lix. 16–19 ; Wisd. v. 17–20 ; 1 Thess. v. 8. He does not
mention the *pilum* or heavy javelin, but the soldiers would not be likely to
carry this into a guard-room.
[2] Ps. i. 1.   [3] i. 3–20 ; ii. 6.   [4] iv. 1, 17 ; v. 2, 8–15.
[5] vi. 11, 14.   [6] vi. 20, ὑπὲρ οὖ πρεσβεύω ἐν ἀλύσει.

the manner in which (as in the Colossians) chord after chord of feeling is struck, and all of them seem to vibrate in unison before the ones first struck have trembled into silence;—all this must be studied with close and repeated study before it can be appreciated. In the depth of its theology, in the loftiness of its morals, in the way in which the simplest moral truths are based upon the profoundest religious doctrines —the Epistle is unparalleled. In it you see Paul the theologian and Paul the man at their greatest and their best. He has risen as into some purer atmosphere far above all controversies and all personalities. The mingled prayer and paean of this magnificent Epistle is inspired throughout by a sense of opposites, " of the union of weakness and strength; of tribulation and glory; of all that had been and all that was to be; of the absolute love of God, of the discovery of that love to man in the Mediator; of the working of that love in man by the Spirit; of the fellowship of the poorest creature of flesh and blood on earth with the spirits in heaven; of a canopy of love above, and an abyss of love beneath, which encompasses the whole creation." The Apostle would have rejoiced in the high words of the modern poet :—

> " I say to thee, do thou repeat
> To the first man thou mayest meet
> In lane, highway, or open street,—
> That he, and we, and all men, move
> Under a canopy of love
> As broad as the blue sky above."
> —ARCHBISHOP TRENCH.

NOTE I.

OUTLINE OF THE EPISTLE TO THE EPHESIANS.

1. Greeting, i. 1, 2.

2. General thanksgiving, into which is introduced the general thesis of the Epistle, the fore-ordained election of all members of the Universal Church, united in the Risen Christ, by the work of the Father, the Son, and the Holy Spirit, i. 3–14. Prayer for their growth in the full knowledge of this mystery (15–23).

3. DOCTRINAL. Unity of Jew and Gentile in Christ, ii. 1–22. Fuller explanation of this mystery, as preached by St. Paul, with prayers for their full comprehension of it (iii. 1–19), concluded by a doxology (iii. 20–21).

4. PRACTICAL. Exhortations to walk worthily of this ideal unity of the Catholic Church in love (iv. 1–16), and to perform the duties of the new life in the conquest over sin (iv. 17–24).

The duties of sincerity (25), gentleness (26), self-control (27), honesty and diligence (28), purity of speech and mutual kindness (29–32).

Special duty of love and purity and walking in the light, with spiritual fervour (v. 1–20).

Duty in social relations—children and parents; wives and husbands; slaves and master (v. 22–vi. 9).

The armour of God (vi. 12–17).

5. Personal (18–22).

6. Final salutation (23–24).

NOTE II.

AUTHENTICITY OF THE EPISTLE.

The authenticity of this Epistle has been seriously impugned on the following grounds:

1. "It has many new and rare expressions, such as *the heavenlies* (i.) ; *world-rulers* (vi. 12) ; *purchased possession* ($\pi\epsilon\rho\iota\pi o\iota\eta\sigma\iota s$, i. 14) ; *incorrup-tibility* ($\dot{a}\phi\theta\alpha\rho\sigma\iota a$, vi. 24) ; *devil* ($\delta\iota\dot{a}\beta o\lambda os$, iv. 27 ; vi. 11),[1] *richly varied* (iii. 10)."[2]

---

[1] St. Paul elsewhere uses "Satan," except in the Pastoral Epistles.

[2] It is also urged that he uses $\ddot{a}\phi\epsilon\sigma\iota s$ for "remission" (Eph. i. 7 ; Col. i. 14), not $\pi\dot{a}\rho\epsilon\sigma\iota s$, Rom. iii. 25 ; and uses Church in a more abstract sense. Minor criticisms are hardly worth noticing.

The argument has no value. Unique expressions (ἅπαξ λεγόμενα) occur even in St. Paul's most undoubted Epistles. The phraseology of Christianity was at this epoch in a fluid condition, and St. Paul, like all men of highly susceptible temperament, constantly enriched his vocabulary with new words and "turns of expression."

2. "It abounds in recurrent phrases, such as "the heavenlies," and "the riches of his glory."

This is rather a mark of genuineness than otherwise. We have repeatedly noticed the same phenomena in the Second Epistle to the Corinthians.

3. "The style is weak, diffused, and embarrassed."

Some of the best judges of style in all ages—men like Chrysostom and Theophylact in ancient days, and Luther, Calvin, Grotius, Coleridge, Maurice in modern days—have, on the contrary, felt or recorded the very highest admiration for the style.

4. "It speaks of 'the holy Apostles' (iii. 5); a phrase which could not have been used by the writer of Gal. ii."

The phrase belongs to the σεμνότης—the overflowing fulness of the style, and the word "Apostles" is here combined with "prophets" in a perfectly general sense, and the epithet merely means that they, like all Christians, were consecrated or "saints." The word ἁγίοις is not found in all MSS., and may not even be genuine. It may have originated from a reminiscence of Col. i. 26 ; but if genuine it is official and impersonal, and there is no reason whatever why St. Paul should not have used it in such a letter as this.

5. "It contains traces of advanced Gnosticism, and therefore must be later than St. Paul's time."

This rests on mere assertion. Simon Magus, the father of all Gnosticism, was the contemporary of St. Paul. There was an incipient Gnosticism long before the days of the Gnostics. To press into the argument such common words as "aeon," "mystery," and "wisdom," is absurd. The words *Gnosis* and *Pleroma*, though beginning to be technical in Ephesians and Colossians, are not used in the senses afterwards attached to them. They were borrowed by the Gnostics from St. Paul, not by the writer of this Epistle from the Gnostics. Tertullian, when he uses the word προβολὴ, and is afraid of the objection that the word is tainted with Valentinianism (*adv. Praxean.* 8), answers that heresy has only *borrowed* the word from truth to fix to it its own bad stamp.

6. "It expresses un-Pauline views of marriage."

This quite baseless objection arises from overlooking the fact that in 1 Cor. vii. (with which Eph. v. 22-23, is supposed to conflict), St. Paul is only speaking of marriage under one special aspect, and in answer to definite questions, and with reference to special exigencies. Nor is there anything strange even if on that subject his thoughts had widened and deepened as they did in many other directions.

7. The advanced Christology of the Epistle, and its developed conception of the Church are due to the rapid growth and enlightenment of Christian thought in the most germinant period of the Church's life, and amid the most marked outpouring of spiritual gifts. At supreme epochs of human enlightenment, the writings of a few years seem to be separated by whole centuries of thought. St. Paul has already left far behind him the now settled controversies of a few years earlier.

Even if the objections were as valid as they are in reality weak, they could not counterbalance the positive proofs that the Epistle is genuine. The external evidence in its favour is strong and ancient, and it was received by the whole Church without question from the days of Ignatius to those of Schleiermacher. In every essential particular it is admittedly Pauline. It abounds in the most fundamental conceptions of St. Paul—the relations of Christianity to Judaism ; the universality of sin ; the prominence given to faith and love ; the freedom of grace ; the moral necessity for good works ; the exaltation of Christ. No forger could have developed the thoughts which St. Paul had already expressed in Colossians, with the intimate knowledge, and yet splendid originality and independence which are seen in every clause of this Epistle. There was not a single writer in the first three centuries, except St. Paul, who could have written this deepest, loftiest, and most final utterance of his special Gospel. If any one but Paul wrote this letter there must have been two Pauls. We may confidently assert that no Christian of whom the Church has ever heard was capable of either forging the style or expressing the deepest thoughts of St. Paul. "Non est cujusvis hominis," says Erasmus, " Paulinum pectus effingere."

NOTE III.

LEADING WORDS OF THE EPISTLE.

Leading words—which indicate the characteristics of the whole Epistle.

GOD'S WILL ($\theta\epsilon\lambda\eta\mu\alpha$, i. 1, 5, 9, 11 ; v. 17 ; vi. 6) and *purpose* ($\beta\text{ου}\lambda\acute{\eta}$, i. 11; $\epsilon\mathring{v}\delta\text{οκ}\acute{\iota}\alpha$, i. 9, $\pi\rho\acute{o}\theta\epsilon\sigma\iota\varsigma$, iii. 11), and *dispensation* ($\text{οἰκονομ}\acute{\iota}\alpha$, i. 10 ; iii. 3). There has been no reversal of God's plans respecting the unity of Jews and Gentiles in the Church. All has been *foreordained* ($\pi\rho\text{οορ}\acute{\iota}\sigma\alpha\varsigma$, i. 5 ; $\pi\rho\grave{o}$ $\kappa\alpha\tau\alpha\beta\text{ολ}\hat{\eta}\varsigma$ $\kappa\acute{o}\sigma\mu\text{ου}$, i. 4 ; $\pi\rho\text{οορισθ}\acute{\epsilon}\nu\tau\epsilon\varsigma$, i. 11 ; $\pi\rho\text{ο}\acute{\epsilon}\theta\epsilon\tau\text{ο}$, i. 9 ; $\pi\rho\text{οητοι}\mu\acute{\alpha}\sigma\epsilon\nu$, ii. 10).

GRACE. The word occurs no less than thirteen times (i. 2, 6 (*bis*) 7 ;

EPHESIANS. ii. 5, 7, 8 ; iii. 2, 7, 8 ; iv. 7, 32 ; vi. 24) ; and may be regarded as the most prominent conception of the Epistle.

THE HEAVENLIES. (τὰ ἐπουράνια), i. 3, 20 ; ii. 6 ; iii. 10 ; vi. 12. The word does not occur in Colossians, but four times in 1 Cor. xv.

SPIRIT AND SPIRITUAL. Thirteen times in this Epistle (i. 3, 13, 17 ; ii. 18, 22 ; iii. 5, 16 ; iv. 3, 4, 23, 30 ; v. 18 ; vi. 17, 18). Only once in Colossians (i. 8, 9).

MYSTERY. i. 9 ; iii. 3, 4, 9 ; v. 32 ; vi. 19.

PLENITUDE. "Pleroma," i. 10, 23 ; iii. 19 ; iv. 10-13. The Plenitude of the Godhead is in Christ, and is in His Church.

GLORY. δόξα, i. 6, 12, 14, 17, 18 ; iii. 6, 21.

TRUE KNOWLEDGE as opposed to false.[1]

The prominence of thoughts respecting the *grandeur* of the revelation and the *unity* of the Church is shown by the prevalent compounds in ὑπέρ, "exceedingly," (i. 19, 21 ; iii. 19, 20 ; iv. 10, &c.) and σύν, "together." [2]

(SPIRITUAL) WEALTH. i. 7, 18 ; ii. 4, 17 ; iii. 8, 16.

LIGHT. v. 8-15.

LOVE. iv. 3-13.

NOTE IV.

LEADING THOUGHTS OF THE EPISTLE.

The new aeon of God's ideal Universal Church (ἓν σῶμα καὶ ἓν πνεῦμα, iv. 4), according to a fore-ordained dispensation, of which the benefits are extended to all mankind, Jew and Gentile indifferently. This perfected idea is a mystery, once hidden, now revealed.

It is the result of unsurpassable love and inexhaustible grace.

It centres in the person of the Risen Christ. The Epistle is emphatically the Epistle of the Ascended Christ (iv. 8, 9). "The idea of *catholicity* is here raised to dogmatic definiteness and predominant significance." Pfleiderer, *Paulinism*, ii. 164.

The Church is represented as the House (ii. 20-22) ; the Body (iv. 12-16) ; and the Bride of Christ (v. 25-27). Indeed we might take as the essence of the Epistle, the words which Paul addressed to the elders of

---

[1] γνῶσις, iii. 19 ; ἐπίγνωσις, i. 17 ; iv. 13 ; σύνεσις, iii. 14 ; φρόνησις, 18 ; σοφία, *ib.* ; ἀποκάλυψις, iii. 3 ; φωτίζειν, iii. 9.

[2] συνεζωοποίησε, ii. 5 ; συνήγειρε, συνεκάθισεν, 6 ; συμπολῖται, ii. 19 ; συνοικοδομεῖσθε, 22 ; συγκληρόνομα, σύνσωμμα, συνμέτοχα, iii. 6 ; σύνδεσμος, iv. 3 ; συμβιβαζόμενον, συναρμολογούμενον, 16.

Ephesus at Miletum, "the Church of God, which He purchased with His own blood."

Pfleiderer calls the writer of the Epistle (which he does not regard as genuine) "the first dogmatist of Catholicism." He points out that whereas the Epistle to the Colossians is directed against a speculative, ascetic, mystic Judaism, mixed with Oriental elements, the "Ephesians" is directed against the libertinism and exaggerated Paulinism of Gentile Christians mixed with Gnostic and dualistic theories.

NOTE V.

THEOLOGY OF THE EPISTLE.

The exposition of the plan of salvation in Romans is *psychologic*. It is built on moral facts—the universality of sin; the insufficiency of man; God's appointed method of justification by the union of the believer with Christ.

In this Epistle the statement is *theologic*. It expresses the idea of God's eternal plans realised in the course of ages, and the unity in Christ of redeemed humanity with the family of *heaven in the heavenlies*.[1]

In Hebrews we have the idea of reconciliation viewed especially in the light of Christ's Eternal Priesthood.

In this Epistle and Colossians, Christ stands forth as the Central Being of the Universe.

[1] See Reuss, *Les Epîtres Paulin.* ii. 146.

EPISTLE TO PHILEMON.

WRITTEN IN ST. PAUL'S FIRST IMPRISONMENT, ABOUT A.D. 63.

"Evangelico decore conscripta est."—JEROME.

"Epistola familiaris mire ἀστεῖος, summae sapientiae praebitura specimen."
BENGEL.

"Ein Muster von Takt, Feinheit, und Liebenswürdigkeit."—HOLTZMANN.

"Here we see how St. Paul layeth himself out for poor Onesimus and pleadeth his cause with his master, and so setteth himself as if he were Onesimus and had himself done wrong to Philemon. Even as Christ did for us with God, His Father, thus also doth St. Paul for Onesimus with Philemon. We are all his Onesimi to my thinking."—LUTHER.

"No longer as a slave, but more than a slave, a brother beloved."
PHILEM. 16.

PHILEMON.

DURING St. Paul's long stay at Ephesus he had made the acquaintance of a Colossian named Philemon, who, with his wife Apphia, and his son Archippus, had been converted to Christianity. They seem to have occupied a good position, and they lent their house as a meeting-place for the little Christian community in their native city. Thus Philemon and Apphia [1] became "fellow-workers" with St. Paul. Archippus seems to have entered the Christian ministry as a deacon [2] or a presbyter, either conjointly with Epaphras at Colossae, or at the neighbouring town of Laodicea, for St. Paul calls him not only his "fellow-worker," but his "fellow-soldier."

---

[1] The Phrygian name Apphia must not be confused with the Roman name Appia.
[2] Col. iv. 17. Εἴπατε Ἀρχίππῳ, Βλέπε τ ὴ ν δ ι α κ ο ν ί α ν ἥν παρέλαβες ἐν Κυρίῳ.

In this household thus converted to Christianity there was a slave—probably, as we gather from the tone in which he is spoken of, a young slave[1]—named Onesimus. His name meant "Profitable," but he had proved himself very much the reverse; for he had certainly run away from his master, and probably, if we rightly interpret St. Paul's delicate references, had either stolen something from him, or had in some other way inflicted on him an injury.

The poor dishonest fugitive escaped from Colossae, and through we know not what perils and hardships, made his way to Ephesus, and then as best he could across the Aegean and the Adriatic, to the common drain of all the misery and vice of the ancient world, the city of Rome. In that city, as in London, there were multitudes of lodging-houses—called *insulae* or "islands"—where the swarming myriads of slaves and paupers and escaped criminals lived a precarious and miserable life.

Any one who had drifted into such abodes of wretchedness might sink to all conceivable depths of squalor and degradation. If Onesimus had stolen any money from Philemon it would soon be exhausted in such haunts and taverns as would alone be open to a runaway Phrygian slave. But the adventures of Onesimus must be left to the imagination. Could we but read them they might throw no little light on the condition of ancient society; but we can only hope that they were less deeply dyed in infamy than the adventures of others of his class as described to us in romances of that age which are still extant.

We do not know how he was snatched out of this perilous abyss. It is very probable that in former days he may have been in attendance on his master Philemon at Ephesus, and there, in the school of Tyrannus, or in some private gathering of converts, he may have seen and heard St. Paul. It is, at any rate, likely that he must have been known by sight to

---

[1] St. Paul calls him his "child," and uses of him the word σπλάγχνα ("son of my bowels") which was applied affectionately to sons.

Epaphras, who was now in some sense a "fellow-captive" with St. Paul at Rome, and who, as a native of Colossae, must have been very familiar with Philemon and "the Church in his house." Perhaps Onesimus, when he was at the lowest ebb of his worldly fortunes, had met and been recognised by Epaphras or Aristarchus, or had of his own impulse come to seek St. Paul. Those who are familiar with misfortune are quick to recognise the countenances and the characters of kindly and sympathetic men. Onesimus, in the house of Philemon, must have caught some glimpse at least of the love and tenderness and respect for the bodies and souls of men which were ruling principles in the Christian society. He must have been well aware that if he appealed to such a man as Paul, he would not appeal in vain. For Paul "received all that came in unto him . . . teaching those things which concern the Lord Jesus Christ." [1]

To whom else could he apply? At Rome for the ordinary fugitive there were no means of earning a living except by vice and crime. Unless the Asiatic slave could turn gladiator, or thief, or sell himself into slavery again, how was he to earn his bread? He was not of the slightest value in the market, and the terrified instincts of the slave were too strong in him to permit of his return to his offended master. Slavery was a legal and a universal institution. Onesimus had no means of judging how it would be affected by Christianity. If he returned to Colossae, Philemon, even if he were a kind-hearted man, would in no sense be transgressing the most ordinary customs of the day if he had branded Onesimus or sent him to work in chains in some stifling and horrible ergastulum, or tortured, or resold him into slavery for anything which he would fetch from a fresh master, who might treat him with the worst extremes of Pagan cruelty. He might fall into the hands of some owner, who would, without compunction, fling him into a fishpond to feed the lampreys or even nail him to a cross to feed the ravens and the kites.

[1] Acts xxviii. 30, 31.

Even the elder Cato, that model of Pagan virtue, had habitually sold innocent and faithful slaves when they were too aged to be of any further use to him. At that very period there had been in Rome a recrudescence of the worst severities of slavery. The multiplication of slaves, which had been progressing for nearly two centuries, had now become so overwhelming that the slaves in the wealthiest houses were to be counted not by hundreds, but by thousands. The natural Nemesis of that vile institution had ensued. Everywhere there was terror; everywhere there was enervation, misery, and corruption. Wherever Onesimus moved among the thronged haunts of the mob, he would hear discussed the burning question of the wrongs of slaves. Very shortly before his arrival in Rome the city had witnessed one of the indescribable horrors of a decadent civilisation and an imperial absolutism. A Senator, named Pedanius Secundus, a man of high rank, a Consul, a Praefect of the city, had four hundred slaves; and in the condition of morals which then prevailed and which, as Seneca said, made vice a necessity to those who were not free, one of these slaves—a rival with his master for the love of a fellow-slave—had murdered Pedanius in his bed. The murder struck a thrill of terror into the heart of Roman society. Such an event had not occurred within living memory. The slaves were so completely trodden down under the iron heel of force, they were so securely kept in control by their own vices and mutual jealousies, that the murder of a master by one of his own slaves seemed a portentous omen of future possibilities. The sleep of many a Roman was disturbed and haunted by the sense that so many slaves only meant so many enemies. A slave might be only "a live chattel," [1] "an implement with a voice;" [2]—a slave might seem something lower than the mire beneath a Roman's feet—but somehow these slaves seemed to have an awkward

---

[1] ἔμψυχον ὄργανον.—Arist. *Pol.* i. 4. The Greek etymologists of the *Etymologicum Magnum* connect δοῦλος with δόλος, ἀνδράποδον with ἀποδόσθαι.

[2] "Instrumenti genus . . . vocale."—Varro, *De Re Rust.* i. 17.

PHILEMON. way of showing that they were human, that they too were made of flesh and blood, that they too were capable of love and envy, and hatred and desperate revenge. At the splendid banquets, when the slaves had retired to a safe distance, men whose lightest word might have handed over scores of human beings to the prison or the torturer—ladies who by a nod might have their slave girls branded for putting a wrong fold in a robe—whispered to each other their terrified confidences about the black looks which they had seen, or the stern murmurs which they had heard among the slave population. We may be quite sure that, at this very period, grim stories flew from lip to lip about the possible recurrence of massacres and rapine, such as those which had occurred in the Servile War under a Eunus in Sicily, or had long afterwards been inflicted by a Spartacus in Lucania and Bruttium.

There existed in Rome an old and ruthless law which had long fallen obsolete, that when a master was murdered his whole "family" of slaves should be put to death. This Silanian law was founded on the principle that no master could ever be murdered without the complicity of a number of his slaves, and it was meant to strike terror into the vast numbers of these wretched dependants by making their common safety depend on their protecting the life of their owner. Pedanius had 400 slaves—a number by no means unusually large. It was debated in the Senate whether or not the Silanian law should be put into execution. One of the most eloquent and eminent of the Senators, C. Cassius Longinus, had argued that it should. "The rich and the noble," he said, "at Rome were few among the many. Their only safety lay in the terror of their inferiors, or, at any rate, in the certainty that if they perished they would never perish unavenged." So spake Longinus.

> "and with the tyrant's plea,
> Necessity, excused his devilish deeds."

His appeal to a terrified selfishness carried the day. The Senate voted that the Silanian law should be carried out.

The Roman populace, worthless as it had become—ever " the lewd people of the baser sort," the scum of the forum and the tavern, surrounded as they were by every influence which could deprave and harden them, and

> " Cruel, by their sports to blood inured
> Of fighting beasts, and men to beasts exposed—"

had yet enough humanity left in them to feel horrified at the inexcusable butchery of four hundred innocent human beings, of whom three hundred and ninety-nine were avowedly innocent. Every one knew who had murdered Pedanius, every one knew the desperate feelings of revenge and lawless passion by which the murderer had been instigated. There was no pretence at hinting that there had been any conspiracy among these four hundred slaves. They were of different ages and sexes ; they came from different nationalities ; they had different interests. There was probably not one of them who would not, if it had been in his power, have arrested the murderer's hand, and protected their owner—not out of love, but out of fear and self-interest—even at the expense of their own lives. To butcher them merely in order to strike terror was shocking even to the *faex Romuli*—the dregs of the capital of the world. Wrathful menaces were heard among the populace. They should not die. They should be rescued.

But Nero sided with the Senate. The golden quinquennium, such as it was, was over. The imperial tiger had long ago tasted blood, and relished the taste. He ordered the execution to be carried out by military force. In the sight of the whole city—whose merchandise was not only of gold, and silver, and pearls, and precious stones, and fine linen, and purple, and silk, and scarlet, and ivory, and incense, and wine, and thyine wood, but also of slaves and souls of men— in the sight of the whole city that long line of slaves—old and young, men and women and children—had been led forth to die.[1]

[1] In the *Miles Gloriosus* (i. 4, 19) of Plautus, a slave touchingly exclaims, " I know the cross will be my sepulchre ; all my ancestors are buried there."

At such a time there was not a slave in Rome who must not have felt his slavery more bitter and galling than ever. Never had the chasm between slave and freeman seemed to be more immense. When a slave was emancipated the Praetor had but to turn him round and touch him with his wand, and the most worthless stable-boy in Rome—the *non tressis agaso*—might assume his master's praenomen, and spring into the full dignity of a man. But Onesimus was a slave—a slave of the lowest class, for he was a Phrygian[1]— and, more than that, he was a dishonest Phrygian slave, a pilferer and a fugitive. But in a happy hour Onesimus came, or was brought, to St. Paul. He learnt that Christ died for all, that God is no respecter of persons; that in Christ there is neither Jew nor Greek, there is neither barbarian, Scythian, bond, nor free, but Christ all and in all. The good tidings—good for all—had for slaves a yet more indescribable and infinite sweetness. Onesimus became a man and a Christian. He was no longer Onesimus, the worthless Phrygian fugitive, whose very name had become a satiric contrast to his character, but Onesimus the brother faithful and beloved. Free indeed he was not. His conversion did not change the then universal constitution of society. But if he was not free outwardly he enjoyed inwardly a freedom such as he had never conceived before. He was freer than those who, while they thought themselves so free, were inwardly slaves.

And this inward freedom involved so glorious an exaltation of condition that it seems to have educed all that there was of sweetness in the youth's natural character. Jeremy Bentham once said of a nobleman who had been kind to him, "He drew me out of the lowest abyss of humiliation; he first taught me that I could be something." Onesimus had been raised from an unspeakably lower depth to a then

---

[1] There was a contemptuous proverb, Μυσῶν ἔσχατος, Menander, *Andro*, 9, 7. Cicero (*pro Flacco*) quotes two others — "Phryges sero sapiunt;" "Phryges plagis meliores fiunt."

undreamed-of height. He earnestly tried to repay to St. Philemon.
Paul the great debt of gratitude which he owed. He made
himself so useful, so truly " profitable," that St Paul cannot
refrain from playing on his name. He treated Paul like a
father, and Paul loved him as a dear son—as his own very
" heart " [1]—and would gladly, in his bonds and loneliness, have
kept him by his side for the sake of his company and help.
But this he could not do. It would have been contrary to
the ordinary rights of society and ownership. It would have
been a selfish encroachment on the property of another,
however gladly such an encroachment might have been
conceded. Paul was not a man to take a liberty with a
friend. As a gentleman,[2] as a man of honour, above all as a
Christian, he felt himself obliged to send back the fugitive to
his lawful master. He would not give any occasion for
abusing Christianity by an illegal interference, nor would he
presume on the generosity of even so beloved a convert as
Philemon of Colossae.

And therefore, though he could not part with Onesimus
without a severe wrench, he sent back the runaway to his
former home. He sent him back under the kind care of
Tychicus, and with a letter which he knew would insure
forgiveness, kindness, probably even emancipation. He does
not utter the word " emancipation," though, as has been said,
it seems to be almost trembling on his lips. But he wrote of
Onesimus in such terms as would make Philemon view him
in a favourable light, and receive him, if not with affection,
at least with pardon. He could not retain Onesimus, but
what he could do he did by appearing as his intercessor
(*precator*), and throwing over him the shield of spiritual
adoption. He felt that the " timid Phrygian " (as proverbs
called the slaves of this country) would thus be more than
safe.

---

[1] Philem. 12, Σὺ δὲ αὐτὸν, τουτέστι τὰ ἐμὰ σπλάγχνα, προσλαβοῦ.

[2] " Luther—not by any means such *a gentleman* as the Apostle was, but
almost as great a genius."—Coleridge.

PHILEMON.   The letter which he wrote to render this service to poor
Onesimus is the "Epistle to Philemon." It begins with
1-3. the usual greeting and a thanksgiving in which he grate-
4-7. fully acknowledges the liberality and goodness of his friend.
He then proceeds at once to tell him the object of his
letter.   He has tidings to give of Onesimus, his runaway
slave. He might lay an injunction on Philemon, but he will
not do so; he will only plead with him as an old man and a
prisoner.

In past days "Profitable" had shown himself profitless,
useless, and un-Christian; now he is useful and a good
Christian. Paul would gladly have retained his services, but
would not do so without Philemon's leave. He was not the
man to extract from a friend a compulsory kindness. He
therefore sends him back, and entreats Philemon to receive
him, not only as a slave, but as a dear brother, yes, even as
he would receive Paul himself. If the youth was in Philemon's
debt, Paul bids Philemon regard his autograph as a bond that
he would be surety for that debt, without mentioning that
Philemon owed him his own self besides. "Yea, brother,
may I 'profit' by thee in the Lord. Will *you* be *my*
Onesimus, my Profitable? Refresh my heart in the Lord."
Paul is sure that he will do this, and even more, and asks
him also to prepare a lodging in view of a speedy visit
8-22. which he hopes to make when he is set free. Then with
salutations and a blessing the Epistle ends.

1. We may notice first its infinite charm. This has been felt
by almost every reader. Casual as it is, slightly written,
entirely unpremeditated, simple and unartificial in style, it is
yet a little "idyll of the progress of Christianity." It has
been compared by Grotius, and since his time by many others,
with a much-admired letter of the younger Pliny to his
friend Sabinianus, to ask pardon for a young freedman who
had given Sabinianus some offence. Pliny was one of the
most eminent writers of his day; he had spent a life of culture
and literary ease among men of the highest rank and refine-

ment; and he was celebrated for the polished style of his
correspondence, which was specially written for publication.
Yet with all its noble carelessness of expression, the incidental
note of the poor despised Jewish tent-maker is more moving,
and more beautiful, and of incomparably more importance.
For the elegant little letter of Pliny is not enriched by any
deep underlying principle. It is the petition of a kind man
on behalf of a young and once deeply-loved freedman, not a
request for a criminal and fugitive slave. Pliny pleads only
the youth and the tears of the freedman, and the love which
Sabinianus once bore for him. Paul pleads only the broad
eternal claims of humanity redeemed in Christ. Pliny has
to beg that Sabinianus will not put the young freedman to
the torture. Paul has no need to make such a request.
With perfect confidence he asks Philemon to receive Onesimus
no longer as a slave but as a brother beloved in the Lord.

2. Then we may notice the beautiful light which this letter
throws upon the character of St. Paul.[1] We see him here in
private life; in the sweet and genial intercourse which he
held with the friends whom he loved. We see how very far
Christianity is from interfering with the exquisite courtesies
and refinements of daily intercourse. We see—let us repeat
it—in the best and truest sense of the word what a gentleman
Paul was.

> " For look who is most virtuous alwaïe
> Prive and apert and most intendeth aye
> To do the gentle dedes that he can
> And take him for the greatest gentleman."

3. We note further how vast was the change introduced
into the world by Christianity. It taught as one of its
central and most essential doctrines the dignity of man as
man. It gave honour to man simply as man. It saw in
every man a possible Christian, and in every Christian a true
brother. So deeply rooted is the respect of persons, so
inveterate the prejudice of man's innate pride of circumstance,

---

[1] Even Baur calls it a "short, attractive, friendly and graceful letter."—
Paul. ii. 80.

that, even four centuries later, there were Christians who thought very lightly of the Epistle to Philemon, and argued that it was beneath the dignity of an Apostle to trouble himself about a runaway slave.[1] But St. Paul had learnt from the example of Him who was a friend of publicans and sinners, not only that all men are of one blood, and that

> "There's a red stream beneath the coarse blue doublet,
> Which warms the heart as kindly as if drawn
> From the fat sources of Assyrian kings
> Who first made mankind subject to their sway ;—"

but far more than this, that God is no respecter of persons, and that to be a Christian is much more than to be a king.

4. It has been said, but falsely, that these principles came to the world from other sources than Christianity. From what other source could they have come ? Not certainly from Paganism. All that Paganism—all even that Pagan philosophy had contributed to the slave's cause was a few fine theoretic sentiments of late writers which rang hollow on the lips of those who were themselves slave-masters, after centuries of brutal cruelty and boundless oppression. All that even Judaism contributed was the belief that slavery was both permitted and inevitable. "It is forbidden," said the Rabbi, "to teach a slave the law." When a slave of Rabbi Eliezer died, and his slaves came to condole with him, he first tacitly discouraged and then openly rebuked them with the words, "Have I not taught you that these signs of respect are not to be shown at the death of slaves ; and that nothing may be said but what is said when oxen or asses die : 'May the Lord replenish thy loss' ? " When R. Jose allowed people to say, "Alas, a good and faithful man ! " other Rabbis thought that he had gone too far. The lesson of the inherent sacredness of humanity was effectively taught by Christianity alone.

---

[1] In Chrysostom's days, some called it περιττὸν εἴγε ὑπὲρ πράγματος μικροῦ ἠξίωσεν, ὑπὲρ ἑνὸς ἀνδρός. (*Comment in Ep. Philem.*) In Jerome's days, some said, "*aut epistolam non esse Pauli aut nihil habere quod nos aedificare possit.*"

5. Lastly, this casual little Epistle teaches us the deeply important lesson how Christianity dealt, and was meant to deal, with vast social problems. The broad experience of humanity has proved that slavery contains in itself almost inevitably the deathful elements of corruption; that it is in the long run ruinous alike to the enslavers and the enslaved. The conscience of humanity, touched and quickened by Christian truth, at last awoke, however slowly, to the truth that slavery is a radical and inherent injustice. Christianity was meant to teach these lessons. But it was not, and could not be, revolutionary. It was "a kingdom not of this world." Had it attempted to interfere by violence and open opposition with the facts of the established order it would have inevitably perished in the storm which it would have kindled. It was not meant to pour upon the midnight a sudden and blinding noon, but it was a beam of light shot into the darkness, which was to broaden gradually into boundless day. It inspired a sense of freedom, which became ultimately fatal to immoral tyrannies. It proclaimed a Divine equality, a universal brotherhood, which, without at once interfering with the established order of things, left slavery impossible in enlightened lands. By Christianising the master it emancipated the slave. It emancipated the slave still more by rescuing him from the worst slavery of self. It did not need to *preach* emancipation, for it *was* emancipation—an emancipation more complete than any Praetor or owner could bestow. Slaves who were Christ's freedmen were free indeed.

6. And thus, by the principles which it expressed, by the results which it involved, this little letter became the Magna Charta of freedom throughout the world. "Through the vista of history we see slavery and its Pagan theory of two races fall before the Holy Word of Jesus, 'All men are the children of God.'" [1]

We know that Sabinianus at Pliny's request forgave his

[1] Mazzini, *Works*, vi. 99.

young freedman; we may be quite sure that Philemon not only forgave his profitless Onesimus, but took him to his heart as a brother in Christ. We never hear of him again. There was an Onesimus who was Bishop of Beroea (*Constt. Apost.* vii. 46), and another who was Bishop of Ephesus (*Ignat. ad Ephes.* i. 8), with both of whom he has been identified by Christian tradition. In two of the MSS. of the Epistle there is a postscript which says that he was martyred at Rome by having both of his legs broken upon the rack.

NOTE I.

SPECIAL WORDS AND PHRASES IN THE EPISTLE.

Verse 2. The true reading probably is "*to Apphia the sister,*" not "the beloved." Theodore of Mopsuestia hints that the epithet "beloved" had given rise to coarse sneers in his age, and it may have been so far the case at this period also as to make the title "sister" appropriate (Comp. 1 Cor. ix. 5, "to lead about a Christian sister as a wife").

Verse 5. This verse should be rendered "*the faith which thou hast towards the Lord Jesus* (πρὸς, Vulg. *in Domine Jesu*) *and* (manifested) *unto* (εἰς) *all the saints*" (Vulg. *in omnes sanctos*). Comp. Col. i. 4 ; there the phrase is varied.

Verse 7. *The bowels of the saints.* This literal translation has been very wisely altered by the R.V. into "the *hearts* of the saints." This Epistle is characterised by the repetition of this metaphoric term σπλάγχνα three times (verses 7, 12, 20). It is the Greek equivalent of the Hebrew *rechamim.*

Verse 8. Not "though *I might have* much boldness ; " (as in the A.V.), but "though I *have*" (ἔχον).

Verse 12. "*Thou therefore receive him.*" These words (σὺ δε προσλαβοῦ) are probably spurious, and were only added to complete the sense of St. Paul's careless, natural, epistolary *anakoluthon.* The verse should really run, "I send back to thee in his own person, that is my very heart." Compare the Latin term of endearment, "*Corculum,*" "my little heart ; " and *viscera,* used of sons. Οἱ παῖδες σπλάγχνα λέγονται, Artemid. *Oneirocr.* i. 44.

Verse 11. "*Onesimus, who was aforetime to thee unprofitable.*" There is clearly a play on the name Onesimos, "Helpful," as also in verse 20, ὀναίμην, "yea, brother, let me have *help* of thee." Baur acutely surmised another play of words in ἄχρηστον . . . εὔχρηστον. "Christus" was often pronounced by Pagans *Chrestus,* so that the adjective *achrestos euchrestos,* would suggest the meanings of "non-Christian" and a "good Christian."[1] (Compare Whitfield's pulpit appeal to the comedian Shuter, who had often played the character of Ramble. "And thou, poor Ramble, who hast so often rambled from Him, oh, end thy ramblings and come to Jesus.") Such paronomasias were quite in accordance with Greek, Latin, and Semitic taste.

---

[1] This play on words occurs in Just. Mart. *Apol.* i. 4 ; Tert. *Apol.* c. 3 ; Lactant. *Instt. Div.* iv. 7 ; Theophil. *Ad Autolyc.* l. i. and i. 12, &c.

A A

PHILEMON.　Verse 18.　From the phrase "*reckon*" or "*debit that to me*" (ἐλλόγει), and from the term "*partner*" (κοινωνὸν) in verse 17, some have (precariously) inferred that St. Paul had pecuniary relations with Philemon, perhaps connected with his trade of tent-maker.

NOTE II.

FRIENDS OF ST. PAUL.

Most men who kindle against them the intense hatred of enemies are gifted with qualities which win for them the warm love of friends. St. Paul seems to have made some friends in nearly every city which he visited.

Among them we may mention :—

Barnabas of Cyprus, the friend of his youth.

Silas of Jerusalem, the faithful companion of his second journey.

Luke of Antioch, his beloved physician and friend.

Timothy of Lystra, his "dear son" and most beloved pupil.

Titus, probably of Corinth, a vigorous and practical helper.

Mark of Jerusalem, who after some wavering, became profitable to him for ministering.

Philemon, Archippus, Epaphras, Onesimus of Colossae.

Aristarchus of Thessalonica.

Aquila and Priscilla in Corinth and Ephesus.

Tychicus and Trophimus of Ephesus.

Apollos of Alexandria.

Erastus of Corinth.

Besides these mention is made of Andronicus, Junias, Demas, Crescens, Herodion, Epaphroditus, Onesiphorus, Tertius, Zenas, and others.

SLAVERY.

One of the best books on ancient slavery is Wallon, *Histoire de l'Esclavage.* An admirable sketch of the Scriptural bearings of the subject may be found in Channing's *Remarks on Slaves*, and in Mr. Goldwin Smith's pamphlet *Does the Bible Sanction American Slavery ?* In Boissier *La Religion romaine*, ii. 345–405, many of the ancient *loci classici* are collected. Materials for the picture abound in Plautus, Horace, Seneca, Petronius, Juvenal, Tacitus, Suetonius, and both the elder and younger Pliny.

THE FIRST EPISTLE TO TIMOTHY.

WRITTEN FROM MACEDONIA, A.D. 63 OR 66.

"This charge I commit to thee, son Timothy."—1 Tim. i. 18.

WHEN Timothy, still in his early boyhood,[1] had once left his Lycaonian home, and been swept into the vortex of St. Paul's fervid activity, he seems to have lived a life of toil and travel as the almost inseparable companion of his beloved master and father in Christ. Eunice, his mother—probably his widowed mother—and his grandmother Lois, were faithful Christian women well known to St. Paul. The boy had "followed from the first St. Paul's teaching, conduct, purpose, faith, long-suffering, patience," and had witnessed the bitter sufferings and persecutions, which he had to endure at Antioch, at Iconium, at Lystra. It was during the second mission journey that his mother made the brave sacrifice of her son to the cause of Christ. St. Paul, in order to fit him for work among Jewish synagogues, had performed the rite of circumcision,[2] which the youth's Greek father had hitherto neglected or opposed. By this act, which had a purely national and not

[1] This appears from the fact that he is still addressed as a youth nearly sixteen years later, in 1 Tim. iv. 12; 2 Tim. ii. 22. A critic sneeringly says that "the Timotheus-legend endowed him with the gift of immortal youth"; but nothing is more natural than that St. Paul when old would still regard as a youth one who was still young for his high duties, and whom he seems to have loved from a child. The only known dates in the life of Timothy are those in the life of St. Paul. They were together in the second mission journey, at Philippi, Corinth, Ephesus and Rome.

[2] 2 Tim. iii. 10, 11.

a religious significance, Timothy sided as it were openly with the faith and the countrymen of his mother. The circumcision was followed by ordination, in which he made a solemn profession of his faith before the assembled Church, and when St. Paul and the elders had laid their hands upon his head, prophetic voices marked him out for a great work, and the Grace of the Holy Spirit descended like a fire into his heart.[1]

During the rest of St. Paul's journeys Timothy was generally with him, though he was occasionally left behind, as at Thessalonica, or despatched to some other nascent Church to consolidate and continue the work which had been begun. The name of the young evangelist is associated with that of St. Paul in the superscription of both the letters to the Thessalonians; in the second letter to the Corinthians; and in those to the Philippians and Colossians; and to him are addressed two of the three Pastoral Epistles. He is therefore connected with each of the four groups of St. Paul's letters; special use was made of his services in organising the Churches of Thessalonica, Corinth and Ephesus. He was at Ephesus as " Overseer " or Apostolic commissary when this first letter was addressed to him, and from Ephesus he hurried at the Apostle's urgent request—bringing with him the cloke and books which St. Paul had left with Carpus at Troas—in order to receive the last instructions, and solace the last hours of his friend. And thus, "as a son with a father he slaved with him for the Gospel."[2] The effort was all the nobler because, as we judge from various allusions, he was naturally of a timid and shrinking temperament.[3] This may have been partly due to weak health and frequent attacks of

---

[1] 1 Tim. vi. 12, "Thou didst make the fair confession *before many witnesses.*" 1 Tim. iv. 14, "The charism which was given thee by means of prophecy with the laying on of the hands of the presbytery." (2 Tim. i. 6, "by the laying on of *my* hands.") 1 Tim. i. 18, "According to *the prophecies, which went before on thee.*" 2 Tim. i. 6, "To *fan into flame* (ἀναζωπυρεῖν) the charism of God which is in thee."

[2] Phil. ii. 22, ἐδούλευσεν εἰς τὸ εὐαγγέλιον.

[3] So we infer from 1 Cor. iv. 17; xvi. 10, 11, and from the general tenor of all St. Paul's personal exhortations to him in 1, 2 Tim. (1 Tim. iv. 14-16; vi. 20; 2 Tim. i. 14; ii. 1-7; iv. 1, 2, &c.).

illness, which in their turn may have been caused by months of hardship in many lands and under many trials. But his friend and teacher saw the depths of self-sacrifice and the capability of energetic work which were latent in his blameless character.[1] He knew of no one else who was so absolutely unselfish, or whose heart beat so entirely in unison with his own.[2] This was the reason why he sent him with perfect confidence to console the persecuted Churches of Macedonia, to face the conceited turbulence of Corinth, and to rule the Church of Ephesus with its many troubles alike from the worshippers of Artemis and the adherents of Jewish priests.[3]

When St. Paul, in accordance with his own anticipation, had been liberated from his first Roman imprisonment[4] he visited Macedonia and on his way left Timothy in charge of the Ephesian Christians. The task thus imposed upon him was the more difficult, because, in addition to all other sources of peril, the growth of heresy in Asia became daily more alarming. It was in order to lighten these difficulties that St. Paul, from some resting-place in his last missionary travels, wrote this letter.[5] His object was twofold. He wished to give Timothy practical advice about the way in which he should deal with the various classes of men and women in the Church, and he wished earnestly to put him on his guard against the false teachers who were constantly acquiring a more formidable power. Against these heresiarchs St. Paul had already raised his voice in his farewell at Miletus and in his encyclical letter to the Ephesians. St. John had spoken with yet sterner denunciation in his letter to the Angel of the Church of Ephesus which is the first of the seven letters in the Apocalypse.

---

[1] Acts xvi. 2. [2] Phil. ii. 20.

[3] Acts xix. 22; 1 Thess. iii. 2; Phil. ii. 18–20; 1 Cor. xvi. 10; 1 Tim. i. 2.

[4] See note at the end of the discourse.

[5] The place from which the letter was written is entirely unknown. The various idle guesses of the unauthorised superscriptions say, "from Laodicea;" "from Pacatiana the capital of Phrygia;" "from Nicopolis;" "from Athens;" and "from Macedonia."

The first Epistle to Timothy passes from subject to subject with all the ease and familiarity of a private communication written by an old man to a favourite disciple. Its outline is as follows :—

After the greeting (i. 1—2) St. Paul at once proceeds to renew the warning, which he had already given orally to Timothy, against the babbling and vain speculations of gnosticising Judaists (3—7). He lays down the true functions of the law (8—11), and thanks God with a glowing doxology, for the grace which had removed his own former ignorance and revealed to him the true Gospel (12—14). After these parenthetic, but deeply important, remarks, he repeats his warning against those who were undermining the faith (15—20).

The second chapter is devoted to rules about the regulation of public worship. Prayers are to be offered for those in authority, (1—3), a rule from which St. Paul digresses, according to his wont, into the expression of precious truths respecting the universality of God's offered grace (4), the unity of God, the redemption of Christ (5—6), and the solemn sanctions of his own apostolic office (7). The men are to pray in every place, fearlessly uplifting holy hands (8); the women are also to pray in shamefastness and simplicity, remembering alike their condition and their hopes (9—15).

The third chapter deals with the qualifications for the Christian ministry. It sketches the ideal of the pastor and presbyter (iii. 1—7), of deacons (8—10, 12—13) and of ministering women (11). After a personal message to Timothy (14—15), the chapter ends with a rhythmic confession which may possibly be the fragment of one of those ancient hymns (16) which from the earliest days have formed so blessed a part of Christian worship.

The fourth and fifth chapters contain advice respecting the government of the Christian community. Timothy is bidden to counteract the dualistic heresies, the exaggerated

asceticism, and the anile speculations of false teachers with
zeal, study, and diligence (iv. 1—16). He is taught how he
should bear himself towards elders, and towards women (2),
especially towards widows, both aged and young (3—16). A
few words are added about the maintenance of presbyters
(17—18), about the manner in which offenders are to be
treated (19—20), and about ordination (21). The chapter
ends with two personal directions (22, 23) and a solemn
remark about the nature of different classes of sin (24—25).[1]

The sixth chapter, after touching on the duties of slaves
towards their masters (vi. 1, 2), reverts to the false teachers,
denouncing their insolence, their factious sophistry, and
above all their avarice (3—10). After a solemn adjuration
to Timothy to continue steadfast (11—16) and parting
references (by way of postscript) to the duties of the rich,
(17—19) and to the false teachers (20, 21)—both of which
were pressing considerations to a presbyter of Ephesus—the
Epistle ends with the brief blessing "Grace be with thee."

Among many noticeable features of this familiar and
friendly letter we may call attention to the following:—

1. The difference between it and some of St. Paul's other
Epistles is very marked, and yet it furnishes striking internal
evidence of its own genuineness. It is absurd to suppose
that St. Paul could be always at his greatest, or could never
write anything less powerful and epoch-making than the
Epistles to the Galatians, Romans and Ephesians. This letter
is exactly what we should expect a letter to be which was
written by an old man to an intimate friend much younger
than himself. The manner is that of an old man. While
there is not a trace of senility or garrulity in any bad sense,
the digressive style is so exactly what we should expect of one
who wrote under St. Paul's circumstances that it would have
required the genius of a Shakespeare to imitate the Apostle's
ordinary manner with such perfection and yet to retain the

---

[1] The connection of thought has been variously, but not successfully
explained.

wide differences caused by the change of themes and outer conditions. Take for instance the sixth chapter. With what familiar ease does St. Paul break off his warning against the love of money to pour forth his personal exhortations! In how thoroughly Pauline a manner do these exhortations end in one of those rich spontaneous doxologies in which the Apostle relieved his over-burdened heart! And there we should naturally have expected the Epistle to end; but, just as in the Epistle to the Galatians, the Apostle cannot help diverging again for a moment into remarks about the right use of riches which were suggested by his recent denunciation of covetousness, he reverts in a similar manner to the warning against babblings and Gnostic errors which he has so repeatedly denounced. Or again, take the intensely individual digression in i. 12—17 with its closing doxology, both so entirely in St. Paul's manner, since all his theology is, in ultimate analysis, the reflex of his personal experience.[1]

Much stress has been laid on what are stated to be un-Pauline expressions. But may we not ask, on the other hand, whether a *falsarius* would not have been sure to keep closely to the matter and phraseology of St. Paul while it would have been impossible for him so remarkably to reproduce his individual manner? Would a forger have gone out of his way to add the touching word "mercy," to St. Paul's recognised greeting of "grace" and "peace"? Would he have ended his very first sentence with an anacoluthon, as in verse 4?[2] Could he have caught the digressive and personal style of the allusions and asseverations in i. 11, ii. 7, which seem rather due to past conflicts[3] than to any present necessity? Would he have been so bold as to make St. Paul call himself "the chief of sinners," which is

[1] Reuss. *Les Épitres Paulin.* ii. 352. For similar digressions and doxologies, see Gal. i. 12 ; 1 Thess. ii. 4 ; 2 Cor. iii. 6 ; iv. 1, &c.; and Rom. xv. 33 ; xvi. 7 ; Phil. iv. 20, &c.
[2] Comp. Gal. ii. 4, 5 ; Rom. v. 12.
[3] Rom. ix. 1, 2 ; Cor. xi. 31.

far stronger than his former saying that he is "less than the
least of saints"? Would he purposely, by way of mere
literary imitation, have lost the thread of his subject as in
ii. 3—7? Would he have said anything which *prima facie*
appears to contradict what St. Paul had said to the Corinthians
(1 Cor. vii.) about marriage, as in ii. 15 v. 14? Would
he have written as though he had meant to end the Epistle
at iii. 14—16, and then had begun again?[1] Could he have
introduced so casually the personal directions to be pure, and
"not to continue drinking water," as in verses 22, 23?
Could he have imagined that St. Timothy would need such
directions? Is not the latter advice just the opposite to
what we should naturally have expected from the former?
Would any one but St. Paul have addressed Timothy,
who was now a full-grown man, as though he was still a
youth? Would he have left unaltered the singular, but
quite Pauline confusion of metaphors ("treasuring up a
foundation") in vi. 19? Would he not have tried to
end with some great climax or doxology and not with a few
stray and disconnected remarks? May it not be safely
assumed that the writer who had the piety to write this
Epistle and the skill to forge it must have been one who
neither could nor would have forged at all? And where in
the second century is the writer to be found who either held
the same sentiments as these or had the power to set them
forth with a literary skill which, if he were indeed a forger,
must be pronounced to be little short of Shakespearian in
the insight which it must have required?

2. For it is a thoroughly Pauline characteristic that the
Epistle "abounds in memorabilia." It seems as if St. Paul
was one who could not write the simplest letter without
uttering in the course of it some priceless truth which has
become to the Church as familiar as household words.

Here are a few of these gems:

[1] The same phenomenon is found markedly in 1 Thess. iv. 1; Phil.
iii. 1.

1 TIMOTHY.

i. 1. "God our Saviour and Christ Jesus our Hope.[1]

i. 5. "But the end of the charge[2] you are to give is love out of a pure heart and a good conscience and faith unfeigned."

i. 15. "Faithful is the saying,[3] and worthy of all acceptation, that Christ Jesus came into the world to save sinners; of whom I am chief."

ii. 3—6. "For this is fair[4] and acceptable in the sight of God our Saviour; who willeth that all men should be saved, and come to the knowledge of the truth. For there is one God, and one Mediator also between God and men, himself man,[5] Christ Jesus, who gave Himself a ransom for all; the testimony to be borne in its own due times."

iii. 16. "And confessedly great is the mystery of godliness; He who was:[6]

> "Manifested in the flesh,
>
> "Justified in the Spirit,[7]
>
> "Seen of Angels,
>
> "Preached among the nations,
>
> "Believed on in the world,
>
> "Taken up in glory."

v. 6. "The wanton, though alive, is dead" (ἡ δὲ σπαταλῶσα ζῶσα τέθνηκε, an epigram at once profound and brilliant).

---

[1] The attribution of the title "our Saviour" to God is one of the peculiarities of the Pastoral Epistles (1 Tim. iv 10; Tit. i. 4; ii. 10, 13; iii. 4, 6). The omission of the article with this word shows that it was beginning to be regarded as an appellative. St. Paul perhaps adopts both these striking expressions from Ps. lxii. 6, 7. "God our Saviour" also occurs in Jude 25; 2 Pet. i. 11. (Comp. Luke i. 47.)

[2] τῆς παραγγελίας refers back to ἵνα παραγγείλῃς in verse 3.

[3] πιστὸς ὁ λόγος. This phrase is characteristic of the Pastoral Epistles (1 Tim. iii. 1; iv. 9; 2 Tim. ii. 11; Tit. iii. 8, comp. 1 Kings x. 6). By this time (as we should naturally have expected) many of the most striking truths of Christ had been compressed into brief formulae. Comp. Rev. xxi. 5; xxii. 6.

[4] καλόν.

[5] Here the word *one* may be emphatic (Col. ii. 15-18), and the word *man* may be aimed at Docetic views.

[6] There can be little doubt left that ὅς not Θεὸς is the true reading in the passage. The "Mystery of God" is Christ. Col. ii. 2. (On the hymnic form see Eph. v. 19). The passage is closely analogous, line for line, with 1 Pet. iii. 18, 19, 22.

[7] See Rom. i. 4.

vi. 6. " But godliness with contentment is great gain."

vi. 10. " For a root of all kinds of evils is the love of money."

vi. 12. " Fight the good fight of the faith; lay hold on the life eternal, whereunto thou wast called."

Might we not ransack all the extant writings of the first, second, and third centuries, and yet fail to find such pearls of great price as these ? Could an equal number of sayings of the same value be collected in all the writing of Confucius ?

3. Among expressions which characterise this and the other Pastoral Epistles we may notice (besides " God our Saviour" and " Faithful is the saying ")—

a. " *The faith,*" to express a body of Christian truth (i. 19, iii. 9, iv. 1-6, v. 8, vi. 10, 12, 21).

β. " *Grace, mercy, peace* " (i. 1, 2).

γ. " *Doctrine,*" " *teaching,*" " the *sound doctrine.*" The word means both " instruction " (Rom. xv. 9, 1 Tim. iv. 13, 16, v. 17) and the doctrine taught (i. 10, iv. 6, v. 17).

δ. " *Godliness* " ($\epsilon \dot{v} \sigma \acute{\epsilon} \beta \epsilon \iota a$, ii. 2, 10, iii. 16, iv. 7, 8 ; v. 4, vi. 3, 5, 6, 11) ; $\theta \epsilon o \sigma \acute{\epsilon} \beta \epsilon \iota a$, ii. 10. This word occurs ten times in these Epistles, and only five times in all the rest of the New Testament, four of those instances being in 2 Peter and one in Acts.

ε. " *The devil* " (iii. 6, 7. Comp. Eph. iv. 27, vi. 11). Elsewhere St. Paul uses Satan.

ζ. The word " *Mediator* " as applied to Christ. The idea however is Pauline (Rom. v. 10, 2 Cor. v. 19), and the word itself (Gal. iii. 19, 20). Compare Hebrews viii. 6, xii. 24.

η. The abverb " *really* " ($\check{o} \nu \tau \omega s$) : " that which is really life," vi. 19, " really widows," v. 3.

The word *neophyte* occurs for the first time in this Epistle, iii. 6.

We may also notice the bold universalism of the expressions in ii. 4, " whose will it is that all men be saved," and iv. 10, " the Saviour of all men, specially of the faithful " (comp. Tit. ii. 11). To these we must add such words as " other-teaching;" " myths ; " " boundless genealogies ; " " vain talking;" "profane emptinesses of speech," "profane anile (γραώδεις) myths," and others which are used to describe and denounce the false teachers. What is the exact meaning of ' myths" and "genealogies" we cannot say, since we are ignorant of the condition of heresy at this epoch. All that we can say is that "legendary stories," to which the name "myths" might well be given, seem to have abounded among the Jews since the days of the captivity. "*Myths*" might be the Greek rendering of the Jewish "*Hagadoth*." Those who doubt the genuineness of this Epistle think that "boundless genealogies" applies to the system of emanating and inter-marrying Aeons invented by Valentinus. But, on the one hand, if this Epistle had been aimed at these later heresies it would have been far too vague to be efficacious, and it has no allusion to a developed Gnosticism; and on the other there are in the Jewish Kabala genealogies of various kinds which may have had their prototype in very early days. When Timothy is bidden to avoid "oppositions of the falsely-named gnosis" (vi. 20), Baur and others think that there is an allusion to the book of Marcion called *Antitheses*, in which by a series of parallel quotations—much after the fashion of Abelard's *Sic et non*—he tried to show the irreconcilable antagonism of the Old and New Testaments.[1] But there is no allusion whatever in this Epistle either to this or to other special views of Marcion, and it is doubtful whether "anti-theses" here means anything more than the oppositions of false-called knowledge to the true knowledge and full know-ledge (ἐπίγνωσις) of the faith of Christ. When Baur tries to extort an allusion to Valentinianism out of the casual expression "to the king of the ages" (of the aeons, *i.e.* of the world as manifested in time) he finds hardly any one to see any force in his suggestion. The phrase may very possibly have been derived simply from Psalm cxlv. 13, " Thy kingdom is a kingdom of all ages."

---

[1] Tert. *c. Marc.* i. 19; Hippolytus, *Philosophumena*, vii. 30. The frag-ments of Marcion's *Antitheses* have been collected by Hahn, 1823.

There are one or two passages which require special
explanation of the difficulties which have been raised
respecting them.

a. One of these is ii. 15, "But *she shall be saved through
the child-bearing,* if they continue in faith and love and
sanctification with sobriety."

"The child-bearing" may mean no more than "child-
bearing" regarded in the abstract. St. Paul perhaps merely
meant to say (in accordance with the general meaning of
the context) that a married life, together with the duties of
motherhood, is, as a rule (Gen. iii. 16), the appointed path
for woman, and will end in her salvation if it be pursued
in humble holiness.[1] Most ancient and modern commentators make it mean "through *the* child-bearing," *i.e.* the
Incarnation. This surely would be to lay a very undue
emphasis on the article, and the truth would then be expressed very obscurely. As the "faith" and "love" which
he speaks of must have an object no one could mistake St.
Paul to mean that motherhood *in itself* had any saving
power.

β. iii. 13. The curious expression, "*a good degree,*" seems
to mean no more than "a fair standing-point," "an honourable position." Comp. vi. 19.

γ. iii. 15, "That thou mayest know how to behave in the
house of God, which is the Church of the living God, *the
pillar and ground of the truth.*"

This verse offers several difficulties. It may mean "how
thou oughtest," or "how *men* ought" to behave in the house
of God; and it is by no means clear whether "the pillar and
ground of the truth" is in apposition to "the Church," or
whether the verse should be rendered and punctuated, "how
to bear thyself in the House of God—seeing that it is (*ἥτις*)
the Church of the living God—as a pillar and basis of the
truth."

If *the Church* is here called "the pillar and stay of the

[1] Comp. v. 14, βούλομαι οὖν νεωτέρας γαμεῖν, τεκνογονεῖν.

truth " (for such in any case must be the meaning of ἑδραίωμα), the expression is one of the least Pauline, the most difficult and the most modern in these Epistles. It is so unlike anything which St. Paul anywhere says, that it would certainly add to the strength of the suspicions which attach to the genuineness of the Epistle. In that case this verse might have led Schleiermacher (for the first time in many centuries) to feel a hesitation on the subject far more naturally than the word " to teach a different doctrine," [1] which excited his doubts. It would, moreover, be an excessively clumsy anti-climax—amounting to positive confusion of thought—to speak of the Church first as the House of God and then as a pillar and stay of the House. On the other hand, all difficulties vanish if we refer the words to Timothy, who is here bidden to bear himself as an upholder and support of the truth. The parallel expressions in Gal. ii. 9, Eph. ii. 20, Rev. iii. 12 are in each case used with reference to persons ; and these very words were applied to the martyr Attalus in the letter of the Church of Lyons and Vienne (c. v.).

δ. v. 18. " *The scripture says*, Thou shalt not muzzle a threshing ox " (Deut. xxv. 4). " And, The labourer is worthy of his hire."

It has been urged that St. Luke's Gospel (x. 7) is here quoted as Scripture, and that therefore the Epistle must be later than St. Paul's day. " But the Scripture saith " may only apply to the first clause. The second seems to have been a current proverb.

ε. v. 21. " *In the sight of . . . . the elect angels.*"

This appeal is unusual, but is quite in accordance with St. Paul's training and beliefs.[2] It is also in accordance with the ideas of this epoch, for King Agrippa invoked " the holy angels " in his appeal to the Jews not to rebel.[3] The

---

[1] i. 3, ἑτεροδιδασκαλεῖν.
[2] 1 Cor. xi. 10 ; 1 Pet. i. 12. Comp. Tobit xii. 15.
[3] Jos. *B. J.* ii. 16.

word "elect" seems to be no more than a general epithet of 1 TIMOTHY. excellence.

The passage in iv. 4, "Every creature of God is good, and nothing to be rejected, if it be received with thanksgiving," is interesting because, as Dr. Field has pointed out, it is possibly a proverbial expression which had its origin in Homer.[1]

The "delivering to Satan," in i. 19, is probably a form of excommunication, which was believed to be accompanied indeed by penal bodily suffering, but which was mercifully designed as a means of leading back offenders to repentance.

The genuineness of the Epistle will further be examined in the note, and we have every reason to accept the ancient testimony of the Muratorian fragment : " An Epistle to Titus and two to Timothy, written out of personal feeling and regard, are still honoured in the respect of the Catholic Church in the arrangement of ecclesiastical discipline." [2]

---

[1] *Iliad,* iii. 65.

[2] See Westcott on the Canon, p. 217. The original is, " Et at titu una et ad tymotheii duas pro affecto et dilectione in honore tamen ecclesiae catholice in ordinatione ecclesiastica."

NOTE I.

ST. PAUL'S SECOND IMPRISONMENT, AND THE GENUINENESS OF THE PASTORAL EPISTLES.

It has for centuries been the common belief of the Church that after having pleaded his cause before Nero, or before those whom Nero left in charge of Rome during his disgraceful expedition to Greece,[1] St. Paul was acquitted and set free. This must have taken place early in A.D. 64. Had it been later, St. Paul must inevitably have perished in the fiery horror of the Neronian prosecution.

The belief in his liberation at least accords with his own confident and twice-expressed anticipation to the Philippians (i. 25, 27), and to Philemon (verse 22). So strong were his reasons for expecting an acquittal that he even requested Philemon to provide a lodging for him on his expected visit to Colossae.

Of course this hope may have been disappointed; but if St. Paul's trial was finished before the Fire of Rome, the deficiency of evidence against him, or the testimony of Festus, Agrippa, Lysias, and the centurion Julius, may have secured the recognition of his innocence. Further, he may have been aided by the very favourable impression which he had made on the soldiers of the Praetorian guard, or by some of the humble converts in the households of Caesar and Narcissus—if the latter be the famous freedman of Claudius.[2] We might even conjecture that the case against him practically collapsed, if any of the witnesses or documents were on their way to Rome in that vessel in which about this time Josephus sailed to secure the release of certain Jewish priests. The prosecution of St. Paul may have been a subordinate object of that expedition. But the vessel foundered at sea, and out of 200 souls, eighty alone—of whom Josephus was one—were rescued, after having floated or swum all night in the waves.[3]

While, however, there is great probability in the belief that St. Paul was liberated, and that he enjoyed two years of missionary freedom before his arrest at Troas and his second imprisonment at Rome, the external historic evidence in favour of these events is unhappily weak.

---

[1] Clement of Rome says that he "bore witness" (μαρτυρήσας) "before the rulers" (ἐπὶ τῶν ἡγουμένων). The verb μαρτυρέω may here have its ordinary sense. Ἡγούμενοι may be a general word, but, if meant to be taken strictly, may refer to Helius and Polycletus, or Tigellinus and Nymphidius Sabinus who were regents during Nero's absence.

[2] Narcissus himself by this time was dead.

[3] Jos. *Vit.* 3.

B D

St. Luke, who could so well have informed us, suddenly drops the
curtain upon St. Paul with the one emphatic word *unmolestedly* (ἀκωλύτως), when he describes the comparative lenity of the early part of
St. Paul's imprisonment. Perhaps the prisoner's sufferings were aggra-
vated when the upright and honourable Burrhus had been superseded
in the Praefectorship of the Praetorian guard by the villainous
Tigellinus.

The only other evidence we have is

(1) A vague and rhetorical passage of Clement of Rome in the first
century (Ep. 1, *ad Cor.* 5), in which the liberation is perhaps implied,
but which is too general and uncertain to have much weight.

(2) A phrase in the fragment of the Muratorian Canon (about A.D.
170), which perhaps implies his voyage to Spain, but in which the text
is corrupt and the meaning uncertain.

(3) A direct statement of Eusebius in the fourth century, and of St.
Chrysostom and St. Jerome in the fifth.[1]

Unhappily the historic value of this evidence is almost *nil.* If, then,
we believe that St. Paul was liberated, our belief rests on other
grounds.

Those grounds are the intrinsic probability of the fact; St. Paul's
own confident expectation that it would be so; the generality of the
tradition; and above all, the Pastoral Epistles.

If the Pastoral Epistles be genuine they must have been written
after his liberation; the First to Timothy, and that to Titus during
fresh travels; and the Second to Timothy during his second imprisonment, just before his death. No other place can be found for them in
the records of St. Paul's life. If they were not written *after* A.D. 64,
we must then be driven to the reluctant conclusion that they are not
from the hand of St. Paul.

To the present writer the conviction that those Epistles are genuine
certifies the tradition that St. Paul was set free, and escaped the Neronian persecution to meet his final martyrdom about A.D. 68.

In the first place the Epistles are well authenticated by external evidence. It is said that the First Epistle to Timothy bears marks of
spuriousness, and therefore drags the other two into the same condemnation. On the contrary, it seems to me that the other two, especially the
Second to Timothy, are quite indisputably genuine, and that they carry
with them the acceptance of the First. But, even in favour of the First
we can quote a clear allusion in Clement of Rome, and quotations by
Ignatius, Polycarp, Hegesippus, Athenagoras, Irenaeus, Clemens of
Alexandria, Theophilus of Antioch, and perhaps Justin Martyr. It is
accepted by the Peshito, and mentioned in the Muratorian Canon, while

---

[1] Chrys. *ad* 2 *Tim.* iv. 20; Jer. *Catal. Script.* See also Tert. *Scorp.* 15;
De Praescr. 36; Lactant. *De Mort. Persec.* 2.

1 TIMOTHY. there is little or no significance in its rejection by the heretics **Marcion** and **Tatian**.

From internal evidence it is argued that

1. *They are inferior to St. Paul's greatest writings.*

This is an argument of no value. No author is always at his best and greatest, and these were private letters to dear friends. They stood on quite a different footing from the letters to great Churches on controverted themes. Yet no one has said that the style differs from that of Paul. Almost any reader can see in the original the radical difference of style between St. Paul's Epistles and that to the Hebrews ; and between the first and the second Epistles of St. Peter ; and between the Apocalypse and Gospel of St. John. In the latter instance the difference can be accounted for, and in the former it may perhaps be explained. But no one can read the Pastoral Epistles without admitting that *if* the style be an imitation it is an imitation transcendently skilful, and without suspecting that those flashes of deep feeling, those outbursts of intense expression, those majestic doxologies, those simple and beautiful ideals of work and character, those swift, perfect, unfaltering summaries of Christian truth could only have come from the master's hand. It is remarkable that not a few critics who have rejected the Epistles as a whole, have yet been driven to plead for the authenticity of certain parts of them, which they feel could only have been written by St. Paul.

2. But *they abound in isolated expressions not found elsewhere in St. Paul's writings.*[1]

This in no way proves spuriousness, since there are similar unique expressions (*hapax legomena*) in every one of St. Paul's Epistles, three in the Romans, and six even in the few sentences addressed to Philemon. St. Paul was linguistically susceptible. Like other men of genius he often assimilated new words and phrases. "In a fresh and vigorous style," says Alford, "there will always be *librations* over any rigid limits of habitude which can be assigned ; and such are to be judged of, not by their mere occurrence or number, but by their subjective character being or not being in accordance with the writer's well known characteristics."

---

[1] Such as "piety" (εὐσέβεια, εὐσεβῶς, εὐσεβεῖν). The word may (as Pfleiderer suggests) have been taken as the fundamental idea of the Christian life, as the word "faith" became gradually appropriated to express a body of doctrines.

"Soundness" (ὑγιής, ὑγιαίνειν) 1 Tim. i. 10 ; vi. 3 ; 2 Tim. i. 13 ; Tit. i. 9, 13 ; ii. 2, 8 ; and as natural antitheses, νοσῶ, γάγγραινα. These words, as well as the new phrases, παραιτεῖσθαι, προσέχειν τινι, may have been picked up from intercourse with St. Luke.

Master (δεσπότης), 2 Tim. ii. 21, for κύριος, Lord. As κύριος became more and more a proper name, δεσπότης was wanted.

"To deny" (ἀρνεῖσθαι), 1 Tim. v. 8 ; ii. 12, 13, &c., in the sense of renouncing truth.

For other expressions see the Note to the Epistle of Titus.

Technical terms, due to special subjects, fall under a different head.

3. *But the theology of these Epistles differs from that of Paul.*

This assertion is not true. It is absurd to stigmatise the dominantly practical tendency of these Epistles as "utilitarianism and religious eudaemonism," when good works, though profitless to deserve salvation, are insisted on as a moral necessity in every one of St. Paul's Epistles. To say that a difference of theology is involved in the new use of "Saviour" as applied to God ; in the greater objectivity of the word "faith ; " and in the phrase "the sound doctrine," is to ignore the simple fact that the circumstances of the Church progressed with great rapidity during its earliest days, and that even in St. Paul's day, and through his powerful influence, the struggle between Paulinism and Jewish Christianity gave way to the deadlier struggle between heresy and the Church.

4. *But these Epistles betray the existence of an ecclesiastical organisation more developed than that which existed in the days of St. Paul.*

So far as this is at all true it is exactly what we should expect. Every year that a Church existed there would be a more pressing necessity for Church government and order. On the other hand the simplicity of the organisation alluded to in these Epistles, the fact that there is no trace of predominant episcopal authority, and that the names "bishop" and "presbyter" are still synonymous (1 Tim. iii. 1–19 ; Tit. i. 5–7), furnish the strongest proof that these letters could not possibly have been written in the second century. The "crushing despotism" of an irresponsible Episcopate had not yet begun. The directions given to the presbyter-bishop are ethical, not hierarchic.[1]

5. *The Epistles are aimed at phases of gnosticism which did not exist till the second century.*

The proof that this is the case wholly fails. It is founded on the flimsiest inferences from such words as "aeons," "gnosis," "antitheses," which were borrowed by gnosticism from Scripture. The germs of gnosticism—the systems and ideas prevalent in that vague form of heretical teaching—have existed in many ages, and countries, and religions, and philosophies. They were familiar to the Essenes, to the Greek philosophers, to Oriental mystics, to Alexandrian theosophists, to Simon Magus, to Cerinthus, and many others. We find traces of them in the Epistles to the Ephesians, Colossians, Philippians, and even in those to the Corinthians, as well as in the letters of St. Peter, St. Jude, and St. John. This argument, like the last, rather tells the other way. If these Epistles had been second-century forgeries, they would not have dealt so vaguely with such definite errors as those of Valentinus, Carpocrates, &c.

The Gnostics as a body were, in the second century, intensely anti-

[1] The argument founded on the fancy that "*the widows*" of 1 Tim. v. 11–14 meant, as in later times (Ignat. *Ad Smyrn.* 13), a sort of celibate order of virgins is contradicted by the plainest facts.

1 TIMOTHY. Judaic. The incipient Gnostics of these Epistles are, on the contrary, Judaisers, who have affinities alike with the Kabalists, the Pharisees, and the Essenes.[1] Lipsius [2] sees in the false teachers of these Epistles " a development of the same Essene Jewish Christianity as that of the false teachers of the Colossians." In theory they were ascetic (i. Tim. iv. 3, 8) and dualistic (1 Tim. iv. 4 ; Tit. i. 15, 16 ; 2 Tim. ii. 18) ; in character they were impure, covetous, disorderly, and given to idle disputes (2 Tim. iii. 1–7 ; vi. 6 ; Tit. i. 10, 11 ; iii. 9 ; 2 Tim. i. 23 ; vi. 20). It was needless for St. Paul to *discuss* their views. He is not writing to them, but to his apostolic delegates Timotheus and Titus, who were perfectly well acquainted with all his views. To the heretical doctrines of opponents he has only to oppose the sound doctrine of the Church of God, and to their moral aberrations the rules of practical piety.

The Epistles stand or fall together. Even the most "advanced" and hostile critics are prepared to admit the genuineness of the Second Epistle to Timothy.[3] But if that be genuine, St. Paul must have been liberated before the Neronian persecution, and the case in favour of the two other Epistles is greatly strengthened. The power, beauty, and value of the Epistles is their best attestation. Dr. Wace says truly that " the sacred writings are throughout characterised by a wonderful combination of the loftiest faith in the mysteries of godliness with profound practical wisdom ; and it is a combination of which no instance can be shown in those apocryphal and forged productions among which it has been attempted to range these Epistles."

[1] "*Jewish* myths," Tit. i. 14. "Teachers of the law," 1 Tim. i. 7. "Strifes about the law," Tit. iii. 9 ; 1 Tim. i. 8.

[2] *Der Gnosticismus* (in *Ersch. u. Gruber*)

[3] The *extreme* frivolity of some of the arguments urged against these Epistles is illustrated (1) by Baur's suggestion on 1 Tim. ii. 2 that "*kings*" (a common term in the provinces for local dynasts and even for the Roman Emperor) refers to the times of the Antonines, when emperors took associates into the empire ! and (2) by Pfleiderer's remark on the same verse (*Protestanten Bibel*) that it refers to the time of Hadrian, who befriended Christians.

THE EPISTLE TO TITUS.

WRITTEN PROBABLY FROM MACEDONIA ABOUT A.D. 66.

'"Speak thou the things which become the healthy teaching."—TIT. ii. 1.

IF St. Paul was enabled to carry out the plans which he
had formed in his first imprisonment, he sailed to Ephesus
shortly after his release, and then for the first time paid his
promised visit to Colossae and the other cities of the Lycus
valley.   Leaving Timothy at Ephesus to preside over the
Church, he set out for Macedonia.   His work in Syria was
finished.   It is most unlikely that he ever again saw Caesarea
or Jerusalem.   Persecution was at this time raging in the
Holy City.   The Sicarii—a band of zealots who resorted to
secret assassination—were filling the whole country with
terror.[1]   James, the Lord's brother, had recently been
murdered.[2]   The Apostle could never again have visited the
Temple with impunity.   His life could not have been safe
for a moment in the recrudescence of Jewish fanaticism
which marked the outbreak of the last rebellion.   If the
"many thousands" of Christian Jews had not raised a voice
or lifted a finger for him when he was nearly torn to pieces
in A.D. 60, they would certainly have been powerless to
defend him in A.D. 66.   If even James had fallen a victim,
what chance would there have been for Paul ?

We do not know the circumstances which took the Apostle
to Crete.   From Macedonia he would in all probability take

[1] Jos. *B. J.* ii. 14, § 2.
[2] A.D. 63.   Jos. *Antt.* xx. 9, §§ 1, 2.

his old route to Corinth, and from thence it would have been an easy sail to the great island. Christianity had already been established under the shadow of the ancient Ida, in all probability by some of the Jews who had been converted on the day of Pentecost.[1] But the Church needed organization, and for this reason St. Paul left Titus to superintend the infant communities, and "to ordain elders in every city."

During the last year of his missionary activity we only catch an occasional glimpse of him. We see him still burdened with the care of all the Churches. We still find him surrounded by a little band of devoted friends, whose presence and support were more than ever necessary to him in his broken health and advancing years, and one or other of whom he constantly despatched from his side on some errand of importance. The immediate occasion for writing this letter to Titus was to announce that he meant to send either Artemas or Tychicus to replace him in Crete. He wished Titus to rejoin him in Nicopolis—the famous Epirote city which Augustus had built to celebrate his victory at Actium. At that city, which he may have visited in the journey which took him as far as to Illyricum, he intended to spend the winter.[2]

Of all the companions who surrounded St. Paul, Titus seems to have been the most respected for his practical vigour and efficiency, though Luke and Timothy may have been more personally beloved. It is a remarkable proof of the fragmentary character of the Acts of the Apostles that his name does not once occur in those memoirs, probably because he was frequently despatched in various directions, and was not much with St. Paul at the special crises narrated in the memoir and itineraries of St. Luke. There is no evidence whatever to identify him with the Titus or Titius Justus of Acts xviii. 7 (even if that reading were more than

[1] It seems idle to suppose that St. Paul could have founded any Churches during the days of storm which he passed as a prisoner on board the Alexandrian vessel at Lasaea and Fair Havens.

[2] Rom. xv. 19; Tit. iii. 12.

dubious).[1] All that we know of him is that he was a Gentile
convert who accompanied St. Paul on that memorable visit
to Jerusalem from Antioch which had ended in the emancipation of the Gentiles from the thraldom of the circumcisionists. The presence of an uncircumcised Gentile in
Jerusalem, and in close personal connexion with Jews, excited such tumultuous emotions that there is much reason
to believe that in the acme of the struggle, and pending the
final decision, Titus made a purely voluntary sacrifice, and
accepted circumcision in order to allay the immediate excitement. By such a sacrifice, which afterwards gave room for
bitter taunts against Paul, as though he too had once been a
preacher of circumcision, Titus at least qualified himself for
work in Churches so largely composed of Jewish elements.
Even bigoted Judaists would be favourably inclined to one
who was thus not only a proselyte of the gate," but " a
proselyte of righteousness." [2] All that we further know
about him is drawn from allusions in the Epistles. Since
Titus was made of sterner stuff than Timothy, St. Paul had
on one occasion countermanded a mission of the latter to
Corinth, and had sent Titus in his place. Indeed, on three
separate occasions Titus had been sent to introduce order
and submission into that turbulent and distracted Church.[3]
Towards the close of St. Paul's life he was despatched to
Dalmatia.[4] After this he disappears from history, though
we have the usual vaporous ecclesiastical legends that he
returned to Crete, and there died at an advanced age as
a "Bishop" or "Archbishop"—terms which, as Dean
Alford says, are, as applied to that period, mere "traps for
misconception "—of the Church of Gortyna in that island.

---

[1] There is reason to think that he had been converted by St. Paul, who calls
him "his genuine child in the faith" (Tit. i. 4). There is an apocryphal
biography of Titus in Fabricius, *Cod. Apocr.* ii.

[2] As this is not the usual opinion, and as it cannot here be argued out, the
author must refer to the full discussion of the question in his *Life of St. Paul,*
i. 407–420.

[3] 2 Cor. vii. viii.

[4] 2 Tim. iv. 10.

It is a probable conjecture that he may have béen converted during the first journey of St. Paul.[1]

The outline of the Epistle to Titus is as follows:—

After a singularly condensed greeting, rich with such characteristic Christian terms as "faith," "full knowledge," "hope of eternal life," "manifestation," "salvation," "grace, mercy, peace" (i. 1—4), the Apostle tells him what sort of elders he ought to appoint (5—9), with special reference to the bad reputation of the Cretans and the prevalence of a Judaic form of gnosticism,[2] which substitutes myths and ceremonies for holiness towards God (10—ii. 1). He then gives directions for the conduct of aged men (ii. 2), of aged women (3—5), of young men, to whom Titus is to set an example (6—8), and of slaves (9, 10). These directions are based on a beautiful summary of the principles of Christian conduct (11—15). He then enforces the lessons of gentleness and submission (iii. 1, 2) as a direct result of our Christian faith and calling (3—7), and urges Titus to devote himself to these practical duties, while avoiding idle speculations (8—11). After a few personal messages and salutations, he ends with a brief blessing (12—15).

No such summary can give any adequate picture of this admirably practical and dignified letter. To those who have ventured to describe it as meagre, colourless, and monotonous, I oppose the consensus of the Christian world, which has recognised in it a priceless and unrivalled manual of pastoral advice. Luther was accustomed to declare himself with extreme freedom as to the merits of various books of the New Testament. He never hesitated to express his depreciation of any Epistle which did not come up to his loftiest and most spiritual ideal. And yet of the Epistle to Titus he

---

[1] See Gal. ii. 1, 2 ; 2 Cor. vii., viii. 6, 16, 17, 28.

[2] That it was Judaic appears from i. 14 (μὴ προσέχειν), Ἰουδαϊκοῖς μύθοις, and iii. 9, μάχας νομικάς. Judaic Christianity did not at once lose all the elements of Judaism, and the Judaism of that day, no less than of the days of the *Talmud*, abounded in discussions (ζητήσεις) both foolish (μωραί), empty in their own nature (κεναί), and void of all results (μάταιοι), as well as in discords (ἔρεις, μάχαι) and "genealogies."

said, "This is a short Epistle, but yet such a quintessence of Christian doctrine, and composed in such a masterly manner, that it contains all that is needful for Christian knowledge and life."

The following are some of its characteristics:—

1. It is completely dominated by a few leading conceptions, as is shown by the constant repetition of the same words and phrases in the short compass of three chapters.

a. One of these words is "*Saviour.*"

Thus we have—

i. 3. "In the proclamation wherewith I was intrusted, according to the commandment of God our Saviour."

i. 4. "Grace and peace from God the Father and Christ Jesus our Saviour."

ii. 10. "That they may adorn in all things the doctrine of God our Saviour."

ii. 11. "The grace of God was manifested, bringing salvation to all men."

ii. 13. "Looking for . . . . the appearing of the glory of the great God and our Saviour Jesus Christ."

iii. 4.. "But when the kindness of God our Saviour . . . was manifested . . . . according to his mercy he saved us."

iii. 6. "The Holy Ghost . . . . which he poured upon us richly through Jesus Christ our Saviour."

Thus, in three chapters, we have the epithet "Saviour" given no less than seven times—four times to God the Father, and three times to our Lord Jesus Christ. To whom the epithet applies in ii. 13 has always been uncertain. The words may either be rendered as in the Authorised Version and the margin of the Revised Version, "the great God and our Saviour Jesus Christ," or as in the Revised Version, "our great God and Saviour Jesus Christ."[1] It is taken in this latter sense by most of the Greek Fathers; but the majority of versions ancient and modern, and most modern critics, understand it in the former, and this rendering ("the

[1] See Dr. Kennedy, *Ely Lectures*, p. 83.

great God and our Saviour Jesus Christ") certainly seems in accordance with the analogy of other passages.[1]

β. Another dominant conception is *soundness in doctrine.*

i. 9. "Holding to the faithful word which is according to the teaching (διδαχὴν) that he may be able . . . . to exhort in the sound doctrine (ἐν τῇ διδασκαλίᾳ τῇ ὑγιαινούσῃ)."

i. 13. "Rebuke them sharply that they may be sound in the faith."

ii. 1. "Speak thou the things which befit the sound doctrine."

ii. 2. "Sound in the faith."

ii. 7. "Uncorruptness in this doctrine."

ii. 8. "Sound speech."

ii. 10. "The doctrine of God."

Thus we have "teaching" or "doctrine" spoken of seven times, and six of these times connected with the ideas of "healthiness" and "soundness." It is further noticeable that (as we have seen) in the Pastoral Epistles "the faith" has acquired a sense which can hardly be paralleled in St. Paul's earlier writings, namely, the general body of Christian truths.[2] This is, however, exactly what we should expect to find in the gradual progress of the Christian Church.

γ. As "soundness"—a new metaphor with St. Paul, and one which he may have caught up from his constant later intercourse with Luke—indicates the standard of doctrine, so "*sober-mindedness*" is the rule of practice.[3]

i. 8. A presbyter is to be "sober-minded."

ii. 5. Aged women are to be "sober-minded," and "to sophronise" the young women.

ii. 6. Young men also are to be sober-minded.

---

[1] 1 Tim. i. 1, "the commandment of God our Saviour, and of the Lord Jesus Christ"; v. 21, "Before God, and our Lord Jesus Christ." (Comp. vi. 13; 2 Pet. i. 1; 2 Thess. i. 12; Jude 4, &c.)

[2] 2 Tit. i. 13; ii. 2.

[3] The word σωφροσύνη (which in one form or another occurs ten times in these Epistles) is a very beautiful one. It is derived from σώζειν and φρήν and represents the many-sided excellence of practical conduct and character which is represented by the Latin *frugi.* Elsewhere in St. Paul it is only found in Rom. xii. 3; 2 Cor. v. 13; and (in a speech) Acts xxvi. 25.

ii. 12. The grace of God trains us to live sober-mindedly.

The combination of soundness in doctrine and soberness in practice constitute the " *godliness* " (εὐσέβεια) which is also a prominent conception in the Pastoral Epistles.[1]

δ. In close accordance with the object of this Epistle, which is to teach the application of Christian doctrine to daily life, an unusual prominence is given to " *good works.*"

i. 16. "Disobedient, and to every good work reprobate."

ii. 3. "Teachers of good things " (καλοδιδασκάλους).

ii. 14. " Zealous of good works."

iii. 1. "Remind them . . . . to be ready to every good work."

iii. 8. " That they . . . . may be careful to maintain good works."

iii. 14. " Let our people also learn to maintain good works " (καλῶν ἔργων προΐστασθαι).[2]

This prominence of " fair works," thus urged many times indirectly, and six times verbally in three chapters—in a phrase not found except in the Pastoral Epistles—has been sometimes represented as un-Pauline. How little this is the case may be seen at once from—

iii. 5. " Not by works (done) in righteousness, which we did ourselves, but according to His mercy He saved us."

If any proof were needed that the insistence upon good works as the natural and necessary fruit of true faith is essentially Pauline, it is found in the fact that rules of moral conduct occupy so large a part of all his Epistles, even those to Rome and the Galatians, and that in this Epistle of good works he lays it down so clearly that we are " justified by grace " (iii. 7). But St. Paul, it must be remembered, is neither writing this letter to a Church nor to a novice. It is a familiar private letter, not a formal theological treatise. It was needless for him to lay the foundations which had

---

[1] Tit. i. 1; ii. 12; 1 Tim. *passim.* Ten times in these Epistles, but not elsewhere in St. Paul.

[2] The epithet καλὸς occurs seventeen times in 1 Tim. and only sixteen times in all the previous Epistles.

been already so surely laid in the mind of Titus during many a year of intimate association.

ε. Owing to the self-asserting independence of the Judaists against whom he is warning Titus, he lays special stress on the virtue of *submission*.

i. 6. The children of a presbyter are not to be disorderly (ἀνυπότακτα).

i. 7. A presbyter is not to be self-willed (αὐθάδης).

ii. 5. Women are to be subject (ὑποτασσομένας) to their own husbands.

ii. 9. Slaves are to submit (ὑποτάσσεσθαι) to their own masters.

iii. 1. The Cretans are to be submissive to constituted authorities.

2. But among these dominant and reiterated conceptions it is interesting to come upon passages in which St. Paul, with the firmness of absolute conviction, and the fulness of long familiarity, compresses into a few lines a majestic summary of his Christian faith.

Two such summaries—worthy of the Apostle in the zenith of his spiritual power—occur in this Epistle, and they are not, so to speak, dragged in, but arise from the general train of thought with a spontaneity which is inimitably Pauline. One of these is in ii. 11–14 :—

"For the grace of God hath appeared, bringing salvation to all men : training us that denying impiety and worldly lusts, we should live soberly, and righteously, and piously in this present age ; looking for the blessed hope and appearing of the glory of the great God and our Saviour Jesus Christ, who gave Himself for us that He may ransom us from all lawlessness, and may purify for Himself a people for His own possession, zealous of good works."

Another of these swift summaries of Pauline doctrine, unparalleled for beauty and perfectness, yet free from all polemical elements, is iii. 4–7 :—

"But when the kindness of God our Saviour, and His love

toward man appeared, not by works of righteousness which we did, but according to His mercy He saved us, through the laver of regeneration and renewal by the Holy Ghost, which He poured upon us richly through Jesus Christ our Saviour, that, being justified by His grace, we may become heirs, according to hope, of eternal life. Faithful is the saying."

Those who deny the genuineness of the Pastoral Epistles may well be asked which of the Fathers of the second century could have written two such passages as these ? Are they equalled, or even approached, in grandeur and completeness by anything which could be culled from the writings of Clemens Romanus, or Hermas, or Justin Martyr, or Ignatius, or Polycarp, or Irenaeus—nay, even of Tertullian, or Basil, or Chrysostom, or Gregory of Nyssa, or Gregory of Nazianzus ? If the mind of Sophocles was recognised in a single chorus, and the pencil of Apelles in a single thin line, and the eye of Giotto in the sweep of one flawless circle—are passages like these insufficient to prove the power and authenticate the workmanship of St. Paul ?[1]

3. Among passages which may be specially noted are—

a. The very severe remark about the Cretans—

"The Cretans are always liars, evil wild beasts, lazy gluttons," which is quoted (i. 12) from the poem "On Oracles" by the Cretan poet Epimenides, whom St. Paul calls "a prophet of their own." St. Paul adds that the witness is true. Of course his words are not meant to be taken *au pied de la lettre*, as though the Cretans were indiscriminately wicked. No more is meant than that Titus has to deal with a population of general bad repute. The ancients used to say that there were "three worst K's," namely Kretans, Kappadocians, and Kilicians.[2] "To Kretize" meant "to lie;" and the ancients accused these islanders of drunkenness; of general sensuality;

---

[1] Among many minor touches of genuineness we may point to the obscure names Artemas and Zenas ; the uncertainty as to whether he shall send Artemas or Tychicus ; and the title "the lawyer," which Titus would understand, but which may mean either Roman jurist or Jewish scribe.

[2] Κρῆτες, Καππάδοκες, Κίλικες, τρία κάππα κάκιστα.

TITUS.

and of greed, which makes Plutarch say of them "that they stuck to money like bees to their combs." "The Cretans," wrote Leonides, "are always brigands, and piratical, and unjust. Who ever knew justice among Cretans?"[1]

The quotation is often adduced as a proof of St. Paul's classic culture. It does not in the least prove this. The line was quoted by Callimachus in his *Hymn to Zeus,* and St. Paul seems to have seen the poems of Callimachus, perhaps in the same book as those of his countryman Aratus. But, independently of this, the verse had become proverbial. It was as universally current as "*perfide Albion,*" or "canny Scotch." or "drunken Swabian." St. Paul had probably learnt a little of Greek rhetoric and logic in the schools of Tarsus, and if so he must have often heard the syllogistic puzzle founded on this line, and known as "the liar." It was this: "Epimenides said that the Cretans were liars; but Epimenides was a Cretan; therefore Epimenides was a liar; therefore the Cretans were not liars."

β. Another curious passage is iii. 13, 14.

"Set forward Zenas the lawyer and Apollos on their journey diligently, that nothing be wanting to them; and let our people also learn to maintain good works" (or, possibly, "to profess honest occupations") "for necessary uses" (or "wants"). What is meant by "*our people also*" (καὶ οἱ ἡμέτεροι)? It cannot possibly mean "other Cretan Christians as well as you and me." Such a meaning would be inconceivably vapid, and would not have been so expressed. Does it then mean that Zenas and Apollos belonged to some assembly or gathering of Christians other than those over which Titus was to preside? It is a question of great interest, for the answering of which we possess no data. But its very obscurity—which could not have been obscure to the recipient of the letter—is one of the many marks of an authentic document.

[1] Liv. xliv. 45 ; Plut. *Paul. Æmil.* 23 ; Polyb. vi. 46. See Clem. Alex. *Strom.* i. 14 ; Jer. *ad loc.*

γ. Of the particular errorists whom St. Paul had in view I need add nothing to what has been already said, but we may touch for a moment on iii. 10 : "A man that is heretical (αἱρετικὸν) after the first and second admonition refuse." It has been said by some that in the Pastoral Epistles *haeresis* acquires its later sense of " heresy," and loses its original and Pauline sense of "faction." [1] Doubtless " heresy" and "factiousness" might often be combined, but there is nothing to show that in this passage the "heretic" is one in the modern sense. And even if αἱρετικὸν here means the same as our "heretical," there had been plenty of time to allow for the growth of this new shade of meaning.

[1] In St. Paul the word αἵρεσις only occurs in 1 Cor. xi. 19 ; Gal. **v.** 20. Elsewhere only in the Acts six times—viz. once of the Sadducees, once of the Pharisees, and four times as applied by the Jews to Christians.

THE SECOND EPISTLE TO TIMOTHY.

WRITTEN SHORTLY BEFORE ST. PAUL'S MARTYRDOM AT ROME, A.D. 67.

"Testamentum Pauli et cycnea cantio est haec epistola."—BENGEL.

"Non tanquam atramento scripta, sed ipsius Pauli sanguine accipere convenit. Proinde haec Epistola quasi solennis quaedam est subscriptio Paulinae doctrinae eaque ex re praesenti."—CALVIN.

"The cloke that I left at Troas with Carpus, when thou comest, bring with thee, and the books, but especially the parchments."—2 TIM. iv. 13.

MANY have regarded this verse as one of the least important in the whole Bible. Many have been perplexed by its appearing there at all. They consider it unworthy of what they imagine should be the dignity of inspiration. Many, again, have used its supposed triviality to point a sneer at the sacred book. Others, like Calvin, have suspected that it contained some hidden mystery. All these views have their root in one and the same error;—the error which consists in men bringing to the Bible their own self-made dogmas and artificial theologies, instead of learning, from its own simple and noble truthfulness, what the Bible is. It must be ever so while partisans make use of it, not as the rock on which to build their own faith, but as a heap of broken missiles to hurl at the heads of others. Incredible is the misery and ruin which has been caused by misinterpretation of Scripture founded on the superstition that every passing word which it contains must have been miraculously infallible and supernaturally inspired, and must therefore involve enigmatic and mystic senses. Infidelity is the natural outcome of false and exaggerated dogma. Widespread scepticism is the certain Nemesis of arbitrary superstition.

But if the Bible be what it seems to be, what it professes to be; if we do not thrust it into a position which it never claims; if it be, like the Saviour of whom it tells, both human and divine; if its inspiration be an illuminating wisdom, a dynamic energy, not a mechanical penmanship, or a miraculous dictation; if it be best honoured by manly faithfulness, not by grovelling fetishism; if we are taught by its own direct words, and by the manner in which our Lord always treated it, to receive it as the straightforward utterance of men whose souls had been taught of God, not as a kabalistic enigma to be deciphered by methods which bear no relation to ordinary criticism—then this verse is just what it professes to be—a message of St. Paul, in a letter to his friend Timotheus, to bring him a cloke, and some books, from Troas. It is that, and nothing more. St. Paul would never have dreamt that any divine instruction lay in it; he would probably have been amazed beyond expression could he have been told that it would be made the theme of a discourse to a Christian congregation in the then wild, far-off island of Britain, 1800 years after he was dead. And yet there is instruction, even divine instruction, in it, if we treat it as exactly what it is—no cryptograph, no oracular utterance—but just a simple message of one Christian brother to another, which acquires its pathos and its wholesomeness neither from impossible supernaturalism, nor Gnostic allegorising, but from the circumstances, and from the man.

1. The man we know. We know him doubly, from the picture of a friend in the Acts of the Apostles, and from his own thirteen letters. It is that "man of the third heaven," —the worn, bent, scourged, exiled, shattered missionary, who, persecuted but not forsaken, cast down but not destroyed,

C C

2 TIMOTHY. flung wide open to the Gentiles the gates of the Christian Church, and showed to all men that in Christ Jesus circumcision is nothing and uncircumcision is nothing, but a new creature.

2. And we know the circumstances. When the curtain falls upon him in the Acts of the Apostles, we see him at Rome during his first imprisonment, in custody indeed, but in immediate expectation of his acquittal and deliverance. That acquittal came, and it came not one hour too soon. A few months after his release there burst forth at Rome that frightful conflagration, which raged for six days, and laid a vast region of the city in ashes. It was darkly rumoured that the guilt of that conflagration rested on the head of the Emperor himself—of Nero, the imperial monster, who at that time disgraced, not only the name of Roman, but the name of man. Just as the great fire of London was falsely attributed to the Papists, even in the inscription on the Monument—

> " Where London's column, pointing to the skies,
> Like some tall bully, lifts its head, and lies—"

so, in order to avert the suspicion from himself, Nero laid the charge upon the innocent Christians. Multitudes 'of every age, of every sex, were arrested. They were slain with the sword; they were exposed in the amphitheatre; they were covered with the skins of wild beasts to be torn to pieces by dogs; they were wrapped in sheets of pitch, and tied to stakes, and set on fire. Nero threw open his own gardens for the revolting spectacle, and when the dusk of evening fell, only too literally

> " Commanding fires of death to light
> The darkness of their scenery,"

he drove about among the people in his chariot, by the flare of these hideous human torches, of which each was a martyr in his shirt of flame. Such was the diabolical horror of heathenism in its dregs; and he who, more than any man, helped to free the world from such horrors—he who dispelled, by the radiance of the Gospel, these demon shadows of a dying paganism—had he, the great Apostle, at that time been still in prison, and in Rome, it is thus that in all probability he, as a leader of the Christians, would have been among the first to fall.

3. God had ordered otherwise for him. We are enabled by the Pastoral Epistles to catch at least a misty glimpse of his final movements and read his state of mind as death drew very near. Set free in time, wherever else he had gone, we may be sure that he had visited Philemon at Colossae, and seen the dear slave Onesimus, now a true Christian, and therefore now doubtless beloved and free. He had wintered at Nicopolis. He had written his first letter to Timothy as his delegate at Ephesus, and to Titus as his delegate in Crete; and then, after revisiting his kind and noble Macedonian churches, he seems to have been arrested a second time, at Troas. Since the Fire of Rome, Christianity had been no longer a *religio licita*, or tolerated religion. Like all brave and good men, Paul had many an enemy—all the mean, all the base, were his enemies; all the conventional Judaisers, all the slander-mongering worldlings; Jews, whose opinions he offended; Gentiles, whose gains he checked. Such a one as Alexander the coppersmith, or any other angry and designing Jew, could easily have procured his arrest, and when suddenly seized by the lictors at Troas he could have had no time to take away his few possessions. He was conducted to Ephesus, and as he lay there in prison he experienced the generous kindness of Onesiphorus.[1] After a preliminary trial there he may perhaps have appealed once more to Caesar and been once more despatched to Rome. Though no St. Luke has recorded it for us, we can trace step by step the journey of the wearied prisoner. At Ephesus he bade farewell to Timotheus with

---

[1] 2 Tim. i. 18, ὅσα ἐν Ἐφέσῳ διηκόνησε. Onesiphorus may have been, as Wieseler suggests, a *deacon* (διακονέω).

2 TIMOTHY. many a streaming tear.[1] At Miletus, Trophimus fell sick. At Corinth, Erastus stayed behind. But the weak health of the Apostle needed attendance, and one or two, with Luke the beloved physician, were with him still. As they neared Rome along the Appian Way, no brethren, young and old, came this time in deputation as far as Appii Forum to meet him. Over the blackened ruins of the city, amid the squalid misery of its inhabitants, perhaps with many a fierce scowl turned on the "malefactor" (ii. 9), he passed to his gloomy dungeon. There, as the gate clanged upon him, he sat down, chained night and day, without further hope, a doomed man. His case was far more miserable than it had been in his first imprisonment, two or three years earlier. He was no longer permitted to reside in "his own hired room." To find him was difficult, to visit him dangerous.[2] He was in the custody not as before of an honourable soldier like Burrus, but of the foul Tigellinus, whose hands were still dripping with Christian blood. To see friends was perilous, to preach Christ was death. One by one they of Asia deserted a prisoner whom it was deemed a disgrace to own. The first to leave him were Phygellus and Hermogenes.[3] Titus and Crescens were called away to mission work. Demas deliberately deserted him. Tychicus was sent, perhaps with this letter, to Ephesus. Luke only stayed. The warm-hearted Ephesian Onesiphorus took

---

[1] 2 Tim. i. 4, μεμνημένος σου τῶν δακρύων.

[2] The difficulty of finding him is shown by the expression, "he sought me very diligently (σπουδαιότερον ἐζήτησέ με) and found me" (2 Tim. i. 17). He who wished to visit a hated prisoner had to face the insolence of the soldiers (Juv. *Sat.* xvi. 8–12). The danger is obvious. At this time the Christians —since the fire of Rome—were not only "everywhere spoken against," but savagely persecuted. In fact the mere profession of Christianity became an offence. Yet the total neglect of St. Paul, and the loneliness in which he was left by the Roman Christians is a strange circumstance. Were they at this time almost exclusively Judaists who had but little sympathy with his views? Or had they been almost exterminated by the martyrdom of that "*ingens multitudo*" in the Neronian persecution? Or had they not as yet acquired that sympathy with martyrs, confessors, and prisoners which was so remarkable in later days, and which Lucian mentions with admiration in his account of the worthless impostor Peregrinus, who at one time professed to be a Christian?—Lucian, *De Morte Peregr.* 13.

[3] "They who hurt me most," said Luther, "are my own dear children—my brethren—*fraterculi mei, aurei amiculi mei.*"

the trouble to find the aged prisoner, and often refreshed his
soul which scorned all hardship, but yearned to its inmost
depths for human sympathy. But now, it seems, Onesiphorus
was dead,[1] and when the Apostle was brought for trial in his
first appearance before Nero, no man stood with him. It was
an awfully perilous matter to face that human Antichrist.
"No man—no patron, no advocate, no *deprecator*—took his
place by my side to help me; all abandoned me; God forgive
them!" He felt that it was God alone who had enabled him
to face the gleaming axes, the *vultus instantis tyranni.* God
had saved him from "the lion's mouth."[2] He knew that it
would be but a brief respite. During that brief respite—
which would have been technically called the *ampliatio* of his
trial—he wrote once more to his own dear son in the Gospel,
the shrinking but faithful Timothy. There was no one whom
he loved so well. Since the day when the young Lycaonian
boy had come to share his travels and dangers, Paul had
grappled him to his soul with hooks of steel; and if he has
one earthly wish left it is to see again before he dies that
dear friend of earlier days. He writes therefore to urge him
to do his best to come—to come with all speed—to come
before the winter storms have closed the Mediterranean, or
else, as he intimates not obscurely, he will find him dead.
For the time of his departure was at hand. In reading the
Second Epistle to Timothy we are reading the last words of
St. Paul. It is amid those last words that he asks for his
cloke and books. In his hasty arrest at Troas he has left
them behind with Carpus to take care of them, and he wants
them now.

---

[1] 2 Tim. i. 16, πολλάκις με ἀνέψυξεν. That Onesiphorus had died either in
Rome or on his return to his family in Ephesus is a natural inference from
1 Tim i. 16, 18, iv. 19, where St. Paul prays for, and salutes, "the *household*
of Onesiphorus," but not himself.

[2] 2 Tim. iv. 17. The "lion" was in all probability Nero. Λέοντα τὸν Νέρωνά
φησι διὰ τὸ θηριῶδες, Chrys. When the jailer announced to Agrippa the death
of Tiberius, he did so in the words, "The lion is dead" (Jos. *Antt.* xviii. 6,
§ 10); and Esther (Apocr. Esth. xiv. 3) in entering before Xerxes goes "before
the lion." For "the mouth of the lion" see Amos iii. 12. "Save me from
the lion's mouth" (Esther, in *Megillah*, f. 15, 2).

The Epistles.

4. The word rendered cloke—the φελονὴς—was one of those large, sleeveless, travelling garments which we should call an "over-all" or "dreadnought."[1] Perhaps St. Paul had woven it himself of that *cilicium*, the black goats'-hair of his native province, which it was his trade to make into tents. Paul was a poor man.[2] He, like his Lord, had often known what it was to work night and day for his livelihood, and barely to earn it then; and he had felt, for many a weary year, the pangs of hunger, and thirst, and cold, and nakedness. Doubtless the cloke was an old companion. It may have been wetted many a time with the water-torrents of Pamphylia,[3] and whitened with the dust of the long roads,[4] and stained with the brine of shipwreck, when, on the rocky cliffs of Malta, Euraquilo was driving the Adrian into foam.[5] He may have slept in its warm shelter on the chill Phrygian uplands, under the canopy of stars; and it may have covered his trembling limbs—bruised with the brutal rods of the lictors —as he lay that night in the dungeon of Philippi. And now that the old man—who is (as with a passing touch of self-pity he calls himself) an "ambassador in a chain"—sits shivering in some gloomy cell under the Palace, or it may be on the rocky floor of the Tullianum, and the wintry nights

---

[1] The notion that it was a book case (γλωσσόκομον) is given up. It may be a transliteration of *poenula* (Syriac פלינ).

[2] That St. Paul often had to struggle with poverty, and sometimes even with positive want and hunger, appears from many passages of the Epistles. Whether he had any private means is an interesting question which we cannot solve. It appears from his ability to hire a room of his own at Rome (Acts xxviii. 30), and to be responsible for the debt of Onesimus (Philem. 19), that some small resources were at his disposal. The expression, "I was mulcted of all" (ἐζημιώθην τὰ πάντα), in Phil. iii. 8, might imply a sudden loss of what he once had possessed. His other means of livelihood may have been derived in part from his relatives at Tarsus and Jerusalem (Acts xxiii. 16), from his Macedonian converts (Phil. iv. 15), and especially from his own exertions at the trade of tentmaking, which, in Thessalonica at any rate, earned sufficient not only for his own maintenance but even for that of his comrades also (2 Thess. 8). Obviously the trade would not be equally flourishing at all places, and in prison St. Paul would not be able to work at all.

[3] κινδύνοις ποταμῶν, 2 Cor. xi. 26.

[4] ὁδοιπορίαις πολλοῖς, 2 Cor. xi. 26.

[5] κινδύνοις ἐν θαλάσσῃ, 2 Cor. xi. 26. τρὶς ἐναυάγησα, *id.* 25. ἄνεμος τυφωνικὸς ὁ καλούμενος Εὐρακύλων, Acts xxvii. 14.

are coming on—he bethinks him of the old cloke, and asks Timothy to bring it him,—the cloke in which in former days

> "Yes! without cheer of sister or of daughter,
> Yes! without stay of father or of son,
> Lone on the land, and homeless on the water,
> Passed he in patience, till the work was done."

"The cloke that I left at Troas with Carpus, bring with thee."

5. "And the books; but especially the parchments." The *biblia*, the papyrus-books—few, we may be sure, but old friends. Books in those days were life-long possessions. Perhaps he had bought them in the school of Gamaliel at Jerusalem; or received some of them as presents from wealthier converts. Perhaps among them may have been poems of Aratus, a Cilician like himself, or pamphlets of Philo, or the Wisdom of Solomon.[1] The papyrus-books, "but especially the parchments"—the works inscribed on vellum. What were these? Was there any document among them which might have been useful to prove his rights as a Roman citizen? Were they any precious rolls of Isaiah, or the Psalms, or the Lesser Prophets, which father or mother had given him as a life-long treasure, in the far-off days, when, little dreaming of all that awaited him, he played a happy boy in the dear old Tarsian home? Dreary and long are the days, longer and drearier still the evenings, in that Roman dungeon; and often the rude legionary, who detests to be chained to a sick and suffering Jew, is coarse and cruel to him; and he cannot always be engaged in "the sessions of sweet, silent thought," either on the hopes of the future, or the remembrance of the past. He knows Scripture well, but it will be a deep joy to read once more how David and Isaiah, in all their troubles, learnt, like his own poor self, "to suffer, and be strong."

---

[1] If these be fancies, they are at least fancies founded on real indications. St. Paul quotes from the Cilician poet Aratus in Acts xvii. 28. It is certain from many passages that he was not unfamiliar with the conceptions of Philo. There are several passages in his Epistles which resemble the Wisdom of Solomon. St. Paul was so completely a student that Festus thought his studies were driving him mad (Acts xxvi. 24, τὰ πολλά σε γράμματα εἰς μανίαν περιτρέπει).

And therefore—"The cloke that I left at Troas with Carpus, when thou comest, bring with thee, and the books, but especially the parchments."

And who, as he reads this last message, can help recalling the toucning letter written from his prison in the damp cells of Vilvoorde by our own noble martyr, William Tyndale, one of the greatest of our translators of the English Bible ? "I entreat your Lordship," he writes, "and that by the Lord Jesus, that if I must remain here for the winter, you would beg the Commissary to be so kind as to send me, from the things of mine which he has, a warmer cap. . . . I feel the cold painfully in my head. . . . Also a warmer cloke, for the one I have is very thin. Also some cloth to patch my leggings. My overcoat is worn out, my shirts even are worn out. He has a woollen shirt of mine, if he will send it. But most of all I intreat and implore your kindness to do your best with the Commissary to be so good as to send me my Hebrew Bible, grammar, and vocabulary, that I may spend my time in that pursuit.—William Tyndale." The noble martyr was not thinking of St. Paul, but history repeats itself, and what is this over again but "The cloke that I left at Troas with Carpus bring with thee, and the books, but especially the parchments"?

6. A simple message, then, about an old cloke and some books, nothing more, but is it not pathetic and human ? Would we willingly part with it ? May we not with profit consider what it can teach us more ?

i. Does it not show us, first of all, that this great and holy Apostle was a man like ourselves, a tried and suffering man with human wants, and human sympathies, ay, and with human limitations and human weaknesses, and though with transcendently severer trials, yet with no greater privileges than we enjoy ? The hero-worship which would elevate the Apostles into demi-gods, on pedestals of supernatural superiority, is a false hero-worship, which Scripture itself sets at naught, and by which those who profess to honour

Scripture, most flagrantly contradict it. Take Paul's own
account of himself, "the least of the Apostles, not meet
to be called an Apostle;" "less than the least of all
saints;" "the chief of sinners;" one who does "not yet
count himself to have apprehended;" engaged still in an
earnest struggle with the flesh; undelivered even yet from
"the body of this death."[1] Yes, a fellow-sinner, a fellow-
sufferer with us; but, like us, forgiven; like us, redeemed.
Like us;—and yet, with no higher grace to help him than we
may have, how unlike us! And if he was but a man like
ourselves, and yet such a high saint of God unlike ourselves,
from those heights of Christian holiness to which he had
followed the footsteps of his blessed Lord—yea, from those
heavenly places to which he had risen in spirit with the
risen Christ—does he not call to us with more clear
encouragement, "Faint not; I too was weak, I too was
tempted; but thou, no less than I, canst do all things
through Christ that strengtheneth us."

ii. And then in how fine a light of manliness, good sense,
contentment, does this message bathe the Apostle's character!
The sword, he well knows, is hanging over his head, whose
flash shall slay him; but life is life, and till the Lord calls
him there is no reason why life should not go on, not only in
its quiet duties, but also in such small blessings as it yet may
bring. There is no flaring fanaticism, no exaggerated self-
denial here. He has been telling Timothy to study, and to
take due care of his health. Incidentally he sets him the
example of doing both. The winter nights will be cold and
dull. There is no sort of merit in making them colder and
duller. That is why he writes for the cloke and the books.
God, for our good, sends us trials enough to bear; but it is
only for our good. There is not the least reason—it is not
even right—to create tortures and miseries for ourselves

---

[1] 1 Cor. xv. 9, ὁ ἐλάχιστος τῶν ἀποστόλων, κ.τ.λ. Gal. i. 13, τῷ
ἐλαχιστοτέρῳ πάντων τῶν ἁγίων—Eph. iii. 8 (St. Paul here in his humility invents a double comparative, "less-than-least"), Phil. iii. 12–14, Rom. vii. 24.

which He has not sent us. We are allowed to take, we ought to take, every harmless and innocent gift which He permits to us, and to thank Him for it. Let us never think that our sorrows as such, or our hardships as such, are pleasing to God. "The cloke that I left at Troas with Carpus, when thou comest, bring with thee; and the books, but especially the parchments."

iii. Then look at the matter in one more light. What is it that a life of ceaseless ungrudging labour has left to Paul! What earthly possessions has he gained as the sum-total of services to the world, unparalleled in intensity, unparalleled in self-denial? Perhaps he wants to leave some small memento behind him, some trifling legacy by which some true heart may remember him, ere the rippled sea of life flows smooth once more over his nameless grave. Just as the hermit St. Anthony left to the great bishop St. Athanasius his sole possession, his sheepskin cloke, so Paul would like to leave to the kind and faithful Luke, or the true and gentle Timothy, the cloke, the books, the parchments. But how small a result of earth's labours, if earth were everything! Worth far less than a dancer gets for a figure in a theatre, or an acrobat for a fling on the trapeze. The heavenly work and the earthly reward are not in the same material; it is not for such rewards that the best and purest work of the world is done.

> "Where are the great, whom thou couldst wish to praise thee?
> Where are the pure, whom thou couldst choose to love thee?
> Where are the brave, to stand supreme above thee,
> Whose high commands would cheer, whose chidings raise thee?
> Seek, Seeker, in thyself; submit to find
> In the stones bread; and life in the blank mind."

Nay, seek, Seeker, not in thyself but in Christ, in whom are hid all treasures bodily.

The singer who has a fine note in her voice may blaze in diamonds; the speculator who makes a lucky venture on the Stock Exchange, or the distiller who manufactures some horrible intoxicant, may, in a year or two, have his carriages and his palace, his title and his estate. But the thinker who has raised the aim of nations may die unnoticed, and the poet who has enriched the blood of the world be left to starve. Paul pours out his life, a libation on God's altar, in agonies and energies for his fellow men. He cleanses the customs, he brightens the hopes, he purifies the life, of men. He adds for centuries to the untold ennoblement of generations; and what is the sum-total of his reward ? What is the inventory of all his earthly possessions, as he sits upon his prison floor ? Just "the cloke that I left at Troas, and the books, and the parchments." Do we think that he sighed when he contrasted his sole possessions—that cloke and books—with the jewels of Agrippa, or the purple of the vile Nero, or even with the gains of any buffoon or parasite in a rich man's house ? Such rewards he had never sought. He sat loose to earthly interests. He knew that on earth the cross is often the reward of nobleness, the diadem the wage of guilt. No ! he will thank God for such warmth as he may find in the cloke, for such consolation as the books may bring; and for the rest he will trust death, he will throw himself on God.

7. Thus much, surely, of instruction lies, without any pious fraud or exegetical jugglery, in one of the most despised verses of Scripture. These are plain lessons to which it lends itself without any effort. Let us only ask you in conclusion whence Paul derived this supreme nobleness, this divine contentment ? What was the source of this heroic faithfulness, this absolute indifference to the dross and tinsel, the passing fashion and fading flower, of the world ? Read this his last Epistle, and you will see. It was because he could say, "I am now ready to be poured forth, and the time of my departure is at hand. I have fought the good fight; I have finished my course; I have kept the faith. Henceforth there is laid up for me the crown of righteousness which the Lord, the righteous Judge, shall give me at that day." It was because he saw all life resting on one foundation of God,

2 TIMOTHY. standing sure, with a seal on it, and on the seal these two divine legends—one, "The Lord knoweth them that are His," the other, "Let every one that nameth the name of Christ depart from iniquity." It was because he could say with all his heart, "Faithful is the saying"—the saying which perhaps he quotes in all its rhythmic beauty from some ancient Christian hymn—

> "If we died with, we shall also live with Him ;
> If we endure, we shall also reign with Him ;
> If we deny, us also will He deny ;
> If we are faithless, He abideth faithful ;
> For He is not able to deny Himself." [1]

---

[1] ii. 7-13. The words are certainly rhythmical, perhaps liturgical.

NOTE I.

OUTLINE OF THE SECOND EPISTLE TO TIMOTHY.

1. Greeting (i. 1, 2).
2. Thanksgiving (3-5).
3. Exhortation to steadfastness in the Gospel (6-14).
4. The kindness of Onesiphorus (15-18).
5. Continued exhortations to steadfastness, and rules of pastoral conduct (ii. 1-26).
6. Warning against false teachers (iii. 1-iv. 5).
7. Personal details. Consciousness of approaching death (iv. 6, 7). His loneliness and desertion (8-18).
8. Salutations (19-21).
9. Blessing (22).

The *motive* of the letter is the desire for Timothy's presence : Haste ! Come ! (Σπούδασον !) :—

iv. 9. " *Haste to come* to me quickly."

iv. 21. " *Haste to come* before winter."

iv. 13. " When thou comest" (ἐρχόμενος).

i. 4. " *Yearning* (ἐπιποθῶν) to see thee."

iv. 5. " My *death is near* at hand " (ἐγὼ γὰρ ἤδη σπένδομαι).

The letter is St. Paul's last will and testament.

Be brave ! be faithful to the truth as I have been ! Do not be misled by false teachers. Come to me, for I am alone, and doomed to die.

There are hints and allusions that Timothy, perhaps in his grief at the loss of his teacher—was in danger of yielding to timidity, fear, and sloth. St. Paul writes to urge him to " fan into a flame " (ἀναζωπυρεῖν) the graces which he has received by imposition of hands (i. 6) because God has not given us the spirit of cowardice (δειλίας). He knew the unfeigned faith of Lois and Eunice, " *but*" he is persuaded (πέπεισμαι δὲ) that it is in Timothy also (i. 4). Timothy is "not to be ashamed of Paul and the Gospel"; he is to endure hardship (κακοπάθησον, i. 8, iv. 5) ; not to forsake Paul or to waver in doctrine as others have done i. 8, 12, 15), but to strengthen himself (ii. 1), and toil like the soldier, the wrestler, the husbandman (ii. 3-6), and not to be misled but to *abide by* the truth (i. 13 ; ii. 23 ; iii. 14).

It can I think, hardly be doubted that deep as is the tone of affection there is yet an undertone of anxiety and misgiving.

Among the more remarkable passages are—

i. 9, 10. An epitome of the Gospel.

ii. 7–13. The rhythmical expression of perfect confidence in Christ.

ii. 19. The double inscription on the one foundation.

iii. 1–9. The prophecy of Gnostic corrupters of the Church.

iii. 16. The profitableness of all inspired Scripture. "Every scripture inspired by God is also profitable," &c.

iv. 6–1. The retrospect of his life.

Among the more remarkable expressions we may notice—

i. 9. "*Before times eternal*" (πρὸ χρόνων αἰωνίων). It shows that αἰώνιος means "epochal," "age-long."

ii. 9. "*I suffer as a malefactor.*" The two robbers are regarded as "malefactors," Luke xxiii. 32. At this period it was a political crime to be a Christian.

ii. 14. The uselessness and danger of religious disputes (μὴ λογομαχεῖν).

ii. 15. "*Rightly dividing*" (lit. "cutting straight," (ὀρθοτομοῦντα, Prov. iii. 6, LXX.), the word of life."

ii. 16. "*Profane babblings*" (βεβήλους κενοφωνίας).

ii. 17. "*Will spread as a gangrene* (ὡς γάγγραινα νομὴν ἕξει.")　Medical terms. The beloved physician was at this time his sole companion, Comp. κνηθόμενοι, iv. 3, ὑγιαινούσης, iv. 3.

ii. 26. Lit. "*That they may become sober from the snare of the devil, after having been taken captive by him* (ὑπ᾽ αὐτοῦ), *to do* (εἰς) *His* (*God's*) *will* (τὸ ἐκείνου θέλημα)."

iii. 4. "*Lovers of pleasure rather than lovers of God.*" The Pythagorean Demophilus said that no man could be at the same time a φιλήδονος and a φιλόθεος.

iii. 8. "*Jannes and Jambres.*" Names derived from the Jewish Haggada.

iii. 15. "Thou knowest from infancy (ἀπὸ βρέφους) the *sacred writings*."

THE CATHOLIC EPISTLES.

The Epistles of St. Peter, St. John, St. James and St. Jude are called "Catholic Epistles." They seem to have acquired this name in the second century. Clement of Alexandria speaks of the Synodical letter of the Church of Jerusalem (Acts xv.) as "a Catholic Epistle." Properly only three of the seven letters are "Catholic" in the proper sense, *i.e.* General or Encyclical.

The use of the word to mean "Canonical," and its rendering by "Canonical" in the Western Church seem to arise from mistake.

THE EPISTLE OF ST. JAMES

WRITTEN FROM JERUSALEM ABOUT A.D. 61 OR 62.

> "A document like the Epistle of James shows completely how the full consciousness of possessing God's love and forgiveness accustomed to itself all reflection upon the means by which they were obtained."—WEISS. *Cap. i. 4.*

> "James put this Epistle into the hands of the Jewish Christians that it might influence all Jews, as it was a missionary instruction to the converted for the unconverted and the half-converted for the half converted."—LANGE.

> "Thy works and alms and all thy good endeavour,
> Staid not behind nor in the grave were trod;
> But, as Faith pointed with her golden rod,
> Followed them up to joy and bliss for ever."—MILTON.

"But be ye doers of the word."—JAS. i. 22.

TRUTH is many-sided. We can best apprehend it when it is presented to us in the different aspects which it assumes to many different minds. It was doubtless for this reason that in the Old and New Testaments God has revealed Himself in many fragments and many ways.

We can see quite clearly from the New Testament and from early Christian history that there were in the Church two parties or schools of thought—the Jewish-Christian and the Pauline. The views of both were due to the natural growth of the Church, and were alike compatible with perfect faithfulness to the Gospel of Christ. The thoughts of the Jewish-Christians were deeply rooted in the past; the more progressive and expansive views of the Pauline

THE EPISTLE OF ST. JAMES.

WRITTEN FROM JERUSALEM ABOUT A.D. 61 OR 62.

"A document like the Epistle of James shows completely how the full consciousness of possessing God's love and forgiveness subordinated to itself all reflection upon the means by which they were obtained."—WEISS, *Life of Christ*, i. 4.

"James put this Epistle into the hands of the Jewish Christians that it might influence all Jews, as it was a missionary instruction to the converted for the unconverted and the truly converted for the half converted."—LANGE

> "Thy works and alms and all thy good endeavour
> Staid not behind nor in the grave were trod;
> But, as Faith pointed with her golden rod
> Followed thee up to joy and bliss for ever."—MILTON.

"But be ye doers of the word."—JAS. i. 22.

TRUTH is many-sided. We can best apprehend it when it is presented to us in the different aspects which it assumes to many different minds. It was doubtless for this reason that in the Old and New Testaments God has revealed Himself in many fragments and many ways.

We can see quite clearly from the New Testament and from early Christian history that there were in the Church two parties or schools of thought—the Jewish-Christian and the Paulinist. The views of both were due to the natural growth of the Church, and were alike compatible with perfect faithfulness to the Gospel of Christ. The thoughts of the Jewish-Christians were deeply rooted in the past; the more progressive and expansive views of the Paulinists were mainly occupied with the future of the kingdom of God.

The acknowledged head of the Jewish Christians was James, the first recognised presbyter-bishop of the Church of Jerusalem, whom, without any controversy on the subject, we may here call by the name under which he was known to the Apostles and to the Church of the first century,—" James the Lord's brother."

During the lifetime of Jesus, " His brethren did not believe on Him." Immediately after the Ascension they appear in close union with the Apostles as faithful Christians. The change was wrought by the Resurrection. We find the clue to that change in the passing reference of St. Paul— " then He was seen of James." [1] Seven or eight years later James is incidentally mentioned among those whom St. Paul saw when, after his return from Damascus, he spent fourteen days in Jerusalem. [2] Six years more elapse and we find that in the year A.D. 44, when James the son of Zebedee had been martyred by Herod Agrippa the First and Peter had been thrown into prison, Peter on his escape sends a special message to James—" Tell James," he says, " and the brethren." [3]

That expression shows that on the death of James the son of Zebedee, James the Lord's brother became the recognised ruler of the Church of Jerusalem.

An old and probable tradition says that the Apostles had been bidden by the Risen Christ to make Jerusalem their head-quarters for twelve years, and then to preach the Gospel far and wide to all nations. [4] When the Apostles had thus separated in fulfilment of their high mission, it was natural that the stationary superintendence of the Christians at Jerusalem should be intrusted to James. His force of character, his near kinsmanship to Christ after the flesh,

---

[1] 1 Cor. xv. 7.   [2] Gal. i. 18, 19.   [3] Acts xii. 17.
[4] Clem. Alex. *Strom.* vi. 5, § 43 (quoting the Κήρυγμα Πέτρου) and Apollonius *ap.* Euseb. *H.E.* v. 18.

pointed him out as a natural successor to the son of Zebedee.

The choice was eminently wise. The mother-Church was composed exclusively of Jewish Christians, among whom were not a few converted priests and Pharisees. The Christians, who, in many thousands,[1] visited Jerusalem at the yearly Passovers, were also strict Judaists. We shall not understand early Christian history, and much of the New Testament will be dim to us, if we do not bear in mind that Christ had not formally abrogated the Mosaic dispensation; that Judaism was the cradle of Christianity; that the first Christians had been trained in adoring acceptance of the old Levitic law; that the Temple was still standing, the feasts still observed, the sacrifices still offered; that the Apostles lived in rigid obedience to these rites and ceremonies; that the vast majority of the early converts in Palestine, and large numbers even in the Churches of Europe and Asia, were Jews first and Christians afterwards. The wine was new, but the wine-skins were old. The Jewish Christians, who had thus barely stepped into the Church out of the portals of the synagogue, did not understand—it was not natural that at first they should be able to understand—the mystery of evangelical freedom which had been revealed to the daring genius of St. Paul. James the Lord's brother to a great extent shared in their views. He saw indeed more clearly than most of them that it was right, nay inevitable, that to a great extent the Gentiles should be left free; but in all other respects he was a Hebrew of the Hebrews, a rigid observer of the Mosaic ritual, a regular worshipper in the Temple, a man who intensely valued the privileges of the chosen people. Men knew that the blood of David, perhaps also the blood of Aaron, flowed in his veins. He was all the more a pillar of the Christian community because even the Jews looked up to him with reverence. So

---

[1] Acts xxi. 20, Θωρεῖς, ἀδελφὲ, πόσαι μυριάδες εἰσὶν ᾽Ιουδαίων τῶν πεπιστευ-κότων.

strict were his legal observances that they called him "the righteous one," and *Obliam*, "the bulwark of the people." They told how he was often found prostrate in the sanctuary in earnest supplication for the people of God, and that his knees were hard with kneeling in prayer. More than all this, he was a Nazarite and an ascetic. He was clad only in white linen, and the long unshorn locks of the vow of his youth streamed over his shoulders. As he rose to speak the grandeur of his appearance, the mysterious awe which clung about him as the heir of the line of David and the earthly brother of his Lord, the stern sanctity of his life, the ascendency of his powerful character, the spell of his life-long vow gave to his words a force which exceeded that of all the other dwellers in Jerusalem. If there was any man who could have won back his countrymen to the Messiah whom they had rejected, this was he whose mission was most likely to be favourably accepted.

His antecedents, his training, his position, all that we know of his personal character and history furnish us with the sole clue to the difficulties of his Epistle.

That Epistle was probably written shortly before his martyrdom at the hands of the Jews in A.D. 63. All the allusions which it contains, and the general tone of it, correspond well with this date. The sins which he so sternly rebukes were the very sins which sprang into such terrible prominence during the closing days of the Jewish nationality. The denunciations of the rich accord with the eight-fold curse, traditionally remembered, and in the Talmud thrice repeated, against the Sadducean priests who at that time horrified, oppressed, and betrayed the Jewish Church. Sins of the tongue, feuds and factions, wars and fightings, worldliness and presumption, insincerity and double-mindedness, were the vices which at that epoch were rife among the Jews throughout the world, and were tending to the swift destruction of their place and nation. As were the priests so were the people. There was but one remedy possible;

there was but one chance left for the Jewish race. (It was that they should learn to see in Christianity the true theocratic inheritance) This St. Peter had tried to teach them. It was that they should turn from the shadow to the substance, from the transient to the permanent, from the Aaronic to the Eternal Priesthood. This the author of the Epistle to the Hebrews had tried to teach them. It was that instead of trusting to a dead profession and an external conformity they should learn to obey from the heart the royal and perfect law of liberty. This was the lesson which is here enforced upon them by St. James.

His faithfulness precipitated his death. In all other respects the Jews loved and reverenced him, but they did not forgive his emphatic testimony to the Messiahship of Jesus, or his bold rebuke of their refusal to look on Him whom they had pierced. It was this, if we may trust the testimony of Hegesippus, which led to the murder of the unresisting Just One. His Epistle was written almost certainly from Jerusalem.[1] It reads like the pastoral of some ideal "Prince of the Captivity" to all the faithful. It was the last appeal addressed to the Jews in the tones of ancient prophecy by one whom early legend described as "a Christian High Priest wearing the golden mitre." It was a missive like that which was despatched from time to time to the Jews of the Dispersion by the great Hierarch of the Temple.

We will first consider the message and outline of this memorable Epistle, and then try to account for its many peculiarities.

It is addressed to the "twelve tribes that are in the Dispersion"—in other words to Jews scattered throughout the world. There can, however, be no question that by the twelve tribes are meant primarily not Jews but Christians, for St. James begins by calling himself "a slave of God and of the Lord

---

[1] This view is favoured both by what we know of St. James's history and by all the local allusions to oil, wine, figs (iii. 12), the Kausôn, or Sirocco (i. 11), the earlier and latter rain (v. 7) &c. St. James was doubtless familiar with Joppa also (i. 6 ; iii. 4 ; iv. 13).

ST. JAMES. Jesus Christ," and in the only other passage in which the name of Christ occurs he assumes that he is addressing Christians, for he says, " My brethren, hold not the faith of our Lord Jesus Christ, the Lord of the glory, with respect of persons." Yet from the whole tone of the Epistle, and from its special allusions, it seems highly probable that he took advantage of the honour in which his name was universally held as a bulwark of the people to address Jews also while he is addressing Christians. To Gentiles he does not once allude. To him the Church (v. 14) is still the synagogue (ii. 2). He is speaking through the converted to the unconverted and the half-converted among his own people. Jews were to him Christian catechumens; Christians were to him ideal Jews. He is writing throughout with a sort of dual consciousness, and is mentally addressing his contemporaries at Jerusalem while he is nominally speaking to Christians throughout the world. He could only judge of Jewish and Christian communities by the state of things which he saw during his many years of residence in Jerusalem. The significance of his Epistle becomes more marked if we remember that it derived much of its colouring from the condition of Judaism in the ferment of its fierce hopes and on the eve of its final overthrow.

The Epistle scarcely admits of an analysis. One of its characteristics is the extreme abruptness with which the writer plunges into each new subject, following no other order than that suggested by mental associations which he has not explained.

Ewald divides the Epistle into seven sections, followed by three appendices, and it is quite possible that St. James, no less than his brother St. Jude, his kinsman St. John the Evangelist, and the author of the Book of Wisdom with which he was familiar may have been influenced by Concinnity and the Kabbalism of sacred numbers.

1. After the brief greeting (i. 1) the first section speaks of the endurance of trials (2-18).

They should be borne with joy, being meant to test faith. The wisdom to use them aright can be obtained by prayer, steadfastness, single-heartedness. Alike wealth and poverty are trials, but they only become perilous as temptations when men yield to their own lusts. Every good gift—above all our new birth by the word of truth—comes from God alone.

2. The next section deals mainly with hearing and doing God's word (i. 19-27).

To hear is nothing unless it result in doing, and the true ritual is active love.

3. The next section is on respect of persons (ii. 1-13). After sharply and sternly rebuking the undue partiality shown to rich men, even when they were tyrannous, unjust, and godless, he shows that such conduct, involving as it does a deep injustice to the poor, is a violation of the perfect law of liberty and of the supreme prerogative of mercy.

4. The next section is the controversial part of the Epistle in which he treats of the relation between faith and works (ii. 14-26).

He shows that a fruitless faith, which consists in idle professions, and which performs no deeds of mercy, can profit no man, and he points out that both Abraham and Rahab were saved by works. This section was probably suggested by the last, because St. James saw that the selfish arrogance of the rich and the abject servility of their flatterers arose from a reliance on nominal orthodoxy apart from Christian effort.

5. The fifth section deals with the control of the tongue as the true wisdom (iii.).

6. The sixth section sternly denounces the wickedness of strife and evil speaking (iv. 1-13).

7. In the seventh section he reverts to the sins of the rich —their braggart vaunt of independence, their pride, luxury, and oppression—while he comforts the poor, and counsels them to patient waiting for the coming of the Lord (v. 1-11).

Then follow three separate paragraphs.

i. The first speaks of the sinfulness of needless oaths (v. 12).

ii. The next deals with the power of prayer and Christian intercourse, especially in sickness (v. 13-18).

iii. The third abruptly terminates the Epistle with a solemn declaration of the blessedness of converting others, "With a glorious doctrine," says Zwingli, "as with a *colophon*, he ends his Epistle."

Such is the stern, weighty, manly Epistle of the Lord's brother. We may now glance at some of its specific features.

1. Its style is remarkable. It combines pure, and eloquent and rhythmical Greek with Hebrew intensity of expression. It has all the fiery sternness and vehemence of the ancient prophets, while it is chiefly occupied with inculcating the truths of the "Sapiential" literature—the wisdom of the gnomologists. It is at once fervid and picturesque. It abounds in passionate ejaculations, rapid questions, graphic similitudes. It is less a letter than a moral harangue stamped with the lofty personality of the writer, and afire with his burning sincerity. "What a noble man speaks in this Epistle!" exclaims the eloquent Herder. "Deep unbroken patience in suffering! Greatness in poverty! Joy in sorrow! Simplicity, sincerity, firm, direct confidence in prayer! How he wants action! Action, not words, not dead faith!"

2. Its leading idea is that faith without works is dead. He has flashed the lightning of this conviction into every one of the several sections. It is the one thought which gives unity to all that he has said about endurance; about temptations; about the rich and the poor and their mutual relations to each other; about prayer; about perfection.

3. It is marked by abruptness. It plunges *in medias res* from point to point with no connecting sentences. It begins with no thanksgiving, it ends with no benediction. Clause is attached to clause, something in the manner of St. John by what is called *duadiplosis*,—*i.e.*, by the repetition of a previous word.[1] The writer will not throw away any superfluous words;

[1] See i. 1, "giving thee *joy*"; 2. "Count it all *joy*":— 3. "Trial worketh patience: 4. "But let patience have her perfect work;" and so on, throughout.

he does not care for preambles or formulae. His stern, ST. JAMES.
unbending character is reflected in his manner of address.

4. It contains, as do the writings of St. Luke, an element of
what has been called Ebionism. The word *Ebion* means
"poor," and the Ebionites were deeply impressed by the
beatitudes of voluntary poverty. Some readers have been so
much struck by the severity of St. James's denunciations
against the rich that they have argued in favour of giving a
metaphorical sense to the words "rich" and "poor." The
supposition is impossible. Without being an Ebionite St.
James from his Nazarite vow, from the simplicity of his life
and training, from the early communism of the Church of
Jerusalem, and from the lessons of the Sermon on the Mount
may have looked with admiration on contented poverty. At
the same time, the greed, the cruel injustice, the insolent
violence of the hierarchy whose shameful doings he daily
witnessed were more than enough to suggest his burning
denunciations against godless wealth. A man who had
witnessed the gross misconduct of the Sadducees who then
ruled at Jerusalem—the gluttony of John, son of Nebedaeus,
the blows inflicted by the adherents of Ishmael Ben Phabi,
the viper-hissings of the House of Hanan, the "bludgeons" of
the Boethusim, the libels of the Kantheras—had cause
enough to exclaim amid the impending ruin of his country,
"Go to now, ye rich men, weep and howl for the miseries that
shall come upon you."[1]

5. This Epistle furnishes an unusual number of parallels
to other writings.

It reflects more than any other book of the New Testament
the language of the Sermon on the Mount, and offers many
close resemblances to the Proverbs of Solomon, and the Books
of Ecclesiasticus and Wisdom. St. James had evidently been a

---

[1] St. James has been called an Essene because of his views about "help"
and "mercy" which were the special duty of Essenes, together with his
lessons about riches, and the virtue of silence, and the duty of checking
wrath (Jas. i. 19 ; ii. 5-13 ; iv. 13 ; v. 12. Comp. Joseph. *B. J.* ii. 8 § 6.
Philo, *Quod omnis probus liber*, § 12). But any Christian who had studied
the Sermon on the Mount might have written on these subjects.

close student of what the Jews called the *chokmah*—the literature about "Wisdom." [1]   Most of the early Christian writers show traces of the effects produced in their minds by the words of others; but St. James is no mere plastic borrower, like Clemens of Rome for instance.   Into all that he borrows from others he infuses an individual force which makes it original.

6. The Epistle is more wanting than any other in distinctively Christian and spiritual elements.   Twice only does he mention the name of Christ.   Not once does he use the word "Gospel."   Not once does he allude to the work of Redemption, or to the Incarnation, or the Resurrection, or Ascension.   Even the rules of morality are inculcated without any of those constant references to specifically Christian motives, which are never wanting in the writings of St. Paul, and which constitute the basis of all appeals in St. Peter and St. John.   The morality of St. James is indeed "touched by emotion," but it is urged with no constant and immediate reference to the highest Christian sanctions.

The reason of this peculiarity is not far to seek.   It lies in the fact that the Epistle was intentionally and avowedly a moral appeal, not a theological treatise; partly also in the character and past training of St. James, and in the fact that he is constantly thinking of the state of things which he saw around him among unconverted Jews.   He saw on every side hollow professions of religion, gross partiality, idolatry of riches arrogant evil speaking, factious partisanship, unblushing worldliness, sensual self-indulgence.   These were the sins which he had to denounce; and if he met them without direct reference to the deepest mysteries of Christian theology it was partly because that theology was already fully known to his Christian readers, while it would have had no weight with the Jews whom he also desired to teach.   His object is ethical.   He has to set forth an ideal legalism—the legalism of the royal and perfect law of liberty as it had been set forth in the Sermon

[1] There are six allusions to the Book of Job, ten to Proverbs, five to Wisdom, and fifteen to Ecclesiasticus.—Immer, *Theologie*, p. 428.

on the Mount—in opposition to the Judaic legalism which left room for Antinomian license and prating sloth. What he had to counteract was the barren predominance of a subjective dogmatism which was dissevered from practical activity. What he had to obviate was the dangerous falling asunder of knowledge and action.

Nor must it, on the other hand, be overlooked that, besides the preciousness of this Epistle as a protest on behalf of the necessity for what is idly called "mere morality," it is (a) more full than any other of thoughts drawn from the discourses of Christ; [1] (β) it has one passage of deep and comprehensive theology (i. 18); and (γ) it contains a sketch of heavenly wisdom almost worthy to be hung side by side with St. Paul's immortal picture of Christian love.[2] Little as he touches on specific dogmas he has shown the glory of Christian ethics, and "a Church which lived in sincere accordance with his lessons would in no respect dishonour the Christian name." Moreover his allusions to Christian truth are quite distinct. He would not have called himself "the slave" (i. 1) of any one whom he regarded as merely man ; nor would he have given to any man the title of the "Lord of the Glory."

7. It has been asserted that the passage about faith and works is a polemic against the doctrine of St. Paul.

It is on this ground that the Epistle was so strongly condemned by Luther as "a downright strawy Epistle, which lacks all Evangelical character;"[3] as "wholly inferior to the Apostolic majesty;"[4] as "unworthy of an Apostolic spirit;"[5] as "flatly (*stracks*) contradicting Paul and all Scripture."[6] On similar grounds it was disparaged by Erasmus, Cajetan, the Magdeburg centuriators, Grotius and Wetstein. Ströbel said that, "no matter in what sense we take the Epistle, it is always in conflict with the remaining parts of Holy Writ."

---

[1] There are ten allusions to the Sermon on the Mount.
[2] See also ii. 1, ii. 7 ; v. 6, 14.
[3] Preface to New Test. 1524, p. 105.
[4] Seventh Thesis against Eck, 1519.　　　　[5] *De Captiv. Babyl.* 1520.
[6] Preface of 1522. See too Postills, where it is spoken of as "nowhere conformable to the true Apostolic character."

Luther, as Archdeacon Hare says, "did not always weigh his words in jewellers' scales," and it is impossible not to admire the noble independence of a spirit which was free and bold because it was living and because it felt the Spirit of God as a fresh power. But his condemnation of the Epistle rose from his not possessing the right clue to its comprehension. "Many," he says, "have toiled to reconcile Paul with James . . . . but to no purpose, for they are contrary. 'Faith justifies;' 'Faith does not justify;' I will pledge my life that no one can reconcile those propositions, and if he succeeds he may call me a fool." [1]

It is obvious to say that the propositions cannot be reconciled if St. James and St. Paul meant the same things by "Faith," "Justification," and "Works." But if it is demonstrable that they meant different things—if those three terms in the mouth of St. Paul connoted something quite unlike what they connoted to St. James—the synthesis of their apparently opposing views may be quite easy.

For, in brief, by "faith" in its highest sense St. Paul meant mystic union with Christ; and St. James meant only theoretic belief.

By "works" St. Paul mainly meant Levitic observances and ceremonial externalism, or at the very best servile naked duty; St. James meant works of love and mercy, wrought in conformity with the royal and perfect law of liberty.

By "justification" St. Paul meant the righteousness of God imputed to guilty men; St. James meant the righteousness manifested in those whose life is in accordance with their belief; just as St. Paul himself meant when, in the very Epistle which he devotes to the doctrine of "Justification by Faith," he says (Rom. ii. 14) that "the doers of the law shall be justified," without in the least intending to contradict his own words that "from the works of the law shall no flesh be justified in His sight."

[1] *Colloquia*, ii. 202.

It is not even certain that St. James intended in any way to correct the views of the followers of St. Paul. For the question of faith and works was constantly discussed in the Jewish schools, and constantly illustrated, on both sides, by the cases of Abraham and Rahab. But even if his remarks were intended to have the character of a polemic they in no wise touched St. Paul's real position, while yet they might be both valid and useful against those who perverted his formulae and misrepresented his real meaning.

This at any rate is certain, that even if the Apostle of the Gentiles and the Bishop of Jerusalem misunderstood each other's phraseology there was between them a fundamental agreement. For St. James writes of faith in i. 3, 6, ii. 1, 2, 5, 6, 22, 26, in terms which might have been adopted *verbatim* by St. Paul; and St. Paul in 2 Cor. ix. 8, Eph. ii. 10, Col. i. 10, 2 Thess. ii. 17, and in multitudes of other passages, writes of works in terms which might have been *verbatim* adopted by St. James. Both Apostles would have freely conceded that faith without works is barren orthodoxy, and works without faith are mere legal righteousness. And both would have agreed that all apparent and superficial discrepancies vanish in such broad truths as those expressed by St. John, when he says that "if we say we have fellowship with Him, and walk in darkness, we lie and do not the truth."

Those then who have spoken depreciatingly of the Epistle have done it grave injustice. The Apostles have taught us in different but not in discordant voices. It therefore becomes the duty of Catholic Christianity to adjust one truth with another, and to place apparent contraries in their position of proper equilibrium.[1] We may rejoice that the wisdom of God is manifold, and that the Church of God is *circumamicta varietatibus*—clad in raiment of rich embroidery. St. Peter is the Apostle of Hope; St. Paul of Faith; St. John of Love; St. James completes the ideal of Christian life, when he

[1] Baur, *Ch. Hist.* pp. 128-130.

stands forth as the Apostle of Works. For, as St. Paul also says, " In Christ Jesus neither circumcision availeth anything nor uncircumcision, but faith working by means of love," and "a new creature," and "a keeping of the commandments of God;"[1] and again "the end of the commandment is love out of a pure heart, and of a good conscience, and of faith unfeigned."[2]

[1] Gal. v. 6 ; vi. 15 ; 1 Cor. vii. 19.
[2] 1 Tim. i. 5.

NOTE I.

LEADING WORDS IN ST. JAMES.

Endurance, Patience, Submission (ὑπομονὴ, i. 3, 4, 12, v. 11; Μακροθυμία, v. 7, 8-10; ὑποτάγητε, iv. 7; ταπεινώθητε, iv. 10; Κατήφεια, "downcastness of face," here alone, iv. 9).

Temptation (πειρασμὸς, i. 2, 12, 13, 14).

Perfection (τέλειος), i. 4, 17, 28; iii. 2. Comp. Matt. v. 48.

Prayer (i. 5-7, iv. 2, 3, 8; v. 13-18).

NOTE II.

PECULIAR EXPRESSIONS IN ST. JAMES.

i. 1. "*To the twelve tribes in the dispersion.*" The word *diaspora* only occurs in John vii. 35; 1 Pet. i. 1; and in the LXX. Ps. cxlvi. 2; Deut. xxviii. 25. St. Paul uses the phrase "our twelve-tribed nation" (τὸ δωδεκάφυλον, Acts xxvi. 7). The fiction that the lost Ten Tribes still existed as a body first occurs in 2 Esdr. xiii. 39-47. Even the Talmud recognises their complete dispersion (Sanhedrin, f. 110. 2). But many individual Jews kept their separate tribal genealogies.

i. 1. "*Greeting*" (χαίρειν), "giving them joy." This was the *Greek* method of address, and elsewhere occurs only in Gentile letters (Acts xxiii. 26; 2 Macc. ix. 9). The Hebrew greeting was *Shalôm*, "Peace!" It is singular that St. James, both here and in Acts xv. 23, uses only χαίρειν, but the LXX. render *Shalôm* by χαίρειν in Is. xlviii. 22; lvii. 21.

i. 3. "The *testing* (τὸ δοκίμιον) of your faith." The phrase is adopted by St. Peter (i. 7).

i. 8. "*A two-souled man*" (ἀνὴρ δίψυχος). Also in iv. 8, comp. Ps. xii. 2; "a double heart," lit. "a heart and a heart." Ecclus. i. 28; Matt. vi. 24.

i. 1. *Unstable, restless* (ἀκατάστατος, comp. iii. 16, ἀκαταστασία). This word, with the metaphor of waves driven and tossed by the wind, well expresses the state of excitement, political and Messianic, which then prevailed in Palestine.

i. 11. *The Kausôn*—the burning, scorching wind; the *Kadîm*, or *Simoom* was the worst form of it, Jon. iv. 8; Hos. xiii. 15, &c.

i. 13. "*Untempted of evil.*" "God is always in the meridian." He is out of the sphere of evil.

i. 14. *Enticed* (δελεαζόμενος, 2 Pet. ii. 14, 18. Prov. xxx. 13, LXX.); a metaphor from a fish caught with a bait or lure.

i. 17. "*The Father of the Lights.*" Probably "the Creator of the heavenly bodies."

"*No variableness nor shadow of turning.*" The words used are technically astronomical, but the meaning is the same as that of St. John, "God is light, and in Him is no darkness at all," 1 John i. 5. "Though the lights of heaven have their parallaxes, yet for God He is subject to none of them."—BISHOP ANDREWS.

i. 26, 27. "*Religious, religion*" (θρῆσκος, θρησκεία). The words refer to external and ritual service. This is the old sense of the word "religion," as in Milton's

"Gay *religions* full of pomp and gold."

The verse means that the true ritualism of Christianity is active service. "Morality itself is the service and ceremonial of the Christian religion." —COLERIDGE.

ii. 1. "*Of our Lord Jesus Christ, of the glory.*" Christ is here perhaps identified with the Shechinah. Comp. John xvii. 5.

ii. 7. "*The holy name by which ye were called.*" Lit. "the fair name invoked over you." The name of Christ given in baptism (Cor. iii. 23).

iii. 1. "*Be not many masters.*" This condemns the itch of teaching, and the spirit of "other-peoples-bishops" (ἀλλοτριοεπίσκοποι, 1 Pet. iv. 15).

iii. 5. "*How great a matter*" (ἡλικὴν ὕλην, perhaps "how much *wood*," or "how great *a forest*").

iii. 6. "*The wheel of being*" (or "of nature," or "of birth"). Some understand by this "the orb of creation;" but it is a phrase of very uncertain meaning.

iii. 10. "*These things ought not* (οὐ χρὴ) *so to be.*" The word χρὴ occurs here alone in the N. T. or LXX. The word for "ought" elsewhere is always δεῖ, which expresses moral fitness.

iii. 17. "*Without partiality*" (ἀδιάκριτος). The word (which occurs here only) may mean "without variance:" *i.e.* true wisdom is not Pharisaic and separatist; or better "without vacillation" (διακρίνομαι "doubt").

v. 9. "*Murmur not against one another.*" Lit. *Groan not* (μὴ στενάζετε). "Grudge" (A.V.) once meant "murmur." (See Prayer-Book version of Ps. lix. 15.)

NOTE III.

SPECIAL PASSAGES.

Besides the passages specially touched on in the previous discourse we may notice

i. 18. " *Of His own will He brought us forth by the word of truth, that we should be a kind of firstfruits of His creatures.*"

This verse is of great theological importance.

It implies the *need* of a new life.

It repudiates the fatalism of the Pharisees, and the self-dependence of the Sadducees, by stating that God, by one great act of will (βουληθεὶς), bestowed this new life upon us, and was Himself the cause of His own mercy.

It tells us that the instrument of this new birth was "the word of truth," *i.e.* the Gospel (John xvii. 17 ; 1 Pet. i. 23 ; 2 Tim. ii. 13)

It implies that by this new birth we are as a dedicated first-fruit in Christ (Rom. viii. 19-22), to be completed by the offering up to God of all His creatures.

iii. 17. The seven qualities of *heavenly wisdom.* Seven colours of the Divine rainbow.

iv. 5. " *Or think ye that the Scripture saith in vain, Doth the spirit which He made to dwell in us long to envying ?* "

Neither this rendering (of the R.V.) nor that of the A.V. is intelligible.

Many other renderings are suggested, all of which are liable to objection except either

"God yearns jealously (πρὸς φθόνον, adv.) over the spirit which He placed in us ; " or,

" *The spirit which He made to dwell in us jealously yearneth over us.*"

The quotation is unidentified. It is either a terse summary of *several* passages (see Gen. vi. 3-5 ; Num. xi. 29 ; Ezek. xxiii. 25 ; xxxvi. 27, &c.), or is from an apocryphal book (see Ecclus. iv. 4 ; Wisd. vi. 12-23), or from some book no longer extant.

NOTE IV.

IS THE EPISTLE A TRANSLATION ?

There is every reason to believe, from the freshness, force, and special turns of the Greek, and from the absence of all trace or tradition of an Aramaic original, that we possess the Epistle in its earliest form. If

E E

ST. JAMES. there be any difficulty in the supposition that a Galilean peasant could have expressed himself in a Greek vocabulary so forcible, varied, and poetical, it is easily conceivable that he, like St. Peter,[1] may have availed himself of the services of an interpreter. Prof. Wordsworth has, indeed, suggested that there may have been an Aramaic original, because the supposition might account for some of the strange variations of the Corbey Latin MS. of St. James (Codex ff¹) recently edited by Mr. Belsheim at Christiania.[2] This Latin text, which is entirely different from the Vulgate, furnishes a new testimony to the recognition of the Epistle in the Western Church (though it did not obtain *early* recognition, Jer. *De Virr. ill.* 2, and is not quoted by Tertullian or Cyprian), The divergences of this Latin text exceed the ordinary limits of variation. Prof. Wordsworth refers to certain peculiarities of tenses, and conjunctions, and certain Hebrew turns; to the rendering of δελεαζόμενος, (i. 14), by *eliditur* (as though from *nâdach*); of ἱματία (v. 2), by *res* (as though from *Kêlim;* of iii. 6, by " et lingua ignis *saeculi* iniquitatis," for which he accounts by the fact that *êsh* "fire" does not change its form in the construct state; of μὴ κατακαυχᾶσθε by *quid alapamini* as though *tithhallelû* ("boast yourselves") had been confused with *tithchallelû* (wound yourselves); and so on. There are, however, other variations which do not admit of these somewhat facile and seductive, but highly precarious explanations; and Mr. Wordsworth admits that there are counter improbabilities. The suggestion deserves more thorough study, but at present the argument in favour of an Aramaic original is far from strong.

Of the authenticity of the Epistle there can be no reasonable doubt. It was early accepted by the Syrian Church, and has the important evidence of the Peshito in its favour; though it was not finally accepted by the Greek and Latin Churches till placed in the Canon by the Council of Carthage, A.D. 397. On the other hand its *apparent* contradiction of St. Paul, and its *apparent* silence as to the essential doctrines of Christianity, together with its close resemblance to what we should have expected from the writer and his surroundings, are strong evidences in its favour. Dogmatic prejudices which might have been an obstacle to its acceptance were overpowered by the proof of its Apostolic origin. The fact that it was (probably) known to St. Peter[3] more than outweighs any other deficiency of external testimony.

---

[1] St. Peter is said to have used the services both of St. Mark and of a certain Glaucias.

[2] A paper in the *Guardian* signed J. W., Jan. 9, 1884.

[3] See 1 Pet. i. 6–7, 24; iv. 8; v. 5–9; as compared with James i. 2–4, 10; v. 20; iv. 6, 7, 10.

THE FIRST EPISTLE OF PETER.

WRITTEN ABOUT A.D. 67.

"Habet haec epistola τὸ σφοδρὸν conveniens ingenio principis apostolorum."
—Grotius.

"Mirabilis est gravitas et alacritas Petrini sermonis, lectorem suavissime retinens."—Bengel.

"When once thou hast turned again, stablish thy brethren."—Luke xxii. 32.

Each book of Scripture, as we read it, seems to possess a supreme claim upon our love and admiration. Each book has its own unique lessons, its own special beauties. The First Epistle of St. Peter is full of noble thoughts and striking characteristics which we will now endeavour to seize and to understand.

The genuineness of the book is proved alike by external and internal evidence.[1] Of all the writings of the New Testament it is perhaps the most anciently and the most unanimously attested. The internal evidence is no less strong. The Epistle abounds in indications of genuineness which no forger could have imitated. In clause after clause we can trace the subtle, the indirect influence of events in which St. Peter took a prominent part. Without mentioning, or even referring to those events, he shows that they have left their deep traces in his memory. Thus Christ had said to

---

[1] It is attested by Papias, Polycarp, Irenaeus, Clement of Alexandria, Origen, &c., and by the second Epistle, which is (in any case) a very ancient writing. There were many spurious works attributed to St. Peter, such as the "Gospel according to Peter," used by the Nazarenes (Theodoret *Haer. Fab.* II. 2); the "Preaching of Peter" used by Judaisers; the "Apocalypse of Peter," &c.

him, "Thou art Petros, and on this rock (*petra*) will I build my Church;" and He calls Christ "a rock," and the corner-stone of a spiritual house into which Christians are to be built as living stones.[1] On the very same day that his Lord had alluded to him as a man of rock, He had called him "an offence" ($\sigma\kappa\acute{a}\nu\delta\alpha\lambda o\nu$), and St. Peter here unites those two words—"a rock of offence."[2] In directing him to pay the Temple didrachm Jesus had taught him that nevertheless the children were free; and here St. Peter tells Christians that though free they must yet submit to every human ordinance.[3] Our Lord had told him to forgive his brother seventy times seven, and here he says that "Love covers a multitude of sins."[4] He had seen his Master, in an acted parable of intense humility, gird a towel round Himself and wash His disciples' feet, and here he bids Christians "to tie on humility like a slave's apron."[5] From what our Lord had then said about washing he has learnt to look on "baptism" as not only an outward cleansing, but "the inquiry of a good conscience seeking after God."[6] He speaks of Satan as an ever-watchful adversary ($\dot{a}\nu\tau\acute{\iota}\delta\iota\kappa o\varsigma$),[7] using a word which Christ had used in the Gospels. He had been one of the very few who had seen the derision and scourging in the halls of Caiaphas and Pilate, and he alludes both to Christ's silent meekness, and to the weals which He bore for our sakes.[8] He had seen the dead weight of the Cross, and he speaks of it as "the tree."[9] He had been bidden to tend the flock of God, and he repeats the exhortation, and thinks of Christ as the chief shepherd.[10] He had been told that

---

[1] 1 Pet. ii. 4–8. [2] $\pi\acute{e}\tau\rho a$ $\sigma\kappa\alpha\nu\delta\acute{a}\lambda o\nu$, 7; Matt. xvi. 18, 23.
[3] Matt. xvii. 24–27; 1 Pet. ii. 13–16. [4] Matt. xviii. 22; 1 Pet. iv. 8.
[5] John xlii. 1–6; 1 Pet. v. 5, $\dot{e}\gamma\kappa o\mu\beta\acute{\omega}\sigma\alpha\sigma\theta\epsilon$. [6] 1 Pet. iii. 21.
[7] Matt. v. 25; Luke xviii. 3; 1 Pet. v. 8.
[8] 1 Pet. ii. 20, $\kappa o\lambda\alpha\phi\iota\zeta\acute{o}\mu\epsilon\nu o\iota$; 23, $o\dot{v}\kappa$ $\dot{a}\nu\tau\epsilon\lambda o\iota\delta\acute{o}\rho\epsilon\iota$; 24, $\mu\acute{\omega}\lambda\omega\pi\iota$.
[9] 1 Pet. ii. 24; Acts v. 30; x. 39 (in his speeches). For the remarkable analogy between St. Peter's speeches in the Acts and this Epistle see Acts iv. 11; ii. 32–36; iii. 19–26; (The rejected cornerstone, "witness," Prophecy, the Resurrection, &c.).
[10] 1 Pet. ii. 25, v. 2. To these we may add 1 Pet. i. 13; $\dot{a}\nu\alpha\zeta\omega\sigma\acute{a}\mu\epsilon\nu o\iota$ (Luke xii. 35); i. 12; $\pi\alpha\rho\alpha\kappa\acute{v}\psi\alpha\iota$ (Luke xxiv. 12), ii. 15; $\phi\iota\mu o\hat{v}\nu$ (Luke iv. 35); $\sigma\kappa\acute{o}\lambda\iota o\varsigma$, ii. 15 (Acts ii. 40).

when he had himself turned to Christ he must strengthen ($\sigma\tau\eta\rho\iota\zeta\epsilon\iota\nu$) his brethren and the strengthening of his brethren is from beginning to end the object of this letter.[1]

Further than this, we see in this Epistle the true Peter, with his fervid mind and picturesque utterance—his large charity and the open-hearted magnanimity which enabled him to embrace new truths. The character of St. Peter was very early distorted by ecclesiastical tradition; but the Peter of this Epistle is neither " the wretched caricature of an Apostle, a thing of shreds and patches which struts and fumes " through the Ebionite romances of the pseudo-Clement, nor the haughty autocratic Pope who, with infallible opinions and withering anathemas, lords it over God's heritage, and claims the two swords of temporal and spiritual power. He is a simple fellow-presbyter of those to whom he writes. The Bishop of Bishops barely even mentions the word " Bishop." The assumed head of all ecclesiasticism and sacerdotalism does not use the word " priest," or the word " Church." He is the true Peter, but a Peter who has learnt to know himself; a Peter who, though no less vigorous than of old, is mild, fatherly, conciliatory; a Peter who no longer repudiates the notion that his Lord should suffer, but knows all the glory and the blessedness which that suffering involves; a Peter who oscillates no longer between error and repentance, but who is humble and immovable in his Master's strength; a Peter who, though he is a chief Apostle, is still the simple, warm-hearted fisherman of the Galilean lake.

One of the noblest features of his Epistle is its catholicity; not a catholicity which is exclusive, self-asserting, and damnatory, but which is gentle, tolerant, comprehensive. Hence there is a light and a sweetness in his tone which show how thoroughly he had learnt to follow the example of his Lord. He has the authoritative dignity of St. James, but none of his threatening sternness. He has the swift insight of St. Paul into the heart of Christian truths, but none of his

[1] 1 Pet. v. 12.

dialectic subtleties or controversial passion. He has the serene gentleness of St. John, but never breathes that accent of uncompromising severity which comes from regarding all truths in their purest·ideal, and yet at the same time in sharp contrast with their antitheses.

His relationship to his brother Apostles is that of indebtedness and yet of independence. St. James was the acknowledged head of the Church of Jerusalem; the sternest and narrowest Judaisers claimed the sanction of his authority. St. Paul was the acknowledged head of the Gentile Church; the party of freedom claimed him as their champion. The views of the saintly Bishop and the strong Apostle were thrust into violent antagonism by their respective partisans. St. Peter sided with neither school. As the Apostle of the Circumcision, and yet as the first who had admitted uncircumcised Gentiles into full fraternity, he had sympathy with the views of both. The day had been when, in the "consistent inconsistency" which rose from his natural impulsiveness, he had been too anxious to stand well both with Judaists and Gentiles; but long before he wrote this letter he had seen that the unsystematic but practical synthesis of complementary truths lay in Christian holiness and Christian love. It is clear from his letter—and it is a fact of·the deepest interest—that he had read and was even familiar with St. Paul's Epistles to the Romans and Ephesians, which he would have been sure to see during his stay in Rome.[1] It

---

[1] Compare i. Pet. i. 5, "who are being guided by the power of God through faith for a salvation ready to be revealed in the last time," with Gal. iii. 23 (πίστιν . . . ἐφρουρούμεθα . . . ἀποκαλυφθῆναι).

1 Pet. ii. 6, 7, with Rom. ix. 23, where two quotations from Isaiah are similarly combined.

1 Pet. ii. 11, with Rom. vii. 23 (the same metaphor of *warring* passions).
,, ii. 13, 14, ,, ,, xiii. 1–4 (the same main verbs and nouns).
,, iii. 9, ,, ,, xii. 17.
,, iii. 18, ,, ,, vi. 9, 10.
,, iii. 21, ,, ,, vi. 4.
,, iv. 10, 11, ,, ,, xii. 6, 7.
,, v. 1, ,, ,, viii. 18.

Also compare 1 Pet. i. 1, 3, 14, with Eph. i. 3–8; 1 Pet. ii. 18, with Eph. vi. 5; 1 Pet. iii. 1, 2, and v. 5, with Eph. v. 22, i. 20, v. 21.

All these references are by way of *reminiscence*, not direct quotation.

is almost equally certain that he had read and been influenced by the Epistle of St. James, a copy of which must naturally have been lent to him by the Church of Jerusalem.[1]   It would have been easy for him, as for others, to distort the views of the two Apostles into irreconcilable opposition.   St. Peter, on the contrary, embraces the truths which were the common possessions of them both.   He is at once a Judaist and a Paulinist.   He is a Judaist, for the metaphors and titles which he applies to the Christian community are all derived from the old dispensation,[2] and yet he never once mentions the Law, not even as a law of liberty, but identifies all law with the will of God.[3]   He is a Paulinist, for he adopts the fundamental conception of the Pauline Gospel, but he entirely strips St. Paul's thoughts and expressions of their antithetical character, and thereby rescues them from their polemical appearance.   He dwells more predominantly than St. James on Christian verities, more continuously than St. Paul on moral rules.   St. Paul devotes all his skill to prove the doctrine of justification by faith; St. Peter, while accepting the doctrine, does not enter upon the arguments, and abandons the terminology.   St. James, while he enforces Christian duties with magnificent energy, barely alludes to a single event in the life of Christ; St. Peter, while no less impressive as an ethical teacher, makes everything hinge on the sufferings, the cross, the resurrection, and exaltation, the descent into Hades, and the second return of his Lord.[4] "Christ," he says, "suffered on our behalf, leaving us a copy (ὑπογραμμὸν) that we should follow in his traces (ἴχνεσι)."

---

[1] Compare 1 Pet. i. 6, 7, 24, iv. 8, v. 5, 9, respectively, with Jas. i. 2-4, 10, v. 20, iv. 6, 7, 10.

[2] 1 Pet. i. 1 ; ii. 9, 10.

[3] This is quite in accordance with his speaking of the Law as an intolerable yoke (Acts. xv. 10).

[4] Cross, i. 18, 19 ; ii. 24 ; iii. 18.
Sufferings, ii. 21 ; iii. 18 ; iv. 13.
Resurrection, i. 3.
Manifestation (*Apokalupsis*), i. 7, 13 ; φανερωθέντος τοῦ Ἀρχιποιμένος, v. 4.
Descent into Hades, iii. 19, 20 ; iv. 6.
Exaltation, iii. 22 ; iv. 11 ; v. 10.

And yet he does not in so many words, nor of set purpose, try to reconcile the separated parties. His Epistle has no resemblance to a tendency-writing. His catholicity, his conciliatoriness, are due to the natural and happy temperament which acts as a solvent to all religious asperity. He is not writing a theological disquisition. He had no intention to compose an Eirenicon, or to offer himself as a mediator between contending controversialists. His object from first to last is didactic and hortatory. The Church was passing through one of its earliest storms of persecution. Under the stress of that fiery trial it was above all things necessary that all schools of Christians should close their ranks against their common enemies. They needed neither impassioned arguments nor elaborate syllogisms, but they needed mainly to be taught the blessed lessons of resignation and hope. Accordingly resignation and hope are the keynotes of this Epistle. As his brethren in Christ stood defenceless before their enemies, he, their fellow-sufferer, reminds them of One who, when He was reviled, reviled not again, but intrusted all things to Him who judgeth righteously. Patient endurance would in time disarm even their persecutors; the hope of the future crown would transmute their very sorrows into exultation. They might be happy even amid trials if they sought their happiness in innocence and in hope.

In accordance with these objects he views even theological truths primarily in their moral aspect. He often speaks of redemption; but without entering into transcendent mysteries speaks of it chiefly as a deliverance from sin and worldliness. He often speaks of faith, but with him it is not mystic oneness with Christ, but the conviction of unseen realities. Good works are so prominent in his pages that "to do good" (ἀγαθοποιεῖν) occurs no less than nine times in his Epistle, yet it would be impossible to deduce from his pages the technical notion of "justification" either by faith or by works. Even when he touches on baptism his thoughts are mainly

fixed not on its sacramental aspects but on the vow by which
an upright conscience binds itself to God.

It must not however be supposed that St. Peter is only a
moral writer, and that he merely echoes the thoughts and
phrases of others. Nothing is less justified than the sneer
that he is "second-hand and commonplace." The vivid force
of many of his expressions would alone defend him from this
charge, and, besides this, he has several conceptions which are
peculiarly his own. Thus he has the striking remark that
"the angels desire to stoop down and look" into the scheme
of redemption (i. 12). He alone speaks of Christ as the
Chief Shepherd in that character in which the early Christians loved to represent Him on the walls of the catacombs
(v. 4). He alone points to Christ's sufferings as being not
only for our deliverance but also for our example (ii. 21).
From him we learn the beautiful expression "strangers and
pilgrims" (ii. 11), the duty of silencing attacks by silent
blamelessness (ii. 12, iii. 16), and the predominant conception
of Christian hope.

And there is one doctrine of capital importance for which
St. Peter is our chief authority, and which well accords with
his large and hopeful heart. It is the doctrine of Christ's
descent into Hades ; the doctrine of the Gospel to the dead.
In his statement of that doctrine St. Peter is thoroughly
original, and lays down the glorious truth that men "may be
judged according to men in the flesh, but may live according
to God in the spirit." To the Apostle, on whose agency and
confession, as on a rock, Christ built His Church—to the
Apostle who first admitted Gentiles as Gentiles into the full
freedom of the fold—was further vouchsafed the high honour
of revealing clearly to us that Christ "went also and preached
to the spirits in prison." By thus telling us of a Gospel to
the dead—by thus extending the all-embracing blessedness
of Christ's atoning work even to dead men who once were
disobedient, St. Peter enlarged the circle of life and light,
and flung one gleaming ray from the Sun of Righteousness

to the farthest circumference of that illimitable circle which includes the spirits of men beyond the grave.

And thus in all respects the Gospel of St. Peter is the Gospel of an eternal hope—that is, of a hope which transcends the limits of time, and embraces those spiritual conditions of man's relationship to God which in this narrow life we can neither see, nor measure, nor fully apprehend.

St. Peter wrote to console, to testify, to exhort. We do not know the circumstances under which he went to Rome, but he may either have been arrested in the provinces, or may have gone spontaneously to the great city to console the Christians in their hour of peril. There he was seized, and there he suffered martyrdom. This Epistle was written towards the close of his life. That it was written in Rome, which he calls by its mystic name of Babylon, is all but certain; and this agrees with the mention of Mark as his companion, for St. Mark had been summoned to Rome by the wish of St. Paul, and all early tradition regards the two Apostles as having suffered in that city, and at about the same time.

The intensest fury of the Neronian persecution did not last long. The suspicions of the people were not only satiated by the butchery of a "huge multitude" of Christian victims, but their sympathies had even been to some small extent enlisted on behalf of the sufferers. But when the executioners had been sated with blood, the after-throes of the persecution still continued, and it is perfectly idle to suppose that they could have been confined to the capital. They had the effect of exacerbating the whole heathen population against a sect which long before had everywhere been spoken against. Hence even in the provinces, to which St. Peter addresses his letter, Christians were exposed to threats, insults, and unjust prosecutions. The very name of "Christian" became a synonym for malefactor, and even persons of refinement and literary culture, blinded by their own fatal disdain, looked down upon the faith as a 'deadly' and 'execrable' superstition. Such were the circumstances in which the Apostle who had been so close an eye-witness of the sufferings of Christ and the glory which followed, wrote to these persecuted communities a letter of which the central message is, Submit and endure in cheerful innocence, for you are heirs of salvation.

The letter, which is addressed both to Jews and Gentiles[1] falls into two great divisions, of which the former is general and doctrinal, the second more special and practical. In the first division (i. 1—ii. 10) he speaks chiefly of the blessings of Christians; in the second division (ii. 11—v. 14) of the duties of Christians.

I. After the greeting (1, 2) follows a rich and comprehensive thanksgiving, in which he shows that salvation embraces alike the past, the present, and the future :—the future, in that it is a living hope of an unfading inheritance (3—5); the present in that it is a source of exultation, love, and faith, even in the midst of trials and sufferings (6—9); the past in that it was the ultimate end of all prophecy (10—12).

They ought then to gird up the loins of their minds, to abandon the past, to hope for the future, to obey in the present (13, 14), because of God's holiness and the fear they owe to Him (15—17), and the price of their redemption, so that their faith is also hope towards God (18—21). And this purification of the soul by hope should lead naturally to love and obedience, as consequences of the new birth by means of the living word of God—to a life not transient but eternal (22—25). In accordance with this new birth they should, as new-born babes, desire the spiritual and unadulterated milk, and in lives free from all stain of malice and hatred realise the preciousness of their holy unity as stones in one spiritual temple built on the corner-stone of Christ, and united to Him in living union (ii. 1—11).

---

[1] The address to "the elect sojourners of the dispersion" shows that he was addressing Jews as well as Gentiles; Gentile readers are distinctly implied in ii. 9, 10; iv. 3; i. 14, 18.

II. When he has thus laid upon the great truths of Christianity the foundation of hope and comfort and holiness, he exhorts them to live pure and blameless lives in the midst of their heathen persecutors (ii. 11, 12). Then he proceeds to urge on them due submission, in all things lawful, to the civil government (ii. 13—iii. 7), in order that, whether as freemen (16, 17), or as servants (18—20), or as women (iii. 1—6), or as men (iii. 7) they may endure cruelty and injustice by specially considering the example of Christ's meek sufferings (ii. 21—25).

III. Passing to a third series of exhortations (iii. 8—iv. 19) he urges them to unity (8), meek endurance (9), the government of the tongue (10), and a spirit of general peacefulness (11), because our case is in the hands of God, who knows all things, and because there is a beatitude in unjust persecution (12—17). These lessons are once more enforced by the example of Christ, who not only died, the just for the unjust, but even descended to Hades to preach to the spirits of them who were disobedient in the days of Noah. Then the few were saved through water as now the few are saved by lives in accordance with their baptismal vows; but even to those who perished Christ made His Gospel known (18—22).

They should therefore put on as armour the resolve of Christ, and make suffering the death-blow of past concupiscence, remembering Him who shall judge both the quick and dead, and who Himself preached His Gospel to the dead (iv. 1—14). The end of all things was at hand, and therefore their attitude should be one of sobriety, watchfulness, mutual and active love, and the right stewardship of God's diverse gifts. Let them feel at home in the conflagration (πυρώσει) which was burning among them, for to suffer unjustly as a Christian is to share in a beatitude. To do well, and to commit their cause to God, was to rejoice in sharing the sufferings of Christ, and to exult in the glory which should follow (iv. 10—19).

IV. He then enters on a fourth series of more special exhortations to elders (v. 1—4), and to younger and lay members of the Church (v. 5—9), pressing on both classes the duties of humility, submission, and watchful faithfulness. He ends with a doxology (10, 11), a few personal salutations, and a blessing (12—14).

Such are the characteristics, and such the general tenor, of this beautiful Epistle of hope and consolation. With lofty and happy sweetness the Apostle views the truths of Christianity in their comprehensive unity. He applies them to inspire the courage and direct the efforts of suffering Christians by pointing them to the example of Christ's humility and endurance, and he bids them fix their steady gaze on that exaltation of His glory which should be to them the sure pledge of eternal happiness when the brief trials of life were past.

NOTE I.

The keynotes of the Epistle are :—

1. HOPE, founded on the resurrection of Christ ; a living, life-giving hope of which the resurrection is "not only the exemplar but the efficient cause."

   a. " Who begat us again *to a living hope*," i. 4.

   β. " Set your *hope* perfectly on the grace that is being brought to you in the revelation of Jesus Christ," i. 13.

   γ. " So that your faith is also hope towards God," i. 21.

   δ. " To him that asketh us concerning the hope that is in us," iii. 15.

   See the topic enlarged on in v. 1, 4, 6, 10.

2. Faith, in St. Peter's point of view, is nearly allied to *hope*, i. 5, 7, 9, 21 ; v. 9.

3. SUBMISSIVE RESIGNATION in accordance with Christ's example.

   a. "*Submit yourselves* to every human ordinance for the Lord's sake," ii. 13.

   β. " Servants, *submit yourselves*," ii. 18.

   γ. " Likewise, ye wives, *submitting yourselves*," iii. 1, 5.   Compare ii. 13-25 ; iii. 18-iv. 1.

4. WELL-DOING (ἀγαθοποιΐα), ii. 12, 14, 15, 20 ; iii. 6, 11, 17 ; iv. 19.

5. OBEDIENCE (ὑπακοή), i. 2, 22 ; "as children of obedience," i. 14. Salvation, i. 5, 9, 10 ; ii. 2.

NOTE II.

SPECIAL WORDS IN ST. PETER.

1. " *To the sojourners of the dispersion* " (παρεπιδήμοις διασπορᾶς), i. 1 ; comp. ii. 11.   Both words are Jewish, and technically "sojourners" corresponds to *Toshabim*, the dispersion to *Galootha*. Even in writing to Churches which were largely Gentile, St. Peter writes with the feelings and habits of a Jew.

2. " *To sprinkling of blood*," i. 2 (ῥαντισμόν), comp. Heb. xii. 4, and Ex. xxiv. 8.

3. " Who hath *begotten us again* " (ἀναγεννήσας), i. 3.   The word is peculiar to St. Peter ; but comp. Jas. i. 18, iii. 3 ; and Tit. iii. 5 ; Eph. ii. 10.

4. "*That fadeth not away*" (ἀμάραντον), i. 4; comp. ἀμαράντινον 1 PETER.
   "amaranthine," v. 4 (Wisd. vi. 12).

5. "*Impartially*" (ἀπροσωπολήπτως), i. 17; comp. Acts x. 34.

6. "*Spiritual, unadulterated milk*" (λογικὸν ἄδολον γάλα), ii. 2. Milk
   even in those days was frequently adulterated with gypsum, as
   is mentioned by Irenaeus.

7. "The *praises*" or "excellences" (ἀρέτας, Is. xliii. 20, LXX.).

8. "An *example*" (ὑπογραμμὸν), ii. 21. A copy over which other words
   are to be written.

9. "Those who *revile*" (ἐπηρεάζοντες), iii. 16.

10. The *slough* of dissoluteness (ἀνάχυσιν), iv. 4.

11. *Busybody* (ἀλλοτριοεπίσκοπος, "other-people's-bishop"), iv. 15.
    The only word like it is ἀλλοτριοπραγμοσύνη, "*meddlesomeness*,"
    in Plato. Hilgenfeld (*Einleit.* p. 630) and others take it to
    mean "informer" (*delator*).

12. "*Fiery trial*" (πύρωσις), iv. 12. The word occurs in the LXX. of
    Prov. xxvii. 21, for "furnace." St. Peter might have possibly
    thought of the great fire of Rome which had been the cause
    of the first great persecution.

13. "*Gird yourselves with* humility," v. 5. The word ἐγκομβώσασθε,
    is derived from κόμβρωμα, an apron worn by slaves, and tied on
    by strings (κύμβοι). The word is a much more picturesque form
    of "put on" (ἐνδύσασθε, Col. iii. 12), and is an unconscious
    reminiscence of the scene recorded in John xiii.

14. "Neither as lording it over *your allotted charge*," v. 3 (τῶν κλήρων).
    From this word *clerus* is derived "clergy"; here however οἱ
    κλῆροι means the same as "your flock" (ποιμνίον). The Church,
    like the Holy Land, was divided "by allotments" (Jos. xiv. 2).

NOTE III.

SPECIAL PASSAGES IN THE EPISTLE.

(*a.*) ii. 3. "If ye tasted that *the Lord* is *gracious*." It is not impossible
   that there may be in these words a latent paronomasia. "The
   Lord," stands for Christ, and *Christos* was constantly confused
   both in pronunciation and meaning, by Gentiles, with *Chrestos*,
   "kind." The words would then mean "if ye learnt by personal
   experience that He whom you call *Chrestos* is indeed what that
   word implies, 'gracious.'"

(β.) ii. 16. (i.) *As free*,
   (ii.) *And yet not using your freedom as a veil of baseness*,
   (iii.) *But by love be slaves to one another.*

The verse is an exact parallel to and obvious reminiscence of Gal. v. 13 :—

(1) Ye were called *for freedom,*

(2) Only not freedom as *a handle for the flesh,*

(3) But *as slaves* of God.

St. Peter shows a generous nobleness in thus referring to an Epistle in which his own conduct is so strongly condemned. There is another marked reference to Galatians (ii. 19, 20), and that to a passage addressed to himself at a moment of deep humiliation, in 1 Pet. ii. 24.

(γ.) ii. 24. "*Who Himself, in His own body, bore up our sins to the tree.*" The word "bore up" (ἀνήνεγκεν) cannot here mean "offered up," as in Heb. ix. 28 ; Jas. ii. 21 ; for "sins" cannot be a sacrifice. The meaning is that Christ carried up (Mark ix. 2 ; Luke xxiv. 51), our sins with Him to the Cross, and as it were slew them there by nailing them to it. "Tree" for Cross, Deut. xxi. 23 ; Gal. iii. 13.

(δ.) iii. 4. "*The hidden man of the heart.*" Comp. Rom. ii. 29, vii. 22 ; 2 Cor. iv. 16 ; Eph. iii. 16 ; though St. Paul uses the word not of "the Christ within us," Gal. iv. 19, but of the inmost soul.

(ε.) iii. 18–20 ; iv. 6. The preaching of the Gospel to the dead.

(ζ.) iii. 21, "*which also, in the antitype, doth now save you, even baptism,—not the putting away of the filth of the flesh, but the interrogation of a good conscience towards God by the resurrection of Jesus Christ.*" 'Αντίτυπον means "baptism as an antitype of the deluge," and may be paraphrased as in the R.V. by "*after a true likeness.*" The meaning of ἐπέρωτημα, and of the parenthetic clause, is very uncertain ; the word has been explained (1) "pledge" or "vow" ; or (2) "question and answer," "anima non laxatione *sed responsione* sancitur." Tert. *De Resurr.* 48 ; or (3) "the *inquiry* after God of a good conscience" ; or (4) "*the request to God for a good conscience.*" The latter seems a possible view (comp. 2 Kings xi. 7 ; Dan. iv. 14, LXX.). "The word intends the whole correspondence of the conscience with God."—LEIGHTON.

(η.) iv. 16. "But if a man suffer *as a Christian* let him not be ashamed." The word "Christian" had not yet been adopted by the Church, but was only used by enemies or Gentiles (Acts xi. 26 ; xxvi. 28). It was originally a name of scorn, and began from that time forward to be a criminal designation. See Plin. *Ep.* x. 97 ; Tac. *Ann.* xv. 44 ; Suet. *Ner.* 16 ; comp. *Basilides ap.* Clem. Alex. *Strom.* iv. 12 ; Just. Mart. *Apol.* ii. 2. μήτε μοιχὸν κ.τ.λ. μήτε ἁπλῶς ἀδίκημά τι πράξαντα ἐλεγχόμενον, ὀνόματι δὲ Χριστιανοῦ προσωνυμίαν τὸν ἄνθρωπον τοῦτον ἐκυλάσω.

(ι.) v. 13. "*The co-elect in Babylon saluteth you.*" Babylon is the
common cryptograph used by the Jews and Christians of this
epoch for Rome (Rev. xiv. 8, &c.; *Orac.* Sibyll. v. 143, &c.),
just as in the Talmud Rome is called Babylon and Edom.
The fathers are unanimous on this point.[1] The notion that
ἡ συνεκλεκτὴ (=your sister Church) means "*Peter's wife*,"[2] or
that an obscure Galilean woman would send a greeting to the
Churches of Asia, is out of the question. There is not the
faintest tradition that St. Peter had ever visited Babylon; and
Mark, if the Evangelist be meant by "Marcus my son," was at
this time at Rome (2 Tim. iv. 11).

(κ.) v. 12. "By Silvanus, *our faithful brother, as I esteem him.*" There
is nothing to show whether the Silvanus thus incidentally mentioned was or was not the Silas of the Acts. The words ὡς
λογίζομαι, "as I account him," are due to some under-current of
thought. Some imagine that Silvanus was the amanuensis, and
that he modestly added those two words.

---

[1] Euseb. *H.E.* ii. 15, § 2; Jer. *De Virr. illustr.* 8; Hippolytus, *De
Christo et Antichristo*, 36.

[2] Peter was married, and there is a touching legend that in passing his wife
on the road to his martyrdom he bade her "remember the Lord" (Μέμνησο
ὦ αὕτη τοῦ Κυρίου). Clem. Alex. *Strom.* vii. 11, § 63.

THE EPISTLE TO THE HEBREWS

WRITTEN BY AN UNKNOWN AUTHOR, PERHAPS APOLLOS, ABOUT A.D. 68.

"Nihil interesse cujus sit, dum ecclesiastici viri sit, et quotidie ecclesiarum lectione celebretur."—Jer. *Ep.* 129, *ad Dardanium.*

"Auctor Epistolae ad Hebraeos, quisquis est, sive Paulus, sive, ut ego arbitror, Apollo."—Luther, *ad Gen.* xlviii. 20.

"Das ist eine starke, mächtige, hohe Epistel."—Luther.

"Of this ye see that the epistle ought no more to be refused for a holy, godly, and catholic epistle than the other authentic scriptures."—Tyndale.

"He is the mediator of a better covenant, which hath been enacted upon better promises."—Heb. viii. 6.

HEBREWS. THE Epistle to the Hebrews, apart from those deep and sacred lessons which, like every book of Scripture, it addresses to our souls, is interesting and precious on many grounds for the history of the Christian Church. It is (1) the only work in the New Testament canon by an independent follower of the school of St. Paul; it is (2) the only early specimen of Alexandrian Christianity; it is (3) a profound and original attempt to co-ordinate the relations between the new and old dispensation, between the Law which was given by Moses and the grace and truth which came by Jesus Christ.

(1) That it was not written by St. Paul himself, and not by any Apostle (ii. 3), is a conclusion supported by an over-whelming mass alike of external and internal evidence, and that evidence has been so often stated, and remains so entirely

untouched by counter arguments, that it is now the all but universal opinion of critics and theologians.[1] Without again entering on the controversy, it must suffice to say that, as has been abundantly shown, the writer of the Epistle to the Hebrews cites differently from St. Paul; he writes differently; he thinks differently; he argues differently; he quotes from a different edition of the Septuagint;[2] he constructs and connects his sentences differently; he builds up his paragraphs on a wholly different model. His Greek is different; his style different; many of his phrases different;[3] his line of reasoning wholly different; his tone of thought in many respects different. St. Paul is rugged and impetuous, this writer is elaborately and faultlessly rhetorical. He never abandons his calm and sonorous euphony, and he delights in amplitude and rotundity of expression. Even his theology, though fundamentally the same as St. Paul's, as was that of all Christians, is presented in different terminology and under different aspects.[4] St. Paul was the Apostle of the Gentiles, and spent the greater part of his life in establishing their privileges; this writer ignores the Gentiles almost as completely as if there had been no such thing as a Pagan in the world. St. Paul had bent the whole efforts of his dialectics to prove the nullity of the Law, and his contrast between the Law and the Gospel is that between command and promise, between sin and mercy, between the threat of inevitable death and the gift of eternal life. This writer treats of the contrast as one solely between type and reality. One of St. Paul's main subjects had been justification by faith; this writer never once uses either faith or righteousness in the specifically Pauline senses. St. Paul, in dwelling on the redemptive work of Christ, regards Him chiefly

---

[1] "Quis porro eam composuerit non magnopere curandum est, sed ipsa dicendi ratio et stylus alium esse quam Paulum satis testantur."—CALVIN.

[2] The Vatican, not the Alexandrian, as Bleek proves, *Hebr.* 338.

[3] These are pointed out by Bleek, Tholuck, &c. See *Early Days of Christianity*, i. 297.

[4] St. Paul uses "Christ Jesus our Lord," or "our Lord Jesus Christ," sixty-eight times; this writer not once, and only once even "our Lord Jesus." He speaks of "Jesus," "Christ," or "the Lord."

as the sacrificial victim; this writer mainly as the sacrificing Priest. The Epistle has therefore a special interest as a representation of Paul's Gospel by one who had with perfect independence embraced his general views.[1]

(2) It is our only canonical specimen of Alexandrian Christianity.

Owing to the revivifying contact of Judaism with Greek philosophy and culture, there had grown up at Alexandria a school of liberal thinkers, represented by such writers as Aristobulus, the translators of the Septuagint, the author of the Book of Wisdom, and above all by Philo, who, while they continued to be faithful Jews, found room in their theology for thoughts which they had not derived from Moses or from the Old Testament. By using the potent instrument of allegory they were able to make Moses express the thoughts of Plato and to turn a religious philosophy into something which they considered to be a philosophic religion. Their method was the source of many absurdities, and much of their system of interpretation was fantastic and valueless, but they were led into some thoughts which in the providence of God became part of the preparation for Christianity. Among these was the doctrine of the Logos or Divine Word, and the general conception that a wider and less exclusive dispensation was at hand. St. Paul and St. John were probably acquainted, if not with the actual writings of Philo, at least with some of his conceptions. The author of the Epistle to the Hebrews was certainly familiar with some of his numerous treatises, and in not a few passages has been directly influenced alike by his views and his expressions.[2] He is one of the

---

[1] The Epistle has resemblances to 1 Thess. i. 3 ; Rom. xi. 36, xii. 18, 19, xv. 23 ; 2 Cor. iv. 2, &c. He dwells on three of St. Paul's great topics, Judaism and Christianity, Faith, Redemption, but handles each of them in quite a different way ; on the fourth great topic of St. Paul, the Universality of the Gospel, he does not even touch.

[2] Twenty-two passages may be quoted in which the writer resembles Philo, (see Credner, Bleek, Hilgenfeld, &c.), and as regards some of these it is simply impossible that the resemblance could be accidental. He also has close resemblances to the Book of Wisdom (Wisd. vii. 25, 26 ; xviii. 22, &c.), and many words in common with it.

links between the Jewish and Christian schools of Alexandria. The Christian school, which was Alexandrian not only in its locality but in many of its fundamental views, continued the traditions of the Alexandrian Judaists; founded by St. Mark it was carried on by the labours of Pantaenus, Clement of Alexandria, Dionysius, Pierius, Peter Martyr, Didymus, and was above all enriched by the learning and genius of the glorious and indefatigable Origen.

The character of this Epistle is Alexandrian in its learning, its culture, its theosophy, its method of exegesis. The writer shows Alexandrian influences in the exclusive regard which he pays to the Chosen People;[1] in his manner of treating Scripture, which deduces mysteries from its symbols and latent meanings even from its silence; in his application to Christ of many of the terms and conceptions which Philo had applied to the Logos; in his conception of the Word of God as more cutting than any two-edged sword;[2] in the uncompromising sternness and unconditional condemnation with which he speaks of apostates; and above all in two fundamental conceptions which run throughout his Epistle. One of these is the Melchizedek priesthood of Christ;[3] the other is that philosophy of ideas which Philo borrowed from Plato. The keynote of the reasoning of the Epistle is found in the quotation, "See that thou make all things[4] after the pattern showed thee in the mount."[5] He regarded the visible world as only the shadow of the invisible. To him the reality of all phenomena depended exclusively on the unseen, pre-existent, eternal Noumena. The world of sense was but a reflex, as a Persian poet said, of the world of

---

[1] "The People" always in this Epistle means the Jews, v. 3; vii. 5, 11, 27; viii. 10, &c. See ii. 17; iv. 9; xiii. 12. He even speaks of the Incarnation as "a taking hold" not of humanity, but "of Abraham's seed."

[2] Heb. iv. 12, 13. *Quis rer. div. haer.* § 26.

[3] Philo *De Somn.* § 38; *Leg. Allegg.* iii. 25.

[4] The reading "all things" for the "*it*" of the Hebrew and LXX. is borrowed from Philo. *De Leg. Allegg.* iii. 33.

[5] The less cultivated and more literalising Rabbis regarded this pattern as *material* not as *ideal*.

HEBREWS. spirit.[1] Throughout the Epistle he represents Pauline views, but coloured by Alexandrian influences, and leaning as far as was possible for a Paulinist to the standpoint of Jewish Christians.[1]

(3) It is on this conception that his whole argument is based. He shows that Christianity is a nearer (and on earth the nearest attainable) approximation to the Eternal Archetype. He thus furnishes a " thoroughly original attempt to establish the main results of Paulinism upon new presuppositions and in an entirely independent way." St. Paul's arguments, from the very fact that they were so sweeping and irresistible, awoke the bitterest antagonism of the Jews, and stirred up all their frantic patriotism against the man who ran counter to all their most cherished prejudices by speaking of the Law as consisting of "weak and beggarly elements," and saying that it was given "for the sake of transgressions." The argument of this writer was far less shocking to Jewish convictions. It was the argument *a minori ad majus* (first formulated by Hillel) with which their own Rabbinic methods had made them familiar. The words "how much more" (πόσῳ μᾶλλον) might almost be taken as its pivot. He treats the relation of Christianity to Judaism not from the ethical point of view, as St. Paul does, but from the meta- physical. He does not say one wounding word against Levitism. He does not dwell, as St. Paul does, on its accidental and subordinate character, its frivolity, its menace, or its deathfulness. On the contrary, he recognises it as a sacred and essential part in the unbroken continuity of God's economy. He views Mosaism not as St. Paul does as an inferior intermediate between the promise to Abraham and the Gospel of Christ, but as a copy between the Eternal Archetype and the Final Reality; as a material symbol of the Idea which should hereafter be subjectively realised. He is able to speak of it with respect as a genuine revelation

[1] "L'Épitre aux Hébreux est incontestablement l'œuvre la plus étrange du Nouveau Testament. C'est une tête de Janus à deux faces, dont une est pauli- nienne, mais dont l'autre trahit les traits véritablement juifs."—FRIEDLÄNDER.

(i. 1, ii. 2, iii. 9, iv. 12, xii. 19, &c.), while yet he can lead his
readers to see that Christianity offers a better hope (vii. 19);
a better covenant (vii. 22); a more excellent service (viii. 6);
a better and more perfect tabernacle (ix. 11); better sacrifices
and better promises (ix. 23); and above all a great, sympathetic, atoning, glorified Eternal Priest.[1]

He was able thus to avail himself of Jewish feeling by
regarding Judaism less as a law than as *a system of worship*.
He seizes upon Priesthood and Sacrifice as the central point
of his treatment. He treats the Temple and the High Priest
with profound respect. Christianity is represented as a
sublimated, completed, idealised Judaism. He dwells with
loving detail on the imposing splendour of the Tabernacle,
and shows us the High Priest entering the awful darkness of
the Holiest Place and clad in the pomp of his gorgeous and
jewelled robes; and then—as with one wave of the wand—
sets all this aside as a symbol, a picture, a transient shadow,
while he draws aside the blue curtain of the heavens and points
to the High Priest for ever after the order of Melchizedek who
has passed with His own blood once for all into a Tabernacle
not made with hands eternal in the heavens.[2] The Jewish
Tabernacle was a material pattern of that ideal archetype
which is partially realised in Christianity now, and will be
attained in heaven hereafter. It was a shadow of salvation
which now is subjectively enjoyed in Christianity, and will
hereafter be objectively realised in heaven.

The Epistle was either written by Apollos—a friend of
Timothy, and a follower of St. Paul, an Alexandrian with Jewish-
Christian antecedents, eloquent, courageous, independent, and

---

[1] The Christology of the Epistle, though the writer dwells so prominently
on Christ's sufferings and humiliation, is no less lofty than that of St. Paul.
"The writer does not however think of Christ as the 'Second Adam' any
more than St. Paul thinks of Him as 'the Captain and High Priest of our
profession.'"—See Holtzmann in Schenkel Bibel-Lexicon.

[2] "A pattern," viii. 5; "a shadow," ix. 1, 23; xi. 1, 3; xii. 18, 27. "A
parable," ix. 9; "antitype," ix. 24. The "visible" (xi. 3) is capable of being
shaken (xii. 27), and is tangible (xii. 15), but the archetypal world, the true
house of God (x. 21), the genuine tabernacle (viii. 2), is based on firm
foundations, unshakable, heavenly (xi. 10; xii. 22-28).

learned in the Scriptures—or else the name of the author is unknown to us.   It can be decisively proved that it could not have been written by Aquila, Titus, Silas, Barnabas, Luke, Mark, Clement, or any other of those companions of St. Paul whose names are preserved for us in the Epistles or the Acts. The probable date of the Epistle is about A.D. 68, shortly after the martyrdom of St. Paul and the subsequent liberation of Timothy, and certainly before the Fall of Jerusalem (in A.D. 70).   It was addressed exclusively to some community of Jewish Christians (ii. 3, 4, iv. 14, v. 11, vi. 1, &c.), but we know neither the place at which it was written nor the city to which it was addressed.[1]

Unlike the Epistles of St. Paul, no name is mentioned at the beginning, there is no greeting, and no thanksgiving. The writer plunges at once into his subject, in one majestic sentence, in which he summarises the religious history of the world before Christ and shows that in the manifestation of this supreme glory the final aeon of God's dispensations has begun.

His object is to save the Jewish Christians from apostatising under the stress of persecutions and amid the glamour of a pompous ritual,[2] and this he strives to accomplish by showing them the unique transcendence of Christ and of Christianity by a comparison between the Law and the Gospel under the double aspect of the mediators by whom they were administered, and the blessings which they were meant to bestow.

The first seven chapters are devoted to the supremacy of Christ; the eighth, ninth, and tenth to the superiority of the New Covenant. Having thus contrasted Judaism and Christianity in their agents and their results, he devotes the rest of the Epistle to exhortations (xi.), warnings (xii.), and

---

[1] The Apollos-authorship, suggested by Luther, is accepted by Osiander, Clericus, Heumann, Semler, Dindorf, Bleek, Tholuck, Credner, Reuss, Moll, Lange, Rothe, Bunsen, Feilmoser, Lutterbeck, De Wette, Lünemann, Norton, Alford, Plumptre, Moulton, Davidson, &c.

[2] The common opinion is that "Hebrews" must mean Palestinian Jews, but Wieseler shows that this is an error (*Untersuchung.* ii. 3), and the opinion that the letter was written to Jerusalem is now untenable.

the inculcation of practical duties (xiii. 1—17), and ends with a few brief personal messages, a prayer for them, and a word of benediction (xiii. 18—25).

Although the divisions are not always distinctly marked, it will be seen that the general object of the Epistle is very clear, and that the argument is managed in a manner which does not offer the smallest resemblance to the dialectics of St. Paul, but which is yet in its own way immensely effective. With admirable method the writer first states his magnificent thesis, and then proceeds to prove it in three great sections: on the superiority of Christ to all Mediators (i.—iv.); on Christ as the High Priest after the order of Melchizedek (v.—vii.); on Christ's new and better Covenant (viii.—x.). The rest of the Epistle enforces the practical results which spring from these great principles. The noble chapter on the heroes of faith is meant to carry out the lessons of the earlier sections by showing the Jewish Christians that there was no discontinuity in their religious history, and that the glories of their past annals, so far from being dimmed and disgraced for them, had only been enriched and glorified by their conversion to Christianity. The new dispensation was not the ruinous overthrow of the old, but its ideal fulfilment, its predestined and eternal consummation.

Among specially noticeable features of the Epistle we may observe—

1. The section about Christ as a Priest after the order of Melchizedek.

All that we know of Melchizedek historically is contained in exactly two verses of the Book of Genesis.

From that allusion we learn that he was the priest-king of the little town of Salem, who, with kind hospitality, brought forth bread and wine for Abraham and his allies when they returned victorious from the defeat of Amraphel, king of Shinar, and his vassal kings. He is called a priest of El Elion, and though there was a Phœnician deity of the name Elion, it is clear that by that title here as elsewhere is meant

Jehovah, as is indeed explained in verse 22. Melchizedek means, or may mean, King of Righteousness, Salem means Peace. On these etymological facts, together with the circumstance that, in the midst of idolatrous Canaanites, the king of the little town had retained a knowledge of God, and was a priest of God, his name was invested not only with a deep interest, but also with mysterious sanctity. Hence, in the 110th Psalm, some unknown Hebrew poet had seized upon the noble and ancient figure of this priest upon his throne as the type of the Royal Priesthood of the Messiah, since it was a priesthood anterior to that of Aaron and superior in dignity even to the patriarchal position of the Father of the Faithful. Slight as are these two Scriptural allusions to Melchizedek—the only two in all the literature of the Old Testament—the Hagadists founded on them an entire mythology. In the Bereshith Rabba, Rabbi Samuel Bar Nachman says that Melchizedek taught to Abraham the ordinances of the law, since the bread which he brought forth was a type of the shewbread and the wine a type of libations. Other Rabbis referred in this connection to Prov. ix. 5, where Wisdom says, " Come, eat of my bread and drink of the wine which I have mingled."

The Rabbis generally identified Melchizedek with the patriarch Shem. They tell us that God had intended that the priests should descend from him, but since, in his benediction over Abraham, he had the carelessness to mention Abraham's name before the name of God (" Blessed be Abraham by the Eternal "), an error which Abraham corrected, God took the priesthood from Melchizedek and gave it to Abraham. It was thus that they explained Psalm x. " The Lord said unto my lord (Abraham), Sit thou at my right hand "; and Psalm cx. 4, " The Lord sware and will not repent, Thou art a priest for ever after the order of Melchizedek." [1] Further they say that the expression, " He

---

[1] The Talmudic passages in which Melchizedek is referred to are Nedarim, 32, 2 ; Sanhedrin, 108, 2 ; Avodath Hakkodesh, iii. 20 ; Genesis Rabba, 44 ;

was a priest of the Most High God," means that his priesthood ceased with him, and was not handed down to his descendants.

Since the Jews had thus interested themselves in the venerable figure of the king, peaceful and righteous, the mysterious priest among idolaters, who flashes into light for a moment out of the dim patriarchal records, and then disappears to emerge only in one single allusion hundreds of years later—it was natural that the writer of this Epistle, trained as he was in Rabbinic and Alexandrian methods, should found upon his priesthood the perfectly sound argument that the allusion of the Psalmist implied a priesthood older and more permanent than that of Aaron, which was a type of the Eternal Priesthood of Christ.

Nor is it strange that he builds on the silence of Scripture an inference which enhances the dignity of Melchizedek, when he calls him "fatherless, motherless, without pedigree, having neither beginning of days nor end of life." In using those expressions he was adapting a well-known method of Kabbalistic exegesis to an idiom familiar in all languages. He argues that Scripture, by not recording the father, mother, or descendants of Melchizedek, casts on him as it were a shadow of Eternity.

If this reference to Melchizedek has been the excuse for the wildest conjectures—if an ancient Gnostic sect called itself Melchizedekian[2] and set Melchizedek above Christ—if Melchizedek, the unknown priest-king of a little Canaanite town to which the Book of Genesis, when allegorically explained, has

---

Levit. Rabba, 25 ; Numb. Rabba, 4, &c. Friedländer, *Revue des Études juives.*

[1] So Philo, *De Ebrietate*, § 14, speaks of Sarah as ἀμήτωρ, "*without mother,*" because her mother is not recorded ; so we find in Bereshith Rabba= f. 18, 1 : "A Gentile *has no father.*" Eurip. *Ion.* 850 : "Quibus nec pater nec mater est," Cic. *De Nat.* ii. 64 : "*nullis* majoribus ortum ;" Hor. *Sat.* i. 6, 10.

[2] On the Melchizedekians our chief authorities are Marcus Eremita, Epiphanius, *Haer.* lv. 7, lxvii. 3 ; Philastrius, *Haer.* 52, 148 ; Augustine, *Contra Melchizedechitas* ; Theodor. *Haer.* ii. 6 ; Ambrose, *De Abraham,* i. 3.

See Friedländer, *Le Secte des Melchisédec et l'Épître aux Hébreux. (Rev. des Études juives*, 1883, vol. v. pp. 1–188.)

given a typical eternity, has been identified even by modern commentators with the Holy Ghost, " the Angel of the Presence," "the Captain of the Lord's Host," the Metatron, the Jewish Shekinah, God the Word previous to his Incarnation— such guesses are only due to the fact that Scriptural exegesis has often been founded on an absolute ignoring of all linguistic analogies and all literary methods. Others again have identified him with Shem, with Ham, with a reappearance of Enoch, and with the Phœnician god Sydik or Saturn! But in all ages, both among Jews and Christians, there have been writers of eminence who took more sober and reasonable views. Josephus merely speaks of Melchizedek as " a chief of the Canaanites"; [1] and even among the fathers, Hippolytus, Eusebius of Caesarea, and others saw in him simply what he was—the casually mentioned Sheikh of a little town in Palestine, peaceful among the cruel, pure amid the corrupted, a priest of the one true God among idolaters—to whom, though in all other respects he lived and died unknown, his meeting with Abraham has given a symbolic rather than a personal or historical importance.[2]

2. Certain passages of the Epistle were misunderstood, and were the chief cause why it was so long rejected in the Western Church.

In the Muratorian Canon we are told that " it cannot be received in the Catholic Church for it is unsuitable that poison should be mixed with honey." Even in the fifth century Philastrius (*Haer.* 89) says that it was rejected because heretics had made additions to it. Even Luther, while he admired the Epistle as a whole, said that as the author was not one of the Apostles, to whom it appertained to lay the foundations of truth, we must not be shocked if he perhaps mingles in the superstructure some elements of hay and straw (*Streu oder Heu*).

[1] Jos. *B. J.* vi. 10.
[2] Modern writers might draw precisely the same inferences as the author of this Epistle does from the same *data*; the difference would not be in the *point of view* but only in the *method of statement*.

The passage at which the Church took most alarm was iii. 2,
" Jesus Christ who was faithful to Him that *appointed* Him "
(τῷ ποιήσαντι αὐτὸν, literally " to Him that *made* Him "), as
also Moses was in all His (God's) house." Taking the expression literally, some heretics, as we learn from Philastrius
(*Haer.* 89), distorted it into an assertion that Christ was a
created being. Even Athanasius understood it of the Incarnation. But it simply means that Christ as our Apostle
and High Priest was faithful to Him who *made Him such.*
Theodoret and other Greek Fathers rightly saw that " made "
here means " appointed," and the particular verb (ποιῶ) is
probably used from a reminiscence of the LXX. version of
1 Samuel xii. 6, " who made Moses." [1]

It is, however, a curious circumstance that, in dealing with
other subjects also, the author uses language which, while
capable of explanation, lent itself easily to the possibility of
being misunderstood. Thus in vii. 27, and x. 11, he seems to
say that the high priests *daily* offered sacrifices; in vii. 5, he
says that the *priests* received tithes of the people; in ix. 3, 4,
he half implies that the golden altar of incense (θυμιατήριον)
was in the Holy of Holies. His language is never demon-
strably wrong, but unlike St. Paul he makes use of expressions which appear to go to the verge of inaccuracy, or at least
give rise to natural misapplications.

3. Another remarkable point in this Epistle is the tone of
utter sternness which the writer adopts towards those who
swerve from the faith.

It was because of these " hard knots " that the Epistle
appeared to Luther to present a grave difficulty. He says
that in the 6th and 10th chapters it refuses to sinners
the benefits of repentance, and states, in xii. 17, that Esau
though he repented was not forgiven. That, he truly says,
appears to be contrary to all the Gospels and to the Epistles
of St. Paul. Explanations of these passages may, he adds, be

---

[1] Comp. Mark iii. 14 ; Acts ii. 36.

furnished, but, considering the precise language of the Epistle, he doubts whether any explanation is sufficient.

The three passages in which this tone of absolute and unconditional condemnation is adopted are vi. 4—8, x. 26—31, xii. 16, 17. They were seized with avidity by the Montanists and Novatians, and all the more because no such passages occur in St. Paul's Epistles. It is true that if the language thus used did not admit of the large qualification which it demands, it would stand in flagrant contradiction to the rest of Scripture. Meanwhile it may, in part at least, be due to Alexandrian views, for Philo also says that a soul "once unyoked and separated from the Logos will be cast away for ever, without possibility of returning to her ancient home."

But no uncatholic dogma can be based on these passages, whether as to the "indefectibility of grace" or "final reprobation." In vi. 4, "impossible" cannot, with the Arminians, be pared down into "very difficult," nor can παραπεσόντας be rendered with the Calvinists and our A.V. "If they fall away," but "on their falling away." But the author is only thinking of earthly conditions, and of what is *impossible to men*. He means that for deliberate apostasy and defiant wretchlessness no human, no ecclesiastical, no earthly remedy is provided. But that which is impossible with men is possible with God.

In xii. 16, 17, the true rendering is, "For ye know that afterwards, when he was even anxious to inherit the blessing, he was rejected ; for he found no opportunity for repentance —though he sought it (the blessing) earnestly with tears." Unless we are to give to the passage a sense which contradicts the rest of Scripture, we must understand "place for repentance" to mean such a change of mind (whether in himself or in his father) as would reverse the consequences of his profane levity. Scripture, at any rate, knows nothing whatever of the hideous and heretical dogma which refused absolution to all post-baptismal sin. If Esau sincerely repented, he was forgiven. The Targum on Job says that he never did repent. If there was in him any *metanoia* which yet proved to be ineffectual, it was of the character of mere remorse for unalterable consequences, and it could not have been that genuine repentance to which the gate of pardon is never closed.

" Who with repentance is not satisfied
Is not of heaven or earth." [1]

---

[1] Want of space prevents me from adding any special notes to particular difficulties and expressions in this Epistle. They do not admit of very brief treatment. I may therefore be permitted to refer to *Early Days of Christianity*, i. 266-483, and my edition of the Epistles in the Cambridge Bible for Schools.

NOTE I.

ANALYSIS OF THE EPISTLE.

 I. Fundamental thesis (i. 1-4).
 II. Christ is superior to Angels (5-14).
  Exhortation (ii. 1-5).
  Christ raises humanity above angelhood (ii. 6-16).
  For He was our High Priest (ii. 17, 18).
 III. Christ higher than Moses (iii. 1-6).
  Exhortation (iii. 7-19).
  Christ and not Moses leads His people into rest (iv. 1-13).
  Thus He is our High Priest (iv. 14-16).
 IV. The High Priesthood of Christ.
  A. Qualifications for High Priesthood.
   a. Power of sympathy (v. 1-3).
   β. Due appointment (4-10).
  B. Digression on their spiritual backwardness, with appeals
   warnings, and encouragements, since our hopes are based on
   Christ's High Priesthood, which was not Aaronic, but eternal
   after the order of Melchizedek (v. 11-vi. 20).
  C. The Melchizedek Priesthood superior to the Aaronic.
   a. Because it is eternal (vii. 1-3).
   β. Acknowledged by Abraham (4-10).
   γ. Recognised in the Psalms (11-14) ; and involving a change
    also in the Law (15-19).
   δ. Founded on an oath (20-22).
   ε. Continuous, not hereditary (23-25).
 V. A. Christ is the minister of a new and better Covenant (viii.).
  B. Superiority of the New Covenant shown by a comparison of
   Christ passing into the heavens, once for all, into the immediate presence of God, sinless, through His own blood, to make
   an eternally efficacious atonement, with the repeated, in-
   efficacious, symbolic ministry of the High Priests on the Day
   of Atonement (ix.).
  C. Recapitulation and summary (x. 1-18).
  Solemn warning (x. 19-39).
 VI. The Heroes of Faith (xi.)
 VII. Final exhortations, warnings, messages, and blessing (xii.-xiii.).

NOTE II.

CHARACTERISTIC WORDS OF THE EPISTLE.

The word "BETTER" (κρείσσων) occurs more often in this Epistle than in all the rest of the New Testament—namely, thirteen times; whereas elsewhere it only occurs twice in St. Peter, and three, or perhaps four, times in St. Paul.

i. 4.   "Better than the angels."

vi. 9.   "We are persuaded better things of you" (vii. 7).

vii. 19.   "A bringing in of a better hope."

vii. 22.   "Jesus hath become the surety of a better covenant."

viii. 6.   "He is the mediator of a better covenant which hath been enacted upon better promises."

ix. 23.   "With better sacrifices than these."

x. 34.   "Ye have yourselves as a better possession" (in some readings).

xi. 16, 35.   "A better country"; "a better resurrection."

xi. 40.   "God having provided some better thing concerning us."

xii. 24.   "The blood of sprinkling which speaketh better than that of Abel."

Besides this we have "*more excellent*" (διαφορώτερος, **i.** 4; viii. 6), which does not occur elsewhere in the New Testament; and "by so much," "by how much more" (τοσούτῳ . . ὅσῳ), and similar phrases, i. 4; iii. 3; x. 25, &c.

It may thus be truly said that the essence of the Epistle is an argument *a fortiori;* a comparison *a minori ad majus.*

THE EPISTLE OF JUDE.

OF UNCERTAIN DATE.

Ἰούδας ἔγραψεν ἐπιστολὴν ὀλιγόστιχον μέν, πεπληρωμένην δὲ τῶν τῆς χάριτος ἐρρωμένων λόγων.—ORIGEN, *in Matt.* xiii. 55.

"Quia de libro Enoch assumsit testimonium a plerisque rejicitur: tamen auctoritatem vetustate jam et usu meruit ut inter sacras Scripturas computetur."—JEROME, *Cat. Script. Eccl.* 4.

"I was compelled to write to you, exhorting you to contend earnestly for the faith once for all delivered to the saints."—JUDE 3.

THE Epistle of Jude certainly presents more surprising phenomena than any other book of the New Testament. It is in many respects altogether unique.

In style it is original and picturesque.[1] In tone it is intense, vehement, denunciative. In its point of view, it is Judaeo-Christian.[2] In structure it is Aramaic, abounding in triple arrangements. In matter it abounds in strange allusions to Jewish Hagadoth and apocryphal incidents. In some respects it resembles a passionate page of one of the old prophets when they denounce apostasy and idolatry: in others, it has affinity with Apocalyptic literature, except that it does not develop its isolated metaphors into continuous symbols. Another curious fact is the relation which it holds to the

---

[1] Like the style of the Book of Wisdom it is lexically rich and poetic, but structurally unclassical. It is Greek as learnt by a foreigner, and partly from books ; and it is mixed up with Hebrew phrases (*e.g.* θαυμάζειν πρόσωπα).

[2] The Levitic training of the writer is shown by the fact that he twice alludes to a peculiar form of Levitic pollution, verses 8, 23. Both allusions are omitted in 2 Pet.

second chapter of the Second Epistle of St. Peter, but as it may now be regarded as all but certain that the author of that Epistle is the borrower, and St. Jude the original writer, we need not here allude further to that circumstance.

Who was the writer?

1. He calls himself Jude, "a slave of Jesus Christ and a brother of James."

The expression "slave of Jesus Christ," first used by St Paul in the Epistle to the Romans, is found also in the Second Epistle of St. Peter and in St. James. If the writer adds that he is "a brother of James," this can only be to enable his readers to identify him. Among the Jews there was an extreme paucity of names, and Jude was one of the very commonest of those few names. There are six Judes in the New Testament alone and very many in Josephus and among the Rabbis. The name at once marks the nationality of the writer; he is so completely a Jew that he has not even adopted the almost universal practice among his countrymen of choosing another name for the purpose of intercourse with the Gentiles. But the name "Jude" alone would convey no definite information. There are at least three Judes in the very narrow circle of early believers. Judas Iscariot was dead; there was another Apostle who with the name Jude also bore the names Lebbaeus and Thaddaeus. This three-named Apostle was the son of a James of whom we know nothing (Luke vi. 16; Acts. i. 13); and is himself entirely unknown to us except by a single question (John xviii. 3), and by the tradition that he laboured in Syria and died at Edessa. There was also a Judas Barsabbas (Acts xv. 22). The writer of this Epistle distinctly intimates that he was not himself an Apostle (verses 17, 18), and as he was in other respects unknown he describes himself as "the brother of James."[1]

At this period, after the early death of James the son of Zebedee, there was but one James who was universally known

---

[1] Hegesippus, *ap.* Euseb. *H.E.* iii. 19. There was also a Jude, Bishop of Jerusalem in the days of Hadrian.—Euseb. *H.E.* iv. 5.

throughout the Church, and that was James the Lord's brother, the author of the Epistle, and the Bishop of Jerusalem. When "James" was mentioned, the early Christians knew that he was meant (Gal. i. 19, ii. 12). Jude identified himself sufficiently for his purpose when he called himself "the brother of James."

But if he was "the brother of James," why does not *he* also call himself the Lord's brother ? (Matt. xiii. 55 ; Mark vi. 3.) For the same reason that James does not. Awe and humility prevented him. Their relationship to Jesus of Nazareth in the earthly life gave them no right to speak of themselves as brothers of Him who now sat at the right hand of the Majesty on high. I believe that both James and John would have repudiated with something like horror and indignation the title of *adelphotheos*, "brother of God," which was sometimes applied to them in the early Church, and which is even found in late inscriptions of this Epistle.

We know nothing more of this Jude except that he was married, and that he must have been dead before the reign of Domitian (A.D. 80). We learn these facts from the anecdote recorded by Hegesippus (*ap.* Euseb. *H.E.* iii. 20), that the grandsons of Jude, the Lord's brother, were summoned before Domitian, whose jealousy had been excited by rumours about Christ's kingdom. These earthly kinsmen of our Lord were known among Christians as the Desposyni, and they were summoned from Palestine into Domitian's presence. When he saw that they were poor peasants, whose hands were hard with labour, and heard that they had only seven acres of land between them, which they farmed themselves, he was content with their assurance that the kingdom of Christ was neither earthly nor of this world but heavenly and angelical. He dismissed them with contempt, and with them (so far as we know) ended the race of the family of Nazareth.

2. What was the date of this Epistle, and by what circumstances was it called forth ?

All that we can say of the date is that it must have

been written before the accession of Domitian (A.D. 80), because
at that time Jude was dead ; and indeed before the destruction
of Jerusalem, because otherwise that awful catastrophe must
have been alluded to among the retributive events to which
the writer appeals. For the genuineness of the Epistle may
be assumed. It is among the best attested of the *Antilegomena*.[1]
The name of Jude was far too insignificant in the Church to
tempt any forger or—to use a milder term—*falsarius* to adopt
it. The object of pseudepigraphy was not deceptive but literary. It was meant to claim the authority of some weighty
and distinguished name for opinions which might otherwise
fail to attract the same attention. But opinions would gain
little from the name of one who was so obscure that he can
only mention himself as the brother of some one else. Besides
this, the phenomena of the Epistle itself are too surprising to
have come from a forger's hand. He would have defeated his
own object by the adoption of an unusual style and unprecedented allusions. A forger would not have referred to strange
legends, or have introduced into the compass of a few verses
a mass of unique words and phrases. But St. Jude himself
tells us the circumstances under which this strange impassioned outburst was written.

He tells us that he was very earnestly meditating a letter
($\sigma\pi\sigma\nu\delta\grave{\eta}\nu$ $\pi\sigma\iota\sigma\acute{\nu}\mu\epsilon\nu\sigma\varsigma$ $\gamma\rho\acute{\alpha}\phi\epsilon\iota\nu$) to Christians about the common salvation, when he felt himself under a sudden and im-
mediate necessity ($\grave{\alpha}\nu\acute{\alpha}\gamma\kappa\eta\nu$ $\acute{\epsilon}\sigma\chi\sigma\nu$ $\gamma\rho\acute{\alpha}\psi\alpha\iota$) to write to them
at once to contend on behalf of the faith once for all delivered
to the saints. For he finds that persons whom he will not
name ($\tau\iota\nu\epsilon\varsigma$ $\acute{\alpha}\nu\theta\rho\omega\pi\sigma\iota$), who had long ago been fore-pictured
for this doom, have slunk into the Church ($\pi\alpha\rho\epsilon\iota\sigma\acute{\epsilon}\delta\nu\sigma\alpha\nu$)—
impious men, transforming the grace of our God into wan-
tonness, denying our only Master and Lord, Jesus Christ.

It was to Jude a strange and an appalling phenomenon.

---

[1] It is not in the Peshito, and is not quoted by Justin Martyr, Irenaeus, or
Theophilus of Antioch ; Theodore of Mopsuestia rejected it. But it is recognised in Tertullian and Clement of Alexandria and Origen.

JUDE.

These men who had insinuated themselves ("slunk in") into the Christian body were marked by two frightful characteristics—impious apostasy and wanton license. He wishes then to remind the faithful,[1] once for all, though they know all things, (πάντα) that Jesus [2]—the Angel of the Lord in the wilderness—first saved from Egypt the chosen people, and then destroyed those that proved faithless. The fall of the angels who kept not their own principality through sensual sins, and the overthrow of the cities of the plain pointed the same warning lesson. These apostates in their insolent independence defile the flesh and "rail at glories." The example of even Michael, who would not rail at Satan when he was contending with him for the body of Moses, might rebuke their insolence ; [3] and the irrational animals, who do not fall into their abysses of corruption, might rebuke their lust. They combine the violence of Cain with the corrupting influence of Balaam and the rebelliousness of Korah. "These," he says, "are the sunken reefs in your agapae ('love feasts'), banqueting dauntlessly with you, pasturing themselves; waterless clouds swept hither and thither by winds, autumnal trees, fruitless, twice dead, deracinated (ἐκριζωθέντα) ; wild waves of the sea foaming out their own shames; wandering stars for which the mirk of darkness has been reserved for ever." Then, after applying to them a quotation from the Apocryphal Book of Enoch,[4] he charges them with murmur-

---

[1] Those who are "kept for Jesus Christ," comp. John xvii. 11. The verb τηρεῖν occurs three times in this Epistle, verses 1, 6, 13.

[2] The readings here adopted often differ from those of the A.V. They are generally noticed in the R.V.

[3] It seems clear, though we may think it strange, that these Antinomian libertines are here reproved for *railing at fallen spirits*, which even Michael would not do, comp. Rev. xii. 10. Milton makes Gabriel say to Satan,
  "*Satan, I know thy strength*, and thou know'st mine.
    Neither our own, but given."
Clearly, as Dr. Fraser says, St. Jude would not have approved of the tendency of modern literature to speak of Satan with contemptuous jocularity, as in Ben Jonson's "The Devil is an Ass," or Burns's "Address to the Deil."

[4] "Enoch the *seventh* from Adam." We should say "the sixth," but the Jews counted inclusively. Besides this quotation there are references to the language of the Book of Enoch in verses 6, 7, 13, &c.

ings, discontent (μεμψίμοιροι), sensuality, vaunting language, and designing partiality.

The faithful must remember that the Apostles had prophesied of these scoffers, these egoistic (ψυχικοί), unspiritual separatists (διορίζοντες). They must keep themselves secure by prayer and watchfulness. Some of these errorists they must convince by discussion; some they must, so to speak, snatch out of the fire; others they must pity but must shun their contaminating contact.

He ends with a blessing which seems to be modelled on that at the end of Romans (xvi. 25—27), but is marked by some of the peculiar expressions which Jude adopts at every turn :—

"Now to him that is able to guard you unstumbling, and to set you before His glory blameless in exultation, to the only God our Saviour by Jesus Christ our Lord be glory, majesty, might, and power, both before all the aeons, and now, and to all the aeons. Amen."

Such is the strange Epistle of St. Jude, which is full of valuable moral lessons, though they are conveyed in so peculiar a form.

It shows us at once how false an estimate we form when we imagine that the Church of even the first century was in a state of spotless purity. Hegesippus says that the Church was a virgin till the days of Symeon, son of Clopas, second Bishop of Jerusalem, and that then Thebuthis—apparently a kind of personified heresy [1]—began to afflict the Church. But from the very first the dragnet of the Church contained bad fish as well as good, and in the field of the Church tares grew as well as wheat. There is scarcely one of the Apostles who does not show us that there existed in the Church from the first some men who had not abandoned their heathen practices,[2] and others who made their spiritual freedom a cloak

---

[1] Rufinus has "Theobutes quidam." The word is possibly connected with תֶּאָב, "filth."

[2] 1 Thess. iv. 6 ; Eph. v. 3 ; 1 Cor. v. 1–11 ; 2 Cor. xii. 21.

for carnal lust.[1] The notion that this Epistle was meant for a venomous attack on Pauline Christians becomes absurd when we see enough in St. Paul's own writings, to show that he would have denounced the very same offenders with a flame of indignant zeal no less intense than that which burned in the breast of St. Jude himself.

It may be perfectly true that some of these offenders had adopted Pauline watchwords and had perverted Pauline arguments. We know that in very early days there were many who did so.[2] The Marcionites did so with the writings of St. Paul, the Valentinians with those of St. John. And this abuse of the truths which it was his special mission to reveal was sure to be turned by the enemies of St. Paul into a weapon against him. It may even have had the effect of making Christians who had been unable to abandon their own Judaic prejudices look on St. Paul himself with suspicion and dislike as a dangerous and unsound teacher. This, however, does not reflect the smallest discredit on the great Apostle. It is only another specimen of what invariably happens when some great original teacher—a Paul, a Huss, a Luther—is commissioned by God to break down the barriers of immemorial prejudice.

The persons whom St. Jude so vehemently denounces find their exact analogue in the days of the Reformation. They are the invariable product of an epoch of religious ferment and excitement. Their abuse of the preaching of St. Paul exactly resembles the abuse of Luther's teaching by men like Storch, and Matthys, and Rothmann, and even Carlstadt. Such men would have been denounced equally by Judaeo-Christians like James and Jude, or by St. Peter, or by St. Paul himself, just as the Anabaptists were by men like Cardinal Cajetan, or like Erasmus, or like Luther. The narrow school of Christian Pharisees at Jerusalem might hold Paul respon-

---

[1] Eph. iv. 19 ; 1 Cor. vi. 9–18 ; Gal. v. 13 ; 1 Pet. ii. 16 ; 1 Tim. vi. 5 ; 2 Tim. iii. 2 ; Acts. xx. 29 ; 1 John iii. 7–10.
[2] Rom. iii. 8 ; 2 Pet. iii. 15.

sible for these excesses, and might say or insinuate that he taught "apostasy from Moses," just as the Romanists might have charged Luther and do still charge him with having sown the seeds of Antinomianism and revolt. New truth is always liable to misinterpretation and to perversion; but, as an ancient Father wisely and bravely said, "It is better that truth be preached even if some pervert it than that for fear of its perversion, truth should be suppressed." We cannot be surprised when the old wine-skins are bursten by the new fermenting wine.

When we read the history of the Anabaptists and the career of men like Thomas Münzer and John of Leyden, we see a reproduction of the very features of crime and heresy which St. Jude condemns in these immoral Gnostics of his own day.[1] They too built up the most monstrous abuses on the doctrine of justification by faith. They too combined the inflated, boastful, insolent language (ὑπέρογκα, verse 16) of wild and fanatical enthusiasm with extreme religious pretensions. They too were apostate and Antinomian Pharisees.[2] They too had *agapae* in which they were as "sunken reefs," and in which they rioted with shameful and shameless self-indulgence (verse 12). They too "railed at glories," making "death to all priests and nobles" their common cry. They too plunged into the grossest excesses of sensuality, like Bochelson who took fifteen wives at Münster and said that he would have 300, or his agent Knipperdolling, who, with the words of Scripture for ever on his lips, danced indecent dances in the market-place, and taught the doctrine of "holy sensuality."

The Epistle of St. Jude draws a picture which might be applied line by line, and word by word, to the obscure wretches (ἄνθρωποι τινες)—the Bochelsons and Knipperdollings, the Krechtings and Hoffmans, the Stübners and Münzers—of the years 1521 to 1535; and something of

---

[1] Such men—Nicolaitans, Cerinthians, Ophites, Cainites, Carpocratians, Antitactae, Adamites—abounded a little later, and in the second century.

[2] διορίζοντες = Separatists = Pharisees. See Hooker, *Serm.* v. 11.

JUDE.   Jude's own tone rings through the eight sermons which
Luther preached at Wittemberg on the days after his return
to that city in 1522. The Anabaptists, no less than these Antinomians, were murderous like Cain, corrupted others with
sensuality like Balaam, and like Korah set at defiance all
constituted authorities.

As for the Rabbinic and Hagadistic allusions of St. Jude,
we must leave them where we find them. It is undeniable
and undoubted that he makes a direct citation found in the
Apocryphal Book of Enoch; that he attributes the fall of the
angels (as the Book of Enoch does) to their sins with mortal
women ; that, like Philo, he apparently identifies the pillar
of fire with a manifestation of Jesus (verse 5) ; that he refers
to a singular Jewish legend about a dispute between Satan
and the Archangel Michael about the body of Moses, which
Origen says was quoted from an Apocryphal book called "The
Assumption of Moses," and which is alluded to in the Targum
of Jonathan. These peculiarities were sufficient to cause the rejection of the book by many as uncanonical ;[1] and the omission
of these very elements by the writer of the Second Epistle of
St. Peter shows that they were felt by some to be anomalous
or open to objection. We can throw little or no light on the
matter because we are ignorant of the arguments which would
have told most powerfully among those to whom the Epistle
was addressed. All that can be said is that the Church has
accepted the Epistle as a portion of the canonical Scriptures,
without at the same time receiving the Book of Enoch, or
pronouncing any opinion on such subjects as the fall of angels
or the contest of an Archangel with Satan about the body of a
man. All speculation on such subjects is vain and useless, but
the moral lessons which St. Jude inculcates belong to all time.

---

[1] The words of Jerome are remarkable:—"Et quia de libro Enoch, qui
apocryphus est in eâ (epistolâ), assumsit testimonium, *a plerisque rejicitur :
tamen auctoritatem vetustam jam et usu meruit,* ut inter sacras scripturas
computetur."—*Catal Script. Eccl.* 4. Didymus of Alexandria felt the same objection.   The Book of Enoch is now well known from the translation from the
Aethiopic by Lawrence (1821), and Dillman (1853). "The Assumption of
Moses " has perished.

NOTE I.

PECULIARITIES OF STRUCTURE AND PHRASEOLOGY IN THE EPISTLE OF ST. JUDE.

Arrangements by threes.

Mercy, peace, love, vs. 1.

The Israelites; the Fallen Angels; the Sodomites, vss. 5-7.

Corrupt, rebellious, railing, vs. 8.

Followers of Cain, Balaam, Korah, vs. 11.

Murmurers, discontented, self-willed, vs. 16.

Boastful, partial, covetous, vs. 16.

Separatists, egoistic, unspiritual, vs. 19.

To be refuted; saved by effort; pitied with detestation of their sins, vss. 22, 23.

Saints to build themselves in the faith; to keep themselves in the love of God; to await the mercy of Christ, vs. 20.

Glory to God in the past, present, and future, vs. 25.

Unique expressions, "to contend for"; "slunk in"; "going after strange flesh"; "naturally"; "poured themselves forth"; "love feasts"; "sunken reefs"; "autumnal"; "foaming forth"; "wandering stars"; "murmurers"; "blamers of their lot"; "separatists"; "unstumbling"; "before all the aeons," &c.

"Archangel" occurs elsewhere only in 1 Thess. iv. 16.

Michael only in Dan. x. 13; Rev. xii. 7.

THE SECOND EPISTLE OF ST. PETER.

OF UNCERTAIN DATE.

"Stylo inter se et charactere discrepant structuraque verborum. Ex quo intelligimus pro necessitate rerum diversis eum usum interpretibus."—Jer. *Ep. ad. Hedib.*, cxx. 11.

IN reading the Second Epistle of St. Peter we are face to face with a book which is indeed an acknowledged part of the canon, and which contains many great and sacred lessons, but of which the genuineness is less certain than that of any book of the New Testament. It is an Epistle for which we can offer the smallest amount of external evidence, and which at the same time presents the greatest number of internal difficulties.

The evidence in its favour becomes all the weaker when it is contrasted with the all but unanimous acceptance of the First Epistle. Setting aside some dim and dubious signs that it may have been read by Hermas and by Melito of Sardis, there is no certain proof that it was known to any writer of the first or second centuries. By Polycarp, Ignatius, Barnabas, Clement of Rome, Justin Martyr, Theophilus of Antioch, Irenaeus, Tertullian, and Cyprian it is ignored, as also by the Peshito, the Itala, and the Muratorian canon. By Clement of Alexandria and by Origen, by Eusebius, by Theodore of Mopsuestia, by Gregory of Nazianzus, it is controverted or regarded as of uncertain authorship; by Didymus of Alexandria and by the Syriac school at Nisibis it was rejected as " spurious and not in the canon."[1] It was not till the fourth century that it was accepted, and it was only by late Councils in the fourth century that it was declared to be canonical. If it was indeed in the hands of the Church and the Fathers of the second and third centuries, the tardy and hesitating recognition of an Epistle which bore, alike in its structure and on its forefront, the claim that it was written by the chief Apostle is unfavourable rather than otherwise to its asserted genuineness. The Church of the fourth century was in no respect better able to decide upon critical questions than we are—in many respects far less so ; and though the Councils of Laodicea and Carthage declared it to be canonical,[2] Jerome, who, by admitting the Epistle into the Vulgate, did more than any man to further its acceptance, yet admits that it was in his day rejected by most Christians, and that it differs from the First Epistle in style, character, and structure of words.[3] In fact, he can only accept the partial genuineness of the Epistle by supposing that " from the necessity of things St. Peter made use of different interpreters ; " which practically means that, while the thoughts are those of the Apostle, the words and the style belong to some one else.

After the fourth century, during long centuries of critical torpor, scarcely any one ventured to question the current tradition. But at the Renaissance, when the Reformation broke " the deep slumber of decided opinions," and Churchmen were no longer able to suppress inquiry by violence, the old doubts immediately revived. They were freely expressed by Erasmus, Luther, Calvin, Cajetan, Grotius, Scaliger, Salmasius. In modern times the genuineness of the Epistle has been denied without hesitation, not only by Semler, Baur, Schwegler, De Wette, Hilgenfeld, Meyerhoff,

---

[1] For details see Davidson, *Introd.* ii. 474–484. Westcott, *On the Canon.* Charteris on *Canonicity.*

[2] Laodicea, A.D. 363 ; Hippo, A.D. 393 ; Carthage, A.D. 397.

[3] " A plerisque ejus esse negatur, propter styli cum priore dissonantiam." —Jer. *De Script. Eccl.* 1.

Bleek, Mesnier, Reuss, Immer, Pfleiderer, Renan, Davidson, Abbott, but even by such conservative theologians as Neander, Weiss, Huther, De Pressensé, and in part by Bertholdt, Ullmann, Bunsen, and even Lange, who hold that it has, in any case, been largely interpolated.

And indeed when we take up the Epistle we can hardly wonder either at the tardiness of the ancient recognition or at the strength of the recent doubts, for there is hardly a single paragraph of the letter which does not abound in the most startling phenomena.

In the first place, the style—as was noticed more than fifteen centuries ago—is totally unlike that of the First Letter. It is true that some of the same phrases and expressions—such as "conversation"; "eye-witness" (ἐπόπτης); "to carry off as a prize"; "to walk in lusts"; "spotless and blameless"; "lawless" (ἄθεσμος); "ceasing from sin"; and "putting away"—occur in both.[1] But this fact goes only a very little way to counterbalance the opposite phenomena of a style radically different, and expressions as unique as they are extraordinary. For it is in any case admitted that the writer of the Second Epistle was perfectly well acquainted with the First; and if indeed he was a *falsarius*, who, for religious purposes, adopted the name, as he believed himself to express the sentiments, of St. Peter, he shows an extreme anxiety to speak in the person of the great Apostle,[2] and he would therefore naturally familiarise himself with the genuine expressions both of his Epistle and of his speeches as recorded in the Acts of the Apostles. But his parsimonious constructions, combined with a vocabulary sparse yet sonorous, leave a very different impression from that produced by the finer periods of St. Peter's genuine Epistle.[3]

---

[1] Add the words ἐπιχορηγέω, φιλαδελφια ἀσέλγεια, εὐσέβεια (Acts iii. 12), "the Day of the Lord" (Acts ii. 20). The Deluge and Prophecy are prominent in both. All that can be urged under this head may be seen in Professor Lumby's papers in the *Expositor*, iv. 372, 446.

[2] i. 1, 13, 14, 15, 16–18; iii. 1, 15.

[3] A certain literary difficulty is shown by the incessant repetition of words,

But while it is easy to borrow certain phrases, it is supremely difficult to assume the whole individuality, and style, and tone of thought of the person who has used them; and the style of the Second Epistle is stamped with a separate individuality of its own, and abounds in expressions so unusual that it is difficult to regard them as being other than eccentricities of language. If St. Peter wrote the Second as well as the First Epistle, how is it that in the earlier letter we find nothing analogous to such terms as "to acquire faith by lot"; "giving things which tend to life and piety"; "greatest and precious"; "bringing in besides all haste"; "to furnish an abundant supply of virtue"; "to furnish an abundant entrance"; "receiving oblivion"; "the present truth"; "they shall bring in besides factions of perdition"; "the judgment is not idling, the destruction is not drowsily nodding"; "to walk behind the flesh"; "eyes full of an adulteress"; "insatiable of sin"; "a heart trained in covetousness"; "the mirk of the darkness"; "treasure stored with fire"; "pits of gloom"; "calcining to ashes"; "hurling to Tartarus"; "blaspheming glories"; "hurtlingly"; "to the day of the age"; "the world compacted out of water, and by means of water";[1] and many more. Most of these depend in no wise on the peculiarity of the subjects handled. They are not unique terms due to strange matter, but peculiarities of structure wholly different from the Apostle's acknowledged manner, and due in part to the writer's difficulties in expressing himself in an unfamiliar language. The First Epistle is smooth and flowing; but the Second is full of ruggedness, of tautology, and of phrases

---

e.g. i. 3, 4, διὰ τῆς ἐπιγνώσεως. . . διὰ δόξης. . . δι᾽ ὧν· i. 2, 3, ἐπίγνωσις· ii. 1, 2, 3, ἀπώλεια· ii. 12, φθορά· iii. 12, 13, 14 ; προσδοκᾶν, &c.

[1] λαχοῦσι πίστιν, i. 1 ; τὰ πρὸς ζωήν . . . δεδωρημένης. i. 3 ; μέγιστα καὶ τίμια, i. 4 ; σπουδὴν πᾶσαν παρεισενέγκαντες, i. 5 ; ἐπιχορηγήσατε τὴν ἀρετήν, i. 5 ; λήθην λαβών, i. 9 ; ἐπιχορηγηθήσεται . . . εἴσοδος, i. 11 ; ἡ παροῦσα ἀλήθεια, i. 12 ; παρεισάξουσιν αἱρέσεις ἀπωλείας, ii. 1 ; τὸ κρῖμα οὐκ ἀργεῖ, ἡ ἀπώλεια οὐ νυστάζει, ii. 3 ; ὀπίσω σαρκός, ii. 10 ; μεστοὺς μοιχαλίδος, ii. 14 ; ἀκαταπαύστους ἁμαρτίας, ii. 14 ; γεγυμνασμένην πλεονεξίαις, ii. 14 ; ὁ ζόφος τοῦ σκότους, ii. 17 ; ῥοιζηδόν, &c.

which to a classical Greek ear would—in prose writing at any rate—have sounded little short of grotesque.

It is indeed perfectly possible that a writer's style may differ in different books which are separated from each other by long periods of years, and wide differences of circumstances. It is thus that the Judaic tone and rough style of the Apocalypse is modified twenty or thirty years later in the Gospel written after the fall of Jerusalem and after long years spent in travels among the Gentiles and in the polished capital of Ionia. It is thus that the Epistle to the Colossians differs from the Epistles to the Thessalonians. It is thus that Plato's *Epinomis* differs from the *Laws;* and Virgil's *Ciris* from the *Aeneid;* and the dialogue of Tacitus *De Oratoribus* from his *Annals;* and *Twelfth Night* from *Hamlet;* and the *Paradise Lost* from the *Paradise Regained;* and Burke *On the Sublime and Beautiful* from Burke *On the French Revolution.* But if both the Epistles of St. Peter are genuine, we know that they were written under similar outward conditions, and within a year or two—at latest—of each other.

And yet differences between the two meet us at every turn. The "Peter" of the First becomes "Symeon Peter" in the Second. The persons addressed are different. Christ's descent into Hades—so capital a point in the First—is not so much as alluded to in the Second, even in passages where it would have been specially apposite. In the First St. Peter shows that his thoughts are full of Isaiah, the Psalms, the Proverbs, the Epistles to the Romans and Ephesians, and the Epistle of St. James; in the Second there is barely a single allusion to any of these writings, and if two passages (ii. 22, iii. 8) be quotations, they are introduced in a wholly different way. In the First our Lord is usually called "Christ," or "the Christ," or "Jesus Christ," in the Second He is always called "our Lord," or "our Lord and Saviour Jesus Christ." [1] Then again there are differences

---

[1] Σωτήρ does not occur in the First Epistle. Κύριος in 1 Pet. is only applied to Christ in ii. 3. The Second Epistle also differs from the First in using ἐν

of expression as regards the Second Advent. In the First it is called the "Apocalypse," in the Second the "Parousia" (i. 16, iii. 4), or "Day of the Lord"; in the First it is regarded as near at hand, in the Second as possibly relegated to an indefinite distance; in the First it is regarded as the glorification of the saints, in the Second as the destruction of the world.[1] The postponement of the expectation of the Second Advent is surprising in an Epistle which, if genuine, must have been written before the Apocalypse, and it is unlike any other passage in the New Testament. Even as late as the days of Justin Martyr there was still the expectation of an immediate return of Christ.[2]

Again, in the First Epistle, the writer reveals his personality by minute, accidental, unconscious allusions; but in the Second there is at the utmost only one touch of this kind, while on the other hand the writer seems anxious to establish his identity by direct assertions.

Once more, in the First there is constant reference to the sufferings, death, resurrection, and ascension of the Lord; in the Second, where, from the nature of the subjects handled, these topics might have been expected to have still greater prominence, there is not a single allusion to them.

Again, the tone of the letters is obviously different. In the first it is full of sweetness, mildness, and fatherly dignity; in the second it is anxious, denunciative, and severe.

Again, even the keynotes of the Epistles are very markedly different. The keynote of the First is hope (i. 3, iii. 15); that of the Second is full knowledge ($\epsilon\pi i\gamma\nu\omega\sigma\iota\varsigma$).

Lastly, there is the peculiarity that the false teachers are spoken of sometimes as future (ii. 1—3, iii. 3), sometimes as present (ii. 10, 12, 13, 15, 17, iii. 5, &c.); there is the strange allusion to "the earth compacted out of water, and by means

pleonastically, and in not using a pleonastic $\dot{\omega}s$. Credner in his *Einleitung*, Davidson, &c., point out many other peculiarities.

[1] iii. 9, 10, 12. In other passages of the New Testament the Second Advent is not identified with the Day of Judgment.

[2] In the second century this expectation was chiefly retained among the Montanists.—Baur, *First Three Centuries*, i. 247 ; ii. 45 (E. T.).

H H

of water;"[1] and there are phrases which wear an obvious appearance of comparative modernism. Such are "*your* Apostles" (iii. 2); the description of Mount Hermon as "the holy mount";[2] the phrase "since the fathers" (apparently the earliest generation of Christians) "fell asleep," which seems to mark an age later than that of Peter; the recognition of St. Paul's collected Epistles, and the placing them (in a manner quite unparalleled in the New Testament) on a level with the Scriptures of the Old Testament.

But there is more even than this to awaken some misgiving. It is the unprecedented relationship of a large section of this letter to the Epistle of St. Jude, and the all but certainty that it is a copy from, not the original of, that peculiar and half-apocalyptic letter.

The "impious persons" of St. Jude, and the "false teachers" of St. Peter are described by exactly the same characteristics, pictured by the same metaphors, compared to the same Old Testament offenders, warned by the same examples, threatened with the same retributions. But the writer of this Epistle is less impetuous, more elaborate and restrained. He omits, he modifies, he softens. He seems to be writing from vivid memory of what St. Jude has said, but without the Epistle actually before him, so that sometimes he has been as it were magnetised only by the *sounds* of the words rather than by the words themselves. Thus for St. Jude's "sunken reefs" (*spilades*) he substitutes the more natural metaphor, but similar-sounding word, "spots" (*spiloi*); and for St. Jude's unique "love feasts" (*agapais*)—a word which might have suggested many erroneous notions—he uses the word deceits (*apatais*). Again, for St. Jude's impossible "*clouds* without water" he has the more accurate "*founts* without water." For the lyrically bold expression "chains (*seirais*) of darkness,"

---

[1] This verse (iii. 5) seems to imply not only the notion of Thales that water was the ὕλη, the *material* cause, but also that it was the *instrumental* cause of the world.

[2] In the New Testament there is no other instance of this reference to localities as "holy."

suggested to St. Jude by passages in the Book of Enoch, he substitutes the less daring phrase "pits (*seirois*) of darkness." He prefers not to touch on such dubious matter as the lusts of angels, and the dispute of Michael and Satan about the body of Moses. He omits St. Jude's double allusions to a particular form of Levitic pollution. He sets aside St. Jude's quotations from the apocryphal Book of Enoch and the "Assumption of Moses," and to the latter he gives an ingenious turn which seems intended to remind us of the well-known scene in the Book of Zechariah (iii. 1, 2). In general he treats with consummate judgment the burning material before him, but in one or two passages his tacit reference to what St. Jude has said leaves his own language obscure. Thus he speaks of the teachers "for whom the mirk of the darkness has been reserved for ever," without adding to it the vivid comparison of them to "wandering stars," which had added so much picturesque force to the earlier expression. In ii. 10 he says (with the abruptness which marks other parts of the Epistle), "Daring, self-willed, they tremble not when they rail at glories, in cases wherein angels, greater though they are in strength and might, do not bring against them" [the "glories" before spoken of] "a railing judgment." Here all is obscure. There is nothing at all to show who the "glories" are, or that by the word is meant a fallen angel, who even in his fall is not

> "Less than Archangel ruined, or excess
> Of glory obscured."

It is only when we turn to the parallel passages of St. Jude, and see that the original reference was to Michael and Satan that we are at all able to fathom the allusion. In the next sentence again we find a curious turn, for which we could hardly be able to account if we had not St. Jude's words lying before us. St. Jude says quite intelligibly (verse 10) "These rail at all things which they know not (οὐκ οἴδασι); but all the things which, like the reasonless animals, they understand naturally (φυσικῶς), in these they corrupt themselves" (or are destroyed, φθείρονται). The writer of this Epistle says, " But these, as reasonless natural (φυσικὰ) animals, born for capture and destruction, railing in things of which they are ignorant (ἀγνοοῦσι), shall be destroyed (καταφθαρήσονται) in their own destruction (or corruption φθορᾷ)." It is clear that he remembered some of St. Jude's words, but has given to the sentence a form which by no means explains itself. There is a sort of *antanaklasis* or play on the double meaning of φθορὰ (corruption and destruction), but the pregnant moral warning and coherence of St. Jude's sentence has in great measure disappeared. The words are partially identical, but the force of them has in great measure evaporated, and the meaning is at once different and very inferior.

But even now we have not exhausted the perplexing facts which must be taken into account. Dr. Abbott has recently pointed out for the first time a series of parallels between this Epistle and passages in the *Antiquities* of Josephus,[1] such as occur in no other book of Scripture, and such as cannot be accounted for except on the supposition that one of the two writers had seen the work of the other. Now, if the writer of this Epistle had read Josephus, he could not have been St. Peter, for the *Antiquities* were not published earlier than A.D. 93, long after St. Peter was dead. On the other hand, it is, to say the least, curious that this Epistle should have fallen into the hands of Josephus, and should in some passages have exercised an influence over a style which shows no trace of influence from the First Epistle, or from any other book of the New Testament.

No one, I think, who has carefully examined all the evidence, of which I shall here only give the merest sketch, can doubt as to the conclusion that Josephus and this writer cannot have written independently of each other. The proof

---

[1] Dr. Abbott's papers were published in the *Expositor*, Jan. 1882. While fully admitting the importance of his discoveries, I disagree with Dr. Abbott entirely in his very slighting estimate of the Epistle. My reply to this was also published in the *Expositor*.

depends on the identity in both writers (1) of nine or ten words which occur nowhere else in the LXX. or New Testament;[1] (2) in the use of groups of words in close juxtaposition;[1] and (3) in the occurrence, among these words, of some very peculiar conceptions.[1]

Thus, in the Proem to his *Antiquities*, Josephus, quite in his natural style, says that Moses thought it right to consider "*the divine nature*" (θεοῦ φύσις), without which he could not promote the "virtue" of his readers; that other legislators "*following on the track of their myths*, transferred to the gods the shame of their human sins," but Moses, having shown that "*God was possessed of perfect virtue*," thought that men should strive after virtue; and that the Laws of Moses contain nothing contrary to the *greatness* (μεγαλειότης) of God.

In this passage the peculiar expressions which are unknown to the Old Testament and the LXX. arise quite spontaneously from the nature of the subject. The same can hardly be said of the similar passages of this Epistle. In i. 4 the writer speaks of "greatest and precious promises" (ἐπαγγέλματα) given, that by them we may be "partakers of the divine nature" (i. 4). In i. 16 he speaks of "following after cunningly elaborated myths" (σεσοφισμένοις μύθοις ἐξακολουθήσαντες), and of the "greatness (μεγαλειότης) of Christ. In i. 3 he says that God "called us by His own glory *and virtue.*" Now the word "virtue" is very rare in the New Testament. It only occurs in Philippians iv. 8, and in this passage. The ideal of the New Testament is not virtue, but holiness. It is so astonishing to find "virtue"—the cold, lower, human ideal of virtue, as distinct from righteousness and holiness—ascribed to God, that the strangeness of the phrase has actually frightened the Authorised translators into the impossible mistranslation, "who hath called us to glory

---

[1] Among these words and phrases are βραδυτής (iii. 9, as applied to Divine retribution) ; ᾧ καλῶς ποιεῖτε προσέχοντες (i. 19) ; λήθην λαβών (i. 9) ; σπουδὴν παρεισενέγκαντες (i. 5) ; καταστροφῇ κατέκρινεν (ii. 6) ; ἰσότιμον (i. 1) ; ἐπάγγελμα for ἐπαγγελία (i. 4) ; σεσοφισμένος (i. 16) ; ἔκπαλαι (ii. 3).

and virtue." And yet in Josephus the attribute explains itself, for he has been led by the nature of his subject to speak of *a God of virtue* in contrast with the vicious deities of heathen mythology.[1]

When again we find in Josephus's account of the last words of Moses seven or eight phrases which scarcely occur elsewhere in the sacred writings, including some so marked as "*departure*" for "death" (i. 15), and "*the present truth*" (i. 12), there can be no doubt left that such resemblances are more than accidental.

It may serve to illustrate the features of the Epistle if we take a single passage.

After appealing to the voice of which "we (emphatic) heard *borne* (ἐνεχθεῖσαν) from heaven, when we were with Him in the Holy Mount," the writer adds:

"And we have the prophetic word (made) more sure, whereto ye do well in taking heed, as unto a lamp shining in a squalid place, until the day dawn, and the daystar arise in your hearts; knowing this first, that no prophecy of Scripture is of private interpretation. For no prophecy was ever *brought* (ἠνέχθη) by the will of man, but men spake from God, being *borne along* (φερόμενοι) by the Holy Ghost" (i. 19—21).

In this passage we have the emphatic "we"; the phrase "the Holy Mount," applied to the Mountain of the Transfiguration which is nowhere else so called; the thrice-repeated verb "to be borne or carried along," implying impetuous spiritual utterance or influence; and besides this we have direct parallels to three writers, Josephus, Philo, and the author of the Fourth Book of Esdras. "Ye do well in taking heed" is found in Josephus,[2] "A lamp shining in a

---

[1] It is true that in 1 Pet. ii. 9, we find ὅπως τὰς ἀρετὰς ἐξαγγείλητε τοῦ ἐκ σκότους ὑμᾶς καλεσάντος, κ.τ.λ. But even if the reference there be to God, and not rather to Christ, the parallel is purely accidental and deceptive. For ἀρετή means virtue, but ἀρεταί has no such meaning. It is a *pluralis excellentum* and means *excellences* (as in R. V.; "praises," A.V.), and is merely a translation of the Hebrew.

[2] 2 Pet. i. 19, ᾧ καλῶς ποιεῖτε προσέχοντες. Jos. *Antt.* xi. 6, § 12, οἷς ποιήσετε καλῶς μὴ προσέχοντες.

squalid place " is found in Esdras;[1] and the unusual word "to be borne along," as applied to prophecy is found in a passage of Philo, together with the words "private," "day-star," and "dawn."[2]

What then are we to say respecting this accumulation of abnormal phenomena?

It would indeed be perfectly easy to offer a speciously plausible account of many of them singly, but I doubt whether the confluence of so many points which require defence or explanation can fail to leave an uncertain impression. Even the supremely improbable hypothesis that the Epistle is a translation from the Aramaic helps us very little. In the Second Epistle of Timothy we are certainly reading the last words of St. Paul. It is impossible to be equally assured that in this Epistle we are reading the last words of St. Peter. It still remains just possible that we are reading thoughts to which, though not wholly penned by himself, he lent the sanction of his name and authority.

But whether it be genuine, or only partially and indirectly genuine, or only expressive of thoughts such as St. Peter might and would have used, we must dismiss from our minds all the connotations of the words "forger" and "plagiarist." "Pseudepigraphy," and the free use of previous writers, was common in antiquity. Pseudepigraphy in many, perhaps in most, cases, neither did deceive, nor was intended to deceive, the readers who were originally addressed. It was only a well-understood literary form to give imaginary weight to a writer's thoughts by placing them under the assumed shadow of a great authority. Whatever be the ultimate verdict respecting the direct authenticity of the Second Epistle of St. Peter, it will remain to the end of time a writing full of instruction, which is undoubtedly superior to all the writings of the second and third centuries.

---

[1] " For you have survived to us from all prophets, as a lamp in a dark place."—4 Esdr. xii. 42.

[2] θεοφόρητος, φωσφόρος, ἴδιος, ἀνατέλλει . . Philo, *Quis rer. div. haer.* p. 52. This parallel is pointed out by Dr. Abbott.

It has come down to us from the Apostolic age. It does not touch on a single specific feature of the later and more elaborate systems of Gnosticism. It shows no trace of the ecclesiastical organisation or the ecclesiastical spirit which were so rapidly developed after the death of the Apostles. Whatever be its peculiarities, it expresses thoughts of which many are akin to those of St. Peter, and worthy of the great Apostle ; and on the ground of its intrinsic value we thankfully acquiesce in the decision of the Church Councils which assigned to it a place in the New Testament canon. "In all parts of the Epistle," says Calvin, "the majesty of the spirit of Christ displays itself."

NOTE I.

OUTLINE OF THE EPISTLE.

1. Greeting, i. 1, 2 ; into which is introduced the keynote of ἐπίγνωσις "full knowledge."

2. Exhortation to the attainment of this full knowledge (i. 3–11), which he makes the more urgently from the certainty that his end is near (12–15), and as a witness of the Transfiguration he can give them a testimony (16–18), which is rendered yet more sure by inspired prophecy (19–21).

3. Warning against false teachers, who are described in the same manner as by St. Jude (ii. 1–22). Special warning against those who scoffed at the second coming of Christ,—who are reminded that, as the world once perished by water, it shall hereafter—though it may be ages hence—perish by fire (iii. 1–10).

4. Exhortation founded on this longsuffering of God (11–14) in accordance with the teaching of St. Paul, the difficulties of whose Epistles have been perverted by many (10–16).

5. He repeats his warning (φυλάσσεσθε) and his exhortation (αὐξάνετε ἐν χάριτι καὶ γνώσει), and ends with a brief benediction (17, 18).

It is an Epistle, therefore, of mingled exhortation and warning.

Its keynote is knowledge and full knowledge in contradistinction to "cunning myths" (i. 16) and "feigned words" (ii. 3).

THE FIRST EPISTLE OF ST. JOHN.[1]

WRITTEN PERHAPS IN PATMOS, *circ.* A.D. 97.

> " This is he who lay
> Upon the bosom of our Pelican ;
> This he into whose keeping from the Cross
> The mighty charge was given."—DANTE, *Parad.* xxv.

" Sumtis pennis aquilae et ad altiora festinans de Verbo Dei disputat."—Jer. *ad. Matt. Prooem.*

"Transcendit nubes, transcendit virtutes coelorum, transcendit angelos, et Verbum in Principio repperit."—AMBROS. *Prol. in Luc.*

" Aquila ipse est Joannes, sublimium praedicator, et lucis internae atque aeternae fixis oculis contemplator."—AUG. *in Joann. Tr.* 36.

INTRODUCTORY.

ALTHOUGH this Epistle resembles a theological treatise and a religious homily, it was yet evidently intended as an encyclical letter. The words " I write " (γράφω, and the epistolary aorist ἔγραψα) occur thirteen times ; the words " to you," " you," occur thirty-six times ; " my little children " (τεκνία, παιδία) six times ; " beloved " six times. The unconstrained style, the informal transitions, the mingled exhortations, all show that it is a letter. At the same time it is the most abstract and impersonal, the most independent of place and time and circumstance, of all the writings in the New Testament.

[1] Dr. Westcott, whose edition of the Epistles of St. John I had not the advantage of seeing till these pages had been written, calls it " a Pastoral."

It is extremely probable that it was meant to accompany copies of the Gospel as an appendix to it and a practical commentary. " The Gospel," says Hoffmann, " seeks to deepen faith in Christ; the Epistle sets forth the righteousness which is of faith." Apart from the Gospel, neither the prologue nor other parts of the Epistle could have been easily understood. It seems to assume throughout in all readers a familiarity with the order of thought (*e.g.* respecting " witness," " the Truth," " the Word," Communion, Life, Light, &c.) with which the whole Gospel is occupied. Above all, the passage about the Spirit, the water, and the blood (v. 6-8) would have been absolutely unintelligible to readers who had not received a clue to the meaning in John xix. 34.

There are fully thirty-five parallel passages in the Gospel and the Epistle. In the Gospel we see the origin of various thoughts ; in the Epistle they are generalised and practically applied. The Gospel gives us the historic manifestation of the Word ; the Epistle shows how that manifestation bears on Anti-Christian errors and Christian lives.

The notion that it was addressed either " to Parthians " or " to Virgins " (compare Revelation xiv. 4) may be dismissed as due to some clerical error or some inexplicable blundering ;[1] but whether Parthians (Πάρθους) and Virgins (Παρθένους) have been confused together, or whether either word has any connection with Pathmios (dwellers in Patmos), is only a matter of conjecture. There can be little doubt that the letter was addressed, like the Apocalypse, to the Churches of Asia, in which St. John for the last thirty years of his life exercised so preponderant an influence.

The Epistle derives special interest from the circumstance that it is practically—perhaps even absolutely—the latest utterance of Apostolic inspiration.

The Fall of Jerusalem had entirely changed the conditions

---

[1] Bede, *Prol. ad. Ep. Cath.* attributes this assertion (*ad Parthos*) to Athanasius, and we find a similar statement in Idacius Clarus and Augustine (*Quaest. Evang.* ii. 39). Πρὸς Πάρθους is found in some late cursive MSS. of the *Second* Epistle.

of the Church. The Gospel had been spread far and wide. The liberty of the Gentiles, for which St. Paul had battled all his life, was now established. The prerogative influence in the Church had passed from Jerusalem and the followers of St. James to Ephesus and the followers of St. John. Such controversies as those about circumcision, and clean and unclean meats, had passed away. No one dreamed any longer that it was necessary for a man to become a rigid Jew before he could become a perfect Christian. The questions which now occupied men's minds, even in the bosom of the Church (ii. 18), were different and far more abstract. They were questions about dogmatic truth. They turned chiefly on the nature of Christ. St. John's witness combats at every turn the dawning spirits of heresy and error.

Was Christ, as the Ebionites believed, a mere man ? (iv. 2 ; ii. 22, &c.)

Was the suffering Jesus to be separated, as Cerinthus held, from the sinless Christ ? (1 John v. 6 ; Epiphan. *Haer.* xxviii. 1 ; Iren. *Haer.* iii. 9, 3).

Was His human life, as Docetists pretended, a mere phantasmal semblance ? (v. 6).

Was evil an eternal attribute of matter, as the incipient Manichean Gnostics began to whisper ?

Was there no real distinction between the moral and ceremonial law ? or, as Nicolaitans and Antinomians asserted, did faith and knowledge emancipate men from moral obligations ? (1 John ii. 4) Clem. Alex. *Strom.* iii. 4, 31 Iren. *Haer.* i. 6, 2). Since such questions were already beginning to be discussed the dangers with which St. John had to deal were not assaults from enemies without, but false types of orthodoxy and false types of goodness which were springing up within the Church.

St. John met such heretical tendencies, not by Pauline dialectics, for which he was wholly unsuited by nature and temperament, but by the lofty tone of inspired authority, and the presentation of positive truths in sharp contrast to nascent

error. On all doubts and difficulties "Christ's own eagle," as
Dante called him, seemed to gaze downwards as from a
supreme height. To him history is the invisible translated
into the visible. "The central characteristic of his nature is
intensity. He sees the past and the future gathered up in the
presentation of the Son of God. He had no laboured process
to go through; he saw. He had no constructive proof to
develop; he bore witness. His source of knowledge was
direct, and his mode of bringing conviction was to affirm." [1]

To St. John the central object of all faith, the supreme
counteraction of all unbelief, is the Word made Flesh; communion with Him, and with the Father through Him, and
with all mankind in Him, is Eternal Life, and all life apart
from this communion is not life but death.

Oporin, the first theologian who gained the credit of seeing
and demonstrating the consecutive and systematic character
of this Epistle, showed much insight when he named his
tract *De constanter tenenda communione cum Patre et Filio.* [2]

"The Word was God." "The Word became Flesh."
"Without Him was not anything made that is made."
These words, as Haupt says, constitute the signature of the
Johannean writings. The theme of the Epistle, says Dr.
Westcott, is "the Christ is Jesus," the theme of the Gospel
is "Jesus is the Christ."

There is something in the supreme and authoritative finality
of St. John's utterances which seem to solve all antinomies.
Contradictions find their harmonious synthesis in sublimest
truths. The controversy about Faith and Works, for instance,
disappears in such words as "He that doeth righteousness is
righteous, even as He is righteous." The controversies
between Jews and Gentiles are merged in the unity of the one
Church, which is the antithesis to the World. All difficulties
about forensic and sacrificial aspects of the Atonement are
lost in the simple sentence, "The Father sent His Son to be

[1] Westcott, *St. John, Speaker's Comment.* p. xxxv.
[2] Joachim Oporinus *Joannis Ep. e nodis interpretum liberata,* 1741.

the Saviour of the world." In the region of the Idea there is no room for jarring conflicts. This Epistle, with the Gospel, sets the final seal to Revelation.—It does so

a. In its teaching about Eternal Life, as a state, not an extension of time; as an ethical condition, not as an endless continuance. "The horologe of earth," as Bengel said, "is no measure for the aeonologe of heaven." St. John does not mention "Heaven" in his Epistles. Heaven is the true Christian's eternal Now. "The road to heaven lies through Heaven, and all the way to Heaven is Heaven."

β. In its teaching about the Word.

γ. In the teaching about God. "God is righteous." "God is Love." "God is Light."

δ. In the simplification of the essentials of Christian truth. St. John moves in the sphere of a few ultimate verities. He is, in the highest sense, a mystic, a realist. With him ideas are the only Realities. *Universalia ante rem* is the principle of his philosophy.

St. Paul is discursive, St. John is intuitive. St. Paul deals with Justification, St. John with Life. St. Paul is human and practical, St. John's divine realism is mainly occupied with the abstract conceptions of Love, and Life, and Light.

There is no clue to the date of the Epistle beyond the certainty that it was written after the Fall of Jerusalem, and at a period when the Church was free from persecution. This would point to some time before A.D. 95, or between the persecutions in the reigns of Domitian (A.D. 95) and of Trajan (A.D. 98). Ewald suggests A.D. 90.

THE FIRST EPISTLE OF ST. JOHN.

"And these things write we unto you that your joy may be full."—1 JOHN i. 4.

THE Epistle of St. John differs greatly from most of the other Epistles. There is in it nothing of the passionate personal element of St. Paul's letters; none of the burning controversy, of the subtle dialectics, of the elaborate doctrine, of the intense appeal. Nor has it anything of the stately eloquence and sustained allegorising of the Epistle to the Hebrews; nor does it enunciate the stern rules of practical ethics like St. James; nor, again, does it throb with that storm of moral indignation which sweeps through the Epistles of St. Peter and St. Jude. Its tone and manner are wholly different. It was written under different circumstances, and at a later time. In St. Paul we can rarely lose sight of the fact that Christians are in a double world of deadly antagonism—partly Jewish, partly Pagan. In St. John neither Jew nor Pagan is so much as mentioned; their distinctive hostility to the Church has melted into the one dark background of "the world." The Church is older, more instructed, more conscious of herself. It was the task of the other Apostles to plant; it is the task of St. John to water; it was theirs to teach, it is his to remind; it was theirs to lay the foundations, it is his to build the superstructure. His recurring formula is "ye know," "we know," "that ye may recognise;" and he says to them that he has not written to them because they know not the truth, but because they know it; nay, he even tells them that they have an unction from the Holy One, and know all things.

Why then does St. John thus write to remind them of truths which they had been already taught? what was the general object of his first Epistle?

1 JOHN.

On that question we need have no doubt, for he twice tells us. He tells us once at the beginning of the Epistle, where he says that he declares unto them that which they have heard, and seen, and handled of the Word of life—of Christ, the life of the Father manifested unto us—in order that he and they alike might have fellowship in the Father and the Son, and, so, that their joy might be full. Again, at the close of the Epistle he says that his object was that they might know that they had eternal life, and might believe on the name of the Son of God, and have confidence that God hears every prayer which is in accordance with His will. To give full joy; to impart unshaken confidence,—confidence in God's love, joy in the present possession of eternal life; to show that Eternal Life is in Christ Jesus and can only be realised by union with Him—such was the grand purpose of the Evangelist; and the Epistle fails in its object if it does not impart to us, as to his first readers, some share at least in that unshaken confidence, that perfect joy.

But besides this grand general motive, St. John, like the other Apostles, was induced to write by special motives. We find these special motives in the two passages (ii. 18 ; iv. *sq.*) about antichrist, and in the last warning to his spiritual children to keep themselves from idols. The immediate, or the worst, peril of the Churches of Asia did not arise from Jewish malice or Pagan violence, but from inward error and corruption ; their enemy was not the open Satan of Judaism or Heathendom, but the disguised Satan—the Satan transformed into an angel of light—of idle speculations. Now in St. John's view the victory of the Christian over evil depended solely on his confessing Christ, on his believing Christ, on his thus gaining fellowship with, and therefore reflecting, the life of Christ. The belief that the life of the Christian is a life " in Christ," that each true Christian is a member of His body, a branch of His Vine, a stone on His foundation, which was the heart of the theology of St. Paul, was no less the heart of the theology of St. John. But St. John saw with alarm that there were some who were taking away his Lord, substituting for Him another Lord altogether; one who was not perfectly man, or was not truly God. And these foes were within, not without the walls; men who, not denying but simulating holiness, were introducing the spirit of the world into the Kingdom of Heaven, the spirit of darkness into the sphere of light. These, then, are the immediate dangers, which, so late in life, when he was already an old man, first led St. John to break his long silence and to write, as he expressed it, with paper and ink.

And how does he deal with them?

i. St. John meets the heresies of his day by the assertion, not of speculative, but of practical truths. He does not complain of, he does not theorise about, the antagonism of the world to the Church, or of Antichrists to Christ. He simply mentions and accepts them as facts. He does not argue, he testifies; he does not denounce error, he teaches truth. There is the kingdom of Satan—darkness, sin, death; and over against it is the Kingdom of God, which is Light, Righteousness, Life. He has no theory as to how this kingdom of Satan began; he has no express statement as to how it will end. Enough for him that it began before, and independently of, the creation of man; enough for him that because God is God, it cannot permanently triumph. St. John is what would be called a Realist. He sees things only in the light of great ideas. He regards individual men and particular actions only as they are affected by those ideas. The Church and the world are to him exhaustive antitheses. He does not even stop to define what righteousness is, or what love is; he only lays down the broad general principles; all details will be learnt easily if the great principles reign in the hearts of Christians. The weapon which he puts into their hands for their eternal warfare is the ennoblement of their interior life. He sets before his Churches a work so high, a love so warm, as may leave them no heart for idle controversies. The object, then, of the Epistle is to check the subterranean growth of error by the statement of practical, eternal, universal truth—even by declaring the life which has been manifested in Christ, and has overflowed upon all His people, the life which alone matures our fellowship with God and with man.

ii. Such is his theme, and such his method. And what is the tone which he adopts? The main point about it is that it is memorably tranquil and peaceful. There is in it no trace of excited vehemence. The sternness and passion indeed of the Son of Thunder shows itself in the intense sharpness, the awful decisiveness, of that line of ideal severance which he draws between the kingdoms of light and darkness. He speaks of every sin—even the slightest—as essentially Satanic. Yet, strange to say, under this breastplate of dogmatic inflexibility we can feel the beatings of the human heart of love. We trace the Apostle of Love, the bosom disciple, him who played with the little partridge, and won back with tears the youthful robber, and laid his head on Jesus' breast. Even over the Alpine summits of his ideal holiness there breathes " a breath of most pathetic and most inward affection, from a spirit overflowing with love, and strong in peaceful rest." In reading the Epistle it is beautiful to see this consummate repose in the presence of Satanic hatred ; this infinite serenity amid the noises and agitations of the Church and of the world. He regards the world, it has been said, without wonder and without sorrow. It is but a transient semblance. *Crux stat, orbis volvitur.* Heretics spoke of Christ as a phantom ; it is the World which is the phantom, Christ is the only reality. St. Paul in the conflict with error bursts into plain thunderings and lightnings ; St. Peter "flings himself back with an energy of love into the days when he had lived with the Son of Man, and forward with an energy of hope into the days of His perfected kingdom;" St. Jude, breaking into passionate invective, calls the heretics filthy dreamers, waterless clouds, withered trees, raging billows, wandering stars ; but St. John seems merely to fix his intense gaze on

Him whom he had seen, as He was on earth, and whom he hoped to see, as He is, in heaven. He speaks the language not only of a father to his children, but of a soul at peace with God, of a soul which lives in the Eternal. His accents are as of a glorified saint speaking to men from a higher world. Just as the Epistle of the imprisoned Paul to the Philippians overflows with loving joy, so the words of St. John breathe a serene tranquillity, born like the fragrance of night flowers, of darkness and trouble. The exile of Patmos is as one who, standing on the shore, sees the ships toss indeed in the storms and billows of the offing, yet knows that they are moored, by anchors sure and steadfast, to the eternal rock. Hence comes it that his thoughts are so transparent, so ingenuous; unfathomable even to the deepest thinker, yet intelligible even to the little child. All this makes it very probable that the letter was written in the seclusion of the little rocky islet, which he may often have visited, and that it was sent to Ephesus to accompany the Gospel, with which it is essentially one in tone and doctrine. The fundamental thought of both is that Jesus is the Word of God, the Son who revealed the idea of the Father. In the Gospel we have the historic testimony to those fundamental facts by which the revelation of God has been introduced into this earthly life; in the Epistle it is shown how, on the ground of these truths, the life of individual men may be strengthened by confidence, and filled with joy. The truth which he has thus stated thetically, *i.e.* as revealed in fact, is here stated antithetically, *i.e.* in opposition to theoretic errors. And thus St. John is removed immeasurably above the vulgar style of religious controversy. He is too near the Great White Throne to be *agitated* by the existence of heresy; he is far too sure in his grasp of truth to mix it up with hostile ambitions, or personal dislikes. He had arrived at that stage in which

> " Love is an unerring light,
> And joy its own security."

1 JOHN. We may say of St. John as the poet says of the raised Lazarus:

> " Whence had the man the balm that brightens all ?
>
> He holds on firmly to some thread of life
> Which runs across some vast distracting orb
> Of glory, on either side that meagre thread,
> Which, conscious of, he must not enter yet,
> The spiritual life around the earthly life.
>
> This is the man as harmless as a lamb;
> Only impatient, let him do his best,
> At ignorance, and carelessness, and sin—
> An indignation which is promptly curbed."

St. John's love came from the source to which he would direct us for ours. He loved man and he loved God, because he loved Him who was the Son of Man and the Son of God. " By loving Him we learn to love all men with unfeigned love; not with the transient precarious love which comes and goes, comes while good-will is shown us, and goes directly ill-will and disfavour meets us ; not with the feeble love which is extinguished by the first evil word, blown away by the first injury; not with the self-righteous love which will love none but the good, the excellent, the perfect; but with that love wherewith God first loved us. . . Where this love dwells—a love which at the same time is joy in the Lord— there the heart never freezes nor withers. It remains perpetually young, for the glow of eternal life streams through it."[1]

" St. John's point of view is in many respects new and final. To St. James the salvation brought by Christ presented itself under the form of an accomplished work; to St. Peter under that of a promised glory; to St. Paul it was a righteousness secured; to St. John it was life in full possession. Work, glory, righteousness, life—these four things are included in the salvation which Christ offers to the world. We may almost say that they exhaust its contents, nor is it possible to possess one of them without in some measure possessing all. Yet in the personal aspirations and past history of the

[1] Bishop Monrad, of Denmark, *The World of Prayer.*

individual man there may be that which predisposes him to receive the whole through the medium of one of these elements rather than another. And Providence willed that the four chosen men, who by their writings were to transmit the salvation in its totality to all the world, should each of them perceive it under one of these four characters, which in their combination constitute its fulness."

"Paul fixed his eye on righteousness accorded to faith. John on life found in communion with God. Thus these two Apostles disengaged themselves more completely than the other two from their Jewish past. To James and Peter salvation in Christ was a flower yet folded in the bud. To Paul and John a flower opened wide, and the fruit forming within the flower."

We have seen the general and the special object of this beautiful Epistle—its practical aim, its calm tone, its positive method—it only remains to say a few words as to its plan and outline. In the old traditional way in which for ages the Bible has been dealt with, this Epistle has been treated as though it had no order or method. "He is going to say much," says St. Augustine, "and almost all about love." "The main substance of this Epistle," says Luther, "relates to love." "It contains," says Calvin, "doctrine with exhortations, but in no continuous order; he especially insists on brotherly love, but touches also briefly on other things." But on the contrary, so far is this Epistle from being, as some have said, aphoristic, or a series of loosely connected thoughts, that you will find in it steadily worked out from the first verse to the last the thought of man's brotherhood to man, resulting from man's fellowship with God, and both rendered possible by the revelation of God in Christ. The fundamental theme of the Epistle is communion with the Father and the Son as the source of love to our brethren. You will easily trace also a threefold division in the Epistle. Three times St. John warns against error; three times he bases the refutation of all error, and the possibility of all holiness, on some deep utterance respecting the nature of God. The thoughts interlace one another—the predominant melody of one section is heard by anticipation in the undertones of the others—but the divisions are discernible, and there are three distinct movements in the general music.

i. Thus the first two chapters are dominated by the melody of the grand utterance that God is Light; not the light of earth, which is but His garment and His shadow, but its eternal prototype—

> " Holy light, offspring of heaven firstborn,
> Bright effluence of bright essence uncreate
> Whose fountain who shall tell ? "

And since this Light of God is all-pervading, all-illuminating, therefore, where ignorance, darkness, sin, and falsehood are, there God is not ; and where God is there is truth, goodness, purity. Hence they who are in communion with God must of necessity be walking in the light—in the light of sin forgiven; in the light of holiness sincerely loved, and ever more and more attained.

ii. And the next great utterance, in the last verse of the second chapter, is that God is righteous. This definition, mingled with the truths that He is our Father, that we are born of God and have confessed Christ, and that this confession is possible only through the Spirit of Christ, and therefore that, ideally, unrighteousness is impossible to us as God's true children, dominates through the next chapter. Of this section the one great lesson is that we are bound to righteousness by the very law of our being, and that thereby we gain the blessing of confidence, and the knowledge that God abideth in us.

iii. The third section, which begins at iv. 7, turns on the divine truth that God is love. As the colours of the rainbow melt imperceptibly into one another, and are not to be divided one from the other by sharp lines, so this thought has already been lending its glow and colour to the last section ; but it is only in the grand utterance that God is

Love that it bursts into its own full and proper splendour. That little sentence has brought to the world more sweetness than all the world can bring besides. And from it springs at once the clear truth for us to grasp, and the certain test for us to apply, that every offence against the law of love is a sin; that all and every form of hatred, whether it be the serpent glance of malice, or the sidelong look of envy, or the glare in the murderer's eye; whether it be the curse of the enemy, or the lie of the calumniator, or the slander of the gossip; whether it be the detraction of the Pharisee, or the anathema of the inquisitor, or the rivalries of the partisan; whether it be the animosities of the politician, or the jealousies of the religionist, all and every form of hatred is a positive proof that we are not of God and not of Christ. For sinlessness is the life of Christ, and sinlessness means obedience and love. God is Love. When the Christ for us is Christ in us we shall know the meaning of that truth. After this there is nothing essential to add. All is said. The last word of revelation has been spoken.

The Epistle simply closes with a swift recapitulation, which is, however, enriched with new elements, and ends with perhaps the most pregnant exhortation ever uttered : " Little children, keep yourselves from idols."

Idols still exist. Most of them are not idols *instead of* God, but idols set up as though they were God. But every true Christian must fling them to the moles and to the bats ! Those idols—not material idols, but εἴδωλα, vain subjective images—idols of the forum, the cavern, and theatre —which would represent Him as a God of arbitrary caprice, making Him treat men as though they were mere dead clay to be dashed about and destroyed, or made and marred at His will; the idols which would represent His justice as alien from ours, or things as being good in Him which would be evil in us;—those idols are shattered on the Rock of Truth that God is Righteous. Idols which represent Him as one who delights in the aggressive ignorance, self-satisfied narrowness, and bitter exclusiveness of religionists ; as making of dull and acrid bigots His sole elect, but hating the brighter, bolder, and more trustful natures—as though He loved the jagged thistles and dwarfed bents better than the rose of Sharon and the cedars of Lebanon—idols of the sectarian, idols of the fanatic, idols of the Pharisee, idols of the partisans who would label themselves as the only Christians, and all others as infidels—are shattered by the ringing hammer-stroke of the Truth that God is Light.

Idols which represent Him as living only a life " turned towards self, or folded within self "—caring only for His own glory, not caring for the creatures He has made, delighting in the smoke of unending torments, deaf to the endless shrieks of an unimaginable agony, burning as with implacable wrath against little deviations of opinion, regarding even the sin of a child as deserving of infinite punishment, be- cause though the child be finite yet He is infinite—the idols of many a schoolman, of many a theologian, of many a priest—idols of the zealot, idols of the ecclesiastic, idols of the inquisitor, who think that their wrath can work the righteousness of God—these are dashed to pieces by the unlimited force of the truth, that God is Love.

" Little children," says St. John, " keep yourselves from idols." God is Light; God is Love ! With those hammers of the word dash in pieces the Ignorance that takes itself for Infallibility, and the Hatred that forges on its phylacteries the signatures of Love.

In Himself God is Light : when His Light disperses itself in colour, it is the Universe ; when it passes in one unbroken ray, it is He who was the brightness of His glory, the Eternal Son ; reflected upon us, it is the self-communication of perfect love. The unfathomable and inconceivable fulness of life which is implied when the Evangelist tells us that God is Light is, from eternity to eternity, existent only, manifested only to us, under the modality of Love.

God is Righteous, and therefore what is morally revolting

cannot be theologically orthodox, what is morally indefensible cannot be commercially expedient, what is morally wrong cannot be politically right.

God is Light, and therefore folly, and ignorance, and prejudice, and stupidity, and superstition are to Him alien as children of the darkness.

God is Love, and therefore cold and selfish hearts can be none of His; suspicion and hatred are but unhallowed incense laid on His altars; hands which are presumptuous and fierce do but pollute the Ark which they are professing to uphold. God is Righteous: shall we be mean and unjust? God is Light: shall we love the deeds of darkness? God is Love: shall we make no sacrifice for Him who has done so much for us?

It is perhaps the very last utterance of revelation—"Little children, keep yourselves from idols!"

NOTE I.

OUTLINE OF THE EPISTLE.

In the previous discourse I have spoken of the Epistle under the three heads suggested by the great utterances, God is Light, God is Righteous, God is Love. A formal analysis of the Epistle cannot, however, be made under these heads. They throw light on the order of thought, but are not the pivots of arrangement in the writer's mind. Huther who, at De Wette's suggestion, adopted this division in Meyer's commentary, abandoned it in his second edition. Still less can we adopt Bengel's divisions made with reference to the Trinity, into which he was misled by the spurious verse about the Three Heavenly Witnesses. Certainly the Epistle illustrates the famous remark of St. Augustine, *Ubi Amor ibi Trinitas ;* but the reference to the Trinity belongs to the essence of the subject, not to the writer's intended plan.

The Epistle consists of an Exordium (i. 1-4) ; the treatment of the subject (i. 5-v. 12), and the conclusion (v. 13-21).

The general outline is as follows :—

INTRODUCTION (i. 1-4)

A. ETERNAL LIFE MANIFESTED BY THE WORD.

B. ASSURANCE OF THIS AS A CERTAIN TRUTH.

The object of setting it forth being to fulfil the joy derived by the fellowship with God and with one another of which it is the ground.

A. ETERNAL LIFE, i. 5-v. 5.

I. The evidence that we have Eternal Life is Fellowship with God, demonstrated by Walking in the Light ; for God is Light (i. 6-ii. 2).

This Walk in the Light must show itself,

    i. *Towards God*—by freedom from sin and forgiveness of past sins through the blood of Christ (i. 6-ii. 2).

    ii. *Towards man*—by brotherly love (ii. 3-13).

    iii. *Towards the world*, by severance from it, which is secured by the knowledge derived from the Spirit's unction (ii. 15-27).

II. The confidence of sonship which springs from the possession of Eternal Life (ii. 28–v. 5).

    1. The *evidence* of sonship seen in conduct (iii).

        i. Towards God, by righteousness (iii. 1–10).

        ii. Towards man, by love (iii. 11–18).

        iii. Recapitulation (19–23).

    2. The *source* of this sonship, the Spirit of God, who

        i. Saves us from false spirits by teaching us to confess (iv. 1–6), and thereby

        ii. So teaches us to love one another (7–12).

        iii. Recapitulation (14–16) and retrospective conclusion (17, 18).

III. Final Illustrations.

        Love and Faith.

        a. The idea of love embraces love both to God and man (iv. 19–21).

        β. The idea of faith involves love both to God and man (v. 1–3).

        γ. And this is victory over the world (v. 4, 5).

B. ASSURANCE THAT ETERNAL LIFE IS MANIFESTED BY THE WORD (v. 6–12).

        i. The witness of God (v. 6–9).

        ii. The witness echoed from within (10–12).

C. CONCLUSION.

    a. The conscious possession of Eternal Life—Faith, Assured Prayer, Love (v. 13–17).

    b. The signatures of sonship—sinlessness, assurance, communion (18–20).

    c. The practical aim of the Epistle (21).

Professor Westcott arranges the Epistle differently, as follows :—

INTRODUCTION (i. 1–4).

A. The Problem of Life, and those to whom it is proposed (i. 5–ii. 17).

B. The conflict of truth and falsehood without and within (ii. 18–iv. 6).

C. The Christian Life ; the victory of faith (iv. 7–v. 21).

He adds, "The thought of a fellowship between God and man, made possible and in part realised in the Christian Church, runs through the whole Epistle. From this it begins " *Our fellowship is with the Father, and with His Son Jesus Christ*" (i. 3). In this it closes : " *we are in Him that is true, in His Son, Jesus Christ* " (v. 20).

NOTE II.

STYLE.

The prevailing triplicity of arrangement is equally marked in the Epistle and in the Gospel. Owing to the Jewish training of the Apostle it was the order in which his thoughts naturally grouped themselves. Yet though the Epistle is thus obviously written by a Jew, it does not mention the Jews, nor does it once quote the Old Testament.

The style is plain ; the manner contemplative. The sentences have none of the periodic structure of classical Greek, but have an Aramaic simplicity. The method of reasoning has been called "cycloidal." It flows on by constantly taking up the chief word of the previous clause (*Anaphora*). The words are easy but the meaning is profound. St. John seems to think in antitheses ; and, in the Aramaic fashion often states truths, first positively, and then negatively. Each chief word is like a stone flung into a smooth lake, making ripples which extend to the shore in concentric circles, and these circles are broken and interlaced by the influence of other words. The difficulty of understanding St. John is due to the depth of meaning involved by his use of ordinary words ; his causal particles are often puzzling, but in his *constructions* there is generally no difficulty at all.

NOTE III.

SPECIAL PASSAGES.

ii. 6–11. *The Commandment both new and old.* The commandment "Love one another" was old as the Gospel, and even as the Old Testament ; but it became new and was invested with a new significance under the circumstances in which it was illustrated and renewed by Christ (John xiii. 34, 35, 1–20).

ii. 12–14. A six-fold appeal to Christians.

ii. 15 -19. *Antichrist and Antichrists.* The word is peculiar to St. John. The Antichrist which the Church had now to dread was no longer a Roman emperor, but the spirit of Heresy.

iii. 6. *Ideal* sinlessness.

iii. 19, 20. *God greater than our hearts.* The rendering is "We shall assure our hearts before Him, *whereinsoever* (ὅτι ἐὰν) our hearts condemn us, because God is greater than our hearts;" or else, "because, if our hearts condemn us, God is greater," omitting the second ὅτι with some MSS., or regarding it as superfluous. There are instances in Xenophon and other writers of a second ὅτι superfluously repeated, but in these cases ὅτι always means "*that*" not "because." Another way of accounting for the ὅτι has been suggested by Dr. Field in his valuable notes (*Otium Norvicense*, p. 127). It is to *understand* δῆλον (it is evident) that God is greater than our hearts. He quotes two instances from Chrysostom in which δῆλον is thus omitted before ὅτι, and another instance in 1 Tim. vi. 7, where the δῆλον of the received text is spurious, but must be understood.

iv. 3. "Every spirit which *severeth* Jesus . . is the spirit of Antichrist" (reading ὅ λύει, which has disappeared from the MSS., but existed in ancient MSS., and is so quoted by Irenaeus, Tertullian, &c.). If this reading be right, it alludes to that Antichristian element in Gnosticism which *severed* the one person of Christ by isolating either the Divine or the human nature.

v. 6–8. *He who came by means of water and blood* (one a λουτρὸν and one a λύτρον). Christ manifested Himself by virtue of the regenerating and atoning power of which the water and the blood were symbols (John xix. 34). "Why water? Why blood? Water to cleanse, blood to redeem."—AMBROSE (*De Sacr.* v. 1).

v. 7. The spurious verse about the "*Three that bear witness in heaven*" first printed (perhaps from an ancient marginal note, possibly by St. Cyprian, which had found its way into 16th century MSS.) in the Complutensian edition of 1514. It was unknown to the Greek Fathers, and does not appear in a single ancient version. It breaks the reasoning of the passage, and belongs to a totally different order of ideas. "Let them make good sense of it who are able, for my part I can make none."—SIR I. NEWTON.

v. 16. "*There is a sin unto death: I do not say that he should make request for that.*" No definite sin is meant, but some interior quality (undiscernible by man) of sin in its most desperate stage; a sin which cannot be remedied by man's prayer, though it cannot be beyond the reach of God's mercy.

NOTE IV.

GENUINENESS OF THE EPISTLE.

The genuineness of the Epistle is proved by overwhelming external evidence. It was "universally acknowledged" (Euseb. Jer.), and is referred to by Papias, Polycarp, and Irenaeus. It is mentioned in the Muratorian fragment, and found in the oldest Syriac and Latin versions. Its independent resemblance to the Gospel at once proves that it is by the same author.

It has been asserted that this Epistle differs from the other Johannine writings, because,

i. It speaks of the approaching end of the world (ii. 18, "It is the last hour"), whereas the Gospel is the only book in the N. T. which does not allude to this subject. There is, however, no real disaccord. The allusion is only a passing one and need imply no more than "the final dispensation." The writer does not speak of the personal Antichrist of Jewish eschatology (2 Thess. ii. 3–12 ; Rev. xiii.-xix.), but heretical belief is to him the Antichrist (ii. 18-22 ; iv. 3).

ii. He applies the term "Advocate" (Paraklete) to Christ (ii. 1), not as in the Gospel, to the Holy Spirit (John xiv. 16). But the *different offices* of "Advocate" belong alike to both Persons of the Blessed Trinity.

iii. He uses the word "propitiation" (ἱλασμὸς), which occurs here alone in the N. T. (iv. 10). But this word, though not used in the Gospel, belongs to the ordinary language of Christianity (Luke xviii. 13 ; Heb. ii. 17 ; Rom. iii. 25), which expressed the relation between the death of Christ and the pardon of man by this among other metaphoric expressions which describe the results of Christ's death as regards ourselves, while they never attempt scholastically to explain it *in reference to God.*

iv. He uses the word *unction* (χρίσμα), ii. 30. There is nothing strange in the fact. This term also belonged to the metaphoric usages of the Old and New Testaments (2 Cor. i. 21).

THE SECOND AND THIRD EPISTLES OF ST. JOHN.

OF UNCERTAIN DATE.

"Amor non modo verus amor est, sed veritate evangelicâ nititur."—
BENGEL.

"Superscripti Johannis duas in catholica habentur."—MURATORIAN
FRAGMENT.

THE Second and Third Epistles of St. John are in all probability specimens of the free and unreserved religious correspondence which in all ages has been interchanged between Christians. In St. Paul's letter to Philemon, and in these short missives, we have the first extant specimens of letters like those which were thenceforth constantly written by religious teachers. They begin that branch of literature which has been subsequently enriched by men like Basil, and Gregory of Nazianzus, and Gregory of Nyssa, and Jerome, and Augustine, and Gregory the Great, and Luther, and Rutherford, and Cowper, and Wesley, and Robertson, and Maurice.

There can be little doubt that the letters are genuine. There would have been no adequate reason for their forgery Their leading thoughts are so fully expressed in the other writings of St. John that they contain very little that is original or that possesses any independent dogmatic value. There is but one passage in each Epistle that can be quoted as distinctive (2 John 10, 11; 3 John 9, 10), and out of the thirteen verses in the Second Epistle eight are to be found in the first. They are chiefly interesting as giving us a glimpse of Christian correspondence in the earliest days. It may be said of them, as the Muratorian Canon says of St. Paul's letters to Timothy and Philemon, "that they were written out of private affection, and yet to the honour of the Catholic Church."

Their brevity, their casual character, and the fact that they are so unmarked by characteristic features, accounts for the circumstance that they were comparatively unknown in the early Church. Irenaeus, however, quotes from the Second Epistle. They belong as Eusebius says, to the number of the Antilegomena—the writings which were widely but not unanimously accepted as genuine.

In the school of Alexandria they were quoted by Clemens, and perhaps commented on by him in his last work, the *Hypotyposes.* Origen mentions them among the Antilegomena but does not quote from them. Dionysius of Alexandria spoke of them as being currently assigned to St. John.

In the school of Antioch they were rejected by Theodore of Mopsuestia, and are not noticed by Theodoret.

The Pseudo-Chrysostom says that the Fathers reject them from the canon (ἀποκανονίζονται). Gregory of Nazianzus mentions them doubtfully. They were not translated in the ancient Syriac version, the Peshito, but were received in the fourth century by Ephraem Syrus.

Tertullian does not quote them, nor Cyprian. In the Muratorian Canon the text is corrupt, and the testimony somewhat dubious. St. Jerome received them, but says that there were very many who attributed them to a supposed " John the Presbyter."

Perhaps no stronger external evidence could be expected, and internal evidence is strongly in their favour. They abound in Johannine phraseology, which yet is used in an independent manner; and they show the singular mixture of sternness and tenderness which arose from St. John's habit

of looking at all things at once antithetically and in the
ideal.

The analysis of the Second Epistle is very simple. After
a kindly greeting (1—3), St. John expresses to "the elect
lady" his joy that some of her children are "walking in
truth," and then enforces the new and old commandment
of Christian love (5, 6), which is all the more necessary
because of dangerous antichristian teachers against whom the
lady is warned (7—9), and to whose errors she is not to lend
the sanction of her hospitality or greeting (10, 11). The
Epistle ends with the expression of a hope that the Apostle
may soon visit her, and with a greeting from the children of
her Christian sister (12, 13).

The keynotes of the little letter are the words "Truth,"
which occurs five times, and "Love," which occurs four
times. The word "commandment" is also repeated four
times, and "walking" thrice.

Besides the general exhortation to Christian faithfulness
in doctrine and character, the motive in the letter was to
warn "the elect lady" not to welcome or to be misled by
"deceivers" and "antichrists."

The occasion of the letter was to convey the kindly
messages suggested to the Apostle by his meeting with
the lady's sister, and some of her children.

Three questions are suggested by the letter :—

1. Who is meant by "the Elder"?

2. Who is "the elect lady"?

3. What is the meaning of the distinctive message in
verse 10?

1. In the early Church there was a vague notion—perhaps
originally suggested by the title in these letters, increased by
the ambiguity in a passage of Papias, and fixed by Dionysius
of Alexandria and a remark of Eusebius [1]—that there were two
great religious teachers in Ephesus at the close of the first
century, John the Presbyter and John the Apostle. The

---

[1] Euseb. *H. E.* iii. 25 : εἴτε καὶ ἑτέρου ὁμωνύμου ἐκείνῳ.

subject is not without difficulties, but I have elsewhere given reasons for believing that this "nebulous Presbyter," this "spectral duplicate" of St. John had no real existence, and that "John the Presbyter" was none other than "John the Apostle" himself.

Without again entering into the controversy I may say that in the famous passage in which Papias gives us an account of his oral sources of information there is nothing to show that "John" and "the Presbyter John" mean two different persons. The contrast is not between two persons, but between what he heard *second-hand* as being stated by St. John and what he heard *from his own lips.* As he calls other Apostles (Andrew, Philip, Matthew, Peter), by the name "elders," in the previous clause, there is no reason (except such as arose from his own confused and simple style) to assume that he meant another John when he speaks of "John the elder." The general meaning of the passage of Papias in telling us how he composed his book is that, "he used to inquire about the discourses of the elders, what Andrew, or Philip, or John, or Matthew said, or any one of the Lord's disciples ; and to take notes of what Aristion and John the Elder say." The testimony which he derived from John—the Apostle, the Lord's disciple, the Elder—was two-fold : (*a*) reports of his conversation furnished by others, and (β) his own "living and abiding voice." Eusebius knew and states[2] that Papias had been an actual hearer of John the Apostle, and if he and others were anxious to believe that there was also another John—John the Elder—it was because they disliked the Apocalypse, and wished to find another John who might have written it.

Dionysius of Alexandria was avowedly influenced by this motive and supported his view by the fact that "some said that there were two tombs in Ephesus, each of which was called the tomb of John."

---

[1] *Early Days of Christianity,* ii. 553–586.
[2] *Ap.* Euseb. *H. E.* iii. *sq.*

Thus, then (1) we have a confused passage of Papias; (2) the guides at Ephesus had duplicate sites for the tomb of John; (3) Dionysius, writing about the middle of the third century, when John had been at least a century and a half in his grave, conjectured from this circumstance that there were perhaps two Johns; (4) Eusebius half inclines to accept the conjecture :—that is literally all the evidence we possess to show that there was any "John the Presbyter" as apart from John the Apostle! The fathers had the work of Papias in their hands and there is scarcely one of them, either Greek or Latin, who is even for a moment misled by the specious suggestion of Dionysius and the bolder implication of Eusebius.

But why does St. John call himself "The Elder"?

The term has three meanings.

a. It is used to express the dignity of age.

β. It is used to express the office of a Presbyter.

γ. It is used, especially by Papias and by later writers who refer to him, to describe the latest survivors among those who had been the actual Apostles or disciples of Christ.

The retiring character of St. John led him entirely to suppress his name in the Gospel and First Epistle. In the private letters he was naturally compelled to describe himself, but instead of choosing the high title of "Apostle," which it was not necessary for him as it was necessary for St. Paul to claim, he calls himself "the Elder" in all three of the senses mentioned above. He was a Presbyter by office, just as St. Peter calls himself the fellow-Presbyter of those to whom he wrote (1 Peter v. 1); he was an Elder by age just as St. Paul calls himself "Paul the aged";[1] and he was the last survivor of "the Elders" who could say "I have seen the Lord." The title was humble, but on the lips of St. John it connoted a position of exceptional dignity; on the other hand it would have been presumptuous for a mere Elder to

---

[1] Philem. 9. But there ὁ πρεσβύτης *may* mean the ambassador.

write as "the Elder" as though he had any special title to a then universal designation.

2. Who is the Elect Lady?

The text is not absolutely certain, but the best supported reading is τῇ ἐκλεκτῇ κυρίᾳ.

i. Athanasius says, "he is writing to Kyria and her children." Can we then render it "to the elect Kyria"? There was such a name as Kyria, for it is found in an inscription, and it might be a Greek form of the Hebrew "Martha." But St. John would then (almost certainly) have written not "to the elect Kyria" but "to Kyria the elect."[1] Further than this, in verse 5, "I beseech thee, Kyria," would have been a most unusual mode of address.

ii. Clement of Alexandria understood it to mean "to the lady Eclecta." He says, "It was written to a Babylonian lady named Eclecta." But in this case verse 13 ought to mean, "The children of thy sister Eclecta greet thee," and both sisters could hardly have had the same name. The name Eclecta does not seem to occur anywhere, and further St. John would then have written "to Eclecta the lady" (Ἐκλεκτῇ τῇ κυρίᾳ).

iii. The rendering therefore, "to the Elect lady" is correct. But is the letter addressed (a) to a lady; or (β) to a Church called by this title; or (γ) to the Church in general?

γ. That the letter is addressed to the Church in general (though suggested by Jerome, who fantastically referred to Cant. vi. 9 LXX.), may be dismissed at once. It is rendered impossible by verse 13.

β. The notion that a single Church is addressed is suggested by Œcumenius and Theophylact, and adopted by Huther, Ewald, Wordsworth, and many modern editors. It is supported by a reference to the uncertain allusion in 1 Peter v. 13, and it has even been (on no ground whatever) conjectured by different writers that the Church referred to is Corinth, or Philadelphia, or Jerusalem, or Patmos, or Ephesus, or Babylon!

---

[1] Comp. 3 John i., Γαίῳ τῷ ἀγαπητῷ. Rom. xvi. 13, Ῥοῦφον τὸν ἐκλεκτόν.

If a Church was intended we can give no reason whatever for the adoption of a style so needlessly euphuistic, so alien from Apostolic simplicity. A Church certainly might be called " the bride of Christ," but the word "Lady" is nowhere applied to the Church, still less is there any trace of correspondence between Churches under the title of "ladies."[1]

a. It is most natural therefore and simple to take the letter in its obvious sense, and to suppose that the Apostle is writing to a Christian lady and her children "whom," he says, " I love in the truth." The " I," is emphatically repeated in the original (οὕς ἐγὼ ἀγαπῶ) but it cannot be safely inferred from this that others regarded this family with different feelings. In one of his visits of supervision among the Churches of Asia he had stayed at the home of this lady's sister and there met " some of her children." Pleased to find that they were faithful Christians, and worthy of a family which (speaking in ordinary language) he says that " all Christians know and love,"[2] he writes to the Christian mother to congratulate her. Women like Priscilla, Lydia, Phoebe, and Persis played no small part in the early spread of the Gospel, and St. John would naturally feel a deep sympathy with them as he did with the young. The delicate suppression of the individual name in a letter which might probably be read aloud in the Christian assembly is perfectly explicable.

3. But St. John thought it right to give a special warning to this lady, and through her to the Church to which she belonged. Many " deceivers " and many " Antichrists " were abroad. By those terms St. John meant men who taught false and heretical views about Christ; as that He was a mere man; or that "Jesus" and "Christ" were different beings; or that the human life of Jesus was a mere illusive semblance.

---

[1] Hilgenfeld, *Einleit.* 686, thinks that the name κυρία might be applied to a Church from a misunderstanding of the LXX. in Is. xl. 10, μετὰ κυρίας.

[2] This expression has been used to show that St. John cannot be writing to a lady. Why not? Why, for instance, might not any religious teacher say to an esteemed and beloved correspondent "you whom all Christians love"?

Now the Church was full of wandering teachers, some of whom were designing men who deliberately spread erroneous doctrines. St. Paul, St. Peter, St. Jude had all raised against such teachers a warning voice. But they were specially apt to creep in unawares, and most of all into the houses of widows, and of those whom in a passage of intense severity St. Paul calls " womanlings, laden with sins, led away by divers desires " (2 Timothy iii. 6), whom they " took captive " by their wiles. Not to such a class of women did " the Elect Lady" belong ; but since it was the rule and the duty of Christians to support and to receive into their houses the missionaries of the Gospel, St. John warns her that she must not show this hospitality, nor give the deeper fraternal greeting, to those who would claim it as a sanction, and abuse it for the furtherance of fundamental heresy.[1]

This text—torn from its context, severed from its historic meaning—has been terribly abused. It tells ill for the spirit of Christians that from the earliest days the one verse almost exclusively quoted from this Epistle of love by the Apostle of love has been a verse which has been perverted into a plausible excuse for religious hate.[2] It is so easy to fulfil *this* precept, so difficult to obey the new and old commandment which is the end of all the law ! On the strength of this text John a Lasco having been expelled from England with his congregation in the reign of Queen Mary in 1553, was refused admission into Denmark. On the strength of this text, among the misguided fanatics of Münster, " all intercourse with the ' pagans ' was strictly forbidden. Those who received the new baptism alone were ' Saints.' " It is thus that Cornelius à Lapide, in a spirit the very opposite to all the teachings of Christ and all the lessons of the New Testament, quotes this text to forbid " all conversation, all

---

[1] In verse 9, the true reading is πᾶς ὁ προάγων. "Every one who goes in advance" *i.e.* who enters into unauthorised and misguiding speculations such as those which St. Paul condemns (1 Tim. vi. 4 ; 2 Tim. ii. 14, 16).

[2] It was quoted by an African Bishop, Aurelius, in an African Council in Cyprian's days.

intercourse, all dealings with heretics," an inference which if it were not (happily) set at naught by the common sense and right feeling of Christians would prevent all Roman Catholics and all Protestants from being even on speaking terms with each other. It is thus that the ocean of evil passions excluded by the whole spirit of the Gospel is suffered to come flooding in through the narrow aperture of a misinterpreted text. It is thus that,

> "The devil can quote Scripture for his purpose,"

and, in Scriptural phrase, lay at Heaven's door his evil off-spring of wrath and strife.[1] It is thus that we teach aliens to blaspheme; but

> "Having waste ground enough,
> Shall we desire to rase the sanctuary
> And pitch our evils there?"

---

[1] Sceptics, eagerly adopting the exaggerations and misapplications of texts by Christians, exult over these passages as breathing "the deplorable spirit of dogmatic intolerance" (Renan); and others quote it as a proof that the Epistle must be spurious, as proving that St. John had failed to learn the lesson which Christ Himself had inculcated (Luke ix. 50). Such remarks and inferences would be perfectly justifiable if we were obliged to understand St. John in the sense which religious partisans have given to his narrowly limited and perfectly intelligible caution.

THE THIRD EPISTLE OF ST. JOHN.

"Ex operibus cognoscitur valetudo animae et hanc prosequentur vota sanctorum."—BENGEL.

THIS Epistle is even slighter in texture than the former, and much of it resembles other passages of St. John (John xix. 35, xxi. 24, 2 John 12, &c.).

It is addressed "to Gaius the beloved." After a greeting and a prayer that he may prosper in all respects,[1] and be in health, the elder commends his sincere faithfulness (2—4), and especially his hospitality (5—8).[2] After a complaint and warning to domineering Diotrephes (9—10), whom Gaius is not to imitate, St. John bears testimony to the worth of Demetrius (12, 13), and then ends the letter with a salutation, because he hopes soon to see Gaius and does not wish to write any more (13—15). The closing words "salute the friends by name," if they be the last words which we possess from the pen of St. John, accord well with his last famous and beautiful traditional utterance :—

> "Filioli, diligite alterutrum.
> "Little children, love one another."

Who Gaius was is entirely unknown. It was the commonest of Roman names. It was used in the Roman law books for "so-and-so," like our John Doe and Richard Roe. In St. Paul's letters we have no less than three Gaiuses: Gaius of Macedonia (Acts xix. 29), Gaius of Derbe (Acts xx. 4),

---

[1] περὶ πάντων. Not "above all things" as in A. V.
[2] Both φιλαδελφία and φιλοξενία (verse 5).

and a Gaius of Corinth (Rom. xvi. 4) who, like St. John's
correspondent, was famous for the necessary duty of Christian
hospitality.[1] The Gaius to whom St. John writes may be
the Bishop of Pergamum mentioned in the Apostolic
Constitutions.[2]

The word "Truth"—reality, sincerity, orthodoxy—occurs
no less than six times in these few verses.

From this Epistle, as from various allusions in St. Paul, we
get an interesting glimpse of the early missionaries. Some
who called themselves by this name were false teachers,
against whom in the last Epistle, the Christian lady is warned.
Some, as we see from what St. Paul says to the Corinthians
(2 Cor. xi. 26), acted with an insolence and rapacity truly
outrageous. But the true missionaries were full of self-
sacrifice "for the Name" and, like St. Paul, would take
nothing from the Gentiles (verse 7). Hence it would have
been impossible for them to do their work at all, if the houses
of Christian friends had not been freely opened to them.
Gaius is justly praised for his ready hospitality. He has
sped them on their journey ($\pi\rho o\pi\acute{\epsilon}\mu\psi as$) "worthily of God"
($\grave{a}\epsilon\acute{\iota}\omega s\ \tau o\hat{v}\ \theta\epsilon o\hat{v}$). It is a truly Christian task to further the
good work which we cannot personally undertake.

This little note furnishes us with two contrasted pictures
which St. John etches in a few words with the same masterly
pyschological skill which we see in the Gospel.

1. One is domineering Diotrephes. He is represented as a
turbulent intriguer who rejects St. John's authority; babbles
($\phi\lambda\nu a\rho\hat{\omega}\nu$, garrulous) against him with wicked words; refused
to receive the friends and messengers who came with com-
mendatory letters from him; and not content with this, did
his best to prevent others from receiving them and even
wished to excommunicate them. St. John had written
something to the Church of which this man was a Presbyter,

---

[1] Rom. xii. 13 ; 1 Tim. iii. 2 ; Tit. i. 8 ; Heb. xiii. 2 ; 1 Pet. iv. 9.
[2] St. John prays that he may be "in health." This was a common Stoic
greeting, but was not common among Christians. Perhaps Gaius had weak
health.

but apparently Diotrephes had suppressed it. St. John warns him that when he comes, he will bring his ill-doings to remembrance before the Church. Perhaps his special reason for writing to Gaius was that Gaius had welcomed the travelling brethren whom Diotrephes had tried to turn away.

It has been thought impossible that any Presbyter should have had the audacity to act in this way towards an Apostle of the age, dignity and supreme authority of St. John. But early Church history is full of surprises, and the figure of Diotrephes is recognisable in the Church in all ages. If St. Paul had to contend with a Phygellus and an Alexander (1 Timothy i. 20), a Hymenaeus and a Philetus (2 Timothy ii. 17, 18), and with other nameless opponents actuated by the most virulent spirit of antagonism, in Rome, Corinth and Galatia, why should not St. John have met with a Diotrephes? If there were men who could forge letters which purported to come from St. Paul (2 Thess. ii. 2, iii. 17), why should not a Diotrephes suppress a few lines (ii. verse 9) written by St. John? The brief missive has been lost like many others which the Apostles must have written.[1]

2. A very different person was Demetrius, possibly the bearer of this letter. All bore witness to his character, and St. John himself ratified the universal testimony.

Thus even in these few lines we have vivid presentations of Gaius, Diotrephes, and Demetrius. They also afford us an interesting glimpse into the history of the early Church, its missionary activity and its hospitable unselfishness, but at the same time the growth of factions and of self-asserting ambition among its leading teachers. If we are surprised and shocked to see this early fading of the orange-flower and staining and rending of the white and seamless robe of the Bride of Christ, we have at the same time a valuable indication that room was left in the Church for a spirit of independence, and that

---

[1] 3 John 9. There is a reading ἔγραψα ἄν, and the Vulg. has *scripsissem forsitan.* The change of reading is probably due to the desire to exclude the notion that any letter by an Apostle could be lost.

while the abuse of that spirit was repressed by the high personal authority of the last Apostle, the independence itself is left unrestrained, because where the Spirit of the Lord is, there also is and must be liberty.

St. John would have had much more to say, but prefers to say it "mouth to mouth," not by "ink and reed." Probably he was unaccustomed to, and disliked the physical toil of writing, specially in his old age. He has said the same to the Elect Lady. Possibly too it may not have been always easy to procure papyrus, especially if St. John was writing from his little isle of retreat in Patmos.[1]

[1] The newly-discovered teaching of the Twelve Apostles shows us a state of society which in many respects resembles that described in this brief Epistle.

THE REVELATION OF ST. JOHN.

THE REVELATION OF ST. JOHN.

WRITTEN IN PATMOS PROBABLY ABOUT A.D. 68.

"Poi vidi . . . . . un vecchio solo
Venir dormendo, con la faccia arguta."
—DANTE, *Purgat.* xxix. 142, 143.

πάντα δὲ ταῦτα ἀρχὴ ὠδίνων.—MATT. xxiv. 8.

"Sub Nerone damnatio invaluit."—TERTULLIAN.

"The poet says, 'Dear city of Cecrops;' wilt thou not say, 'Dear City of
God'?"—MARC. AURELIUS.

"*Rome shall perish!* write that word
In the blood that she has spilt ;
Perish, hopeless and abhorred,
Deep in ruin as in guilt."—COWPER.

"Yea, I come quickly."—REV. xxii. 20.

THE Apocalypse, or Revelation of Jesus Christ to St. John, REVELATION.
though it stands last in the order of our Canon, was the
earliest, not the latest, of the writings of the Evangelist.
Misled by an ambiguous passage of Irenaeus, in which it is
not impossible that he fell into some confusion between
Domitius (Nero) and Domitian, many ancient and modern
writers have regarded it as the last utterance of special
inspiration. But the whole force of modern criticism tends
to correct the ancient error.[1] Internal evidence sufficiently

---

[1] If Irenaeus made a mistake in this matter it is by no means his only one.
In matters of fact he is very far from being a certain guide. It is, however,
possible that he is assigning the date of *St. John's closing days* to the reign of
Domitian, and not the date of the Apocalypse. Tertullian, Epiphanius, a
Syriac MS., Theophylact the author of the *Life of Timotheus*, of which ex-
tracts are preserved in Photius, Andreas and Arethas (the earliest Apocalyptic
commentators), probably also Clement of Alexandria and Origen indicate the
reign of Nero as the epoch at which the Apocalypse was written: and this is

REVELATION. proves that the book could not have been written after the fall of Jerusalem, and the writer all but states in so many words that he is writing in the brief reign of Galba.[1] It must be regarded as a psychological impossibility that St. John should have written the Gospel in extreme old age in Greek, which, though unidiomatic in structure, is comparatively pure ; and yet, some years later, should have written the Apocalypse in Greek, more rugged and solecistic than that of any other book in the New Testament, and even than all but the very worst parts of the Septuagint. It is still more impossible psychologically that St. John should have retrogressed from the supreme calmness and absolute spirituality of the Gospel and the first Epistle to the cruder symbolism, the tumultuous agitation, the intenser Judaism, the fiercer denunciations, the more human tone and the more imperfect treatment of the Apocalypse. It would be nothing short of a retrogression to pass from the abstract and absolute forms in which the Gospel and Epistle set forth to us the conflict of good with evil, to the kabbalism of numbers and the symbolism of strange figures; from the most ethereal regions of Christian thought to scarlet dragons and hell-born frogs; from realms of spiritual assurance, in which the pure azure of contemplation seems to be unstained by any earthly cloud to dim images of plague and war, in which cries of vengeance ring through an atmosphere which is lurid with fire and blood. The last words of the New Covenant Inspiration were not heard in this tumultuous record of eclipse and earthquake, even though the Divine tragedy (as Milton says) shuts up and intermingles her solemn scenes and acts with a sevenfold chorus of hallelujahs

the view of Grotius, Hammond, Lücke, Schwegler, Baur, Hilgenfeld, Züllig, De Wette, Bunsen, Neander, Auberlen, Ewald, Bleek, Krenkel, Volkmar, Stier, Weiss, Düsterdieck, Schaff, Reuss, Réville, Renan, Aubé, De Pressensé, Maurice, Moses Stuart, Desprez, Dr. S. Davidson, Bishop Lightfoot, Westcott, and many others.

[1] Rev. xiii. 3 ; xvii. 10, 11. The former of these passages alludes to the death and resuscitation of Nero (partially fulfilled at least in Domitian, who was regarded as *Nero redivivus*) ; the latter to the five Emperors who preceded Galba, namely, Augustus, Tiberius, Gaius, Claudius, Nero. This would give the date in the summer or autumn of A.D. 68.

and harping symphonies; but the voice of the Spirit, as REVELATION. heard in Scripture, breathed its last tones in the two united books which tell us that "The Word was made flesh," and that "God is Love." In the Apocalypse[1] John was still a Son of Thunder; in the Gospel the red flames of youth have become a pure and steady glow of love.[2]

It must not be thought for a moment that in thus speaking we are disparaging the Apocalypse, which, in its own proper sphere, in its own historical connexion, in its proper interpretation, in its own due place in the economy of revelation, shines with a splendour of its own. It is a book of war, but the war ends in triumph and peace.[3] It is a book of thunder, but the rolling of the thunder dies away in liturgies and psalms.[4]

---

[1] The fundamental theology of the Apocalypse and of the later writings is the same, as has been carefully and fully shown in Gebhardt's *Doctrine of the Apocalypse*, and as even Baur admits when he calls the Gospel a spiritualised Apocalypse (*Die Evang.* p. 380). In both Christ is represented as the victim Lamb. (The ἀρνίον of the Apocalypse is perhaps chosen, rather than the word ἀμνὸs of the Gospel, as the best antithesis to θηρίον.) In both He is called "the Word." In both we read of the Living Water. Both give prominence to the prophecy of Zechariah (xii. 10), "They shall look on Him whom they have pierced"; both, in this quotation, diverge in the same way from the LXX. There are many isolated resemblances of phrase and construction (see xiii. 13, 16), and in relation to many doctrines an identity of essence underlies the dissimilarity of form. Yet there is also a wide difference between these writings. The material eschatology of the Apocalypse becomes in the Gospel and Epistle a spiritual consummation. In the Apocalypse Christ is rather the Judge and the Avenger than the Good Shepherd. The Antichrist of the Apocalypse is Nero; the Antichrists of the later writings are incipient Gnostics. In the Apocalypse Heaven is a future splendour; in the later writings a present and living realisation of eternal life. In the Apocalypse the persecuted Christians are consoled with the promise of what shall be; in the later writings with the knowledge of what is. See among others, Lechler, *Apost. Zeitalt.* 199-201. Reuss, *Hist. de la Théol. Chrét.* ii. 564-571. Ewald, *Johan. Schriften,* ii. 1, 52, 53, 62, 63; Düsterdieck, pp. 73-80, and *Early Days of Christianity,* ii. 179-323. These differences, on the hypothesis of the same author, can only be accounted for on the supposition that more than twenty years elapsed between the time when St. John wrote the Apocalypse when he was, so to speak, emerging from the synagogue (Rev. ii. 9; iii. 9; xi. 1, 19, &c.), and the ripe old age when after the Fall of Jerusalem, and with all the enlightenment which dawned on his mind, in consequence of the development of Christian history, he left to the Church the precious legacy of his last writings.

[2] Weiss, *Leben Jesu,* i. 101.

[3] "War" occurs in the Apocalypse nine times; and only seven times in the rest of the New Testament. "To war" occurs six times, and only once (Jas. iv. 2) in the rest of the New Testament.

[4] Comp. Renan, *L'Antichrist,* p. 381.

We could ill afford to lose—all Christian thought would be the poorer if we lost—this superb and stormy protest against the apparent triumph of evil ; this magnificent and tempestuous assertion of hopes which no darkness could extinguish, no seas of blood could drown. Each part and each form of revelation has its own necessary function, and must be considered relatively to the whole of which it is an essential part. The apocalyptic form of literature, so popular in the first century, was acknowledged by the Jews to be generically inferior to the prophetic. They did not dream of placing the Book of Daniel on a level with the Prophecy of Isaiah. The Apocalypse is the "Daniel" of the New Testament, and we shall wilfully throw away the sole key to its interpretation if we do not interpret it by the well-recognised principles which dominate the whole literature of which it is a specimen. In its imagery, in its scope, in its expressions, it is closely analogous, not only to the Book of Daniel, but also to the nearly contemporary apocalypses of the Books of Enoch, Esdras, and Baruch, the Assumption of Moses, the Shepherd of Hermas, and the Pseudo-Sibylline oracles. Every one of these books, without exception, describes, in certain recognised cycles of imagery, events which were either actually or nearly synchronous with the publication of the books themselves. Their vaticinations were never intended to be understood as anticipated history. The predictive element belongs only to their literary form. They were, and were only meant to be, applications of eternal principles to contemporary facts. Their object is didactic and practical, not predictive. An Apocalypse is essentially and of necessity a cryptograph to the uninitiated, though it would have been valueless and would have entirely failed of its purpose if it had not been intelligible to the readers for whom it was meant. The form of these writings was due originally and chiefly to the dangers of the times. We see in reading Josephus how constantly he has to be on his guard against the peril of awaking the jealous susceptibilities of his Roman readers, although he stood to them in so friendly a relation, and was under the REVELATION. immediate protection and patronage of the Flavian emperors. If a traitorous Jew like Josephus had to be careful when he stood merely on the neutral ground of history; if even Peter has to allude to Rome under the name "Babylon;" if St. Paul could only refer dimly to "the checker" and "the check," and "the man of sin" in language of studied reticence and obscurity; if (as has been conjectured) St. Luke broke off the Acts at a point beyond which it became perilous to describe the relation of Christianity to the Empire—how could St. John have possibly written of such days as those of Nero without the utmost peril, not only to himself, but to the whole Christian community, if he had not veiled his conceptions in a form which would have seemed grotesque and meaningless to heathen informers? If these circumstances had received their proper weight—if the necessary conditions of all apocalyptic literature had been duly borne in mind—this book would not have been treated as a repellent enigma which could only be abandoned to fanatical interpreters. The shocking series of misinterpretations to which it has been subjected—the reactionary sense of impatience, and even of dislike, which it has inspired—its positive and determined rejection, not only by Alogi and Antichiliasts, but by some eminent Christian writers in all ages, from the days of the Presbyter Gaius, Dionysius of Alexandria, and Eusebius of Caesarea, to those of Erasmus, Zwingli, and Luther, and from the Reformation down to Scaliger, Lowth, South, Schleiermacher, and Goethe [1]—have been due to the rejection

---

[1] Dionysius of Alexandria says that the Alogi "jeered" at the Apocalypse (χλευάζοντες), and that many criticised and condemned it with extreme severity. Gaius and others attributed it to Cerinthus. It is omitted from the Canon of the Council of Laodicea (A.D. 363). Junilius tells us that the Eastern Church had great doubts about it. Primasius in the sixth century confesses that there was much in it which he could not comprehend. Jerome and Augustine speak of its obscurity. The dislike of the ancient Church to the narrow literalism of the Millenarians prejudiced them against the book. Cardinal Cajetan says that he could not interpret it literally. Zwingli regarded it as non-Biblical (*"Dann es nit ein biblisch Buch ist"*). Tyndale wrote no preface to it. Luther calls it "a dumb prophecy," and said that Christ could neither be learnt nor recognised in it. Gravina thought that its exegesis involved danger. De Wette said that whole chapters of it were like

by the instinctive feeling of Christians of the conflicting schemes of exegesis which have distorted this book, page after page, into a clumsy, fantastic, and impossible approximation to events, religious and secular, during the nineteen Christian centuries. Men have felt that the very conception of prophecy would have been degraded by a minute praedescription of future history, and that the very basis of charity was overthrown by the "loud-lunged anti-Babylonianisms" of "heated pulpiteers," each hurling at the other the conflicting anathemas of their religious partisanship. Nothing but offence and degradation could be the issue of principles of exposition—the outcome often of confident ignorance and bitter intolerance—which applied "the single eagle" or "angel" of Rev. vii. 13 to the Holy Spirit, to Pope Gregory the Great, to St. John, to St. Paul, and to Christ;—which interpreted the fallen star of ix. 1 as an evil spirit, or the Beast, Eleazer, or Arius, or Origen (!), or Romulus Augustulus, or the Emperor Valens, or Hildebrand, or Mohammed, or Napoleon;—which made the locusts imply Saracens, the mendicant orders, Jesuits, or Protestants;—and in which the Seven Thunders were the seven Crusades, or seven Protestant kingdoms, or the Papal Bull of Leo X. against Luther! Such systems and such methods of interpretation are things of the past. We may be confident that no such anachronism will again be perpetrated by any competent writer. It is now becoming a more and more universal conviction that the Book of Revelation deals with the events by which its composition was suggested; that its symbols have no direct connexion with the accidental analogies for which modern history has been ransacked; that it is not an enigmatic anticipation of Gibbon, or Milman, or Neander and Gieseler, breathing of theological hatred and sectarian animosity; that in writing to the Churches of Asia about the "three frogs"

empty vials. Düsterdieck calls it deutero-canonical. Adam Clarke said that he could not pretend to explain it. Robert South even ventured to say in one of his sermons that "the more it was studied, the less was it understood, as generally either finding a man cracked or leaving him so."

which came from the mouth of the Dragon, the Beast, and REVELATION.
the False Prophet, St. John was not indicating either the
French Revolution or " the growth of Tractarianism ; " finally,
that if the anticipations of the Seer have " germinant and
springing developments," it is because his book describes the
never-ending conflict of Christ with Antichrist of which the
world's history is full, and because all eternal principles are
capable of infinite applications. As the key to the Book of Daniel
lies in the recognition of Antiochus Epiphanes as " the little
horn," so the key to the contemporary interpretation of the
Apocalypse has not been flung either into the Sea of Patmos
or the Maeander, but lies in the identification of Nero with
the Wild Beast, which is now accepted by almost every one
of the leading critics in England, Germany, and France.[1]

The true grandeur of the Apocalypse lies in its applicability
to the terrible days in which it was written, and in the fact
that it expressed the inextinguishable hopes and indomitable
courage of Christianity when Christians first found themselves face to face with such perils as had never before been
dreamt of. " Without tears," says Bengel, " it was not
written ; without tears it cannot be understood." It is rather
a paean of exultation poured forth out of the midst of
anguish than " a *miserere* wrung from mighty grief." The
words in which it was written as they sprang fresh and burning from the heart of the Seer, passed, fresh and burning, in
all the full force of their then intelligible symbols, into the
hearts of those to whom they appealed. It was not written
to inflate the spiritual pride, and gratify the speculative
curiosity of handfuls of Christians in Smyrna and Laodicea,
by setting forth in a mass of fantastic enigmas and monstrous
symbols the career of Theodosius or Mohammed, or the
Mediaeval Papacy, but—in exact conformity with the laws
which governed the strange form of literature to which it

---

[1] The healing of the death-wounded head, and the phrases " which was, and
is not, and is about to come out of the abyss," and " he is an eighth, and is
of the seventh " are allusions to the universally believed escape or future
resuscitation of Nero. Ideally it was more than fulfilled in Domitian.

belonged—it was meant to tell them in what spirit they should face the human Antichrists of Pagan Rome—"the world rulers of this darkness"—the deadly combination of a Judaism and a Paganism, each at the nadir of their degradation, yet arrayed side by side in their sanguinary decadence to overwhelm and murder them. It was a rallying cry to the armies of Christ, at the moment when they seemed to be trampled in irremediable defeat; it was meant to show them in what light they were to regard the Neronian Persecution and the Jewish Rebellion. It expressed the thoughts of men who had seen Peter crucified and Paul beheaded. It is "the thundering reverberation of a mighty spirit" struck into stormy music by the plectrum of apparent overthrow. To understand it rightly we must read it by the lurid light of the bale-fires of martyrdom as they flared upon the palace-gardens of the Beast from the abyss. We must try to feel as Christians felt when they saw their brethren torn by the wild beasts of the amphitheatre, or standing as living torches, each in his pitchy tunic, on one ghastly night at Rome. Such a book was needed in the awful days when men saw an Antichrist, a wicked human god, sitting absolute, and slavishly adored upon the throne of the civilised world; when the Devil, the Beast, and the False Prophet, were holding foul orgies in the streets of the mystic Babylon, red with the blood of the martyrs of the Lord. It was written in days of earthquakes, and inundations, and volcanic outbursts, and horrible prodigies. Emperor after emperor was perishing by poison, suicide, or slaughter. Alike Rome and Jerusalem had been deluged with massacre. Men were gnawing their tongues with pain and terror. The sun of human life seemed to be setting amid seas of blood; the air was full of the vultures of retribution as they gathered to the carcass of decadent societies with the rushing of their abominable wings. At such an hour—perhaps the dimmest and the most disastrous which ever fell upon an afflicted world—the Seer still prophesies triumphantly of the coming dawn.

At such an hour of visitation—while earth seemed to reel REVELATION. under the stroke of her judgments, and the stars of heaven to be shaken from their places as the fig-tree sheddeth its ripe figs—when the little bands of the faithful were fleeing to the mountains from the horrors of doomed Jerusalem, or being crushed to earth under the iron heels of murderous Rome—he sings the dirge of expiring anarchies and dead religions, but the simultaneous birth of a new order, the brightness of a new heaven and a new earth, the ultimate victory of peace and holiness, the descent from heaven of the New Jerusalem, like a bride adorned for her husband. The agonies of his time were but "the woes of the Messiah"— the travail-throes of the future age. The key to the whole Apocalypse is the repeated promise, "The time is at hand!" "Behold, I come!" "I come quickly!" "Maran atha— The Lord is at hand!" The Book by its very title implies a manifestation of Christ.

The essential ideas and entire structure of the Apocalypse show us those deep and subtle resemblances in the midst of difference which deepen our conviction that in reading the Apocalypse we are reading an earlier book by the author of the Gospel. It was the mental habit of St. John to regard all the facts of life and religion in absolute antitheses, and this book is from end to end the development of an antithetic parallelism. It shows us the struggle of good and evil, of light and darkness. Every Divine archetype has its hideous or blasphemous parody. There is God and Satan; there is the Lamb and the Wild Beast; there is the Harlot City and the New Jerusalem; there is Michael and the Dragon; there is heaven and the abyss; there are the armies of the saints and the armies of idolaters: there is the Trinity of Heaven and the "Triad of anti-Christianity," the Trinity of Hell.

The outline of the book is as follows:

After the Prologue, which occupies the first eight verses, there follow seven sections.

1. The letters to the Seven Churches of Asia (i. 9—iii. 22).

2. The Seven Seals (iv.—vii.).

3. The Seven Trumpets (viii.—xi.).

4. The Seven Mystic Figures—

The Sun-clothed Woman; the Red Dragon; the Man-child; the Wild Beast from the Sea; the Wild Beast from the Land; the Lamb on Mount Sion; the Son of Man on the Cloud (xii.—xiv.).

5. The Seven Vials (xv.—xvi.).

6. The Doom of the Foes of Christ (xvii.—xx.).

7. The Blessed Consummation (xxi.—xxii. 7). The Epilogue (xxii. 8—21).

The letters to the Churches are normally sevenfold, consisting of the address, the title of the speaker, the encomium, the reproof, the warning, the promise, and the solemn appeal. Each Church represents a different phase of Christian life. Two—Smyrna, faithful amid Jewish persecutions, Philadelphia, faithful and militant—receive unmingled praise; two—Sardis, slumbering, though not past awakenment, Laodicea, proud and lukewarm—receive unmitigated reproof; three—Ephesus, faithful, though waxing cold, Pergamum, faithful amid heathen persecutions, but with Antinomian temptations, Thyatira, faithful, but too tolerant of Antinomian seductions —are addressed in terms of mingled praise and blame.

Then begins the Apocalyptic section of the book. A splendid vision burns before the eyes of the Seer. He sees the Throne of God and the Immortalities (ζῶα) of Heaven. On the right of Him who sat on the throne lies a seven-sealed book, which none is found worthy to unseal but the Lion of the Tribe of Judah, the Lamb that was slain. Amid an universal outburst of triumph and blessing He takes the book, and opens it seal by seal.

As each seal is opened there is a fresh vision.

The first is opened, and a crowned rider springs forth on a white horse conquering and to conquer, armed with a bow, to smite his enemies, not as yet in close conflict, but from afar. It is the symbol of the Christ.

The second is opened, and War rides forth on a fiery horse. REVELATION. It is a symbol of the internecine conflicts which at that epoch raged alike in Judea and in the Roman world.

The third is opened, and Famine on a black horse rides forth unarmed, but with a balance in his hand, and uttering an edict of awful scarcity. It indicates an epoch scourged by famines severe and almost continuous, which filled Rome with alarm and misery, and reduced Jerusalem to the horrors of murder and cannibalism.

The fourth is opened, and Death rides forth on a livid horse, followed by Hades to receive the prey. It is the symbol of pestilence and other scourges. In Rome in the days of Nero a pestilence slew 30,000 of the inhabitants in a single year. At Jerusalem from this and other causes there was " a glut of mortality," from which it is calculated that during the siege there perished not less than one million souls.

The fifth is opened, and the souls of the martyrs in the Neronian persecution—which is called " the great tribulation"—cry for vengeance, and are bidden to wait a while.

The sixth is opened, and there is an outburst of signs lurid and terrible, which usher in the Day of the Lord, in the imminent destruction of Jerusalem, and the close of the Old Dispensation.

Before the seventh seal is opened the servants of God are sealed upon their foreheads, and there is an awful pause. Then to the seven great Angels are given trumpets to blow the signal blasts of doom. A censer filled with fire from the altar is hurled down to earth, and thunders and voices echo its crashing fall. The judgments which follow the blast of each trumpet represent the widening spread and more tragical incidence of judgments similar to the former—which however are neither definite nor continuous nor rigidly historical. These visions—retrogressive and iterative, like those of Pharaoh and of Joseph and of Daniel—no longer affect a fourth part but a third part of the earth ; that is, they afflict the Roman Empire as symbolising the whole Pagan world.

They recur in cycles, but constantly deepen in intensity. The trumpet-judgments represent in terrifying and colossal images the catastrophes which marked that epoch. We read in the history of that period about storms and inundations, earthquakes and devastations of hail, internecine civil wars, the bloodshed of battles which stained the rivers and seas, the poisoning of springs and fountains, the overthrow and assassination of rulers, the carnage, the riotous wickedness, the demoniac frenzy and indescribable anguish, the gathering hosts of cavalry and infantry, the siege of Jerusalem, the anticipated Parthian invasions, the epidemics of massacre unparalleled in all the rest of history. What else can we make of these burning mountains flung down into seas of blood; the great star Absinth, which makes the waters bitter; this smiting with darkness of the sun and moon and stars;—these scorpion-locusts swarming out of the abyss; these two hundred million horsemen, breast-plated with fiery jacinth, and riding on lion-headed steeds, who, with their flames and amphisbaena-stings, slay the third part of men who do not repent? These strange scenes are described in symbols suggested by the Plagues of Egypt and the old prophets, and are repeated in other Apocalyptic books of this period. They either imply nothing to which we can attach any definite significance, or they are pictures of events synchronous, or imminent, or anticipated, seen through the lurid and blood-red mist of cryptographic images, and described in the familiar hyperboles of Semitic metaphor. The trumpets are a sketch of contemporary calamities written in language which is a hundred-fold reverberation of the woes depicted by Isaiah and Joel, and the prophets of Judah and Israel in ancient days.

Then follows an episode which has never been fully understood. An angel of sun-like face, robed in clouds, and crowned with the rainbow, descends with a little book in his hand, and when he speaks in the voice as of a lion seven thunders utter things which the Seer is forbidden to write. The Angel swears with uplifted hand that at the seventh trumpet-blast the mystery of God shall be finished. The REVELATION. Seer is bidden to eat the roll. In his mouth it is sweet as honey; in his belly it is bitter. This imagery seems to imply that much of the future is to be left in mystery, and that the things which are to be revealed will have commingled the bitterness of judgment and the sweetness of consolation. The six seals have affected the fourth part of all mankind; after the sealing of the servants of God (*i.e.*, the members of the Christian Church) the six trumpets affect only Jews and Pagans. Before the seventh trumpet, after the measuring of the Temple, the preaching, martyrdom, and resuscitation of the two witnesses, and the great earthquake which shakes down a tenth part of their city, the remnant of the Jews repent and give glory to God. The total failure of any Christian commentator in any age to do more than guess at the significance of these symbols, and the complete variance of the explanations suggested for them, shows that they belong to the subordinate and less essential elements of the book. If neither Irenaeus the hearer of Polycarp, nor Polycarp the hearer of St. John, nor the learned schools of Alexandria and Antioch, nor Augustine, nor Jerome, nor Andreas, nor Arethas, have succeeded in throwing the least light on the definite historic meaning of these symbols, it is impossible—and therefore must be needless—for us to do more than to try and grasp such eternal principles as they, no less than the rest of the book, consistently imply.

The next vision, on the other hand, is retrospective and perfectly clear. A star-crowned woman, representing the ideal Church of Israel, brings forth a man-child, who symbolises partly the Messiah, partly the Christian Church. A scarlet dragon, with seven diademed heads and ten horns— an emblem of Satan as represented by the Roman Empire with its seven successive Emperors and its ten Provincial-Governors—endeavours to devour the Child. But the Woman, the Mother-Church of Jerusalem which had rocked the cradle of Gentile Christianity, flies to the Wilderness—to

REVELATION. Petra, on the edge of the Arabian desert, and is there safe for
1,260 days, *i.e.* during the horrors of the three and a half
years between the time when Vespasian began his dreadful
work in Judea, and A.D. 70, when city and temple perished
in fire and blood. The Dragon is overcome by Michael, and
the Woman, aided by the eagle-wings of divine protection,
escapes in safety.

Then in the vision of the Wild Beast from the Sea,
St. John intimates, as clearly as any Apocalypse could
possibly intimate, that he is speaking of Rome and Nero.[1]
He describes this Wild Beast by sixteen distinctive marks,
every one of which points to Rome and Nero, and most of
them to Nero only ; and then, in a very common form of
enigma, known to the Jews as *Gematria,* and to the Greeks
as *isopsephia,* he gives the numerical equivalent of the Wild
Beast's name. That equivalent is three sixes—6 6 6—three
numbers symbolic of earthliness and imperfection. In the
same way in the Sibylline books the name of Rome is
isopsephically represented in the number 948, and the name
of Jesus is indicated by three perfect numbers—8 units,
8 tens, 8 hundreds—888. This suggestion of numerical
equivalents for the letters of names had in it nothing
essentially mysterious. In itself it was as easy to decipher as
when Dante prophesies in the *Purgatorio* (xxxiii. 43) that 500,
10, and 55 should slay the harlot and the giant. In Dante the
three numbers stand for DXV, *i.e.* Dux, and refer to Can Grande,
Lord of Verona.[2] Any ordinary reader would instantly (and

---

[1] For a further elucidation I must refer to my *Early Days of Christianity*,
ii. 281-301. In the Sibylline verses Nero is called "the Beast," "the serpent,"
&c. The belief that 666 = Nero Caesar קסר נרון is adopted by Fritzsche, Benary,
Reuss, Hitzig, Volkmar, Ewald, &c. In the ancient various readings 616 is
the correction of some reader who dropped the final *n* in the word Neron.

[2] The only difference is that in Dante's enigma the word *Dux,* "leader," is
not expressed isopsephically but with reference to the Roman numerals, D, X, V.
And yet simple as is the solution he adds,

> E forse che la mia narrazion buia,
> Qual Temi e Sfinge, men ti persuade,
> Perchè a lor modo lo intelletto attuia ;
> Ma tosto fien li fatti, le Naiade
> Che solveranno questo enigma forte,
> Senza danno di pecore e di biade.

for the Christian community very perilously) have deciphered REVELATION. the riddle had not St. John intentionally made his Gematria correspond to Hebrew letters and not to Greek. In Hebrew letters the names Neron Kesar—Nero Caesar—give 6 6 6. Even to the early fathers—who guessed the solution *Lateinos* —it was known that St. John meant by the Wild Beast Nero and the Roman Empire. Of course, *Lateinos,* "a Latin man," could not possibly be the real solution, but it pointed in the right direction. Nor were they far wrong when they guessed *Teitan,* for Titan was an old name for the sun, and Nero affected the attributes of the sun, and had himself represented as the sun-god with radiated head in the huge colossus of himself which he reared at Rome. Another ancient guess, *Euanthas,* is probably also intended to indicate Nero, who prided himself on the long hair which grew down his neck. If the early writers failed to discover the *exact* equivalent, it was only because most of them were entirely ignorant of Hebrew. and it did not occur to them as it occurred simultaneously to many modern scholars, to try the solution of the isopsephia in Hebrew.[1]

The second Wild Beast, also called the False Prophet, is described by ten indications.[2] No breath of tradition as to

> " And haply my narration dark like those
>   Of Sphinx, or Themis, credit may not claim,
>   Since o'er the mind like them a cloud it throws,
> But soon this hard enigma to explain.
>   Events shall be the Œdipus ; nor blade
>   Nor flock therefrom shall injury sustain."—WRIGHT.

[1] If it be objected that Nero neither returned to life nor reappeared, the answer is twofold, (1) At this epoch both among Jews, Christians, and heathens, there was a universal expectation that he would, an expectation that lasted centuries later (Suet. *Nero.* 40-57 ; Tac. *Hist.* i. 2 ; ii. 8, 9 ; Dion. Cass. lxiv. 9 ; Lactant. *Mort. Persec.* 2 ; Aug. *Civ. Dei.* xx. 19 ; Sulpic. Sever. ii. 36 ; Jerome on Dan. xi. 28 ; Chrysostom on 2 Thess. ii.). (2) Domitian was regarded and universally spoken of as a second Nero (Suet. *Tit.* 7 ; Tert. *Apol.* 5 ; *De Pall.* 4 ; Juv. *Sat.* iv. 35, &c.). Moreover Otho at the beginning of his short reign not only allowed himself to be saluted as Nero, but even *wrote to the Provinces* in Nero's name. Further, as Thiersch says, the popular legend involved an ideal truth. Symbolically speaking, Nero did return, and every Antichrist, from Antiochus Epiphanes downwards, has had Neronian characteristics.

[2] They will be found detailed and explained in *Early Days of Christianity* ii. 301-330.

the meaning of this symbol has come down to us, but a study of the hints thrown out point almost with certainty to Vespasian. The symbol is, however, in all likelihood, a composite one, as is the case with so many other apocalyptic figures; and it is far from improbable that into the main symbol are infused subordinate touches which point to two False Prophets—Simon Magus and Josephus, who, in their way, were representatives of the sorcery and superstition and false religion which helped to support an abominable tyranny. Vespasian, who was himself a worker of lying miracles ("signs"), upheld the power of Nero. By this composite symbol is perhaps intended every element of influence— Pagan, Jewish, and heretical—which aided Nero in the two cities, Rome and Jerusalem, which are perpetually before the eyes of the Seer.[1]

The following chapters are more general, and for the most part explain themselves. Intermingled with resplendent visions of the Lamb on Mount Zion, with the virgin multitude, and the Angel with an eternal Gospel in his hand, the millennium of the Saints, and the jewelled glories of the New Jerusalem, through whose streets flows the River of the Water of Life, and wherein there is no more curse, are seen the awful Visions of the Judgment, the vintage of the wrath of God; the seven diamond-clad Angels who empty their vials of divine wrath; the Battle of Armageddon; the siege of Jerusalem, and the doom of the mystic Babylon.

A careful examination will show that in these closing chapters we have three great conflicts, each described in three sections, of which the first describes the foe, the second the victory, the third the final issue.

1. First conflict and triumph.

 a. The enemy is Rome, the harlot-city, in her power and splendour (xvii.).

 β. She is doomed and overthrown (xviii.).

---

[1] This dual symbolism is found in the Apocalypse in the seven heads of the beast, which indicate both seven hills and seven emperors; in the dragon, which is both Satan and Rome, &c.

γ. The Hallelujahs over her defeat (xix. 1-10).

2. Second conflict and triumph.

   a. The enemies are the Beast and False Prophet, representatives of Pagan empire and Pagan religion, aided
by the Devil (xix. 11-19).

   β. They are defeated and flung into the abyss (xix. 20-
xx. 3).

   γ. The Millennial triumph (xx. 4-6).

3. Third conflict and triumph.

   a. The enemy is Satan unloosed, heading the nations
Gog and Magog (xx. 7-8).

   β. They are defeated and destroyed (xx. 9-10).

   γ. The final victory, the new heaven and earth, the
Heavenly Jerusalem (xxi.-xxii. 5).

The Book ends with an epilogue in which we have the triple
attestation of the Angel, of Jesus, and of St. John, to the
truth of these prophecies (xxi. 6-7), and after the adjuration
to those who copied the Book to keep it in its integrity, it
closes with the words of the Lord—which are practically the
idea of the whole prophecy—" Yea, I come quickly." The
Seer answers, " Amen! come, Lord Jesus," and concludes with
the brief blessing, " The grace of the Lord Jesus be with the
Saints." [1]

It is deeply to be deplored that while Christians have so
often and so anxiously employed years of study in the attempt
to explain details by methods of exegesis wholly inapplicable
to this or to any other of the numerous extant Apocalypses—
or, indeed, to any book or prophecy of Scripture—they have
succeeded in throwing general discredit on promises and
encouragements which were meant to be precious to the
Church in all ages, but most of all during times of persecution. No one can understand the Apocalypse aright who
does not begin with studying this form of literature in
general, and understanding its common characteristics, the

[1] In the Epilogue the Triple Attestation is twice repeated. The Angel
speaks twice in verses, 6, 9-11. The Lord twice in verses, 7, 12-17. St.
John twice, 8, 18-20.

nature and limits of the imagery in which it revels, and what he should expect from it. He must abandon the rash fanaticism of ignorance and narrowness. He must refuse to be led into the quagmire of private interpretations after the *ignis fatuus* of narrow religious hatred. He must bear in mind that it is always the primary object of a writer to be understood by those whom he addresses, and that he writes with reference to events which stir his own heart and the hearts of those among whom he lives. He must discount the oriental hyperboles which were partly necessitated by the perils of the time, and were partly congruous to the grandiose form of these ancient allegories. He must neither criticise an Apocalypse by the canons of Hellenic taste nor of Aristotelian logic.

The two cities which towered so vast before the imagination of the Seer, and which formed the terrible antithesis to the City of God, were Rome and Jerusalem. The main events which at that epoch crowded the horizon of the world were the Fire of Rome, the setting of the sun of the Julian line into seas of blood, the revolt of Judea, the burnings of the Temple of Jehovah in Jerusalem, and of Jupiter Latiaris in Rome. The events which crowded the horizon of the Church were the Neronian Persecution, the Fall of Jerusalem, the close of the Old Dispensation, the Coming of the Lord. Amid minor details this is the double series of events which is dealt with in the book of the prophecy. It is the book of the Second Advent. It is the consolation of martyrdom. It is the burden of Jerusalem. It is the burden of Pagan Rome. It is a stormy comment—dictated by its commencing accomplishments—upon the great eschatological discourse which Jesus uttered to His disciples on Olivet, in which He had told them that that generation should not pass away till all things were fulfilled. It is a paean and a prophecy over the ashes of the Neronian martyrs. It breathes an infinite defiance against all tyrannies, whether they assume the garb of religion or of the world. It is the tremendous counter-

manifesto of a Christian seer, uttering the language of immortal confidence in God, and assured certainty of triumph,
as he stood face to face with the bloodstained fury of imperial
heathendom. The writer himself tells us—though he has
not been attended to—that he is going to write " the things
which are," and "the things which must speedily come to pass."[1]

But meanwhile,· amid these contemporary allusions, the
book from end to end reminds us of eternal realities and
immeasurable hopes. The visions of Christ which precede
each crisis of horrible judgment, the psalms and harpnotes of
heaven which are heard amid the cries and the fury of men,
all point the same lesson. Fear not, even in the midst of
anguish and persecution, ye true saints of God. Christ shall
triumph! Christ's enemies shall be overthrown! All who
hate Him shall be hurled into ruin; all who love Him shall,
after this brief spasm of anguish, be blessed everlastingly. On
Judea and Jerusalem, the strongholds of a false orthodoxy
and a false religion—on Rome and Nero, the representatives
of earthly oppression—the doom has gone forth. Old things
are vanishing away, but the things that cannot be shaken
shall remain. Before the seals are opened, before the
trumpets are blown, before the vials are poured forth, heaven
is opened for us that we may see the King in His beauty.[2]
An awful darkness is falling on the earth, but already the
grey secret of the East is beginning to reveal the new and
never-ending dawn. Maran atha—the Lord is at hand! Even
so, come, Lord Jesus! Abide with us, for the day is far
spent! And thus from first to last the object of the book is
simply practical. It is to encourage Christians to endurance
by the lessons of Hope. It is to keep them faithful to all
that is good by showing them the destined overthrow of all
that is evil.

[1] Rev. i. 1. ἐν τάχει, ii. 5, 16 ; ταχὺ, iii. 11 ; xi. 14 ; xxii. 20. Almost
every fragment of ancient traditional interpretation refers the allusions of the
Apocalypse to events of the epoch in which it was written.

[2] See iv. 5 (before the Seals) ; viii. 2–6 (before the Trumpets) ; xv. (before
the Vials).

REVELATION.
And thus, understood in its general outlines, the Apocalypse ceases to be a great silent Sphinx propounding at the outer gate of the New Testament its menacing and insoluble enigma, and it becomes in its essence a series of glorious pictures " wherein," as was said by Herder the great poet-theologian, " are set forth the rise, the visible existence, and the general future of Christ's kingdom in figures and similitudes of His first coming to terrify and to console." [1] It is a " precious vessel in which the treasury of Christian hope has been deposited for all ages of the Church, but especially for the Church under the Cross." [2]

[1] The practical aim of the writer is expressed again and again. See (besides the seven letters) vi. 9–11 ; xiii. 9, 10 ; xiv. 4-7, 12, 13 ; xvi. 15 ; xix. 9 ; xx. 6 ; xxi. xxii. *passim.*
[2] Godet.

NOTE.

APOCALYPTIC SYMBOLS.

A synoptic glance at the series of the Seven Seals, of which the Seventh seems to include the Seven Trumpets, and the Seven Trumpets, of which the Seventh seems to include the Seven Vials, will shew their parallelism. It will also be seen how largely the images are borrowed from the Twelve Plagues of Egypt, from the Eschatological discourses of Christ, from Isaiah, Joel, Ezekiel, Daniel, &c.

THE SEVEN SEALS. (vi-viii. 1.)	THE SEVEN TRUMPETS. (viii. 1-xi. 18.)	THE SEVEN VIALS. (xvi. 1-21.)
1. The white horse. The conqueror Christ armed with a bow.	Hail, and Fire, and Blood.	A grievous sore on the Worshippers of the Beast.
2. The red horse. War.	The Burning Mountain. The sea turned to blood.	The sea turned into blood.
3. The black horse. Famine	The star, Wormwood.	The rivers turned to blood.
4. The livid horse. Pestilence.	Sun and stars darkened.	Scorching heat from the sun.
5. Martyred souls crying for vengeance.	Pause. An eagle crying woe. The scorpion—locusts.	Darkness in the kingdom of the beast.
6. Earthquake.	Four angels loosed. Two hundred million horsemen in breastplates of fire.	Drying of the Euphrates.
7. *Episode.* (vii.) The sealing. The great multitude. Silence. The seven trumpet angels. Censer hurled to earth. Earthquake. Thunders. Voices.	*Episode.* (x-xi. 14.) The little book. The measuring reed. The two witnesses. Great voices, thunder, hail.	*Episode.* (xvi. 13-16.) The three frogs. Lightnings, thunders, earthquake.
	THE THREE FOES The Devil, the Beast, the False Prophet (xii. i.-xiii. 18). Anticipations of the Final Catastrophe (xiv. 1-xv. 4).	The three combats, victories, and results (xvii. 1-xxii. 5).

Apocalyptic symbols must only be criticised under the conditions in which the Eastern imagination works. We ought not to seek in them the severe beauty, the pure forms of classic poetry, still less the charming outlines and lovely pictures of modern taste. It is the burning breath of the East which animates these figures ; it is an unbridled imagination which, everywhere sacrifices grace to boldness, proportion to the necessity to strike and dazzle, and which, influenced by the desire to abandon the limits of prosaic reality, does not recoil from what seems to us grotesque and revolting. That which gives to the Apocalypse its special peculiarity is the endless personifications, each more daring than the last ; the embodiment of abstract ideas in visible forms to the astonished eyes of the spectator, who contemplates them with a curiosity mingled with terror. With all this the descriptions are not clear and lucid ; the drapery is cloudy, the outlines vague and indistinct. All the attempts, for instance, in the illustrated Bibles of the sixteenth century, to paint the scenes of the Apocalypse are inevitably caricatures in proportion to their fidelity to the text. No one can paint symbolised ideas. An angel whose legs are pillars of fire ; the Christ out of whose mouth comes a sword and in whose hand are seven stars ; a Lamb with seven horns and seven eyes who opens a book ; how can these be painted ? What we have to do is to fix our eyes on the ideal signification and not at all on the material symbol.[1] In these eagles with human voices, altars which speak (xvi. 7), angels clothed in precious stones, single stars which fall on all rivers and infect them with poison, sting-armed locusts, army-collecting frogs, and millions of horsemen in breastplates of hyacinth, we must see, not material figures, but only symbols. In the book of Enoch "stars" eat, and have hands and feet. The image of the star is immediately superseded by direct references to the personality which it represents.

The characteristics of Apocalyptic literature are—

1. The cessation of normal Prophecy.

2. Visions poetically described.

3. Symbols which, unlike those of the ancient Prophets, need special explanation.

4. The Kabbalism of numbers.

5. " *Gematria*," " *isopsephism*."

6. Imaginative hyperbole.[2]

The date of the Apocalypse is definitely fixed by i. 9 ; vii. 9–17 ; xi. 1–2 ; xii. 6 ; xvii. 9–11 ; and that date (as we have seen) is the age of Galba, about A.D. 68.

[1] See Reuss, *L'Apocalypse*, pp. 21, 22.
[2] See Immer, *Theologie des N. T.* 445, Schürer, Neutest. Zeitgesch. 449.

breath of the East which animates these figures; it is an unbridled imagination which, everywhere sacrifices grace to boldness, proportion to the necessity to strike and dazzle, and which, influenced by the desire to abandon the limits of prosaic reality, does not recoil from what seems to us grotesque and revolting. That which gives to the Apocalypse its special peculiarity is the endless personifications, each more daring than the last; the embodiment of abstract ideas in visible forms to the astonished eyes of the spectator, who contemplates them with a curiosity mingled with terror. With all this the descriptions are not clear and lucid; the drapery is cloudy, the outlines vague and indistinct. All the attempts, for instance, in the Illustrated Bibles of the sixteenth century, to paint the scenes of the Apocalypse are inevitably caricatures in proportion to their fidelity to the text. No one can paint symbolised ideas. An angel whose legs are pillars of fire; the Christ out of whose mouth comes a sword and in whose hand are seven stars; a Lamb with seven horns and seven eyes who opens a book; how can these be painted? What we have to do is to fix our eyes on the ideal signification and not at all on the material symbol.[1] In these eagles with human voices, altars which speak (xvi. 7), angels clothed in precious stones, single stars which fall on all rivers and infect them with poison, sting-armed locusts, army-collecting frogs, and millions of horsemen in breastplates of hyacinth, we must see, not material figures, but only symbols. In the book of Enoch, "stars" eat, and have hands and feet. The image of the star is immediately superseded by direct references to the personality which it represents.

The characteristics of Apocalyptic literature are—

1. The cessation of normal Prophecy.
2. Visions poetically described.
3. Symbols which, unlike those of the ancient Prophets, need special explanation.
4. The Kabbalism of numbers.
5. "Gematria," "isopsephism,"
6. Imaginative hyperbole.[2]

The date of the Apocalypse is definitely fixed by i. 9; vii. 9-17; xi. 1-3; xii. 6; xvii. 9-11; and that date (as we have seen) is the age of Galba, about A.D. 68.

[1] See Renan, L'Apocalypse, pp. 21, 22.
[2] See Immer, Theologie des N.T. 7. 445, Schürer, Neutest. Zeitgesch. 446.